JAMES CARVILLE
SCOTT TROST
DE TREE A WE

CARVILLE & TROST

DE TREE A WE

JAMES CARVILLE
& SCOTT TROST

GR8 BOOKS

A DIVISION OF GR8 MEDIA

GR8 Books, June 2017

First Edition

Copyright ©2017

All rights reserved under International and Pan-American Copyright Conventions. Published in the United States by GR8 Books, Los Angeles.

Carville, James, Scott Trost

De Tree A We: The Remarkable Lives of Sanford Meisner, James Carville & Boolu

ISBN 978-0-9993327-9-5 (pbk.)

Library of Congress Control Number: 2017912961

Manufactured in the United States of America

Acknowledgments

My acknowledgment and gratitude for anecdotes and information I squirreled away through the years from Paul Morrison, Stella Adler and her cousins Pearlie and Lulla Rosenfeld, Harold Clurman, and Edith Ross. My thanks also go to Sandy's mother, Bertha, sister, Ruth Post, and of course Sanford "Sandy" Meisner himself as well as to Julian "Boolu" Martin and his sisters, June Phillips and Grace Reno. Lastly but not least I am forever grateful to my own loving and understanding family.

Magazine articles by Steven Harvey, Arthur Seidelman, and Gene Terruso were helpful. The Lincoln Center Library and Harold Clurman's *The Fervent Years* were resources I leaned on for information.

My fondness and affection for Rita McDowell and Lou Keane of Bequia are boundless. They helped and encouraged me when I needed it most during the early days of this endeavor. Rita went over every word to make it presentable. I must mention my brother Hugh Carville and my high school buddies Robert Gottuso, Richard Bryant, and Dennis Carney whose input was invaluable. I know those crude early drafts made it a daunting task. I want to thank you guys for your time-consuming efforts. Lastly, I must graciously thank the renowned writer Frank De Felitta for his keen professional advice before I even began.

Words cannot express my luck in finding, through Rosemary Billings' good graces, my editor, the tireless, indomitable "Ms. Picky," for picky, picky, picky was the bane of my existence from the very start, for over two years. She darn near drove me bats, she was such a stickler over every damn comma and semi-colon and her "What do you mean by this?" Yes, I refer to my beloved editor, Judith Hammill, without whom there would be no book, such as it is. Thanks to Trudie Kessler for proofreading. And special thanks to Scott Trost for getting this project to the finish line.

I must not leave out my friend Sydelle Engel. From the time "we tree" met her, her belief in me, in Sandy, and mostly in Boolu, never wavered. We thank you, Sydelle, from the bottom of our hearts for all your support and effort. We send much love to you and yours always. I know that to you and all who had a hand in the progress of this work, "De Tree a We" will be eternally indebted.

Love always,

Jimmy, Boolu, and, I am sure, Sandy wherever he may be. 2017

Contents

Preface	11
1 Himself	15
2 Love Enters	41
3 Myself	62
4 To St. Vincent and the Grenadines	87
5 And Boolu Makes Three	100
6 Reconnoitering	117
7 Transition	136
8 Freedom	144
9 Survival	162
10 Bruises and Hard Knocks	168
11 To Bequia or not to Bequia	181
12 Sandy Hellbent on Bequia	190
13 Cinnamon Buns and Silverballi	214
14 Coming Together	227
15 Adventures Across the Water	239
16 Fait Accompli	249
17 Bells A'ringing	262
18 Metamorphoses in the Making	275
19 The Ides Betide	287
20 From Webber to Mozart	304
21 The Requiem	324

Contents cont.

22	Life is a Bumpy Ride	345
23	Exaltation and Dejection	363
24	Culture, Culture and More Culture	374
25	To the Land of Saints and Scholars	387
26	For the Record	404
27	A Near-Death Experience	417
28	The Wonders of New York	434
29	Blow by Blow	449
30	Boo, He, and Me Full tilt	471
31	One Thing Leads to Another	490
32	Reaping the Rewards	504
33	Life is Sweet	523
34	On the Road Again	531
35	The Sun Rises in the Far East	548
36	Ups and Downs	572
37	Bonbons	581
38	Hanging by a Thread	596
39	Bodies in Motion	609
40	All Shook Up	621
41	Shaken and Stirred	636
42	Annus Mirabilis	645
43	The Grim Reaper Slowly Pulls the Curtain	668
	Appendix	682

Preface

By Arthur Seidelman

This is a love story. In fact, it's a few love stories.

The first is the story of two men, Sanford Meisner and James Carville, who found inspiration, comfort, and sanctuary in each other. When you were with Sandy and Jimmy, even briefly, you knew you were in the presence of a deep bond of devotion and care. They were keenly aware of each other's vulnerabilities and were there to offer protection and courage when needed. In the world of theater, protection and courage are the essential elements for survival.

Sandy's last decade and a half were difficult for him physically. Illness and a car accident exacted a heavy toll. Jimmy kept Sandy alive by motivating him to adhere to his calling and teach. Jimmy understood that teaching was

Sandy's passion and the source of his identity and pride. Relinquishing that would have been like dying. Jimmy gave Sandy the moral fortitude to persevere emotionally and the physical support he needed to get to class even when he could barely walk. Jimmy encouraged Sandy to speak to his students, even when he had no voice. In this process of their mutual accommodation, Sandy and Jimmy became one in spirit to a degree few couples ever achieve.

Jimmy was and is a gifted actor. His gift is simple and honest. More complementary words cannot be spoken about any actor. But he chose to devote more of his life to Sandy than to a conventional career. It was a selfless choice.

Jimmy and Sandy's bond was so strong that they were able to extend it to embrace their adopted son, Boolu. Disabled from birth, Boolu found himself a virtual orphan in his village on the island of Bequia, where Sandy and Jimmy had built their getaway house. Jimmy and Sandy opened their hearts and their home to Boolu, and gave him the companionship and guidance of true parents. As he grew older, Boolu became as much caregiver as child in this extraordinary family as they traveled between New York, Los Angeles, and Bequia.

It was on Bequia that Sandy found the respite from show business that he needed to periodically gather his wits and his wisdom. But he could not stay away from his calling for long. Each summer he would bring with him to their Bequia home a group of students, and this lucky band would pursue the illusive art of acting for a few magical months in an idyllic island setting.

Those are the human love stories in the tale of these lives. There are others, more abstract but no less profound.

Foremost is the love of art, theater, and music. These men built their lives on that foundation, and the love was so profound that the art needed to be held to the highest standard. When you truly love someone or some thing, you expect, even demand, the maximum from it. Sandy was passionately committed to the theater, but not to the theater of cheap tricks and prostituted emotions. He revered the theater of truth, of untrampled artistry. He had no patience for pretense, for ego-driven self-indulgence that called itself acting. Truth was the goal -- the truth that shed light on the dark corners of the human soul. And if one wasn't always able to get to the truth, one could, at least, stay on the right road, taking pride in the journey. Sandy passed that love on to generations of students. He put us on that right road, and his voice in our heads challenges us to stay on it, regardless of the temptations or distractions.

If you were fortunate enough to be a student of Sandy Meisner, you were changed forever. Your sense of truth was refined, your ability to listen was honed, your realization that the scene isn't about you was born. Even if you weren't able to scale the heights, you left Sandy's tutelage with a sense of how glorious, deep, yet simple, acting could be.

Sandy Meisner's love for the art of acting changed it. Other teachers might

Preface

have received more public acclaim because of their penchant for publicity, but it was Sandy who quietly set the standard for incisive truth in acting which every other practitioner had to strive to meet.

His teaching methods, like his persona, allowed no room for nonsense. " Acting is being real under imaginary circumstances." " Acting is living moment by moment." "Listen!" No psychological game-playing and parlor tricks were allowed. Only the respect for truth in art.

Sandy often joked, almost ruefully, that after he had gone, his name would become a noun. Teachers would talk about teaching "Meisner." His prediction came true. Teachers good, bad, and mediocre adopt the Meisner mantle around the world. Some, often those actually trained by Sandy, wear it with honor. Others exploit the brand without the understanding. Jimmy has endeavored to protect the meaning inherent in Sandy's name, but one thing is clear: wherever young actors gather to search for truth through the art of acting, Sandy's voice will forever be heard.

Jimmy's memoir tells an adjacent but also profound love story – that between America and the theatre – through Sandy's personal history with the Group Theater. Not since Harold Clurman's *THE FERVENT YEARS* has the story been told as intimately. The insights, the character portraits, the behind-the-scenes tales are vivid and insightful. And they shine fresh light on America's most daring attempt to create a national theater. Were it not for Sanford Meisner, Lee Strasberg. Cheryl Crawford, Harold Clurman, Clifford Odets, Luther Adler, Stella Adler, and their colleagues, we would never have had Elia Kazan, John Garfield, Montgomery Cliff, Marlon Brando, Paul Newman, and their artistic descendants. This, too, is a love story of heroes and villains, jealousies and ambitions.

With this honest volume, Jimmy has accomplished the daunting task of capturing a life on paper and portraying the inner workings of human and artistic passion. In so doing, he honors the memory of the man he loved and inspires others to pursue and fulfill their own personal and artistic destinies.

1 Himself

He Knew What He Wanted

In 1924 Sanford "Sandy" Meisner was a well-read, musically-inclined 19-year-old working at his uncle's lace factory on 17th Street and 5th Avenue in Manhattan. To keep from going stark raving mad pushing bins of lace around, he would practice his pitch recognition and sight reading, going over solfège in his mind, that is, practicing his do-re-mi's. One day his buddy Monkey Tobias told Sandy to get uptown to the Theatre Guild. The Guild was a theatrical society that had been founded in New York City six years previously for the production of high quality, non-commercial American and foreign plays. They were holding auditions for Sydney Howard's play *They Knew What They Wanted* starring Pauline Lord. Sandy was hired on the spot to play a farmhand and that same year he was ushered into the Theatre Guild School on scholarship. Finally he had a reason to get up in the morning.

The Theater Guild Years

Nineteen twenty-four was the most prolific year ever for Broadway productions, with over 228 openings, a record that hasn't been matched since. It was a time of plenty for an actor.

That year, Aaron Copland, Sandy's long-time piano buddy and childhood friend in Brooklyn, who went on to compose some of this country's greatest music, brought Harold Clurman to *They Knew What They Wanted* to meet Sandy. Harold was destined to become one of America's outstanding theatre commentators, as well as a successful producer and director. In later life he turned to teaching actors. But back in 1924, Aaron and Harold had just met in Paris where they were students, Harold at the Sorbonne and Aaron with Madame Nadia Boulanger studying composition. While in Paris, Harold had attended lectures at Jacques Copeau's school, Le Théâtre du Vieux-Colombier. Now he was back in New York trying to break into the New York theatre scene. He wasn't having much luck. Harold and Sandy soon became friends, and Harold managed to get a job as an extra in the Guild's 1925 production of Caesar and Cleopatra. Shortly thereafter, Sandy invited him to a special presentation for Guild subscribers of Pirandello's *Right You Are, If You Think You Are*, in which Sandy had his first real part. Harold felt he was very "picturesque" in the role but he was more intrigued by the rather disagreeable though effective lead performance by Lee Strasberg. Strasberg, it turned out, had studied at the American Laboratory Theatre where, for the first time, the technique of acting according to the Moscow Art School was being taught by Richard Boleslavsky and Maria Ouspenskaya.

While Sandy and Lee were playing in John Howard Lawson's *Processional*, which opened January 12, 1925, they were cast in Dick Rodgers and Larry Hart's review, *The Garrick Gaieties of 1925*, which was to open June 8 at the Garrick Theatre. Sandy landed a job singing and dancing in the chorus. His partner was Libby Holman, who was to become a famous chanteuse of the thirties. It was said that the show *Mame* was patterned after her life. Sandy remembered he was so inept that every night Libby had to tell him which foot to start out on. Just telling him "the left" wasn't enough; she had to give him a swift poke with her fist on the side of his hip while she verbalized, "This one." Lee was in some of the sketches and Sandy remembered him stumbling through a Spanish tango. Harold was the stage manager and became friendly with Lee. Lee, because he was familiar with backstage requirements, was a big help to the novice Harold.

On October 11, 1926, Sandy opened as the Blasio in a historical drama, *Juarez and Maximilian*. A year later, on September 19, 1927, he played Sid in *Four Walls*. Subsequently in 1927, he was picked from class at the Guild's school by his teacher Winifred Lenihan, who had been the original actress in the New York production of George Bernard Shaw's *St. Joan*, to play the Newsboy in Shaw's revival of *The Doctor's Dilemma*, running the complete season of '27-'28.

Harold Clurman, in his memoir *The Fervent Years*, tells of two important happenings in the mid-twenties. The first occurred when he went downtown to see Lee Strasberg rehearse John Masefield's translation of Racine's *Esther* at the Christie Street Settlement and saw Lee following an acting technique that he had learned at the American Laboratory Theatre, familiarly known as "the Lab". The second important happening took place in a conversation with Sandy. Sandy told Harold that he was not altogether satisfied with his training at the Guild School and thought perhaps he needed extra work. Harold recommended Meisner get a part in the Strasberg production at the Settlement. Harold became a frequent visitor at the Settlement rehearsals to see how his friend Sandy was getting on and to see how Strasberg worked. I believe these events first sparked the idea that was to catch fire through the thirties.

Clurman, after a couple of unsuccessful stabs at producing with Sydney Ross, began rehearsing Waldo Frank's *New Year's Eve* on the roof-top garden of Ross's building at Riverside Drive and 85th Street. Besides Sanford Meisner and Morris Carnovsky-at twenty-nine an older member of the Guild-Clurman called on other young actors he had not yet met in the course of his experience at the Guild. He also brought in a young Franchot Tone, fresh from Cornell University and a looker. Clurman engaged Strasberg to direct. After seventeen weeks of rehearsing, while the actors were still working at their regular jobs, Sydney Ross reneged because of the impracticality of the proposed plans. They then chose a delicate fantasy, a slight comedy called *Balloon* by Padraic Colum. After six weeks they gave a run-through, and zilch, nothing happened. Clurman's experiment with producing was finished.

The Guild packaged two shows starring Alfred Lunt, Henry Travers, Sanford Meisner, Morris Carnovsky, and Albert Van Dekker. In *Marco Millions* Sandy played the Papal Courier and Ghazan Khan of Persia. In *Valpone* he eventually played the Judge and, earlier in the

---

The Theatre Guild of New York Presents
THE THEATRE GUILD ACTING COMPANY
(Under the Auspices of the Art Alliance)

—in—

"VOLPONE"

A Sardonic Farce Based on
Ben Jonson's Famous Comedy
By Stefan Zweig

Translated by RUTH LANGNER

Production Directed by PHILIP MOELLER

Settings and Costumes by LEE SIMONSON

CAST (In order of appearance)

First Singer .... Walter Franklyn
Second Singer .... Vincent Sherman
Third Singer .... Paul Yost
Fourth Singer .... George Lamar
First Groom .... Louis Veda
Second Groom .... Sanford Meisner
Mosca (The Gadfly) .... Earle Larimore
Volpone (The Fox) .... Claude Rains
Slave to Volpone .... John Henry
Voltore (The Vulture) .... Philip Leigh
Corvino (The Crow) .... Whitford Kane
Corbaccio (The Raven) ...... Henry Travers
Canina .... Ruth Chorpenning

run, a groom. They hit the road in 1928, crisscrossing the country until, with the Crash of '29, the road company closed in Chicago. The complete company found themselves at the station about to board the New York Central heading back to New York, wondering where their next check would come from. Everyone was accounted for except Paul Morrison, an understudy. A minute before departure, there was still no sign of Paul. Then, just as the train lurched to a start, he jumped aboard. He had been somewhere in the bowels of South Chicago looking for a Black woman who had a magic potion to prevent baldness. Sandy, who developed a lifelong friendship with Paul, observed, "That's Paul. The whole country is facing devastation and Paul is out there spending his last cent on blackstrap molasses."

By January 1, 1929, Harold Clurman was working with Cheryl Crawford at the Guild. She had started there as an assistant stage manager and had had executive experience with the Guild by now. She seemed to know how to deal with such people as board members. She was practical, shrewd, and tactful, a hell of a lot more so than either Harold or Lee, the arcane, esoteric idealists.

Teresa Helburn, who was on the board of the Guild, invited Harold to read and report on some plays. He agreed. When she approached him with the Guild's wish to produce plays at special Sunday night performances for the 'scribers (subscribers) with Herbert Biberman as stage-manager and Cheryl Crawford as casting director, Harold as play-reader suggested *Red Rust*. Though Biberman directed, Harold brought in as many of the actors from the Riverside Drive fiasco: Franchot Tone, Sanford Meisner, and even Lee as an actor. *Red Rust* was favorably received and was given a regular production under the auspices of the Theatre Guild Studio.

Although this production and its performances were not associated with the yet-to-be-established Group Theatre, I am positive it was here that the spark was fanned. Shortly afterward, Harold Clurman, Cheryl Crawford, and Lee Strasberg started holding little gatherings of like-minded parties in the ballroom of the Steinway Building on West 57th Street, the subject of which was the plight of the American theater, with Harold Clurman often holding forth. Harold said of Cheryl Crawford, "She was capable of being roused to fine action when she was confronted with a sound idea or a noble motive. She had determination, moral perception, and a desire to learn and grow. She was immediately caught by my analysis of the theatre situation, struck by my passion, intrigued by my praise of Strasberg's ability as a stage director."

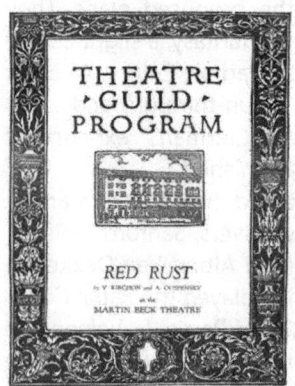

Sandy didn't share this opinion, seeing Crawford in an entirely different light. But then, he thought, what did he know? He was just an actor and that was all he wanted to be.

The Group Theatre Years

With the establishment of the Group Theatre in '31, Sanford Meisner found a home for himself and really came into his own. Meisner was the first member by virtue of his relationship with its founders and also their finest disciple as time went on. The leaders were Lee Strasberg, Harold Clurman, and Cheryl Crawford, with founding member Sandy as well as Morris Carnovsky, Alexander Kirkland, Clifford Odets, Art Smith, young Phoebe Brand, and Dorothy Patten all at the Guild. From Broadway came Margaret "Beanie" Barker, and from downtown came J. Edward Bromberg, who was at the Civic Repertory Theatre, and Stella Adler, whom Harold had first met at the American Theatre Laboratory.

Lee Strasberg   Sanford Meisner   Harold Clurman   Stella Adler

Stella Adler had already established a name for herself in her parents', Jacob and Sara Adler's, Yiddish Theater Company downtown on the Lower East Side. Her desire to move uptown to Broadway had led her to the Lab where she met Harold. He convinced her to join the Group and, eventually, to marry him. In the 1940s she would establish the Adler School of Acting on upper Broadway. Stella was to become the grande dame of realistic acting, a style of acting the Group was credited with.

The Group also included from the *Red Rust* cast, Franchot Tone, Ruth Nelson, and Eunice Stoddard. Most members of the Group had worked together at the Theatre Guild at one time or another. Many had just finished a production of their own at the Guild that eventful year of '29.

It was no secret that the Sandy's and Cheryl Crawford's personalities clashed. No love was lost between gays and lesbians at that time. Sandy was still struggling with his own darker sexual contradictions and inconsistencies, which were very much unresolved within him then. A woman with her qualities just didn't sit well with a temperament as sensitive as his. An in-your-face, strong, masculine woman wielding authority, no matter how slight, was more than he could cope with. He found her personality offensive and did little to conceal it. He knew she didn't want him in the Group and had voted him out, but her maneuvering had made little difference to Clurman and Strasberg. Sandy appeared in seventeen Group productions, including the first, *The House of Connelly*, backed by the Theatre Guild, even though Cheryl Crawford had left him off the list, no surprise to him or anyone else in the company.

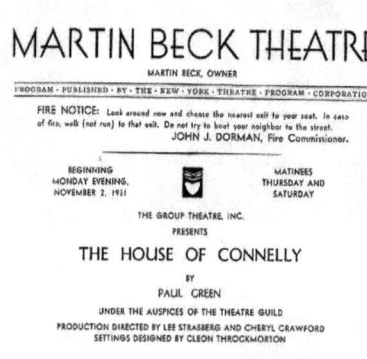

The show was very well received at the Martin Beck Theatre on September 28, 1931, and an exciting new type of theatre, based on an ensemble approach to acting, was presented to the New York public. Individual actors playing individual parts were no longer most important. The ensemble approach afforded a highly personal and cooperative way for the cast to focus. For audiences it was the beginning of a revolutionary experience of the theatre. The realism of what was on the stage began to attract a whole new audience from Brooklyn and the Bronx.

Nevertheless, the Group Theatre's second production, *1931* by Claire and Paul Sifton, which opened at the Mansfield Theatre on December 10, 1931, closed in nine days. "A failure, then, a total failure," one reviewer captioned his notice. "The year 1931 would be remembered but not the play." Unfortunately the Group proceeded with three bombs, one bigger than the next, and they lost the backing and sponsorship of the Guild. Maxwell Anderson's *Night over Taos* opened on March 9, 1932, with the reviewers expressing respect, but

1 Himself

boredom. It was ready to close after the first Saturday night of its run, but the determination of the actors managed to keep it running for a month in spite of the reviews.

After a nervous summer up at Dover Furnace, where they had gone to workshop productions for the fall season, the company presented two shows: John Howard Lawson's *Success Story* directed by Lee Strasberg, and Dawn Powell's *Big Night* directed by Cheryl Crawford. Fortunately, Sandy was spared both shows. Strasberg badly miscast *Success Story*. It opened in the fall of '32 to moderate reviews and managed to stay afloat for four months. Harold described Lee's condition after *Success Story*: "The effect was frequently a loss of strength, and though he remained dogged, he also was somewhat lamed." The results left Harold himself in a similar state. Cheryl's *Big Night* production bombed with a vengeance on January 25, 1933. The actors had been rather critical of Cheryl Crawford as director and she had grown weary of the fractious company, so that Harold had had to step in and take over rehearsals for the last few weeks.

Although Sandy had mercifully been spared, the company was licking their wounds after the negative outcomes of *Success Story* and *Big Night*. Many in the cast had had great expectations for *Success Story* in particular, and they were all depressed and surprised by its mediocre reviews. Curiously, the whole company seemed to spiral into a state of withdrawal and dejection, with the apparent exception of Clifford Odets, who was holed up in his room busily working on two plays of his own. The honeymoon was over and the Group was experiencing its first growing pains. The Guild had reneged on their support after the second play, leaving the Group penniless. Many members were living in what some of them called the "poorhouse," a badly neglected, dilapidated ten-room brownstone over in the far reaches of Hell's Kitchen on West 57th Street next to the New York Central Railway. Sandy was still living with his family out in Flatbush, in the bowels of Brooklyn, so he was spared the experience of the Group's dire communal existence.

The first drafts of his friend's plays being finished, Sandy read them and found them promising. He spoke to an acquaintance of his, Mrs. Bess Eitingon, whose husband was willing to provide her with $50,000 for a theatrical investment. Sandy told Lee about the lady with the money, and Sandy the actor suggested Lee the director give her a call. Lee was in such a funk that he believed people were no longer parting with their money, not even as an investment, certainly not a theatrical investment. Perhaps the state of the Depression was getting the better of him or maybe Lee thought this was all wishful thinking on Sandy's part. Whatever the case, he never called the fine lady. Not hearing from Lee, Mrs. Eitingon called him herself. His rude, offhand manner was such a put-off that she concluded from his conversation that the Group had all the money they needed. She told Sandy that Lee had been so contemptuous of her money and had treated her so badly that she would be taking her investment elsewhere. And so director/producer Frank

Merlin wound up the beneficiary, able to sink the $50,000 into two productions of his own.

So much for astute leadership, Sandy thought. At this point Sandy began to question other aspects of Lee's nature, his unyielding, uncompromising ways. He was by now also questioning Lee's method of teaching as well as his manner of direction. Lee's martinet approach to life did not sit too well with Sandy's more egalitarian ways. Sandy never allowed himself to become embroiled in personality disturbances. It went against his nature. He saw himself as merely an actor and wanted to keep it that way. He left the Group, but only temporarily, and went into rehearsal for the Theatre Guild production of *American Dream*. The play, written by George O'Neal, staged by Philip Moeller, and starring Claude Rains and Josephine Hull, with Sandy playing Henri, opened February 21, 1933. It was a play in three time periods: 1650, 1849, and 1933. Sound strange? Maybe that's why it ran less than a month.

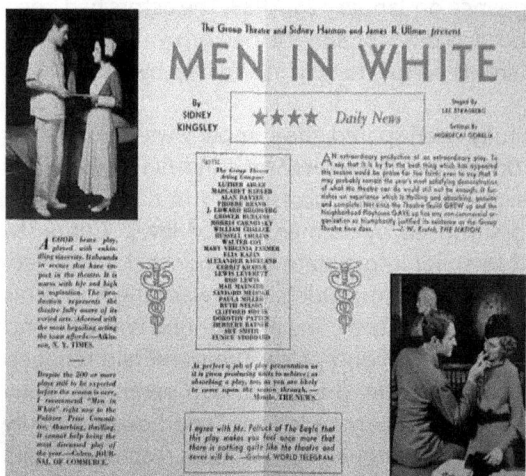

In the fall of that year, the Group Theatre mounted the Pulitzer Prize-winning show *Men in White* written by Sidney Kingsley. It opened at the Broadhurst Theatre on September 26, 1933. It was a hit and ran 351 performances, with Sandy playing Mr. Wren and Mr. Smith.

From *Who's Who in the American Theatre*:

"The cast, directed by Lee Strasberg, in a truly ensemble performance, included Luther Adler, J. Edward Bromberg, Alexander Kirkland, Sanford Meisner, Robert Lewis, Morris Carnovsky, Art Smith and Ruth Nelson... The production's precision and finish, particularly in the operating room scene, which achieved an almost ballet quality, helped establish the reputation of the Group Theatre."

Brooks Atkinson of the *New York Times* wrote:

"After two years of real hardship, the Group is not only still in existence, but still determined to keep the theatre in its high estate. This time they have a play worthy of their ambition, and they have adorned it with the most beguiling acting the town affords. It is a good brave play and it is just the play to summon all the latent idealism from the young players of the Group Theatre."

Critic Joseph Wood Krutch called *Men in White* "a work of art."

Nevertheless, Meisner was becoming disillusioned with Strasberg's work.

1 Himself

It was now a couple of years into the Group and Stella Adler, a dear friend of Sandy's by this point, had also, along with others in the group such as Robert Lewis, become disenchanted with Lee. Sandy had admired Lee ever since their days together in the mid-'20s at the Theatre Guild. He had even considered Lee his mentor at the Christy Street Settlement long before the Group was even an idea. But now Sandy felt Lee's teaching had become stiff and unchanging, and Sandy knew stagnation was sure death to artistic development. Because Stella had not been cast in *Men in White*, she was able to go with Harold and Lee to Moscow that year. It was a short stay, but Harold was impressed by the range of the Moscow Art Theatre's repertoire. In Paris, Harold and Stella called on Constantine Stanislavski who was there recuperating. He was warm, simple, urbane, and thoughtful, a relaxed, fine human being. They took walks with him to the Bois de Boulogne where both asked many questions that Stanislavski cordially answered. Stella had been worried over the Stanislavski system as taught by Strasberg. She no longer found any joy in acting, she avowed; perhaps this was due to that cursed Method.

Constantine Stanislavski

Stanislavski immediately said, "If the system does not help you, forget it. But perhaps you do not use it properly." He worked on a scene Stella found difficult in Lawson's *Gentlewoman*. She came back day after day and worked five weeks under his private tutelage.

When Stella returned to a mountaintop in the Catskills that summer, she reported to Bobby Lewis and Sandy Meisner, confirming Sandy's notion that Strasberg's use of the Stanislavski system had been incorrect. Stella felt that Strasberg introverted the already introverted, a very serious and dangerous practice. As well, an undue emphasis on the exercises of effective memory had warped the work. Strasberg's reaction to Harold upon this declaration was to charge that Stanislavski had gone back on himself. But others argued against Lee that Stanislavski may well have, and so what? They argued that art is forever changing as nature itself.

With Stella's return from Moscow, the conflict was reaching a critical point for Sandy. After the opening of *Gold Eagle Guy* at the Morosco Theatre on November 28, 1934, in which Sandy played Ortega and Guy Button Jr., it looked as if the Group had hit the skids—at least as far as Lee was concerned. In Boston, Luther Adler was quoted as saying, "Boys, I think we're working on a stiff." The press loathed the play. It was bad.

The egomaniacal Strasberg was a sore loser. According to Clurman, this disaster sent Strasberg, the play's director, into a state of depression, impassivity, and pessimism. He was the same as he had been after the disaster of Cheryl Crawford's bollixing of *Big Night* and his own failure with *Success Story*.

Lee was also losing his hold over the actors as his teaching prowess came gradually into question after Stella's return from Europe. It wasn't to happen for a couple of years yet, but I think this was the beginning of the finish of Lee in the Group.

About this time Clifford Odets was playing hooky from Lee's rehearsals when he wasn't on call, affording him time to work on writing *Waiting for Lefty* and *Awake and Sing*. Though the workouts with Lee were turbulent, with a third of the ranting directed at Clifford, Odets still remained loyal to Lee and his approach to acting. Sandy chose to keep his cool, remain silent, and do his own thing.

If the Group were to survive, they were in dire need of a property. At a meeting in the basement of the Belasco Theatre, Odets spoke up on behalf of his *Awake and Sing*, and offered to raise the money for the production himself. Exasperated, Strasberg broke out fiercely, "You don't seem to understand, Cliff. We don't like your play. We don't like it!" What Strasberg was truly saying was, "I don't like your play."

In spite of Lee, Clifford read the play to the company, and as the last words of the final act were being spoken, the actors' faces were aglow. The enthusiasm was unanimous. After the closing curtain of *Gold Eagle Guy*, Harold announced their next production was to be the work of their own Clifford Odets. The actors gave out a shout of joy and threw their costumes into the air. Some of the company immediately went into rehearsal for *Awake and Sing*, a nine-character play, while most of the others were preparing *Waiting for Lefty* under Sanford Meisner's and Clifford Odets' co-direction.

On January 5, 1935, at the Civic Repertory Theatre down on West 14th Street among the union halls of the area, an event took place at the modest proletarian collective that developed into the Theatre Union that would be noted in the annals of American Theater. So said Harold Clurman. For some unknown reason, from the first two minutes of the first scene of *Waiting for Lefty*, an instant empathy rushed through the audience, and the place went wild. Actors and audience fused into a single unit, Harold said, the likes of which he had never before witnessed in the theatre. Throughout the performances there were shouts of kinship, whistles, and bravos. At the end, after the militant question, "Well, what's the answer?" the audience rushed the stage with a spontaneous roar of "Strike!! Strike!!" a cry of hunger for constructive social action. A new American author was born and the voice of the 1930s was heard.

Harold sat next to Lee in the audience, and said the whole experience seemed to be lost on Lee. Sandy told me he felt Strasberg suffered from "a prophet is not without honor save in his own country" syndrome. Simplistically speaking, perhaps Strasberg saw Odets as an actor and after so many years could not nor would not picture him under any other hat.

Whatever the case, *Awake and Sing* opened on February 19, 1935 to favorable reviews, with Sandy playing Sam Feischreibner. In the New York Times, Brooks Atkinson, after calling Odets the Group's "most congenial playwright," went on to say, "To this student of the arts, *Awake and Sing* is inexplicably deficient in plain theatre emotion." Could that have been a compliment?

As early as 1933 when Sandy was becoming disenchanted with Strasberg's Method acting, he had written, "Actors are not guinea pigs to be manipulated, dissected, let alone in a purely negative way. Our approach was not organic, that is to say not healthy."

Meanwhile, Harold Clurman was obsessed with America and the American character. The seed of Clurman's idea took time to germinate, but eventually Sandy realized that if American actors were ever going to achieve the goal of "living truthfully under imaginary circumstances," someone would have to come up with an American approach. He made that quest his own, and the Neighborhood Playhouse was soon to provide him with a venue to pursue it. It would be an association that lasted decades.

And so the times affected Sandy. The disagreement with Lee Strasberg's Method propelled him on a life-long quest to discover how one trains to be able "to live truthfully under imaginary circumstances." Although this goal had been unchanging ever since the idea germinated in the Moscow Art Theatre at the turn of the 20th century under the tutelage of Constantine Stanislavski, Stanislavski, unlike Strasberg, constantly changed and moderated his own approach, endeavoring to improve his teaching to the very end of his life in 1938. Sandy, after almost six years and many talks with Stella Adler, the only American who had worked with Stanislavski, gave up the notion of Lee as his mentor.

As for my take on Lee's work, many years later after studying with Meisner myself, I was an observer at Strasberg's studio up in the remains of the old church choir loft. Sandy told me he would break my legs if I defected and went over to Lee, but I did go to observe, and in my opinion his work, hence his approach, seemed to be chiseled in stone. Sanford Meisner felt that art, any art, should be forever changing and growing and never boxed in. The creative process must be forever free, using whatever works for its creator.

THE GROUP THEATRE, INC.
presents
THE GROUP THEATRE ACTING COMPANY
in
"AWAKE AND SING!"
By CLIFFORD ODETS
"Awake and sing, ye that dwell in dust."—Isaiah 26:19
Production directed by HAROLD CLURMAN

While in the Group, Meisner was no joiner, though the Group had its little cliques that people identified with and gravitated toward. There was the college group from places like Smith, Cornell, and Princeton (the preppies of their day). There was the Jewish group led by Morris Carnovsky with Phoebe Brand and their crowd. The younger, inexperienced apprentices banded together, a bit starry-eyed I would think and just tickled to be there. Ruth Nelson eventually became the mother of the Group. Stella, now Harold Clurman's wife, and Harold, Lee, and Cheryl were a group unto themselves. Sandy said he belonged to none. He drifted, rather aloof, from one group to the next, playing the piano now and again or when requested.

Awake and Sing ran concurrently on Broadway with the double bill *Waiting for Lefty* and *Till the Day I Die*. *Lefty*, directed by Sandy, moved to Broadway with the companion-piece, which Cheryl directed, with still no Lee in the picture. He wouldn't even co-direct with her. Paul Morrison, technical helper, adviser, and apprentice since the second season at Dover Furnace, designed the sets. It opened at the Longacre Theatre on March 26, 1936, and ran till the end of the summer. *Till the Day I Die* was based on a letter from Germany and was one of the first anti-Nazi plays presented on the New York stage. It was respectfully received by the press and a popular success, becoming the talk of the town and running for five months. The double bill played all over the country simultaneously in many of the larger cities.

Paradise Lost
Sanford Meisner & Stella Adler

In the late summer of 1935, the Group took a brief hiatus. They opened on Broadway on September 9 at the Belasco with a double bill of *Awake and Sing*, directed by Clurman with Sandy playing Sam Feinschreiber, and *Waiting for Lefty*, staged by Meisner who also played the Henchman. They shortly took the shows on tour to Philadelphia, where they ran for five weeks. Harold noted at the time that Strasberg was no longer fighting for his opinion much.

Since the failure of *Gold Eagle Guy* the previous year, Strasberg had slipped into a state of depression. Sandy was directing *Waiting for Lefty* now, and when it came time for Nellise Child's *Weep for the Virgins* rehearsals, Lee refused to direct, so the job went to Cheryl Crawford who needed it personally after the *Big Night* catastrophe. Her confidence had not been altogether restored by her work on *Till the Day I Die*. *Weep for the Virgins* opened November 30, 1935 to gloomy results and it didn't last a month. The play about a depressed family in San Diego had very little going for it and probably never should have been acquired in the first place.

Harold Clurman next directed Odets' *Paradise Lost* at the Longacre, opening December 9, 1935, with Sandy portraying the ailing Julie opposite Stella Adler. The play, a hard-hitting, realistic drama was a departure from the more urbane style of the time and created a furor in theatrical circles. The press was generally disappointing and Clifton Fadiman wrote, "As it is practically impossible to make oneself heard amidst the hurly-burly of the Odets controversy, this department wishes merely to mutter doggedly that with all its faults, *Paradise Lost* is a pivotal American drama." Many people were devoted to the play without being explicit about their reasons why.

Strasberg was still in a funk, refusing to fight for a say in any proceeding, according to Harold, and this wasn't the usual Strasberg. Who knew why? Was it the loss of Maxwell Anderson's *Winterset*, which he had wanted to acquire for the Group—a loss for which he blamed Harold—or was it just Odets' ascendancy? Whatever it was, when Milton Shubert put up the cash for Erwin Piscator's *The Case of Clyde Griffiths*, Lee finally agreed to direct. But he seemed to go at it half-heartedly, Harold said. On March 13, 1936, the play opened at the Ethel Barrymore Theatre, with Sandy Meisner playing Wiggham. The reviews were ambiguous.

In April of 1936, Sandy went on the road playing the part he had created in *Awake and Sing*, Sam Feinschreiber, for the third time. The play toured to Baltimore and points west, to Chicago and Cleveland, to rave reviews from the heartland. In spite of the raves, it turned out not to be a lucrative venture and left Harold fatigued.

In need of a rest, Clurman took a six-month leave of absence and headed to Hollywood for the first time. While out there he spent time with members of his Group Theatre who had defected to Hollywood. With them, he experienced what it was like to live in the lap of luxury next to a pool under the luscious California sun, all paid for by the outrageous paychecks the defectors were getting. Still, Harold found himself encouraging those who would listen, like Franchot Tone, Joe Bromberg, and Clifford Odets to return to New York and the Group and, in Clifford's case, at least to consider continuing to write for the Group.

While in Hollywood, Harold realized that the Group was adrift primarily because the "Troika Leadership" of Lee, Cheryl, and himself was just too loose. He proposed a new plan whereby the benefits of a new Group democracy might be combined with a strong central leadership. He drafted this plan on his way back to New York, presented it to Crawford and Strasberg, and nominated himself managing director. Harold said they were altogether willing to adopt this arrangement now, but I am sure neither Cheryl nor Lee was any too happy about it.

The Group had already started on Paul Green's musical play Johnny Johnson two weeks before Clurman's return. He found his job as central head all too overwhelming so he relinquished the direction of the play, asking Lee Strasberg to take over. With too little time, the company was under-rehearsed, and the house was too big for such an intimate production. Their singing voices were weak in such a barn of a place, but the directing was weaker. Sandy, a non-singer, played Captain Valentine, who has a solo. When I told Sandy I couldn't imagine him delivering that song without the amplification we have today, he said neither could he; that was why every night he had asked Lehman Engel, the conductor, to cut his number, but he never would.

There were many outbursts and arguments. Dress rehearsals were costly and, with no money, the rehearsals were cut. The actors were lost and previews were disastrous. They were not ready for the opening on November 19, 1936. But opening night proved to be the greatest shock. The performance went smoothly and the audience was enthusiastic. It looked like a hit, but the press was bad. This unnerving experience led to serious unrest within the company mostly directed at Lee. The members wrote:

> There is no doubt that it was Lee who gave the first artistic shape to the Group Theatre. For example, the thing that most of the actors in the Group still call the Method is in reality Lee's own method of work—at least up till Gold Eagle Guy. In this respect, we believe that in actual influence exerted, Lee has been a great artistic force in the American theatre during the last five years. Six years ago with the inception of the Group, the revolutionary task was his to do. He had to break down the whole tradition in thirty different individuals and this really necessitated (as it tended to further harden and bring out) Lee's great courage, his doggedness, his arbitrariness, his need to be right, his cold scorn of artistic compromise, his clannishness, his removal from life, his historical force (used as a threat) and above all the brute domineering of his will [...]. Lee filled the need of that time [...]. But today the same qualities that once were necessary seem unhealthy. We believe that Lee under the new organization should be relieved for some time from all but purely artistic tasks [...]

All three leaders met and agreed to present their resignations to the company. It was now time for a break.

Sandy was teaching at the Neighborhood Playhouse and he just did his thing. Harold Clurman and Elia Kazan took off for Hollywood, and many of the Group followed. Harold made some connections and took on a few jobs of his own with generous remuneration. Walter Wanger put most of the Group under contract, but not Julius Garfinkle or Stella Adler. Going along with Hollywood practice, they changed their names to John Garfield and Stella Ardler and signed on to other studios. Garfield joined the cast of Arthur Kober's play, *Having Wonderful Time*, and was signed by Warner Brothers to do the film *Four Daughters* (1938). Stella signed on with Paramount and did a few B-movies.

Sandy teaching at Neighborhood Playhouse with assistant Charles Conrad

John Garfield had come to the Group in the mid-'30s, after some drama studies in New York and one bit part in Hollywood. As assistant director, Sandy would coach "Julie," as Sandy always referred to him, in *Golden Boy* that established him among the stars of Broadway. Sandy also worked with Julie on his technique before he left again for Hollywood and international recognition. Despite his success, Garfield would be unhappy in Hollywood. He was never satisfied with his work and what was demanded and expected of him there. Eventually, after being blacklisted for refusing to name names to the House Un-American Activities Committee (HUAC) in the early 1950s, he and his wife came back to New York, never to return to Hollywood. Unfortunately, Julie met an untimely death in 1952 due to heart failure. At the very moment of his demise, Sandy and his wife Betty were waiting for Garfield with Roberta, his wife, at their apartment on Gramercy Park East.

While so many of the Group were decamping to Hollywood in the mid- to late '30s, Sandy Meisner stayed contentedly in New York. He was teaching at the Neighborhood Playhouse, doing occasional radio gigs, and performing in a play here and there. He was cast as the neighbor to Gertrude Berg's Molly in the Goldberg's radio show.

Harold had left New York with instructions to the Group that they should continue with Cheryl and Lee without him. The folks in Hollywood felt the Group would continue one way or another. But Harold's participation was pivotal, and Harold himself knew they would not get together again. What happened in April 1937 should not have been a surprise. Cheryl sent a letter of resignation to Hollywood because she was not getting any collaboration from Harold. A resignation letter followed from Lee Strasberg stating his feeling that the Group had destroyed the leadership.

Plans in Hollywood didn't work out for various reasons for members of the Group, and they all started returning to New York, except Tone, Bromberg, and Stella Adler. On August 23, 1937, Harold returned and started working on Odets' *Golden Boy* with Sanford Meisner as assistant director and starring Luther Adler, John Garfield, Morris Carnovsky, and Frances Farmer, a "star" imported from Hollywood. It opened that fall at the Belasco to enthusiastic press and general admiration. *Golden Boy* was the greatest success in the Group's history, and Sanford Meisner, Stella Adler, Robert Lewis, and Elia Kazan were among the actors sent to England for the London production, produced by Kermit Bloomgarden. The theatre critic of the Times wrote, "The acting attains a level which is something we know nothing at all about."

Throughout the years many accusations had been lodged against Harold because of his partiality to the men of the Group. It seemed he spent more time with their development at the expense of the women's. If not, then why had he imported Frances Farmer all the way from Hollywood? This was a group and what of all the women already in it? If Frances was the best of all actresses for the part, was that not the "commercial theater's" way of doing it? Later in Hollywood, after *Golden Boy*, why was Harold wooing the Hollywood actress Eleanor Lynn for *Rocket to the Moon*? It was no secret that Clurman, and Odets for that matter, were womanizers. Why didn't the actresses in the Group protest and rebel?

Cheryl Crawford and Lee Strasberg, now on their own and no longer part of the Group, decided to produce under Lee's staging Hardie Albright's *All the Living* with Leif Erickson and Sanford Meisner, who portrayed Gilbert Kromer. It opened on March 24, 1938 at the Fulton Theatre running a mere fifty-three days to dull reviews. Despite all that had preceded, Lee and Cheryl cast Sandy. Lest we forget, Sandy never took sides. He once told me that he tried to remain true to his profession: he was an actor only looking for work, whatever it was, wherever it was.

Rocket to the Moon opened November 24, 1938 at the Belasco with Sandy playing Willy Wax. The show was not a success. Harold seemed desperate to do plays to keep the Group in operation, plays that Sandy had nothing to do with. Irwin Shaw's *The Gentle People* opened in '39 at the Belasco starring Hollywood's Franchot Tone and Sylvia Sydney with movie fans screaming in the street for autographs. Was this the Group's kind of theatre? The press didn't like the show and neither did the Group. Nevertheless, because of the stars, it had a fair run.

Still desperate, Harold mounted a revival of *Awake and Sing*, which brought Sandy back to the stage as Sam Feinschreiber. Joe Bromberg and Stella Adler came back from Hollywood in their old roles as well. It opened at the Windsor Theatre on March 7, 1939 to very good reviews. The next production was a stylized interpretation of William Saroyan's *My Heart's in the Highlands* directed by Robert Lewis. The audience didn't show up despite the excellent press

In the summer of '39, the Group gathered for their last summer at Winwood School at Lake Grove near Smithtown, Long Island, to lick their wounds and possibly regroup. In an attempt to save the Group that fall, Elia Kazan directed Robert Ardrey's *Thunder Rock*, to less than lukewarm notices. Despite cries of "Don't close it, don't close" from the audience closing night, it closed.

Clifford then came up with *Night Music* directed by Harold Clurman with Elia Kazan, Jane Wyatt, Morris Carnovsky, and Sanford Meisner as Gus-the-Hurrying-Salesman and Mr. Gilbert. It opened in Boston and played to a miserable box office. It then moved to the Broadhurst, opening on February 22, 1940, and was greeted very badly by the press. This was the de facto end for the Group, but Harold still fumbled on with one last feeble attempt, Irwin Shaw's *Retreat to Pleasure*. He directed it himself, and he himself said, "It was worse than bad." Stella's single comment: "Sad, isn't it?"

So although no official announcement was made, after ten momentous years, 1941 saw the final curtain fall for the Group with the closing of *Retreat to Pleasure*. Then Clifford came up with one last "unofficial" production of his own with Strasberg directing. It also bombed. Everyone went their separate ways. It was the end of a beloved theatrical institution, one that left its mark on American actors ever after...

Group Theater 1938, left to right, back row: Art Smith, Walter Fried, Sanford Meisner, Ruth Nelson, Lee J. Cobb, Leif Erickson, Roman Bohnen, Morris Carnovsky, Lee Strasberg Kermit Bloomgarden; middle row of three: Luther Adler, Phoebe Brand, Harold Clurman; front row: Irwin Shaw, Eleanor Lynn, Frances Farmer, Robert Lewis, Elia Kazan.

The Neighborhood Playhouse Years

Back in 1935, Clifford Odets was the man of the hour, with *Waiting for Lefty* being produced all over the world and everyone wanting him. Everyone included Mrs. Rita Wallach Morgenthau, who wanted him to teach at her school at the Neighborhood Playhouse. But with all the success and fame being bestowed on him, he wasn't interested. Instead, he suggested his friend Sanford Meisner for the job and the rest is history.

The Neighborhood Playhouse provided a place for Sandy to hone his craft unencumbered by the industry's crass commercialism. He was also for the most part unhampered by Mrs. Morgenthau, the director of the Playhouse. Both were headstrong and astute. He, ever conscious of his mission, knew what he had in the Neighborhood Playhouse, and she, in spite of her separate vision, saw the extraordinary talent in her acquisition. So over the years they agreed to disagree on some issues, as much as they could. Only on rare occasions did it become too much for both sides. One could say it developed into a love/hate relationship.

Sandy continued at the Group Theatre, playing on Broadway at night and teaching at the school by day. He even went off to London in the 1938 production of *Golden Boy* in which he played a feature role. In those years, his only true friends (besides Paul Morrison) were Clifford Odets and Stella Adler.

In the late 1930s, he started dating, and, in his mid-thirties, married out of the Group. Peggy Meyer was a young Irish woman from Buffalo who was playing on Broadway at the time. He could cope with this alignment, as he put it, until her jealousy, which was fierce and implacable, made things between them irreconcilable. As he began to be recognized and heralded with every new Odets play, Peggy's career was waning, and fighting and drinking became a serious problem.

Cast of Odet's *Golden Boy* aboard ship to London. Robert Lewis, Sanford Meisner, Stella Adler, Kermit Bloomgarden, Ellen Adler, Harold Clurman. Standing - Elia Kazan

One night Sandy was on his way home after an opening night party of an Odets play, an opening Peggy would not attend. After getting off the Seventh Avenue subway, the review with its glowing mention of his performance tucked under his arm, he was walking down West 55th Street when he spotted it. Halfway down the block, across the street from the City Center, his easy chair lay helter-skelter about the sidewalk, smashed to smithereens. After reading the review, Peggy had shoved his chair out the fifth floor window. Sandy realized it was time to part company.

When the Group closed in '41, Sandy continued teaching at the Playhouse and acting on Broadway. In *They Should Have Stood in Bed* in '42, Sandy played Sam Simpkins. He directed *I'll Take the High Road*, which opened on November 9, 1943, and in December he staged *Listen Professor*. Then he starred in *Embezzled Heaven* as Bichler opposite Ethel Barrymore, doyenne of America's outstanding theatrical family and one of America's reigning icons of stage and screen in the first half of the twentieth century. *Embezzled Heaven* opened on October 31, 1944, and ran through the winter of '45.

The Whole World Over with Sandy in the cast opened on May 27, 1947 for four months. Opening on December 22, 1947, Sandy played Simon Zaharitch

Marmeldoff opposite another icon, Lillian Gish, in the revival of *Crime and Punishment*. Gish, of the famous Gish sisters, Dorothy and Lillian, was recognized as "the first lady of the silent screen." Many still remember her as the archetypal young damsel in distress clinging to that ice floe rushing toward Niagara Falls in *Way Down East* (1920), executing the act herself in the days when no stunt-double relieved her of the danger. She had a long and illustrious career both before her appearance with Sandy and after, and her work, in *The Birth of a Nation* (1915) for instance, is still seen from time to time at silent film festivals.

Crime and Punishment
Lillian Gish & Sanford Meisner

The Actors Studio

After the demise of his Broadway production of Maxwell Anderson's *Truckline Cafe* in 1947, Elia Kazan started his Actors Studio with Cheryl Crawford and his friend Robert Lewis. Kazan invited Sandy to join them and asked for his help. Not only did Sandy join him, he also brought many of his most talented former graduates from the Neighborhood Playhouse. He taught at the Actors Studio with Bobby Lewis for almost two years while director Kazan was busy with the success of Tennessee Williams' *A Streetcar Named Desire*, and celebrating his new find Marlon Brando, a student from his first class. Bobby then took a job on Broadway and left Sandy alone at the Studio.

The work at the Studio then became too much for Sandy with his full-time commitment at the Playhouse. When he told Kazan he couldn't handle it alone, Gadge, as he was affectionately called, suggested Strasberg. So Sandy and his new wife at the time, Betty, went to Lee's apartment to ask if he would come and help. Lee hadn't taught in years but nevertheless accepted, saying, "Just remember, Sandy, who the teacher is."

Sandy, who had been teaching for the past fifteen years, was livid. He turned to his wife and said, "Come on, Betty, we're wasting our time here. Where's the lift?"

The last Sandy was ever to see of Strasberg was his head sticking out the door as he yelled, "In America we call it an elevator."

Sandy went back to Kazan and told him he could not work with the man. He was much too egomaniacal. But what else did Lee have to do? Sandy knew that Lee wasn't teaching or committed elsewhere. Better Kazan should hire Strasberg, reasoned Sandy, and let Sandy go back to the Neighborhood Playhouse where he belonged. He left his former students to work at the Studio in spite of Strasberg because by now Kazan, after his huge success on

Broadway, had many connections that could prove beneficial to them in their careers.

But Sandy lived to regret it. For him, Strasberg was not only wrong-headed in his approach to acting; he also turned out to be prone to seducing Meisner's own prize pupils to switch allegiances. It galled Sandy that Lee took and got so much credit for the achievements of so many of his own theatrical progeny. In later years, I heard Sandy addressing teachers at UCLA on the teaching of acting. He explained that the Meisner Technique and Strasberg's Method could not be blended; they negate one another. "They are like oil and water; they just don't mix," Sandy stressed. Over the years, many actors encountered and struggled with the antithetical nature of the two approaches, some knowingly, others unaware.

Barbara Baxley in the 1940s and June Carter Cash in the 1950s were two who recognized the conflict between the approaches. Barbara became a serious dissenter from Strasberg's Method. Sandy had brought her to the Actors Studio and consequently she had been there before Lee's arrival. She said she continued to work and act there in spite of Lee. She fought insistently over technique, forever saying, "But Sandy says..." Lee would tenaciously stand firm or more often simply clam up. Barbara's dissent was most vehement during the London production of Chekhov's *Three Sisters*. At one point she retreated to her hotel room and refused to go back to work until Lee left the rehearsal hall and ceased "mucking me up," as she put it.

When Lee was at the height of his popularity at the Actors Studio, Elia Kazan brought June Carter Cash to study with him. He had found this authentic talent in the hills of Tennessee and brought her to New York. But June couldn't for the life of her work under Lee and she told Kazan so. He said, "I'm sorry. I should have sent you to Sandy." He did, and till the day she died, June was grateful. She and her husband, country music legend Johnny Cash, became lifelong friends of Sandy. Johnny even generously offered to give a benefit concert for the Duke University Eye Center, a charity Sandy devoted much time and energy to in the 1980s.

A prime example in later years was the case of Kim Stanley, with all her God-given talent. Working with Lee's Method took its toll; she could well have done without Lee Strasberg's gobbledygook. Just as Stella Adler had once described Strasberg's Method: "He introverted the already introverted, which was a very dangerous practice."

Another interesting case to ponder is that of Marilyn Monroe. Sandy told me that playwright Arthur Miller, once married to Marilyn, felt that if she had only studied with Sandy instead of Lee, she would still have then been alive because Sandy would have set her head straight. As it was, it is questionable whether Strasberg gave or got more from his association with the famous and vulnerable Hollywood icon.

Strasberg was not averse to publicity; in fact, Kazan told us Strasberg had engaged a publicist who was with him for over thirty years. Sandy's reaction to that news was, "What does a teacher need a publicist for?"

As late as the 1960s, Strasberg was still wooing them in Hollywood. Somehow he coaxed three of Sandy's most high profile former students of the time—Lee Grant, Mark Rydell, and Sydney Pollack—to serve as board members and teachers at the Strasberg Institute. They may have agreed to disagree on almost everything, as Lee Grant described it. But who knew? Certainly not the prospective students of the Lee Strasberg Institute. From Sandy's point of view, it wasn't the Meisner Institute, so how did these defections look to him?

So the clash between Sandy's philosophy of teaching acting and Lee's approach lasted for decades, with its roots going back as early as the 1930s and '40s.

The Juggling Years

Sandy had met the woman who was to be his second wife, Betty Gooch, one day in 1948 as he was hurrying along Seventh Avenue to catch the 57th Street crosstown bus. She was with Martin Waldron, a recent graduate of the Neighborhood Playhouse. Martin had spent the past summer playing in a stock company at the Barter Theatre in Virginia, and Betty, a young southern belle from Memphis, Tennessee, was an apprentice there that year. Martin introduced them, but it was a short encounter as Sandy was in a rush. As soon as Sandy had boarded the bus, she turned to Martin and in her deepest, thickest accent said, "Ah'm goin' to marry tha-at ma-an."

Well, she was a fast worker. Soon after that first encounter, she had Martin arrange a second rendezvous at the Wellington Hotel where Sandy was living at the time. Martin remembers that in no time the two were wending their way across the country to Reno so Sandy could acquire a divorce from Peggy Meyer, immediately after which Betty and he were married with no fanfare, folderol, or waiting time, a common practice back then.

They then went on to Hollywood where a studio wanted to sign Sandy to a seven-year contract. Sandy believed they were searching for a Peter Lorre type. In the '40s, the studios built up their stables with types, one movie company matching the other. Sandy wanted no part of it. He had visions of playing Peter Lorre for the rest of his career. He could not think of a worse scenario. So back to New York they went, hunkering down in an apartment on East 14th Street at Peter Cooper Village next to their neighbors, former student Val Rothschild and her husband George, and Frances and Tony Randall.

Back at the Playhouse, with the novice students he preferred, Sandy felt he belonged, despite the differences in policy between him and Mrs. Morgenthau. She was a little old-fashioned and from the upper classes of the East Side. Her vision of the school consisted of a strict, authoritarian, no-nonsense, upper-class, private finishing school for girls that would provide them with art and culture. It was a vision unchanged from the founding principles of the school down on Grand Street in 1928.

Sandy's interest, on the other hand, was in the talent and ability of the students. He strove to give them what they needed in their careers. He felt what they principally needed was to be able to get in touch with their emotions and to be able to live truthfully under an imaginary circumstance. His dream was of a school where only the work mattered.

The love/hate relationship had festered between the two for years. The differing visions and values collided spectacularly in the case of Steve McQueen. In 1950 Mrs. Morgenthau threw McQueen out for obstreperous behavior, and Sandy insisted he be reinstated because of his talent.

On February 22, 1950, Sanford Meisner was back on Broadway playing Ferdy in *The Bird Cage*, directed by Harold Clurman. In 1955, Sandy directed Gloria Vanderbilt in *The Time of Your Life*, which opened on January 19 at the New York City Center. Sandy recalled a kind of charming vignette between two big stars. One day while he was working with Gloria at home in his apartment, the doorbell rang. Opening the door, Sandy saw Frank Sinatra standing there asking if he could come in to wait for Gloria.

Opening on December 8, 1958, Sandy played the role of Norbert Mandel in S. N. Behrman's *The Cold Wind and the Warm* at the Morosco. Of the play John Chapman wrote, "There is a broad vaudeville performance of Sanford Meisner, as a middle-aged peacock who wants to buy a wife." Walter Kerr concurred in the *New York Herald Tribune*, referring to "Sanford Meisner's well dressed frog of a neighbor, letting his riding-crop dangle from his wrist to make his rich-man's gestures more imposing."

After twenty-two years of many successful students and more or less pleasantly putting up with one another, in 1958 Mrs. Morgenthau and Sandy decided to call it quits. Sandy accepted a position with 20th Century-Fox. It was an offer he felt he couldn't, or at least shouldn't, refuse.

The late '50s were taking a toll on his marriage as well. He and Betty had been trying to have a baby, with no success. Sandy remembered the day she walked in clutching a big hatbox from Mr. John's of East 57th Street. She opened the box, clapped the hat on her head, and asked, "What do y'all think? Y'all like it?"

Sandy replied, "Betty, you know very well we can't afford that on my salary."

Her retort "Well, if Ah can't have a baby, Ah sure as hell am entitled to a hat ba Mr. John," made it obvious that she held their inability to conceive against him. It is probable he was the one who was infertile. It bothered him immensely, and he was devastated by it, whether true or not.

Sanford Meisner
The Cold Wind and the Warm

1 Himself

The Hollywood Interval

The move to Hollywood wasn't a wise one for Sandy. He had been offered three movies to direct, but the deal turned out to be extremely disillusioning. The three movies never materialized. All were dropped because of the dire financial straits 20th Century-Fox found itself in after the disaster of Elizabeth Taylor and Richard Burton's *Cleopatra* (1963). So Sandy missed out on his directing dream. Couple that with the starlets he was hired to teach, many of whom were manipulable naïfs who cut classes on the advice of their agents and managers ostensibly because Sandy was spoiling their image. God forbid they should learn how to act! Hearing this nonsense, Sandy became disillusioned with the whole project.

On top of the disappointments of work, out there in Hollywood his personal life went from bad to worse. Betty started acting up. It had something to do with Patricia Neal, and whatever they did with whomever, I have no idea. Sandy would never discuss their antics, but it was so bad he immediately sent Betty packing. Back in New York, she promptly took up with a man named Kaufman and became pregnant. Sandy would have been ecstatic if the baby had been his, but alas it was Kaufman's and Sandy demanded a divorce. I remember Sandy had pictures of the child all over his apartment. She resembled Sandy to the extent I thought she might be his. When I asked Paul Morrison about the possibility, he said, "Not on your life. All you would have to do is get a gander at Kaufman and you would see why you would think that. The resemblance between him and Sandy is uncanny—they could pass for twins." Paul assured me, "No, the baby was not Sandy's."

There is a God, however, because the personal and professional debacle expedited his return to New York, where he resumed teaching actors.

One good thing about Meisner's sojourn in Hollywood was the fantastic paycheck he got there. The 20th Century-Fox contract was in another stratosphere. But even though his New York salary was oceans apart, money alone couldn't keep him in California. Another positive thing was that he got to act in two marvelous movies while there. In 1959, he appeared playing the prosecuting attorney in *The Story on Page One* with Rita Hayworth, Gig Young, Mildred Dunnock, and Anthony Franciosa, written and directed by Clifford Odets. The press said, "This by no stretch of the imagination could be called a think-film yet Mr. Meisner's performance strikes me as a very interesting job indeed, and his sharp, savage strokes almost manage to pull the film out of its doldrums." In 1961, he played an Austrian psychiatrist in *Tender Is the Night*, with Jennifer Jones. A few years later in 1970, Sandy again acted for the screen, playing the Jewish mob don of Philadelphia in *Mikey and Nicky*, with John Cassavetes and Peter Falk, directed by Elaine May. It wasn't released until 1976 and became a bit of a cult film. So his sojourn in Hollywood wasn't a total loss. If he had stayed, he almost certainly would have been asked to do many more. Who knows? As it was, when his three-year contract was up for renewal, he returned to New York.

Back Where He Belonged

Sanford Meisner felt at home back on the east coast. He was a New Yorker in every sense of the word. He had been born and bred in New York. He saw the first light of day across the East River in Green Point. There he could view the expanse of Manhattan all the way down to Kips Bay where it jutted out into the East River just below Bellevue Hospital. Further off in the distance were the skyscrapers around Wall Street. He could look almost across to 44th Street where the United Nations complex now stands and over to Sutton Place and the East Side which would one day be his stamping grounds.

Farther up past the 59th Street Bridge and out of sight to the northwest was the East Bronx where he played as a child. His family of four soon moved up to the Southeast Bronx on Hunts Point Avenue. It was a mixed immigrant neighborhood of Jews and Irish. The gang of kids hung out beyond Lafayette Avenue and Edgewater Road along the banks of the Bronx River where Sandy became very adept at skipping flat stones across the water's surface. On summer days there were trips to the sound at the end of Hunts Point Avenue and across East Bay Avenue to the water.

One afternoon he hiked across the Bronx with his Irish buddies to a church where, just inside the door, they all splashed water in their faces, so he did too. Then they all tramped up the center aisle en masse where each of them bent down on one knee, and he did too. They all very slowly and solemnly approached a glass-covered coffin in which lay a lady all decked out in black with a funny-looking bonnet on her head. After much gawking and whispering, all the boys slowly filed back up the aisle clutching their caps in their hands, until they got outside.

Once out in front of Mother Cabrini's, the boys started jumping about and laughing as they needled Sandy, telling him he was now a "Cat-lick." Sandy bolted all the way across the Bronx to Hunts Point and home where he hid in the closet sobbing his heart out. Bertha, his mother, couldn't get him out until his father, Herman, got home from his little furrier factory downtown in the Seventh Avenue district and coaxed him out.

When he was still very young, his mother used to take him downtown to the Yiddish Theatre on

*Sandy, Herman, Bertha Meisner
Ruth in perambulator*

1 Himself

the Lower East Side to see the Adler family and also over to Walter Damrosch's School for his piano lessons. He attended PS 75 where Miss Pierson was his teacher in IB. He sat directly in back of Arthur Meckenberg, who, in turn, was seated behind Seymour Lazarus. Miss Pierson liked her pupils to sit and be questioned in alphabetical order. Young Sanford found the long dull wait before she reached the M's very annoying.

The time came when she asked her students what they wanted to be when they grew up. The responses had been mostly conventional—doctors, nurses, lawyers, a dentist. Arthur Meckenberg said he wanted to be a scientist. Sanford's turn was next. "An actor," he said proudly. "Why?" Miss Pierson demanded disapprovingly, and Sanford tearfully replied, "Because 'actor' begins with A and A's are always first." Throughout his life he swore that this incident planted the seed. When I recalled that his uncle had been a rather well known actor on foreign stages, he denied the influence. He told me his father had never liked his uncle's acting. Sandy said, "My dad used to say no matter what the role was, my uncle played it so it turned out to be a Cardinal. That frightened me."

I once told a friend of mine who played the piano that I was going to study with Sanford Meisner. She told me that she had lived next door to him on Hunts Point. She remembered him as a quiet chap, a little stand-offish, a bit of a loner. He was always sitting on the stoop, his nose in a book with two more at his side and one eye on the boys playing stickball in the street. He was frail and slight and to her he seemed somewhat troubled even then.

His favorite pastime was going across town on Saturdays with his friends to the Yankee games at the Stadium. He was a Yankee fan all his life. He had a happy childhood, happier than he would lead you to believe, but nevertheless he wasn't spared that demon of demons—Jewish guilt.

When he was no more than five years old, lying in bed one night in his room off the kitchen, he heard his mother weeping and wailing. Through her sobs he heard her cry out to his dad, "Herman, if it wasn't for Sanford, Jacob would still be alive today. If we hadn't spent the summer in the Catskills, his little brother would still be here." Because of Sandy's frailty and ill health, the family had gone to the Catskills so he could benefit from the fresh country air. There, his brother Jacob, who was no more than three at the time, came down with an infection from drinking raw milk, which was the practice in rural America at the time, and he died. If Jacob had been back in the Bronx, he would have been drinking pasteurized milk.

Herman Meisner

Burtha Meisner

In telling this key event, I had trouble remembering

Jacob's name because even more than fifty years later Sandy could never bring himself to speak of him. Sandy carried his brother's death as a burden for the rest of his life, among other burdens I might add.

Later, during the family summers on the beach at Far Rockaway, Sandy used to hide in the bushes in the evenings and scare the daylights out of his sister Ruth as she passed by. Ruth felt the sun rose and set on her older brother. For the rest of their lives, she thought the world of him. His brother Robert was a late-in-life baby born 16 years after Ruth. Sandy left for Manhattan when Bobby was just a baby.

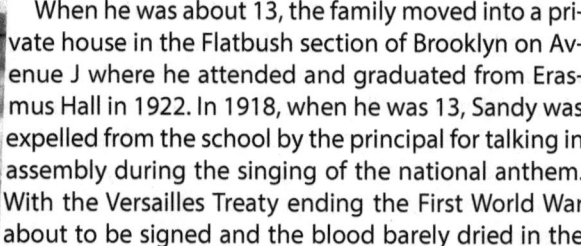
Nat & Ruth Meisner Post

When he was about 13, the family moved into a private house in the Flatbush section of Brooklyn on Avenue J where he attended and graduated from Erasmus Hall in 1922. In 1918, when he was 13, Sandy was expelled from the school by the principal for talking in assembly during the singing of the national anthem. With the Versailles Treaty ending the First World War about to be signed and the blood barely dried in the fields of France, this irreverence was considered un-American. But soon, the principal had to eat crow and not only ask him back to school but also designate him the equivalent of the class of 1918's valedictorian! As Sandy put it, "I found great pleasure in watching that principal suffer through my valedictory speech on The Privilege and the Responsibilities of Being an American."

After high school, Sandy had no interest in continuing his studies at college or university, much to his father's disappointment. He spent two years at the Damrosch Institute where he started to knock about with Spivy, a heavy-set girl with a heart of gold. On the weekends, they would shoot across to Manhattan on the subway and head up to Harlem to all the hot jazz hangouts and smoke weed. Madame Spivy became a character actor on Broadway and eventually established herself as a restaurateur in a penthouse on 57th Street attracting all the young gay blades of the forties. Sandy saw little of her then, perhaps because he was living the straight life at that time. After two years at Damrosch, where he had studied piano for years, he dropped out, and his mother's dream of having a son who was a musician was dashed.

But all this time, Sandy had been studying theatre on his own, devouring everything about it he could get his hands on. It was an interest that he'd had since childhood when he used to direct his cousins in plays and little skits whenever they got together. They would present them in the back yard or sometimes in the living room of his uncle's home in Washington Heights where the double doors of the dining room would conveniently slide open to begin the performance for the family assembled in the living room.

So when his friend, Monkey Tobias, rescued him from his uncle's lace factory and sent him uptown to audition for the Theatre Guild in 1924, Sandy's raison d'etre began to crystallize.

2 Love Enters

Jimmy Carville 1962 at AMDA

Back to School

When Sanford Meisner returned to New York from Hollywood in January of 1962 to start teaching classes at the American Musical and Dramatic Academy on East 23rd Street, he was back in his element, doing what he loved to do best. Here I came into the presence of the "Master" through the generosity of Broadway Music Incorporated, which awarded me a scholarship to study with him. Getting to work with Sandy was just a fluke. But then how many milestones in life are triggered by pure luck? Speaking for myself, my life has been full of chance events.

There I was on a cold January morning in 1962, standing on the corner of 2nd Avenue and 23rd Street waiting for the cross-town bus, when a gust of wind swept along 23rd Street. It was a cold, damp wind bringing with it sheets of driving rain, the kind of wind that cuts right through to the bone. I was making my way to the Actor's Equity office up in the theatre district just off Broadway on 48th Street to check out the audition schedule for the week. I had just finished a workout on the arias from Mozart's *The Abduction* from the Seraglio with Frank Fulton, my accompanist, on East 19th Street.

When the harsh wind swept along 23rd, there was absolutely nowhere to run for cover— except the door of the building on the corner, which I knew had been unoccupied for a long time. But I was desperate. I ran to the door and tried it anyway. To my surprise, it was unlocked. I scurried inside for shelter. I immediately realized that some company was in the process of moving in.

The building on the northwest corner of 2nd Avenue and 23rd Street was old building, constructed before the Civil War. During that war it had served as an army hospital and now, I thought, who was in here was anybody's guess. I looked up at the newly painted white walls of this small vestibule I stood in, which led up four steps to a larger common entrance hall. Hanging there on the walls were many colorful blown-up posters of musicals of the fifties. I must say this piqued my interest. What was this place and who was moving in? Was it some big theatrical agency? No, no chance of that, not in this part of town.

I turned to open the door a crack to see if a bus was coming. I could see across the avenue to the other side of the stoplight, but there was no bus yet. Then I heard a voice coming from the larger hall. I turned around, looked up. At the top of the stairs stood a tall, thin, dark and handsome man in his early forties, the assistant to founder Noel Ben, as it turned out.

He asked again, "What time is your audition?"

I told him, "I have no audition. I just took the liberty of stepping in out of the driving rain." It was now a downpour and I wasn't about to go anywhere until it let up. "I'm waiting for a crosstown. What is this place?"

"It's a musical-dramatic school."

"A what?" I stammered. I had never heard the phrase before.

"You could say it's a school that concentrates on the 'triple threat,'" he answered, laughing.

"Oh, singing, dancing, and acting, like Vaudeville," I offered.

"You said it." He went on, "You sing and dance? We teach you to act. You act and sing? We teach you to dance—."

"OK, OK, I get it," I said, stopping him. What was this spiel he was handing me?

He went on with his pitch. "New York's first-rate teachers are going to be here. Sanford Meisner is coming from LA, and plenty more."

"Who's he?" I asked.

"Well, I guess you're not an actor, or you would know—"

I interrupted him, "No, I'm not. I'm a singer."

"Why don't you look at our brochure?" he suggested.

"No, no, I'm already working in musicals, thank you. That is, I've done a few since 1955, but I'm not in one just now. You could say I'm between jobs. Ho-ho. In fact, I'm on my way up to Equity to check on the auditions for the coming week." For some reason I was babbling on.

Now he went on, "If you're out of work and your time is your own and you want to learn to act, what better way to spend your free time than working with the best there is, like Meisner?"

"No matter." I said, "I haven't got a dime to spare. You see, I'm on unemployment insurance."

"Too bad. As I said, we're going to have some terrific teachers. Do you know Philip Burton? Lehman Engel?"

"Lehman Engel," I thought, "from West Side Story! He did wind up conducting it."

The name took me back to 1956. My fisherman's story about the one that got away unreeled in my mind. I was just starting out and, with some kind of beginner's luck, I was at Cheryl Crawford's office. I didn't even know who she was. She was producing *West Side Story* at the time, before the Kermit Bloomgarden Office took it over. She was looking for a Tony with a high C and two of us were there that day. He looked like me only he had blond hair, and I looked like him only I was a brunette. He was a Jim, and so was I.

They were all there, Sondheim, Lawrence, Robbins, and Bernstein, and I didn't know one of them. I was absolutely dead in the water, and the other Jimmy was in the same boat. The part was really written for a top tenor. I was later told they wrote the high note out of the show. Maybe they did, maybe they didn't, who would know? Anyway they gave the part to Larry Kurt, Sondheim's friend. He lived in Sondheim's house over in the East Forties or Fifties, that much I knew. You go figure.

Still reflecting, I thought, that's the stuff long careers are made of—a lead in a hit show in your twenties. I really came close that time. One needs that reassurance once in awhile. As time passed, both the other Jim and I sang the show under Lehman's baton, but that doesn't make a career. No, working for minimum, being paid less than the stagehands and electricians, is a job, not a career. Never mind that we both could have done the high note that Bernstein wanted. That was the way of the business, I learned early in the game.

I was standing gazing at the posters on the wall when I realized that it had stopped raining. I was turning around and about to leave when the guy at the top of the stairs said, "You say you're a singer and you've already worked

Meisner in '62 at AMDA

in musicals? You're just what we're looking for. We hope to start a permanent off-Broadway musical company in the near future. Why don't I introduce you to my boss and see if we can waive the audition fee? What have you got to lose?" I thought, Lehman Engel, that's what I have to lose, indeed. At least, I thought, I'll get to sing for him again. So I said to myself, To hell with Equity today. It will be there tomorrow, and up the stairs I went to the boss.

The rest is history, at least my history. I didn't know it, but at that moment my life did an abrupt 180-degree turn. In the office I met Noel Ben, the president and founder, who did waive the audition fee. And within the week I sang for Lehman Engel, danced for Honya Holm of *My Fair Lady*, and had an interview with the "Master," Sanford Meisner.

At the meeting with Meisner, I almost blew it. Up until then, all I had ever done to get a job was to sing my best eight bars and either I got the job or I didn't. As a dyslexic, I found reading for a part at an audition frightening. I knew reading was paramount in acquiring a role, but it was my Achilles' heel. So when Mr. Meisner asked me why I was willing to come back to school after working in the industry for seven years, I didn't have enough sense simply to say I wanted to learn how to act.

That would have been a good answer, but not me, oh no, not me. All I wanted was to be able to get a job. What did I care about acting? I didn't give a fig about studying acting. I wanted to learn how to do cold readings, though I didn't even know that's what actors called it. So I said, "I have to work on my sight reading."

To a trained musician like Meisner, this meant reading music on sight. So he must have thought it made sense for a singer like me, and what better place to perfect it? If I had had an actor's savvy, I would have told him I wanted to brush up on my cold reading technique so I could get jobs. In Sandy's mind, those words were death. To him, that's exactly what they were: cold! All they showed was that the actor could read and if he could indicate that would be good, too. If you happened to be looking for a good reader, cold reading would be a good way to find one. If there's one thing you don't go to Meisner for, it's cold readings.

Thank God for small favors. Not knowing what his attitude toward cold readings was and not knowing the right term for them saved me. Sandy completely misunderstood me. And so I met the "Master" who changed my life.

On my way out of the audition, I passed Mr. Ben's assistant who asked, "How did it go?"

"Ok, I guess, but I still don't have a dime to pay for any of the training." Chalk it up to experience as I headed down the stairs, I thought. At least I got to sing for Lehman. There would be another time, I was sure of that. Within two weeks, Noel Ben called to say, "I'm setting up a dinner date for you and another prospective student to meet Erwin Y. Harburg, commonly known as Yip. He's the president of BMI, and they're giving a full scholarship to the school." I thought, Fine, two students and one scholarship. With my luck, where is that going to leave me?

When I got to the restaurant on the corner of 23rd and 3rd, in walked a tall, slender young woman with flaming red hair flying all over the place. She looked like a young Ann Margaret. So before the dinner even started, I knew where that left me. I'd be doing the dishes. I don't know what ever happened to "Ms. Margaret," but as it turned out I wasn't left doing the dishes. BMI's President, Yip Harburg, eventually presented the scholarship to me with Noel Ben's approval. Harburg had an impressive background. Among other things, he had penned the lyrics of the Depression-era anthem "Brother, Can You Spare a Dime?" and won an Academy Award© for Best Music, Original Song for "Over the Rainbow" from *The Wizard of Oz* (1939).

John O'Shaughnessy, the Broadway director whom I worked for in *Cut of the Axe* starring Thomas Mitchell, had directed for Sandy at the Neighborhood Playhouse. When he heard I was going to study with Meisner, he said, "Jimmy, he's either going to kill you or cure you." I remember thinking, "Now what in hell does he mean by a statement like that?"

My first day in Mr. Meisner's class I thought was going to be my last day in his class. To begin with I was petrified, so intimidated by the Master and the other actors I could barely breathe. I sat in the last seat in the farthest row from Mr. Meisner: I couldn't get any farther away without leaving the room. I felt like a fish out of water. This class had nothing to do with music and there was no song for me to hide behind. You stood out there in front of the class feeling as naked as the day you were born with the man studying you like a hawk, ready to pounce.

Yet he didn't. As couple after couple got up to perform the basic repetition exercise, he seemed to treat them gently. I didn't really want to be called upon, and I wasn't, at least not until everyone else had been up there. Then I was next with the only other untried student as my partner. We did what I thought everyone else did: repeat the initial words back and forth until we were finished. Then Meisner got up and descended on us hammer and tongs, tearing our little exercise to shreds. It seemed everything we had done was wrong, except breathe. I don't remember ever being raked across the coals like that in a class. Yet I felt that what my partner and I had done was not that different from what the other twosomes had done.

All I could think was, my God, was I that bad?

As we were the last couple, the class was over, and I couldn't wait to get out of there. I told my partner I wasn't going back into that class again.

"Who needs that shit? Not me."

She told Sandy's assistant, Ed Moore, who came over to me and asked, "What's the problem?"

I told Ed we hadn't done anything different from anyone else, so why, I wanted to know, was Meisner raking me over the coals?

"But he wasn't," Ed stated.

"Oh, yes he was," I insisted. "And I don't need that crap."

"Jimmy," he said, "that's your name, right? He was just teaching the exercise by explaining what everyone was doing wrong, not just you. It wasn't personal. He was just using your work to explain the correct way to do the exercise. You were no worse than anyone else. Listen, don't quit, promise me you won't. This is a chance in a lifetime for you."

As I walked away, I wasn't convinced. "I don't know. I don't think so."

"Think it over, Jimmy, give it some thought," I heard him say as I turned and headed downstairs to my next class.

He caught me leaving the building at the end of the day and stopped me, asking, "Will I be seeing you on Monday?" I just shrugged.

Over the weekend, I was troubled as to what to do. I had never come across a man as keen as Meisner, and if Ed was telling me the truth, it was worth another try. I also knew it was Meisner's class or nothing, and I could kiss Lehman Engel's class good-bye, too.

When Ed saw me on Monday morning, he said, "Good, you're here."

I told him, "If I'm going into that class again, it's with the attitude that I know absolutely nothing about this stuff. I don't care what anybody else does; I'm going in there like a bright-eyed schoolboy back in kindergarten, questioning nothing. I'll be leaving myself wide open as a receptacle for whatever he can dish out. If he tells me to crap, even if I don't have to, I squat and grunt. Whatever he tells me to do, I will do or give it my damnedest." Ed said, "Jimmy, you do that and I can guarantee it will work for you. You will never be sorry."

All I can say after the fact is—I did, and it did, and I wasn't.

I was fortunate to have cottoned onto Meisner's manner of teaching, and my encounter with Ed encouraged me to give it a second thought. My approach to class was what Mr. Meisner was looking for in every student. He didn't care about nor was he interested in the personal baggage you brought with you to class. He wanted you to leave it at the door and start fresh as a newborn baby. You could leave your thinking there at the door too, for Meisner was clear: acting was not about thinking; it was about feeling.

One also had to be willing to give over to him 100%; there was no half measure with Meisner. It was imperative to give up every notion one had about acting and be willing to start over again at the beginning. Such surrender was hard on the ego and almost impossible for the self-centered. But when you gave over to him and trusted him, then voilà, progress. It worked.

To begin with, Mr. Meisner gave us all the same simple exercises. They only became difficult to execute if you complicated them. All you had to do was what he asked you to do, and not a hair's breadth more. Everyone did the same exercise working with, or rather working off, a partner. We advanced along in class en masse from exercise to exercise, not progressing until most were ready to move on. Then the group effort ended.

When it came to critique, Meisner handled each and every one of us individually. What was good for one actor to work on might be bad for another. It was as if we had our very own private tutor. He could be tender, patient, and

Jimmy Carville and Sally Shiffer singing "Big D" from *Most Happy Fellow* - AMDA's first commencement show

understanding when called for. But he was stern and he could be harsh. He suffered no nonsense when it came to slackers and know-it-alls.

That first year we were into the third month of class, building on the repeat exercise with an independent activity and the three knocks. My partner was to be doing an independent activity while I was to be outside at the door delivering the three knocks. Gail was to open the door and react to and work off the last knock. I instinctively wanted to be emotionally alive when she opened the door but I didn't know how to go about achieving it. Mr. Meisner hadn't worked on that with us yet. So I gave myself an imaginary situation: I was being chased by cops after doing a drug deal. I would toss the dope in a trashcan and run into my building but, not wanting to go to my own apartment, I would head to my neighbor's and wait there till I was in the clear.

Not knowing how to get in touch with my emotions, I decided to run downstairs to the first floor, head out of the building, and tear up 2nd Avenue to 24th Street and back again into the school and up the stairs to the classroom. There, out of breath and sweating like hell, I knocked on the "neighbor's" door three different ways. The last set of knocks was desperate and urgent. She opened the door, took one look at me gasping for breath with my clothes all disheveled, turned around, and went back to her easy chair.

"Come in. Do you want a cup of coffee?" she asked.

"A cup of coffee?" I repeated incredulously.

And I heard Meisner yell, "Stop! What is this, Gail? What are you doing?"

"I'm watching TV," she replied.

"Where's the TV?" he roared.

"Over on that dresser," she answered, a little defiantly.

Meisner turned to the class and asked, "Do any of you see a TV over there? Because I sure don't." Then he added, "Look at him, Gail. What do you see?"

She was silent.

"Sit down, Gail," he told her. Looking over at me he added, "and you, too." After a rather long and uncomfortable pause he said, "Well, I guess it's time for preparation."

And he segued into the Charles Laughton story. The story may or may not be apocryphal, but Meisner always used it as an example of how an actor conjures up emotion. It seems Laughton was playing a lowly bank clerk who finds out he has won a great deal of money. He is required to feel alive and on top of the world. Instead of daydreaming about the money, Laughton fantasized that a handsome young man was all his very own. The point is that the imagining can be anything that gets to you, turns you on, or jiggles your juices and consequently brings you alive emotionally. These fantasies or daydreams are yours alone, never to be shared. You never reveal them to anyone.

I was aware that what I had done was for the birds. For whatever reason, Mr. Meisner now felt it was time to move us to the next level, preparation. I was ready and beginning to feel more at ease in his classroom.

I attended school living off my unemployment check, and took in a roommate to helpdefray expenses and share my bed—I only had one. I was also working in shows during the summer. I did Ed Peterson in Judy Abbot's production of Harold Prince's *Fiorello!* The next winter I played Pat-the-Irish-Cop and the Fireman in *Wonderful Town* at City Center with Kaye Ballard, with Lehman Engel conducting. With Lehman again that summer, I sang the second tenor role in *Brigadoon* in Washington with Sally Ann Howes. I asked myself at the time, "Why didn't I know him seven years ago?"

More Than Friends

In the telling of how the relationship between Sandy and me unfolded, Paul Morrison's story is an important subplot. Shortly after meeting Sandy, I became aware that Paul had been carrying a torch for Sandy for as long as he had known him, years before Sandy ever married. For Paul it started the very first day they met at the Theatre Guild in 1927. Paul's college days at Bard were full of trips to New York to attend plays. I believe that when Paul spotted Sandy in a Theatre Guild production, his interest was piqued, long before he ever moved to New York.

I would say that the greater part of Paul's life was patterned around Sandy, from the Theatre Guild, to the Group Theatre, through the Bob Hope USO shows of World War II and Robert Whitehead's productions, right on through the days of the Neighborhood Playhouse. Of course, Paul had friends and people who periodically entered his life, spent time, and eventually left, as people have a way of doing throughout one's life. Lenny Bernstein numbered in the mix.

Paul was a very attractive young man and Sandy always seemed to be at the center of Paul's life, like an older brother. From the time he met me, I had the feeling Paul thought of me as nothing more than an interfering interloper, just short of an opportunist, who would eventually fade away. Sandy was well aware of Paul's attitude toward me, though he never made it an issue by verbalizing it. He just carried on as if there were no problem at all.

Paul Morrison

It wasn't until Paul died at the age of 74, and Sandy, as the administrator of his estate, had me go through Paul's papers, that I gleaned the magnitude of the problem that my presence in Sandy's life had been for him. Paul was a prolific writer of letters and kept all the ones he received, and there were many. I saw then how threatened Paul had been and just how aware Sandy was of Paul's feelings. I saw the lengths Sandy went to, to keep all this from me, because, I must assume, Paul's affections were not reciprocated by Sandy.

Another plot thread in Sandy's life at this time was his ex-wife Betty. By the early 1960s, when I came on the scene, Betty was living with Kaufman over at the London Terrace on West 23rd Street. I can remember while I was studying at AMDA on East 23rd Street, Betty would barge into the middle of class at any time, disrupting the proceedings, with the little one in tow. With the child in a stroller, it was just a quick jaunt across 23rd Street to 2nd Avenue, any time she felt like it. She would sit in the front row next to Sandy, with him making a fuss over the baby. One could see he was infatuated with the little girl. Not another person on earth would or could pull this stunt off except Betty and then only because of the little tyke. I am sure Betty was well aware of it.

By 1963, I was a graduate student of Sanford Meisner's program at the American Musical and Dramatic Academy of New York and had been invited to the Neighborhood Playhouse to attend an advanced third-year study of the classics under Meisner. For Meisner, the classics included Henrik Ibsen, George Bernard Shaw, Anton Pavlovich Chekhov, and Sean O'Casey.

Shakespeare, however, wasn't his cup of tea. He thought that playing Shakespeare demanded more from the actor than just realistic acting. And although Meisner felt Shakespearean style wasn't beyond us, he also believed that, even though we Americans spoke the same language, the style was foreign to us and created a different set of problems. He wasn't about to waste his time with it; he had other fish to fry.

His mission was to teach truthful, realistic acting. He wanted actors to get at truthful human emotions based on the moment and not on words systematically arranged and delivered in measured rhythm in verse. He held that Americans shouldn't touch Shakespeare unless they were ready to take the time and trouble. By that he meant a good deal of time and trouble, at least five years, to get a handle on it. Iambic pentameter renditions were, he felt, better left to the English; they were good at it because they were immersed in it from kindergarten. Oh! When done correctly, it is very beautiful, like opera.

The classes were to be held at the Neighborhood Playhouse on East 54th Street. Sandy had taught these advanced work classes twice before. The first time was in the late '40s with actors such as Eli Wallach, Jo Van Fleet, Tony Randall, Barbara Baxley, James Broderick, Marian Seldes, Montgomery Clift, and Richard Boone. The first group was held at Elia Kazan's Actors Studio with Robert Lewis and Sandy teaching before the days of Lee Strasberg.

Sandy held an advanced class again in 1956 and 1957, this time to work on the classics. Martin Waldron had introduced Sandy to Richard Burton's foster father, Philip Burton, formerly of the BBC in London, as well as to the renowned voice coach Henry Jacoby. They all three embarked on a new third-year program of the classics. This time on the scene, besides Martin Waldron, were notables such as Sydney Pollack, Mark Rydell, Joanne Woodward, Marian Winters, Jack Lord, Elizabeth Wilson, and Peter Falk, among others.

In 1963, he did it for the last time with Lainie Kazan, Louise Lasser, Marge Champion, Shari Lewis, Jon Voight, Bill Alderson, and Eva Gabor. I was in this class and remember working on Nikolai Gogol's The Inspector General with the actor who was playing one of the female roles in Superman on Broadway at the time. While I was in this program, Sandy asked me to accompany him to Monday night philharmonic concerts at Lincoln Center. He held two season's tickets and had lost his concert companion for the rest of the season.

These outings were extremely enjoyable for me, a former music student, and I was spending an evening with the man I held in such high esteem and admired most in the world, bar none. I'd had a secret crush on him ever since my early days at AMDA. A couple of times over the years other students had teased that Sandy liked me, but I had never really thought anything about it. It was an unrequited love that I never expected to be returned.

One evening, while we were talking during intermission, he asked me if I would be interested in finding a brownstone he could afford and do the fixing up for him. He felt it would be a good investment for him at the time. He said he couldn't pay me much, but whatever he could manage should be of

2 Love Enters

some assistance to me just now. I was strapped for cash and he knew it. Aren't most unemployed actors, most of the time? (Or should that read aren't most actors unemployed most of the time?)

What he didn't know was that for him I would have done it gratis. Sandy had been to my apartment in 1963 where we held a graduation party and he had asked me who had renovated and decorated my coldwater flat. I had done it of course, who else? I had also helped quite a few of my less fortunate friends who were strapped for cash. I enjoy doing it on the cheap. I remembered Sandy had seemed quite impressed at the time. Suffice it to say I took on the job.

This project marked the beginning of a long and close friendship that was to last a lifetime. Well, the rest of Sandy's at least.

At 207 East 83rd Street I found a five-story brick brownstone built in 1866 that had seen better days. Sandy would occupy the first three floors and the upper two would become an apartment he could rent out. I set out to restore it to its earlier grandeur. We gutted the place down to the brick walls on either side, put in a couple of steel girders for support, laid new flooring, and rearranged the rooms to suit Sandy's needs.

I decorated it in the style of the mid-Victorian period from whence it came. When everything was finished, my brother Ed and his brother-in-law, Nick Fuchs, came down from Utica to paint the place from top to bottom. It was quite a change from the former rundown rooming-house condition it had been in when Sandy purchased it. We put in three modern kitchens, three baths, two powder rooms, seven period working fireplaces, and four period crystal chandeliers. Iris Whitney, the actress-decorator, helped me with the period pieces. We also added a second-floor terrace off Sandy's bedroom, which I designed and my brother Leo built. We landscaped the backyard garden as well.

If I do say so myself, the effort was well worth it. It really suited Sandy's elegant taste. It was like walking back into the 1860s.

When we started on the project, Sandy temporarily moved into a two-bedroom apartment on Park Avenue and I moved in to save expenses. That was when we became intimate. I was sure Sandy was bisexual, and we did start an affair. Then I found out that he was going to his old psychiatrist whom he had spent eight years working with earlier in his life. When I asked why, he told me sex with me seemed to bring out a darker side of him, of which he was afraid.

Sandy had a darker element in his psyche that festered for years and he couldn't come to grips with it. He saw it as a problem and was willing to go to a psychiatrist to work it out. I felt our bond certainly didn't need this. In truth, it freaked me out a bit. I didn't trust psychiatrists and was afraid of them and of psychiatry, so I turned away from the problem. Was I wrong? I probably was. I hoped our love and respect for one another would prevail over his problem. He wanted me to understand that his difficulty was no reflection on me or of how he felt toward me. It was a serious problem he had within himself. I told him whatever the problem, I didn't need or want anyone going to a psychiatrist in order to have sex with me.

I told him it didn't change my feelings for him, I still loved and admired him, but Sandy expressed concern about our relationship lasting without sex. He couldn't bear living alone and he was certain I would just take off sooner or later, leaving him a lonely old man. I insisted he needn't do anything but be himself, that he was the man I loved just as he was. I knew even then we were soul mates, and I also knew he still had to be convinced.

He wasn't getting any younger nor was I, and I was damn well aware that I was ready to settle down. I hadn't been sitting around playing tiddly-winks with manhole covers. I had sowed my wild oats already, and was looking forward to a quiet uncomplicated life as much as Sandy was. Time was the only thing that would prove it to him, and in time, it did.

The problem Sandy was manifesting all started in his early teens with his unwillingness to accept himself. He wanted no part of his homosexual urges even though one of his earliest recollections was of a brief encounter with an older man who worked in the office building on 5th Avenue and 23rd Street across from the Flatiron Building, just up the street from his Uncle Dave's lace factory on 17th Street.

In high school, he was not attracted to girls. He busied himself with friends like Aaron Copland and with piano practice, developing a fondness and proficiency for German Lieder. Whenever the storm windows needed changing, he was always at the piano. His father Herman wasn't any too happy. A job at the furrier's would have made him a lot happier.

Eventually Sandy's total interest was directed to the theater, any- and everything about it. He was a ravenous, insatiable reader and just devoured material about theater. To him, it was a respectable subject and more deserving of his efforts and interests than the deep-seated drives of his psyche. Perhaps it was an escape.

The Harlem School of the Arts

Though the house renovation was completed, we wouldn't get the building occupancy certificate for six months. So in the summer of 1965, Sandy took me on a trip to Portugal and Spain as a celebration. We sailed from Lisbon back to New York on the final voyage of the *Mauritania*.

On our return, we both moved in downstairs and rented the apartment upstairs. Sandy went back to work at the Playhouse, and I went to work auditioning for jobs. At this time Sandy was asked if he would set up an acting department at a school up in Harlem. He offered me the job of Director of the Department, promising me he would procure teachers for me. I accepted and he made good his promise.

It had all started not entirely auspiciously one Sunday evening. The concert singer, Dorothy Mainer, and her husband, a reverend at the St. James Church on St. Nicolas Avenue in Harlem, were coming to dinner. The guests hadn't arrived yet as I went into the kitchen for a final check. I couldn't believe the sight I was beholding! Nora, our German shepherd pup, had eaten most of our meal. And what she hadn't touched was pushed off onto the floor, plate and all. The countertop was clean but the floor was a mess of broken plate, wine, and bits of steak.

RMS MAURETANIA NEW YORK — LISBON, 1965

What to cook now? The only thing in the freezer was the meat I got from the butcher for the dog. Sorry, Nora, you moved in on us, now we're going to move in on you! I ran out to the delicatessen, the only store open on a Sunday evening back then, bought some sour cream, and rushed back to the house. When Nora's meat was ready (I used my fast-thaw method), I chopped it up quite small, slapped everything together, and made Sandy's mother's Sekateen Goulash. Little did I know at the time that Ms. Mainer had attended the Cordon Bleu School in Paris with Julia Child and that they were still the best of friends. If I had known, Sandy would have been taking us out to dinner that night.

So up I went to Harlem with my band of teachers, with the best of good intentions and Sandy's blessing. It all went like clockwork until Los Angeles and Detroit started burning and the riots finally came to Harlem. The Department had been moving along splendidly until then. We were working on a demonstration for the parents. Barbara Ann Teer, one of my teachers, was working on a piece for the teenagers called *Lenox Avenue Sunday*. The action of the piece took place in the middle of Harlem as the title indicates, and the actors recited modern poetry readings as well, written by a young black poet who was a friend of Barbara's. As I see it now, it could be considered the forerunner of our modern-day rap. It was really a substantial piece and very well executed.

At the same time the students were studying Greek theatre in their theatre history class. I thought for contrast they could do a Vachel Lindsay poem entitled "The Congo" and perform it in the Greek theatre tradition. They had made papier-mâché Greek hairpieces and long gray robes as in a Greek chorus that made them look like Greek statues. They all seemed to be enjoying the preparations immensely. Then, all of a sudden it seemed, Black was Beautiful. Whites and white culture became anathema; the term honky came into wider use. The first thing I noticed was the hairpieces were discarded. When I asked why, the students said something to the effect that they shouldn't cover up their blackness. So I said fine, so be it. When they showed up for dress rehearsal with their Greek robes ripped into rags, I couldn't believe what I was looking at. So much for Greek theatre! I found that they hadn't come up with this idea all on their own. A teacher at the school had instigated it and encouraged them. I was positive I knew who the culprit was— Barbara. Only months before she had asked me to see if Sandy would work privately with her on an English Restoration comedy piece she was planning to audition at Lincoln Center. Yet, at the same time that she was preparing her own piece, to our students she was disparaging anything that wasn't Black-oriented.

One day I heard a teacher singling out Jewish landlords as part of the present problems, and this during class time. My biggest shock was to find out that even the better-educated parents—doctors, lawyers, and teachers—were telling their children not to bother with "white man's" speech and his theater, that they didn't need it. I washed my hands of the whole production right then and there, and I started to pull out the whole department.

At the same time, I was hearing "No, no, don't go. We're just doing our own thing." What they were really saying was, "Stay and keep the money coming in." Some people at Newsweek had a two-million-dollar proposal with ideas for a new building and everything that goes with it. It was all very tempting and inviting. Yet I just could not or would not have any part of this real estate venture, with the students being encouraged to keep their ghetto speech and not wanting to hear anything about Shaw, Ibsen, and Greek theatre or to work on their craft.

Our aim was to apply Sandy's work, the Meisner Technique, and be true to the work. We were not willing to lower Sandy's standards. From a personal point of view, I knew these were my productive years. I wasn't going to sit around wasting those years on anyone not ready to buckle down seriously so they could learn and better themselves. Nor was it fair to expect anyone else to waste those years sitting around making like we were teaching. They didn't need good serious people for that; anyone could goldbrick the scene that way. In short I felt we would be wasting time and money. Waste is waste no matter where it is. The only conclusion I could come to was—another time, another place.

So I told Sandy in 1967 I was leaving. He said, "If you go, I go, so go ahead and pull out the whole damned Department." I spoke to the teachers in the Department and they all agreed except two. I told the two that they were welcome to stay and the rest of us made plans to leave. Dorothy Mainer wanted us to stay and weather it out. Her heart was in the right place, but unfortunately it wasn't a time for Ibsen, Chekhov, or Shaw. Either we were ten years too early or ten years too late. All I knew was I felt rejected and out of place and that they neither needed nor wanted what our Department could give them. So we folded our tents and slipped out. I couldn't then have seen the episode as a harbinger of what lay ahead for me a world away.

Darkening Times

During this time at the house on 83rd Street, we held a lovely birthday party for Sandy's mother. It was the first really big party we ever held at the place. All her relatives and friends in the greater metropolitan area were there. The house looked beautiful. I went down to the flower mart on 6th Avenue and came back with enough large white chrysanthemums, red roses, potted palms, and ferns to fill the house.

We had lots of parties in those years. There were the backyard parties Sandy held every spring for his professional students. Very often there were sit-down dinner parties held for Sandy's theatre friends in the grand room with the fireplaces at either end. Many of his friends had been anxious to see the results of the renovation. Dinner parties were exchanged back and forth with Sandy's friends, people like the producer Bob Whitehead and his wife Zoe Caldwell, Paul Morrison of the Playhouse, Kate Reid, Uta Hagen and Herbert Berghof, Bob Fosse and Gwen Verdon, Maureen Stapleton, Carol Saroyan and Walter Matthau, Eli Wallach and Annie Jackson, Phillip Burton, Elizabeth Wilson, Lehman Engel, Rosemary Edelman, Marion Winters and husband Jay Smolin, David Craig and Nancy Walker, and Kathleen Nolan.

Still, these days Sandy was becoming disturbed, short-tempered and upset, but mostly with himself. His students' behavior bothered him. The seeming instant fame and overnight success of TV and movie actors was getting to them. So many of them were only interested in stardom, expecting it to happen yesterday. He wasn't accustomed to the attitude. In a conversation about the problem, Stella Adler said, "Sandy, I don't see why you let it upset you so. I know when they come to me, most are only doing it to be able to put 'Stella Adler' on their resumes, and I couldn't care less—because I get my money first."

That wasn't Sandy's nature. He was never that way nor could he ever be. It hurt him that many of his most talented students would never get a fair chance at the craft they lived and would even die for because of their sizes and shapes, i.e. their looks. It was all about being the right type or already having a "name," any kind of name even a football hero, a daredevil, or a financier. That's what Hollywood was all about. They had a name for it— typecasting. And acting had little or nothing to do with it. TV was no different, just faster, demanding on-the-spot acting, with no time for artistic development.

Instant acting was not the kind of acting Sandy Meisner was about. When Sandy was asked by Vivian Matalon, the actor-director, why he, who was such a good actor, became a teacher, Sandy explained, "If it wasn't for the Group Theatre I would never have developed into an actor. I would have ended up back at my uncle's lace factory down on 17th Street. The mainstream theater back then had absolutely no use for a little Jew from Brooklyn."

Now things are somewhat different—there's Woody Allen after all. Some stars can act, but the truth is, it's not a prerequisite; even Woody is a writer. No, you don't have to be an actor to be a movie star. Sandy wished "movieactor" were all one word and that people used it more and left the word "actor" for the theater, such as it is. He would tell his students no matter what becomes of our theater, never forget what it could be, and perhaps one day...

Then came Vietnam, Nixon, student unrest, flower people, dope addicts, Black riots. The Blacks were in upheaval, the feminists were in upheaval, and so were the gays. The Stonewall Riot in the Village hadn't happened yet but the instances that triggered it had been festering for years. Closer to home there were bureaucrats, break-ins, fire inspectors, and police intrusions ignored by their departments. These hassles worked against the New York landowner, a group of which Sandy was now a member.

A-Hunting We Will Go

One day in 1966, while I was still teaching up in Harlem, out of a clear blue sky Sandy asked me to go to Puerto Rico. The previous summer he had spent a month there with Michael Locascio, a former student and director. Sandy was working on an acting book. While there, he had met a German fellow who planned to open a hotel and wanted Sandy to join him in the venture. Sandy liked the idea and wanted to see what I thought.

To be honest I couldn't have cared less about the project and Puerto Rico, but when he told me Bob Raison, the Hollywood agent, was coming down to spend a week, it changed the whole picture for me. "Sure, I'll go," I said, thinking, I get to meet Raison!

The German seemed OK and the hotel idea wasn't bad, but it wasn't for me. Neither was Puerto Rico, and I said so. Bob Raison was another story. I spent the whole week he was there trying to impress him. Yet the notion that I was an actor and a former student of Sandy's never came up. Nor did Sandy himself ever broach the subject. I was introduced as the director of his theater school in Harlem, and that was it.

All Raison wanted to talk to Sandy about was this young actor, Jon Voight, who had been a student of Sandy's. He wanted to know what Sandy thought of his talent and what his chances of getting Jonny as a client were. I was so envious I really wanted to puke. All I heard all week was Jon Voight this, Jon Voight that. As luck would have it, the end of the week was New Year's Eve, and plans were afoot to have dinner at the Condado Beach Hotel and catch the show. Being "Meisner" and a "Hollywood agent" got us a ringside table. The headliners were "The Hits of Broadway."

As dinner progressed, there was more of "Jonny." This guy was persistent and I could tell Sandy was getting bored. I had not met a Hollywood agent before, much less seen one operate. He wasn't going to let the investment of this trip go for naught. Even though Raison was absorbed in his quest for Jon, he was still an agent and was keeping an eye on the show as well. The restaurant was filled to capacity.

As the show progressed he couldn't help but notice that the players in the show were directing the whole show toward me. He finally let up on Sandy about Jon and turned to me to say, "Hey, wait a minute, you know these people, don't you?" I thought to myself, "You bet I do. Yeah! at last! I'm here and I'm human. Now is the time to make a pitch." I simply said, "Yes, I do. I was in the original cast, and that guy in the white tennis outfit was my understudy. They didn't know I was coming tonight; in fact, I didn't know for sure it was the same show. They've been touring the gambling casinos for over five years."

I then turned to Sandy. "That was before I studied with you."

Raison butted in and asked, "Sandy, you mean he's an actor? He studied with you?"

"Yep." That's all Sandy said.

Raison turned to me and stared. I could see he was looking at me with his beady little eyes for the first time. He seemed at a loss for words.

Sandy then said, "And a damn good one, too. He can sing and dance as well, as you can see from the show."

Raison just shook his head, looking over at the performers once again and then at Sandy. At this time, I was thinking to myself, "WELL?"

Raison then looked me straight in the eye and said, "Aren't you lucky you don't have to do this shit anymore."

Racing through my mind went, "You snake-eyed, mean-spirited, flesh-peddler of an agent."

I never spoke to him again that night, right up until he left. I don't believe he even noticed. If he did, he never knew or cared why. To me the only saving grace in this whole matter was he never did get Jon as a client.

We weren't home long before Sandy asked if I would take my vacation with him in August to St. Thomas. My answer to that was, "On my salary?"

"No," he said, "on mine."

"Sure, why not?" I said. "Why the island of St. Thomas?"

"I seriously want to price land there. My friends David and Nancy have a place there, and David said he would be there and would help us look."

August came, both schools were closed, and off we went. We were going to be at Morning Star Beach Hotel for a month. It didn't take us long to see that St. Thomas's prices were already off the grid. The place was out of the question for Sandy's pocketbook. We went over to St. John and St. Barts and found nothing affordable there either. We went back to St. Thomas and a little cottage for two on the beach.

Once at a party at David's, an overbearing woman tried to impress Sandy, a very hard thing to do. She was carrying on about what Sandy thought was some "nobody" dancer and he heard the name "Imakitchen." Sandy said half-heartedly, "Oh, yes, yes, I remember him, 'I'm a Kitchen.'"

Whereupon she abruptly stood up and put her hands akimbo on her hips. She was so upset, she sputtered, "Well, I'm he!" and she bolted into another room. Later, Nancy Walker told Sandy gleefully that the woman had been Iva Kitchell, the dancer.

"So who is she?" he asked.

"Nobody," said Nancy, "except Iva."

Sandy said, "You know, Jimmy, it's hard to listen when you're bored. I really shouldn't go to parties anymore."

While we were at our Morning Star cottage, so close to the beach the sand came right up to the door, we heard hurricane warnings. The storm was headed straight for our island! We went to the manager who told us not to worry and put us on the upper floor of some two-story units farther back from the water but still down on the beach. As late afternoon came upon us and evening began to approach, so did the winds and the sea. The ocean was raging. We had no flashlight, we had no radio with us, and there was no radio or telephone in the room.

"Now, you go to the office and tell the manager that we insist on being moved to higher ground," Sandy urged.

Off I went as dusk descended, amid the roar of wind and the sea, only to return almost immediately to the room and Sandy. Rushing in out of pelting rain, soaked to the skin and breathless, I announced, "Sandy, the place is deserted, not a soul here! Everything is locked up and boarded and barricaded." We were the only two in the hotel in the first place. "What should we do? What can we do?"

I was amazed at Sandy's cool. He said, "They must know more than we do and feel we're OK right where we are. So let's just hunker down, read, and go to sleep. At least we still have electricity."

Reading helped keep the storm off our minds, and eventually we read ourselves to sleep. I woke suddenly to a mighty crash, like a tree cracking, or a boulder smashing, or something smacking up against the building in the wind—and the lights were still on! We had fallen asleep with them on and now they were still lit up. To me that was a good sign. Sandy hadn't heard it, since he was still sleeping. I went back to sleep.

We woke up in the morning to a beautiful sunrise. The afternoon before, the storm had been raging head-on for southeastern St. Thomas, placing us in its direct path, but late that afternoon it veered north, heading right into Drake's Passage, north of St. Thomas. Were we an oversight by the staff in all the confusion? I tried to find out the next day, but to no avail. We had spent that storm right at sea level, and the sea came right up to the building we were in. With a slight turn in the storm, it could have been curtains for us.

Back in New York, the idea of a place in the Caribbean was becoming an obsession with Sandy. He was relentless. Now he wanted me to go on my own and look for him. I wanted no part of that.

"Count me out," I said. "I can't keep up with you. First the house on 83rd Street—it's not even cold yet. Now you want me to go to the West Indies and search for a place to design and build you a house for your retirement. Retirement! West Indies! Caribbean! Are you crazy?" He wouldn't let up, and I ranted on. "Oh, I see! You're getting older and ready to throw in the sponge. Well, this is just fine. I'm glad you know what you want to do, but what about me? I see, I just pack and get out and get on with my life, is that it?" I went on with my tirade, as I have a way of doing.

Sandy's answer was calm and peaceable: "No way, Jimmy, no way. I love you and you know that. No, no, no. I've given it a lot of thought."

"Have you thought about my career?" I snapped.

Looking me straight in the eye, he said, "Jimmy, you're thirty-nine, almost forty. What career? Jimmy, do you remember back in class when you were complaining about Jon Voight and I told you to never mind him, that he wasn't your problem? I told you he was going to be a star. You, in this commercial typecasting business, weren't going to get to work until you were fifty. You asked me why, and I told you."

"Yeah, you sure did. I'll never forget it. It hurt like hell."

"I said that you had a leading man's head on a character body," said Sandy. "Somebody had to tell you, and I cared enough to. Besides, sooner or later, you would have had to accept it. That's why I gave you that job up there in Harlem, aside from the fact that I knew you could do it. Trust me. Just think it over, give it some time. I know you'll see the sense in all of this."

In a way, I knew he was right, but it had still hurt like hell. I remember I couldn't breathe. But everything has a way of fading and that moment did as well. So I did take some time and I did think it over, a lot.

I began to realize that ever since we had moved to 83rd Street, any free time Sandy got from the Playhouse we'd made tracks for the Caribbean. The first stop had been Puerto Rico, the next, St. Thomas, St. John, St. Martin, St. Barts, and Saba. Sandy had been to many of the larger islands to the south in earlier times with both Peggy and Betty. This notion of the Caribbean had been percolating in Sandy's head for a long time. A little more time and a little more thought, and I was coming around. Maybe Sandy was right. Maybe, I thought... but there were no maybes about it. Sandy was usually right, and why should it be any different this time?

Soon, I was off to St. Martin. It wasn't easy to get government clearances to buy land on this island without having plenty of bread or crossing somebody's palm. Sandy's advice: "Forget it."

On the next trip, I went to some islands an Englishman on St. Martin had told me about. He was a world-traveling salesman who sold watches and jewelry to all the backwaters of the world. "The place is called the Bay Islands about thirty miles off the coast of Honduras," he said. "It's suspended in time, and I'm sure you'll both fall in love with it, as I did."

Before I left for Roatán, the largest of the Bay Islands, in early summer, Sandy said, "You go, spend three months if you have to. Take all the time you need to find out all you can about this place."

So I did, and reconnoitered like I have never reconnoitered before. I felt like Jungle Jim. The people spoke English. Roatán was given to Honduras in a treaty with England in the 1860s. The island was twenty-eight miles long and three miles wide with a reef that ran the length of the island along the north shore and entombed thirty-some sunken galleons. I couldn't believe it. I found myself digging up Mayan ruins with a tablespoon. The place was unspoiled, un-traveled and off the beaten path. It was a lovely island although difficult to get to from America. After three months, I found that land was available, cheap and easy to buy. I discovered some on the west end of the island, and I had Sandy come to look at it. He loved it.

Now we had to get government permission to buy. When we took off on a trip to the capital, Tegucigalpa, on the mainland, Sandy asked, "How far do you have to go 'to-goose-a-galpa'?"

I laughed and answered, "How the hell would I know?"

Tegucigalpa was an old, untouched, Spanish colonial settlement from the 1700s way up in the mountains in the middle of coffee and banana plantations. The trip there and back is a story in itself. We got permission to buy in a day from the government and went back to finish the deal with the owner.

About 6 PM the evening we got back, Sandy went for a long walk along the beach in his bathing suit. Shortly after he got back, we had dinner and then sat on the veranda overlooking the ocean. The house was a one-room bamboo structure with palm fronds from the coconut tree for roofing. We were given plastic sheeting to pull up over us in bed when it rained, which it did, pat-pat-pat, as we were going to sleep.

Forget it! Sandy hadn't been settled in more than an hour or so when he began to itch. It became unbearable. He woke me up, and I could see, as dim as it was in the hurricane lamplight, that he was covered in huge welts. I had nothing to help him. All I could do was rub sand, and ice from the kerosene fridge on the welts to soothe him.

In the morning the fisherman's wife explained that sand fleas had attacked Sandy. The locals were mostly immune to them and didn't spend time on the beach in the evenings or when the tide changed from low water to the high water marks. But there had been cases where foreigners were severely affected and had to get back to civilization and into a hospital.

"They must be the type one encounters on the unspoiled beaches of the Yucatán in Mexico," I said nervously.

Whereupon Sandy snapped, "Never mind on the beaches of Mexico. Right here the goddamn critters have been all over me, and what the hell are we going to do about it? It's driving me wild. What can we do?" he pleaded with me plaintively. He also saw the implications. "Great, if we have guests they would have to stay for two years to become immune before they could go near the water. The place is out of this world, and maybe that's where it belongs. Let's get the hell out of here, and I mean right now."

We took off the next morning in a South American dugout, the kind you find on the rivers in Brazil, just a big log with the insides chiseled out. Then we were out in the open ocean, luggage and all, the fisherman in the back with a little side motor and Sandy sitting behind me. I sat in front to break the onslaught of oversized swells and block the water from Sandy as best I could. He kept rubbing the back of his hand up and down my back. It was only adding to my nervousness and irritating the hell out of me.

Finally, I yelled sharply, "What the hell are you doing?"

"I'm just keeping my watch dry," he snapped back.

By noon we were on another perilous trip, bouncing up and down, gripping our seats as we took off on a rickety Tan Airlines plane across a bumpy grass field. We were, at last, on our way back to San Pedro Sula on the mainland. There we boarded a larger plane to Miami via San Salvador. The following day we were winging it home, thankfully on our way back to New York and medication. When we got back to the city, I said I was finished with the whole idea. Sandy agreed, for a while.

Then one morning over breakfast he said, "I was reading the *Saturday Review* last night and came across a short article about this little island." When he said short he meant short. The article was no more than an inch-and-a-half by three at the most. "I would like to go there, to Bequia, over Christmas, just to have a look. Whaddya say?"

I was resistant at first, but there was something about the name "Bequia" that struck a familiar chord, and it kept bugging me over the weekend. I knew deep down that I knew this place, but how? The faraway geographical placename kept running through my head. Then—light bulb—that's it, *geographical*, the *National Geographic*.

I started poring through the back issues that Sandy kept. It was the summer of 1968, and I went through copy after copy from '68 back to '65, and then there it was: an article on Bequia by Tom Johnston. I remembered when I'd first read about Bequia, I thought it sounded and looked like paradise. But I thought that even if it were, it was miles away at the other end of the world. If I ever got there, I'd have to die there, because how would I ever get back? I had turned the page and forgotten about it. Now, here it was back in my life. Somebody was trying to tell me something!

3 Myself

Jimmy Carville

The Magic of the West Indies

"Look! Here it comes. Don't take your eyes off it! The flash happens just after the sun disappears into the sea," she said. She was standing in her overworn, under-washed, postage-stamp bikini, one arm and one leg wrapped around the rigging. She was the distaff side of a pair of hippies, England's answer to one of James A. Michener's drifters, gone adrift in the West Indies.

Bruce, the other side, was a little more appealing. He was muttering about the tide being with us, the wind being at our back, and the possibility of cutting our time by twenty minutes. Bruce had introduced his lady fair and himself in a thick English accent. Her name was easy; it was either "On" or "Ann." But his was tougher. It was Loose, Moose, Spruce, or Goose. I had settled for Bruce. You try saying these five names with six marbles in your mouth and you'll get the idea.

Sandy, my former teacher and boss, my mentor, life partner, and friend, was sitting in the cockpit of the boat fidgeting, a cigarette hanging from his mouth. He was fumbling about his person looking for his lighter, no easy feat under the circumstances. I wondered how he had got the cigarette out of its pack and into his mouth in the first place. I was busy staring at a big red ball called the setting sun, waiting for the green flash as advertised by "Ann." I had looked for it many times before to no avail, although I had been blessed for my efforts with several breathtakingly beautiful sunsets. I was perched on the edge of the seat in the cockpit next to the door to the cabin. Thus situated, I kept myself quite stable.

Sandy was not so fortunate. With every lurch of the boat, I could see him sliding back and forth on the vinyl-covered cushion. As he fumbled for his Dunhill lighter, he was also occupied with the business of keeping his Burberry coat from falling onto the wet deck of the cockpit. He had it rolled up ball on the seat next to him. He was miserable not only because of his present situation but also because of the bad flu bug he'd been fighting for the past week. His throat was raw and sore. He was having his annual bout with laryngitis, probably caused by a cold on top of the smoking and abusing his vocal cords in class with too much talking. Overexertion left him short of breath due to a heart condition that he was being treated for, and added to those problems he had a minor case of emphysema. We were both hoping a few days in the tropics would help.

I busied myself putting Sandy's coat in the cabin, where it would keep dry, and I had him slide over into my seat next to the door where he could brace himself. I then sat on the starboard side where the seat was about six inches from the wash coming in over the gunwale. My ass was beginning to get soaked, and Sandy's cigarette was taking on the look of a soggy mush. It wouldn't light even if had did find his lighter.

In the middle of all this, Ms. Great Britain let out a shriek. "That's it! Did you see? Did you see it, Bruce?" Bruce let out a grunt, busy fiddling with his various knobs and snatching glances at the sea up front. She then turned to us and, in her broadest Oxford English, said, "Mista Carroll, did you evha see such a lovely flash?"

I said, "No, I didn't see the 'lovaly' flash."

"Pity, pity."

"Ah... I... ah excuse me, but do you think Sandy could have a drink? Ah... before it gets too dark?" I stammered.

"Oh, sorry, sorry, of course, but of course." She then scurried down into the galley. The sound of a refrigerator door, ice clinking in a plastic glass, and then a pause. Her head appeared at the cabin door. "Scotch or gin?" she yelled up at us.

"Do you have vodka?" I asked.

"No plum out. How about a beer... lime squash?" she asked.

"One gin and lime and a lime squash, please," I answered.

Bruce chimed in, "I'll 'ave a beer, luv."

With that done we settled back and tried to get comfortable. I don't think another word was spoken until we reached Bequia. Sandy was savoring the cool drink as it soothed his sore throat. If it had been laced with a double shot of vodka, it would have been even better. Only God knew what was occupying his mind, probably fatigue. We had been up since five that morning.

Up at the crack of dawn, out in the street with snow and slush underfoot, we had hailed a cab. The taxi ride from Manhattan to Kennedy Airport, the luggage, the ticketing, and the flight to find out seats had all been too much. The plane, of course, was overbooked, as it always is on December 15. Our flight was more than an hour and a half late getting off the ground. Our connecting flight in Barbados a on LIAT was scheduled to depart for St. Vincent just a half hour after the intended arrival. We had known we would be cutting it close. Would Pan Am radio on ahead to LIAT? You worry to get on, worry to get off, and worry to make the change.

When we landed in Barbados, the LIAT people were holding the plane and waiting to escort us directly from one plane to the other. We only hoped our luggage wouldn't end up in Trinidad. "Not to worry," they told us. Not to worry? We wouldn't know if we should worry until we reached Arnos Vale Airport in St. Vincent.

We could face one more little tribulation. The sun sets early in the West Indies and very fast at that. Arnos Vale at that time had no runway light for night landings. If it should happen to cloud over before we approached St. Vincent and it got dark, the plane would have to about-face and high-tail it right back to Barbados. Because of our late take-off, we could be back at square one, having to go through Customs, luggage and all, and make a cab trip to a hotel for the night. Then we would have to be up at first rooster crow, if we could get to sleep at all with all the barking dogs, and be on a flight at 6:15 AM or "thereabout." Who needed this?

Well, the clouds were kind and we were able to land. As luck would have it, probably beginners' luck, the baggage arrived with us. Just part of the magic of the West Indies.

The pier in St. Vincent where we had boarded the yacht was only a fifteen-minute ride from Arnos Vale. The sun was low in the western sky and partly hidden behind clouds, turning them into great globs of pale cotton candy. The far side of the clouds, the side of the setting sun, looked like a soft pink-on-blue baby's blanket. It was shedding a rosy glow over everything in sight, Sandy and me included. The eastern side toward us was getting darker by the minute, changing from white to dirty-dull whit to a pallid gray, the clouds strung like a strand of so many black pearls on a necklace that would have sparked the envy of Mikimoto himself. The spectrum was awesome. It recalled to my mind a little jewelry shop at the Imperial Hotel across the street from Hibiya Park in Tokyo, Japan, where once many years ago I had seen displayed in a low glass-incase many strands of pearls running the gamut of color from pure white through pink to luscious, soft bluish-grays. Behind us, Kingstown was all awash in a bath of dusty rose that completely transformed the rusty galvanized roofs of the old, broken-down cobblestone buildings and the drab, paintless wooden shanty shakes, their pilings like so many outstretched claws clutching precariously to the steep, rocky hillside. It was right out of a child's dream. Standing there engulfed in all this beauty, I let myself bask in the evanescent beauty of nature.

Now, as we pushed through the salty brine, I left Sandy to his innermost self or his stupor, whichever it was. My brain began swimming with thoughts that floated back and forth through time. We had been darting around the Caribbean for three years seriously looking for a spot where the weather suited our clothes and the climate matched our dispositions. The reasons we each had for looking for a place in the sun were as different as day and night, as we ourselves were. True, many of our tastes were similar. We had studied at the same music school, Sandy, the piano and I, voice. Modestly, one could say were both into drama, and both of us were of the same political persuasion, etc. I don't mean to be Pollyanna, or give the impression that we were completely compatible like peas in a pod, because we weren't. One doesn't have to look further than our accomplishments and our basic human drives. My sexual orientation toward my own sex was the same and had never wavered for as long as I can remember, as early as my preschool days. It was a huge part of my identity, and my early mission in life had been to learn to accept who and what I was and to be proud of how God made me, even if no one else was. I felt this way regardless of anyone else at an early age. My family taught me how to live with myself as I was, mostly by not interfering. I feel they left the rest to God and for that I thank God and am eternally grateful. Still, out of this laissez-faire upbringing grew an insatiable need to be accepted. My thoughts turned to my past and my family and the big move to Shaw Street when I was a child and about the different paths that had brought Sandy and me to the point of embarking on what would no doubt be a life-changing move for both of us.

Recollections: My Story

I remember the first big move for the family that made a real difference in our lives—the move into our house, in a nice neighborhood of Utica. We now had a garage and a huge backyard. The property abutted Lincoln Playground, a five-level stretch uphill. At the base of the hill on Lincoln Avenue were a football field and a baseball diamond. Up five cement steps were five clay tennis courts, and on the next level off to one side along Watson Place were two paddle tennis courts. The fourth level held two volleyball nets. On the top level stood the field house. This level was the kiddy's area with many strapped-in safety swings, a merry-go-round, and a big tall shooter-chute that would be outlawed today for safety reasons. But they were magical to a seven-year-old, as were the trick bars that overlooked all four levels to the west and the magnificent sunsets all summer long. Many a night we sat up there absorbing this loveliness, and in the early fall we were blessed with the colorful spectacle of the aurora borealis. In the center of all this stood a mammoth covered sandbox that had been there for years. I know because in the field house was a big banner that Lincoln Playground had won in 1912. Little did I know on my first visit that I would be spending most of the long hot days of summer up on that hill. All in all, the move to 906 Shaw Street made for happy times.

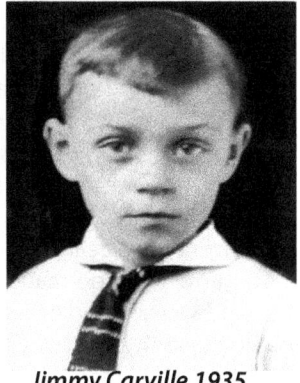

Jimmy Carville 1935

And Before

Things hadn't always been so rosy for my Mom and Dad. This move was scarcely their first. They had had their lean years coming to America in 1922. Dad came with his younger sister Josephine to their Uncle Joe in Utica, New York, while Mom braved the trip alone as an indentured servant to work for the Proctors of Utica. Neither had much education. England, as Ireland's supposed protector, wasn't too keen on supplying it. Mom finished her schooling at fourteen but her mom, Mariah, sent her back. What was she going to do with a fourteen-year-old around the house? Her teacher put her to work teaching math. Even with her limited education, years later when Tom and Joan were studying trigonometry and calculus in high school, she was able to help them with their homework.

Dad's case was totally different. His home in Monaghan was on the border of Armagh, a strongly Protestant county, and the teacher was Protestant. Dad, being Catholic, was dumped in the last seat of the last row. To his dying day he insisted he hadn't been able to see the blackboard because he needed glasses and had ended up flunking in every subject because of it. His father, Ned, brought in a tutor for all his children, but Dad ignored the schooling, left it to his sisters, and spent his time in the stables. As soon as he could, in third grade, he dropped out altogether. Now, I suspect his real problem was dyslexia. He said that when he came to America he couldn't read a street sign. What kind of job could he hold as an illiterate?

At first he found a job with his friend Pat Devaney, who would one day be my uncle and godfather. The job was on the assembly line at The Savage Arms, a rifle factory. For Pop the job was dull, boring, and going nowhere. So Mom and Pop, after their marriage in Utica in 1925, took off for Rochester with Aunt Jo and Uncle Jerry to try their luck at Northeastern Electric. Here their first son, Edmond, was born. Homesickness set in, and longing for their relationships and friends led them back to Utica. A little over a year later, in 1927, their second son, Thomas, made his appearance, and thirteen months later on March 18, 1928, just missing St. Patrick's Day, Hugh was born.

In Utica jobs were scarce in the middle of winter and Dad took a job shoveling snow for the school board. It wasn't long before his mechanical aptitude was discovered by the Superintendent of Schools, Mr. Dillon, who gave Dad Horatio Seymour, a grade school in North Utica, to care for all by himself. It was a job he was to stick to all through the Depression. From shoveling snow, and in spite of his dyslexia, he rose to Head Custodian of city schools in less than twenty-five years.

To get the job permanently, however, he was expected to pass the Civil Service Exam, He had never been required to take an exam before and he was petrified. So my brother Hugh helped him. As luck would have it, during all those dark chilly mornings all by himself in the boiler room stoking the fires before the students arrived, he had slowly started to read books. Without his realizing it, he had outgrown his dyslexia, as some do. Still, under great stress he took the first test in his life, and with all those years of experience he managed one of the highest marks ever in the state on that particular exam.

Tom Malloy, a friend at the time, bought a bar and grill in a rough and tough derelict neighborhood and asked Pop to move upstairs rent-free to be the night watchman. Prohibition was rearing its ugly head, and he needed Dad to unlock the place in the wee hours of the morning to enable the bootleggers to make their clandestine deliveries out of sight of the police station, which was just at a slight angle to the west across the street. To Pop, free rent was a bonanza. How could he turn it down?

1929 The Year of the Crash

Pop's windfall didn't last long for a couple of reasons. One evening after work, he came into the bar to find my brother Tommy sitting on the bar with the well-oiled patrons making a fuss over him. Pop was furious. If there was anything he wanted for us kids, it was an alcohol-free environment. Because alcoholism ran rampant in his family, he was a teetotaler and a member of the Pioneers of Ireland, an association founded by a Catholic priest in the 1800s to battle the alcoholism that was destroying one Irish family after another. Dad knew he had to move for the sake of his children no matter what the cost to him.

And the other reason? The sheer seediness came to be too much for my mother. I had been born in this rundown part of town. I spent the first summer of my life at the playground in my mother's arms with the roughnecks and toughies going after my brothers and she trying to break up fights. Eddy was so frightened he wouldn't go to school alone. So Mom sent Tommy with him even though he was but three years old. She would put his pacifier in his shirtwaist pocket and off he would trek to the Potter Street School with Eddy holding his hand. Then there was the night a rat ate the nipple off my bottle while I was sleeping. The next day Mom saw the flat was infested with huge, dark gray rats. She was knocking them silly with the handle of the broom while Hughie was crying his head off. This was the catalyst that made our move imperative. When Pop came home that night, Mom delivered an ultimatum, which she was very good at. A day or two later a mammoth fire broke out in a large abandoned warehouse across the street, and it burned to the ground. The rats in our flat, Pop said after the fire, were like rats leaving a sinking ship. They seemed to have sensed a catastrophe before it happened. Mom said, "I don't care about ships or warehouses. All I know is that I don't want any rats in my house." That very night, plans were afoot to move out. But where?

As luck would have it, when Dad's boss heard about the fire, he thought of all the empty city houses scattered about town. Because of the Depression, foreclosures were happening every day. At the same time, Seymour School needed a night janitor, and Mr. Dillon, the school board superintendent, asked Pop if he would take on a second job. They couldn't pay him two salaries, but in lieu of a paycheck the city would let the family live in one of their unoccupied houses, rent-free. Pop jumped at the offer.

With Mom pregnant again—Joan was on the way—we moved up to Hungry Hill. The house was a two-family flat with a store in the front on the corner of Oak and City Streets. We moved into the back half, which consisted of two small bedrooms, a bath, and a kitchen, with a potbelly stove in the living room.

Pop got a loan and bought foodstuffs for the store and Mom was to run it. But soon Dad realized she was handing out everything on credit. Because of the Depression, customers had no way to pay for what they needed, and she couldn't let them go away empty-handed. "Why, some of them have babies," she would say. Pop understood why they couldn't pay, and in these times would never pay, so he shut it down.

Ed got some rabbits and put them in the empty glass cases of the store. He would let them run free around the living room, their droppings all over the place. These were my first memories.

The advent of Joany in 1931 had me in a fury. I must have been afraid the squalling little brat was going to usurp my position as baby of the house. Apparently one day I pushed her off my mother's bed and she was saved only by a thick throw rug. I remember being impossible, throwing tantrums and screaming fits to get my way. Mom could only pacify me by telling me I was still the "baby boy." I seemed to accept this explanation.

1933

The small back rooms of the store were getting too crowded for the growing family. Only a year later, Mom was pregnant once more, with Madeline, and Mr. Dillon had us move next door to 1438 City Street, a one-family house of gray stucco with a basement for Dad's workbench. He loved working in the cellar. In his free time he made a trailer for the Ford and a boat. I remember when he finished the boat he couldn't get it out of the basement so he had to dismantle it and reassemble it in the backyard. The house had an attic I loved to play in. On the ground floor were the living room, dining room, and kitchen on one side, and three bedrooms and a bath on the other. We now had more than enough space.

Daddy Bert played a significant role in my young life. I called Bert Hayes that because, having no son of his own, he spent time with me. Who had time for needy kids in our family? He used to take me to work with him where he built houses. He would give me a piece of wood, a hammer, and a nail, and I would play with them all day. We used to stop and have lunch together and I liked

Standing - Hugh, Ed & Tom
Sitting - our dog Lindy, Joan & Jimmy

that. Daddy Bert lived next door and was reorganizing his family. His wife had died, his oldest daughter had taken off down valley with her boyfriend, and he was sending his youngest daughter, Tooty, to live with her aunt in Rome. He asked Mom if she would take Lizzy. Of course, Mom would never say no to a request like that. Lizzy moved in with all her things. Some of her stuff was put up in the attic with all our things in steamer trunks that Pop and Mom had brought with them from the Old Country.

Elizabeth Hayes had graduated from 8th grade at St. Pat's and, as was not unusual for girls in these dire times of no jobs and little money, she wasn't planning to go on to high school. Mom had her look after me. With her friend Eleanor Kane, she used to take me on outings. We would often go just two and a half blocks over City Street and down Thorn across the tracks to Lincoln Avenue and the playground. I loved the outings, playing in the mammoth sandbox and being fussed over by the girls. Sometimes she and Eleanor would dress me as a girl. Years later, when I asked her why, she said, "With your deep dimples, you were prettier than most."

Unbeknownst to the rest of the family, I would play up in the attic by myself for hours. In Lizzy's suitcase one day, I found her white Swiss eyelet graduation dress. It fitted me like a gown. I would spin, swirl, and twirl around in it, having a ball, being ever so careful, even at that tender age, not to be caught. I had enough sense to know being discovered in that dress would spell disaster. So began my secret life, which was to last another thirty-one years.

Sister Joan at 6 months with old Ford in the backyard

I was also bullied. My uncle taught me not be afraid, to stand and fight no matter the inevitable outcome. Uncle Pat and Aunt Kathleen lived across the backyard on Oak Street with their two sons, Joseph and John. Uncle Pat was forever putting the boxing gloves on us kids, and he would play referee after matching us up. I was always matched with Hughie who was slighter than I but so fast and wiry that he always got the better of me. I learned how to take a beating and when to duck. I never did learn when to run—Uncle Pat wouldn't let me. The running came much later.

Walt Matica and Gordy Kane lived in the neighborhood. They were just a little older than our gang but they liked hanging around because Dad took them fishing at Delta Dam on the Mohawk River north of Rome. Pop was one of the few around who still had a flivver of a car. He would also kick a ball around the neighborhood field in front of the school with them, and they liked to fool around in the cellar at Dad's tool bench. Gordy had a habit of making us kids share whatever candy, cookie, or cake we might be munching on and it was driving Hughie wild. He was fed up and said to me, "I'm going to get this guy. You just watch me."

I said, "How can you? He's bigger than us."

"You just watch me," he insisted.

A day or two later, Hughie and I were sitting on the front steps doing nothing in particular. Hughie had a two-penny brown paper bag all rolled up and sealed tight. Gordon happened by and said, "Hey, Hughie, whatcha got there?"

"Nothing."

Gordy insisted, "Oh, yes you do, I can see. What is it? Candy? Come, Hugh, give me some."

Hughie still said, "No, no, it's not. I don't have any candy," pulling it in to himself as he said this.

Gordy, being the bigger of the two, snatched the bag from Hughie and stuffed his fist into it only to sink his hand in a hot, soft ball of horseshit. Horse balls were plentiful in those days; the streets were covered with them. Let me tell you, Hughie took off down City Street like a bolt of lightning, laughing all the way. Gordy followed like a bat out of hell, but Hughie was faster.

One day I saw the Brody boys, David and Irving, come out of Hugel's, each licking an ice cream cone. I crossed the street and asked them nicely for a lick. I'd have done the same for one of my brothers. They started running even though they were older than I was. I began to chase them, and in the excitement Irving dropped his ice cream, cone and all. I picked it up, licked off the cinders and dirt and spat them out. What was left tasted pretty damned good to me. A few days later I was in Hugel's standing up on the wooden box so I could get a good look at all the sweet, wonderful, colored penny candy behind the curved glass case, and me without a cent to my name, when in walked the Brody boys with their mother. Somehow, she knew who I was and asked the boys, "Is it this little fellow who chased you?" They both nodded their heads sheepishly. She gave me a once-over and said, "You should both be ashamed of yourselves. Why, you should be able to lick the tar out of him."

Sensing trouble, I jumped down off the box and ran out of the place. When

I got home, I asked, "Do I have any tar in me? What is it, Mom?"

She said, "Why, that's the black stuff they pour on the roads in the spring to fill up the holes after a tough winter. Remember last year I caught Tommy and Hughie chewing on it?" Why?" she asked.

"Mrs. Brody told her boys they should be able to lick the tar out of me."

One day the McCabe girls were all on their front porch screaming and laughing as they pointed up Oak Street at me and my very first girlfriend, Rita Hartman, who lived up Oak directly across from the school. There we were walking down the street hand in hand and me naked as a jaybird swinging my little elastic-waistband shorts in my hand. I guess I thought it was too hot even for my little shorts.

Other days, I used to skip down Oak Street's steep hill to Mrs. Kane's across from the Baserts' smelting factory. Her husband had died and she took in laundry, washing and ironing shirts for fancy doctors. She would let me come in and bang away on the old upright piano until my fingers ached. Sometimes I crossed the street to stare through the bars of the open factory window and watch the hot presses molding big pieces of steel into all kinds of shapes.

One day, heading down the hill, I must have stopped to rest. My only mistake was sitting on the curb with my feet outstretched in front of me in the gutter. I was right in front of a little Model A coupe. Unbeknownst to me—I must have been daydreaming—a couple got into the car and started off down the hill, rolling over both my shins with the front and then the back wheels. I let out one screech as if I had been stabbed in the chest, and I didn't let up. The couple found my mom and dad, an easy thing to do on that hill. Mom told me they took me to Dr. Jim Douglas who, after examining me, told my parents that there didn't seem to be anything wrong, not even cinder marks, but still I kept howling as if my legs had been broken in twelve pieces.

The obviously clever nurse said, "Just a minute, doctor," and left the room. She came back with a big, luscious navel orange all the way from California and, holding it up in front of her, said, "Look, Jimmy, I have something for you."

I immediately stopped screaming, jumped off the gurney, and ran over to her, reaching for the orange. Mom looked at the doctor, shaking her head. "That's our Jimmy. Thank you, doctor, thank you."

A drama queen already, at that early age. I guess I wasn't easy.

I remember once when I wasn't quite four, a Saturday morning when Pop was taking the boys to school with him. They helped him sweep the halls and polish the desks. I couldn't go because he was stopping at the gasworks to pick up two burlap bags of coke and had taken out the back seat of the old Model T to make room for them. Consequently there was no room for me. I was so furious at being left out that I jumped on my little blue tricycle and took off after them. I managed to get more than a mile from home, reaching Varick and Columbia Streets between St. Joseph's and St. Pat's Churches. At this point I saw one little guy getting trounced on by a bigger bloke. I jumped off my little blue mean machine to go to the little guy's defense. I felt the two of us should be able to finish off the big bully pronto, only when I started clouting him, the little guy ran off and left me to battle alone. The morning was over by now and it was into early afternoon. Pop and the boys were on their way home. As they passed Columbia Street, Tommy, sitting in the back on top of the burlap bags of coke, spotted my blue tricycle and saw me fighting with someone.

"Stop, Pop," he shouted, "That's Jimmy's bike over there—and there's Jimmy!"

Pop stopped the car and the fight. He stuffed the bike in the back between Tommy and Hughie on top of the bags of coke and sat me between him and Eddy. I could see he was madder than blazes at me for pulling such a stunt. Pop would never blow up in public at me or anyone else—he was too much of a Carville for that—but I knew I was going to catch hell when I got home. When we got there, it was Mom who scared the hell out of me. She told me that, if I had only gone a little farther over on Oriskany Street, a big fat Gypsy lady who sat in a storefront window would have stolen me and sold my bike and made me suck her big teat in the window for all to see. Well, that was enough to cure me! There were no more jaunts across town after that.

For the older boys, Pop took a long 2"x12"x12" plank and attached four wheels and a steering device with a little motor on the back. We all used to ride it up to the school and back down Oswego Street to the house. When the motor sometimes conked out, we would all jump off and push up Oak with Hughie steering, then jumping back on and coast down Oswego, hoping the motor would kick over. It often did. Pop was always doing things like that for us. He would also pick up the odd orange crate for us to which we attached a two-by-four with roller-skates on either end. We pushed it along with one foot like a scooter. These toys were just as much fun as any fancy scooter today and they cost little or nothing to make.

I did get to spend time over at our dad's school in the summertime when the older boys went to help with the work. I, still being small, was relegated to the playground adjacent to the school. I won an amateur contest dancing while singing "Pennies from Heaven" and "Little Old Lady Passing By." The next year Wes Keyes and I danced in the Field Day Celebration across town at Murnane Field. We danced as a couple of Dutch boys. Yet back then, out of the whole city, we were the only boys dancing. Who could have foreseen then that one day I would wind up singing and dancing all over New York, and Wes would tap at the Roxy movie house at Seventh and 50th for years?

1934

The '30s and prohibition generated many neighborhood speakeasies. Even our neighborhood had one—Fuch's on Maple and Lenox across form Basert's Refinery. But many preferred house parties to the speakeasy, and our house was often the scene. Mom and Pop, even with all the activities and responsibilities of their busy lives, still had time for fun for themselves. Young immigrants forging a new life in their adopted home found a welcome mat at our door, and many of the greenhorns came and went as if it were a clubhouse. It made for an interesting life for us kids as well. So why not a dance?

The adults would gather on a Saturday night about once a month. The furniture, including the dining table, was put on the front porch and the rugs would be rolled up and then they would strike up the music. By this time we kids would be snug in our beds, the boys in the middle room and the girls in the back. Uncle Jerry played violin, Jack Croghan and Mick Prendergast would begin pulling in and out on their squeezeboxes, their Irish button accordions, and the fun would begin. They would set up two Irish square sets. No matter where they were from in Ireland, everyone knew the sets by heart. After the sets would come some slow numbers or "Stack of Barley," popularly called "You put your little foot right out." It was an Irish schottische. At midnight Mom brought out the ham salad sandwiches, and beer was served. In the kitchen a bottle of Irish whiskey would show up from nowhere, and a group of the serious drinkers would always be out there knocking back a few. It was now time for us kids to be marched out in our nightgowns to be ooh'ed and ah'ed over, all of us on our best behavior, I might add. We would be given a sandwich and a soft drink of ginger ale, sarsaparilla, or homemade root beer. When we were finished, we were sent back to bed to drift off to sleep to the strains of a familiar Irish air.

The summer of 1934 was our first real big outing away from home. Dad was taking all of us to visit his sister Josephine and her family in Framingham, Massachusetts, a little town west of Boston. Lindy, our dog, and my cat were coming along. The old Model T was not very comfortable but it would get us there. We tied everything onto the roof and to the running boards. Mom sat in front with Mandy on her lap, and Hughie sat in the middle. In the back Lizzy sat with baby Leo in her arms, while Eddy and Tommy sat and Joany and I stood hanging on to the front seat with Lindy and my cat at our feet. When we got tired we switched with Eddy or Tom. I swear a weirder sight you never saw, unless it was the Joad family in Steinbeck's The Grapes of Wrath, only they were heading west and were going east. We cruised along Route 5S to Albany, then farther into Massachusetts on Route 2, north of the Berkshires, and down into Framingham with no fatal accident. It seemed to take us a lifetime to get there.

Both families took a trip into Revere Beach on the ocean where we all experienced our first dip in the sea. I can still see Lizzy in her woolly black bathing suit with the white stripes around the skirt. God, was she skinny. She must have been all of ninety-five pounds sopping wet as she stood there, her back to the sea, with a big wave about to engulf her and send her head over heels onto the beach while all we kids laughed with glee.

One day the gang of us headed over to the playground across a railway trestle bridge. The trestle passed over a swamp, and my little legs didn't make the step from one wooden tie to the next. One leg slipped between but fortunately my other leg slipped down the other side of the tie. I sat there crying my head off. One of the older local boys said I was damned lucky I hadn't fallen into the swamp.

The summer of '35, Eddy and I spent two weeks on the Goggins' farm in Holland Patent. It was a pretty rustic place with dirt roads for miles. With no electricity and no running water, it was kerosene lamps and a hand pump at the well that served us. Mrs. Goggins was Mom's cousin, making her seven kids our second cousins I guess. It was my first time away from home, and what an experience it was. Her kids called us city slickers from the big city. Eddy milked cows but I wouldn't go near them. One cow stepped on my sneaker-shod foot and would not let up. I was stuck under her until she moved and I was scared to death. There was the day the bull broke into the cow field, and I watched the big, snorting, huffing and puffing bull chase Eddy and John down the field till they made it over the fence just in time. One big turkey used to lie in wait for me every time I headed for the cow barn. He would gobble like mad, fluff up his feathers, and chase after me like a demon. He never bothered anyone else.

One afternoon, Cathleen, Mary, Alex, Helen, John, Eddy, and I got pails and went berry picking down by the ice pond. When the pond froze over in winter, blocks of ice would cut out with a big saw and stored in a wood-insulated shed appropriately called the icehouse. The ice would then be covered in plenty of sawdust to keep it from melting. We were down there picking berries when John and I got into a fight over nothing. I knew I couldn't get the better of him since he was a lot stronger. When he set the big pail down to move back the bush, I took on swift kick at it and sent the berries flying. I ran like hell back to the house, where I knew his mother would take my side. She did, until Mary, who couldn't believe what I had done, told her mom what had happened. After that even their mother thought I was a spoiled city slicker. Life was tough for them on the farm and berries were precious food, but I was mad and I didn't give a damn. For days Mary couldn't get over what I had done.

When the two weeks were up, I knew I would remember that summer for the rest of my life. For both Eddy and me, it was marvelous and indelible.

When it came time for me to start school, Mom took the older boys out of the Washington Grammar School and sent us all down to St. Pat's. To me the Sisters of St. Joseph back then, with the peak their veils made over their starched-white-wimple foreheads, looked like huge black birds with pure white breasts. They scared the hell out of me and sent my bullying to kingdom come.

In good weather we walked the mile to and from school, but when it rained or snowed, Mom gave Gordy Kane ten cents and all five of us, because Bernie Kane, Gordy's brother, was also with us, would pile onto the trolley car. Bernie had caught polio when he was small and was paralyzed from the hips down.

He managed to get about with leg braces and crutches and he would get on first. Gordy, getting on last, would drop the dime in the slot and off we would go in style on the Lenox trolley car all the way to Columbia Street. Tommy and Bernie were in the same class, and on good days Tommy would pull him in his little red wagon all the way to and from school.

Pulling the same little red wagon, we four boys would head down Thorn Street to the Delaware Lackawanna Railroad to try to fill a couple of burlap bags with coal that had fallen off the open boxcars. Sometimes a train would pass by with the railroad dicks, as we called them, threatening to chase us, but they never did. Sometimes one would encourage an avalanche of coal by starting it up with a kick of his foot. On days like that we had no trouble filling up the two bags.

In the second grade I started tap dance lessons and found one good reason to go to school. There was also a second good reason and her name was Jane Curley. She lived off in the other direction from my house, up Columbia Street just off Columbia Square beyond Shaheen's orthopedic shoe store. Though we boys all took off for school in the family group, coming home was another matter. We all found our way home with our own class friends. At six I was no exception. One could do such a thing in those days. It was safe then. I would parade up Columbia with bright-eyed Jane, a little Irish girl with dark hair and green eyes. She was the sunshine of my life. I loved being around her and walked her home many times. I would leave her in front of her door a half a mile out of my way and proceed up the hill to Court Street and Lenox Avenue and then trudge on up to City Street and home an hour and a half after school let out. Kids had much more freedom then.

I was held back in second grade with a reading problem, a real chip off the old block. The nuns thought I was lazy, undisciplined, or just uninterested. I truly was none of those things. They knew I wasn't dumb because I managed 90s and 100s in catechism, and when Mrs. Kirkland came in as a special music teacher, I was an honor student, first in her class.

In third grade I remember being the last one picked for spelling bees and I was always the first to be forced down. When I finally refused to get up when I was picked last again—I wanted no part of this fiasco—the teacher was vexed and asked, "Why don't you get up?"

I said, "Why get up when I'll be the first to sit down? This is all a joke."

She sent me to the Mother Superior who didn't know how to handle the problem any better than the third grade teacher did and gave me detention. Well, at least I wasn't hit with a rod.

The mid-'30s with the Depression were devastating to everyone. No one seemed spared. Roosevelt and the Democrats were doing everything they could to help the destitute. Social Services was there helping the needy, but no matter how much we needed at this time, we as a family did not qualify because Dad had a job and many were worse off than we were. Catholic Charities, realizing Pop's pitiful salary at the time and knowing now he had a family of eleven to feed, felt they should do something to assist. They got Mom an assistance card from the city authorizing her to partake of the food assistance program held every Saturday morning in the back basement entrance to City Hall. Her card allotment was for a family of eleven, a pretty big hand out. It was mostly government food surplus: corn, flour, vegetables, fruits, and cheese. I especially remember the grapefruit, something I had never had before. Even the prunes were good served hot on a cold frosty morning. There was one small problem with this windfall—Pop was too proud to partake of the offer. He was a Carville, remember. Well, my mom certainly wasn't and she and I would go, along with Hughie and Tom, who would go with her to help carry. But Pop would not let us off next to the building. He would let us out a block and a half from City Hall and make us walk, lest he be spotted and it became known. He was embarrassed to think he couldn't provide for his family without help. I am sure that that food helped and, with all Mom's canning in the fall of "bushel produce" bought at the open farmers market, got us through those long, lean winters.

1936

One day when I was seven I was kept home from school with a toothache. At that time, I knew we were all being forced out of our homes but why or when I didn't know. Mom and Pop never talked over their problems with us kids. So no one had told us our house was being torn down to make room for a playground. Several families were being evicted, and most had been making plans to move for some time, although not us. Dad had combed the city for months now, but no one would rent to eleven people, Freddy being the new addition. The situation was hopeless, and both Pop and Mom were beside themselves. The two houses on either side of us were empty and their demolition was underway. The day I stayed home from school in excruciating pain, they started tearing the shingles off our roof even though we were still living there. The noise was tremendous and my tooth ached like hell. Mrs. Edith Hayes, from over on Oak Street, came to the house and told Mom I should go stay in Donald's room as they hadn't started razing her house yet.

Back Row - Ed, Jimmy, Hugh, Thomas Jr.
Middle Row - Nora (Mom), Madleline, Leo, Joan, Thomas Sr. (Dad)
Front Row - Fred, Carol, Gerald, Anita

3 Myself

With so many people not having the money to pay their mortgages, foreclosures ran wild and any number of houses went up for sale. But who had the money to buy them? Pop found houses going for a song but no matter how well he sang, he didn't have the money for a down payment.

Then out of the woodwork sprang two unlikely angels. Both were friends of the family, both were unmarried women, and both were housekeepers. Ann Doherty and Ann Hunter came up with a hundred dollars each, which met the $200 down payment. It was a fourteen-room house in a delightful neighborhood for growing children. But alas, Pop came up with the down payment too late. A barber down Lincoln Avenue beat Pop to the draw. He got the house for $1500. When he heard Pop actually needed it, he offered it to him for $1800. Dad jumped at it. It became Hugh's job to take the $18 mortgage payment each month to his barbershop. Eventually, Eddy turned sixteen and began helping with the payments.

When we finally left City Street already being demolished, they had put our furniture out on the street. I remember riding with Tommy and Hughie to our new home in Eddy Prendergast's Model A coupe in a rumble seat for the first time.

So it was that in 1936 we made the big move to our own house on Shaw Street. Now we had fourteen rooms, counting the upstairs flat that Dad had foreseen taking over as the family grew. It turned out to be more than adequate for our brood of fourteen plus whomever Dad and Mom were taking in because they need a place and TLC. Mom and Dad had an abundance of both to spare and share. There was always room for one more. Once, Pop's sister Jo and her husband Jerry Ruddy came up from New York with their three kids, and later his sister Tessy and Hugh Rooney followed with three kids, looking for a better life. Pop just turned the upstairs summer kitchen into a bedroom, and we kids tightened our belts and doubled up until they found a place of their own.

We were hardly settled in before our next addition, Anita, was squalling in Mom and Pop's bedroom. It was a sound one got used to in our house. Anita was as tiny as they come and she was skinny all through adolescence. Pop called her his little bird and feared one day she would just fly away. I have a memory of her sitting at the dining room table doing her homework and crying her heart out as she tried to answer Mom's questions. Mom was saying, "Anita, just spell out the word slowly and then say it." And through her sobbing and tears I heard "W... A... G... O... N... Cart!"

My God! I thought. Another one. Don't tell me it isn't hereditary. I guess an apple doesn't fall too far from the tree. Anita had a tough time all through school, as I did, with little or no help back then. They didn't know what the problem truly was, not even what to call it. It wasn't until the mid-'50s that they started to cotton on to it.

Anita and I shared another event in our youth. In the fall, she too, while playing in a bunch of dried leaves next to the curb, was struck by a car when the driver didn't see her as he started up. The impact dislocated her shoulder. To Mom, dislocated shoulders, broken arms, deep infections from rusty nails, unexplained earaches, high fevers, and cracked teeth were common occurrences and she faced them head on like a Florence Nightingale.

Until, years later, the big one happened two days before her 55th birthday on February 20 in the middle of a fierce winter. Joan went flying through the front window of a car; they had no seat belts back then. It was a freak accident on an icy road in a telephone company car driven by her trainee on the way from Albany, New York over the Northern Catskill Mountains to Oneonta, where they both lived at the time. Joan was in a coma for three months, and Mom, still Florence Nightingale, though all her children were fledged, immediately went back to work. It was a job that was to last thirty-five years. I could see Mom and Joan turning into sisters. Mom had a stroke at ninety-four, and Joan stayed with her until she finally passed away at ninety-six.

The new neighborhood offered us new opportunities. I spent my pre-adolescent years on the upper level of Lincoln Playground. I became captain of the safety patrol and spent my time seeing to it that the youngsters played fairly and safely. In my early years from the age of nine to twelve, I was happier than a June bug up there on the hill; I didn't even take the time to go home for lunch. It was a self-motivated nine-to-five commitment. Lizzy would send Mandy over with a fried egg and lettuce sandwich and a jar of cocoa. I was given three citations from the mayor on Field Day at the end of each summer.

The football field and the baseball diamond at the base of Lincoln Playground were a bonanza for Tommy and Hughie, though I knew by now I wasn't interested. Down at the foot of our yard and over the fence, the Nameless Eleven football team reigned supreme. They were my brothers' heroes. Eddy Dugo befriended my brothers, and at the end of every season the team's cast-off equipment would find its way to our front porch. Thus encouraged, my brothers carried on the tradition when the Nameless Eleven disbanded. Tommy founded the Utica Raiders, and they too came to reign supreme down on Lincoln Flats. Pop was the unofficial manager. He built a shower in the basement, and the cellar was turned into a clubhouse. Mom was out there on that field every weekend on the cold, frosty, snowy days of December with hot coffee and homemade sugar- and plain-donuts. All this stopped every year because of the "lake effect," when the big snows came drifting across the state from Lake Ontario and settled at the foot of the Adirondacks in the swamps of Utica. But until then, it wasn't unusual on a Saturday or Sunday to find a big bus parked out front waiting to take the team to an out-of-town game in Norwich, Dolgeville, Little Falls, or sometimes as far away as Saugerties down on the Hudson River. Cousin Joe played on the team displaying his mettle, for he later outdid himself in high school on the basketball court. Mom and Pop and the younger kids, Leo and Fred, would go along for the ride, and sometimes Joan would go and make one hell of a cheerleader. But never me, I had found my way to the Munson-Williams-Proctor Institute of the Arts where I listened to music. I fell in love with Bach's "Contra Dances" and kindled an affair with Mozart that has stood the test of time, for he still holds a precious place in my heart. I was realizing by now that in my family I was different and I was going to have to find my own way.

1938

Roosevelt was president and the New Deal was having an effect. Government projects like the food assistance program had been initiated and were beneficial to families like ours. The WPA and Civil Conservation Corps were providing jobs for the unemployed. Unions like the CIO and the AF of L were springing up everywhere. After much strife and bloodshed, laws were passed forcing up wages in the steel industry and in the coalmines. Artists were now getting assistance, with the WPA funding theatrical companies as well as roadwork around the country. Gordy Kane and his buddies joined the Conservation Corps and went off to the CCC camp to work on forestry projects. One fine Sunday in the spring of '38, Pop drove all of us in the big green Nash to the CCC camp to visit Gordy and Walter. Soon after, Gordy joined the army and was sent to the Canal Zone in Panama where he stayed until the war was over in 1945.

1939

The county dentist had been working on my teeth for months. I had a serious case of pyorrhea: my gums were a mess. One day a doctor decided my four front teeth needed to come out and he extracted them right there and then, one after the other. When I walked into the kitchen with my cheeks and upper lip swollen, puffed out like a chipmunk missing his two front teeth, my mother screamed. She hadn't been warned ahead of time. I was all of ten years old and God only knows what a front upper plate would cost. Pop knew the city school dentist, Dr. Griffith. When Dad told him of my misadventure at County, Dr. Griffith said he wasn't surprised and that I should come to his private office on Bank Place. As I sat there overlooking the Gold Dome Savings Bank with a panoramic view of the foothills of the Adirondacks, he proceeded to prepare me for an upper plate. My mom came the last day with her purse in her hand, wondering if she was going to have enough to pay for it. When she asked, "How much?" Dr. Griffith answered, "Did you see that lady walk out of here in the fur coat, Nora? Well, she's paying for them. But she doesn't know it yet."

That same summer, I was being sent to YMCA Camp at Lake Mernain. A week was being set aside for the underprivileged. I was picked by the Kiwanis Club, compliments of Catholic Charities. My dad drove me to the "Y" with my very own cardboard suitcase holding my two brand new bathing suits and a couple of new pajamas. For a hand-me-down kid, this was luxury. Though there were just the two of us in the car, I sat in the back and said in my best English accent at the time, "To the station, James." And Dad laughed himself silly.

We were always piling into cars on a Sunday to go off somewhere. Sometimes we went on a picnic next to Sauquoit Creek in Ridgewood in South Utica. One Sunday a little Italian boy drowned there. Pop, who was one of the searchers, found him under the falls. When he pulled the boy out of the water and laid him out on the ground, he was already dead. I was too young to know what to make of it. Sometimes we went off in the other directions, near Poland, to swim in West Canada Creek. Often we took the long, thirty-five-mile trip to Sylvan Beach on Oneida Lake with its expanse of sand and its exciting midway next to Barge Canal. We were always accompanied by another car loaded with my parents' Irish friends. One of the trips was on my seventh or eighth birthday with a cake and all.

Times were getting better and Dad at one point junked the little old Ford and bought a big, fancy, green, second-hand Nash with a large outside trunk that stood straight up on the back of the car. In the '40s Dad bought a Chevy and he still had the two-wheel trailer he had made, which he attached to the back. Mom designed a canvas cover for it with room for a dressing area that went right down to the ground behind the trailer. It looked like a covered wagon, a prairie schooner snatched right out of the Old West. Mom, Pop, and little Carol slept in the car trailer in a mattress. Mom also ran up a large regular tent on her old reliable Singer for Lizzy, baby Dickie, and the girls, and the smaller boys. The two oldest boys slept in the car. We spent Dad's two-week vacation camped in these up next to the Barge (in earlier times called Erie) Canal, across the street from the midway at Sylvan Beach. We did this every summer right up to and including our high school years. Very often our school buddies would hitchhike out to spend a day or a weekend with us.

1940s

It was 1940 and Dad was busy writing his Irish operetta *The Lost Cathleen* or *Gypsy Rest*. For the past ten years he had been performing in and around Utica, singing the familiar Irish ballads of John McCormack. When we kids were old enough to carry a tune or turn a step, we were shoved out on stage and told to strut our stuff. In the operetta little Joany was cast as Cathleen, and Dad planned to use the rest of us where needed.

He enlisted the help of two English teachers, Bea Conlin and Miss McCarthy, and of three music teachers, Miss Fleeger, Miss Gardner, and Miss Woods, all from the school system. He used Gordon Hood's high school band and former graduates of Seymour Grammar School whom he had worked with vocally. Many were now dispersed among the various high schools: Utica Free Academy, Utica Catholic Academy, Proctor High, St. Francis, and even out in the

Whitesboro Central High. Others were already out in the workforce.

We gathered together nightly at Seymour and produced one hell of a show. It was so successful that other Parent and Teacher Associations had us do fund-raising performances for them. We also played at many military installations in the area throughout the war.

SEATED - Carol STANDING - Thomas Sr., Jerold (Dickey), Jimmy, Joanie, Leo, Anita, Freddie, Mandy

After the war, Dad continued presenting shows and eventually broadcast a half hour Irish show every St. Patrick's Day over WKTV.

As we children grew up and left the nest, Pop just replaced us with grandchildren. Once on our way to do a show, I remember a grandson who was joining us for the first time whining, "Why do we have to do this anyway?" I heard Dick John, who was all of seven years old, replying, "Because you're a Carville, that's why." I thought to myself, Good answer.

In 1941 it finally happened. Pearl Harbor was bombed by the "Japs," as we called them at the time, and America was sent headlong into all-out war in both theaters. I was in sixth grade and the Monday morning after the attack I remember before serving mass sitting in a cold, unheated boys' lavatory, as the nuns called it, wondering whether I would ever be sent to war. Would it last another six years? It looked like a sure thing that my cousin Joe and brother Eddy would be going soon enough.

For many years, Mom had had her hands full, but eventually Carol and Dickie grew old enough to be cared for by Lizzy, who treated them as her own. They were inseparable and she paired them up as twins. She would spend hours dolling Carol up, combing her hair and doing it up in ringlets and sausage curls. The two would go out to play in the backyard, Dickie looking like little Lord Fauntleroy and Carol looking like a little Shirley Temple doll, lace collar and all. Within an hour or two, they would be at the door hand in hand, Carol like a warthog all covered in mud and Dickie standing there looking as if he had just stepped out of a band box, not a hair out of place. That's how they were, as close as thieves and as different as night and day. Just a few years later, when Joan captained the high school cheerleading team in 1946, Carol was right at home out on the football field, tumbling, twirling, and leaping as the UFA's cheerleaders' mascot.

During the war, Mom took a job down on Court Street in the Globe Mills making army blankets. She and I walked together on my way to school as the mill was very near St. Pat's. Then as the war went on, Horrockibbiston's, who used to make fishing rods on Oriskany Street, shifted over into the war effort like most everyone else, and she was offered a job buffing M1 rifles on the 3-to-11 swing shift. It paid too well to turn down, and the swing shift timing was better. With Dad home at five, it would work with the supervising of us kids and the running of the house. Pop went down at 11 PM to pick her up, and some of us kids would go for the ride. One night she came out with a huge helmet and facemask pulled over her head, looking like Rosie the Riveter, all black around her ears and neck and on her forearms, to tell us she would be thirty more minutes. All Pop said was, "Take a good look, kids—that's your mother." Years later she was given a citation from Washington for her war effort.

With Mom at work and Pop home with us, it was natural that he would line us up and give us voice lessons. The oldest were not too interested at first. I loved it and luxuriated in the attention. Even little Leo had a ball trying. Joany started piano lessons on the new-to-us upright piano that Pop thought was essential though it took up precious living room space. He would spend hours pushing in and out of his Irish button Boxeen but as an accordionist he was one hell of a singer. Tommy thought he could get out of the voice lessons by studying the trumpet. Fred followed suit and wound up marching in the prestigious South Utica Drum and Bugle Corps. Before long Leo took up drumming and had his own high school dance band. He played for my father's Saturday night dances all through the '40s down on Devereau Street and later up on South Street.

It was through South Street that, in 1951, Lizzy met her sad demise. She had been spending her Saturday nights at Pop's dances there and took up with a man who, unbeknownst to her, was married with kids. She got pregnant, and because she was such a slightly built young woman with undeveloped veins, it was a difficult birth. The Catholic Charities were in charge and at the crucial moment decided to save the baby at Elizabeth's expense, in spite of my mom's wishes. She died giving birth to Frederick Joseph. That was the way of things then. Catholic Charities then had Frederick adopted by a "good Catholic family," again against my mother's wishes. She wanted to bring the baby up as one of her own, but she didn't have a legal leg to stand on. Mom took the sorrow to her grave. Our whole family took Lizzy to Watertown and laid her to rest next to her mother. They were all there, except for me. By then, I was in an Army Hospital in Massachusetts in the process of being medically discharged.

During the war life went on as usual. We were all in school now and soon would be. Life-as-usual included putting up with food and gas rationing, counting stamps, saving paper and tinfoil, giggling through blackouts, peeking through the curtains during trial air raids, listening to war news on the radio, saving up to buy a War Bond, and waving goodbye at the railroad station to friends and relations on their way to the war. Eventually, Joe and Eddy were among them.

I was growing older and changing from the wild-headed child who was always looking for a fight. I was teeming with emotions. All kinds of frustrating questions remained unanswered because I never dared ask them—I was afraid of the answer. In spite of it all, I was ever so slowly turning into a fairly levelheaded boy in his early teens.

During my last year at St. Pat's, I was a member of our Boy Scout troop. We were working on our merit badges for First Class Scout, and it was time for the big 25-mile hike. We had been on others but this was the big one that we had to make to qualify. But at the last moment, I missed out on the hike. After many sore throats, I was sent to the hospital for a tonsillectomy. When I got better I was going to have to make the hike alone on my scout's honor, since no one wanted to make the grueling trek again. I was behind the eight ball until Joany, all eleven years old, said she would do the hike with me. Mom packed us a lunch with colored hard-boiled Easter eggs and hot cocoa in a jar covered with a big woolly stocking to hold in the heat, which it did, a little.

We took off up Thorn Street to State Hospital and over the halfway bridge into Whitesboro. West of town, we crossed the bridge over the New York Central tracks and the Mohawk River and followed the river as it turned north through the flats. Then we crossed over the Barge Canal Bridger and the railroad tracks to the River Road. We were now at the junction called Carrie's Corners that led west to Rome and north to Marcy and Holland Patent. After the war, at this junction the Kallet Theater, a movie drive-in, would be attracting carloads of people for all over. But now we turned west on the Rome road to where a lovely babbling brook crossed the road at the foot of a steep hill leading to a plateau and the Utica Airport. This establishment was considered the halfway mark to Rome and about twelve-and-a-half miles from home. This distance, and the return journey, would now qualify me for my merit badge. We crawled in under a fence along the brook and had our lunch, cracking open a few eggs and drinking our barely warm cocoa. The stream water was still like ice. We had had a freezing cold winter with mounds of snow. After lunch we trudged up the hill to the little airport, which boasted private planes and a pilot school. We hung around the observation area where many people used to drive up in their cars to watch the landings and take-offs. After a long rest, having become bored with watching planes, we chucked our garbage into the trashcan and headed back down the hill and home.

It was an uneventful trip back home—except for one thing. I noticed tire tracks where cars had parked out of sight behind trees. This didn't strike me as unusual, but I noticed something odd among the discarded empty beer and whiskey bottles, napkins, and toilet paper. Also strewn around here and there were little dried-up balloons. I had never seen balloons that looked like this before, all white with a gigantic rubber mouthpiece ring. I knew they were not kids' balloons. I had absolutely no idea what they were or what they were for but I had enough sense not bring any attention to them. This is something Joan need not contemplate, I thought.

DE TREE A WE

We made our way home through Whitesboro Town, Yorkville, and a part of New York Mills and lastly went through Hungry Hill and the State Hospital grounds before arriving home. Walking up Shaw Street, I saw Mom on the porch waiting for us. It was minutes to six. It had been quite an outing for us, and I did get my merit badge on my scout's honor. I remember no one talking to us nor did we to anyone on the way. But we were in rural upstate New York in the early '40s and in those times, children seemed much safer.

In 1943 I graduated from eighth grade, and Father Legault gave me a scholarship to Catholic Academy. The nuns, I am sure, had a notion I was a good candidate for the priesthood and had me pegged for the monastery at an early age, as was the custom then. I was sure father couldn't agree more, but my mom and I knew I had other plans. I turned down the scholarship and joined my brothers at the Utica Free Academy where I planned to major in music.

I was now in high school and in choir and Mom was shelling out two dollars a week for voice lessons. Mandy and I also took dance classes with Vinnie Rajerrio.

The big bands are what I remember most from that time—Glenn Miller, Tommy and Jimmy Dorsey (I actually met Tommy Dorsey at the Hotel Utica in '44), Guy Lombardo, and Xavier Cugat. Gene Krupa on drums and Harry James on trumpet were unforgettable. I was a jitterbug nut and didn't miss a high school dance in the area. Sometimes I attended two in one night. My passion for dancing culminated at the War Memorial Fund-Raising Bazaar held at the big old World War I armory on Rutgers Street. There, in 1946, Carol Curtin and I won the Central New York Jitterbug Contest and were crowned the Jitterbug Queen and King. As a result of the title, we toured the area high schools and all the military establishments giving dance exhibitions accompanied by Lizzy Jay, our high school music teacher.

My gonads began to activate about this time. I was sexually precocious at thirteen but I certainly was not attracted to my girlfriends in school, in that way. They were fun to be with and they were great dance partners, but that was as far as it went. I would walk home from a date with a girl, after which there was always a teacher, store clerk, shoe salesman, or married man I knew one way or another looking for diversion. They call it "cruising," but I didn't know it had a name. It all started innocently enough with a married man in our church choir. Often I would indulge myself, treating it like a little experiment, satisfying my inquisitive, sexual nature, always telling myself it was nothing serious. It all presented itself so easily, with little or no effort on my part. It was just there for the taking and I took it. The thought of safety never crossed my mind. I knew if the football players were to find it this easy with girls, without all the chaotic foreplay, they would jump at the chance and probably did.

I wouldn't mess with any of my buddies in high school. I felt that would be too risky. When I first felt the urges, I hit on my only true friend, Bob Gottuso.

3 Myself

He only laughed at me, insisting he just wasn't interested and definitely not that way. He was bright and well read—he would eventually go on to Syracuse University—and he was well aware of what I was going through. He told me I should read a book called Butterfly Man about a young man like me who ran off to New York and had the heady experience of being the belle of the ball dressed up in drag at the famous, or rather, given the times, the notorious Phil Black's Thanksgiving Day Ball in Harlem. The good times didn't last, however, and he wound up committing suicide by jumping off a building. Is this what I had to look forward to, the bottom of an airshaft on the Upper West Side of Manhattan? From this cautionary tale, I learned I had to be careful and levelheaded and make damn sure I didn't let such a thing happen to me. Thus began my clandestine second life, a life I kept entirely to myself, sharing it with no one. Let me tell you, it was a very lonely existence.

If it hadn't been for the friends I made while working part-time as a busboy at the lunch counter in Woolworth's, I don't know what would have happened or how it would have ended. Part-time help was hired from all six high schools in the area. Consequently a loose group formed as members wafted in and out through the years. A core group developed and to this day some of us have remained friends. I guess our main purpose was to get together and laugh. If you couldn't laugh, you didn't belong. Not surprisingly, some did tire of us. But I am here to tell you that the core group had a ball as we still do today whenever we get together. In the group were Betty B., Tommy H., Merlyn O., Bob I., Polly K., Denny C., Terry M., Tom McC., May Marie M., Dick B., Ruthie K., Wes K., Carol C., Bob P., Mary H., and Jean M. The one thing most of us had in common was that we loved to dance. Others came and went but whomever we were with at the time, we laughed till we wet our pants; just ask Poll. I still remember her laughing her ass off while she balanced on a rock mid-stream in Prospect Park screaming to Denny Carney to throw her a hotdog so she could row herself in. She was laughing so hard that her lovely light mauve pants turned dark purple. We were like a band of comics, one endeavoring to outdo the other.

In 1946 I was sent to Westminster Choir School in Princeton on scholarship. That summer I finally got to New York for the third time when Carol and I did an exhibition dance at the Taft Hotel. I began counting the days until I could get out of Utica and on to New York. I was tired of living behind a façade, and the constant fear of exposure was oppressive. Exposure would mean dragging my family through all the degradation a small town could and would conjure up, and for that, I would never have been able to forgive myself.

In my last year of school, I took a job at the Utica State Hospital for the mentally disturbed. I could make good money there. And it was money I needed to make the move to the city.

1950s

One day I got a call from my brother Hugh asking me to come home. Hugh had met Kevin Gruchy, an Icelandic composer who had agreed to write some new music for a revival of Pop's operetta, *The Lost Cathleen*. He was knocking out one number after another. He was up to seventeen or eighteen and almost finished. The entire family had decided to take a sabbatical from whatever they were doing at the time. Since none of us were that far into our careers at that point, it wasn't a great sacrifice. Everyone was doing this to launch the show for Pop. It was going to be a mini-musical with only twenty performances, just the immediate family including in-laws and the baby, if Equity would allow it. They formed a company with John Huss, Mandy's husband, as president, Joan as secretary, and Hugh as treasurer. I was designated choreographer and was hoping to be director but that hadn't been decided yet. I was already working on numbers in my head by the time I got home.

It was all going great guns until Hugh discovered Kevin had previously signed with a manager who demanded 20% of the profits before we had even begun. He had contributed absolutely nothing to the effort and would be contributing nothing because he was useless. Hugh was very disappointed in Gruchy for not telling him up front. Hugh told him he would have to dissociate himself from the manager before we moved any further. Apparently it was a long-term contract, and Gruchy didn't have the money to break it. Consequently *The Lost Cathleen* project went up in smoke, taking Dad's dream with it. But that didn't stop him. He went right on producing shows with grandchildren up to and throughout the '60s, culminating in a show featuring his first great-grandson, Michael Carville, son of TP. Pop's first grandchild.

Posthumously Thomas J. Carville was inducted into the Irish Hall of Fame in Dublin for advancing Irish culture in America.

For the next ten years I sang, danced, and cavorted in shows in New York and around the country until that icy, rainy day in January of '62 on the corner of Second Avenue and 23rd Street that changed my life forever.

Fred, Mandy, Leo, Anita, Jimmy, Joan performing their six hand reel at the Annual Irish Counties' FEIS, held at Fordham University in '54

4 To St. Vincent and the Grenadines

1968: Two Troubled Souls

Now here I was drinking lime squash, bouncing around on a sailboat racing across the Caribbean Sea to yet another home, another life. And we were just a little family of two. Although our stories are different, Sandy's and mine, perhaps what led us to form a family bond are the convergences— both of us born in New York State the first-generation sons of immigrants, both struggling with issues of sexual identity in adolescence, both pursuing musical and theatrical interests as livelihoods, and more, both of us reaching this state of disillusionment at the same time. I didn't know him of course in his formative years. Suffice it to say, I knew his mother and his family and I can say with all assurance that he was loved deeply by all of them.

He spent more than twenty years married to two different women, and I can add that he would have been married still had his choice of women been more in keeping with his needs than with theirs. Sandy loved the second wife deeply, but that love was not for a man as sensitive and giving as he. Avaricious behavior in both these people convinced him not to make the same mistake a third time. Yet this decision didn't relieve him of his insatiable need to share his life. He couldn't bear the thought of life all by himself.

Out of experiences in his youth, he had the notion that he was bisexual. He may have been, but I can say his homosexual tendencies didn't boil up in him as naturally as his heterosexual tendencies. So this was not just a little matter we had to deal with. It was obvious we were not comparable, we were different in many ways, but I hoped from the start that we were compatible. I had such great love and admiration for the man he was and I respected and honored him highly for what he had accomplished. He was the most humble, unassuming, righteous, decent, civilized human being one could ever meet, and a man reputed by many to be the most outstanding acting teacher of the last century. He had many a renowned actor's and actress's undying gratitude, and quite rightly so. He was a plain, basic, uncomplicated, effective teacher of a sound acting technique that matures and grows like any sound, basic, living organism.

Be that as it may, our needs were poles apart with Sandy looking for quiet and seclusion and I looking for a fresh new start. We were not so naive as to think we would find Utopia on a paradise island. We had no illusions that being kissed by the soft breezes of the trade winds and lulled to sleep every night to the songs of the surf would solve our problems. But we assured each other the problems of getting established in Bequia would all work out one way or another; after all, nothing is perfect and nothing is forever. I certainly wasn't going there for keeps. I was going there to design and build a retirement home for Sandy, a place where I could hang out intermittently between jobs back in New York. I intended to live in the basement apartment of 83rd Street, where I would continue my professional life.

At that point in our three-year odyssey, our adrenalin was still being pumped by the motivation to get away from the United States of the 1960s, if not totally, completely, and finally, at least from time to time. Both of us were affected by the times, and we each had our personal crises to contend with. We needed to be far enough away to keep our sanity, correction, my sanity. And yet, although I was troubled, I trusted it would work out somehow. Sandy, though not entirely happy, was in a different emotional state from me. He knew exactly what he was doing. He was now in his sixties, with many good teaching years still ahead of him. He had been an actor, director, and teacher in the theater since he was nineteen. Forty-five years later, he knew the American theater well, all too well, and its condition was a source of discontent and constant depression for him.

He had been known to say, "America is nothing more than a vast cultural wasteland."

4 To St. Vincent and the Grenadines

This from a man about whom David Mamet, the playwright and director, once said, "Sanford Meisner's greatness is that for forty years he has been training and preparing people to work in a theatre which he alone saw—which existed only in his heart. The results of his efforts are seen in the fact of the Neighborhood Playhouse School, the work of his students. Many owe a debt to Mr. Meisner and more important, to the same tradition to which he owes a debt—to the tradition of theatre as art. The tradition of theatre as the place we can go to hear the truth."

Even as far back as 1936, Eleanor Roosevelt in her syndicated column "My Day" in the New York Herald Tribune of May 23 said of Sandy's students: "I think they are going to bring a new type of production to the American stage."

Then, in the 1960s, this visionary was asking where was the theater of his dream? He well knew that the rules of free competition that govern industry are not suited to the world of art and culture. He felt that if the only criterion of success is economic, culture is in danger. Producers would choose and were choosing material to satisfy the taste of the common majority—light and worthless.

"Most theater tickets," he said, "are being bought by customers who want a nice evening in New York, with dinner, a show, and if possible good company. What do they care about good experienced theater that confronts challenges? Democratic governments do not seem to understand what totalitarian governments have understood for centuries: we must preserve art. If they will not understand this, it is hard to know where we will go from here."

The theater he saw around him was not the one he dreamed about. With the capitalist system failing the arts, and underfunding cutting into the quality of theatrical production in America, it didn't matter how well he trained his students. The whole situation left him feeling theatrically impotent.

So Sandy was at a point in his life where he welcomed any relief from his futile attempt to make any impression on an impossible situation. A placid beach, a stretch of sand, a palm tree under a tropical sun seemed just the ticket. Even the possibility of retiring altogether in the near future looked appealing. Vietnam, politics, even economics were always kept somewhat remote. As he had in the Group, he tended to keep his opinions to himself. Though he was concerned, he felt it was best left to the professionals. He knew when to accept the inevitable, unlike me. My head was elsewhere in these troubled times. For me, the '60s were a culmination of my dissatisfactions, my dissatisfactions professionally and my dissatisfactions as a citizen of the US.

On the political front, I was ashamed for all those years I deluded myself. I was a member of the silent generation and for this I beg forgiveness. I was almost forty before I began to be politically conscious. Born the year of the '29 Crash and raised during the Depression of the 1930s, I was one of the children saved by President Roosevelt and the New Deal. America was good. Then in the '40s, we teenagers were programmed to wave the red, white, and blue proudly. We ate our creamy cones in a blackout and jitterbugged to Glenn

Miller's "In the Mood" while Dresden burned and Normandy was being invaded. We went about our mundane lives, dreaming of our futures, as if all would work out in the end one way or another.

During the Korean War and the Cold War, I blithely accepted the American way. Questioning nothing and nobody, we believed in the greatest fallacy ever perpetrated upon the American people. When Thomas Jefferson penned that little note of wisdom: "We hold these Truths to be self-evident, that all men are created equal, that they are endowed by their creator with certain inalienable rights..." etc., he made us believe that equality was what America truly represented. Then, in the late '60s, I was much more inclined to believe what my experience had unequivocally shown: "Some men are created more equal than others."

On the professional front, I was exhausted and beginning to recognize my disillusionment. In the mid-1940s when I was still young, I had decided I wanted to become a performer. What else? Remember, the desire was rooted in my insatiable need to be accepted. I started my serious studies at the age of fourteen as a sophomore in high school and ended them with Sanford Meisner in 1964 at the age of thirty-five.

Jimmy (on left) and a couple of friends in Tokyo 1950

The only break in the routine was the few years I spent in the US Army. But I put in twenty years of study and work mastering theater craft, ten of these years while working professionally. I was an active member of five performing unions and yet I was still expected to work for the meager union minimum wage. Why? Because I wasn't a "star." That was just the way of it. The concept of seniority, which exists in so many other industries, held no sway in the theater world. If you were not fortunate enough to become a "star," you were expected to live out your life as a beginner with nothing more than a starting salary. You could never raise your living standard, and you were expected to feel lucky if you had a job at all!

Year after year I kept playing the game, blaming myself for my situation. I really believed if I had integrity, was industrious, diligent, persuasive, and persistent, sooner or later—assuming I had a semblance of talent in the first place—my career would work out well. All these adjectives seem almost Victorian to me now, right out of the 19th century. I must have forgotten, or dismissed as not applying to me, what Lehman Engel once said in class, "Remember, many are called, but few are chosen."

It took a man of Sanford Meisner's stature in the business to convince me it was the system and not of my making. He wanted to know if I was willing to waste what was left of my life waiting for a fluke to happen. To him, situations like mine were the most debilitating and depressing part of being an acting teacher. Here he was preparing talented young actors for a business that would never use them, all because they weren't lucky enough to become a star or feature player. He had been teaching for what seemed like a lifetime, and it had all come to seem so futile to him.

When I mustered up enough courage to ask him what my particular problem really was, he very simply told me that I had a leading-man's head on a character body, and what is any casting director going to do with that? I had turned into a "man-boy." I was difficult to cast—how many Mickey Rooneys does the industry need? Sandy knew what the core of my problem really was. I was thirty-five years old and still playing sixteen- and seventeen-year-olds.

When Lighta Virginia Parker came up to Harlem to head the Speech Department at the School, she said, "My God, Jimmy, you can't be the Director. Why, you're just a kid."

I said, "I hate to disillusion you, Lighta, but I'm thirty-five years old."

In *Bye-Bye Birdie*, my partner was fourteen and I was already thirty-three. Once, when I was doing Bobby in *The Boy Friend* at the Fred Miller Theatre in Milwaukee, a high school senior lived next door to where I was billeted. One morning I was out in the yard looking over a script while he was shooting baskets through a wire hoop over a garage door. Between shots we got to talking. He had seen the show the night before so we went through the usual banter of compliments for the show and myself. He then asked me where I was going next and what show I would be doing and so forth. He even said he would like to go off and do summer stock somewhere himself, maybe paint the scenery and do the little parts. He told me actors must have one hell of a time and those "show-broads" are something else.

He took a long look at me and said, "Yah know, I mean, yah know man, yah know like... what are you going to be when you grow up?" His question was serious. He had no idea of my real age, and he really wanted to know the answer. I was taken aback by the question and I didn't really want to answer. He had stopped dribbling and was looking at me, waiting for a reply. I said, "Man, I've been doing this for sixteen, seventeen years ever since I was eighteen, even longer."

He scratched his head for a minute and then, without another word, grabbed the ball with both hands, bounced it on the tarmac a couple of times, and aimed for the wire hoop, leaving me to my script. For me, that moment was the turning point. I could now see that Sandy was right. I told Sandy about this incident when I got back off tour, so he was well aware that I too was ripe for change—even if I wouldn't admit it yet. Sandy, if he was anything, was a patient man.

I credit most of my personal and professional awakenings to Sandy, my mentor, my better half. So we were both going through our separate but converging disillusionments professionally. What with the racial disturbances in Harlem, the Mafia element one had to deal with in the building trades, and the graft and corruption among city officials over the building codes, the fire department and police on the take, etc., the life we lived was full to the brim with disillusionment. Add to that the mess on the larger political stage—Vietnam and Nixon's election—and even the country looked to us to be in total disarray. We had both just about had it. I wanted out, only I couldn't verbalize it quite yet as Sandy had been doing for quite some time. But I really wanted out, way out!

Way Out With Bequia Up Ahead

Well, now we were way out all right, not a sign of life, just the dark and stillness hanging over us like a shroud. All of a sudden Sir Francis Drake, our sailor friend at the helm, came to life and jumped into action. We had reached the harbor, and it was time to navigate in between the other yachts. Bruce was having the time of his life. I might have also, if I had been able to see what was happening. Everything was as black as pitch, save for the little lights on the boats moored about the harbor, which were a welcome sight. For the past half hour all we had been able to see was a land mass swelling out of the darkness like the back of the Loch Ness monster, black and bleak like something out of a horror film. Not a soul seemed to inhabit it; not even a teeny tiny flicker from a match pierced the darkness, let alone candles or a lamp. What in the hell were we doing here? I asked myself.

Sandy was sitting there in a semi-comatose state not uttering a word or moving so much as a finger. I wasn't about to distract him or bring him around from whatever trance he was in. I could tell from Bruce's and Ann's actions that we didn't have headlights or a roving spotlight to light our way. This was one experience Sandy would do well to miss, at least until it was made unavoidable by our boat ramming into the side of a dark, steel-hull ship or tangling up on somebody's drag line.

Ann was up on the bow with a flashlight in one hand and a long hooked pole in the other. I could just about make out what she was doing. She was guiding the boat through the maze of boats up ahead. When we reached a designated spot, after we sideswiped a boat or two and skimmed over an anchor line here and there, Ann began to jab into the darkness with the spear

4 To St. Vincent and the Grenadines

as if she were going after Moby Dick. Now I'm no yachtsman. I had sailed only once before and that was only on Long Island Sound. But I could see she was in trouble and needed help. Our admiral at the helm couldn't leave his post. I already had my shoes and my soggy socks off, so I rolled up my pants, got up, and worked my way forward to the bow, hanging on for dear life to the stainless steel rope wires that served as guard rails.

"I don't know much about all this, but I can at least hold the flash," I said.

"Thanks awfully," was her reply, not taking her eyes off the black onyx-like sea stretching out before us into nothingness. From her squatting position she thrust the seaman marine torch at me managing to hit me with it right smack-bang in the balls. I had all I could do to keep myself upright, hanging on to the rigging with both hands.

"Christ!" was all I said. She said nothing, as if it had never happened.

The *Luna Quest* was no old boat, and for the longest time I couldn't understand why such a brand new, lovely yacht was having trouble with the electricity. The battery wasn't run down, that was obvious—the motor was running, and the refrigerator worked. I heard later from many a boat captain that electricity and the sea just don't mix. I came to realize nothing much does mix with the sea, except fish, and only live ones at that. I was to learn eventually that anything else becomes part of the sea in time, if you don't keep vigilant fighting the endless battle. Dead fish, boats, piers, wharfs, stone walls, jetties, trees, houses near the sea—sooner or later everything in or around it loses the battle with that champion of champions: Mother Nature.

As we neared shore, everything was a hustle and a bustle, this had to be done and that had to be done, with Sandy and me not understanding any of it. All we could do was make ourselves as small as possible and try to keep out of the way, an impossibility on such a narrow boat. The *Luna Quest* was made for racing, not for transporting landlubbers and much too much oversized luggage. Then, before we knew what was happening, we were off the boat, into a dinghy, and dumped out on the beach—not exactly on the beach, about one foot from the shore. We had to jump, our shoes in hand and our pants rolled up to the knee with the surf splashing well up to and even over our knees as we stumbled from the sea onto the dry sand. Our trousers were soaking wet and our wet feet picked up every grain of sand they came in contact with. Neither of us were nautical people, nor were we down here for the joys and the thrills of the surf and the sea.

"Doesn't this mother island have a pier?" I muttered half to myself for not a soul was in sight and I knew Sandy couldn't see any farther than I could.

We had been left to ourselves as Bruce returned to shut and lock up the boat, then come ashore with Ann and our luggage. My question was answered later when I found out that there was a pier just off to our left and a little farther down the beach. Reaching it would have meant a little more rowing on the part of our ever-obliging sea captain.

Stumbling about, Sandy had found an old wooden dinghy. He was sitting on the end of it with his right foot cocked up on his knee, wiping sand off it with his pocket-handkerchief. His face revealed not one shred of emotion I might pick up on. I shot him one look and he, on the other hand, could read every word I didn't say: it was your idea to come here; I wasn't keen on the idea from the start.

He finished his left foot, shook out the hanky, and handed it to me. I got in the old boat and sat down. Sandy was still sitting on the edge, pulling on his cigarette and staring off into space. It was very dark. Most of the few houses about had only one little kerosene hurricane lamp flickering through the window. Off to the left, here and there, a few houses had what seemed like electricity, some kind of fluorescent light. Far off down the road, I could see one streetlight with one bare light bulb all of seventy-five watts under a saucer-like galvanized shade.

"I read there was no electricity on the island," Sandy said, directing his statement to the feeble glow off in the distance. How were we to know that the island had opened a diesel powerplant just weeks before?

"You call this electricity? What a place." Not very developed, I thought, but then that's exactly what the article in the *Saturday Review* had said: a little bit off the beaten track.

Bequia, we had learned, is one long, undulating hill curving back and forth above the water like a snake from the northeast in the Atlantic to the southwest in the Caribbean. It runs along for approximately six miles and manages to extend for a mile at its widest point. The island's undulating twisting and turning through the water creates thirteen inlets or bays from large to small each offering swimmers a different experience. Currents rush past the island at an angle from the Atlantic into the Caribbean, creating huge waves along some of the beaches. Yet on the leeward side and in some of the bays, the surface is placid and calm.

I knew Bequia had no big tourist hotels like Hilton, Holiday Inn, Radisson, Rockefeller Investments, or a Club Med littering up the place. It was no tourist trap; it was much too small. A few boat people sailed through the Grenadines, but not many. Did it have a university with student unrest? Were there any labor unions with employee and employer disputes? Was there abject poverty and rampant unemployment? Had it a long history of white supremacy, poor US relations? Was the government stable? What about medical facilities and education? Were the people basically independent and self-sufficient? These questions ran through my mind as we sat there waiting for Bruce. We would have to find the answers to them and weigh the yeas and the nays before we took one step in any direction. I could already see the answers to some of these questions before taking another step.

I was still off in my own little world as our captain and crew from the "Royal HMS" *Luna Quest* splashed ashore holding our bags aloft. Ann passed them over to me and I stacked them in the dry sand above the high-water mark. Bruce dashed off in the direction of the more progressive fluorescent-light district, only to dash back a few moments later to tell Ann no taxis were waiting in the Harbour. Then he ran off again in the opposite direction. I could hear Sandy mutter something about a donkey.

"A donkey?" I asked.

"Bruce should have no trouble finding a jackass. At this point anything would do." Sandy was in one of his moods.

"I know where there are two," I jibed.

Sandy laughed. Ann was near enough to detect our discomfort, displeasure, dissatisfaction, disillusionment, and dis-whatever-else, you name it, we had it. Well, I can't speak for Sandy, but that is about where I was. If I know Sandy, he would have given anything at that moment to be home in his own bed on East 83rd Street right in the middle of little old Manhattan.

To ease the situation, and as explanation, Ann said, "Oh! 'e's off to the Frangipani."

"He's off to Fanny who?" I asked.

"The Fran-ji-pan-ni. It's a flower, no, rather it's the name of a guest house down the beach. There should be a taxi over there that will take us to Friendship Bay." She went on. "And here it comes along the beach now."

It was a beat-up Land Rover driven by a man who looked like an East Side hood. Ricky got out of the jeep, said a polite hello, and went to help Bruce. They each grabbed a bag and tossed them into the back of the vehicle. I helped Sandy into the front seat next to Al Capone, Jr., and jumped up into the back of the Rover with the others. We drove along the beach a short distance and turned right onto the smooth cement surface of a narrow road. To the left I noticed a building larger than the rest. "The church?" I asked.

"Anglican," Ann replied.

"Anglican?" I repeated. It sounded English to me.

"Church of England," she explained.

"Oh, like Church of Rome. You mean Episcopal?"

"No, I mean Anglican," she came back.

"In America, we call—" I thought better of it and just left it at that. I sat back to enjoy the smooth ride.

Little did I know how much that building and the church would come to mean to us and what a part it would play in our future! A priest had just been assigned to Bequia, arriving the same week to take up his ministry on the Island. Our paths must have crossed that night as they would many times in the next twelve years.

The smooth ride was too good to be true. It lasted only a short distance and then we started pitching to and fro, bouncing and lurching about like caged balls at a bingo game. I grabbed onto the metal bar with both hands and held on for dear life. I said, "Holy shit, we're off the road. We must be going cross country."

Ann, ever the appeaser, assured me we were still on the road but the government hadn't reached this far with its paving. "They are working on it and some day..." What she couldn't have known was that, although the road is less than three miles long, it was going to take more than six years to complete the project.

"You mean this is the road?" I blustered and spurted out between jolts.

"Oh, yes. See up ahead? The two concrete strips? In some spots they're crumbled to stones with the cement worn away, or they've been washed away by flash floods in the tropical rainy season, but it's the road all right," she assured us.

"'All right?' I've been on better goat tracks."

Bruce, catching the humor, said, "I heard this was a goat track."

"You don't say? Well, I got news for you—it still is," I said.

In due time after many twists and turns we were up and over the back of the huge black serpentine monster that only an hour ago I had seen looming out of the sea. It had looked so foreboding and sinister then, and my feeling hadn't changed one iota as we skimmed across its vertebrae in this beat-up poor excuse for a taxicab.

As we flew over the crest of the hill, Ann said, "Look, this is the most beautiful view you will ever see." I stretched forward, looked out, and saw nothing, not so much as a star. I pulled back and shrugged my shoulders.

"Oh, you can't see it now, the moon's not up yet. It's too dark. But out there is Friendship Bay. It really is a beautiful sight," Bruce butted in.

"If you say so. How far is this hotel anyway?" I asked.

"The Friendship Bay Hotel? Just down this hill to the sea and around to the left. Not far. It's on the beach," Bruce answered.

At the bottom, where we veered to the left, we seemed to turn smack dab into the ocean. It was just an illusion. The next day I saw that the sandy dirt path used as a road came within six inches of the high-water mark before it tapered back into the palm grove that served as an entrance to the hotel. The hotel's concrete strips were in good condition leading from the main gate up and around a slight incline to the main building. It was a fair-sized operation for such a small island. The hotel had many stairs since it was built on the side of a hill.

The staff was standing by, ready to take the luggage. We started up the stairs. The bar was halfway up to the right. Sandy was slowly, very slowly, inching his way up, stopping every other step. We were both beat, but I could see Sandy was in trouble. His emphysema was kicking in and he could not catch his breath. Halfway up the staircase he spotted the bar. It was an open room under the dining room, with a quarry-stone wall behind the bar to the left and open to the bay on the right. Sandy headed straight across the room and sank back into an easy chair.

"God," he said, "this feels good. Please get me a double vodka on the rocks... and a little water, very little water." Well, I wasn't God and I didn't see him in the vicinity nor was anyone else.

Coming up behind us, one of the men lugging a suitcase in one hand with

4 To St. Vincent and the Grenadines

another bag on his shoulder saw me at the bar and shook his head. "De bar she dun close... Come, dey waitin' up de stairs fo ya... Yah see, me de bahtenda but nobody heah jus now."

"Well, we are," I said.

Sandy asked, "What in the world is he saying? Tell him all I want is a little drink, and I'm not moving until I get one."

I went over to our muscular friend and said, "Look, if you are the bartender, how about getting us a drink?"

"De bar she close."

"Come on, be a good buddy. Please put down those bags. Just one little drink?"

He hesitated and shifted from one foot to the other, looked up the stairs and then over at Sandy. "What de hell... Rum and what?" he asked.

"That's the way," I said, slapping him on the back. "No rum. Vodka and water... Me, I'll wait. I don't drink." He didn't seem to understand. He went right ahead and made two. So I took it. It was easier than trying to explain. I figured Sandy could use another one when we got upstairs. After all, he hadn't had a drink since the Pan Am flight. For him, the gin didn't count!

Drinks in hand, we mounted the upper half of the staircase. Sandy's breathing was becoming labored. My ass was dragging, my legs were getting heavy, my feet felt like lead weights, and my eyes were beginning to smart. I felt sticky all over from the salty sea, and the ocean spray made my hair look like a fright wig. Our clothes could have come right out of a Salvation Army thrift shop. I could not begin to imagine how Sandy must be feeling. He really was in a bad way, but he never complained that night, not a word.

As we entered the lounge, three or four heads were poking out from behind the kitchen door. Four waitresses, all dressed up in costume to look like West Indians, which they already were, stood at the entrance to the dining room, and another small group stood in a hallway that I thought must lead to the bedrooms.

A man, about fifty, graying hair, not too paunchy, all dressed in white, had his arm outstretched to shake our hands. A slim, lovely looking, mousy blonde in her early twenties followed just a little behind. She was just a little bit hesitant in a charming way, but he was just the opposite. I could see him sizing up the two of us with the drinks in our hands. He must have thought, ah, just another couple of rummies all the way from the U-S-of-A. Ron Young was English, no question about that. Brenda Punnett looked English enough as well but she wasn't. She was a Vincentian who had been educated in Ireland.

We must have looked a sight, grubby and pale, with Sandy coughing and fighting for his breath. He was barely able to make himself heard because of his laryngitis. Ron and Brenda both later told me they didn't think that Sandy would make it through the night.

Ron, the manager, welcomed us to Friendship Bay and hoped the trip from New York hadn't been too hard on us. "Never mind, a few days out on the beach will do you the world of good. Nothing like the sun to take the kink out of your bones. It will make all the difference," he encouraged.

"I certainly hope so," I blurted out.

Brenda, in her shy, apologetic way, was blushing from ear to ear as she said, "We were beginning to think you weren't going to make it, that you were held over in Barbados or St. Vincent. We had no way of knowing what happened. We have no telephones on the island and that makes it difficult. We use marine two-way radios, but Bruce didn't radio, so we thought his ship-to-shore wasn't working again. Well, no never mind and as we say, 'not to worry'—you made it."

"Better late than never, mates, ha-ha," cheered Ron in his Midlands accent. "I'm sure you'd like to go to your room to freshen up before dinner. We've given you room 15, last room on the right. Nice and quiet that, with a beautiful view of the entire bay. Smashing, smashing." On he went. "It's one of our newest units, just built this August past. You'll be the first guests to occupy it; we ought to have a christening. That would be the fitting thing to do."

"I'll just break this vodka glass on the door, ha-ha," I joked.

Brenda giggled. "No, for God's sake, don't do that. We're in short supply!"

Ron and his brother Stan ran the hotel. They had just taken over the previous April, managing for an American named Bush from New England who had bought the hotel from Noel Agard. Noel was from an old Vincentian family. He had bought the land along the far end of the bay back in '61 or '62 for next to nothing, against the wishes of his headstrong, willful, and rather good-looking redheaded wife. The area was totally undeveloped with no access except by boat or over a small track. He had had to build a road into the property. He had then proceeded to build a twelve-room hotel. This to me made sense. His wife, however, wouldn't leave St. Vincent for Bequia.

I soon discovered most Vincentians wouldn't leave St. Vincent for Bequia, not for so much as a day, even though Bequia has its own particular brand of beauty. Most of them say it's because they do not like the sea, but I think not. I got the feeling they looked on Bequia as some kind of uninteresting backwater, a useless outpost. From St. Vincent, Bequia looked deserted. Its topography, and the southwest angle of the view from St. Vincent, allowed only one light, a kerosene lamp from Moon Hole, to be visible even forty years later. As for Noel Agard, the story goes that while in London purchasing material and supplies for the hotel, he met a pretty little redheaded Irish lass at a five- and ten-cent store lunch counter. He took a fancy to her and asked her to come to Bequia and help run the hotel, since his wife wouldn't. She not only accepted but brought her sister along for good measure. This story could have been and likely was just a rumor, for that is the way of Bequia. Nevertheless, Noel Agard was the typical West Indian male. If he wasn't typical, his brand of the male species certainly was prevalent in these parts. I found most married West Indian men experienced much more sexual freedom than their American counterparts, at least, that is, before the American sexual revolution. I can't say the same for married West Indian women.

The hotel never got off the ground. Noel had no previous hotel experience, and the well-meaning damsels from the Emerald Isle had not a fleeting notion either. It takes more than desires, dreams, and wishful thinking. To Mr. Agard's delight, I am sure, after four or five years he found a buyer and sold it for a profit in 1967 to John Bush for the Young brothers to run. The deal was John's money and the Young brothers' supposed know-how.

Stan Young had met John Bush while sailing in the Caribbean, where Stan captained the charter yacht *Gaivota* working out of Antigua. Stan felt the Grenadines would be opening up to sailing yachts. Bush agreed to set up a small sailing fleet and started by purchasing two slim-lined racing yachts, *Luna Quest* and *Sol Quest*. Stan had heard Friendship Bay Hotel was for sale and conned Bush into purchasing it, too. Stan would operate out of Friendship Bay Hotel chartering the two racing yachts along with *Gaivota*. Stan's brother Ron quit his job, left his wife, and came down from England to manage the hotel. Ron had no experience, not an ounce. He was afflicted with a disease that seems to run rampant up and down the islands. An awful lot of foreigners catch it sooner or later. Many of them wish to live in the West Indies permanently, and out of that wish comes the need to invent something to do to keep them busy or to pay the piper, more often than not both, I suspect.

With so many areas needing development, money was always the primary consideration. Qualifications were pushed to the last, rarely considered at all. The low priority seemed to stem from the foreigners' erroneous belief that they could undertake any endeavor or operation as well as anyone else, certainly better than any West Indian, no proof of credentials needed. Consequently, many businesses were poorly run by unqualified entrepreneurs. The problem was compounded by the lack of trained and experienced personnel at organizational, leadership, and managerial levels on the Islands. You could find experienced experts here and there, and I found most of the time they turned out to be West Indian. These men and women were people of integrity who left the Island to learn their craft and came back home to put it to good use. One can't begin to imagine the frustration they must have endured trying to function productively while being swamped with so much incompetence all around them. Well, all this was not my problem. I just had to make sure, if I stayed here, not to let myself fall into a similar situation.

5 And Boolu Makes Three

Could There Be Such Poverty

Jean, the "room girl" at the Friendship Hotel, guided us down the corridor behind the new units. At the open door at the end of the corridor stood a little fellow who looked as if he were suffering from malnutrition. His stomach was swollen and distended as if he had a bad case of worms. Though his skin was chocolate brown, his hair was bright orange due to vitamin deficiency. His legs, possibly because of rickets, were extremely bowed and hyper-extended, with knees that seemed to bend in the wrong direction. His flashing bright eyes, as glossy as two extra-large black olives, were encased in slanted sockets in a skull a size too large for the bony body it pivoted on. He was scraggly, clothed in mud-caked rags that hung on his tiny body like ruined laundry flapping on a clothesline. I estimated the little ragamuffin to be about eight years old. Was there really such poverty on this island? This tiny tatterdemalion stirred up so many questions in my mind. What was he doing there? Who was he and where did he come from? As we approached the room, Jean shooed the boy away. He sprang like a frightened doe across the clearing into the bush beyond. Where did he belong?

We opened our luggage, freshened up, and changed our clothing. With a little prodding from Brenda, we were hustled off to dinner. It was pretty close to ten o'clock, very late for Bequia. We would learn that as a matter of course, Bequians are up at four-thirty or five in the morning. When she brought us our drinks, I asked "Bet-tee," our very young but oh-so-charming waitress, how many guests were in the hotel.

"No, please...ah, none, please. You be de fost in a long time. Some guests

5 And Boolu Makes Three

dey come Tursday or Friday on we hex-pectin' mo befo Christmas."

Throughout dinner, which was quiet and uneventful, the vision of that little boy pricked away at my mind. Every bite at dinner made me feel shame. I was aware that the sight had bothered Sandy as well. In the middle of dinner, he broke the silence, asking me, "Did you see the eyes on that little waif?" Yes, he too was moved by what we had seen.

Back in the room I checked the windows, ensuring they were mosquito-proof, then went out onto the terrace. I shall never forget the feeling that overwhelmed me then. The spicy sweet smell of the tropical foliage and the feel of the caressing, fragrant, balmy breezes enchanted me. The rhythm of the tree frogs mixed with the rustling leaves of the cedar trees, blending in tantalizing harmony with the melody of the incessant winds wafting softly in off the sea through the whispering coconut palms, all created a symphonic ode to nature, a symphony I had never heard before. Friendship Bay glistened in the silver light of the almost full moon rising over the peninsula to my left, limning the black silhouettes of the islands to the south. The ever-present jet stream had swept away every cloud on the horizon, leaving the sky clear with the isolated moon the sole conductor of this shimmering, silver, tropical fantasia. To me it had to be a fantasy, it could not be totally real. The silvery wavelets out on the bay, the leaves fluttering on the trees, the galvanized roof on the building below, all jumped out at me, taking on a metallic life of their own. It was more than a painting; it was an experience bigger then life.

Sandy came out and looked across the clearing to the left. There, in the midst of all this beauty, the bony, half-starved little boy stood hovering next to a big cedar tree at the edge of the clearing. He was all awash in the silver glow of the nightscape around him. He looked like a tragic nickel-plated figurine on a charm bracelet. Sandy said he looked like a curious little animal. We were both exhausted as we got ready for bed. Sandy said he couldn't stop thinking of the little boy out there in the bush alone and it being so late.

The boy disturbed me too in a way that I had never experienced before. Even in Korea I had never seen the likes of this. I didn't know what to make of it or what to say. I said nothing, but those big, bright, sharp eyes flashing about had pierced through to the very depth of my soul. We would both have been off to sleep before our heads hit the pillow that night were it not for that little tyke at the door. The vision of him was getting to me. Here we were and there he was, with all the questions to be asked: who, why, where, and when? Even if we had asked, no one could have told us the whole true story. For now, we had no answers, nor would we get any.

Boolu

The only living person who knew his story was Boolu himself, and how could he tell us? The boy was deaf and he couldn't speak. Yet in time, little by little, his story unraveled, spilling out over the years from here and there but mostly from him alone. True, his tale may have been altered through time and the fantasies of a small child, but I did my best by checking with knowing Island people at that time as well as with his sister Grace. No one but Grace knew much about him and she knew precious little for she was a child herself. To everyone else, he was just the dummy boy who ran away from crazy Frazeen to live in Ravine.

I must humbly admit by way of apology that I have taken the liberty of changing some of the Islanders' names out of a wish to respect their privacy. I also add my two cents to Boolu's story, my own language, i.e., adjectives of my own to explore the geographical vistas and the complicated physical, cultural, and social mores of Boolu's Island. It would be impossible for Boolu to do justice to the material with his limited vocabulary alone, even after many years of study. So this part of the narration is a joint effort, as it were.

So Let Him Tell It Through Boolu's Eyes: Part I

"Last night, de rats came in again but dey didn't get anytin' dis time because I pulled my feet up under me an', scrunchin' myself inta a ball further away inta de bed, I nestled myself up next ta Boops as much as I could. Me hid my face in my arms; you see, I had nuttin' ta hide my head under. Der was nuttin' but Mommy's bright cloth, if I could get it, de one she carry de provisions home in. It was de one she got from Miz Edmunds who gets dem in de market. I know, 'cause Miz Edmunds take me in she hand once quite down ta de market in de Harbour. Nobody poke or trew anytin' at me dat time because she wouldn't let anyone get at me. Miz Edmunds was good."

Boolu could see the cloth hanging half off the back of the chair. If he could only get over there to get it, he could cover up his head with it. The moon hadn't given up the sky yet. It would begin to slip slowly down, down under the water, way, way out at sea. But no, not yet, the moon was still pushing its light through the large crack of the window shutter. That shutter never did much good, even when it was shut. It let in the wet when it rained and the sharp, sharp cold when the winds came forcing themselves through the cracks.

"Well, de cloth, I couldn't get it ta put over my head even if me dare ta. Me be afraid ta put my feet out on de floor ta go over ta de chair at de table. See, it was Mommy's. Dat is, not my real mommy; my mommy lef me here a long time ago, brought me here from St. Vincent wit Boops an' went off in a boat. Dat was a long time ago.

Anyway, now me be always tied up; Mommy didn't use ta do dat. Now when she go off ta Miz Edmunds', she tie a twine roun my wrist an' secure me ta de bed or sometimes ta de pole. She even tie me up in P.H. Veira's Market, in a corner outta de way while she do her shoppin', so I can't take off. Now, be-

5 And Boolu Makes Three

fore she go ta work at Mistress Wallace's or Miz Edmunds', she leave me in de locked house wit a long rope tied ta my wrist, which she secures ta de post in de middle a de room dat holds up de two-by-four dat runs from wall ta wall."

The post was supposed to be holding back the walls, but the walls looked as if they were slipping, especially the wall on the hill side, because all that rain would wash away the mud from underneath. It was worse during the long wet season when the rain comes down in torrents and the strong winds blow in off the sea.

"It get so cold at night de blanket she so tin dat I shake till de warm sun comes in. Der aren't enough blankets ta keep de cold off my skin. So I keep my head in my arm an' one eye open so I can see each an' every one a dose long white bellies scurry cross de two-by-four down de side a de wall next ta de window, dat's where I be. Der was four a dem, or was it five? No matter, I couldn't count den, but dey sure was big. Dey was about half de length a Mommy's cutlass. One was comin' at me down at de foot a de bed, pushin' his nose dis way an' dat. He never seemed ta take his eyes off me. I pushed back up agains Boops but she was asleep. I couldn't go back any further because der was no more room in de bed. Dose eyes comin' closer an' closer... I began ta tink bout de udders. Where were dey? Me didn't dare ta look, dis one was so close. Everytin' was so still. Even de wind seemed ta stop. Der was jus dose eyes, dat's all dat der was. It was down at de edge a de bed now. I looked down. Me tink it found some bits a bread. I musta dropped dem when I had my afternoon tea. We always had bush tea an' bread when Mommy came home. Well, sometimes we did, when she could get de bread or make some, an' yesterday she did. Yes, it was nibblin' de bread, or sometín' anyway, an its eyes were not on me, an' I knew dat moment was my chance.

De last time a rat came in, it was not at me. It was headed for de salt fish Frazeen had in a tin up on de shelf. Dat time, I be jus sittin' on de bed, Boops be asleep. Frazeen was in she room smokin' de weed an singin' an mumblin' incantation, half awake. De rat was a big gray rat dat came down from de coconut tree. Dat night, wit its bright shinin' eyes an' white, needle-like teeth, just as sharp as a barracuda's only smaller, an its legs splayed out in four different directions each one tipped wit out-stretched claws shaped an' shinin' like de crescent of a new moon, de rat just knocked de tin wit de fish off de shelf an came flyin' down like a bat. Yes, it like de bats dat hang upside-down in de mango trees down off Tony Gibbons Beach. Oh, life! right on ta de fish dat fell outta de tin. I yelled an' yelled an' kicked an' kicked, but it jus scurried away inta de udder room. So dat be how dis time when de rat came inta de house, me knew what ta do an' what not ta do. You don't holler or yell, you quietly wait till it be busy eatin' or pickin' at sometin'. So now when he was eatin' de crumbs offa de bed, I knew dat dis was my chance, me had ta move fas. Dis was de moment ta kick, an' kick I did.

De rat didn't run dis time. It flew cross de room, hit de wall, an' fell ta de floor. Boops rolled over ta face de wall, mumbled sometin', an' went back ta sleep. De rat just laid der still as death. Yet dis was nuttin' compared wit all de rats I seed at night in de children ward at de hospital in town."

The children's ward was right out back of the main building of St. Vincent's Hospital in Kingstown and must have been pretty near the place across from the cemetery where they threw the hospital waste. The waste would get carried off after God knows how long a wait—till someone got around to it—barely before the rats had carted it all away. Boolu remembers being taken to the hospital in an ambulance when he was very little. He was still living in town with his oldest sister June. June was all of thirteen years old when she was pulled out of school and had Boolu and Grace ("Boops") left in her care by their mother before she took off for Trinidad the first time. That was before she came back for him and Grace and took them over to her mother, Frazeen, on Bequia.

One day Boolu had run away from June and was down at the waterfront with the older kids. No one was paying him any mind as he played out on the rocks that stretched out into the deeper waters. Somehow he slipped off and fell in. He remembers his head being down and his feet up as he went down, down, down. Everything was all green. As he described what happened, "Den a porpoise or two come an butt me back up ta de top. It felt like two a dem."

Apparently, a fisherman in a boat spotted him floundering on the surface and rowed over and plucked him from the sea. The man then rowed him in to shore and had someone call for the ambulance. I don't know how long he was kept at the hospital, but he remembers staying in a rather large room with many children and fearing nightfall when the many white-bellied rats would come scurrying across the rafters overhead. He recalls a young fellow next to him named Burton who kept banging his head against the wall and shaking his crib. It is hard to believe he still remembers his name. Burton kept eating all the soap on the sink, and Boolu remembers he eventually died. Later June told me she remembers getting called to the hospital because Boolu had been taken there.

"When Mommy woke me up, de rat was gone. Me knowed den as me looked at de floor where de rat had fallen, sprawled out an still as death, like a dead, cold, dry fish washed ashore in Belmont, wit his milky white senseless eyes starin' at de sky, me knowed like me never knowed before dat I too must get up an go. Go like de rat, but where? Oh, God! Where?"

Boops came in. She had already taken the goats up the road and tethered them just under the second turn up the hill. The grass is always greener there and the big sapodilla tree shades them from the noonday sun. She had her dress on, her only real dress, the one she got from Mrs. Edmunds. Her pencil and book were on the table. Boops would be going down the hill to the Harbour soon, to the primary school in the big building where all the children go every day. But not Boolu.

"I remember when I be a little boy in St. Vincent, me went inta a big buildin wit all de children wit my own pencil an pad-paper. After awhile, when all de children start laughin' at me an' pushin' an hittin' me, dey sent me home wit my big sister June an tol her ta keep me der, an I never went back."

That was a long time ago. Boolu knew that, like Boops, Frazeen would be gone all day, working in Mrs. Edmunds' yard or up Mt. Pleasant washing clothes. They would both leave after they had had their tea. Frazeen used to take Boolu with her, but not anymore. So today would be no different from any other for the past few months. He would not be going down the hill. Boops would be gone, Frazeen would be gone, the goats would be gone, and he would still be there, tied to the pole with the twine knotted and secured to his wrist. He would be able to move about but he would not be able to reach the door to get out.

Their day would begin at 5:30 in the morning. Boolu knew nothing about clock time. But he was familiar with the time when the sun would rise way out on the eastern sea where the breezes make little wavelets that turn white as coconut meat as they tumble over on top of themselves.

"Dis be de time Frazeen poke me wit de bamboo broom ta wake me up. It be still dark in de room, so she light a candle. What time was it? It was time for Mommy ta leave an go down de hill."

By this time the sunlight is reaching over the sea. As the coconut trees and the tops of the big mangos, breadfruit, and sapodillas sway back and forth dancing to the tune of the soft trade winds rustling through their branches, they send off lovely yellow light through their lush green leaves. By about 6:30 or 7:00, Boops would be getting ready to leave for school.

"De sun be jumpin' over de windowsill an inta de room, an de whole house an' everytin' in it changes. Everytin' takes on a new life, just like we do every mornin' when we wake up.

Now de children start comin' down de hill from Mt. Pleasant. And now I have dat sickenin' sense a sometin' happenin'. I couldn't see it, but me could feel it. De pole I was leanin' my back agains while sittin' on de floor shook. It was a quick vibration as sometin' hit agains de pole wit a tud an' shook de pole ta its foundation, which wasn't much in de first place. I didn't have ta figure out what was happenin'. It had happened many times before, at leas once a day, even sometimes twice. Den a rock about de size a my fist came flyin' tru de window an' it land on de table an' bounce off inta de back room.

I stood up ta look out de window ta see who was doin' it dis time. Sure 'nough, it was de same two who been doin' it all week, David an' his brother George, de Bunyan boys. One a dem jus let loose a handful a pebbles dat landed on de roof an' were spillin' off de edge a de galvanize right in front a de window. Dey was standin' out at de edge a de road. Comin' down de road behin de boys were tree girls, all a dem on der way ta de big buildin' in de Harbour. De boys would look at de house an' den back at de girls. De girls stopped walkin' an' just stood der. One was so pretty, her hair so bright, so long, so soft an' light dat it bounced back an fort cross her back an up inta de air wit every move a her body an' every little wisp a breeze. It was jus like de tail a Uncle Mellies' donkey—de exact same color, like straw, an' flippin' in de exact same manner—an' every bit as beautiful. If she could be like Uncle Mellies' donkey fo jus a little moment an' let me pat an' stroke her hair an' neck, I could hold her head soft an' warm next ta me. Her eyes are like de clear sky. No, not exactly. De blue in de sky surrounds de little puff a white dat sails across it, while de blue in her eyes be floatin' in pure white pools. Just de opposite, but just de same—beautiful. De udder girl, de fat one, she shakin' all over wit her lips pulled back an' all her teeth showin', her head goin' back an' fort an' her shoulders shakin' as well.

Dey were all doin' it now. Dey was laughin' at de boys trowin' stones at my Mommy's house. De boys were yellin' at me I could tell; dey was movin' der mouts like de knothole we have in our door. Boops did dat when she wanted me. If she did it real hard an' I was real close, me could hear 'Boo-oo, Boo-oo.' I found out later, much later, it was 'Boolu.' Dey was all doin' it now, even de girls, 'Boo-oo, Boo-oo.' Dey was makin' funny faces, stupid faces wit der lips goin' in an' out. Den dey was laughin' an' shakin' all over. One was knockin' de udder over in de road wit a push while de udder couldn't stop laughin'. What was so funny? Why dey do it? Just like in St. Vincent. How I hate it. Why dey do dat?

I was so busy watchin' dem dat I didn't notice how close dey were comin' ta de window where I be standin'. Den, wap! A stone de siza a fowl's egg bounced off my forehead. I stepped back an sat down outta sight, but before I stepped back me could see de boys an' de girls jumpin' up an' down, clappin' der hands an' laughin' so hard dey were so happy.

As I sat der outta sight, I asked meself why. Me really didn't understan why. Will me ever understan? Rats, dey most a de time run from ya. All dey really want is Mommy's salt fish dat she keep in a tin up on de shelf, an' dat is because dey be hungry. Dogs don't hurt ya or bite ya unless ya go too close ta der house. You can go quite up ta der gates an' walk by an' dey won't hurt ya. Even cats will let ya pet dem, even if some will run if ya try. Udders will scratch, claw, or bite ya, but dat is if ya try ta pick dem up. Goats will not hurt ya an' sheep don't hurt ya. Truth is, I really don't understan people, even Mommy. Why people be so different? Mommy be always beatin' me. Every time I break loose an' she an' Boops have ta come an' catch me an' fetch me back home, or if I come back on my own late at night because me hungry or scared a de dark, she beat me. Sometimes I wait till real late, so dey be asleep, but Mommy never is. She be up watchin' fo me wit de balata."

This balata was a thick rope dipped in tar and dried as was done on ships many years ago. Ships' captains used them to keep their crews in line, doling out punishment by flogging the men with lashes. The origin of this one could have been an old cargo ship or even an old whaling ship; those ships of old came into the Harbour every now and again bringing provisions. It might have been handed down for years through the Gumbs family, Frazeen's people.

Today balatas are more likely to be made from the sapodilla tree. With all its dried juices, it makes for a good strong whip. Frazeen used that old rope balata on Boolu liberally when she felt he deserved it. If he was coming back late on his own—if Frazeen and Boops hadn't dragged him home—he would find the door latched and have to pound on it. Frazeen would open it a crack, take a good look out, and, as she opened it wider, yell out, "Zat you, John?" That's what she called him. When his real Mommy brought him to her mother, Frazeen decided to call him John Reno after her father, Boolu's great-grandfather even though the name his mother had given him was Julian Martin.

"So der she would be standin' over me, holdin' de door open wit one hand an' de balata in de udder. I do believe dat moment, as many times as it happen, was de longest moments a my life. She be so tall, hangin' on de door wit one hand an' de balata in de udder. I can still see her standin' in front a me an' de dark night starin' at my back."

The dark night, the fearful dark night full of jumbies, the Bequian word for zombies, soucouyants, jack-o'-lanterns, and dead people who walk the hill at night, like old John Reno, Granny Lacey, and so many he didn't know nor did he want to know. Then there were the scorpions in the banana leaf, the centipedes in the mud, the steel-gray garter snakes in the trees that jump out and wrap around an arm or your neck, the long black snakes in the tall grass, the brown-and-orange-checkered Congo snakes with their mean bite back in the crevasses of the rocks, and the little black and fuzzy tarantulas that make their home under the rocks beyond Park Bay.

"All dis me tink me could face an' even handle if I had ta. De hardest ta take was de hunger in my belly an' cold wet rain on my skin as well as de sharp cold wind dat pierced tru my clothes at night. It was much worse outside dan inside where I at least had a bed an' de blanket next to Boops ta help keep out de cold."

Need he say more? What choice did he have? Frazeen would slam the door, balata in hand, the tar-dipped rope about a yard long and a half-inch or so thick, and she would start whipping him around the legs, back, his bottom, everywhere and anywhere.

"I would try grabblin' it, but it jus stung my hand. I could never hang on ta it; she was too big, so strong an' so tall. Anyhow, de more me grab, de madder she get an' de harder she hit. Her eyes would go all afire an' she didn't even seem ta see me. Sometimes she would beat me so long dat my head would get dizzy-like, an' de blows would come from far off an' when dey made contac wit my skin, de impac seemed delayed an' far, far away. De hurt would begin ta fade away an' it wouldn't hurt anymore."

Boops would try to stop her but she was small and skinny like Popeye's Olive Oyl, and Frazeen would only shove her against the wall. Boops would sit there crying and hiding her head so she couldn't see anymore. Then it was over. Boolu would often have passed out.

"I would wake up an' open my eyes to see Frazeen lookin' down at me. She would be rockin' me in her arms, cryin', hummin' an' singin' sometin' me didn't know. She would be sayin' over an' over, 'My John, my John, my John.'

Den she would put me ta sleep on de bed next ta Boops. She would wake me in de mornin' wit de broom handle jus like any udder mornin', singin' an' laughin' as if nuttin' had happened de night before."

Only it did happen and he could still feel it. His legs would be swollen, or his face. He wouldn't be able to open an eye, or his lips would be cracked and bleed a little. To Frazeen it didn't seem to have happened at all. The welts would not go away for days and most of those who saw them only pointed and laughed at him. Yet others would look kind of sorry for him—but never interfere. Not one of them would do anything to help him. No one would tell Frazeen to stop.

"I never saw anyone barkin' at Mommy fo what she did ta me. No, Mommy wasn't good ta me all de time." [But she was good to him some of the time.]

When she got work from Murrie Wallace, we would go der an' clean out de field a de ol' corn stocks after de stocks dried an' turned brown an brittle. How I loved dis time a year. Not jus because I got ta go out inta de fields wit Frazeen, but we also got plenty a pumpkins an' tanyas fo soup. I liked workin' in de fields wit Mommy. She be always soft an' gentle den. She sing an' laugh an' pat me on my head an' on my bottom. So did Miz Edmunds, but not Miz Murrie. No, not Murrie. She always had sometin' for me ta eat though."

Still Boolu knew "like I never knew before dat I too must get up an' go. Go like de rat, but where? Oh, God! where?

"She mus be washin' de clothes today because dat's Mommy cutlass over der, on de table. But me can't reach it. If me could reach de leg a de table wit my hand an' pull it closer, I might be able ta get my hand on dat cutlass an cut dis rope... Dat's it, got it. Easy... easy. No, I can't get it; it's not close enough. If I pull de leg some more... a little more... What's dat? De knife fell on de floor... De leg a de table stuck in a knothole in de floor. Now I can't get it, me can't reach it. Wait! I can reach dat broom an' scrape de cutlass cross de floor over ta me. Dat's it, now me got it... A couple a whacks at de rope will do it... My wrist hurts from de rope, but den my head hurts from de stone. I washed de blood off my forehead wit de water Boops lef me. Wait, I better take some out fo drinkin'. Dat is why Boops lef it fo me in de first place. I have it wit me bread when I get hungry. Boops always leaves me sometin.'"

The sun was now way out over the hill and clear out over the sea. Boolu knew the day was half over; it always is when it hits the top of the sky and begins to fall down over the western sea. The mangos were green on the tree outside the window but would become soft and juicy soon. He wouldn't have to wait for that. He could knock them down with a big stone and put them in his pack to eat when they started to get soft. If he were to eat them now when they were hard and green before they got sweet, his belly would get sick. He wouldn't be able to stand up with the pain until he messed himself all down his legs.

"Den I would mess fo days. First de pain, den de mess would come runnin' down witout any warnin' cep de quick sharp pain an' den, swish—all over everytin'. I remember eatin' green mangos down in Belmont. I was workin' wit Mommy at Miz Edmunds'. Mommy was doin' de washin' out back, an' Miz Edmunds was in her fancy front sittin' room sewin'. She had me sittin' on de big long chair, de one wit de tree cushions ta sit on an' de tree cushions ta lay your back agains. I had de cat in my lap, an' we bot were playin' wit a piece a cloth. De cloth was a bunch a pretty colors. I tink she was goin' ta put de cloth up over de windows. Me know because she keep walkin' back an' fort between de windows an' de little machine she be workin' on. She had a long ribbon she would hold up ta de window an den hold it along de cloth. She would den trow de ribbon roun she neck an' go back ta her machine an' work some more.

I felt de sharp quick pain but me didn't know what ta do. I just sat der an' swish—. De cat made one leap from my lap straight fo de window, cep de window be closed. Dat did not stop dat cat, he kep on goin' an' BINGO! Or BANGO! He landed on de floor behin de chair. De curtain fell down on top a me, an' swish—it happened again. I looked up ta see Miz Edmunds standin' up, her machine knocked over lyin' on de floor. My bottom was stickin' ta my pants dat were stickin' ta de cushions a de chair. It was runnin' all over de cushion an' down de side a my legs onta de floor. Well, not on de floor but on de hand-made rag rug dat was on de floor.

She grab my hand an' pull me off de chair, an' again right der in de middle a de room, swish—. She held her nose wit one hand, an' not lettin' go a my hand she quickly led me from de room, tru de dinin' room inta de kitchen an' right out de back door inta de yard. I knew me was leavin' a trail behin me like a goat. I also knew dat a goat's trail would be a lot easier ta clean up dan de mess dat I lef. I might add dat I didn't get back ta Miz Edmunds' house for many a week. Me never did see de inside a her fancy front room again. Nor did I ever fill my belly wit green mangos again either."

So on his own he would know better than to eat his green mangos too soon. But this was it, this was the time. He was ready to go, and he had a feeling that this time was going to be different.

"I drank what was lef in de tin cup my sister lef me an' stuffed de bread she lef inta my pocket, de only one I had lef. De udders were all ripped. I closed de door behin me an' went out ta de edge a de road. I knew dat down de road would be de wrong way ta go."

Boolu used to like to go down to the wharf when the ships came in and unloaded. Everyone met the ships when they came in. They still do.

"I didn't get ta de Harbour very often, because Mommy kep me away from der. I know why—because she tought de people were bad an' she was always fightin' wit dem. Some were bad an' some would hurt me, but not all a dem. Der were some dat would give me sweeties, an' udders would give me a copper or a ha'penny or even a shillin', an' I would jump-up an' dance fo dem an' sometimes I said my words fo dem. You know, I would say, 'Holly poko, diggina potatee, imprim' an' udder words, an' everyone would laugh an' joke, but real nice-like. Dey like me den. Dat is when Frazeen would come an' make me stop what I was doin' an drag me off home."

Much of Frazeen's over-protection of Boolu stemmed from a paranoid streak she had been plagued with for years. But people played right into it. Every time he got loose and went down to the Harbour where all the people were, someone would see his mommy or Boops and tell them where he was or which way he'd gone. Sooner or later they would find him and fetch him home again. If instead he went up the road, all the people in Mt. Pleasant knew his mommy, too. When they saw him up on the hill, they all knew he was running away and would tell her. It made no difference who saw him; if they couldn't catch him, they would get someone else to chase him. They were much better at it than his mommy and Boops. He felt that Mommy was getting too old and Boops did not want to catch him anymore. The boys in Mt. Pleasant seemed to enjoy catching him and bringing him back to his mommy. They would push out their ugly lips and screw up their faces into that stupid look and shout "BOO-OO... BOO-OO," pushing and shoving him all the way home. Boolu would much rather have been caught by Mommy or Boops.

Now he thought that if he went up and quite over that hill, past Mt. Pleasant to the other side, what did they call that place? Nobody goes there anymore. Oh, ya! It's Ravine. Only one double-ender rests there now. It belonged to the Davis boys who used to go out fishing from Ravine. The old one had something wrong with his back. He couldn't stand up straight and he walked with a cane, possibly from the bends, a common malady around here. So they had stopped fishing out of Ravine some time ago. Ravine was left for the animals.

So if Ravine was the place, how to get there? He couldn't go up the road and straight into Mt. Pleasant. That would be stupid, he would never make it. He would have to go up the Quam Gutter, the one that runs down to Tony Gibbons Beach. Quam Gutter would be dry now, and it would give him shelter from anyone on the road. The growth there is thick, with bush and trees growing all the way along it to the top. He would also come out a little distance from Mt. Pleasant. That would be the best way.

Getting there would be tough. The dogs at Lacey's place would hear him, and he would have to get right across their backfield. They had just cleared it and were waiting for the first big rain to finish up their corn holes. If he made it through there, he then had Gun-Munro's dogs to worry about on the far side of Quam Gutter. If they heard him, they would give him a lot of trouble.

Trouble or not, this was it. He took off, keeping to the left side of the road as he went up. When he reached the edge of Lacey's place, he knew he was forgetting something. What was it? Ah, he knew what it was. He turned around and dashed back to the house. Flinging the door open, he went in.

"I picked up a crocus bag from over in de coiner an' walked toward de shelf

5 And Boolu Makes Three

where de tins an' tools an' my little knife lay, de one Boops gave me. I used ta help Mommy an' Boops peel provisions wit dat knife, an' clean fish, an' cut small bush ta start fires. I put it in de crocus bag along wit de tin cup, an' I grabbed de rope Mommy tied me ta de pole wit an' stuffed it in de bag also. I rolled de bag up real small an' tucked it under my arm. Steppin' outta de house, I closed de door behin me. As it snap shut, me felt sometin' snap inside a me as if sometin' broke. I knew it had sometin' ta do wit Boops, but even Mommy, too."

He felt a blush of sadness creep over him as he turned and walked to the road. Just for a second, a slight moment, he thought of his real mommy and St. Vincent. Where was she? Where was St. Vincent where he felt safe and then—?

"Where was I goin'? Oh, ya! Up over de hill ta Ravine, an' I knew I had better get goin'. When I reached de road, me stopped an' turned roun ta take one last look."

There it was—a little faded red shack that had shifted and come to rest on one side, with one window and one door with a knothole in it and a rusted galvanized roof that let in the rain. He went all funny inside. He must have known then that this time would really be the last.

"I took one deep breath an' turned roun an' headed up de hill ta Lacey's backfield."

Boolu was now finally headed up the road to a new and different adventure, whether he was ready for it or not. And whether we were ready for it or not, as we drifted off to sleep in our hotel room near Ravine, Sandy and I would be awakened to a new world, albeit a very small world, a world that would come to mean so much to the three of us—to "de tree a we."

Searching

Since the beach wasn't a priority on this trip, the day after our arrival we took off with Ricky, our "Mafioso" jeep driver, to look at some land that was up for sale. It was part of his family's land up over Ravine. It was just more than a little too far from the beach. It would also cost a great deal to get a road in, and who knew when electricity would reach this far from the powerhouse?

"Beautiful view, but too many negatives," Sandy concluded.

"Turning down Mafia land isn't a smart thing to do," I said aside to Sandy.

Sandy replied, "You'd better make friends with this guy. He may be the Don and prove to be very useful later."

The following afternoon we went over to Lulley's Chandlery. We had heard the owner had land for sale as well as the chandlery. An American, Ross Lulley had visited the Island while on duty as a sailor during the Second World War. After the war, he had come to Bequia on his honeymoon and never left. He built a house and opened a chandlery for fishermen, complete with bar for thirsty patrons, the only chandlery ever on Bequia and the best in the area. Eventually he and his wife had had four or five kids and now he was ready to sell some of the property and the chandlery and retire early. As fellow Americans, we felt it would be prudent to talk to him as he might advise us in our quest.

At the small bar sat a man drinking all by himself. Lulley stood behind the bar. When we told him why we were there, he grumbled, "You need nuggets of gold to buy land on Bequia."

Sandy was taken aback by his gruffness but only a little. He retorted, "We have nuggets of gold, now where's the land?"

When the guy at the bar heard this, he laughed so hard he damned near fell off his bar stool. The laughter obviously disturbed Ross Lulley; apparently he wasn't used to having anyone, especially locals, laugh at his expense. He was, we would learn, a man who always managed to stay on top of a situation by being verbose.

Now he turned to Sandy and said, "Well, I got something for sale. You can have the whole lot for $35,000 US."

"No, no, no," Sandy answered, "we're only interested in an acre or two."

At that point the Bequian at the bar spoke up, wanting to get another one on Ross. "You know, I have land I could sell ya." And looking straight at Lulley, he continued, "It won't cost ya $35,000 US either."

"Jimmy," Sandy said, "I guess we've found something to look at. When can we see it?"

"Tomorrow morning. My name's Verne, Verne Wallace from Friendship Bay down on the beach."

With a "Thank you, thank you," and "We'll see you tomorrow," we were off.

That evening we had dinner at the hotel. No one else was there except the Ford family: Russell, Hope, and their children Holly, Lucia, Kitty, and Rusty. They had arrived to spend a family Christmas together. They had previously bought land from Agard, the last owner of the hotel; it was a piece just up the hill behind the hotel and a little over to the right overlooking the hotel. They expected to be building in a few months.

At dinner that night, we were served Campbell's soup with a whole tomato out of a tin sitting in the middle of the bowl. I don't know what the manager thought he was doing, probably trying to pass it off as homemade soup. All he achieved was to convince me that he knew nothing about food and was certainly no cook. He acted as if he were the owner. He let the kids handle everything in the kitchen. They were teenagers, little more than children. Our waitress, Paulette, was young, attractive, and indifferent. Sandy noticed it and said so.

"Why do you think so?" I asked.

"Because you've had to tell her everything twice."

For dessert she brought a piece of something that looked like cheesecake,

5 And Boolu Makes Three

but I wasn't sure. It was no more than an inch square and frozen hard as a rock. When Sandy saw the size of it, he suggested I have his too. As he had already refused his, and Paulette had taken it back to the kitchen, he asked Bet-tee, who was waiting on the one and only other table in the dining room, to get our waitress to bring back his dessert. Paulette took her good time coming back and then banged it down on the glass tabletop with a sound that reverberated throughout the room. Then she stood there with her arms folded, right next to the table, staring out the window at the sea. Someone in the kitchen must have told her to keep an eye on our table, and this was her version of complying.

At this point Sandy had had it and spoke out in stentorian tones, "Will you get the fuck away from us?"

No matter how furious he was, this was not Sandy's usual choice of expletive. He never would allow this kind of language even in his classes. While he had all the patience in the world in his classroom, he was a man who had little patience with incompetence, no matter where it reared its ugly head, and he refused to suffer indifference. As Paulette scurried from the table, the Ford family stared over at us like we were piranhas.

By that time I had realized what this frozen block really was. It was a little piece of frozen unbaked pie that looked like something dreamed up by Sara Lee. The kitchen help didn't know it needed to be thawed and baked. I showed Sandy and when Ron the manager, checking on Paulette's table, asked what was wrong, Sandy handed him the frozen pie. "This," he said.

The next morning we went to the south end of the beach to Verne's to look at his land. His property extended from the southwest end of the hotel property all the way down the beach, up the hill to the Paget Farm road, across the road and up the hill to the very top of Monkey Hill. It was about thirty-five acres in all. We walked through the magnificent stately palm grove planted in the 1890s by Verne's father and his oldest sister, Doris. The grove was located behind the sea grape bushes that lined the sandy beach forming the perfect crescent of Friendship Bay. On the southwestern end of the grove, we hiked up the steep hill to the main road leading to Paget Farm. We stood on the road, overlooking the Bay and most of Verne's property. The rest of his land continued across the road behind us and up another steep hill to the top of Monkey Hill.

Verne wanted to know, "Well, what do you think?"

"What a view," I said, but then from most anywhere on the Island you could say that.

Sandy asked if the land across the road and up the hill was his, and Verne said, "Yeah, are you interested in a spot up there? How much would you like?"

Sandy answered, "Depends."

"Sandy, what about this end of the grove along the beach?" I asked.

Ignoring me, Sandy asked Verne, "What are you asking for this land?"

"That depends on how much you want. I took a liking to you two. You see, I never sold land to anyone before. I'd sell it to you for the government asking price."

"That sounds fair enough to me," said Sandy, "But we're only interested in building a house, and we only need an acre or so. Ricky told me a foreigner can only buy an acre per person. If it's all right with you, we'll get back to you by Boxing Day. This will give Jimmy and me time to think it over."

Sandy and Verne shook hands on it, and we walked back to the hotel along the beach. I could tell that Sandy felt positive toward Bequia and this spot as well. I liked the spot very much, too. True, Verne's property had a lot of things going for it. It was undeveloped, so no other houses would be near us, making it private. It was on one of the smaller but most beautiful bays in the Caribbean, positioned to take full advantage of the trade winds. It would not be part of a foreign enclave and yet not be in the middle of a local village or settlement. To me this was all so inviting, but for one thing. When we had set out on this venture, I had agreed to accompany Sandy to Bequia only if he would continue on down to Tobago to look at some land an American had for sale, for some reason at a give-away price.

Well, from the 18th through the 26th including Christmas was nothing but—what shall I call it? We couldn't be fighting! We were at a hotel. Safe to say, it was a running dialogue, non-stop. It boiled down to Sandy's seeing no reason to go any further and my feeling it wouldn't hurt to look at Tobago.

"I've already been there with Betty," he said. "I've seen Tobago and it's no contest, believe me."

"Sandy, I think that Bequia may be too small for our lifestyle. OK, maybe for your retirement, but what would I do for the rest of my life?"

"Fish!" Sandy snapped. "Jimmy! Nonsense! I know you, you're resourceful. You'll find something to do. You could run a hotel, open a tourist agency, design houses. Oh, Jimmy, you name it."

"Thanks for the compliments. Sure I could do those things, any one of them, but not here. Maybe on a larger island like Tobago. Let's go," I insisted.

"No, Jimmy. Remember that list we made up? You will never find a place that fits those requirements any better than this. There will be rioting and union unrest in Trinidad before you know it and that goes for Tobago as well. Mark my words."

God, I thought, I have been marking his words for the past seven years and that isn't helping me now. I figured I would wear him down, but he wasn't yielding, no matter what I said.

Christmas wasn't much fun, except for Ruth and Jo. Ruth Derujinsky, a former Ford model, an actual cover girl from the '50s, had been invited down by Stan who was in charge of the hotel's yachts. Her high school friend Jo Ynocencio, from Valley Stream, Long Island, was a costume designer for movies and TV commercials. They were interesting and looked like a hell of a lot of fun. But I was in no mood, so at first I was just polite.

Boxing Day had arrived and the gap widened in our argument, so there was no trip to Verne's. But that day Sandy issued his final word. It was not an ultimatum; it was just a statement. "Jimmy," he said, "it's Bequia for me or nowhere. I know what I need. I've been all over the place and now I need peace. And you know I need you, too."

Well, I knew Bequia wasn't for me. "I have my whole life ahead of me, well, what's left of it anyway. I need you, too, and you know that," I yelled. "But I'm going to pack and go back home," I snapped. "You can stay and rest; you have a whole season of work ahead of you."

I pulled my bag out of the closet, slammed it on the bed, and threw my clothes into it. I was furious. Sandy went out and sat in the lobby. I went out and sat on the terrace. After a while, Sandy came in and lay down. Eventually we both dressed and went to dinner together, neither of us saying a word.

After dinner Sandy went to the room and I went down to the beach bar and spent the evening with Jo and Ruth. When I came back, Sandy was in bed asleep. I went out onto the terrace and sat there looking out over the bay, my mind racing. I was still furious. The interlude at the bar with the women hadn't helped one bit. I got a joint from one of the kitchen hands, and if ever there was a time I needed one more, I sure couldn't remember.

I went over the list we had made in New York. There shouldn't be any institutes of higher learning where there might be student unrest, no industrial complexes with labor disputes, no large cities with their urban sprawl creating problems, no abject poverty, no high unemployment, no large airports or train stations, no freeways, speedways, or turnpikes, no bugs and swamps, no extreme weather such as freezing cold, nor very hot, humid, or incessant rain with days and days of overcast, and not too many seasonal tourists. My God! It flashed on me, Sandy was right!

Virtually everything we were looking for was in this place! Bequia had easy access to and from New York, hospitals in the vicinity on St. Vincent and Barbados, unspoiled, friendly people and a government to match. It was small, English speaking, and had constant temperate weather for the most part. It was a place where foreigners could own, keep, or sell their home if they wished, with a pretty view, and a breeze, and even friendly diplomatic relations with the good old U-S-of-A!

By then the moon hung high in the heavens, big and full right out in front of me over the bay. The lighting effect on the water was eerie. Every ripple gave off a silver glow. Everything was bathed in silver. The breezes were soft and so gentle, and the palm trees swayed in tune with the steel band at the beach bar off in the distance. Was I in paradise or was the smoke just taking over? Whatever, I could not deny the realization. Damn it! Damn it! Damn it! I thought. He's right again. I don't know what the hell I'll do here, but I'll be damned if I won't give it my all! Anything has got to be better than New York and all its rejections. For fifteen years I had been fighting an uphill battle to earn a decent living in the entertainment business and I was tired of coming up against a stone wall. Sandy felt as though he were finished, and at this moment I had to agree with him—at thirty-nine, so was I. I threw my joint away, what was left of it, got up, went into the room, and quietly, very quietly, unpacked and went to bed.

In the morning, as the sun broke gloriously over the hill to our left and bathed our room with a warm lemon-yellow glow, we still didn't speak. It wasn't until we were served our coffee in the dining room and Sandy took his first pull on his cigarette that I looked up and said, "If we're ever going to buy that property, we had better get over to Verne's place and make a deal." Sandy looked me squarely in the face and said nothing. He smiled and then continued eating his breakfast.

That morning we went to see Verne and agreed to buy an acre or so jointly at the government going rate of one dollar (BeeWee) a square foot, equivalent to sixty cents US at the time. Verne asked where. That was the question. I wanted to be down on the flat in the coconut grove on the beach, and Sandy wanted and felt we needed to be above the road. Verne didn't care; either was fine with him. So in the middle of our bickering, he said, "Let's settle the deal, and you guys can go back to the hotel and decide which spot you want, then let me know."

Sandy gave him a traveler's check for the down payment and we left. Now the big question was what spot it should be. This one was much easier to solve. For my part, I wanted to be on the beach because I felt it was more romantic and because I thought more accessible to the beach was not only more valuable but also more likely to be turned into a commercial venture for me in the future.

Sandy's response was to ask what was romantic about putting up with sand fleas and mosquitoes. Where is the accessible view down there? What was the value to us based on our living or working habits, and what commercial venture? "You haven't decided what you want to do here yet. What you're doing is putting yourself in a box before you know what's in the box. Now, if we're up on the hill, we'll have the value of the trade winds so it will be cooler in the hot weather. We'll have no sand fleas and fewer mosquitoes, and the view will be spectacular. It will be much more private, and in truth, how far away from the beach will we be anyway?"

"On the beach," I said.

"On the hill," Sandy said.

Needless to say, in no time Sandy's reckoning won out. Finally, we were able to lie back on the beach and catch the sun. We had our newfound friends, Jo and Ruth, to laugh and play with, and we also now had time to get to know our future neighbors who would be living across the valley beyond the hotel, the Fords.

6 Reconnoitering

Belongers Now

We woke up early on December 28. How could we not wake up with the sun shining into the room brighter than you can imagine, especially if you were from the dark winter canyons of New York City as we were? There we were, as bright as the sun itself, I singing in the shower and Sandy supposedly talking to me through the closed door but not really. He was just sounding off while making plans for us for the rest of the day.

Mr. and Mrs. Ford were the only ones having breakfast in the dining room. It was the only place to have it: the help at the hotel wasn't up to anything as complicated as room service. That was for another time. We planned to get Ricky and his jeep, then cruise the Island for the first time with the eyes of "belongers."

Now that we were buying land there, the place was taking on a completely different meaning for us. It came over us both almost immediately. If we were no longer tourists, then what were we? We must be "belongers"! A more informed person might have said, "Fools rush in where wise men... etc., etc." And it was true; we were so wrong! What we felt was all imaginary, a figment of our over-excited imaginations. We had let the newness of the whole idea carry us away just a little, and Ricky, going along with it that day, humored us. It was going to take years to become really accepted members of this society. Most never do. No matter how many years they spend here, newcomers are looked upon as interlopers.

I must say a few locals were warm, friendly, and welcoming right from the start, like Verne and Mrs. Derrick in the shop in town. Then there was Dovey Nichols whose husband, Henry, was a truck driver who hauled all the stone used to build our place and who was our first auto mechanic. Later, Dovey, as seamstress, sewed our mattress-covers and the costumes for the high school choir activities. She was always volunteering and made herself useful wherever she was needed.

Years later, she told me, "When you first arrived and you two were getting off the boat that dark night, I could see you real good. I was out in front of the Frangipani Hotel down at the water's edge and I saw everything, you know, all that luggage and stuff. I told everyone that you two were Communists." When I asked her why she would think a thing like that, she said, "You guys looked like Communists."

So I asked her, "What do you think a Communist looks like?"

"Well," she said, "you had a head-tie tied around your neck and you were carrying this big book. I know you two are always carrying a book."

"Do you still think we're Communists?" I asked her.

"Oh, go on, of course not," she replied.

This revelation gave me some idea of just what scrutiny we were put under. The head-tie was nothing more than a silk ascot, and the book was James Michener's The Covenant. True, it wasn't a small book, but it should hardly have branded us Communists. When the Communist label didn't stick any longer, to some we became CIA informers. It was like living in a goldfish bowl. But we were never aware of it, and, as the saying goes, "What you don't know can't hurt you." We went blithely on, doing our own "ting," moving from project to project.

But that early morning, we could hear Ricky beeping for us down on the drive. We had finished our breakfast, and it wasn't bad. How can you mess up eggs, bacon, and tropical fruit? Sandy had learned this lesson from all his far-out, off-the-beaten-track travels: always eat a big hearty breakfast because you never know what's being served up for dinner. In places like Bequia, you never find three- and four-star hotels or even two-star ones for that matter. The Prime Minister once said in a New York Times article, "To hell with paradise," referring to the West Indies. "You don't come to the islands for the food."

The point he was making was that places like Bequia can guarantee sun and sea, beautiful beaches and a soft, caressing temperate climate for people who are escaping the freezing snow and rainstorms of the north. But don't come expecting services we can't give you because we do not have them. It was just that simple. Sandy always said the Prime Minister was right. If it is food you're looking for on your travels, you should go to Paris, France.

Sandy and I virtually flew down the hotel stairs and jumped into the jeep, ready for an exciting venture into the unknown, into the unexplored depths of our newly adopted home. I could see that Ricky had the tour down pat. We went up the winding road to Mt. Pleasant. He had taken us up there before Christmas to look at his family's land, which had been too far away from the beach for us. That day we went farther, beyond the huge old water tanks of colonial times, until the dirt road came to an abrupt end at an open field overlooking the Atlantic. A wild, wind-swept landscape cascaded all the way down to Hope, a white sand beach with breakers rolling in furiously, one after the other. It really was breathtaking. The hills and glens behind and off to the left of us resembled the hills and glens of Scotland. This magnificent kaleidoscope of beauty had only the three of us there to appreciate it. Not another soul was even in sight.

On our return down the winding road to Belmont, we could see across the nine-mile-wide strait to St. Vincent where the clouds to the north were hugging the foothills of the island's volcano. La Soufrière had erupted about sixty-five years before, and it could happen again at any time.

We drove down through Port Elizabeth, the main town on the island, but as we had been there a few times before, we stopped only long enough for lunch at the hotel. The Frangipani was crowded. The leftover Christmas merrymakers from the boats in the Harbour strained the capacity of the serving staff, so we were held up. Getting served was one little problem we were going to have to get used to—it went with the territory.

After lunch we went up the road to Spring, passing the commons on the right where the sheep and goats grazed. Along this road, though our guide Ricky couldn't have known it at the time, was the site where the Bequia Anglican High School was to be built one day. Then we drove up and over the pass to the other side of the Island and down through the Island's little and only rain forest. It isn't there any longer: believe it or not, it has been taken over by the dump.

Then we drove through pastureland with a few head of dairy cows. On the right we passed a lovely, well-kept coconut grove and some tennis courts belonging to the Spring Hotel across the road. The coconut trees lined Spring Bay. It was all so very quiet and inviting. As we traveled farther out along the road, it became no road at all, just a stony and sometimes muddy stretch filled with ruts. We were no longer riding; it was more like lurching every which way but backward. As we skirted Spring Bay, where the land jutted out over a small wave-splashed cliff, we seemed to pitch out over water. Then a quick turn and what seemed like out over the water again and another turn to the left and we were at Industry.

In Industry, Ricky explained, Sydney and Enid McIntosh tended to the little tropical farm and land holdings of Raintree for the entire McIntosh family. We were now sliding every which way across Industry in mud caused by the recent rains. We drove behind the coconut grove that curved around the sandy beach. On our right stood a large stone beach house, the only structure on Industry Bay. We got out and walked around. It was wide open with no one there and nothing in it, as if it had been abandoned. I got the impression that it had been built for the future, as a come-on to entice land buyers.

We got back into the jeep and headed for Park, the last bay on the Atlantic side of the Island. The roadway continued in the same condition. Driving out around the headland between the bays was every bit as hair-raising as at Spring, perhaps more so because the spume splashing up against the cliff gave the illusion that the jeep was steering through water. Park Bay had two houses on it. One in the center of Park was occupied by the caretaker-farmer, and in the other at the far end of the bay lived the owner's daughter and her husband, the Kellys.

By then, because of the delay over lunch at the Frangipani, the sun was well over in the western sky. Our afternoon reconnoitering had been brief, but we were feeling a little fatigued and ready for a nap before dinner. So I told Ricky to hightail it to Friendship. We still had Hamilton and the Fort to do on this north end of the Island, and there was still Paget Farm, La Pompe, and Moon Hole to do on the south end. Moon Hole was privately owned; we couldn't get in there without an invitation anyway. So the trip to the southern end of the Island could wait for another day.

When we got back to the room, I turned to Sandy and asked, "Well, what do you say?"

"It's short. It's sweet. It's going to do just fine."

I could see he was contentedly pleased, but I said, "I hope it's going to turn out 'fine.' We've already put out for it. You know, this is the first time in my life that I can remember buying a pig in a poke. I sure hope it doesn't turn out to be a porker. I'll be keeping my fingers crossed... At least, if it doesn't work out, we still have those three rooms and a John in the basement up on East 83rd Street."

"Now, don't be funny. This place is great. We're lucky we found Bequia, mark my words," Sandy said.

"I'll just mark my time, if you don't mind," I snapped. "This is my life and my future that I'm letting you muck around with."

"Don't be like that; just give it time. After all, it's not Borneo or Alaska. Barbados is only four hours from New York. So stretch out on your bed and get some rest before dinner."

Jo, The Devil's Advocate

We had dinner that night with Jo and Ruth. The two of them were getting darker every day. They had spent a couple of days in the sun out on Sol Quest, with Ruth's friend Stan as the captain. Stan was keeping Bush's two boats afloat as well as his own. At dinnertime the conversation centered on our land acquisition across the bay. Earlier, Jo had insisted on going over to the bay windows in the hotel dining room so I could point out the spot to her. We could see Monkey Hill stretching down to the sea, lording over Friendship Bay. I had never looked at the property from here before, but there it was clear as can be, just above the road and to the right of the newly installed telephone pole. The wires from the power plant were not connected because the installation hadn't yet reached this far out from Port Elizabeth.

6 Reconnoitering

"Oh, that looks great! What a view you're going to have from there," Jo exclaimed. "But whatever you do, never cut those trees." The three trees are still there just below the pool, and not so little any more.

Jo wanted to know all about the project. She was full of questions, the usual who, why, where, when, and how much. She couldn't for the life of her see why any New Yorker who had lived in Manhattan for any length of time would give up everything the Big Apple had to offer and settle down on this godforsaken, off-the-beaten-track, lost-in-time backwater of an island that nobody had ever heard of.

"Tell me, Sandy, you don't plan to leave New York for good do you?" Jo asked. "This is just going to be a vacation home, right?" Sandy just sat there smiling at her. "You couldn't leave the Playhouse. You? Stop teaching? Never, never! I can't believe this! What about that big house you have up on the East Side?"

As Jo's baiting went on, Ruth obviously couldn't have cared less. She had something else on her mind. I had the impression the former model was going through an identity crisis at the time. She seemed more intent on being ready to suck in her cheeks so she would look good if someone happened by with a camera, or, for that matter, just happened to be looking at her. I don't mention this to be mean. I really thought this was Ruth! I felt she should have been a movie star, so that she would still be getting the attention she needed. At a later time, in the days of the supermodel, she probably would have. I'm sure it was hard as hell to be a divorced, successful, but over-the-hill cover girl with two young girls to care for on her own. She had been used to living the good life in a big house in Connecticut where it was party time every night and where she was the main attraction. Now all that was gone, already fading into the past, nothing more than a memory. It is fascinating what we hang on to when all else fails us. Her situation with Stan wasn't helping any either.

That night all the interest and attention were directed toward Sandy and me. Jo was in control of the conversation that evening. I didn't know her well enough to be able to read her motivations. Was it sincerity or was it the wine taking over the conversation? At that time I couldn't tell.

"Why, Jimmy, if by chance you should roll out of bed in your sleep, the Island is so narrow you would land up in the ocean, ha-ha-ha," Jo said.

"OK," I said, "OK, Jo, you dyed-in-the-wool New Yorker. Enough."

Still Jo went on. She liked to talk. "Don't get me wrong. I mean, the place is beautiful. But aren't you both going to tire of it? How could you not? You two are so New York."

She seemed more like a yenta than any yenta I have ever known without being a bona fide one at all. Still, there was something I liked about her. Something had drawn me to this woman from the first night we spent alone together at the beach bar. At that point I wasn't sure what it was. Was it her straightforward sincerity, or her innocence? Was it her child-like curiosity? Her vulnerability was charming. I just did not know what it was, but I sure was enjoying her playing the devil's advocate this night at dinner.

On she went. "Well, the whole place is marvelous, it's fabulous, fabulous, I mean super-super. But, and that is a big 'but,' ha-ha-ha..." The last few adjectives were her favorites. Everything was "fabulous" and "super."

"Jo," I interjected.

Ignoring me, she went on. "Sandy, I mean, it's a great place to visit. A cliché, I know. But to leave New York, the New York Times? I don't see how you could leave the big city. Sandy, you're Sandy Meisner! You are New York! You can ask anybody in Hollywood. They'll tell you."

Sandy sat there, elbows on the table, resting his head in his hands, palms cupped under his chin and fingers extended over his cheeks. He said, "Jo, this might be hard for you to believe, but all things considered, New York and Hollywood included, I cannot wait to settle into my own house here and live out my remaining days soaking up the sun and lolling in the sea."

I could see Sandy was beat. After dinner he wanted to go straight to bed. He told me he was going to turn in, that he couldn't remember ever needing a night's sleep more, except for the night we arrived. I think the strain of all the big and lightning-fast decisions we were making was getting to him. Maybe he too was having second thoughts. He told Jo she could wear out a triathlete, wanted to know where she got all that energy, and then bid us good night and headed for our room. As he crossed the dining room, he made a couple of stops to talk to the Fords.

After dinner the three of us hung out down at the beach bar. Jo was in high spirits, but Ruth's affaire de coeur seemed to be on the rocks. I later learned our Ruth had been looking for a commitment from Stan, and commitment was the last thing he wanted at the time, or ever wanted for that matter. To her credit, Ruth had enough sense to get over it quickly and get on with her life. If that woman was anything, she was resilient. She eventually gave up New York and came to Bequia to open a boutique whereupon we became fast friends. We even went at it once. Yeah, we made out, but I blacked out at the crowning moment, and it wasn't because we were so high we were dancing on the moon, so what the hell good did it do me? I always blacked out. Listen to me: "always!" I mean, the few times I tried to make it with a woman, and I mean few, I always blacked out at the crucial moment, as if I didn't want to know what was happening. It was like that from the first time I went at it as a "cherry boy" in Tokyo the year of '49 and I never did know what the hell all the fuss was about. Our friendship, Ruth's and mine, lasted a lifetime in spite of our differences.

Ruth went off by herself this night, but Jo and I sat at the bar and talked and talked then danced and talked some more till the wee hours.

6 Reconnoitering

There He Was Again At The Edge Of The Bush

Back in the room Sandy made ready for bed and crashed before his head hit the pillow. The trip and probably the dinner conversation had beaten him down. He woke up early on the morning of the 29th. He was up and had quietly showered, shaved, and dressed without disturbing me. He was standing out on the terrace breathing deeply, filling his lungs with that pure, fresh, clean sea breeze when, out of the corner of his eye, he spotted that little boy again across the field to the left, beyond the hotel.

The boy was making his way out of the bush that extends up and over St. Hilaire (aka Hilary) and down past the blowhole to the rocks below in Ravine Bay. Ravine was a narrow crevice that led up the steep hill to Mt. Pleasant at the top. No one lived there and few ever passed that way, I was told, "no reason to." The little fellow started plodding across the field through the tall grass. He was staring at Sandy on the terrace, his big, dark brown, almond-shaped eyes popping out of his gaunt, bony face. The strange orange hair that crowned his head was closely cropped, if ever it was cropped at all. I think it just broke off.

Believe it or not, Sandy had never seen the likes of him in his life, except on Save the Children of Africa commercials, the ones where the flies crawl all over the children. Sandy waved at the boy and a wide smile, more like a grin, broke out across his face exposing large white teeth. The waving caused him to scamper just a little faster up and behind the hotel, heading to the kitchen. Sandy had seen him up there on Boxing Day hiding behind a large garbage can. When he had asked what the boy was doing up there, Sandy was told he was looking for food. By now, we knew his name was Boolu. Jean, our "room girl," had told us the night we arrived. As Sandy watched him scamper off up the hill that morning, he couldn't help but wonder what his story was.

All week Boolu would appear from just about anywhere. He always kept at a fair distance, just safe enough to be able to dart away to avoid a confrontation. Sandy noticed that he wasn't always quick enough and some member of the staff, male and female, would grab him and try to hurt him or hit him with a mop or broom or even throw something at him. He was always up for grabs; if they made their mark, they took great glee in it.

One day, four of the young boys on staff had him wedged in and were mercilessly taunting and frightening the daylights out of him. The noises he made were inhuman and upset Sandy so much that he spoke to another older staff member. She acted as if she didn't hear a word Sandy was saying. She just stood there smiling at the whole incident. It was as if he were talking to a stone wall. So he called me and told me to go break it up and make them stop. It wasn't a hard thing to do. I just told them to stop and they did, laughing as they walked away and went about their hotel chores. The boys didn't seem to bear any malice toward the child, or me for that matter. They didn't seem to see it as anything serious; it was as if it were mere tomfoolery, except all at the little fellow's expense. I approached the child to soften and soothe the situation, but he didn't give me a chance. He darted off quicker than a frightened rabbit.

Sandy and I had just finished breakfast and were again waiting for Ricky to take us to town. Today was bank day. Once a week, a man from Barclay's came over from St. Vincent and set up shop, sitting at a table under an almond tree near the pier in the Harbour, believe it or not. I for one could not believe it, and even if I had no reason to go to the bank, I had to go to see it for myself. I must add that the bank was in the process of renovating the first floor of a building across the street and expected to open some time that month.

When we jumped out of the jeep in the center of town, there was Mr. Bank Man under the almond tree, doing his business. Sandy changed some traveler's checks for BeeWee, short for British West Indian currency. Then he headed for Mrs. Derrick's, the shop across the street from the pier and the Tourist Bureau. It was a small wooden structure with two entrances, the right entrance into the grocery store and the left into the dry goods shop. Four feet in from each entrance, a counter ran the width of the space. All merchandise was behind the counter, and only one person could be waited on at a time. Peak periods resulted in long waits, outside because of the lack of space. When it was busy and it was raining, it was just tough luck. Today was the day before Old Year's Night, and everyone seemed to be in town. Needless to say, we had to wait, but at least it wasn't raining.

Eventually Sandy got just inside the door, and immediately Mrs. Derrick asked him if she could help him. No one stands in line here. Survival of the fittest and devil take the hind-most rule the day. I must say Sandy had no compunction about taking advantage of this particular local custom.

He spoke up and said, "I want some candy." Mrs. Derrick pointed to a jar of peppermints, but he shook his head no. She then pointed to a large glass jar of brown hunks of something and he asked, "What's that?"

"Sugared coconut," she replied.

He shook his head again, and now she pointed to a pink jar. Sandy asked again, "What is that?"

"The same thing only pink... Wait a minute," she said as she went into the back room. She came out with a two-pound box of Cadbury chocolates in her hand, held them up, and asked, "These?"

"Yep, that's fine," said he, reaching for his money. She bagged the chocolates, took his money, and gave him his change. Sandy turned with a big smile on his face, so proud of his accomplishment.

"You do better here than you do at Saks. Say, you don't eat candy! Who did you buy it for?" I asked.

"The kid, that kid," Sandy replied.

"What kid?" I asked. "That pathetic little boy back at the hotel? Cadbury chocolates! I don't think so! Sandy, I don't think I've ever had Cadbury choco-

6 Reconnoitering

lates before. I know that waif never has. He's probably never had chocolate in his entire life. But," I laughed, "why should I be surprised? I haven't forgotten that Balenciaga dress you were looking at for Betty's daughter, Emily. How old was she? Three or four? Did you ever buy it?"

Sandy didn't even bother to acknowledge my remark. "Come on," he said. "Where's our jeep?"

While on our way to our room back at the hotel, Sandy handed me the candy and said, "Here. When you see that kid, give it to him."

"The whole two pounds?" I questioned. "He'll never get to eat it, and if he does, it will only make him sick. Do you know the staff would only take it away from him? Here, you take it and keep it in our room and when you see him during the day, give him a few at a time," I told him.

"Jimmy, what makes you so smart?" Sandy teased.

"Well, if you really want to know, when I was small and too young to go to school, we lived on the same block as a grammar school where my three older brothers went. My mother said I would cry and carry on, wanting to go with them. She would give me a pad and pencil and tell me to go outside and play. I would sit on the steps of the school with my pad and pencil and cry my heart out to get inside. I remember that the janitor, a Mr. Manley [you see, I still remember his name], would come out on the steps with me. We would sit there and he would talk to me. At some point he would dig down deep in his pocket and he would always say, 'Well, what do we have here?' and he would pull out some candy and say, 'This is for you.' I was always delighted and surprised no matter how many times he did it. In hindsight I know he got as much of a kick out of it as I did. So you see, Sandy, I'm not so smart, I only have a damn good memory."

For the rest of the week, Sandy made it his project to keep an eye on Boolu, fascinated by the boy's every little movement. I could see a strange bond developing. It was slight but nevertheless, it was there. Anytime Sandy would see a staff member giving Boolu a hard time, he would call me to the rescue. A few times he made the trek all the way down to the beach bar looking for me. He would be asking me to run off behind the generator room or over onto the dock to put a stop to some horseplay at Boolu's expense. It got to the point that when the staff saw me coming, they would just include me as part of the shenanigans. I could see they were just fooling. I told Sandy not to worry; it was just their way.

Sandy said, "I don't care about their way. They're frightening him and, damn it, they should stop."

I talked to Ron, who blamed Boolu! He told me Boolu should not be on hotel property and he hoped Boolu wasn't bothering us. So I gave up on looking to Ron for help. By now Boolu was coming up to Sandy for the chocolate, but I must say Sandy was the only one he came near. He was always on guard, even around me.

One afternoon Sandy was telling the young woman at the desk that he felt the staff was insensitive to the little waif from the bush. "Isn't someone looking after him? Is it very Bequian to let a youngster run free like that? You would think the police or the government would step in and do something."

"In Bequia the care of children be left up to each family," she answered.

"Well, where is his family? Where does he live?" he asked.

"The boys on staff say he holes up beyond the bush in the ravine where no one can get at him. His mother left him and his sister with their granny, Frazeen, a long time ago. His mother took off for Trinidad and never did come back. Boolu is a dummy. He can't talk, he can't hear anything, and he isn't all there, y'know? Frazeen herself is a little funny in the head. People leave food out for him and he come get it. That's why he come around here. He come to pick the garbage. Sometimes we even give him food and don't tell Ron."

"That's very nice of you," Sandy said, "but Boolu needs more than food, much, much more."

"I know, I know," she replied. "Food is all we have to give, we have nothing else. So what else can we possibly do? He won't even stay put for anyone."

"It really is an impossible situation," Sandy mused.

We had one week left before going back to reality: the cold, the snow, the Playhouse for Sandy and for me, contract dates with the Schola Cantorum and my modeling agency, Funny Face. I was planning to keep on looking for work until it was time for me to return to Bequia. In the meantime, there was time to play. Sandy loved to swim in the ocean and he would lie on the beach for hours. He was getting darker by the day. We spent most of the day on the beach, but one afternoon we took a trip to Hamilton situated on the northern end of the Harbour beyond Port Elizabeth. We followed the road around and up the hill to the very end. It led to an opening that was once an old fort, albeit a small one. All that remained of it were a few fair-sized cannons with the crest of King George VI embossed across the top of each one. They were strategically placed to protect Admiralty Bay, the main harbor on the Island.

The next day, Ricky, who was by now our buddy as well as our jeep transport, again took us over the Gap to the Caribbean side of the Island. But this time, we took a sharp left turn down a steep winding road to the flat at the bottom of the hill, then cruised along the sea grape bushes bordering the calm Caribbean. Here was a long stretch of beach with absolutely nothing on it but small fishing boats belonging to the men of Lower Bay, the village at the very end of the beach where the two-strips-of-concrete road abruptly ended.

New Year's Eve came and we attended a little party given by the hotel. I say little because, for a hotel with twenty-four rooms, it was a rather small group. Two couples from Massachusetts and three children belonging to one couple, the Fords and their four children from Connecticut, Jo and Ruth from New York, and Sandy and yours truly—that was it for the hotel guests. Ron, Stan, and the hotel staff made up the rest of the party. A sideboard offered food, a rather simple spread, and free drinks. Ron put a tall chef's hat and white jacket on Sammy, one of the kitchen staff, and had him cutting and serving up the ham and turkey as if he were a chef. Yet I doubt that Sammy had ever seen a whole ham or turkey before in his life.

The band consisted of a guitar, bongos, and a bamboo flute, and the staff put on a little show. They sang some calypso songs and danced, one recited a holiday greeting, and another chap did a dance while shredding a coconut with his teeth. One could be kind and say it was innocent fun, very simple and sweet, and then on the other hand one could say it was amateurish, crude and unrehearsed. So be it! We all ate, danced, talked, made merry, and sang "Auld Lang Syne" at midnight.

But underneath it all, I was still wrestling with doubts. I wasn't really convinced at this stage that I wanted to live here. I was afraid I'd be bored to death on this tiny island in the middle of nowhere. For Sandy and me, and for everyone else, for that matter, 1968 was now behind us. For us, all the decisions should have been made, and for Sandy I think they were. But I was still torn between Bequia and New York. Not really New York, but my dream of a career, which was so tied up with New York as to make them seem one and the same to me. Now here I was, making plans to design and build a retirement house for Sandy. But where I stood in the equation was not clear to me. Sandy kept saying, "Mark my words." I was very good at that, I had been marking time for years, always living in the future, working and waiting for the career that might be. "Give it some time," he would say.

"I'm used to giving time. How much more time does one have to give, after fifteen years of trying?" I would say.

Finally, I really had to admit I didn't have much of a career at all. Sandy was right. If at forty there was no career to speak of, what was I doing in New York? The reason I went there in the first place was to get away from Utica and myself and hide in a career. Now if there was no career...? BINGO! It was January 1, 1969, and New York was the last place on earth I wanted to be without a career. Until that point, I would never have admitted this to myself, much less to another living soul... HAPPY NEW YEAR!

Back in our room long after 1 AM of the New Year, while pulling the blinds shut, I noticed our little friend hightailing it back into the bush. I could just make him out through the dim light that shone from the window.

"Didn't you tell me that one of the staff told you there was nothing in that thicket beyond?" I asked.

"Yeah, sure. Bet-tee said there was nothing there except the deserted ravine. No one goes in there any more," he said, pulling off his shirt.

"Well, is that so? Then tell me where is your little friend going at this hour? He's heading right into it as I speak," I said.

"Someone told me he holes up in there; he runs in there to get away," Sandy answered.

"To get away from whom?"

"Whom?"

"Who, whom, what's the difference? What's the answer?" I insisted.

"I don't know. Beats the hell out of me. I can't imagine anyone going in there at this hour or any other hour for that matter. You'll have to ask him. I'm exhausted. I'm going to bed."

"Very funny, 'ask him,'" I countered. "...I'm sure he is the only one who can tell me. That is, if only he could... Good night."

"Good night."

As I said before, Boolu was the only one who could tell his story, and in time he did—many, many moons later when he was well over forty. When he left home for the last time, he had no idea where he was going. He said that at that time all he really felt was the truth of the moment, and the truth was, something was finished and what was up the road was scary and frightening, yet somehow compelling, so compelling that he had fled his misery and headed out.

Through Boolu's Eyes: Part 2

"Only de mommy would be home wit her two picknee. Lacey, Miz Doreen's man, would be gone all day. He wouldn't be back till jus before de sky catch fire an' streaks a red an' pink take over de white cotton sailin' cross de still blue up above, den turn it inta shades a mauve an' deep purple, getting' darker by de minute."

Boolu saw the sky as a great wide space like a lid that seals off Jesus up in heaven. That is where they said heaven was. He always saw them pointing up there or lifting their eyes straight up to the sky, throwing their heads way back, and clapping their hands together as they talked of God and Jesus. By "they" he meant Lacey's missus and all her family and friends. He understood a lot about the religious antics of the evangelical religion of the Island even back then. The physicality of the people's demonstration of faith no doubt made it clear to him.

"Der was really only one picknee. De udder one up der was too small ta pick anytin'. All dat one did was cry an' yell or pound wit bot hands on Miz Doreen's teats. De only time he be quiet was when he be suckin' on Miz Doreen's big fat teat dat hung out over de top a her dress. It was jus like her daddy's big-bagged milker dat I see one time out beyon Raintree. Dat cow was black an' white jus like Miz Edmunds' little cat."

Frazeen, his mommy, called him her "picknee" too, sometimes, like when they were picking row after row of pigeon peas off the tall bushes they hung on. In between the rows, the cassava was planted. It was a highly poisonous plant that had to be processed carefully by squeezing the juices before eating, though its iffy nature didn't detract from its becoming a mainstay at the dinner table.

6 Reconnoitering

"When de pigeon pea bushes be real tall, taller dan Mommy, bout six feet, dey be ready for pickin'. We had our own field back a our house. It was jus up back Murray Simmons' field. Mommy an' me worked der all day. Boops would help before she went ta school, an' when we had a lotta work ta do she didn't go ta school at all. Yes, everyone had a little garden plot, an' so did Lacey. And now I had to get cross it widout dem seein' me.

Der was de house, now if I could jus push dis bush ta one side, I tought, I might get a good look. Der couldn't be anybody home. Der was no dogs roun."

Sure, he knew, the dogs could be sleeping, but they wouldn't be inside. No, it was nothing like that. No one keeps their dog inside around here, no need to. The dogs must have been around the other side of the house. If he were really lucky, it could be they were sleeping. Maybe, just maybe, he would make it. He figured if he went across the road, then into the bush around the far end of the field, straight up the near side across the top, then down the far side into the bush, he could find shelter in Quam Gutter, if he got there safely.

"If dat hill was any steeper an' I slipped, I woulda fallen rass top over bottom quite down ta de big road dat goes all de way down ta de Harbour."

He thought, no wonder the goats go up and down these hills at an angle, first this way then that, zigzagging all the way up. It didn't take much for Boolu to see they knew more about climbing up hills than people do. He would have done it just that way, if it hadn't been for the dogs.

"I wanted ta keep as far as I could on dis side a de house until me get ta de top. Den I be able ta pass de house widout bein' noticed, I hoped. Well, I did. But den I saw Korwin, de big white boy wit hair like corn silk."

Korwin was from Mt. Pleasant and he was down there on the road. Boolu would have been in a whole lot of trouble if he had gone straight up the road to Mt. Pleasant, easy as it was. Korwin would have had Boolu by the scruff of his neck running him and laughing all the way down to Mrs. Edmunds' and Frazeen.

"He wouldn't see me up here. No one looks up much when dey be walkin', outside anyway."

He got to the top of the field. Then all he had to do was get across without those dogs on his tail.

"Me spotted a stick in de newly dug furrows. Dis would make my footin' goin' down easier. I would be able ta run faster an' get off der land away from de barkin' dogs an' inta Quam Gutter beyon where me know de dogs would not chase me. At dis point I saw Miz Doreen. She was trowin' sometin' ta de dogs. Maybe whatever it was would keep dem busy till me pass. She didn't see me, she didn't look up here, an' I didn't know why 'cause she always lookin' up ta de heavens."

God knows she does do that enough, in fact, all the time. She was always looking up, praying to Jesus and preaching to anyone and everyone who would listen, even Boolu and Frazeen. But Boolu knew it wouldn't have made any difference if she had seen him. Miz Doreen never chased him and never would. Miz Doreen never did anything but feed that little one of hers and work the garden. She never went anywhere, neither up the hill nor down, except on a few special days in the year. Then she went with her man and the two children to her parents' up in Mt. Pleasant.

No, wait, Boolu remembered there was one outing she went on and she did it regularly. She went the same place every week. She would get all scrubbed up. Boolu could see her out back in her white dress as she put her black book under her arm and clapped a big white hat on her head. Leaving her man at home with the two little ones, she would start off down the hill flapping one foot after the other, in stiff, just-like-new, hardly worn, lace-up shoes that she never wore anywhere else. She would stretch one leg in front of her as far as she could without ripping herself or her dress into two separate pieces. Those legs, all the way quite up under her dress, would be wrapped skintight in heavy brown stockings no matter the weather. She never looked right or left, or up or down like everyone else, but glared straight ahead as if piercing the air itself with a knife. It looked to Boolu as if she were going off to make everything right with the world, to put everything back in order, just the way she thought her God made it. Yes, to Boolu she looked just like Frazeen when she set herself all straight like a ramrod, grabbed a stick, and set out to find him, wherever he was. The black book under Miz Doreen's arm looked as much like a weapon as Frazeen's stick—the two of them armed and off to fight for what, in their own minds, was right.

Boops had gone off to church just once or twice, with a friend. Grace, Boops's real name, didn't go to pray at the same church Miz Doreen went to, nor did they even go on the same day. Doreen marched down the hill on a Saturday. Grace and her friend went the day after, the very next day after. Boolu thought it strange that everyone went to work on the day Doreen went to church, but nobody worked the next day when Boops went, not even Mommy. Even Doreen's people didn't work on that day. Boops had no white dress, no black book—no weapon at all. All she had was herself and her friend, and they didn't give the impression that they were going to fight a battle. Grace had wanted to take Boolu with her once, but Frazeen would not let her. After that, Grace stopped going altogether.

Once, Boolu did go to that church where Grace went to pray. He didn't go quite inside, but he went up to the door and looked in.

"One mornin' Mommy be still sleepin'. Y'see, she didn't have ta go ta work dat day. Besides dat, she had been up most a de night mixin' an' boilin' plants. She was smokin' de weed an' singin' an' dancin' most a de night. Dat's when she make me drum on de biscuit tins. Boy, did me like knockin' dem tins!

Dat mornin Boops went out somewhere an' she forgot ta tie me, so I lef de house an' went down ta de wharf. On dis day, I pass de prayer house. It was full a people all dressed up in fancy clothes an many wit black books like Miz Doreen's. Dis wasn't Miz Doreen's day though so she wouldn't be der, but

6 Reconnoitering

Grace's friend was der wit her mother an' little brother. I could see she inside. She kep movin' she hand ta me, but very little so de udders der could not see she. I could tell she tryin' ta tell me ta move an' get outta de doorway.

All de udder people kep prayin' an' singin' an' singin' an' prayin', all de while makin' out like dey didn't see me. But I could tell dey all did. You know, dey would dart dey eyes ever so fast ta me, an' den shif dem straight ahead ta de man standin' up front all wrapped up in funny-lookin' clothes as if he be cold, but it was hot, real hot, an' he be sweatin'. Dey never turned dey heads in my direction once. No! Never indicated fo me ta go or ta come in. I don't tink dey want me ta do either; maybe dey want me ta jus fade away, just disappear on de spot. Well, me couldn't do dat, so me stepped in a little further, so me could get a better look at dat man up front. Me couldn't begin ta figure out how he be dressed or why he be dressed in such a way. It looked as if he be all wrapped up in Miz Edmunds' bedclothes, de ones she trow out on de line once a week so bright an beautiful, but me knew dey couldn't be hers because I saw she in der an' no way would dis guy get hers.

I was at de side door, an' in a few seconds me could see dis man comin' right fo me from de back a de place. De man was in a baggy black suit. His tie look more like de rope I use ta hold up my pants. He had on shoes dat were black an' shiny but full a cracks runnin cross dem. His white shirt was very white an' clean but wrinkly, an his skinny neck stuck out from de collar leavin' a big gap all de way roun'. As he came at me, his black book was in his hand an' he was shooin' me way from de door wit it. Me was headin' fo de wharf anyway, so me took off.

As I reach de side gate, de man chasin' me in de black suit reach de side door. At de same time, der was a man at de front door wit two goats in tow. Somehow I feel dat if de man in de baggy black suit hadn't lef his post at de front door because me was at de side door, what was 'bout ta happen would not have happened at all.

Dat man wit de goats be all dressed up like a 'soccer boy'—dat mean very sharp. He be all done up in brown drogin' dose two dumb animals behin him. He parade up de center aisle a de place quite up ta de skinny little man in front. By de time de man in de black suit lef de side door, I ran back ta see. De Soccer Boy an' de man in de bedclothes be standin' face ta face. De goats were not payin' any mind ta either one a dem. All de people in de place jus stood der, some wit der mouths wide open, some dey eyes a-poppin', an' some wit jus blank faces. Ta me dey all look as if de stiffness had set in like dey all died standin' up.

De man in brown promply tied de goat chain roun de rail dat runs cross de front, all de time spittin' out words tru his tight knothole of a mout. Now de little man in de black suit reach de front a de side aisle an' was headin' fo de man in brown but none too fast as far as me could see. When dey met, de man in brown shove de man in black wit such a push dat de little old fellow had ta grab onta de rail ta keep from fallin' all de way ta de floor. All de time, de man in brown was spittin' fort words ta de little man who was prayin' ta de high heaven now. Soccer Boy musta said all he had ta say for he abruptly turned, leavin' de goats tethered ta de rail, an' marched right up de center aisle an' out de back door an' quite over de hill ta Belmont where he lived.

De little man held up de bedcovers wit outstretched arms, an' everyone in de place got down on der knees an' all began ta pray. De little man in black untethered de goats an' headed toward me at de side door. I knew dis was a cue fo me ta get outta de way, so me scurried off ta de wharf in de center a de Harbour."

Much later I did find out the meaning behind the scene Boolu witnessed that day. It seems the man who looked like a soccer boy to Boolu had an important position in the church. He was one of its lay readers, a deacon or leader. He had had a falling-out with the pastor over some church dogma or practice. He was saying by his actions that the priest was only fit to preach to goats and that any- and everyone in the church who was blindly following him was no better. The little man who was the pastor is now dead and the "soccer-boy" man went on to found a church of his own. I wonder what kind of animals he is fit to preach to, or at.

"Well, no matter, taday be nobody's church day, an' der be me at de top a Lacey's place just in line wit de house. Dat day be one a Miz Doreen's slow-movin days an' she was no tret ta me none. Dat brown dog wit de belly full a teats dat hung so low she almos step on dem every time she move was just like she mistress. She also was no tret ta me none, but de big black bull was sometin' else. Oh! he knew me all right but dat didn't make any difference. He never liked me roun der house, even when Lacey himself had Frazeen an' me der clearin' out de dried-up corn stocks or cuttin' down de pigeon pea bushes before de big rain. Lacey always had a time a it keepin' dat black one away from me. Well, whatever de mistress gave dem ta eat dat day wasn't much; I saw dey be finished in no time. God, she so dumb. Den what do you tink she do? Wouldn't you jus know it? She look up, she saw me, and she began ta open her mout and call out ta me. I knew dat damn dog was goin' ta be up der after me. Me had ta get outta der. I could see dey were barkin'. I really had ta get ma rass outta der, an fast."

It wasn't easy to run fast on the side of a steep hill and jump corn holes in furrows at the same time. He thought for sure he was a goner. If he had kept running, the dog would have caught up to him in no time and got a hold of him by "da seat a me pants," as Boolu would say. The dog would have sunk his teeth into Boolu's bottom and then he would have been done for.

"I decided ta stop, turn roun, an' fight him off wit de stick me picked up earlier while I still had some breath lef in me. I let him bark his head off. Dat didn't scare me. I couldn't hear it anyway. Boops would cover her ears wit she hands an' run. It's dat big mouth wit de long teeth so white.

De minute I held dat stick up in front a his face, he stopped, an' me tought, 'Yeah, go ahead, pull your big lip up, an' flash your sharp teeth. Me don't have sharp teeth ta show ya but me have dis big stick. Come on, come on.' I was making noises at de same time at de big black dog. Me was willing him off, 'Go on, go on down der,' keepin' him downhill from me so he couldn't jump me. Whack! 'Run, you slimy snake,' I tought, makin' noise all de while. He be still comin' at me. I would wait till he come one side a me, an' if me be lucky, I'd give him one more whack dat would send him rass over ears quite down ta de main road, me kep tinkin'. OK, I figured, dis be my big chance, an' me better not miss. Wit a bang a de stick on his head an' wit a he-he an' a ho-ho, my big fear was gone."

Boolu then quickly picked up his bag and flew off that hill while he still could. If Miz Doreen saw all this and told her man, he'd be after Boolu for months. He loved that dang dog, or maybe he loved the way that dang dog could scare everyone.

"Now dat dog couldn't scare me, not any more. I trew de stick away. Dat whack I gave dat dog was a whopper an' it split de stick in two. It sent one piece of it flyin' like de dog, end over end halfway down de hill."

Prince, that was the name of the black dog, didn't come back, so Boolu got down and across the Mt. Pleasant road all in one piece, just a little bit dirty and out of breath. He wanted to stop and rest in a cool shady spot under a tree, perhaps the big sapodilla where Boops tethered her goats, but he knew he had better not. The children would be coming with their books soon and no place would be safe around here then, so on he went.

The bush on the other side of the road was thicker and much harder to get through. If he had only had a cutlass like his mommy's, he could have cut his way through in no time flat. His mommy would slash this way and that cutting her way clear through the thickest bush on the Island. But since he had no cutlass, the only way to do it was to scrunch up on his hands and knees, bend way down, and slip in under the splayed-out branches overhead. Boolu knew that dogs, cats, manicou (a possum-like creature), and even rats crawl under that way. He knew because he watched animals closely and saw that often they make more sense than most people. You could move much faster than you would think, working along under the bush. At the same time, no one can see you or even know you are there. The bush doesn't move when you move along under it this way. How did Boolu know all this? He just knew it all by himself. His observation skills were unusually keen. He was out and around the hill and into Quam Gutter in no time at all.

Now, two steep dirt sides hem in Quam Gutter all the way up to the top. The dirt is loose and musty smelling, like the underside of a wide wooden plank left in the field to rot in the rain for a long time. Boolu knew the smell from helping his mommy drag them home whenever they found one. Up the middle of the gutter lay big rocks and boulders worn smooth like... well, they looked like so many babies' bottoms. Some were gray like Frazeen's hair, kind of bluish gray and mauve; some were light, some dark. They were hard to walk on—your footing could slip, causing a perilous trip, sending a boulder below there, while others would slide, rolling out from the side, would start rambling and rumbling all the way down shocking a whole shower of rocks pounding and bouncing, hopping never stopping, all the way down flipping and flying around amidst the roaring sound without a breach until they reached the beach.

"I knew dis was dangerous but dis was de only way fo me at dat time. No matter how hard it was ta walk up de gutter, de only time you could was when it be dry."

It certainly was no place to be when it rained and it was even worse when it poured. Boolu saw Quam Gutter once from the edge when it poured. Down it came, splashing and crashing, dashing and smashing, with no rhyme or reason except it's the season, going down with a roar faster than before, just to rest in the brine and the muddy brown slime, then slip out to sea, slowly floating debris.

There was once a Gooding girl or was she a Lacey? I don't know. In any case, a big storm was approaching. As the rain started pelting down, she went out to get her sheep or goats, only to discover that in the downpour they had broken loose from their stake. She went searching for them. By the time she did or she didn't find them, she probably knew she had better get home—the storm was upon her and it was raging. The sheets of rain must have made it impossible to see. She became disoriented on the top of the hill over Quam Gutter. She must have slipped on the short wet grass into the raging stream and down she went like a rag doll, over one rock and then the other, over and over till she was washed clear out to sea, never to be seen again. Some say it was the spirits that got her, but Boolu thought he knew better. Spirits only come out and work their evil at night, and besides, he knew the power of that gutter when it's full of gushing, roaring water. He had been there; he had seen it. It looked even scarier from up in the breadfruit tree where he got stuck once as a storm raged on. So the girl's tragic demise was very real to him.

"I shouldn't be down here, it could happen. It was dat time a year an' de rains could start at any time. I shoulda been keepin' a lookout fo rain clouds, but me quite forgot about de possibility when me start out dat day. I be down der in de middle a de gutter an' it be too late ta worry bout it, der be little me could do. If I saw rain clouds an' de winds start up or if me felt sprinkles, I was ready ta tear-rass up an' out a dat death trap."

At the time he was more preoccupied with the thought of Gun-Munro's dogs. Could they, would they, become aware of all the ruckus he was causing, all the stone and rocks crackling down on top of each other every time he stepped on one? If they did, they would be down on him in a minute, except for one thing: by then, he was moving away from the place, and they would be below him. That would make the difference. If they came into the gutter below him, he could start rocks a rolling down to them that would send them to kingdom come.

"Me woulda radder been payin' a visit ta de Gun-Munros' instead a away from it. What a beautiful place dat is. De Gun-Munros were away from de place mosta de time, hardly ever der. Dey must live some place else, I tink in St. Vincy where I lived once. Dey had an old Carib livin' on de premises keepin' an eye on de place an' tendin' ta de animals an' de gardens. He was drunk mosta de time or fas asleep, so fas asleep dat even de dogs didn't wake him.

My, what a place dat was, or could be an' would be if it wasn't for de dogs. Der was fowls an' a coupla geese, an' dat mean eggs. Dey had waternut trees, an udder trees: orange, two grapefruit, a lime, a sapodilla, a plum, a big mango plus two or tree udder kinds an' many sugar apple trees. De old gardener grew lettuce, spinach, an' root provisions in boxes up off de groun in row after row. Der was many banana plants an' corn an' pigeon peas in season an' all dis cared fo an' looked after by ol Cicero himself. De Munros pitched in wen dey were on de Island. A few times de ol man after a few rums would let me walk wit him back up ta one a de outhouses where he sleep, stavin' off de dogs from us as we went. He gave me tings ta eat an' all de time talkin' an' talkin' ta me as if me understood every word an' me makin' out as if me did. De ol dogs would leave me alone if I stayed real close ta Cicero as we came near de house. Jus tinkin' bout dat place, me was gettin' hungry.

By de time I neared de top a Quam Gutter, me knew I was safe from de dogs. Dey wouldn't come near me den. It was too far up fo dem. It had been nice an' cool down in der outta de sun, an' still der was no sign a rain."

The bush begins to thin out as you reach the top, and the rocks become stones, then little gravel that turns into dirt until you reach the grass. It got a lot easier for Boolu to walk as he left behind him the rocks and stones and the earthy smell of the gutter so musty and strong.

"I remember askin' meself once, how do all dose good-tastin' tings spring up from under dat strong musty-smellin' dirt? Sometime it vex me plenty ta tink how stupidy I be. Sometime de feelin's burn me way down in me belly an if me get ta eat sometin', de burnin' go way just like when me hungry an' me eat. Well, not ta worry, stupidy or not, I got ta de top dat day an' me was still altagedder an' me was still in one piece."

There, down ahead of him, was Ravine. Looking over to the right, he could see a village way over yonder, beyond a big bay.

"One day, I knew, I was goin' to get me over der, but right den I had ta get myself off dis mountain an' down inta Ravine an' find a little shelter fo meself."

The horizon off to the left looked a little darker than usual that afternoon but no worse than the horizon he had left behind.

7 Transition

January 1969: A Blanket Of White

Back in New York, the winter was upon us with all its snow, sleet, bitter winds, and miserable rain. Snow is so beautiful that first night it falls, and nothing compares to a romp in Central Park the day after. Sandy and I would take Nora to the park. Black as pitch, she was striking against the pure white snow as she jumped around, chasing her tail or one of the other dogs. Those were memorable moments for us both, a part of New York we would miss. But alas, in no time the snow becomes dirty and slushy. Then the traffic problems kick in and the whole town comes to a standstill. At such times, I felt Sandy might be right in wanting to get away from it all.

We couldn't make any decisions and therefore we couldn't make any plans. We spent a lot of our spare time out on the terrace off Sandy's bedroom when the weather was good enough, and when it wasn't, I spent time out there shoveling snow. The terrace had a formal look, faced with decorative tiles we had brought back with us on the boat from Portugal. In fact we had also brought back all the tiles for the front vestibule and all the bathrooms in the house as part of our luggage. The tile had been delivered directly to the boat. Surrounding the terrace stood male and female holly bushes and mixed evergreens, all of which flourished winter and summer. Water in a black marble seashell poured into a small pool. My brother Leo had executed the whole project entirely by himself.

Just two doors away was a Hungarian or Armenian Catholic Church spewing out soot with impunity, unencumbered by any regulation from City Hall. When we had little barbecues on the terrace, Sandy got a great kick out of saying, "Hurry up and eat your hamburger before it gets dirty." That was before the Clean Air Act. Nevertheless, we spent a lot of quality time out there together.

There were nights when Sandy would sit at his Chippendale desk next to the large oak fireplace in his bedroom, doing what I called pushing numbers around. He loved to work with numbers, always making sure he was solvent. One thing about Sandy you could be absolutely sure of: he was a man who never shirked when it came to paying his way. I never bought what I couldn't pay for either. Even in the lean years starting out, in my $27-a-month cold-water flat, at the end of the month when I was left with only fifty cents in my pocket, for me it was peanut butter or plain pasta. Sandy and I both came from a time free of charge cards, and we also still remembered the Depression vividly. No matter what the source or the cause of this practice, there he would be figuring and calculating into the wee hours. Sometimes he would come into my room afterwards and wake me up with a slight nudge. "Are you awake? Come, get up. Let's go downstairs and make some music."

I'd throw on a bathrobe, and splash water on my face to wake myself up. There he would be at the piano seat pulling out all my Mozart, German Lieder, Schubert, and Strauss anthologies. We would go on for hours, finishing up with Irish ballads of John McCormack. Sandy was a fabulous accompanist. His forte was German Lieder. No matter what the hour of the night. One or even three o'clock in the morning, no one could hear us with two feet of brick wall on either side of our building, and the thought of this tickled Sandy. It was as if we were being recalcitrant.

I must admit these nocturnal episodes were the most glorious and memorable hours of my life. I know I shall never forget them, and without being dramatic, I will take them to my grave, as I am sure Sandy did. They were our way of expressing our love for each other. Years later in '94, at Sandy's Gala at the Century Plaza when he was going on ninety, I sang "Danny Boy." No matter how many people were in the room that night, at that moment there were only two of us. We were transported back in time to 207 East 83rd Street. Sandy only wished he were at the piano that night.

The next three months in New York, in the winter of '69, were uneventful except for getting to know our newfound friends Jo and Ruth. You know, the usual routine: we had them over and they had us over. Jo went to an auction with me where I acquired a Georgian easy chair for Sandy. I always bought him something for February 14.

The First Valentine's Present

On that day in 1964 when I agreed to move in with him without any preconceived notions as to what would or could develop between us, I was full of apprehension. I was nuts about him, in awe of him, and scared to death of him all at the same time. Why, the first year at school I never once spoke to him outside the classroom. It wasn't until the third year Professional Program that our association developed into a compatible friendship where we enjoyed going out together and getting to really know each other.

The truth was Sandy was desperately lonely and couldn't stand being alone. My love relations had been on the rocks for six months. After five years, my lover Chad had taken up—notice I said "up" not "off"—with a dancer, and a damned good one. He had been the lead dancer in a show I was in, and Chad had come to see the show in Washington. For him, it was just an affair. But it was an affair I wanted no part of. Though we were living in my apartment, Chad had no plans to move out, saying it was just a fling. So here was

I, miserable as hell, and there was Sandy, desperately lonely living alone and hating it.

One night we sat bitching about our woes, when out of a clear blue sky Sandy asked, "What do you say, why don't you come and live with me?"

I just sat there. All I said was, "Wait, wait." I couldn't look at him; it was so unexpected! Not in my wildest dreams had it ever crossed my mind! Thoughts went racing through my mind. What would this mean? What would it involve? Do I love him? Could I love...? Never mind that. What does this mean? That he has feelings for me? Does he love me? Would he love me? I looked up and said, "Wow, wow. I don't know..."

He took both my hands in his and held them. It was almost as if he were pleading with me. He looked me straight in the eyes and said, "I don't mean here. I'll find another place with two bedrooms. Don't get me wrong. You live your life and I'll live mine. We'll just be sharing a house together. You can have your private life and I mine. We won't even talk about our private moments. We'll keep the sordid details to ourselves." He laughed, a little nervously, I thought. There was so much to think of.

"After all, what do you have to lose?" he asked.

Nothing, I thought to myself. I could leave Chad and my apartment in a shot. The truth was I was desperately in love with the man, this man who was such a public figure. I had sat in his class for three years, hanging on his every word, falling in love with every ounce of help he gave me. He was like a father figure to me, giving me the time my own father never had. Many of the girls in class had fallen for him, too. And although I didn't yet know it, I was ready for a man like Sandy in my life.

Still, no matter what our true relationship was, it would be tantamount to my coming out of the closet, if I wasn't out already. I had never discussed my true self with any straight person since I had talked to my first buddy Bobby when I was thirteen. To him it had been no big thing. He understood me as much as he could at that age and accepted me as I was. He said to me once, "You just got to be who you are." Although we went on to live lives poles apart, I was his best man when he married, and we are still the best of friends. Why couldn't the rest of the world be more like Bobby?

For the past thirty-five years, for the most part, it had been the "don't-ask-don't-tell" approach for me, and that was only to make it easier for the rest of the world. No one had ever asked, and I had never had to tell. I had been accused once several years before but nothing ever came of it. "Coming out" for me just wasn't in the cards. I personally chose not to. That was all.

Considering my mom and dad, I felt it was by far the better choice. To lay something like this on them would have been downright cruel. Remember, it was a time of total non-acceptance and only a minimal amount of understanding. The thought of the number of lives torn asunder on both sides by exposure still makes me cringe. What about Sandy? I thought. What about his wives and the past twenty-five years he's spent with them? All the while, he was reading my thoughts.

"Look, Jimmy," he said, taking my hands and holding them again in his. "Truth! It's all about truth. We owe that to each other. I know I can live it with you." He paused. "And you... you already have it, trust me."

"Give me a little time," was all I could manage to answer. I was so bowled over by it all.

I couldn't breathe. I had to get outside into the air, and all the time I was thinking, thinking, thinking! He knew I was nervous and he didn't press things any further. He even made it easy for me to leave, almost immediately. I literally ran out of the house. I knew this was a big moment in my life and I couldn't afford to make a mistake. How many mistakes are we allowed in life anyway before it is totally ruined? I pulled up my coat collar and buttoned up, tightened up my scarf, and put on my gloves. It was cold, very cold, and a light, powdery snow swirled around my ankles as I walked west on 65th Street. I walked as fast as I could without breaking into a run. When I reached the corner of Fifth Avenue, I turned right and shot up north. When I looked up, I was standing waiting for a green light at 72nd Street. I made a beeline for Central Park and lost myself in it.

I walked and walked, thinking, thinking, thinking. Nothing made any sense. Who was I? What was I doing? Where was I going? Where am I? Who am I, for Christ sake? No one, nowhere, no how, nothing! An absolute zero, that's me. Why me? Why now? Why him? Why us? God help me! Please! I just plowed on further into the park.

Moments passed when I had no thought at all, and it didn't make any difference whether I did or didn't. Sometimes I wasn't even there; I was off in a void. I would come to my senses wiping my eyes, crying like a fool. A well of emotion, years and years of emotion sprang up from within me gushing forth from way back in the second grade, when I went to the Halloween party dressed as a Dutch girl. Why not as a girl? It made no difference to me. The summer before I had danced at the playground field day festivities as a Dutch boy. I had a great time both days, as I did that day twelve years later at the same field when I danced as the first Indian prince of the Mohawks in a sesquicentennial celebration. I knew at the time none of my brothers would have done it, but for me even then I knew I was different.

The truth was whatever my bent was at that stage, it felt natural for me; so then, what the hell is all the fuss about? Nobody, from popes to presidents, including the Muslims, has their head screwed on right when it comes to the question of homosexuality. They are still back in the 10th century before the Age of Enlightenment. Consequently, even today in the 21st century, we have to remain perpetually persistent and vigilant. How troubling it is when a man as influential as Pope Benedict XVI himself can publicly make a statement so inhumane, deplorable, and degrading to a segment of the population, namely Gays, referring to them as "intrinsically evil." Shocking as it was, I heard not one rebuttal, no matter how infinitesimal, from any heterosexual group around the world. The only exception, just a flicker of light in the darkness, was from Bill Maher when on his Politically Incorrect TV program, he broached the subject. Yet even then, not one person on the panel, neither a conservative nor a liberal, would pick up on the subject and discuss it. Was Bill Maher the only heterosexual incensed by such a comment? Yes, a statement from such a man as the Pope condemning, according to Dr. Kinsey's report of the 1950s, 10% of the world's population. Who else has taken the time and money to find out the true figure? It is my belief, some fifty years later, that it truly is even higher.

I Am Here To Tell You I Was Born This Way

Early in life, I was just little Jimmy-boy, no one else. I knew who and what the hell I was better then, at the age of five, than I did these many years later, racing through the park. Or I had known, until society got its grubby hands on me and tried to mold me into its likeness. From then on, it wasn't until I was in Sandy's classes that I learned to free myself enough to dare to be and accept my own true natural depth. I must have been a hell of a good student, damn him. I had been lost, then he had come along, and in class he had tied me in knots to enable me to find myself once more, after all those years. Then he ties me in knots all over again, forcing me to develop the courage to face my true self head-on.

I raced clear on down through the park to 59th and Fifth, passed the World War I Monument across from the Plaza Hotel, then sprinted down Fifth Avenue. I was freezing and the running helped. Sandy was alone for the first time in his life, I thought, and he doesn't like it. And yet he doesn't really know what being alone is. He should try living in a close family of thirteen, no, fourteen, and feel the fear of being exposed for who and what you really are. The warped shame growing in me from the age of six or seven was a living nightmare. When the possibility of entering the priesthood was presented to me in my earlier years, I couldn't see that as the route for me. No wonder so many of my Catholic brothers hid themselves behind the cloth. But there, they were never able to develop sexually naturally throughout their adolescence into adulthood. I do believe that because so many of them remained undeveloped, they turned their sexual attentions inappropriately toward innocent children. Instead I chose to leave home as soon as possible.

Because I had so much love for all my family, an embarrassing exposé would have been dreadful. The thought of degrading or humiliating any of them, or the thought that any one of them would be tainted by who and what I was, had me praying to grow up as fast as possible so I could leave home before a crisis could happen. When that first train ride, the one I had waited and prayed for all through my adolescent years, finally arrived two weeks after my high school graduation, I found out for the first time the difference between doing something motivated by desire and doing it out of a soul-searching need for survival. I realized then I had never wanted to leave my family. I was going because I had to. I was going in order to protect them from me, from

7 Transition

what I was. I planned to go hide myself in a new life.

On the train I was so overcome by the separation that I broke down and had to go hide between the cars and in the toilet all the way to New York City. It was a tricky balancing act, choosing not to submerge who I was, yet choosing to be who I was discreetly. It was a lonely path in the wider world. Sandy should only know what being alone is—not being able to share anguish with another living soul. Oh, Sandy, I thought. How I wanted him to know all this. It was only because God decided to make some of us another way. That was all! It was ever thus in the plant and animal kingdom and it was so with humankind as well. Oh, I am well aware of what some say waving their little black books. Well, they're wrong. What do any of them really know who hasn't walked in our shoes through the twilight zone and had the guts to step out into the light?

God made us all to love everyone and He made the likes of me to do the same. So when in the world are we all going to start? All this mess all of us are in, because of the truth—because of the truth of who we really are. Oh, God! Sandy, if we only could? I cried from the depths of my soul.

By now I was almost home, just a dash across 29th Street to Second Avenue and I would be there. I hoped to hell he wasn't. Chad, that is. I was so numb I could not feel my feet. They were like frozen stumps.

The dark night of my soul passed, but for days I was left in a state of uncertainty and flux. I felt as if I were caught in a cage. Chad didn't know what had hit me, until I announced I was moving out.

February 14, 1964 was upon us, and Sandy had invited me to dinner at his apartment. I had decided to bring him something. He waited till after dinner and Helen, the cook, had left before he opened it. It was a large, red and gold, hardcover Reader's Digest Atlas, the latest edition. I knew that he loved to travel as much as I did and that map reading was the next best thing to it. I waited until he opened it and I saw that he was pleased before I said, "I have something else as well."

"You have something else?" Sandy asked, looking at me quizzically, seeing nothing in my hands.

I waited a moment and then quietly and simply said, "I'm moving in."

Fast Forward Five Years

Now I was hoping the antique chair would arrive before he got in from school. This was going to be a night in because, ever since '64, we had always reserved February 14 just for the two of us, as if we were hot lovers. 1969 was our sixth Valentine's Day and much had changed, and yet nothing had changed. We were both just as happy as we had been six years ago, only now we were not nearly as apprehensive. The chair made it before Sandy did and it looked right at home in the Georgian living room, as I knew it would.

Since we had returned from Bequia, time had seemed to be at a standstill. Our life was like an airplane over Kennedy—in a holding pattern. If the Vincentian government were going to give us permission to buy the land, then and only then would we face decisions. Plans would be made, for both here and there, and then we would have to decide how and when to carry them out. But everything, the lawyer told us, was contingent on approval from the government, and they would first check with the FBI as to our credentials and past record.

"The FBI? My God, Jimmy, you have a top-secret clearance with the US government. As for me, remember McCarthy? I barely squeaked past when a lot of my friends, thanks to Kazan, didn't. I was lucky," Sandy said.

"Well, you could say the same for me. Remember, they estimated 1,300 queers working in Tokyo for General MacArthur and most under top clearance, as I was. A lot of my friends too were sent home then, by the boatload, I heard. By that time, 1952, I was studying at Juilliard. Some officer from the Adjutant General's office came to my place on West 91st Street and asked if I would reenlist under 'The Convenience of the Government Act.' They wanted me to go back to Tokyo and testify for the government in some of the military trials because when they did crosschecks, my name kept coming up in case reports. In other words, they wanted me to be a snitch like McCarthy's Roy Cohn and David Schine and Elia Kazan. Needless to say, my answer to him was simple and brief: 'Not on your life.' Now that I think of it, Sandy, I'm afraid we don't have a chance in hell of getting a place on Bequia."

We joked around like this all the time. Our breakfast and dinner conversations consisted of little else. The breakfast room behind the kitchen overlooked the back garden and was full of early American Colonial furniture dating back to the 1700s. I found the pieces up around the Adirondack region in the Cold Brook area of New York State. Sandy's niece Ellen and her husband Joe Wetherell were always on the lookout, too. They were both antique aficionados. This room was often host to hot and heavy conversations full of disagreements, conflicts, and utter confusion about the pending plans for Bequia. Sandy's mind at least seemed to be made up, but as for me, I was not quite sure. I was trying to keep my mind open to what the future might hold. My uncertainty was grounds for some serious disagreements leading to some memorable discussions. They were never fights. Sandy was too much the gentleman for that. The only stabilizing factor in the house was Nora, our puppy, God love her. Eleanora was named after Sandy's favorite actress who ever lived, Duse, of course. Nora was acquired back in '65 after we moved in together on 83rd Street. She was a solid black German shepherd much loved by both of us. She was sensational.

Now and again we hosted a few informal and formal gatherings. Our close friends were anxious to see the results of the transformation of the house on 83rd, and we took great delight in showing it off. These weekend entertainments, and the time-consuming preparation throughout the week for them, made for a very pleasant existence. Three months passed before we knew it, and I was packing just a few things to return to Bequia to ease Sandy's apprehensiveness.

The night before I was to leave, Maggie Howard, a friend and acting partner of mine from Sandy's class, and I attended the big Anti-Vietnam War march on Washington. One could say it was my last-ditch effort and final act of rebellion in this grand land of ours. Oh, I might add we got a good tear-gassing for our efforts. It was like a slap in the face after forty years of love and loyalty.

I planned to stay in Bequia just long enough to make sure the land got surveyed and to check out which government departments could possibly expedite the process. I would stay for five days and come back right away. You see, Sandy never liked being alone for long. What am I saying? He never liked being alone period. But he was keen to get the ball rolling in Bequia. He had it all worked out. For this year, I would go down for the five days in April, and then again in June to stay. But he wouldn't be coming down when school closed at the Playhouse in June. He would follow only after summer classes ended in August and return in September, in time for his fall classes. The next year, he planned to drop out of teaching summer classes altogether. It would be the first year he would not be at the Playhouse during the summer. He would be able to stay in Bequia for four whole months, and I couldn't wait.

He told me he had to start phasing out sooner or later if he were ever going to retire. When I questioned this intention, Sandy said, "You know, Jimmy, there's no time like the present if I'm ever going to stop."

"I know, but you're stopping before you have a place to go. I think you're rushing things," I said.

"No, I'm not," he answered. "What you need, Jimmy, is trust. Everything is going to work out just fine. Have a little faith."

"Faith! I need faith? I have had faith up to my eyeballs for as long as I can remember, ever since I was five years old when the family sent me off to the nuns. Don't you talk to me about faith, you who know nothing about the inside of a church, sorry, a synagogue."

"Church, synagogue, they're all the same. But don't blame me. So can I help it if my mother and father were progressive? It was important to them I be American. Thank God! I don't know what happened when my younger brother came along sixteen years later. Maybe it was because I became too independent for them. Whatever it was, Bobby attended his Beit Midrash, he was bar mitzvahed, he had faith. What good did it do him? Look at him now. Never mind, you know, you damn well know, what I mean. Bequia is going to work, I say. You want to know why? It's going to work, because I say so."

Well, the day came for me to leave and I did.

8 Freedom

Through Boolu's Eyes: Part 3

Later in life, after Boolu had mastered the English language to the degree he was able, he related to Sandy and me, over a long period of time, anecdotes about his earlier experiences.

"I remember de path down be very easy ta follow, though nobody used it anymore."

The path, which had once been used by the people up on Mt. Pleasant, led down Ravine to the sea. In the dry season, it was uncovered for all to see. Not so in the rainy season. When it rains day after day, the grass grows thick and tall, hiding the path from plain view as if it weren't ever there at all. If it had been used every day, it would be in good enough shape, but a forgotten path would just disappear into the underbrush like a slithering lizard scurrying away to safety, only to reappear later. Eventually the trade winds come and, skirting across the top of the long grasses, they pick up strength and push the rain quite across the sky and out to sea, leaving only the hot sun. The hot, dry sun can burn the grasses brown and make them shrivel up and crumble to bits of dust in less than two weeks, bringing back all the paths, even paths that haven't been used in years.

"I remember when me first started ta run away, where I ran ta was way out beyon Spring Bay, past Industry up over Park, way out der where ya find de

8 Freedom

little black fuzzy tarantulas hidin' under de rocks. It had been dry fo a very long time, everytin' was burnt brown an' dead, an' right der in front a me was a road, a stone road, each stone in place, like de scales on de shell of a turtle's back had come ta life. Der it was, a road dat had been dead ta people fo years. Der was nuttin' out der, nuttin' at'all. Yet der was dis road comin' outta nowhere an' goin' nowhere, just stoppin' dead an' den sippin' back inta de past under de ground ta go back ta nowhere again."

It was a road built as early as the 1700s. Bequia was like that, always full of surprises if you kept your eyes open. To Boolu, everyday things seemed so vivid. He never knew when some new and exciting thing would spring to life right there in front of his very eyes, something that was never there before.

With a few skips, and a jump here and there over a boulder or two, he got down onto the flat. First came the tall coconut trees, then the sea grape bushes that grew like a long wall along the high-water's edge of the sandy beach. That day, the day he ran away from home for the last time, he walked right out onto the warm sand. The late afternoon sun was still reaching its long arm over the tall mountain that splits the Island into three descending land masses, like grapefruit wedges, Belmont, Ravine, and Friendship. When Boolu had climbed up Quam Gutter from Belmont on the Caribbean side of the Island that morning, he saw Friendship Bay beyond Ravine for the first time. Coming out at the top of Quam Gutter, he had made his way down Ravine on the Atlantic side of the Island. From where he stood on the beach that very day he could see the sun stuck up in the sky like a knife cutting the sunlight in uneven segments, giving Belmont at the far other side of the Island the largest wedge.

"Der was jus a little sliver a sunlight left fo Ravine. If I was goin' in fo a sea bat dat day, an' God knows me needed one, I had ta hurry up an' get in an' out before de sun be gone altagedder. I took off my pants an' shirt an' hung dem on a grape bush. Dey would not dry at dat time a day an' me knew it.

De sea was cold an' me didn't like de sea grass. It scared me: ya could not see what was under it. I like seawater, but me don't like de fish out in de deeper dark blue waters. I jumped out, dashed onta de sand, an' ran up an' down de little beach ta dry. De sun was almos gone by de time I reach my clothes. De sun would slip off ta sleep very soon."

He had to get moving, and quick. He had things to do. He hadn't had a thing to eat or drink since he had left the house that morning. It was time to test the water in the well on the flat. This time of year with all the dryness, well water was bound to taste of the sea, and it did, it always did in that big lower well. He had to go farther up the ravine to a small well that would have sweet water, if it held any water at all.

"I checked roun firs fo an' ol powdered-milk tin or a paint bucket, jus in case de well bucket was gone. I didn't fine a milk tin. Dat was too bad because dey were clean inside. I looked fo quite a while, an' when I went over by de old beat-up boat, I spotted a paint bucket hidin' under some palm fronds. Inside was dried white paint, an' when me knocked de bottom wit a rock, it chipped de bottom a de inside clean. I found de lid an figured wit a lid I could keep tings sealed up tight in it also."

This smaller well part way up contained so little water he had to be careful not to muck it up as he dipped the tin cup he had brought into it. For food, he could shimmy up a coconut tree and knock down a couple of water-nuts. A little coconut jelly-meat and coconut water would taste real good with the bread from home that he had in his pocket.

"I den ran up ta de top a de ravine before it got too dark so I could knock down one a dose juicy paw-paws [papaya] dat me saw on de tree before headin' down. Me went back up an' got de paw-paw firs an' den came back down ta de flat an' shimmied up de coconut tree. I could get up an' down a coconut tree wit my eyes covered."

But he must have been a little nervous that night because he did something he had never done before.

"I slid down de coconut tree jus a little bit too fas. Me shoulda known better. Dat is sometin' you jus don't do. One big slip an' you could be finish fo good. De bottoms a me feet were a little sore an' it hurt ta walk on dem."

He forgot about his feet fast enough once his belly was full. He sat at the bottom of Ravine and ate. The paw-paw was sweet and so big he didn't finish it, and the coconut water and jelly from the water-nut quieted his belly. Fortunately, he could only eat half the bread, so he could have the rest the next day when he woke up. He wrapped up what was left of the paw-paw, coconut, and bread in sea grape leaves and stuffed them in his cleaned-out paint tin. With the lid sealing it shut, he would be able to keep out the ants, rats, and all creepy crawlies, and the manicous, too.

Getting through the thick bush and around the boulders to get to the little upper well was tough enough in the daylight but next to impossible at night. But he did manage to do it, because he taught himself to do it. For Boolu, there was always a way. Ravine was like Quam Gutter only a lot wider. When he made that first nighttime foray into it, it was the dry season. The bush was brittle, and the branches hard, dry sticks that scratched and tore at his skin causing it to bruise and bleed. His legs and arms were a mess at first. He kept his hand over his eyes since his sight was useless in the dark anyway.

"All I needed was ta have one a dose stiff sticks chock me in de eye."

Everything looked different in the dark—bushes seemed bigger, trees seemed taller, and everything took twice as long to do.

"Aw, jeezu laud! Dat first night me trip an' fall headlong right over de openin' a de well. It be so dark I could not see it, but me caught myself by grabbin' onta a small tree dat me hit wit my shoulder as I fell. I could tell dat de palm a my hand was bleedin', an' blood was runnin' down one leg. I sat down on a rock an' took de food an' de grape leaves outta de paint bucket an' untied my little cup from my rope. Me den put a little stone in de cup ta sink it an' I scooped out a little water an' used a grape leaf ta pat it on my leg an' hand ta stop de bleedin'.

I remember de water was cool on my skin an' felt good, an' I tought maybe it would stop de blood an' maybe it wouldn't, but me had ta try. Before I put everytin' back an' put de pail way down in de well, I took a big drink a water an' yuck! Me forgot, even from dis upper well, dis water was no good fo drinkin'. I would have ta drink coconut water until de rains came.

I had Mommy's rope an' I needed a stick so I could hang dis pail in de well. I broke a stick off a bush an' used de tick end, so it would be strong enough. I had ta cut a bit wit my knife—da stick was still green an' juicy an' dat was good because dis way it would bend an' not snap clean off. I tied de rope roun de stick an' stuck de big end deep, deep inta de soft dirt nex ta de big stones roun de well till it stuck firm. Den me hid de stick under some stones an' used one a de large loose flat stones dat encircle de top a de well ta cover de hangin' rope from view."

It was all very painstaking, working in the dark. He tied the tin-cup handle to the paint bucket handle and put the paint bucket down into the cool well where everything would stay fresh.

"When I had all dis done, I felt all was safe an' secure, way down at de bottom a de well. I used dat spot fo months. Me kep everytin der."

No one ever went there any more, and most didn't know the little well was there in the first place.

"It was gettin' very late, so I ever so slowly felt my way back down de ravine ta a spot I had picked out earlier when me ate. Der was a huge cedar growin' nex ta a big overhangin' rock dat I could crawl under an' fine a little protection from de cold night wind an' de rain, should rain come."

This sure wasn't the best possible spot, but it would have to do the first night. Boolu felt lucky that night because he had finally done it. He had got away where they would never get him and he had sweet water from the well in the bargain. Sweet, I don't think so.

"Well, passable but not very drinkable. Der had better be rain soon or dat well done finished."

Day two in Ravine started out like most Bequia days. It was bright and sunny with a soft breeze out of the east.

"I busied myself huntin' roun fo foods ta add ta my bucket in de well. Den bout noontime I scurried up de hill ta de top an' went over ta Mt. Pleasant. De Davises would be eatin', an' if I could catch de Missus witout rousin' too much attention, she might give me a piece a bread. Well, me was in luck because she called me over ta de kitchen window an' handed me out a pumpkin fritter still hot from de pan.

As I walked back ta de top a Ravine, I felt a breeze pick up just a little. I looked out over de sea an' I could see dark clouds formin'."

Breezes coming in from the southeast at this time of year could mean nothing but rain and that for him would mean nothing but good. That is, if he could get down this ravine in time to find a little shelter. Those clouds, black as they were, held plenty of rain and they were coming on faster than he could walk. It was not easy getting down the boulder-strewn ravine in the darkening day, and the rain began to pelt down more heavily.

"In my haste I slipped an' slid on de wet leaves. I couldn't stop slidin', an' every branch me grab onta broke. Dey was so brittle. Dis was de way I made it down ta de flat, slippin' an' slidin' all de way down. Well, it was quick, but me had a few more bumps an' bruises after."

The swells out on the midnight-blue sea were becoming monstrous, crashing up against the rocks over on Hilary Point in sprays of daylight white. The rain drummed down steadily once he hit the beach and it was cold on his skin.

"I had all I could do ta keep my crocus bag as dry as possible."

Of course, the rain is never as cold as when the strong winds blow in from the northeast at Christmastime just before the dry season sets in. The night air is cold then whether it rains or not. Of course, the nights on the Island never seem so cold to the people behind their glass windows in their big houses up on the hills, I suppose, but to Boolu out there on the beach with no sleeves in his shirt and his skimpy old pants that didn't cover much, even the more moderate southeasterly winds were chilling.

"I shoulda taken de pants Mommy keep in a box an' dat ol heavy shirt a Boops wit de long sleeves dat she never wore anymore. Once I was at de bottom a de ravine, me spotted a little ol shack way over on de far end a de beach behin some sea grape bushes. I ran down de beach guardin' my crocus sack as best I could considerin' de rain dat was poundin' down on me. When I reached dat little ol hut an' tried de door, it wouldn't open. I first tought it was stuck because a de dampness. It wasn't. It was locked wit a padlock, an' de little window on de side was nailed up tight also. I tought no one was comin' down here fishin' anymore, but me musta been wrong. Den I remembered de paint pail an' dat boat an' after a second tought, I realized it did look like it had been worked over recently.

De rain came down hard an' since me couldn't get in, me quickly got under. Der was enough crawl space an' enough sleepin' room an' de sand was soft an' dry. Me scrunched up inta de crocus sack. If I'd only known me wasn't goin' ta be able ta get inta de ol hut, I would have collected some palm fronds ta spread under an' all roun me ta keep out de cold. De damp wind cut right tru me ta de bone, because me be quite wet. De next day I made dat little spot under dat shack more comfortable.

Before de sun squeezed in between de sea an' de sky like a small flame crackin' tru de brass slit in a hurricane lantern, Mommy used ta chock me wit de broom ta wake me up. Mommy would have dat lantern or a candle lighted long before she get Boops an' me up every mornin.'"

That morning of the third day in the bush, his mommy didn't wake him. He was in the middle of one of his nightmares. Dreaming to Boolu back then was one of numerous mysteries of life.

"In my bed while asleep, way back in my head, everytin' can come ta life, sometimes bright an' beautiful, all colorful an' pretty wit me flyin' all over de place like a big bird, an' at udder times everytin' dark, cold, an' frightenin' wit me unable ta move an inch. Den my legs an' feet would be heavy as lead an' stiff as stone.

Dis was one a dose times when everytin' was scary an' gloomy. In my dream I was lyin' at de bottom of a big pit an' me couldn't move. Der was dese boards over me like me was in a box, like a coffin. De boards were nailed but fitted loose so de light from a lantern seeped in. Me felt as heavy as lead. Between de boards me could see Frazeen standin' over de openin' a de pit. She be twice as tall as I ever saw her. Or I was twice as small—me couldn't tell. Der was someone at her side holdin' a lantern.

Frazeen had a big shovel in she hand an' she was trowin' dirt over me. She was buryin' me like a dead dog. Der was nuttin' me could do. I could see de dirt fall in between de cracks, fallin' in my face an' inta my eyes. I tought I was goin' ta die right der an' den. But at dat moment, I woke up. My mout was wide open an' full a sand an' I let out one yell dat musta outdone a donkey's bray. It ripped me back ta reality. My hands were clutchin' my head an' my eyes were blinkin' out de sand. I was really sweatin', hot an' cold all at de same time.

De last ting I knowed dat was happenin', I be asleep under de fisherman's shack, an' de next ting, der be someone standin' overhead. Der was more dan one person up der, an' dey caused all dat sand ta fall tru de cracks in de floorboards an' onta me face. I could see dat one had a lantern or a flambeau. But dey all turned on der heels an' took off outta dat hut like bolts a lightnin'. Dey were like children caught up a mango tree scared dat any minute one a dem was goin' ta be grabbled in de rass an' each one hopin' all de time it was goin' ta be de udder guy. By de time I shook de sand off my face, squirmed outta de crocus sack, an' crawled out from underneat de shack, de men had taken off down de beach an' had stopped runnin'. All four a dem were turned roun an' lookin' back at de hut where I be standin.'"

They were stretched along the beach in order of their running prowess, the fastest runner farthest away. Perhaps he was the most frightened and the next farther along was the runner-up not only in running ability but in fright as well. Not that they weren't all scared out of their skin. Even the man with the flambeau who brought up the rear was shaky.

"I could see his flame tremblin', but he was de one who was inchin' his way back ever so slowly ta see if what dey tought was happenin' actually was happenin.'"

The others didn't move an inch and seemed not to care to go back and find out one way or the other. They stood poised ready at the slightest provocation to race down the beach and scramble over the rocks into the next bay beyond. When the sand falling in Boolu's face had roused him from his dream, leaving him so confused and terrified that he had let out a bloodcurdling scream like the cry of a banshee, they mistook it for a disturbed spirit. In these parts they are the souls of the dead who have, for some reason peculiar to each and every one, gone to their graves but not their rest. Fit for neither heaven nor hell, condemned to roam the hillside night after night in their own purgatory, they are said to be in search of a victim, or more likely their peace. The people there on Bequia call them jumbies, soucouyants, jack-o'-lanterns, and many other names that I don't know, since I am not versed in Obeah or Voodoo like the fishermen. Who knows what form Boolu's scream took? Was it a jumbie, a soucouyant, or was it one of their victims? Spirit or victim, there stood Boolu, all alone and all in one piece.

"Don't get me wrong, I was jus as frightened a spirits as anyone else an' me still am. Dat is why I be so afraid a sleepin' out at night, an' why I scrunched up in my crocus bag an' covered my head—so dey can't find me when me sleep. Mommy always latch de door an' secure de window shutters, an' so does everyone else on de Island. I always hoped, if me hid myself real good, dey would never find me. I have never seen a jumbie or a soucouyant but me saw a jumbie nest once. I have also seen jack-o'-lanterns many times."

A jack-o'-lantern is a ball of fire like a flambeau that roams the bush out on the bluff and among the rocks where nobody walks at night. Perhaps they could be, as they were in other places around the world, nothing more than ignis fatuus, a light that sometimes appears in the night over marshy ground and is often attributable to spontaneous combustion of gas from decomposed organic matter.

"I hope me never see a jumbie or a soucouyant fo if I do, me done dead."

Boolu waved at the old man with the flambeau, whose first reaction was one of increased fright. The shaking flambeau stopped still in his hand as if he had turned to stone. He looked straight ahead, mouth and eyes wide open, his teeth shining as brightly as the whites of his eyes. It was a good thing that the flambeau man did turn to stone, because if he had taken the tiniest step backwards, he would have startled the others who would have taken off like bolts of lightning again, running till they dropped, or until they hit the sea, never to be seen again. Well, he didn't, and they didn't, and they were all still there.

"I inched forward bit by bit so my stiff friend could get a good look at me. If I had only been able ta talk, it certainly woulda helped. If me ever see a jumbie, I know it would never look any scarier dan dat guy down on de beach, wit de flambeau in his hand."

The flame was flickering across the man's face, casting its lines and hollows into shadows and rendering it as ugly as a gargoyle on some European cathedral.

"I remember back home when Boops would hold a candle under her chin. Her face would turn ugly, like an old Obeah women or a Voodoo witch doctor an' she would scare me half ta death. Den we both would laugh an' laugh. She would trow her head back an' laugh, den grabble me up inta her arms an' roll me over onta de floor. I would scream an' laugh till tears would race down my face. I didn't tink a Boops when me left or a how much I would miss her..."

Boolu was just a little guy, very small for his age and skinny. He looked much younger than he actually was. To the fisherman, he must have looked like a tiny child. The man kept coming closer until he could make out who Boolu was. He straightened up both his arms, still holding his light aloft. He yelled and waved at the others to come forward.

"He ran up ta me, grabblin' me all up inta himself. He trew his arms roun me while he still hangin' onta de flambeau. Dat flambeau was comin' close ta me face an' me ear was getting' hot. I tink he was so glad it was me an' not sometin' else dat he had no idee what he was doin' wit dat red-hot flambeau. I had all me could do ta keep my head away from dat flame. If I hadn't watched his every move, I tink we bot woulda gone up in flames dat night, includin' half a Ravine due ta de dryness, an' right der in front a de udder tree."

If it had played out that way, then let me tell you there would have been some fantastic tall tales racing through the Bequia grapevine the next day. It would have made a great jumbie story for future kids of the Island. Maybe that's what jumbie stories are made of. But then, maybe not...

"Well, he finally let me go an' I be OK, cep for a little scorchin'. He was laughin' now, but de udder men, who be close by now, jus stood lookin' at us. Two a de men looked at me like I wasn't human. So de flambeau man, treatin' me now like a friend, went over ta de men wavin' his hands an' talkin'. Tellin' dem what? Me didn't know. In time, dey all shuffled over ta de shack, some trowin' suspicious glances at me as dey went. Two a de men started ta laugh as dey went inta de shack, but one a dem still didn't like de looks a me. I followed long, keepin' my distance. After dey went inta de shack, I went up ta de door. De most unhappy one saw me at de door lookin' in an' made one jump for me, grabbin' me by de neck. I didn't know what he was goin' ta do, beat me all ta hell, I guess. Before he had a chance ta hurt me, de udder two pulled him off. Now dey all were laughin', cep de one. Dey was laughin' at him now."

In the shack they kept all their fishing gear—nets, lines, bait in tins, sails, water tins, center boards, oars, and rubber coats—everything a fisherman needs out on the open sea. Boolu figured these men had bought the boat from the Davis brothers and would run their fishing operation from this bay now. Who were they? Where were they from? They weren't from Mt. Pleasant, that was for sure.

"I could tell de flambeau man was de top man, an' I was glad we started off on de right foot. I knew me would need him fo a friend if me was goin' ta hole up here in Ravine fo any lengt a time. I stood about watchin' dem as dey loaded der double-ender wit supplies fo de day out at sea, but me be still keepin' well outta de way. Once dey were ready ta shove off, me did grab hold a de boat wit all de udders an' drog it across de sand an' down de beach inta de water. De old man settled himself in de boat, an' I noticed dat he take one last look back at me an', wit a broad smile, he wave. Me jump inta de air an' wave back. Dey was all lookin' at me smilin' an' wavin', dat is, all cep one."

Boolu then walked back to the shack that the men had locked up, but his things were still underneath just the way he had left them. It was still too early to go up the ravine to the old well, so he crawled back in under the shack and into his crocus bag and went off to sleep again.

"My tird day in Ravine was full a activity. It started wit a sea bat at daybreak. It is jus great at dat time a de mornin; everyone should try it. I mus be honest—dis mornin' it was a little later dan daybreak as I slep right tru it."

In fact, it was the sun that woke him up the second time that third day. It shot its hot rays across the foamy sea and up the cool shimmering sand, causing smoke to rise as if it would burst into flame, then bounced off the beach into the underbrush and delved straight under the fisherman's shack and into his eyes.

"I awoke faster dan if it was Frazeen's broom. It was goin' ta be a lovely day an' me felt good. I seemed ta sleep well because it felt so good ta sleep free, an' I mean dat in many ways. My legs an' hands an' even me belly were free a ropes. Even more important me would feel an' be free all day. De first ting I did after my sea bat dat tird day was wash out de crocus sack an' my clothes. I could see it was goin' ta be a dry day, an' all my stuff would dry in de sun in no time an' would smell good again. I left my tings on de sea grape bush ta dry out an' went part way up de ravine in me altagedder ta de old well. Not ta worry, everyting would be dry by de time me got back down. I could see de well was not changed cep de blood me left der dat first night was all gone."

The rain of last night had washed the blood away as if it had never happened. In fact, it had all gone away—no fall, no cut, no blood, and no pain. He couldn't remember where and what the pain felt like. Maybe that was a good sign. He hoped it was. He had to look at the cuts on his hand and the bruises on his leg to make sure that it had ever happened at all.

"I pulled de pail up an took off de lid wit de stick ta check out my food. Everytin' be fine, just as me left it, as I knew it would be. Der was no red ants or even fruit flies like der would be at home. I took de pail, rope an' all. I would need dem down at de big well on de flat where I could give meself a wash-down. De water der is never good ta drink, but it was always good ta give yourself a wash-down ta get rid a de sticky sea salt. It always made me feel better. I wanted to take some drinkin' water down wit me in my little tin cup from de smaller upper well. Me would be wantin' it later wit my food. I took de food outta de tin an' lowered de tin inta de well. Dis time I be able ta fill it because a dose hard rains last night. I would have ta find sometin' ta keep de sweet water in, such as it was. I couldn't find anytin' cep de base of a large palm frond. When dey begin ta dry up, de sides curl up on each udder, an' down at de bottom at de base where it broke off from de tree, it curls up also makin' a long, deep cup. Rain collects in dem durin' de rainy season. But I remember Frazeen tell me dat water be no good. Frazeen show me where de mommy mosquito lay der eggs ta make little mosquitoes in de big palm fronds. Until I be ready ta eat, my little tin cup would be good for holdin' de water in. I was sure I could find better ways ta keep water, but it would have ta wait till later. What I had would do fo taday.

I took my food an' water wit me down on de beach where I had my wash-off. My clothes were dry an' I put my shirt an' pants on, sat down on a log, an' ate. Lef over from yesterday me had bread, coconut meat, paw-paw, an' drinkable water. Not bad, it would at leas hold me fo de day. After my tea—dat's what we call our mornin' meal—I went about col-lectin' sticks, breakin' dem off real dried-out bushes an' trimmin' off de little twigs wit my knife. I cut only de long tin narrow ones, so I could bend dem. Mommy showed me how ta do dis a long time ago. When she add mud, it come hard like cement. You call it mud an' wattle. I would stick de strong ones straight up an' down inta de sand under de shack, runnin' from de sand quite up ta de bottom a de shack. I did dis all along one wall facin' de sea. Dat is where de wind blows in from de sea bringin' in wit it all de rain. When I had all de up-an-down ones in under de shack wit a bit a space between, I took de tinner more bendable ones an', startin' at de bottom, I pushed dem in an' out an' around de straight-standin' ones, like a basket. Oh, I didn't do dis all in one day; it took me some time ta finish it, but I knew I had ta get it started before de real rains started comin'.

When I got all de sticks woven together, I went farther back inta de bush an' got dirt an' clay dat I mixed wit sand an' water from de sea. It was like makin' fry bakes, an' I patted it all over de little wall until it stuck like plaster. When it was finished, I had a hard dry wall ta protec me from de wind an rain."

About mid-afternoon, while he was still working on his wall, the men came back. His back was to the sea and he didn't notice them coming even though they blew a conch shell as they came in to let everyone in earshot know they were coming with fish for sale. There are no homes around this bay, but the women up on Mt. Pleasant still keep an eye out and the people over on St. Hilaire and up over on Friendship can hear the horn. The people from Hilary and Friendship would come to the bay, but the women up on Mt. Pleasant would wait till the men came up the hill on their way to the fish market to sell the fish. If the fishermen had a lot, they would string them on fish-line and carry them to the Harbour to sell to the villagers. These new men fishing out of here now were not from up the hill, and Boolu didn't know them or know what was going to happen when they came in. But before they go to market there is still a lot of work to do if they have any catch at all.

"De first I knew a der return is when me felt a clout de side a my head dat knocked me off balance an' sent me sprawlin' inta de sand. Before I could get back on my feet, witout movin' I twisted my head ta get a look at whoever it was. Der be dat frighten fool who took dat lunge at me dis mornin'. He was kickin' me in de ribs an' den he turned on de shack an' kicked in some a de sticks I had been workin' on all day. It was just one kick an' den he turned on me again. He had me by de neck now an' was droggin' me."

The other men were in the shack stowing their gear and sorting out the fish while the mean one was still holding Boolu with one hand and jabbering away with his mouth, all the time waving his other hand in the air. Boolu had no idea what he was saying, and the other men were only half listening, yet he knew it couldn't be good. Boolu had a feeling it was about taking him back to Frazeen. None of these men were from Mt. Pleasant, they didn't know Frazeen well, and they sure didn't know Boolu at all. In the end, the other men just told him to let the boy go. Then one of the younger guys pulled Boolu away from the bully.

"Dey weren't about ta be dragging me all de way up de hill, dey had work ta do, an dey didn't even know where Frazeen lived. De older man was lookin' under de old hut an' saw where I had slep las night. In his hand he had one a de sticks broken off from my mud an' wattle. Walkin' over ta de udder men, he showed dem de stick, an' he den went over ta de hut an' knelt down ta examine de wall I was buildin'. He was givin' my afternoon's work a good goin' over. He called me over an' pulled me down next ta him an' started ta show me a better way ta do it. When he got up, he patted me on de head an' went on wit cleanin' de fish wit de udder men."

One man was stowing everything away in the shack to be locked up for the night. Another was stringing fish on a line to be hung on a long pole so they could be taken to market. And a third was building a fire. This one got a big pot and a big bottle of water out of the shack and started to make a boilieen. When everyone had finished their work, they all sat around the fire and ate.

"De old man gave me a bowl a de boilieen. When dey finished, dey put out de fire an' loaded demselves down wit der fish an' headed outta de ravine an' over de hill ta de market. As dey went, de old man went over ta de shack fo de last time. He picked up one a my sticks an' walked back ta where I be, handed it ta me, an' motioned fo me ta get back ta work."

Boolu knew then and there that the old man would not let any of the men come after him or send him away. He also knew he was now too far for Frazeen to come after him and besides she was getting old, real old. Maybe Boops wouldn't come looking either. She never did like seeing him beaten and tied up all the time. Anyway at that time she wasn't even twelve years old. That night he had a feeling he was truly free, free at last, free as he had never been in his life.

"My days in Ravine would start very early. I would wake when de fishermen came wit der flambeau an' unlocked de shack ta get out all der gear. I would get up an' help dem set out de rig an' sail. Den wit de men, I helped pull de boat across de beach an' inta de surf."

He would wave them off and then go back in under the shack, crawl into his crocus sack, and go right back to sleep until the sun exploded into his realm under the little shack above the high-water mark. His bed was soft and warm now. The palm fronds he put under his crocus bag made it much softer than the hard bed he had slept on at home. And believe it or not, that mud and wattle wall of his finally got finished, with a little help once in a while from that old fisherman. So he was protected from the wind and the rain.

"When I got up, de first ting I did was ta go fo my sea bat. Dat was one a de best feelin's a de day. Den I would have some fruit an' coconut water ta start off de day. Dat was my usual mornin' tea. When I first settled in, I didn't fo de most part wander too far way from Ravine. I was still afraid ta go near people cep de fishermen."

He depended upon them a great deal at first, especially for food. It worked out very well when they came everyday and when they caught fish. It all depended on the weather, and the weather was good at first, which served him well. Sometimes they would give him a whole fish and even if it wasn't so big, he would keep it in the upper well in case he needed it the next day should they fail to show. The old man not only gave him fish once in a while, he also gave him matches once, so he could light a fire. He kept them dry in a tin under the shack. One day they gave him some line and fishhooks, laughing as they did so.

"I didn't know why dey laugh because me could catch a redhine, a butter fish, a grouper, an' maybe a snapper or an oldwife off de rocks on de point. Even de lagoon where I used ta swim was good sometimes."

Yet other times he would sit all day and not get a thing even though he used island crabs for bait.

"On a moonless night I could catch de big blue land crabs under de coconut trees on de flat behind de sea grape bushes. If it rained a little an' filled up der holes, dey would be forced out an' I would have quite a time collectin' dem in a flour sack me got from de men."

It still wasn't easy because he wouldn't have a light and it would be dark as pitch. He found more by stepping on them than by actually seeing them. The weather began to go from bad to worse as the rainy season set in, and he saw the fishermen less and less. One day it would be the wind and another day it would be the rain. Yet another day it would be because of the high seas, and he would not see them for days.

"It was durin' dis bad spell I went up ta Mt. Pleasant fo de first time in months. Me was very hungry an' didn't have any other choice. Uncle Ky's [Boolu's way of saying "sky's"] woman was very nice ta me."

Boops had taken Boolu up there a number of times a long time ago. When she went up to do the washing, the Missus always had something for them to eat. Like Uncle Lacey, Sky had fished out of Ravine back in the old days, as did others up on the Hill before the oil field days on Aruba. He didn't go near the place anymore. All the same, they all knew Boolu was hanging out down there.

"I went up ta de house one mornin' jus before noon. Dat be de time her children an' Uncle Ky, all a dem, would be gone. She would be cookin' an' if she didn't chase me, she would feed me. I went up ta de back door an' looked in jus ta see what would happen. Dey had a dog but he was old an' he didn't make a fuss. He knew me well because we played a lot together. When me pass de open window, I smell freshly baked bread. Gee, it smelt so good, me went all warm inside an' out, an' me knew I was in luck dat day. When she spotted me at de door wit de dog at me side, I could tell from her smile dat she knew just what me was lookin' fo. She stood at de stove wit one hand on her hip an' in de udder she held a wooden spoon she was stirrin' sometin' wit in a big pot."

Miz Baba [Barbara] was shorter than Frazeen but much wider and built straight up and down, just like a mattress. Her dress was cut simply, just like her, straight up and down, and it was covered all over in flowers just like Miz Edmunds' curtains. The hair on her head was frizzy and cut short. It ran loose in all directions, not tight and kinky like Boops but more like Frazeen's. It was the color of beach wood. Her skin was white, real white, almost translucent, like a gecko, the ones you can almost see through when they're near a light at night, with blue lines running every which way. Her nose was red as was the back of her wrinkly neck. Her eyes were green with brown brows above. Her lips were blue, almost mauve, and her skin was covered in liver spots. One could say Miz Baba was a woman of color. But I don't think she would appreciate it. After all she wasn't a parrot and she was from Mt. Pleasant. Yet Baba embodied still another color, for beneath it all she had a heart of gold. Now, there she stood in her kitchen, arms akimbo and bare flat feet planted firmly apart on the multi-colored linoleum of the kitchen floor.

"She waved her spoon at me ta sit down on de step-up at de door. Den she brought me over a big bowl a pumpkin soup wit chicken wings an' onions. Oh, God! It smelled so fine it made my head spin. She went over ta de sink-counter an' pulled back de dishciot dat she had coverin' de four big, hot, freshly baked loaves a bread. I knew she had been bakin'—me could smell it. Miz Baba cut off a big end piece an' came over an' gave it ta me, an' den she went back over ta her stove."

All the time she was talking as if Boolu understood every word. Every now and again she would point her finger straight at him and shake it up and down in a scolding manner. She talked so fast and so low that even if Boolu had been able to hear, he wouldn't have understood half of what she said. For some reason it didn't make any difference. She just babbled on: he was a bad boy; he shouldn't run away from Frazeen; he should go back; if he didn't, she was just going to have to take him packing home herself. On she went with all kinds of advice and admonition.

"I just sat der lookin' up at her, an' I would smile up at her an' she would go right on talkin' an' me would go right on eatin.'"

Boolu also knew she couldn't really mean whatever she was saying because nothing ever came of it. She must have felt she had to say what she said. If she had really meant it, there were times she could have done something about it. But she never did. Although Boolu went to Miz Baba's house several times in those years, he went only when things got hard for him during certain rough times of the year when he had no place else to turn for food. Sometimes Ba-

8 Freedom

ba's children and Uncle "Ky" would be there and sometimes they would be down in the Harbour. But Baba was always home. She could easily have had one of the family take him back to Frazeen by force but she never did. She might go on about his being a bad boy but she was always glad to see him.

"I knew she was glad ta see me an' she knew me knew. Sometimes in de evenin' before I left de place fo Ravine, she would have me sweep de dirt from roun de house or clean out de chicken coop. One afternoon she handed me a cutlass ta cut de long grass. I remember de day she gave me a paper bag full a provisions. Der was a coupla tanyas, two small onions, an orange an' some plums, even a little rice. Me didn't have rice in a long time. I had a little place under de shack where me kep everytin' in a tight tin."

Another time before he left, she pointed up to where Mickey and Gypsy and Wayne lived with their little sister and made a motion of cutting wood. He knew what she meant by this. Their mommy, Miz Marlene, was always making coals for sale and she would need someone to help her collect the wood in the bush.

One year when Boolu was still in the bush, the winds had been bad most of the month. At this time of year you could lose your galvanize clear off the top of your roof and find it the next morning in your neighbor's corn patch. First the skies go all dark for a day or so, the winds pick up, and so does the sea. Then it happens all of a sudden. The roar of the wind stops and everything goes still, except for the pounding rain. Then even the rain lets up. All is still and quiet. It is like the world itself has stopped breathing. Then the winds start up again, only now they're coming from the other direction, the northeast, in a large circular motion—a sure sign that the storm is overhead.

But at the beginning of this cycle, when the skies go all dark, everyone starts pulling up their boats—I mean all of them and I mean way up, not just above the high-water mark but way up on dry land—and they shackle them down. Everyone runs around hammering down everything that moves: windows, window shutters, doors, everything. And then, little by little, the sea swells get bigger and bigger. The winds get stronger and stronger and the rains start flying in circles, a beating, driving rain that starts taking tons and tons of top soil down with it through the steep crevasses of every ravine and gully on the Island, running, rushing, romping, and racing like Robert Southey's "Cataract of Lodore" down to the sea wildly raging in every bay and inlet.

Everyone is hunkered down in whatever shelter they can find wishing, hoping, and praying with all their faith that the eye of the storm misses the Island by miles. They are hunkered down because they have no choice. Where could they go? No car or plane can help them now. The Island is only one mile wide and six miles long, so everyone tries to find a secure spot, if there is one, and they stay put. In the morning, it's always over. Once it has passed, everyone thanks God as they go about trying to pick everything up and put it all back in place, piecing there lives back together again.

For some time now the winds had been high, and the fishermen had been no-shows at Ravine. Boolu was getting worried. This morning seemed no different. But although the fishermen didn't come at their regular time, they did arrive about three hours later than usual.

"It was long after daybreak when I felt my ol fisherman pullin' at de bottom a my soggy crocus bag. De sack be soakin' wet. It be rainin' all night ever since me went ta sleep. I crawled out from undemeat de shack. Wipin' de sleep outta my eyes, I looked up ta see de udder men pullin' de double-ender way back inta de ravine an' fastenin' each end ta two strong coconut trees. My friend be busy nailin' down de window shutters. I knew what be happenin', but me didn't know what ta do about it. I walked over ta de ol fisherman an' stood next ta him. He finished nailin' up de window an' was lookin' down at me, shakin' his head."

Boolu must have looked awfully funny and scared looking up at the old man. He was soaking wet in the new pants Miz Baba had given him the day before. The pants, too big for him, were all gathered up around his middle and secured with a deck rope that had found its way to him by way of many hands off one of the yachts in the Harbour. He looked more like a little drowned rat than a runaway kid from Mt. Pleasant.

"De ol fisherman patted my head an' got down on his hands an' knees an' pulled out my crocus bag. He motioned me ta go in an' pull out everytin' I had under der. He took each ting I had one by one an' stuffed dem inta my bag. When I scrambled out an' got onta my feet, he took my sack an' slung it over my shoulder. Wrappin' de palm a his broad weather-beaten hand roun de back a my head, he led me ta de path up de hill ta Mt. Pleasant. He wasn't comin' wit me. Der was still work ta be done wit de udder men. Dey lived off in de opposite direction an' dey weren't plannin' ta take me wit dem. It was clear he wanted me ta hurry up de hill alone.

'Go... go...,' he motioned ta me. Go, go, go where? Go home, of course, go home ta Frazeen. After all dis time...? I tought, no, I wouldn't go home, couldn't go home. I turned roun an' shook my head an' took two steps toward de ol man. He was showin' anger now an' I knew it was no time fo talkin'. It would do no good, even if me could."

The winds were getting stronger and the swells out on the bay were getting bigger by the minute. The old fisherman had work to do. No one knew when that storm was going to hit.

"He pulled me roun by de shoulders wit a strong jerk, facin' me up de hill, an' gave me one hard slap on my backside, shovin' me wit such might dat it sent me sprawlin' headlong onta my hands an' knees in de mud a de path. I sat in de mud an' began ta cry. I looked back after de old man tru my tears an' de peltin' rain. I could see dat he was gone, an' so was my crocus bag. It flew inta de bush on de downhill side a de path when I went sprawlin' facedown inta de mud. Wit de rain an' my tears, I couldn't see a ting an' it tore at my soul ta have been pushed an' hit by my friend."

Oh! He looked for his bag all right, but only half looked for it and not for very long at that. He didn't care if he found it or not. He felt so bad at that moment; he didn't care about anything.

"I gave up lookin' an' I continued ta drog myself up de hill. I didn't know where me was goin' or what me was goin' ta do. I still wasn't goin' ta Frazeen, dat was fo sure. When me reached de top a de hill, I could still feel de pain in my warm bottom an' my knees, or was it dat burnin' feelin' in de pit a my belly? Oh, God! I felt so bad, so foolish, embarrassed because it was my fault. Why was I so stupidy? Dat ol man was always so good ta me. He was my friend, why did dis happen?"

On the Mt. Pleasant road, the one that goes all the way down to the Harbour, he could see someone coming leading a nanny goat with little ones stumbling up the hill behind. Up there on top of the hill, the wind was blowing hard; he could hardly stand up on his feet.

"I got behind de trunk of a big cedar tree, an' it kep me from bein' swep right down inta Quam Gutter. I stood der watchin' de figure strugglin' cross de crest a de hill wit de old goat. I could see it be a girl, an' she be havin' a helluva time wit dat goat an' its kids. She by now had decided ta leave de little ones ta make out for demselves. I could see de little ones were not havin' half as much trouble keepin' up wit de old goat as de girl was havin' leadin' dat old goat. She was comin' in my direction, so I didn't move, me just stood der watchin' her as dey approached. When dey passed me, I could see it be Gypsy. She be headin' home wit her goats as she lived just over an' beyon. I tought her brothers, Mickey an' Wayne, must be off gettin' de udder animals.

Wit all de wind an' rain in her face, she didn't see me standin' der, nor did she see me jump out an take hold a de chain ta help her. When she felt me der an' turned roun, she jumped wit such fright but when she realized who me be, she jus laughed an' laughed a nervous laugh a relief. She was glad for de extra help in gettin' her goats in before de real blow came. So we bot struggled along wit de mud up ta our knees on de old dirt road leadin' ta her house over de top a Mt. Pleasant. De rain was beatin' down on us so hard, like it was tryin' ta press us inta de mud, goats an' all, before de winds blew us off dis hill altagedder.

In time we reached de house. I helped her put de goats inta de shed behin. De sheep an' de cow were already in; Mickey an' Wayne had already seen ta dat. When we got dem all in, she closed an' latched de door in a hurry, spun roun, an' made one mad dash ta de house. I stood der an' watched her go an' saw de door slamming behin her."

Well, here he was alone again and he had better find someplace to hole up until this storm passed, and he had better find it soon. He was walking away from Gypsy's when he thought he might go back and stay with the goats in the shed. It was not much protection and it was quite wet in there, but what choice did he have? He was so far away from anything up here. He knew he wouldn't find a better place in the time he had left.

As he went around behind the house, he could see Gypsy's mommy at the back window waving at him. He had no idea what she was saying, so he kept going right over to the shack. Who could hear her in this gale? Certainly not Boolu. He didn't care if she didn't want him in her shed; he was going in no matter what. Let her come out and get him. He also saw Wayne at the kitchen door. He had it open a crack and he was really yelling something. Too bad, thought Boolu. He had to go somewhere for protection, he had to get there right away, and it was going to have to be their shack. He struggled with the latch. It wasn't locked but it was rusty and hard to open with his little hands. Just as he pushed the door in, Wayne grabbed Boolu by his wet shirt and pulled at him. He excitedly motioned Boolu to the house, then shut the door to the shack and latched it.

"Wayne shoved me in front a him wit one hand an' wit de udder he held tight-closed his yellow rubber slicker as it flapped in de wind. De storm at dis point was very close, if not already on us. De sounds a de storm even I could hear in all my deafness. When we reached de house, Gypsy was at de door an' Wayne scurried us into de house an' slammed de door shut behind us."

The house was a good strong "wall house" not a little old wooden house like Frazeen's. Gypsy and Wayne's daddy worked the oil fields of Aruba for years and he had sent money home to build this strong house on the hill. Quite a few had been going up around the Island ever since the '60s. I used to call them Aruba Modern because they all looked alike.

"Gypsy took off my wet clothes an' dried me up an' gave me a pair a pants an' a shirt a Wayne's. De pants went all de way down ta de floor, an' she rolled dem up. She mommy brought in hot fish broth. Dey were all havin' some wit bread an' dey gave me some, too. We were all downstairs in de dinin' room. I went ta sleep in a big chair next ta Wayne as I watched de Missus an' Gypsy pray de storm away. It did go away sometime in de middle a de night."

It had been quite a blow. The storm had come very close to Bequia but fortunately, for Bequia anyway, it made an abrupt, almost unheard-of turn to the south, destroying much of the smaller islands of the southern Grenadines all the way down to Grenada.

When the little group went out the next morning, they saw a big tree had fallen very near the house. Up there on the hill, all the houses are protected from the constant strong winds by tall bush and trees. Everything grows in the same direction, at an angle leaning away from the wind. It is a strange sight like the crooked little man with the crooked little house. But those slanted trees do serve as good protection.

"Dat mornin' I went out wit Mickey an' Wayne an' collected all de fallen branches an' we cut up broken limbs. We den drogged dem ta one spot an' tied dem inta bundles. Dis would make coals fo der mommy. Der was goin' ta be a lotta wood ta cut, an' den der would be plenty a coals fo sale later on. We all worked hard dat day after de storm. When it came time ta eat, dey all went back ta de house, an' me too, I followed long. Nuttin' was said one way or de udder. I followed de kids in an' der mommy handed me de food just like de rest.

At de end a de day was sometin' else. Me didn't know what ta do. One ting I did know was dat Ravine would not be livable fo a few days—it would have ta dry out a lot. Dat night after our tea, everyone sat roun on de porch in front. Dey were all just talkin' an' lazin roun, which I be doin' also, but wit difficulty. I be worried as ta what was goin' ta happen nex. When it came time ta go in, I jus followed de boys an' found a place ta curl up on a chair. Still not a word was said.

De next day all de kids went off ta school down in de Harbour. Miz Marlene went off choppin' wood fo her coal pits an' she had me go along ta help her."

Boolu worked for her for what must have been weeks, stripping and cutting the wood. They dug a big hole into which they placed the long strips of narrow limbs to be smoldered under sand for a day or two with dirt and ash on top, ever so slowly turning the wood into jet-black charcoal. The charcoal was just great for cooking in coal pots and even kitchen stoves. From a distance, on a dark moonless night, the burning charcoal pits looked like so many jumbie graves, burning and smoldering from the depths of hell. Or were they more like jack-o'-lanterns pushing themselves up from their imprisoned graves so they could roam the hillside all night, searching, searching till dawn, for whatever?

When the charcoals cooled, they packed them into crocus bags. Nothing was ever said about how long Boolu could stay or about his going back to Frazeen or to Ravine. One Saturday when they all went off to prayer meeting, and he was left alone, he went for a walk down the Ravine.

"When I reached de bottom a de path an' I approached a clearin' in de sea grape bush an' walked out onta de sandy beach, I could not believe my eyes."

During the storm the sea had risen so high that the strong winds and high tide had pushed the seawater way back up into Ravine. As the rain stopped and the last gust of wind blew up and over the hill, the water had run back down the ravine, onto the flat, across the bush, over the sandy beach, and down into the muddy, murky brown sea. It had run every which way, like so many sand crabs, and finally seeped down into the sand. Everything that had been securely fastened down, even if it was rooted down as well, was carried out to sea: trees, bush, rocks, stone, and soil. Oh, yes, everything was gone, even the fisherman's shack and everything in it, including the boat that had been securely tethered with coil, way up behind the sea grape bush.

"I could see pieces a de boat over on de rocks beyond de blowhole over by Hilary. Nuttin' was left a de foamy, murky lagoon beyon de beach an' behin de sea grape bushes. It had all been der an' now it was gone. Tank de Lord der were coals ta be made."

9 Survival

The Emergency Story

What had happened to Boolu was truly remarkable. It was a long story and no one knew all of it. No one would for a very long time, until Boolu himself was able to speak. Once he could, he would share his experiences with Sandy and me or anyone who would listen, whether they understood him or not. He was eager to share little anecdotes, tidbits, and snippets however embarrassing and hurtful the telling might be. What unfolded was this larger canvas, a canvas that I feel only Boolu could unfurl.

Through Boolu's Eyes: Part 4

It was a grand, bright, and bristling-brisk morning. The sun was still low in the southeastern sky as Boolu made his way across the jagged volcanic rock. The lush green moss that covered it was extra slippery because of the splash from the blowhole, which lay directly ahead.

"If I was ever goin' ta get beyon, up, an' over de blowhole an' onta Hilary, I would have ta wind way off ta de right ta escape its wet salty spray. Me was getting' wet."

He couldn't avoid getting wet, for the ever-reliable trade winds would carry the mist clear across the rock to the dark green of the sea grape bush and the coconut trees. They flourished in the flood of energy from the spray, the sun, and the mineral-rich sediment heaped layer upon layer by storm after storm, century after century. The storms would be over for a while now, and the dry season would descend upon the Island with a vengeance. It was the time of the tourist as well. In the lands to the north, the sharp arctic winds would be blowing south covering everything in their path with swirls of snow. Like the arctic tern, tourists begin their way back, ever so slowly swooping to the south where the earth dries itself off and warms up in the heat of the sun; its perfect timing for an unexplained miracle. The fishermen whose boat had been washed out to sea were on to other things, most likely fishing with others over off Friendship or La Pompe. These were places Boolu had never yet been.

"Ravine would never be de same an' me knew it. It was time ta move on. When I finally made my way ta de crest a Hilary, me see two a de weirdest people me ever see. Ta begin wit dey be neither black nor white. Der faces be pink like de inside of a conch shell. Well, at leas de one was, de udder was redder dan anyting else. One had yellow hair dat hung all de way down her back like de schoolgirls from Mt. Pleasant—straight, soft, an smooth-lookin'. Yeah, like de stuff dat grow outta de corn on de stalk jus out back a Frazeen's shack. De udder one looked like sometin' me never see before. De head was all afire, like a pumpkin, a settin' sun, a ripe orange growin' out Industry way at de McIntosh place. Dat's right, jus like de inside of a pumpkin."

He thought they were both women, decked out in gay colorful togs from head to foot. The wind was swirling around them and blowing right at him where he stood just a little behind them. The sounds he heard coming from them were outlandish, the strangest noise he had yet heard. Though he was deeply deaf, one would have to be stone deaf not to hear the bass burden these two were conjuring up, for it could be heard for miles. You see, they were a couple of Scots, a man and his wife vacationing at the hotel beyond. They happened to bring along with them their kilts and bagpipes. They had risen at the crack of dawn, decked themselves out in their clan's colors, and headed up the winding goat path from the hotel, which led to the summit of Hilary Hill. Their bagpipes were clutched in their arms, and their bonnets, or rather his glengarry and her tam-o'-shanter, cocked on their heads. When they reached the top, they sat on the ground in a clearing watching the sunrise and catching their breath. After a short while, they stood up, then filled their bags with air, secured them under their arms, and marched down off the crest of Hilary, like a couple of corporals in a Highland brigade heading to battle. Only this time they headed for the base of Hilary Point and the sea, playing one of their favorite Scottish airs for all they were worth.

"Dey was bout midway down de hill when I caught up wit dem. When I first heard dem, me couldn't believe my eyes, fo de likes a dese me never saw, not even in my strangest dream."

For him, that experience was next to traumatic; he was hearing music for the first time! Electric rock bands hadn't yet reached Bequia. Why, Bequians didn't even have electricity in their homes. Boolu had heard drumming before, like the sounds he made at home for Frazeen on biscuit tins, but this was different.

"I was hearing beats made by someone else fo de first time. I was really hearing sounds fo de first time as if I had hearing aids on, like I do today. Dey was high an' low, like runnin' up an' runnin' down in rhythm like me on my biscuit tins back home. Ever since I was a little bitty boy back over on St. Vincy, me could feel rhythm in my body. De big people would put me up on a table an' I would move—dance an' jump up an' down, like I see big people do. Everyone would laugh an' clap. Now dat's when I be de happiest, when I knockin' an' movin' ta rhythm."

This time it was all so much fuller than anything he had ever felt before, up and down, swirling around, and jumping about here and there and back again. Then it stopped and started again repeating itself. The couple marched on ahead, their kilts swishing back and forth, unaware of the little waif following along close behind, mimicking their every move as if he had on a kilt of his own. He couldn't help improvising and adding little bits of his own, not missing a beat of the ancient Scottish air that they blasted forth from their ancient instruments. They reached the end of the bluff that dropped straight down to where the sea crashed up against the rocks, out on the point of Hilary. There they stopped and stood silently staring out to sea, ecstatic, and pleased with themselves.

"As dey turned roun, de idee a facin' dem dead on scared de hell outta me. I turned on my heels an' bolted up ta de crest a Hilary, like a frightened orange-eyed manicou. Man, how I ran till I dropped from exhaustion high on de hill up over beside Friendship Bay."

He was just the other side of Florence's little saffron-colored octagon house, which stood directly over the hotel up on the hill. A lonely little West Indian house it was. To me it was beautiful, its proportions were sound, and the design actually sang when you looked at it. Its eight sides were three feet thick and made of solid stone with a smooth finish of saffron-colored plaster. It was topped with an eight-angled walaba-shingled roof. The paint had weathered, as had the shingles. Bleached-out and weather-faded, it looked unreal, like a picture out of Aesop's fables or Hans Christian Anderson's fairy tales. Little old Florence, who lived in the house, withered, dried up, and bent over, could have been a Brothers Grimm character right out of the bowels of the Black Forest.

"I stopped in front a de house. De mornin' was getting' on an' me was hungry. I hadn't put a ting in my belly. Yeah, yesterday all I had ta eat was coconut jelly."

Boodoe, everyone called Little Florence. Boolu had never read that she would stuff him into her oven if she got him inside her saffron-colored cottage. He'd never even heard, much less read, the tale of Hansel and Gretel. In fact he knew Boodoe and had seen her often as she hobbled along with the help of her stick down to the bay for fish.

"I went right up ta de window ta look in, an' not bein' any too careful, I knocked a potted herb off de windowsill."

Little old Boodoe heard the crash and came scurrying across to the door to look out.

"When she saw it was me an' what had happened, she started ta shake her stick at me, rantin' an' ravin' an' me not understandin' a ting. So I took off."

With a hop, skip, and a jump off her water tank, he continued down the hill along a little path that led to Noel Agard's hotel. The path conveniently led right to the kitchen door—obviously little old Boodoe shuffled along here with fair frequency. The kitchen was all hustle and bustle as breakfast was in progress. Aileen, who was not much over twenty, was in charge of a still younger staff. She lived on the Lower Bay road. The rest of the staff was principally from Paget Farm and La Pompe. They were all milling about, bouncing off one another and getting into each other's way, all this bumping and tripping contributing to the overall confusion and commotion.

"I could smell all dose wonderful smells, like outside Miz Edmunds' when Mommy an' I got down der early before she come out ta tell us what ta do round de yard dat day."

Boolu had been up here many times before ever since it had been Noel Agard's place. At this time of the morning, he could detect coffee brewing in a pot, bacon sizzling in a pan, and flat fry bakes cooking on the grill. The aromas wafting their way out the open window were strong and pungent to him.

"Up de hill where I was standin', de smells made my head go dizzy. Dis boy dat I never seed before, he mus be new round der. Now since de Young brothers took over, many changes were happenin'. Dis boy was goin' in an' outta de door from de kitchen. Every time he made for de door, I would hide behin de big garbage tin. I could see from where I was hidin' dat der was a house cross de walkway. It was just one big room full a stuff like Miz Derrick's store in de Harbour. Dis guy was goin' in an' getting' tings fo de lady in de kitchen."

He could see all the way down to Friendship Bay. Samuel, the young man going in and out, spotted Boolu near the garbage tin and he nonchalantly shooed him away with one hand and went about his business.

"I kep comin' closer, very slowly but neverdaless ever so much closer."

The next time Samuel came out, Boolu was in the passageway and Samuel gave him one exasperated look. He had no time for poor little beggar boys. Today was his first day on the job as stock boy. It was no day to screw up. He kept telling Boolu to get the hell out of the way.

"Dis I knew what he meant."

Trying not to attract any attention for fear of Ron, Samuel told him, "Get lost, go to Ugly Island." Not hearing what he said, Boolu just stood there. One of the young women in the kitchen noticed Samuel's dilemma and whispered softly out of the side of her mouth, telling him what to do about Boolu. The next time Samuel came out, he looked behind him into the kitchen to see if anyone was looking and, finding it was safe, he grabbed Boolu by the hand. Gently he shoved Boolu behind the big garbage tin and made him sit down on a flat rock out of sight.

"De big boy made it clear ta me I was ta stay put, so me did."

He just sat there smelling the aromas of all that sweet stuff cooking as they floated out the big long windows. He must have sat there an hour before Samuel came back to him.

"He had a paper bag in his hand dat he gave ta me. I started ta open it, but he motioned to me, no."

He took Boolu down another path that led farther away from the hotel behind the staff quarters. Samuel made it clear that it was safe to sit there and eat. Then Samuel took off like a big bird, all the time hoping he hadn't been missed back in the kitchen. Boolu sat there looking around. There was no one in sight. He opened the bag. Inside were pieces of meat (crumbled up bacon) and something that looked like fry bakes but very thin fry bakes, actually pancakes. Fry bakes is the Bequia name for English scones that West Indians eat regularly with considerable pleasure. This food was left over on the restaurant plates with butter and syrup and salt. Samuel also stuck in an orange and a hard-boiled egg.

"Grabbin' a hold a de egg, I tought a Miz Edmunds again. I collected her eggs from her chicken hut fo her whenever I be down der. Well, it all was sweet an' tasty an' very satisfyin fo der was plenty. I got up on my feet while lickin' my fingers. I scrunched up de bag an' trew it away an' sauntered down ta de beach."

Friendship Bay, and here he is at last. He had never been this far from Ravine before and it was a grand sight to him. It was so large and had so much sand it truly was a magnificent vista. The beach boy or waterfront man, whatever his title, was slowly cleaning up about the place and lining up beach chairs. He spotted Boolu coming down through the coconut grove and began to pitch coconut husks at him.

"I took off down de beach toward Verne an Erma's place, dough I didn't know it at de time. I had a full belly fo de first time in days an' I felt great."

All he needed was a dry head, a full belly, and something to keep out the cold at night. Those basics were all he worked for, full time. His was a constant quest and when he achieved them, Boolu was content. That was all he expected from life then. The basics in life were all he knew or had ever known.

That day was special for him. It was so beautiful on that beach, the sky was blue, and the sun was climbing high. A little way down the bay, he came upon some men hauling logs. Others were sawing and hewing them into crescent shapes. In the center of all this activity was a huge bilge-way that would later be used to support the ribs of one of the finest boats ever built on Bequia. It was to become the ever-reliable, indispensable packet schooner Friendship Rose, which has been running back and forth between Bequia and St. Vincent and up and down the islands of the Northern Grenadines for well over forty years.

Now, reliable and indispensable, and yes, even safe are rare adjectives to bestow on a locally built schooner in these parts, but such was the case and still is with this particular boat. Not to say that there aren't many fine boat builders in the West Indies and on Bequia especially, but there is much more to it than that. Any boat owner knows the constant upkeep is like "a hole in the sea that you keep pouring money into." The Adams family from La Pompe, the builders of the boat and its owners from its inception to this very day, has given it all the care and concern one would expect from a doting parent. It is the safest, cleanest, and best-looking local boat, bar none. Most West Indian schooners fall short of the Friendship Rose in this department. I can recommend the Rose without reservation to any nervous traveler.

When Boolu came upon the site, he realized that these men were strangers to him. Most of them came from the south side, a part of Bequia he had never circumambulated. He was mesmerized by the hustle and bustle of men busy

9 Survival

at work, doing what they knew how to do. He kept at a distance watching and observing every minute detail, like a pup in its master's shop. The few dogs about were keeping at a safe distance, too.

"At noon sharp, an' I always knew when dat was by where de sun be in de sky, de men stopped work an' sat about, each one pickin' out der very own coconut tree ta sit next ta, lean against, an' stretch out."

They were waiting for their lunch pails, which were brought from home by their wife, daughter, small son, sister or mother, or any other family member, possibly even a young neighbor. All the food would be cooked that morning and brought to them in covered steam tins, some three tiers high. In such fashion the breadwinners were fed.

"De dogs slowly moved in closer. Dey knew it was time to sit patiently by an' wait ta be tossed a tidbit or two. I wasn't hungry. I had such a big breakfast dat morning dat it would hold me fa a coupla days. Me still felt full. So I sat where I was. An ol man who was sittin' not too far from me tossed me a chicken wing. I held out my hand ta catch it, but de wing was a little too light ta make de distance and fell short, a little over halfway. I didn't move or jump fo it, but a nearby dog did an' grabbled it up."

Boolu's reticence to jump for the food was misunderstood by the old man. He thought Boolu was too scared to come any closer, so when he was almost finished, he came over to Boolu. He handed the tin to him, and Boolu saw he had left a little food. So he took it and finished it.

"I really wasn't hungry, but I knew that my life was a catch-as-catch-can existence. Dat afternoon was fun fo me, an' no one boddered me all afternoon. Some tried ta talk ta me a little, an' a few pointed in my direction. A few seemed ta laugh at me, but nuttin' more serious dan dat. I had fun sittin' bout watchin' dis one an' dat one measuring dis, hammerin' dat. By dis time it was gettin' hotter an' hotter an' de men were movin' slower an' slower."

The dogs were tending to business, doing whatever dogs do of an afternoon in the tropics. Some were sitting in the shade of the sea grape bush or chasing after lizard tails in the coconut grove. Do you know a lizard can shed its tail in a tight spot? This casting off enables it to slither away to live long enough to grow another one.

At four o'clock, the men stopped work, packed up their tools, and took off in two directions in the blistering hot late afternoon sun. Some tramped up the road to the north. If Boolu's guess was right, they went up over the hill and down to the Harbour. The other group, the larger of the two, trudged south down the sandy beach skirting Friendship Bay toward the far end. There sat the little village Boolu had seen earlier from Mt. Pleasant when he had first left home so many moons ago. He knew these men didn't live in Mt. Pleasant or the Harbour. Obviously they lived in that little village beyond, and for some reason he was intrigued.

"What I didn't know den was dat der be a much larger village bout a mile farther down de road called Paget Farm an' most a de workers came from der."

10 Bruises and Hardknocks

Dreamwork

Back on Bequia, I checked in with everyone I remembered from Christmas and finally relaxed over dinner. The hotel was like a big empty barn, with only one other guest. I turned in early; the trip down with its three separate junkets could wear out a globetrotter! I was up early, well, early for me. The fishermen are in their boats and before 4:30 AM and the locals are up at 5.

Verne was certainly up at 9:30 AM when I surfaced, but for him the day was half over. He had had the land surveyed; in fact, he had had the whole thirty-five acres done and had our price sectioned out on the same survey map, with our names on it. Although he had a copy of it, he explained I would have to go over to St. Vincent to the Government Landholding Office to get our copy.

I called Mr. Campbell, the surveyor, who informed me he would be available only on Saturday. I asked him if the government offices were open on Saturday and he assured me they were.

"Will I also have time to get into the government office for approval then?" I asked.

His answer to me was, "They're open all morning."

I said, "Well, good, I have a flight back to the States on Sunday."

He even repeated himself, "Not to worry, not to worry."

I was lulled by his laid-back attitude and that of absolutely everyone else around me. What a mistake that was.

On Tuesday I trudged up the hill past the three trees to take a 180-degree arc of pictures that, when pasted together, would simulate the panoramic view. I sat down on a rock and dreamed I was sitting out on our terrace taking in the magnificent view of the islands out in the ocean. The trade winds were strong enough to ward off the head of the tropical noonday sun.

10 Bruises and Hardknocks

The Catch Of The Day

I was roused from my daydream by the sound of a horn. I looked about and saw nothing, yet there it was again, that sound. It pervaded the whole valley. I had heard it before and not from an orchestra. Now that I was fully out of my reverie, I remembered. I thought, No, it can't be, not down here! Yet there it was again. It was the sound of a shofar, the call to prayer at Rosh Hashanah. The intermittent sound went on for about twenty minutes.

I decided to walk down the hill and across the beach to the hotel for an afternoon swim. On the road, I ran into a couple of women each carrying an empty pot, and then a couple of kids doing the same. We were all heading toward the beach. Once we had made it down the hill and onto the sand, I saw more people gathering around a group of fishermen who had come ashore with their daily catch. Some men were cleaning fish, others were cutting them into steaks, and one was standing by with a crude scale to weigh the fish and dole it out according to each buyer's request. The was wrapped in newspaper, or just rolled up in a large banana leaf, and dumped into the buyer's container by another fisherman, who took the money. The last man handed out the change, if any was due. This process of commerce had been going on for eons, and I am certain it still is.

Bequia has six or seven bays from which the fishermen take off at 4 AM, returning by mid-afternoon with their catch. That afternoon the fish were selling at one EC (Eastern Caribbean dollar) per pound. In US money, it translated to 60 cents.

Each fisherman took the portion of the catch allotted to him first, before doling out what was left to the buyers. Sometimes there wasn't enough to go around. It behooved a body to be there first or at least to be related to one of the fishermen. Since just about everyone on the Island was related in one-way or another, things could get a little dicey at times.

The mystery of the "shofar" was cleared up. There in the bow of one of the boats was another fisherman intermittently blowing into conch shell. The sound of the conch shell had meant but one thing to the Islanders ever since the first fisherman learned he could make a horn out of a shell. It meant sustenance was forthcoming, food was at hand. The knowledge that their bellies would soon be filled made that sound, like the call to prayer of the shofar, the most comforting sound imaginable.

I sauntered down the beach, took a quick dip in the sea in front of the beach bar, ordered a drink, and then talked to Ernest Williams, the bartender. Not another soul was in sight. Eventually I went up to my room for a nap before dinner. Not a bad day after the snows of the north and the disappointment of the surveyor, Mr. Campbell, and his thoughtless put-off.

Wednesday arrived and the plan was to spend the whole day in the sun. Brenda said, "You're going to get burnt to crisp. Only a little at a time," she advised.

A New Home For Boolu

I remember that afternoon sunning myself on the hotel terrace. There I was, lying on my back with my lime squash, when I heard these god-awful sounds coming up from the bay! It sounded like someone was butchering a pig. I had heard that sound once before, up on Coupe Hill where Mom and dad had retired to a small farm in '56. It's the piercing, bleating sound of a helpless victim being slaughtered.

As I opened my eyes, I saw Joyce Baldwin standing at the top of the stairs. She was an English woman who had recently arrived in the Caribbean with her husband Bill after selling their small farm in Rhodesia. They had seen the writing on the wall there and moved out early before the serious troubles set in. I couldn't help thinking it was a lesson for both Sandy and me to take note of. Now the Baldwins were here chartering in the Grenadines, using Bequia as their base of operations. Joyce was taking a little sabbatical from yachting and spending a month or so on shore at the hotel. She hadn't been feeling well and was "doctoring," as she explained it. Doctoring? What doctor? That was the question in my mind.

Even though it was only April and still in season, we were the only guests at the hotel. To this Ron would say, "The hotel is not on its feet as yet. Give it some time." He had nothing but time, he had all the time in the world, and all he did with it was spend money and more money. He had more ideas than brains, and ideas cost money. All he had done since the day he arrived was build and expand. With little or nothing coming in, the hotel proceeded to go from bad to worse. It was being run into the ground, and he never seemed to realize it. The hotel was too big for the size of the Island.

There Joyce and I were, just the two of us. I was still on my back and she was standing clutching the balustrade. She looked terribly troubled and upset. She came over to me and sat on the edge of a deckchair.

"You won't believe what I just saw. I can't believe what I just saw! Did you hear that?" I most certainly could hear that terrible schreeeeeeee. "Ya hear that?" she asked.

"God, I hear! It sounds like an animal, the cry of a stuck pig. What is it anyway?"

"Well," she said, "it's this kid, this skinny little boy. And he's in rags."

"Joyce, that's Boolu. It's got to be," I said. "I met him last December when Sandy and I were here for Christmas."

"Boolu is he?" she asked.

"Yes, he's deaf and can't talk and on top of that he's living in that bush over there all by himself. I can't get a straight answer from anyone as to how he got there, but he is there nevertheless, and was there last Christmas."

"Well, whoever he is, the staff are dragging and shoving him into the sea, and I swear he is so frightened and skinny, he'll either have heart failure or they will end up breaking some of his bones in the process. Ron should stop this. It shouldn't happen to a dog," Joyce said.

And I said, "They treat him worse than a dog around here."

We both went to the office where she told Ron what she had seen.

Ron said, "That's Boolu. He's a dummy, you know."

"I don't care what he is!" Joyce snapped. "Ron, you must do something. It's your staff that's doing it. Make them stop. You go down there yourself and stop it."

"We will, we will. Where is Samuel?" He directed his question at no one in particular.

"He be in the kitchen," said one of the room girls, who had been standing near the open door to the office watching and not missing a word. Ron went himself to get Samuel. Joyce and I headed down to the beach.

We got there before Ron, and we could see two muscle-bound teenagers dragging Boolu out into the deeper water. They each had an arm, and Boolu was screaming his head off, making sounds that only the deaf can make. About five of the kitchen staff were standing at the shoreline laughing their heads off. One of the girls had Boolu's pants. I could see what looked like the remnants of a little old shirt being washed ashore, tumbling and churning in the sand. I walk over to pick it up, washed the sand off, rung it out, and walked back to where Ron, Samuel, and Joyce were standing. The kitchen staff had scattered when they saw Ron coming, and the two broad-shouldered boys were already bringing Boolu in.

When they came ashore, Ron sent one of them up to the kitchen. He was Buso, in charge of garbage, which, in those days, he was dumping out in the middle of the bay. The other fellow was in charge of the waterfront area, and Ron told him to straighten up the beach chairs. They both strolled off in opposite directions. Boolu, whom Samuel now had by the arm, was naked as a jaybird, shaking and shivering. His arms were flailing in all directions as he just jabbered like a magpie to Sammy. Joyce was wrapping him in a beach towel and trying to dry him. I gave Sammy his shirt to put on and button for him and went over and picked up his pants, which the girl had dropped as she raced off to the kitchen. Ron had turned to Samuel and was asking what was going on, as if he had been part of it. Well, now I was perplexed. How, I wondered, is Ron going to find out what had been going on with no one here except Boolu who knew the whole story, and he could not speak even if he had a mind to? Everyone else had run off or was sent away by Ron himself. And now he was asking Samuel to tell him what had happened? I remember thinking at the time, how English of him to avoid a confrontation at any cost. Much later, after I had come to learn more about Bequia ways, I realized Ron would have gotten absolutely nowhere holding a conference right there on the beach. Every one of those Bequians, or Bequiarians as they call themselves, would have gone dumber than Boolu in a split second.

What actually happened? Early that morning, a shark had been spotted in the bay, a very rare happening in these parts. Boolu, along with Samuel, was there at the time and saw it. Boolu also witnessed all the fright, fear, anxiety, and excitement evinced by everyone around watching from the shore. How much he understood, I don't know. But he couldn't have doubted the danger in the bay that morning. All the staff had been carrying on all day about it, although Ron, Joyce and I knew nothing of it. The trouble started in the afternoon when the hotel girls decided not to take their daily sea bath in the bay on their late afternoon break because they were frightened. One of the boys on staff came up with the idea of throwing some of the girls into the bay where the shark might still be lurking. They harassed the girls for a while until one of them grabbed Boolu. Sensing the magnitude of his fright, everyone, even the girls, joined in, taking great delight in tormenting Boolu. He then became the focus of activity. The shark apparently was long gone, but Boolu didn't know this. All he remembered was that the girls had been frightened, and he was petrified.

Samuel spelled out most of these details to Ron and Joyce, who asked, "Samuel, where does he live?"

Samuel replied, "Right now, he holes up under an old house in La Pompe."

Ron asked, "Where does he eat?" Samuel just shrugged.

Joyce interjected, "My God! Ron, what can you do?"

Ron paused to think the matter over and then said, "Samuel, what about the old generator room? We don't use it any more. We must keep it in working order, but there's still plenty of room in there for a cot." Directing his next thought to Joyce, he verbalized it, saying, "Joyce, you know, he could sleep there and eat with the staff." Turning to Samuel, he said, "You must be willing to take charge of him, look after him, and keep him out of trouble. Now Samuel, are you ready to take on this job?"

Samuel, without so much as batting an eye, answered, "Yeah, yeah, sure. Sure I will, Mr. Young."

"Samuel, good, this is very good. Now, you'll have to take one of these broken beach lounges up there for him to sleep on. And tell Aileen he will eat with the staff and he can use the staff's bathroom. I'll tell Vilna to run up a flower-sack smock or the like. He can't be wearing these rags around this place."

Samuel took Boolu to the staff quarters, and we three went up the path to the hotel. I could see Ron was feeling full of himself as he said, "You see how we solve problems down here, Joyce, simple and easy."

Joyce, feeling pleased with how everything had worked out, said, "Ron that was very good of you to take him in."

I just hoped they were both right. Boolu was no stranger to Ron. Stan and Ron had been around the hotel for over a year now, and Boolu had been coming to the hotel for food for months.

The future for Boolu looked good. He now had a place to sleep and eat, but most of all he had what looked to me like the makings of a real friend in Samuel. Having dinner with Joyce that evening, I was able to fill her in on what I knew of Boolu's past, a story I was to tell over and over during the ensuing years.

Mission Accomplished

In '69, Bequia was still an off-the-beaten-track, laid-back, backwater island, insignificant and inconsequential to the powers that were. Not surprisingly, I might add, at this point in its history it was not very lucrative for them or anyone else, either. Both England and St. Vincent claimed Bequia as a possession but both were extremely neglectful. The lack of concern was plain. I am aware that throughout the world scores of small places are neglected—we know that all too well—but this little Island was the one we picked to be concerned about.

The neglect was blatant right from the start in so many areas that one didn't know where to begin. I'll start with the electricity, since Bequia had only received it less than six months before we came. On a wall in St. Vincent, I saw a picture of Kingstown showing telephone poles for electricity, you know, one of those old photographs that depict many wires strung from post to post. The photo was taken pre-World War I, around 1914. And yet only nine miles away was an Island with over 5,000 people on it that was part of that very country, and they waited almost sixty years for electricity to be made available to them! As another example, the road from Port Elizabeth to the largest village on the Island, Paget Farm, had been started before we arrived in '68, yet it would take six years to finish. The distance from village to village was three miles. Why should the island of St. Vincent worry about electricity or roads on the island of Bequia since it didn't affect them one way or the other? I could go on but I won't, not now, another time. "There is a time for plowing and a time for planting," etc.

The day was lovely—clear sky, soft breezes, and calm seas, a beautiful day for my last day on the beach. Tomorrow I would be spending most of the day in Kingstown. Dinner I spent with Joyce, talking about atrocities in Rhodesia, she wishing she were back in England. I felt if Bill didn't see the writing on the wall, a divorce was imminent. Early to bed and early to rise. The next day at 5 AM, Ricky would take me to the boat.

We—by "we" I mean and a boatload of Bequians who left Bequia that morning on the good old reliable Friendship Rose—set sail at 6:30 for St. Vincent. Off we went across the open sea bucking a crosscurrent between the islands at a weird angle, with the trade winds coming in at another 90-degree angle, so that the sea was choppy. Water splashed over the gunwale and across the deck, tipping the motor schooner way over to port and rocking it back and forth with every wave. We disembarked on hour after departure at the pier jutting out in front of the police station in the center of the bay, with Kingstown spreading out in three directions. We had arrived about forty-five minutes before anything opened. So I had time to find out where the Government Landholding Office was and get there early.

Well, I did get there early but I had to sit patiently, waiting for the clerks to shuffle around taking their own good time before settling down to work. A few people were taken before I was, even though I was there first. It was much like Mrs. Derrick's with the devil-take-the-hindmost attitude.

When I had nudged my way forward, I said that I was applying for a Land Holding license. The clerk told me I would have to find the land first. I told her I had found the land. She said, "Well, you have to get it surveyed." I then told her it was surveyed and she then asked me, "Where is it?" I told her on Bequia. "No, I mean the survey?" she said. I told her Mr. Campbell had surveyed the land he had it. She said, "You will have to go get it before I can give you the application." She didn't know for sure where his office was but it was in Frenches, the same district as this office. I thanked her and set off to Campbell's office.

In time I found it but it wasn't easy as the accents, both mine and theirs, didn't help; it took time to be understood and time to understand. Some people just walked away, turned and walked away without a word! Eventually I got to the office but Mr. Campbell wasn't in yet. "Will he be in?" I asked, holding my breath.

The reply: "Oh, yes, he be in. Just have a seat."

I sat, but very uneasily. I had to get this thing done; I was leaving tomorrow. He arrived, in his own time. He signed the papers and gave them to me. I rushed out and headed over to the Government Land Holding Office. Going back wasn't so easy. At first, I thought I knew the way. But I didn't really. Everything was turned around. There were no cabs as far as I could see. All I saw were mini-buses and vans for long distance rides. Everyone seemed to be walking or in a private car. So I just brazenly shoved my way through walking traffic and asked for directions when I had to.

Eventually I got back to where I'd started. I walked up to the counter and handed the papers to the clerk. She took her time reading them, first eyeing me up and down. I looked at my watch; it was already 10:30. When she finished having her fill of the papers, she handed them back to me and said, "Miss So&So went out. Please sit down, she will be back."

I asked, "Couldn't someone…? Isn't there—?"

She cut me off directly, saying, "No, no, she is just on a break. She be back. Sit."

I sat. I looked at my watch again. It was now going on 10:40. Miss So&So came back, took the papers, and read and read. Eventually she handed the papers back to me and, with a big smile on her face, said, "It doesn't have Mr. Campbell's stamp. You need Mr. Campbell's stamp."

I pleadingly repeated, "His stamp… Stamp?" Looking at the papers myself,

I found his signature and said, "See, there's his signature, he signed it right here."

Still smiling, she said, "Yes, I know, I saw that. But you still need his stamp to make it official."

I looked at my watch once more; it was now minutes to 11:00. I thought to myself, Oh, God! All the way back to him and back here again and then to the boat in an hour? Maybe. No use wasting any more time with her. I flew out of there. I didn't stop to speak to anyone. I had to do this myself. I had a dilemma! The Friendship Rose left at noon and there wouldn't be another boat leaving for Bequia until Monday at noon. If I couldn't get everything done today, I had two options. I could stay in St. Vincent for the weekend and get everything done on Monday and miss my flight tomorrow, or I could leave everything till Monday and go back to Bequia for what was left of the weekend and still miss my flight tomorrow. No matter which way, I wasn't getting back to New York until Tuesday night. All this would cost a hell of a lot more, but what the blazes! I had come down here to do one thing—get the land survey approval—and waited all week to accomplish it.

I reached Campbell's office, and he was gone. I asked the secretary if she had his stamp and if she could stamp the survey. She said she didn't know from any stamp. "Well," I insisted, "I've got to get these papers stamped. Do you know where he is?" I asked.

"Sure," she answered, "he's down leeward."

"Can I get there in a cab?" I asked.

"Sure, but it won't do you any good. He will have gone home for dinner before you get there. Best you go to his home, it's closer."

"How do I get a cab, a taxi?" I asked.

"I better call one for you who knows where he lives," she suggested.

The cab was out front in no time and took me to Campbell's house. His wife informed me that he wasn't coming home for dinner. He was way down leeward and it would take too much time for him to come home and go back. I told the cab to take me to the Government Land Holding Office. The driver said he knew how to get there quickly down the back way, with no traffic.

It was heading for twelve when I walked into the office. I told the clerk I couldn't get his stamp, as Mr. Campbell was way down leeward. She said, "As I already told you, I cannot accept the survey without his stamp. It will not be valid without his two-seventy-five-cent stamp."

BINGO! I thought. "You mean that '275 cent' stamp is a postage stamp?" I asked.

She, hesitating, said, "Well, it's a government stamp tax, and it's Mr. Campbell's responsibility." She stood there and smiled at me.

I couldn't help it, I snapped, "If I put '275 cents' worth of stamps on that paper, it will validate the damn thing?"

"Yes, yes. Yes, of course it would," she muttered, put out by my demeanor and sharp language.

"Where can I buy some stamps?"

"Out there at the cashier's window in the anteroom," she replied.

"Don't go anywhere," I said. Believe it or not, she was laughing. She thought I was joking with her. I went out to the window in the anteroom and bought two dollars and seventy-five cents' worth in five- and ten-cent stamps because that was all they had. I started licking, and my cab driver helped me stick them. I took the survey papers back to my dim-witted friend who took them from me with another big smile and validated the papers with the government's official stamp. I then filled out the application, and she had her boss validate it. I then turned to the cab driver and said, "It's 12:30, I missed the boat back to Bequia."

And he said, "Maybe yes, maybe no, let us see."

We went out to the cab and I jumped into the seat beside him. We went down Front Street while traffic was backed up bumper to bumper on Back Street. As we neared the police station, I could see that the Friendship Rose was still at the dock. I had my money ready for the driver when we stopped. I thanked him many times, waved him goodbye, and ran down the pier. As I passed the police band's headquarters, I could hear sour and shrill sounds penetrating the air. Just a little farther on, I hopped onto the boat and settled myself on deck in front of one of the cabin doors. The boat didn't leave until minutes after one o'clock, as the crew was taking on a load of cinder block. I sat back on the bench, on the leeward or starboard side, you name it, and tried to let myself unwind. I was really tense and upright.

I didn't know, couldn't possibly have known, that this morning was a typical morning in St. Vincent and would be for the next thirty years, any time we tried to shop and get things done, legal or otherwise. The one thing I learned that week was that thinking or planning ahead in the West Indies was futile. Everything, and I mean everything, down here is moment to moment. The one paramount goal in Sandy's classes was "to live truthfully moment to moment" without ever anticipating anything. So, thanks to Sandy, I had already had plenty of training living in the moment. All I had to do now was to put it to good use.

At the end of the day, the one thing I felt good about was all the money I had saved by not having to stay over the weekend. No thanks to Miss So&So and her 275-cent stamp.

Bequia Background

Sunday morning I left with Stan on his sleek, slim-line Sol Quest. The trip back was far more interesting and enjoyable than that first crossing back in December of '68, with the two English hippies. They were now no longer in the Young brothers' employ and long gone. "They didn't last a month," Stan

10 Bruises and Hardknocks

said. "They weren't looking for a job. They were working their way back home to England. 'Boat bums' are what they're called in these waters."

"'Boat bums' are what they're called in any waters," I added.

The sun was barely visible on the horizon, a tiny crescent of flaming red, casting across an awakening sky veins of dark violet-blue, changing into purple, and eventually into a pale pink and reddish glow. The rising red ball of Japan rose over a placid sea and faded as it climbed into the heavens, shrinking into a pale yellow orb.

"Glorious!" Stan exclaimed. "It's a sight I never tire of."

"One can plainly see why," I agreed.

"Look up ahead there. That's what Ron and I call Mother-in-Law's Rock. See the face on her? And all that white stuff? It's bird shit from the booby birds. Makes it look like a fright wig," Stan informed me.

When we got closer, I could see. "She looks mad as hell," I said."

"Ha-ha-ha, you see, don't you?" Stan said, pleased with himself. He went on, explaining the route we were taking. "We're heading northeast up Bequia Head. The current is a little fast here on the Atlantic side and head-on against us, giving us a hard ride up. But it's a hell of a lot quicker from our hotel to St. Vincent this way, especially if you're going to Young Island instead of Kingstown, which is no place for a yacht in the first place. In the second place Young Island is much closer to the airport."

Captain Stan was quite a talker. He had been a charter captain for some time now, first in England out of Cornwall and the Isle of Jersey and later out of Antigua. He had developed a loquacious banter for his shipboard passengers, and I found it amusing myself. It made the trip totally enjoyable.

As we passed Spring Bay, Stan said, "That's the reef were a big slave ship went aground during a hurricane sometime around the seventeenth century, perhaps earlier, and while most souls perished, there were still a great many survivors. The ones who managed to swim to shore through the sharp, jagged coral of the reef and lived through the ordeal, though they may not have realized it at the time, had swum to their freedom! They never did become slaves, as the story goes. They intermarried, interbred, whatever, with the Caribs on the Island. Today, what you see is what you get—voila! Bequians. You can throw in a few whites for color—now isn't that an oxymoron if you ever heard one! Through the years there were estate managers and their flings, as well as some of their fledglings, and traveling, adventure-seeking types from Europe and elsewhere, and there you have it."

This was all part of Stan's banter and also my first abbreviated history lesson of Bequia. One of those traveling, adventure-seeking types was none other than Boolu's great-grandfather, the teacher "Old John" Reno, who happened onto Bequia, probably on his way down islands from Martinique, and intermarried with the Gumbs family, Frazeen's ancestors, who were survivors of that slave ship. Old John Reno came down islands in the 1800s and settled in as one of the early teacher son the Island. Looking back, Captain Stan's was a pretty concise synopsis, and not untrue.

"So," I asked, "you mean to tell me the overseers came from places like Scotland, France and Portugal? If that's a fact, then do you realize that, this being a very small island, Bequia must have been one of the first islands to be integrated? This must be a place where all the families can trace their lineage back to the seventeenth and eighteen centuries, including Carib Indians, Blacks, and whites. It's a true conglomerate, the race of the future."

"That's true. Not bad, I would say," was Stan's assessment.

With Stan's unsolicited shipboard entertainment helping to pass the time, we were already in a cozy harbor behind Young Island. We were disembarking before I knew it and off in a Land Rover on our way to Arnos Vale Airport. Just a short ten minutes away, the airport had only recently been built. To tell the truth, it was small, too small for this day and age. I could see why they had trouble with tourism—no airport, no people. Very simple. How long is it going to take them to wake up? And which comes first, the chicken or the egg?

But this undeveloped state is exactly the way Sandy wanted it. For years he would tell everyone that he was the president of the Keep Bequia Backward Club. Some joke! I laughingly called it the KBB, but I also knew it wasn't going to make my job any easier.

As I waited for the LIAT man and the plane, neither of which was in sight, I started to wonder if maybe the plane had come early and already left. By this point Stan was determining that there was no sense in standing around. He had boat things to tend to, and who knew when or even if that plane—? We said our goodbyes and he was off. Looking at the letters L-I-A-T over the desk, and seeing the way everyone behind the counter moved as they ticketed the passengers (all two of us), I thought, Leave Island Any Time. We were already forty-five minutes late and no one even referred to it, so I didn't either. I was already learning how to deal with this island pace.

The LIAT plane arrived, and I made it back to Barbados in plenty of time to catch my next flight. I even had time to get a bite to eat at the terminal, as the plane for Kennedy didn't depart until 3:30. In there lies a lesson of some sort. Well, I was used to this, having had a lot of practice at hurry-up-and-wait when I was in the army. Little had I known then that one day so many years later it would come in handy.

Barrels Of Questions

We arrived at Kennedy, believe it or not, on time, and Sandy and his friend Paul Morrison met me. I picked up my bags from the carousel, handed the declaration form to the customs official, and went through the double doors where I spotted the two of them down at the edge of the crowd of

10 Bruises and Hardknocks

waiting West Indians. I proceeded to walk toward them. Sandy reached for my bag as he said, "You don't look very tan."

"I got it, Sandy, it's not heavy. And I didn't go down there for a tan," I said trudging along.

"That's right. That's right. How did it go?" he asked. "Did you get it?"

"Wait," I said, "let's get out of here first." I could see he was excited and anxious to know everything at once. His little private dream, held deep down inside him for so many years, could it possibly be...? It just might be coming closer to reality after all.

I acknowledged the polite, cool hello from Paul, who was there because of his deep affection for Sandy, certainly not because of any love for me. After five years and all the work Paul and I had done together on 83rd Street, he still merely tolerated me and I knew it. I didn't need to be a rocket scientist to figure it out and I was certain I knew why. From the very first, I didn't let it bother me.

In the taxi back to 83rd Street, Sandy was all questions, and I tried to answer him as accurately as I could. I described the culture of bureaucracy in the islands and the lack of encouragement on the part of the officials. It was as if they wanted the foreign investment but didn't want to hand over the land outright. Other countries were like this, France being a prime example. I found out much later the Vincentian officials had gone so far as to check us out through the FBI. If I had known that at the time, I would have thought we were completely dead in the water and cut our losses and left. It was as if officialdom wanted to keep us hanging, but at the time I didn't know how to tell Sandy of this because of all the unknowns.

It was getting late as we drove from the airport, so Paul got out at First Avenue and 59th Street and went on home alone. If it had been earlier, we would have made an evening of it. Sandy appreciated Paul's dedication and enjoyed his company and friendship immensely. Sandy couldn't or wouldn't do anything alone; because of this idiosyncrasy, he needed Paul and Paul was always there to alleviate the need. Paul never said no to Sandy and I mean never. Such devotion. Sandy wasn't good at facing deep emotional problems head on; when they hit home, he avoided them. That was just his way. It was all part of his "deep trouble barrel." Sandy used the image of the deep trouble barrel to describe the source of talent. A passage in his book gives a glimpse of his exceptional level of perception and his conceptualization of talent. He developed the metaphor of the two barrels for his psychoanalyst.

All of us have two barrels inside us. The first barrel is the one that contains all of the juices, which are exuded by our troubles. That's the neurotic barrel. But right next to it stands the second barrel, and by a process of seepage like osmosis, some of the troubles of the first barrel get into the second, and by a miracle that nobody fully understands, those juices have been transformed into the ability to paint, to compose, to write, to play music and the ability to act. So essentially our talent is made up out of our transformed troubles. [. . .]

[T]he osmosis between the barrels doesn't work completely. There is always some juice in the trouble barrel, no matter how full the talent barrel is. The trouble cannot transpose itself into talent without leaving some residue behind, even in the most talented of human beings. (On Acting, 190-1)

Sandy himself was a prime example of his deep trouble barrel, and God knows his immense talent could have been the transformation of such complexities.

At home at 83rd Street, Sandy kept peppering me with questions and I tried to answer them. We were not, I explained, out of the woods yet. In fact, this trip had shown me that we actually hadn't even begun our project. I knew now about West Indian rhythm and how you didn't, couldn't, muck with it. We would have to deal with so many little things, like the $2.75 stamps and boat schedules. I hadn't begun to think of building logistics. Why, there wasn't even electricity in our vicinity. I realized we had much too much to work out. All week, we would talk about little else.

But that night, Sandy wanted to know: "How was Verne?... Did you see Lulley?... Is Brenda still at the hotel?... What about Ron and Stan?... I had dinner with Ruth and Jo Saturday night, and believe it or not I cooked a mean meatloaf... Did you use Ricky to get around?... Is Sammy still cooking? I hope not... What about Bet-tee, Jean, and my special waitress, Paulette?... The kid, what about Bobo, Boolu? What is his name anyway?"

"Boolu. What is this, twenty questions?" I asked.

"No, no I just really want to know," he said.

"Well, first," I said, "Boolu is living at the hotel and he has a bodyguard."

"A bodyguard?" Sandy repeated. "Come on, what is this, you joking? Boolu's living in the hotel now? That's so? Good lord! There really is one. How did that happen? Come on, tell me, tell me," he insisted.

"I will," I said, "but it's a long story, not for now, but later."

It went on like that all evening until we went to bed. Now it was eight-thirty of a Monday morning, and I was urging, "Come on now, button up your shirt. You're going to be late for acting class."

"To hell with class, I want to hear what's going on down there," Sandy persisted.

"TO HELL WITH CLASS?! That's a blast, it really is funny coming from you. You don't care if you're late? Now, this is new."

"No," he quipped, slamming the bathroom door in my face. "I'm on to new and better things!"

"Well, I can see the times they are a-changin'!" I yelled back at him through the door.

In order to shut me out, he started whistling. Trouble was, he didn't know how. Never mind. His mother always boasted, "As a baby in his crib, the first thing Sandy ever did was whistle."

"Listen Sandy, you'd better hurry up or you're going to be one late student," I said and went downstairs to make coffee.

11 To Bequia or not to Bequia

Joan On Bequia

In May '69, Sandy was winding up his classes for the school year. The final student demonstrations were followed by the graduation dinner at the Players Club on Gramercy Park where a few alumni of renown came to speak to the graduates. Sandy would then stay in New York to run the summer session; I would go to Bequia to get things moving.

Since I expected to stay longer this time, I wanted to cut expenses. During my stay in March, I had met an older Trinidadian gentleman who lived across the bay. He was an accountant at the hotel, a pick-up job he took to keep busy. And it was he who offered me room in his home. My sister Joan came with me. Carl Miller was a compassionate person and was delighted to have her.

Joan was going to stay for a month. I had been neglecting her and she still depended on me to some degree. For the past decade, Joan and been working her way back from the after-effects of the three-month-long coma that had left her quite disabled. Fifty percent of her body was paralyzed, she suffered a total loss of memory that never came back, and she had visual and verbal aphasia. Although she had progressed a great deal, she still had much to overcome; some doubted she ever would. It was such a slow, petty pace, it was difficult to note any daily improvement.

In the ten years since the accident, I had worked with Joan intensively for the first year and a half, and then on and off for the next several years as well. It was time we went our separate ways. Neither she nor I wanted to, but it was high time she became more independent. Sandy wasn't going to be with us. Our house project was at a standstill and there wasn't anything I could do about it. It would be a good opportunity for Joan and me to get some quality time together.

The delay in the house project followed the sad news that Verne Wallace had died. Now his estate was in the hands of his survivors and an agreement among them would have to be reached.

Friendship Hotel was still empty but Ron was always throwing a party at the drop of a hat to stir up interest. He would invite Vincentian public officials over, who couldn't help him one iota, nor would they if they could. Tourist agents looking for a free romp in the sun were always showing up. He was constantly inviting people over from Barbados and Trinidad. He didn't have a clue as to how to make a hotel a paying proposition. He felt he needed to make the premises look busy and prosperous, so he invited any foreigner hanging about on the Island. Joan and I were part of this group and we just loved being invited over for lunch and a swim or dinner and a dance. Not that Joan could dance very well but she had one hell of a time trying. She would put on a gown and drag herself across the bay, with my help of course, and mix with everyone as if she had no disabilities at all. If anyone had trouble with that it sure wasn't her. She just went on having a grand time. It did my heart good to make this all possible for her.

Here we met "Good Golly Miss Molly" from Moon Hole. Molly Burk was a strikingly beautiful lady in her twenties whose parents had a house there. Molly, like Joan and me, was a frequent guest at the hotel, as were Ruth and her friend Pat, the photographer, who came to Bequia to muster up some PR for the hotel. Then there was Tim Burgess, an English tinker. God knows, they are the best. There wasn't a job he wouldn't or couldn't handle or at least take a stab at. We called ourselves the "Local Planters." We were well aware that we were nothing more than window dressing. Ron or Brenda would call to say, "We're having people in. Come on over and look good."

It was a marvelous month for Joan and me. It was great to take a little hiatus from the pressing job at hand. It also served as a chance for Molly and me to get to know each other. We became fast friends and still keep in touch.

The month cape to an end all too quickly, and Joan was on her way back home. Sandy was finishing up his summer classes at the Playhouse and would be on his way in a week. He would miss my birthday this year but said he would make it up forever after. I said, "So dramatic!"

"No," he told me over the phone, "this is my last summer. Next year my assistants will be taking over the summer school."

Paul wasn't happy about that but I was! Next year after the students' final demonstration, Sandy would pack up and head for Bequia, the place that one day he would be calling home.

The Beginning Of The Long Goodbye

So began the annual ritual Sandy would follow through the seventies, when he gave up teaching the summer school classes at the Playhouse, leaving them to his assistants. It was the beginning of a gradual withdrawal. The total withdrawal would take him another twenty-three years to achieve, or should I say for me to achieve. Obviously, he really didn't want to leave, or at least he had mixed emotions.

In '69 Sandy, Paul, and Oleta D'Ambry, the accountant, were talking of nothing else but what to do with the school when they were ready to retire. The big question was whether they should close it. Then what to do with the endowment? Should they set up some sort of philanthropic institute, nothing more than an office out of which some unspecified usefulness to the theater in general would be generated? Board members like Gregory Peck, Eli Wallach, Tony Randall, and many others wanted the school to stay open. Little did Sandy care what they thought. He felt they made little difference in his life one way or the other, nor, he felt, should they. Since Sandy and his classes were in truth what the Playhouse stood for after thirty-nine years—at least it was now what attracted the students to the school—without him, what would it become? Ideas were being thrown around with no concrete follow-up as Sandy went blithely on making plans with me for his eventual retirement. Paul and Oleta were well aware that they couldn't just abolish it, caput, because, after so many years of service to the school, the question of their security had never been resolved. Where was their retirement income to come from? The question just hung in the balance.

Sandy gave the Playhouse most of his time and effort from ten to six, five days a week, during summer school as well, and yet his remuneration bore no relation to his effort and loyalty. In fact he was grossly underpaid for a teacher of his caliber. I was unaware of his salary at the time but when I found out later, I went berserk. He had student teachers out there making more per student than he was. I just could not believe this inequity. He maintained, "It's a non-profit school, Jimmy, and that's all they can manage to pay me." I thought, this guy is sure not about money or he's just plain crazy. His situation never even crossed the minds of his successful students, much less prompted any concern among them. I would have liked to match their tax returns with Sandy's any day. I never heard any one of them asking him if needed anything, anything at all. Whenever I got onto or even near the subject, he would tell me to forget it. He would say I wasn't taking into consideration the actor's colossal ego, nor that very important phenomenon: "la gratitudine è rara, and don't you ever forget it." He never looked for gratitude, nor expected any, nor wanted any.

No wonder he didn't seem to worry about what was going to happen to the school. It made little difference to him financially one way or the other. But more precisely, he was a realist. He really loved the place. It was his life! But he knew that it was his teaching of his technique that was the school's reason for existing. No one could teach it as he did. So without him, the school didn't need to stay open.

In time Sandy had to deal with all these issues. But now all he was concerned about was getting his plans afoot for his place in the sun. He left worrying about the future of the school to Paul and Oleta and worrying about his future to me, eventually, while he went blithely on teaching.

August 1969—Fallout From Verne's Death

Sandy and I spent a month or so at the Friendship Bay Hotel while we continued the process of acquiring the property. We were the only guests, and I wondered when this hotel would ever make any money. It was not a small place, for this Island anyway. It had more than twenty-four rooms. They weren't filling the ones they already had and yet the Young brothers were still furiously building. We were in one of the new units, the same one we had had the previous Christmas when Boolu used to make his appearances. Boolu was now sleeping in the old generator room; he wouldn't be materializing out of the bush this time. Boolu now belonged somewhere. And he now had Sammy to rely on for support and protection.

With Verne dead, it was up to us and no one else to get this project moving again. We made inquiries about a possible lawyer. It was eeny, meeny, miny, moe for all we knew. Alec Hughes's name kept coming up, so we settled on him. One could say fools rush in, and in my uneasy moments, that's exactly how I felt. Sandy's approach was quite different. He said, "Nothing ventured, nothing gained." It was his dream and his money. You could say at that time I was along for the ride. Little did we know what a hell of a ride it was going to be!

So Sandy and I hurried over to St. Vincent and met with Hughes in Kingstown. He informed us that Verne hadn't owned the property and had had no authority to sell it to us. Why, he asked, did we not go to a lawyer before dealing with an Islander? Well, he was right. What were we to do? The simple answer was to find out who really did owned it.

First we asked Erma, Verne's wife. She told us he was paying the taxes on the property, and she always thought he owned it. He was the last remaining son of the Wallace family who had owned most of Friendship Bay for over a century. Her question to us, since she was living on the property, was, "If it isn't my husband's, whose is it?"

We called the Land Holding and Deeds Office and explained our dilemma. They informed us that paying taxes on property didn't make one the owner, of course. They could find nothing in Verne's name, but if I had the time and wanted to browse through the properties and tax books, I might find something. The Island was only six or seven miles long and one mile wide at its widest part, and they couldn't find the owner of a thirty to thirty-five acre plot! I said to Sandy, "I'm going over and I'm going to find out who is the owner."

11 To Bequia or not to Bequia

So the second week we were there, I could be found in the government offices looking through land titles for the owner. The man in charge started looking but gave up, saying, "If you want to continue looking, search yourself." The books were gigantic. I could barely lift one. All I had to go on was the size of the plot, which was just an estimate, and the approximate location. The Wallace name was no help—it was all over the place.

After much lifting and leafing, I found what I was searching for—about thirty-four acres bordered on one side by the area of Am Boise and on the other by the area of Diamond. The owner was a Bill Wallace, the old whaler from the 1800s. I had seen pictures of him in an old book about the West Indies taken at the turn of the century up on Friendship Gap. He was standing out in front of his house, which, so the captain said, had been blown away right down to its foundation in the 1910 hurricane. So Verne must be a descendant. But then, I asked myself, how many others?

I gathered up all the info and headed back to Sandy with it. It was the correct property all right, and I easily found out that still living were two sisters, Doris Wallace and Winnie Simmons, as well as Erma, Verne's wife, who had a claim to the property, too.

When Erma heard, she was eager to get the whole property resurveyed so her portion and ours could be parceled off. She would then sell us our share. But we now had to get both sisters' approval of the sale. Winnie, her sister-in-law, was living over the hill in Belmont, and Doris, the other sister-in-law, was living in the USA, up on Lenox Avenue just north of 110th Street in Harlem. Winnie readily agreed to the sale, but Doris was another story. She, being the oldest, insisted on returning to Bequia for the first time in sixty years to look into the matter. As it turned out, it was nothing but her avarice that propelled her.

There was on Doris's part, much praying and soul-searching and calling on God to help and guide the family in making the right decisions on such an auspicious occasion. All the other members of the family were at her side. After all, she was a staunch Seventh Day believer, a fact she kept repeating over and over. I do believe that the repetition was a device to convince herself of the fact. It was obvious to both Sandy and me that she was doing very little convincing of anyone else in the room that day. None of her family bought her act for a minute, but the Bequia way is never to let on. We could also see she couldn't wait to get us aside and away from the rest of the family to tell us that she knew, through God, we were good people and she wouldn't be averse to selling the property to us, but we should be aware that she being the oldest should be given all the monies for the property and that it would be up to her as a God-fearing Christian to take care of her loving sister and sister-in-law.

Yeah, sure, I said to myself, you'll take care of them all right.

As this thought was flying through my mind, I heard Sandy saying, "That's right, sister Doris, I'm sure you will. Now let's just get all the necessary papers in order to finalize the sale. We'll leave the taking care of the family to you. After all, you're the matriarch now."

As she drove off in the jeep, she shot Sandy a benign look and then, smiling like a Cheshire cat, she victoriously waved back at the rest of the family standing in the drive. I couldn't wait to gasp out, "Matriarch?"

Sandy looked at me in his calm, even complacent way and said, "We have nothing to worry about. Her insatiable greed has hooked her. I hope."

"Sandy, you played her like a violin," I added.

"Yes, but the concert's not over yet, me boyo. The fat lady has yet to sing!"

All this shuffling of ownership took up precious time. According to the land-holding license, we had to be building within the year after signing the contract or the license would be null and void. So we had to be digging into the hill by May of next year. Sandy wondered if we would ever make it. Finally one evening at dinner, he looked up and said, "Who says it has to be Bequia? There are plenty of islands south of here running all the way to Grenada. We can go reconnoitering if things don't pick up around here pretty soon." Well they didn't, so we made plans to go down to Carriacou, one of the northernmost islands of the Grenadines, belonging to Grenada.

Just Thirty Miles South

The day we left at the crack of dawn, a deluge hit us about halfway across the channel. Sandy did his best to find a little shelter from the driving gale. He didn't like going into the cabin where everyone huddled together sweating and vomiting into basins and holding on for dear life as the ship tossed to and fro. We elected to stay out on deck and weather the gale-force winds next to the main mast. I was standing next to him shielding myself. There was Father McGittigan, the Catholic priest from St. Michael's. He was hanging onto a loose rope, his face meeting the full blast of the wind and rain dead-on as he whistled "Silver Threads Among the Gold." I heard Sandy mutter, "Look at that damned fool standing out there whistling his head off. And here am I running around the world trying to find a decent place to rest this weary carcass of mine. Jimmy, tell me honestly, who is the biggest fool anyway?"

I yelled at him through the gale, "I guess I am. I don't even know why the hell I'm here!"

We made St. Vincent drenching wet with a trip to the airport and a thirty-minute plane ride to Carriacou still ahead of us. Sandy wrote a little verse about this episode in our lives. It gives a peek into his feelings for me. It was entitled "Rose Bud, Rose Bud, Lovely Rose Bud." Rose Bud was meant to be me.

When we reached Carriacou, the sun was shining. We jumped into a jeep and headed for the Mermaid Tavern. The hotel was run by Linton Riggs, an

American from the state of Maryland, a leftover from the Old South and Maryland's horsey set. He was very tall and grubby-looking. Sandy said, "My God! He's a cross between Charles Coburn and W.C. Fields."

The hotel was made up of the main house and five little cubicles in a long rectangular affair stretching down to the beach. Opposite this structure was an open space containing tables and chairs with sheets of galvanize above. That's right, just a roof open to the elements serving as a dining room. Behind this dining room was a cubbyhole of a kitchen. The kitchen was run by Hilda who ran everything else as well.

We walked into Riggs's disheveled office to ask whether he had any rooms. Riggs, never looking up from his desk, yelled out, "Mistress Hilda, do we have any room?"

She yelled back from across the way, "Yes, we do, sir."

"Well, show these fine gentlemen a room." Looking up from his desk, he added, "We have no attendant at the bar, but it's open for your convenience at any time. Just help yourself and write it in the book after your names. We use the honor system around here."

We were led into a cavernous foyer and up a mahogany staircase. Our room was large and totally bare except for one four-poster West Indian bed, with a rickety table next to it, and a straight chair beside an old chest of drawers that pulled out and in with difficulty. The window screen was ripped, but the bed had a mosquito net. The bat was just a huge square room with no hot water.

"Well, one thing this place has plenty of is space," Sandy quipped.

"Yes," I said. "One can easily see we've been given the presidential suite. We must be pretty special."

"We're so special," Sandy scoffed. "Couldn't you see that we're the only ones in this dump? And where does he come off with 'Mistress Hilda, do we have any room?'"

I said, "We never asked how much the rooms were."

"How much can it possibly be? Five dollars?"

We both squared away our things and went for a swim on a beautiful beach. We could row out to have a picnic on a little island just off shore. With its shrubs and a couple of coconut trees, it was a perfect cartoon desert island.

Dinner was served family-style with Riggs holding court in his overbearing, supercilious way. There were just the three of us, and at the end of the meal, I had to ask for coffee. I had to ask for coffee every night until we left! I asked Sandy, "Why do you think I have to ask for coffee every night?"

He said, "Because it's going to cost you five dollars a cup. Ha, ha!" It was just another joke.

After three days, the rather thin bath towels hadn't been changed. Sandy took them downstairs and draped them over the newel post saying, "Mistress Hilda can't overlook them here."

I said, "There goes our room rent, up another five dollars a day."

Sandy retorted, "It'll be worth it."

The second day we took a jeep ride around the island and inquired about land availability from the driver. He asked whether we knew the Kent family, saying they might be of some help to us and that he could introduce us. We felt that was a good idea.

The Kents were an old Grenadian family who owned lime groves and other interests on Carriacou. They grew various kinds of produce and bottled them for shipping off-island.

We finally found land on Sugar Loaf Mountain just south of the airport and bordered on one side by the sea. It was much larger than we were looking for but I felt I could develop the complete site on way or another. Yet I had an uneasy feeling I was getting in deeper than I had expected. We gave the owner a small retainer, very small—after our experience in Roatan and Bequia, we were being cautious.

We then made plans to take the packet boat to Grenada. The trip was a grueling thirty-mile voyage in a dirty, grubby, unkempt schooner. We found a hotel and a lawyer and very quickly started the business of acquiring a land-holding license. It was easy in Grenada compared with St. Vincent, much like in Tegucigalpa. Maybe it was because of the few calls the Kents made in advance.

On the way back from Grenada, Sandy confessed he really preferred Bequia to Carriacou. England obviously didn't give a damn for either's plight or condition, but the situation didn't faze us. We only wanted to be left to our own devices.

When we made it back to Carriacou, we sat up into the night fighting off mosquitoes and discussing the pros and cons of each island. In the end, Bequia won over Carriacou. Looking back, I wonder what it was about Bequia that gave it that little edge. It was nothing more than a feeling, and we both had it.

One night on Carriacou, the driver took me to a dance. Sandy had decided to turn in early. It was not the usual jump-up held at a hotel or rum shop. No, it was held in the living room of someone's house in the middle of a poor village. As we approached, I could see that all the furniture in the house had been removed and stored out back in the shed and yard. The house was packed with people everywhere. Playing inside was a band made up of bamboo flutes, two violins, and a banjo, with a few percussion instruments thrown in. These consisted of hardwood sticks, two glass bottles, coconut shocktras, a kind of cheese grater, and a wooden washboard! Such a sound I had never heard and such merrymaking would be hard to beat. From a distance the house seemed to rock from stem to stern.

Only a kerosene lamp or two flickered uselessly here and there. I could barely make out the dancers through the windows. Enough space had been cleared in both the living room and dining room for two sets of eight people, two by two, to form a quadrille. What I was seeing was something I had seen before in my own Irish-American home at he house parties of the thirties.

Here they were doing Scots-Irish dances I had seen so many times and had taken part in myself, filling up a set with a lovable spinster like Mary Goldrick. It was such fun then, and I was delighted now to be transported miles away in space and time. The songs, jigs, and reels were the same. Only the rhythms and the execution of the figures were West Indian. What a night it was. I shall never forget it.

We had one final meeting with the Fraser family, the owner of the island. We told them we would be in touch from Bequia. We later called to tell them the deal was off and to keep the money.

We checked out of the Mermaid Tavern, and Sandy's and my running joke notwithstanding, we found it to live up to its reputation as the best deal in the Caribbean, if you happened to be looking for one.

A Dream Deferred

September was upon us, time for Sandy to make the trek back to East 83rd Street and the Playhouse. Paul had been on the phone with him all summer long as to the state of affairs at the school. Bequia was like a second command post. Sandy left for New York, as would come to be his routine, the week after Labor Day so he would be at school in time to check the list of incoming students with Paul just one more time.

It was a very apprehensive acting teacher who left Bequia that fall. He wanted our plans to work out so badly and yet he had absolutely no control over the outcome. All I could do was reassure him over and over that I would do everything in my power to make it happen.

"Even move heaven and hell?" he asked.

"Even move heaven and hell," I promised.

"I do believe if anyone can do it, it's you."

I must say he had so much faith in me that it actually scared me. Here he was putting the future of his life solely in my hands. Such faith made me love him all the more.

Yet, what I really wanted was to be back at East 83rd Street myself. It was such a beautiful place to live, even if I do say so myself. My dream of a career was still very much alive—dreams don't die that easily. Now that I had a patron of sorts, I seemed to have New York by the tail. There it was, just waiting to be conquered at last after all those years of plodding away at it and nothing to show for it save experience and struggle. Sandy had moved me into this position and made all this possible, and now he was asking me to help him fulfill his dream. So here I was, off on this backwater island, very perplexed. The one thing I was sure of was that I would stick to this project and give it my all for the one person who saw so much in me and meant so much to me, more than anyone else in the world. Right now it was a time for Sandy's dream, and mine would just have to be deferred.

12 Sandy Hellbent on Bequia

Dreamwork

"No 'ifs,' 'ands,' or 'buts' about it. It is going to work. Everything is going to be just the way we planned it. Jimmy, have I ever let you down? Trust me."

He would go on incessantly. I thought maybe this show of confidence on his part was no more than wishful thinking. We had seen little forward movement on our land acquisition. By the time Sandy had gone back to New York, I truly felt the trip might have been his last, that I would wrapping things up in Bequia and soon be polishing my dancin' shoes once again.

The first letter I got from Sandy after he got home was full of all his New York plans. Without waiting for any news from me, he was starting to make plans to put the house up for lease. He was going to hire an upscale Eastside real estate agent, a Ms. Palmer. I had heard some say she was a real estate barracuda. I was to expedite the Bequia proceedings and keep making things happen. "Good luck," I thought, but I did keep trying.

When Sandy left, I was to have gone over to Mr. Miller's again, but the Young brothers insisted I stay. I would be freeloading and I felt a little cheap. "Oh, life!" as they say here. I knew I couldn't pay the hotel prices over such a long period. Oh, well, a gift horse is a gift horse. Ruth and her two kids were there. What difference would one more make?

I didn't have much to do until the paperwork around Verne's death was processed and the estate was settled among the three women. Now the land had to be surveyed again and split into four sections. The monies from our section were to be split among the three, unless you listened to Doris. I used the time climbing all over the terrain to get a feel for the property and working on the house design. I saw a lot of Ruth, the ex-model, and Molly, "The Beautiful Barkeep of Bequia."

On the phone Sandy told me how the Eastside agent had clinched the deal on one lease. Obviously, the agent was now doing her shtick on Sandy. Land-with-deed or no land-with-deed, Sandy was signing a lease for 83rd Street with a lady who had a chimp. She was planning to rent the triplex. The basement was perfect for her "baby," if his cage could be dismantled to fit through the cellar door. Sand even had a prospect for the upper apartment. He would arrange to move into the Hotel Dover on Lexington until he found a small place for himself near the school since he still planned to teach. She had really hooked Sandy and was reeling him in whether he was ready or not. He had already contacted a mover and a shipper. When I asked him why, he said, "I wanted them to be ready for us when we're ready to make the big move."

"Fine," I said, "but we don't even have a deed yet." He was proud of himself for having already found one tenant for our place. But I couldn't believe what I was hearing. "We're not ready for all this," I said. "And what about our plan to keep the basement apartment? What if I get a job? What then?" I had always thought of it as a pied-à-terre that I could go back to when I had to be in the city and that he could go to as he pleased. He was having none of this. He felt he had to rent the house to get money for Bequia. I said, "Yeah, I thought so too, but the basement? Really, Sandy, what if—?"

He cut me off. "There are going to be no 'what ifs.' Bequia is going to work out. And you are the one who's going to see to it that it does. What if you get a show? Listen to you. You were just as miserable up here as I am. Don't worry about that. If it happens—and remember, that's an 'if,'—we'll work that out together as well" was his retort.

His plans were moving along hell-bent for election, a hell of lot faster than the snail's pace things were moving down on the Island. I was beginning to think he was losing it. I felt he was severing his ties up there much too soon. He would never be able to backtrack if he had to. What he was doing was forcing himself into a predicament that he could only move forward from. He had made up his mind he didn't want a choice.

I knew I could do nothing about it as long as I was down here on Bequia, and yet, did I really want to? I could see this idea of a place in the sun had really taken hold of him. He was aching to have it all pan out. I knew the best thing I could do was to see to it that it did. After all, Carriacou was just waiting a little to the south of us. Not to worry. Boy, did that make me feel Bequian.

Still, as things stood, it was going to take me well over a year and possibly even two to finish his house down here, and he was making so many rash decisions. The next thing he said to me was, "By the way, I've contacted an antique dealer to sell my antiques for me. We won't need them on Bequia."

For some reason, I drew the line at this point. I was already starting to design a house that would call for most of the antiques. I dashed off a letter ranting, raving, and issuing ultimatums as he himself could well do at times.

"Sandy," I wrote,

There is no way that I am going to sit around idly and let you destroy that beautiful house we created on 83rd Street. If I can't stop you, at least I can refuse to be part of it. If you insist on this, I will walk away from this whole shebang right now.

I went on writing him a letter all right, a letter he didn't keep so the following is a reconstruction. Let's see...

You say that you are finished with New York, yet so far you have made no changes at the Playhouse, except to opt out of teaching the summer class next year. That's fine with me, but I'm afraid that I'm not finished with New York, at least not totally, and in truth, you're not either. I can see that. So here is what I propose. If you want to pull everything out of 207 East 83rd Street, I say you go right ahead and destroy it, if you have a mind to. Needless to say, it is yours and you have a right to do with it whatever you wish; you can always change your mind and move back in if you had to. Yet since you are ready to give up the basement apartment, I'd like to remind you that the place was supposed to be put aside for me, or at least I always thought it was for me and for you as well if needed. That was part of the original plan we decided on together many months ago. No, years ago! Now you tell me you are willing to give it up to a gorilla and his or her cage. All right, so it's an oversized chimp. I have heard of a lap dog but an ape? I mean really. What's next? At first, I thought it was a joke, but it's not, so you say. This woman really lives with an ape. All right, so I say go right ahead and rent it to her for her ape. After all, the lease isn't forever and anything can happen. I feel I am being driven out of my own home by an ape. So it isn't my house, but I did live there. Never mind, you go right ahead and rent your house to monkeys for all I care. They are just renters and renters come and go.

However, the antiques we have acquired over the years are a part of my lifestyle as well as yours. Some might say they are just things, material baggage. But they are our things and our baggage, a part of your life and mine. What of all the work Paul, Iris, and I did acquiring and creating what is up there on 83rd Street? And it was less than five years ago. You hand all that over to a dealer and you won't get two cents for it. No, no, no you don't, I won't let you be so foolish.

What you do first is send him packing. Forget the dealer. The next thing you do is pick out what you will need in a one-bedroom apartment, whatever that is. Paul and Iris Whitney will be glad to help with that, I am sure. Then you get that mover you picked and have him pack and store everything else for shipment, so they will be ready to go to St. Vincent when we are prepared to receive them down here.

Now I will change the design down here and create for you, if not another 83rd Street, at least something similar and equal to it. It will be no easy task fitting it in on that damn ski slope you picked. I assure you I will do my damnedest to create for you another 83rd Street in the middle of the Caribbean, so you won't lose all you have now, and all the hard work will not have been in vain. You can get Gerry Russo, Bob Rush, and my brother Leo to help you with the heavy work. Iris and Paul will be a great help picking out what will look good in a small apartment.

The letter went on and on. Suffice it to say, he got the message. He was on the phone the minute he got my letter. The first thing he said was, "What about the chandelier?"

"It's a 17th century Staffordshire," I said. "It's yours, isn't it? Send everything."

"Everything?" he said. "Every—?"

"That's right, everything," I reiterated.

A long pause followed before he quietly confessed, "I can't..." He paused again. "I already sold the Georgian one hanging in the living room, the Coromandel screen, and the yellow Ming desk."

"I know you didn't sell them," I said. "You probably practically gave them away to the first gauche person who asked after them. What did they offer you? Food stamps or a promissory note?" I raved on. "God, Sandy! That rare yellow Ming desk and plum-colored screen were old, ancient and priceless. Stop what you are doing, stop it right now." I knew he didn't care a fig about things any more than he cared about money but he did like nice things, very nice things, and they cost money.

"When this house is finished, if it ever is—and that is a very big 'if'—believe me, Sandy, there is precious little here, if anything, for the getting. In the end, I would have to have most everything made by hand. Sandy, furniture-makers they are not. So please believe me, as God is my witness and as crazy as it sounds, just send everything down here by boat. No matter what it costs, we will still save money. I mean everything, like your mother's antique china and all the dishes. If it isn't nailed down, send it. No, even if it is nailed down, send it, like the crystal wall sconces and hanging lamps. Just replace them with anything. I'm sure the gorilla won't mind in the least bit."

"OK, OK, I got it. I'll do it. Anything, everything, but this phone bill's gonna be... All I ever wanted was a bamboo shack under a palm tree," he moaned.

"Yeah, yeah," I said. "In your dreams."

"Bye-bye for now. Love ya. Take care."

He wrote copious letters to me as I did to him, but we would still get on the phone and yak and yak. The phone bills were so high we decided to include them in the overall expenses along with airfares. It was the beginning of what Sandy came to refer, affectionately and for the rest of his life, to as his "Villa Bankruptcy."

Nine Mornings

When Sandy arrived for Christmas, though I had precious little to tell him, he was full of tales of New York. All the news made my stomach queasy. The big question I had was, what are we getting ourselves into?

Christmas of '69 wasn't very different from the previous year. Ruth was there with her two children, Andrea and Gina, and her friend Pat Field with whom she had worked in New York. They were planning to open a boutique at the hotel. To whom they intended to sell their wares I didn't know, but who was I to judge? The Ford family was there, and the bunch from Massachusetts had come back again. The Mortons from Pennsylvania who were building a house up behind the Fords were there as well as the Dwyers who were also in the middle of construction. Bill and Joyce from the yacht Honey Bird were still at the hotel. Bill was shoving off on a Christmas charter down the Grenadines, and Joyce, still "under the weather" as she put it, was staying at the hotel over the holiday. The hotel was, therefore, almost half full, a much better situation than the previous year. The food had improved, as had the staff. Aileen was a quick learner.

When the Christmas winds from the north start up, they bring rain to the Island. Consequently, "Christmas flowers" bloom, but this year they were running a little late so we could expect flowers about the first week in January.

Sandy found it hard to accept that at Christmastime it was impossible to get anything done—especially anything pertaining to government, legal matters, or self-employed workers. The reason is peculiar to St. Vincent, since it is the only country that celebrates "Nine Mornings." It started as a religious custom when people walked everywhere. They walked to church for services like the novenas of Advent, and at the same time they would stroll in groups from house to house in the wee hours of the morning to give their yuletide greetings over grog and Christmas goodies. Unfortunately, this marvelous, hospitable practice had degenerated. Now all the rum shops, nightclubs, and dance halls would close early, at 11 PM, for the nine days before Christmas and then reopen in the wee hours about 2 AM and stay open until 6 AM. All nine nights, night after night, the loudspeakers would blare incessantly into all the villages of the Island while everyone drank themselves silly. By Christmas most people were in no condition to celebrate much less get to Midnight Mass. New Year's, seven days away, gave them time to sober up and be ready for "Old Year's Night." No wonder they called January 2 "Recovery Day."

Sandy got a big kick out of seeing Boolu in his flower-sack outfit. He did look clean and neat, but some of the staff were still tormenting him. Thank God Samuel now looked after him.

Sandy was leaving on January 15, so one thing was for sure: he wasn't going to see much progress on this trip. The property papers were still at a standstill and I couldn't figure out why. The more they held things up, the madder I got, and yet I had to keep my cool. One thing I had learned by now was that whatever got done was going to get done their way and in their time. There was no way to cope with this laidback attitude. Practically everyone I encountered was so blasé, as if they had the blahs, very uncaring. I wondered how anything at all got done with this attitude. I wondered whether I was treated this way because I was a foreigner or because of a general civil service malaise caused by an unsatisfying paycheck. Who knew?

Yet I met people who couldn't have been more helpful. We kept getting tips on land we could acquire without half the hassle, and there was always Carriacou down in Grenada. The more I persisted in my efforts for this specific piece of property, the more I had a stubborn drive not to give in to their red tape. I told Sandy my feeling, and he said, "Let's dig in and hold out for the hill."

"Do you know what you sound like?" I asked.

"No, what?"

"Like you're in Korea. Remember Heartbreak Hill?" I asked.

"No," he replied. "Now, what's that supposed to mean?"

I was just joking; anyway, I hoped it was a joke.

At first the lawyer said, "Look at something else. Verne's death has really complicated the whole procedure."

I told him, "We are not going to be swayed on this one."

The lawyer offered, "If this is the land you really want and nothing else would please you, as a citizen, I could sign the deed for you and pass it on to you later."

When I told Sandy, his curt reply was, "No way. Not on your life. No one's name is going to be on that deed except ours."

I agreed. "I haven't found many lawyers I trust, and certainly not somebody down here I don't know."

I learned much later that this practice was not uncommon in these parts, and often the lawyer came out ahead with the buyer the loser. If the land deal didn't work out, the lawyer had nothing to lose in the first place.

Our lawyer reminded us that we only had about four or five months left on our Foreign Landholding License and we had to be in the process of building by then.

"So what do you have to say about that, Sandy?" I asked.

"Well, we don't have to be finished by then," he said.

"At this rate, we won't even be started by then," I told him.

"One thing I know is I don't want to be up behind the hotel nor in any other foreigners' enclave, for that matter. Couldn't we start digging in May and take all the time in the world doing it?" Sandy asked me.

"That's a damned good idea. Risky, but good. We would have to get Winnie and Erma's permission and also get them to agree to keep the deed question to themselves."

Both Winnie and Erma wanted us up there and I suspected Doris did, too. So we agreed to move ahead with our plan.

I had heard about a house I could rent for $200 BeeWee a month (US $120 at the time). It was on the far side of Friendship right next to the ocean in the direct path of the trade winds. The landlady was Joan Stowe. It was a three-bedroom house with a long deck facing east overlooking the water. It had only the bare essentials but, although a little crude in a West Indian way, it was adequate and clean. We moved in on January 2 and then went over to Jeff Gunn in Kingstown, St. Vincent, where Sandy and I picked out a Moke. Much like a small army jeep, it was made by the Austin people of England.

When Sandy left on January 15, 1970, he was feeling more positive, thought nothing had changed since he'd arrived a month ago—with the exception of the inexpensive house I had found. It was the tentative plans we had made, I guess. Oh yeah, I forgot, I had completed the house specs and hung them up on the living room wall. Sandy was pleased with them, but I don't think he cottoned on to the extent of the excavation these plans called for on such a steep incline. No matter what we built, it was going to be difficult and costly.

The design I had settled on was a house that was set into the hill as much as possible, but I wasn't Frank Lloyd Wright so my job was cut out for me. The hill was solid volcanic rock with no more than a foot of topsoil. We would have to pickaxe down to quite a depth. Nevertheless, I knew it could be done in time, and time was one thing Bequia had plenty of. Between Christmas and New Year's, I decided it was time to go looking for a contractor, though I didn't really need one. I would be doing all the ordering and taking care of deliveries and tending to all the monies. What I really need was a damn good carpenter and a crackerjack mason. Sandy came along on every interview.

I found a master carpenter who was also a contractor, who had been highly regarded as a fine boat builder. I thought this combination was the best I could find. He said he had a good man who could be our top mason. So, after a few interviews Sandy and I settled oh Japheth Hazell from Paget Farm. I explained I would be on the job most every day but would be running around a lot, so for all intents and purposes he would be considered the contractor and I would not interfere with him and the workers. He seemed to be satisfied with that. In hindsight, I realize we could not have had a better setup. We told him we planned to start in March or May. The dates worked for him because he was still working on David Ollivierre's house less than a quarter mile along our road.

I found Japheth's most pleasing quality to be the relationship he had with the workers. His ability to get the most from the crew was worth his weight in gold. He knew when to push and when to let up. He was by far the most valuable man we had on the job. We were very lucky and the proof was in the quality of the finished work. Japheth was later hired by the city of Baltimore to build their tall ship, The Pride of Baltimore.

On the 15th we were up before the sun. I accompanied Sandy over on the boat and saw him off on LIAT at Arnos Vale. The last thing he said to me was, "You don't have to bother yourself over Doris. When the time is right, I plan to go up to Harlem and put that saintly, avaricious old lady in her place, right in her own back yard."

My Extracurricular Activity

I was spending most of nights at the fabulous Whaleboner Bar owned and operated by the incomparable Miss Molly. I wasn't doing much else; I was just playing the waiting game, waiting for something to happen. The Whaleboner was a bar catering to yacht captains. The beautiful Miss Molly was the magnet that snared them into her den like a black widow spider luring unsuspecting victims into her web. Only victims they weren't, for everyone seemed to enjoy themselves—even old drunk-ass Howell from Mt. Pleasant, who was killing himself nightly, dousing his troubles in Mount Gay rum. He was having an identity crisis. He asked me once, "Mr. Jimmy, what color am I?"

"Why, Howell. No question about it. You're white."

"Then why de hell is it," he asked, "dat every time I leave dis Island, no matter where I go, I'm black?"

This color thing was coming to a head all around the world. Remember, it was the Sixties.

Miss Molly's beauty, brains, and interesting personality collected customers like moths around a fire. They would show up with their charter parties and crews. She treated each and every one of them as if they were the only one. It turned out to be not a bad business setup for her. I enjoyed watching her operate. On Bequia the bars closed relatively early. I would stick around after closing time, and she and I would hang out talking about anything and everything until the wee hours of the morning. During these tête-à-têtes, Molly and I got to know each other well, and a wonderful, warm, and wholesome friendship developed. Many of the Islanders noticed my Moke parked out back of the bar long after closing night after night. The observation made for spicy speculation. Rumor upon rumor about our escapades ran rampant on the Island grapevine. This Island gossip mill was called milly-milly. The talk about us did much to distort my true image, so my initiation into the milly-milly was beneficial to me at this early stage of my Island life. I don't think the Islanders were ready for my lifestyle or my sexual persuasion.

The Night Visitor—Early 1970

One night about 3 AM I swerved down the drive and across the grassy knowll to the house. The headlights lit up the little blue house in the darkness. There, sitting on the steps of the entrance porch, was this little creature. I knew right away it was Boolu. On this cold, damp night he was shivering in nothing more than his lightweight flower-sack outfit with a red and black Scottish plaid zipper-bag at his side. As I approached the house, I could see he was crying and scared half to death. I sat down on the step next to him and put my arm around him to comfort him. I had no idea why he was here and I knew he couldn't tell me. To reassure him, I picked up him and put him on my lap and rocked him in my arms. After a short while, he settled down. I stood him on his feet, got up myself, took his hand in one of mine, grabbing the zipper-bag with the other, and led him to the door and into the kitchen where I sat him down at the table.

If he could only talk! But all he could do was stare up at me with those large, dark, piercingly soulful, almond-shaped eyes, so like a poor little helpless puppy dog. With a towel from the bath, I wiped the tears, mucus, and bloodstains from his bruised face. I put the kettle on and made a big peanut butter-and-jelly sandwich and a cup of hot cocoa for him, which he downed in no time. I took the hot water from the stove, poured it into the bathroom sink, and washed him up with warm water. Then I put one of my pajama tops on him and put him to bed in the front bedroom. I tucked him in under a heavy blanket I found in a drawer, kissed him on his forehead and patted his head, and said, even though he couldn't hear me, "Go to sleep, little man. We'll see about all this in the morning."

Boolu and I were sitting at the table having breakfast when Birdie, Joan's housekeeper, came over to make my bed. I told her how I'd found Boolu. She simply said, "Yes, I know. He was sitting out there all evening. I heard Mr. Young kicked him out of the hotel. Joan told me."

There was a knock at the door. It was Samuel, so I invited him to cover and sit at the table and have something to eat. He said, "No, please. I had my tea dis mornin.'"

"Well, have some more," I insisted.

"No, no, please, nuttin'. I na hungry," he insisted and went on. "Mrs. Stowe told Lancy dis morning she thought Boolu might be inside here, so I have come ta tell ya what happened at de hotel."

"Well, as you can see, Boolu is here all right. I was going over to the hotel to talk to Ron."

"Mr. Jimmy, oh, he be vexed plenty. He fire Boolie an' told him ta get out and don' come back," said Sammy nervously.

"Why?"

"He cut Phyllis in de kitchen. Mr. Ron say Boolu be daft, he be mental like Frazeen," he blurted out.

"Come on," I said. "Ron doesn't even know Frazeen. Slow down, take it easy. What happened? Tell me the whole story."

He stammered and stuttered and was so upset, but after a fashion and many retakes, I got the gist of the story. As best as I could make out, it had all started right after lunch the afternoon before. Aileen had put Boolu to work peeling potatoes at the kitchen door. Phyllis, one of the kitchen staff, apparently plucked a spring of sting-a-nettle. Sting-a-nettle has many jagged thorns on it; even the leaves have sharp-pointed edges that can give a vicious prick or scrape on the skin, causing considerable bleeding, numbing, and swelling. As Phyllis passed into the kitchen, she shoved the sting-a-nettle into Boolu's face. He didn't see or hear her coming in as he was busy peeling potatoes. The sudden shocking pain caused him to strike out with the paring knife, cutting her wrist slightly and drawing blood. She let out one loud scream and ran out front to the office to show Brenda.

Boolu just sat there with the bowl of potatoes still in his lap and blood running down his face. He was used to this kind of treatment, but the stinging and numbness felt strange. He was also frightened at what he had done.

When Ron saw the blood on the girl's wrist, all he heard was Boolu had done it, and he went berserk. Never really looking at the slight abrasion, he ordered Brenda to get someone to clean it up. Then he went to the door of the kitchen and told Aileen to bring Boolu into the office. Boolu came in still wiping his face. Ron never even asked Aileen what had happened to Boolu. He went on ranting, "We can't have things like this going on at this hotel. Boolu, you can't go around cutting people. He'll have to leave. Aileen, please tell Samuel that Boolu is finished here and it's up to him to get rid of the boy." Pulling a $20 BeeWee note out of the cash drawer, Ron said, "Here, Aileen, give him this." Ron turned around to Brenda and said, "I could get myself into a lot of trouble putting up with this sort of thing. We can't have it, Brenda. He's as crazy as a loon."

When he turned back, Boolu, who hadn't understood a word, was standing there finger the $20 note with this face still stinging from the sting-a-nettle. He hadn't moved an inch. Ron said, "What are you standing there for?"

Aileen answered for him. "Mr. Young, he don't know what you told him. He can't hear you."

"Well, you tell him. And get him out of here," Ron ordered her.

She took Boolu by the hand and led him to the kitchen. That $20 BeeWee bill, which was all of US $12, must have been the payoff for ten months of service.

Samuel had been watching all the proceedings from a safe distance. He took Boolu from Aileen to the staff quarters where he transferred his own things from his red and black plaid into his brother Buso's bag. He then walked Boolu over to the generator room where Boolu slept. Sammy pulled Boolu's things out from under the beat-up beach lounge that served as his bed and put them into the bag. Boolu's possessions amounted to nothing more than every flour-sack suit Vilna had made for him these past few months. That's all I found in it anyway. Sammy told me that every month or so Vilna used to make him a new flour-sack suit because no one ever thought to wash the one he was wearing. He would just wear it till it looked so grubby and raggedy that Vilna made him a new one. Yet Boolu kept every one. They were all he had in the world to his name, a bundle of raggedy, dirt-stained, flower-sack shorts and tops.

Sammy took Boolu's pay and put that in the bag as well. When Sammy told me this, I said, "I took everything out of the bag last night, and there was no money in it, nothing except his rags." It was clear to Samuel that someone had taken the money.

The afternoon when all this had happened to Boolu, Samuel couldn't leave the hotel. So he had told Boolu to go home to his house over in Lower Bay Gutter and stay by his mother, Metrius. Now, Boolu knew Samuel's mommy. She sent him food. About six months previously, Ron had decided to stop feeding the staff. He told them they had to bring their own food from home. He never considered where Boolu would get his food from. This new rule required that Metrius Hanson send food for her children, Jean, Buso and Samuel, so she sent food for Boolie, as she called him, as well. She was an uneducated single mother of nine children with no job except whatever she could pick up as washerwoman for other locals like Erma Wallace. Somehow Boolu understood Samuel, but don't ask me how, so he took off across Friendship's field of dried-up pigeon pea pushes and corn stocks, and up into Lower Bay Gutter.

I don't know what or who motivated his next move, but that move would be the move that changed his life forever, although he didn't know it at the time. Arriving in Lower Bay Gutter, he didn't know where Metrius was or why she wasn't home, much less where she might be. So the only thing he could do was to turn around and go somewhere else, and the only place that he knew to turn to was our place over on the point. But on his way he ran into a little trouble. Someone saw two little toughs beat up Boolu over by Sir Anthony Eden's place that day and saw him crying down the road to Sandy and Mr. Jimmy's. Joan Stowe saw him knock on the door and then sit on the steps; he was still there at 10 PM when she went to bed. The rest of the story I already knew.

When Samuel heard about the money, he said he would take care of it. Before the day was out, the police were handing Boolu back his $20 note. Sammy had found out who took the money and then he had Boolu point them out to the police at the station. For the first time in his life, Boolu was having justice doled out in his favor. It must have felt pretty damned good to him after all those years of abuse and neglect and receiving the short end of the stick.

Boolu And Winnie Settle In

Winnie Dewer came to work for us that season as a housekeeper/cook. Japheth our contractor found her for us. She bonded with Boolu quickly and became his surrogate mother. This I liked. She was caring, quiet, and ladylike. Everyone liked her and had a good word to say for her. Every adult and child alike called her Cousin Winnie, as if it were one word, "Cousinwinnie," whether they were related or not. Boolu helped her in the kitchen doing dishes, setting the table, and serving at dinner. At first he ate in the kitchen with Winnie.

He soon became the official water-boy for both our house and Joan's, endearing himself to Joan. The house water system was gravity-based, fed by an overhead tank that had to be manually filled by a hand pump. Keeping the yard around the house looking good and burning the garbage also became Boolu's jobs. These tasks kept him busy most of the morning; then he was free after lunch to do whatever and hang out wherever he chose. He would play with Joan's three young children aged from five to ten and as it happened

12 Sandy Hellbent on Bequia

those ages were good for Boolu then.

I had little or nothing to do except wait for "Vincy," whether that was the government or our lawyers, to get off its tail and do something about the legal papers. Erma and I kept in close contact. I familiarized Japheth with the house plans and we discussed how we would tackle the problem of the sharp incline of the property. He would always stop by on his way home from his job at David's house on the road just past Lower Bay Gutter.

The toughs on the road were still bothering Boolu although not as much. Still I knew I had to put a stop to it one way or another. I just had to wait for the right time. Boolu was also staying out late and coming home at any hour, especially on the nights of the hotels' "jump-ups." I was going to have to curtail this little activity, but how? How do you impose a curfew on a little wild animal? With a dog, you tame him with a rolled up newspaper, but that wouldn't work with Boolu. Remember, he had already had the balata and that didn't work.

One day he came in crying, all disheveled and dirty, his knees scuffed up. It was happening again. Today was a good time to go out and do something about it. The rum shop would be full and all the kids would be around because today the community was having the blessing of the whaleboats. Many would end up at Kenneth's. I put on a dress shirt and my long pants and shoes, combed my hair for I knew they respected appearances, and took Boolu by the hand and headed for the little shop. When I got there, I stood in the doorway with Boolu in tow. I just stood there and once I had just about everyone in the place looking at me, except for the few who were too wasted to notice anything, I said, "I would like your attention. I have something to tell you. Most of you know who I am, and for those of you who don't, I am Mr. Jimmy. I live over on the point at Joan Stowe's place. This is Boolie. You all know him. I want you to take a good look at him. Some of your kids have been beating up on him, and I want it to stop. Why? I'll tell you why. This kid is now my son, and I am now his daddy. I am now responsible for him, and anyone messing with him from now on will have to answer to me. I swear to God I will haul your 'rass' in front of the magistrate, and I mean it. Thank you, Kenneth."

And Kenneth answered, "OK, Mr. Jimmy."

"Come on, Boolie," I said. "Let's go home and I'll wash you up."

I think that Kenneth's "OK" at the end of my little speech was like a seal of approval on the deal to end Boolu's abuse in the village, or anywhere else for that matter. Kenneth Alex was the village political kingpin then. Thanks to the Bequia grapevine, news of the deal spread as if by an AP release to The Bequia Times (if only we had one).

Boolu's life in the community changed drastically after that day. I went over to St. Vincy to the bookstore to pick up a primer and whatever teaching aids they might have. I found a couple he liked. One was the "A for Apple" book with pictures and the other a Dr. Seuss book. We had fun with them. We worked every morning from about ten to eleven-thirty at the dining-room table. He was a willing student and he wanted to please me in the worst way. I found myself working with him for as long as he would concentrate. Sometimes it was longer than I could concentrate, and then we would stop.

We started our classes right after the showdown in Kenneth's rum shop using the "A for Apple" book. I would point to the "A" and say it, exaggerating my lips, mouth, and tongue movements, and get him to mimic me. When he got close to the right sound, I nodded my approval and encouraged him to repeat it over and over and over again, along with me. I would point to the "A" and then to the picture of the apple, accentuating the "A" sound and shape then repeating the word "apple" and so on, with "B" for "boy," "C" for "cat," "D" for "dog," "E" for "egg," and "F" for "fish."

He got a big kick out of what he thought was the meaning of each letter. At first with every new understanding of the connection between letter and word, he actually thought the letter meant the word, that "A" meant "apple." One day he stood up and ran to the refrigerator, pulled a fish, and said "F"—"effa"—and I had to say "no" and hold up the letter "F" and say "effa." Then I took the fish and said "fish" and pointed to the picture of the fish, saying over and over "fish," "fish," "fish." I had to tell myself to stick to the sound problems first and worry about word meanings with flash cards later. We also worked with numbers using little stones in much the same manner.

I will never forget the evening I heard Brugzie and Carmel, the kids from next-door, out on our porch playing a word game with little Roxanne Williams, a relation of theirs visiting from St. Vincy who later went on to become a news commentator on St. Vincent's Channel 11. She was a little younger than Brugzie, about three years old, and the others were teaching her a sweet little word game for kids. In the middle of all the voices, I heard Boolu's, and he wasn't doing badly at all. Joan had come over, and I could hear her encouraging Boolie. I went out and sat on the balustrade. He was having such a ball I joined in as well. The smile he flashed me was worth a million bucks. There really is a God.

The little word game went thus.

All: "Who stole the cookie from the cookie jar? Was it you, Number 1?"
1st Player: "Not me, can't be."
All: "Then who stole the cookie from the cookie jar?"
1st Player: "Number 2 stole the cookie from the cookie jar."
2nd Player: "Not me, can't be."
All: "Then who stole the cookie from the cookie jar?"
2nd Player: "Number 3 stole the cookie from the cookie jar."
3rd Player: "Not me, can't be."
All: "Then who stole the cookie from the cookie jar?"
3rd Player: "Number 4 stole the cookie from the cookie jar."

On it went and what a time we had. Boolu's speech pattern was moving along, albeit at a very slow pace. But you could hear improvement. I wanted to give him a gift for his hard work, so I asked, "What do you want?"

When he understood, he said, "D fo dog."

I believe it was the first thing he ever asked for with words. I got a puppy from Tim Burgess, the English tinker working on the roads out in Industry. It was a little light-tan Bequia dog that Boolu named Rajje and he couldn't love him enough.

Carnival 1970

February was Carnival time and everyone was busy preparing. The Whaleboner Bar was sponsoring a young woman for the Miss Breadfruit contest. Friendship Hotel was sponsoring another. Molly was preparing one young woman and Ruth was helping out the other. Molly had great material for a dress and was working on a big headdress made from breadfruit tree branches. The contestant was short, like Josephine Baker but without the personality or the looks. All Molly's work went for naught against Ruth's contestant for she was the beautiful Paulette, Sandy's favorite waitress from the hotel and the daughter of our housekeeper, Winnie. In spite of the official contestants, it was as if the Beautiful Barkeep of Bequia and the New York Cover Girl were competing. Needless to say, "Rootie's" protégée won.

I shared the running commentary with Eloise Simmons, the cooking teacher from the Harbour school. I felt like a poor man's Bert Parks without the "Here she is—Miss America!" But I sang "Danny Boy" and "Stranger in Paradise" with a West Indian beat and I enjoyed doing that. Winnie, Paulette's mother, was as proud as a peacock that night.

Early spring was upon us and still no progress with the deed. Unless we started to build, our land license would run out and we wouldn't be able to renew it for the same property unless the present legalities were settled. Or, we could wait for that and start all over again, But Sandy said he would be dead before he could move in if that were the case. So he said, "Jimmy, what do you say? St. Vincent doesn't know what's going on in Bequia. They don't even seem to care very much. I say, don't talk about it, don't tell anyone, not even Japheth, and let them all think we have the deed. The only one you should talk to would be Erma. I think we can assume she wants to see this work out for us as much as we do."

So that is exactly what I did.

And Away We Go

The first day, Japheth came with a few men, and we staked out the driveway and the three main sections of the house. Once that was done, he would enlarge the crew and start to dig. I hoped and prayed we were finally on our way. Japheth gave me a list of tools needed to start the job. The

DE TREE A WE

Women Carrying Rocks for House

laborers here, except for Japheth and the second carpenter, had no tools. I had to make a trip to St. Vincy to pick up pickaxes, shovels, buckets, sledge hammers, nails, lumber, and galvanize. We would need a shack for the tools and bags of cement and a strong padlock.

When I showed up the first day on the site, I wasn't prepared for what I saw. Almost half the crew was women. After the introductions, I took Japheth aside and said, "You told me nothing about these women. What on earth can they do around here?

Jay answered, "Just wait and you'll see. They are on every construction site around here."

I found out soon enough that they did all the carrying of stones, sand, cement, and dirt, whatever needed moving except the really heavy stuff. I then noticed a middle-aged, one-legged woman sitting on a large rock with a crutch at her side. Now, I thought, I have seen everything. I went over the Japheth once more and quietly under my breath asked, "What about the lady sitting on the rock over there?"

"What about her?" asked Japheth.

"What about her?!" I repeated. "She's only got one leg, that's what."

"Oh, Lillian. She can do the work as well as anyone." He went on, "Carry stones, sand, everything. You just wait."

"Even if she can, I couldn't let a woman in that condition do such heavy manual labor," I explained.

He said, "If you don't, what's she going to do? She needs the job. She has three young girls at home to feed and care for, with no man. I always give her a job to help her out. She needs this job more than the others. Believe me, she can hold her own against any of the rest."

Naturally, I went along Japheth, but every time I saw her climbing up that steep hill with a crutch under one arm and two stones the size of loaves of bread on her head, it tore at my insides. I couldn't even look at her for the longest time. But I soon saw why Japheth had Lillian on the job. She was charming and intelligent. In spite of it all, she was full of fun. Her attitude was remarkable, and she became one of my favorite people.

12 Sandy Hellbent on Bequia

The work moved along slowly but steadily, inch by inch. At first I thought we would never finish at the rate it was going and it would wind up costing a fortune. That was before I made out the first weekly payroll. I couldn't believe the numbers Japheth gave me. Why the whole crew didn't make what one laborer was being paid in New York City! The government's pay rate for women was a little over US $1.50 a day! I told Sandy, "At these prices, how good can they possibly be? I think I'd better make sure the work is up to standard. That'll be a big job, I'll have to keep an eye out constantly."

Was I ever wrong! One Saturday, when I brought the payroll envelopes to Japheth so he could distribute them, I noticed that one young fellow, Christmas, whom I recognized as one of his best workers, didn't get an envelope. I asked him about it and he said, "Oh, Mr. Jimmy, I don't get no pay," adding proudly, "I am an apprentice." I was shocked but said nothing.

When they all left, I asked Japheth about it.

"That's right," he said. "That is the way of it down here. Apprentices do not get paid."

I said, "Japheth, I'm finding out day by day that there's a lot about this place that's too much like Charles Dickens's England, and I'm going to change some things around here. You know, Japheth, I'm going to start right here and now by giving Christmas a salary. Good God! It's little enough as it is."

"Well, it's you who will be paying him, not me," said Jay.

"That's true, Jay. It's little enough."

With the galvanize shack built it was time to order the cement. In St. Vincent, I bought 500 bags at $2 BeeWee. You never buy more than you need at once because it gets hard fast due to the dampness. Thank God we were having dry weather and we were going to make good use of it. There were plenty of cement pours just waiting to get done on our place.

When Sandy arrived in the summer of '70, he was amazed at our progress and delighted to see walls going up. It prompted him to say, "We have to get those Wallace girls going on their survey so we can get our deed."

I was concerned about how Sandy would take to living in a crude, sparsely equipped local house with no hot water, one thirty-inch army cot, plastic not-so-easy chairs, no pictures on the walls except my house sketches, bare light bulbs, and no lamps. He never complained, never said a word. I could see he was working hard to adjust by pointing out the assets.

"There are great breezes out here on the point," he said. "And the big long deck out back overlooking the sea—once we get comfortable lounges out there, we'll do fine. The spot is private, very private, and now we've got Winnie, our very own cook, cooking our very own food. Remember, Jimmy, the price, the price is right. Who knows how long you'll have to be here. We have to save somewhere, right?"

"Yeah, right," I said.

Boolu was very much in evidence, pumping water, helping Winnie in the kitchen, and doing his lessons with me. Sandy was impressed with his progress under my tutelage. One day he said to me, "We have got to talk, but not with Boolu around when we do."

This statement worried me, but I said nothing. Best I wait for him to take the lead. After Boolu had finished the dishes, he walked Winnie home, as he often did. When they had gone, I looked at Sandy and said, "So?"

Sandy said, "It's about this Boolu thing. Do you know what you're getting yourself into?"

Not knowing where he was going with this question, I said nothing.

He continued, "Don't misunderstand me. I love what you're doing with him, and I'm proud of you both. He has improved so much with your help. It's what the next step will be that I'm referring to. He can walk out of here any time. You don't know anything about him. Why, you don't even know his mother or father. Even you say his grandmother is a little strange at best."

I interrupted him. "So. They're not Boolu."

"I know, Jimmy, I know. But how in the hell is he going to turn out? You have no idea?"

"Who does?" I answered.

"No, Jimmy, listen to me. I don't want you to get hurt. He can do anything. You don't really know this society. He could turn out to be just any other ruffian, thief, drunk, or dope addict. They're all here. The point is he could walk out any time, sooner or later, without so much as a how-do-you-do. If it happens to be later, you'll be that much more attached, and it will leave you with a deep feeling of loss. No matter how you look at it, loss... That is hurt."

I said nothing.

"OK, OK. Just give it some time and think about it," he said, as he got up to go out back onto the deck.

Later, I went out and sat next to him. "Sandy," I said, "if he walks out of here, when he walks out of here, or how he walks out of here—no matter what—he will be walking out of here with more than he walked in with. I'm just going to have to live with that, Sandy. Remember, he picked us, we didn't pick him."

Sandy looked me straight in the eye and said, "If you can do that and have it not tear you up, I say fine with me. It would take a stronger man than I am. I hope to God you're right and I want you to know you have my blessing. I'll back you on this one."

"Thank you." We shook hands, and hugged.

'Tis The Season 1970

Christmas was around the corner and Father Adams and the church board were having a fundraiser for roof materials for the new high school being built. Pam and Nick Myatt, Bill and Jane Brown, the Kelly's from Park, and Tom and Beege were involved in this project. They were planning a costume party on the 15th of December out at Industry. I decided to go as Santa Clause. Joan Stowe said she would run up the suit on her machine, so off I went to Vincent for material. It was the usual Friendship Rose trip, but a little rougher than usual. It always is at that time of year.

I couldn't find any flannel but I did come across some red cheesecloth. Now that was an idea! I could go as the first see-through Santa Claus. See-through blouses and shirts were all the rage, so why not a see-through Santa? I bought plenty of white cotton, some black velvet, and a buckle for a belt, and I finished it off with rubber boots. I took it all back to Joan on Bequia who went to work on it pronto. I was going to use cotton for the beard but I wasn't satisfied with how it turned out. Joan suggested a white mop from the hardware store, which worked out great.

I went to the dance as Santa in his worship, wearing a fancy dress shirt that Rootie designed, not in his red suit. At 10 PM I rushed home. Earlier that day, Joan had sewn up two large sheets on three sides, and before we went to the dance Boolu and I had blown up balloons and filled the big bag with them. When I got home, I quickly changed in to my red suit, stuffed the big bag of balloons in the back of the open Moke, and "tore rass" down the road to Industry Beach again. As I rounded the point between Spring and Industry, I could hear the band playing "Jingle Bells." I gunned the motor and raced as fast as I could, then flew out of the Moke and into the dance hall with the huge bag of balloons on my back while the band was still playing "Jingle Bells." The judging of the costumes was just about ready to start. I won first place. When I got up on the stage, I opened the bag and the balloons all few out over the heads of the crowd, with everyone hooting and hollering.

Jimmy as Santa

Santa Claus had made his virgin visit to Bequia. Until then they had celebrated Christmas only in the churches and the rum shops, with no celebration at home for the children except the family Christmas pork or ham. The people had sense of the spirit of giving or of Santa.

The next day Father Adams hailed me as I passed by in the Moke. "How about bringing Santa to my Sunday-school children? We'll have a Christmas party. You know, children on this Island, and many adults for that matter, have never seen Santa. Oh, they know him from books, songs, and magazines but never in the flesh."

"That's a good idea, Father, but what about all the other children? How many can there be, five or six hundred?" I asked.

"I don't know. I suppose so," he said.

I told him, "I'll look into it, Father. Thanks for the idea."

I immediately went into the Customs Office and presented the idea to Cosmus Cozier, the Customs officer, who greeted it with a big broad smile. I then went into the police station and spoke to Captain Sergeant, and lastly I discussed it with Joan and Winnie at the house. They liked the idea. People on Bequia are never demonstrative, always just a little bit guarded, gun-shy you might say. So I went with my own gut feeling. "OK, that's it!" I said to myself. "I'm doing it."

First I made the rounds of all the businesses and hotels on the Island. They were filling up with guests. I solicited funds, something I had never done in my life. My brother Ed was a hell of a lot better at it, and I am here to prove it—he was always hitting me up for one charity or another.

I got up at 5:30 one morning, no other way, to go over to St. Vincent. I bought cases of bagged sweeties, 100 trinkets of this, 100 trinkets of that. I got boxes of balloons, 300 plastic whistles and 300 plastic necklaces and bracelets. I picked up lots of bubble gum and pencils and small paper pads as well. In total, the number of pieces came to 2400. I bought well over 600 plastic bags to put the goodies in.

Daphne of "Daphne Cooks It" went to the mothers and asked them to make a Christmas cake if they could manage it. Tiare Austin bought a plastic garbage container that she filled with orange Kool-Aid and ice. Teenagers from La Pompe and Kim McDowell and her sister Elizabeth from Paget Farm came to help me fill the bags. Early the week of the event, we set up a Ping Pong table with a mangy simulation of a decorated Christmas tree. Japheth had built us a red, black, and white century box with a striped red and white North Pole and a sign announcing the date and time of Santa's arrival. The century box was big enough to house the cases of toys.

The Big Day Had Arrived

On the big day, we took off to Goff Wallace's in Belmont. He helped Boolu, who was Santa's Helper, and me into a dinghy and put the boxes of bags filled with sweeties balloons, and trinkets into his car. So Sinterklaas and Zwarte Piet took off in the dinghy out to the center of the Harbour, and Goff took off in his Moke for the big almond tree in the Harbour. He put the cases

12 Sandy Hellbent on Bequia

Santa sails into Bequia

into the century box up on the platform while Santa and his helper sailed around the bay ringing their bells, skirting around the yachts in the Harbour before docking at the pier.

This day was another first for Bequia, and hundreds showed up for the occasion. Joan Stowe and the church mothers came early and lined the children up in front of the century box and the pathetic Christmas tree on the Ping Pong table. All the children, both boys and girls, were dressed up in their Sunday best. When Santa arrived at the pier, he was greeted by teenagers asking for their little handout. Santa told them to wait, the little ones came first. That they didn't seem to comprehend.

When Santa disembarked onto the pier and headed over to the century post, he couldn't help but be touched and a little overcome and the sight before him. They were all so beautiful, dressed up in their "Sunday-go-ta-meetins" and full of happy anticipation of what was coming next. The moment was infectious. Then Boolu mounted too and took out a box of plastic bags full of goodies. I said, "Boolu, just one at a time, and keep the door of the century box closed."

Although the scene was peaceful, the crowd was large and the teenagers concerned me. I had a hunch that anything could happen. I asked Mrs. Lynn Joshua to come up and help me. She was a big strong woman with a voice to match, no shrinking violet. I gave her my box, Boolu gave me another, and we started. We handed the bags of goodies to the little ones reaching up for them, and they were then led away over to Tiare for a drink. The second group was led away clutching their bags, which were a little too big for their tiny hands. I was hearing some rumblings in the crowd and so was Lynn because she spoke up, "There is enough for all, if you will just be patient!" I spotted Cosmus, the Customs officer, in his very official uniform and asked him to come up and

Santa's gift giveaway

help. His movement through the crowd caused people to start jostling for position, but he made it to the table and got up. Boolu got a box out for Cosmus, and then the ruckus started in earnest.

Some adults called out to Cosmus to throw them a bag for their kid. When he didn't, they started to push forward. Thank God, the very little ones were gone by now, but the next tranche of children wasn't much bigger. The yelling seemed to incite the crowd to push forward that much harder. The little ones in front were being shoved under the table. I saw one child going and yelled to Lynn Joshua to grab that kid. She did, and slapping a bag into her little hand, she pulled the child up and held her out over the heads of the other children and into and over the crowd of adults, who passed her over their heads, all with the crushing of bodies behind them pushing them forward and no one yielding a mite. By now, women were hollering as well as the men and teenagers. Everyone wanted a bag, and some were even asking for more. Most were afraid they wouldn't get one. Lynn was now grabbing child after child and sailing them out over the heads of the crowd. I was too, but I was leery of letting go of a child. The adults seemed to catch on to what Lynn was doing and reached out for the children to pass them back over their heads, but no one gave up their spot in the crowd.

Cosmus was throwing bag after bag into the crowd now. The crowd was becoming riotous bordering on pandemonium. The teenagers got the idea they could tip the Ping Pong table platform if they rocked it from the back, so we were bouncing up and down. Boolu was frozen to his post, keeping the door closed and steadying the century box as it rocked back and forth. I saw the tall police captain standing in back with some of his men nearby. I called to him to come up and take charge, but he shook his head no. So I yelled for him to take a case of goodies from Boolu to distribute back there so it would disperse some of the crowd.

He yelled back to me over the din of the crowd. "I don't want de sweeties. I want de house before it mash up."

I couldn't believe what I heard. I yelled back, mad as hell, "Well, ya better goddamn well come and get it now, because it's going fast!" as it rocked back and forth on its foundation. Joan heard me and yelled back that she would take a box to pass out behind the crushing crowd, and another strong man said he would, too. "Come around to Boolu and get them," I shouted. They came around to the side of the platform where Boolu gave them each a box that they took to the road at the back of the crowd. There they were able to pass some bags out, thus dispersing the crushing crowd somewhat. The kids were as bad as the adults. Even if they could get out from under the forward-pressing crowd, they wouldn't, until they got a bag. Even as young as they were, they behaved as if it were survival of the fittest.

Lynn Joshua was still picking up kids, slapping bags into their hands, and sending them out over the heads of the adults. I went to Boolu at the side of the platform to see how many boxes were left and, when I turned back to throw out a few bags, I felt a pull on my sleeve. I tried to knock whoever it was off with my elbow, without looking back—who had time? After three tugs, I put both hands together and clenched them into a double fist. I turned around and without looking brought it down on whoever's head, with a few choice four-letter words as well. With whoever still hanging on and bobbing back up again, I heard, "But it's Tantie Tiny, I'm on the committee." She was only seventy-five years young and weighed no more than a sparrow. I took her by both hands and told her to step down because she could get hurt badly.

I couldn't take one step after the other, all three of us were bouncing up and down perilously. Most of the kids were gone now, and the riot had reached a fever pitch. Only two boxes remained. I handed one to Cosmus, still smiling, and one to Lynn and said, "Here, just throw the whole damned box at them." I turned to Boolu and said, "Come Boolu, let's get the hell out of here, and fast, before they eat us alive."

We dashed off down the beach in the direction of the Frangipani and Miz Marie, the hotel accountant and assistant manager. She saw me coming, my cotton trim hanging and flying in all directions and the cheesecloth suit in tatters.

"What do you want me to do?" she asked me.

"Give me the key to your house up in the back," I pleaded.

"It's open," she said.

"Good, I'll see you later," I said, not stopping. "Come on, hurry up, Boolu, Let's get out of sight."

He never said a word, just followed along. He was a real brick.

To this day, I still can't believe that not one child was hurt, or even scraped. There really is a God. If any one of those kids had gotten hurt, it would have been on my head.

The young rapscallions and roustabouts of the Island had it all over the Bequia grapevine the next day that Santa Clause had slept with Miz Marie that night.

Organs And Moonlight

Sandy was back and we all spent Christmas together at Joan's little blue cottage on the point between Friendship and La Pompe. Sandy had missed Boolu and me playing Santa, but it was just as well.

I was getting to know so many people that I felt I could do more in the community. So I offered my services to Father Adams. I said, "I know this is late but I just got the idea. Father, I was a singer for years and if I could be of service at midnight mass, I'm more than willing."

"Well," he said, "we don't have a choir yet—I haven't been here very long myself—but we do have an organist. If she can play your music, I would be pleased to have you sing something at the offertory. Mrs. Benn, our organist, lives just across from the church. You can go over now and talk to her. It's the yellow house. I know she's home. Is it 'Mr. Jimmy'?" he asked.

"Well, it's just 'Jimmy,'" I said.

"From what I hear, it's 'Mr. Jimmy,' and that's what I'll call you if you don't mind."

Mrs. Benn was home and I explained why Father had sent me.

She asked, "What are you going to sing? I'm not that good."

I said, "Not to worry." (God, I thought, I'm speaking Bequian again.) "What about a simple carol like 'O Holy Night'?"

"I know that," she said.

So I said, "Fine. Could you play it up a third? I'm a high tenor."

She smiled at me. "I think so."

That was the gist of our conversation, and of "we rehearsal" as the locals would put it.

When I told Sandy, the first thing he said was, "Did you rehearse with her?"

"No," I said.

"When are you going to?" he asked.

"We don't have to. It's a simple carol," I explained.

"Well, this I have to hear. I'm going to be front and center."

He wasn't front and center. He was in the middle of the congregation right in the center of the church. I was up in the choir loft at the back of the church waiting for the offertory and singing the carols with everyone else. The first thing I noticed was that although Mrs. Benn played the beginning chords all right, she then relied mostly on the right hand melody line, which she was secure in. But the left hand wasn't always there. Or rather, it was there, but not always where it was supposed to be. She was obviously self-taught. When we came to "O Holy Night," she played the first chord in the correct key all right and the first phrase of the melody. Then I began, "O holy night/the stars are brightly shining..." At the point she hit an F#, it stuck like a bagpipe, like the drone of the bass burden on a bagpipe, except it was F# and it would continue until she stopped pumping. But it was a very old foot-pedal organ. Mrs.

Benn didn't stop pumping. If she had stopped, the organ would have stopped altogether and then she wouldn't have been able to play. So she went right on pumping and playing the melody line. I went on too. I could see the back of Sandy's head as he screwed it tightly into his shoulders. Deeper and deeper it sank into his neck socket. Sandy was in misery. His neck disappeared just like I knew he wished he could. I just blocked the steady monotone of the persistent F# and kept going as the organ droned onto the bitter end.

After the service the congregation congratulated me, telling me how much they enjoyed my singing as if nothing unusual had happened. As she was locking up the organ after the service, Mrs. Benn did say, "Sorry, I forgot to tell you the old lady sticks sometimes."

I found Sandy hiding in the Moke. "How did you do it? It was awful."

"Simple," I answered. "Just turned the organ off mentally and went right on singing."

Sandy retorted, "Too bad she didn't."

"Didn't what?"

"Didn't turn the damned organ off as well."

As it turned out, that congregation had been listening to that F# stick for months had been singing through it for God knows how long. If they could do it, then why the hell couldn't I?

Thus I was initiated.

New Year's Eve came and we were staying home. But not Boolu. To Boolu it was Old Year's Night. To me, it had the feel of Halloween with garbage thrown about, rocks in the road, and overturned outhouses. Yet Boolu was going over to Friendship and he was dolling up like a real "soccer boy," as the locals put it.

Pat Field was still here, but not with Rootie any more. She had moved out of the hotel and into Joan's smaller house up by the road with Jane, her girlfriend from New York. During the evening Pat said, "Let's spend New Year's up at the site."

Sandy was all for it, and I agreed. "There's no house yet, but let's go anyway."

We took a flashlight, a hurricane lamp, glasses, and a bottle of wine. We took off at 11:30. A breeze blew softly and the moon, almost full, sat high in the heavens shining so brightly that we didn't need our flashlight at all. We sat on the cement steps that had yet to be tiled leading to the large front doors that were not yet installed. With the incomplete stone walls reaching up into the sky and the rough white concrete columns embracing the moonlight, it looked a Greek ruin.

Minutes to midnight, I said, "The people of the Island say at the stroke of midnight the winds stop and everything is still for the merrymaking and jump-up to start."

As surely as I am writing this, seconds before the stroke of twelve the winds stopped dead and the leaves on the trees stood still. So did we. For that moment, we just stood there looking at each other. Then whooo-wheee, the wind started coming in off the sea again. Happy! Happy! Happy! 1971, here we come. Was it an omen? A good one, I hoped.

13 Cinnamon Buns and Silverballi

Mystique On Mustique Across The Channel

After the holidays, Molly was hearing all kinds of reports coming out of the next island to the south of us called Mustique. As well as a house at Moon Hole, Dick Burk, Molly's dad, owned the yacht *Oh Life*, which enabled her to take trips to the neighboring islands. She had been over on Mustique many times and knew many of the young English employees working for Colin Tennant, the new owner of the island. His wife was Lady Anne, Princess Margaret's lady-in-waiting, which was a royal appointment for life, I am told. Colin formed the Mustique Company and was preparing the island for development. He refurbished the old Cotton House, converting it into a small hotel and adding a pool. He fixed up a little village and built what the Bequians called "Tennant's tenements" to house the workers he intended to employ, mostly from St. Vincent. He had Oliver Messsel, the British theatrical designer, come and design personalized cottages for the rich people he hoped would buy them. In brief, he was attempting to transform it into an instant island paradise. I was told he made a big show of giving Princess Margaret a three-acre plot and the promise of a house as well. It may have been a ploy to attract the jet set to the island as investors. If so, it seemed to work.

The project launch was to be four days of activities and celebrations. The editor of Queen's Magazine came along with the photographer Lord Litchfield, who was a friend of the Princess and her husband, Lord Snowden. Snowden, also a photographer, would not come to Mustique with them, remaining in Barbados because he felt Colin was using his wife. He may have had other reasons, but I wouldn't doubt this was one of them. Princess Margaret later told me she didn't care if Tennant was using her; he had given her a good-sized piece of land and said he would build her a house.

I am sure Colin knew of the tall, beautiful blonde over on Bequia. He may also have seen her photo-spread in Look magazine featuring "The Beautiful Barkeep of Bequia" going about her everyday business on the Island. One of the pictures showed Molly in a revealing macramé dress she had made herself. This photo alone would have warranted an invitation from Colin. Indeed, she got one and asked me to go with her. I asked her, "Where in the hell will we stay?"

Molly said, "No problem. We'll go over on Oh Life and sleep on the boat."

"Sure, why not? We'll show them how hoi-polloi can hobnob with the upper crust without batting an eye," I said.

That first afternoon, we arrived for high tea early because Molly wanted to spend a little time with her friends, the young English women who worked for Tennant, before the others arrived. We were sitting in an out-of-the-way alcove in comfortable overstuffed easy chairs. The English women were discussing royal protocol and one told us, "Remember, when you are talking to the Princess, you always refer to her as 'Mum.'"

I said, "You don't call her by her name or not even Princess? She isn't my mum. She's a Princess, Ms. Margaret, or Mrs. Snowden. 'Mum' is going to be very hard for me. Maybe 'Madam,' I could do that."

One of the young women said, "That's not funny. That's the way it is. So best you don't talk to her."

"We'll, I'll keep my distance. But, Molly, you want to meet her real bad, so just remember 'mum mum mum's the word.'" And we laughed.

Then who approached the group and broke up the laughter? It was Madam herself. All the young women jumped up instantly, so I did too. The talkative Englishwoman did the honors and everyone did the "pleased-to-meet-you, Mum" bit. When it came my turn, I thought I would break the mold and I said, "My pleasure, Ma'am." She chose a chair in the middle of the small group and bent over slightly as if to sit, whereupon we all did, sinking instantly into the overstuffed chairs. She, not sitting all the way down as we all had, was able to pull herself straight up instantly. Then she stood there smiling while all the women tried clumsily to regain their standing positions. I could see she was a very proud Princess who was pleased with her little prank, as she watched the four embarrassed women fumble in their seats trying to get back up on their feet. Well, that's a bitchy act if ever I saw one, I thought. Oh, by the way, I never moved from my chair. The Princess only looked over at me for my reaction and smiled.

After that, the conversation struggled along with the women completely unnerved, until, thank God, Colin came along. I could tell that high tea was turning into a double-vodka fest. Her Royal Highness had arrived with one in her fist. Over her other wrist was looped a huge leather handbag, just like the ones you would see hanging on her big sister's arm back in England. But here in the tropics it truly looked out of place.

One night, sitting around after dinner in the Cotton House lounge playing parlor games that I hadn't played in years, we finally segued into William Tannis from Bequia singing the song from The Brothers Karamazov. Next, an Englishman sang an old sea chantey. Then Colin said, "I'm told you're a fine tenor, Jimmy. Let's hear from Bequia again."

Oh God! I hate this. Singing on stage was one thing, but I was not at all like my father who loved to sing anytime and anywhere. When cornered, I always did an Irish ballad. At another gathering later that weekend, Colin was looking for performers again and Madam spoke up and said, "Come on, Jimmy, you have a big voice."

I thought to my Irish self, "Oh, 'big,' is it? That's all. Well I'll be damned if you'll be getting another 'big' one from me, girl."

"Do you know 'Green Grow the Rashes, O'?" she asked.

I replied, "No, Ma'am, but I do know 'The Wearing of the Green.'" Silence fell, and Colin graciously picked up the ball from there.

The next afternoon a small group was invited to a picnic on Macaroni Beach. We were all told that the Princess would not be available for pictures in her bathing suit. Well, as luck would have it, Lord Litchfield took some of her in her bathing costume anyway and he later sent them to Molly, who gave one to me. I eventually sent it to my "mum" in one of my letters to her. I referred to "PM" as "Nut Meg," a term of endearment bestowed upon her by us locals. My mom wrote back thanking me for the picture and said, "I don't know about 'Nut Meg' but get a load of those cinnamon buns!" My mom, Irish Catholic as she was, still liked and appreciated the Queen Mother, so I feel she was a little impressed by all this.

At the picnic, we frolicked on the beach most of the afternoon. There were beach umbrellas, chairs, ice buckets, and plenty of drinks, but no food. I was getting hungry. We had no lunch because we, Molly and I, had expected a picnic. I thought maybe we had misunderstood and was beginning to give up on the idea until we were led up from the beach to a flat grassy area. There the staff had set up a long dining table with double-damask linen, china, silver and crystal, the whole shebang. It looked like a French Impressionist painting. I said to Molly, "Look, no place cards. Let's sit at the bottom end of the table. That way we can avoid a royal faux pas."

Molly said, "Yeah, and the scintillating conversation. I don't think she likes me anyway."

"Don't feel bad," I said. "I don't think she likes you either. To be honest, I think your looks are a little too rich for her blue blood, ha ha."

We sat opposite each other, the last two at the foot of the long table. Now we could enjoy ourselves at last. After all, we had come together. Down at the other end, or, depending on your perspective, up at the other end at the head of the table, sat "Ms. Mum" with an empty chair on her right. Mum looked up and said, loud enough for all to hear, "Doesn't anybody like me?" And I thought, "Yes, Molly."

Colin, looking up from directing the staff who were busy preparing to serve, asked, "Where's Jimmy? He's supposed to be sitting there on your right."

Molly kicked me under the table and said, "You're on."

"Oh, God, who am I? The guest of honor? I thought she was."

Molly said, "Well, I'm certainly not, so get your ass up there. Your public awaits."

So, felling sheepishly yet trying to be nonchalant, I sauntered up along the table, wondering what the hell we were going to talk about. Well, we talked. We must have, since sitting on her left was the Carnival Queen from St. Vincent and it was obvious Mum couldn't have cared less. She ignored her and left her to the gentleman on her left. I do remember we talked about apples and rainbows. I don't remember why we were talking about apples, but there I was naming all the various types of apples in America. I didn't know if she was having me on or what. She was tickled, if you can call it that, at my favorite: the McIntosh apple.

"McIntosh, a Scott," she said. "In England, to me anyway, an apple is an apple. You Americans have so much of everything even apples have to have names, ha."

For some reason, she asked me if I had ever seen a moon rainbow and I told her that I had, double rainbow up over Friendship Bay, and that it had been an awesome experience. She said, "I saw one on the way to my sister's at Balmoral."

"Sister?" I questioned, blankly. "Oh, yes, of course, Mum."

"Elizabeth's place... Ye-e-es..." and then she went on at great length describing the mystical beauty of it. I had to agree they really are.

That night was the big dinner-dance with many locals invited. It was a night to really mix, drinks and everything else as well. Whether it was really mixing or slumming I wasn't sure, or was I? That was the question, but don't look to me for the answer. As the Frenchman once said, "Not my prob-hub-blem." All I knew was someone was supplying the Princess with one local bruiser after another. One thing I can say about the old girl, she sure looked as if she loved every minute of it. Well, I hoped so for her sake because she danced on and on, all night long.

The next afternoon we were invited to a very small gathering on the beach. We splashed in the sea at Macaroni Bay and intermittently sun-bathed sitting on the sand on beach towels. It was obvious to me who planned this jaunt to the beach. I had noticed very few women.

Now Colin was a foppish, eccentric gentleman but he was bright and well informed and he seemed to be well aware of Milady's tastes. He had quite a brain. He remembered everyone's name and was in control of everything happening around him. He was well versed in whatever subject came up. Lounging around in the sand, he guided the group's conversation. If he hadn't been so foppish, he would have made an excellent diplomat. I could see why the Princess liked to be around him and I could understand Snowden's absence. Colin paid her all the deference and attention imaginable, and she loved every minute of it. She ate it up like luscious fudge.

At one point they were discussing Tom Lehrer, the song-writer and satirist now retired from a very short public career of only six or seven years. Margaret loved his work, as did I. Colin started to recite his works. First came "Be Prepared" with its revised Boy Scout pledge: "Don't solicit for you sister, that's not nice/Unless you get a good percentage of her price." Next, Margaret recited "I Wanna Go Back to Dixie": "Back to the arms of dear ol' Mammy/Her cookin' lousy and her hands are clammy/But what the hell, it's home." Now it was my turn with "The Vatican Rag": "First you get down on your knees/Fiddle with your rosaries/Bow your head with great respect/And genuflect, genuflect, genuflect." And then I added a take-off verse I had heard somewhere. "My shoes are by Dolman and my beads are by Spellman the man elect/And genuflect, genuflect, genuflect." And she would laugh and laugh.

I noticed Colin, Lady Anne, and even the others who were English concentrating their total attention on her every minute. The repartee between everyone and Princess Margaret went on and on. Colin's memory was fantastic and hers was, too. They never let up for a minute. I didn't know about anyone else but I just decided to relax for the first time and before I knew it I was having a good time. By this time the others were getting restless. Princess Margaret stood up and said, "I want to go in again," and as if by some preordained pact, no one moved. She looked at me and said, "Come on, Jimmy, let's you and I go." What was I going to say? No...?

Not waiting for an answer, she took off for the other end of the bay before she entered the water. It was a long way down the beach and I wondered why the distance. She bobbed around on her naturally endowed water wings while I floundered to stay afloat in water over my head. She proceeded to carry on a conversation with me. I thought, God, I could find a better place to be doing this. I felt I was being interviewed. When I said I had worked in musicals for ten years she told me if she had had her druthers she would have loved being on the boards. I thought I should introduce her to Sandy, he's already taught princesses—there was Princess Grace and Princess Radziwill that I know of, not to mention all the movie queens. Sandy would only have said, "Too late." Such is life. She wanted to know why I was retiring so early and all about the house I was building. She told me Colin had given her land and promised her a house, but was trying to renege on the house offer. She said she was going to hold him to it. I told her on my last job I had served as director of a drama school in Harlem. She said, "Harlem." She hesitated, "Blacks, that's blacks."

"Yes, all black."

"That must have been very trying." She added, "It is just as difficult in London, you know. Do you know, if you were applying for a job and I were applying for the same job and a black wanted it, which would get it?"

I wish I had had the chutzpah to say what I was thinking, "Yes. You," but I didn't.

She continued, "That's right, the black would get it." She went on. "It's getting very bad in London, just like the States, and they're barely down out of the trees."

We were out there bobbing up and down, and I thought of Aileen, the cook at the hotel whose boyfriend was a secret service agent for the police in St. Vincent. He was at this very instant hanging up in a tree on her future property on Macaroni Bay, looking after her safety and wellbeing, protecting her from the likes of me. I wished she weren't telling me this stuff; such corny clichés were beneath her. God, that one statement could cause a riot. I never told anyone except Sandy, who said, "Why were you shocked? What would you expect from the likes of her? Why, she's actually no different from any of our upper class, privileged young ladies educated in an ultra-private finishing school in New England. Just because she's a princess doesn't make her any the less human. She has her hang-ups like anyone else."

Funny, during all this personal talk, she never once mentioned Molly. The Princess never asked me about my relationship with my friend. I was positive that Molly's suspicion was warranted, that she was persona non grata.

That evening was the grand cocktail party and dinner. Colin told Molly it was going to be a photo op for Queen's Magazine, so would she please wear her very revealing hand-made macramé gown as featured in Look. She had been planning to wear it anyway.

The Princess stood at the entrance to the Cotton House with Lord Litchfeld and his camera. She was holding court as it were, greeting the guests in the reception line. When Molly and I approached, she took one look at Molly's dress and turned to Litchfield, saying in a voice loud enough for all to hear, "Don't you think it is a bit lesbianish?"

As we passed, she shook my hand and said, "Good evening."

I could see Molly was devastated, totally destroyed. One could see the old girl was expert at this, and Molly, though very beautiful, was too young and inexperienced to handle someone with the long track record "Nut Meg" had. Molly's evening was ruined. We left early with no goodbyes and took off for Bequia and Friendship Bay at the break of daylight.

Twenty-Five Feet Of Volcanic Rock

Back on the job, I could see Japheth was having trouble in the deep sections of the volcanic cliff. The excavation was becoming too hard for the manual pickaxes. Underneath the inner corner of the kitchen area where a nine-foot water tank was to be built, we still had five more feet to go. The driveway at the top called for a twenty-three-foot cut into cliff, and we still had nine feet to go. They were not big areas, and if there was absolutely nothing we

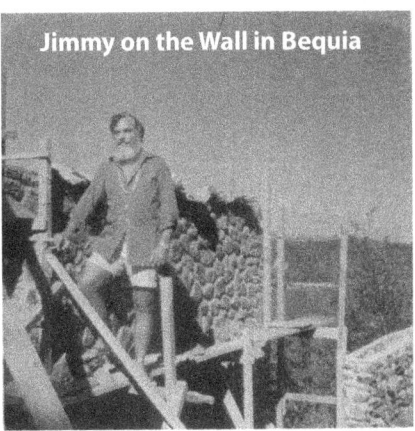

Jimmy on the Wall in Bequia

could use to cut into that dense stone, I would just have to build around them.

As luck would have it, the government was in the process of building roads, after a fashion. "After a fashion" played into our hands. One could say the road progressed in fits and starts. Sometimes it was for want of materials; other times it was a lack of finances; still others, it was just inclement weather. At the job site, an oil-driven, heavy-duty, portable power drill was kept ready, with two government workers assigned to it to operate the compressor. When the road workers worked, the compressor operators worked; when the road workers didn't work, they didn't work either. At least that was the government's way of handling it. Japheth felt that just maybe he could convince the men they could make a little something on the side if they came to our site between the fits and starts.

They agreed. Henry pulled the compressor up the rugged driveway, and the men flattened out a spot for it. The two bruisers only charged me their government pay. They said they were doing the government a favor keeping it running. Sitting idly in the rain and sail wasn't doing the compressor any good. So for a total of US $12 a day, we got two strapping men, the compressor, and the drill bits. They even broke a drill bit on the dense rock in the upper corner in the bargain but assured me the government would replace it, when they needed it. What a windfall it all was! My problems were solved for the month as well. There is a God, even for the little things, only that really wasn't so little to me.

A Family Visit

A couple of weeks after we started work on the property, I had a visit from my younger sister Carol and her husband Jim. We had that extra bedroom in the house so they stayed with us. Boolu was in seventh heaven having company in the house. He went swimming with them every day and showed off with his antics in the water.

Carol and Jim wanted to take Boolu into the Harbour with them shopping. They wanted to get him something, something he wanted and could pick out himself. When they were ready to go, Boolu was nowhere to be seen. We looked and looked but we couldn't find him. So they went without him.

When I asked Joan's little girl Antoinette if she knew where Boolu was, she said, "Oh, Mista Jimmy, he be unda de house."

I went and dragged him out. I asked, "What are doing under there? Don't you know they wanted to take you to the Harbour?"

He looked up at me, shaking his head.

I kept saying, "Why?"

All he said was, "Over der, it be Boo, Boo, Boo."

I knew exactly what he meant. On the other side of the Island where he came from, he might still be ridiculed and he didn't want Carol or Jim to see the way he used to be treated. When they came back, they brought him fins and a spear gun. It was too bad he didn't get to go with them. He would have had a grand time. But he was too proud to have them see him in that light and that made me proud of him.

I was also proud to take Jim and Carol up to the building site and show them the progress of the cut. They went over the whole site as I pointed out where the kitchen, living room, master bedroom, and their guest bedroom would be. Standing where the pool was going to be someday, they were most impressed with the spectacular view. Their stay was much too short, and when they left, I said, "Don't stay away too long, ya hear?" That "too long" turned out to be one month short of thirty years! First their son Jamie was born, then daughter Carrie, then Jim's jobs, first in New York and then in Washington and then back to New York again, kept getting in the way. Finally, once the kids grew up, Carol took a job as assessor to the town of Tenafly.

That was the way of it for all my family and friends except for the ones I made down here. It hurt at first, until I realized that most thought of Bequia the same way I had when I first read about it—the Island sounded and the pictures looked beautiful, but it was much too far away for a short vacation. To most of them, Florida made more sense when it came to taking a vacation in the sun. Mom and Dad and my sister Joan were the exceptions. My mom said she loved it here. It reminded her of the Old Country. She wouldn't have thought twice about moving here if it hadn't been for all those grandchildren and great-children of hers back in the States.

Construction Continues

The stone wall along the back of the guest bedroom on the first floor rose straight up to serve as the back wall of the living room on the second floor and further up to serve as the front wall of the dining room on the third floor. It was over thirty-three feet high at its tallest point. That same wall wrapped seventy-five feet around the curvature of the hill facing the sea and extended to the edge of our property. Behind it one day would be a swimming pool, off the third level in front of the dining room. The front wall of the guest bedroom and the living room above were supported by twenty-two-foot reinforced concrete columns. Building this massive structure was an almost impossible feat,

Construction in Bequia

but the men did it without question and seemingly without inordinate effort. Let me remind you we had no electric power, so no power tools, nor did we even have water on the property yet. All this labor was done manually.

While I was away getting wood, Japheth arranged to pour the ten-foot-wide concrete deck that wrapped forty feet around the living room across the front and around the side. Then the workers would be ready to start the stone steps outside leading from the guest bedroom downstairs up to the front door.

Nor did I have to be present for the completion of the water tank. I knew they could build water tanks in their sleep. It was going to be thick enough and built on solid rock. It was going to be thirty-four feet by sixteen feet by nine feet, with a support wall in the center. I felt safe leaving all this in Japheth's hands.

The Trek To South America

As that work went on, I was making tracks for Guyana to order the wood. I had met Sam Ghanny, who was supplying St. Vincent with South American hardwoods from Guyana. He had stopped on Bequia to talk to Son Mitchell, our government representative, who was planning to build a house next to his Frangipani Hotel. When Son introduced me to Ghanny, I took him aside and asked about the possibility of my going to Guyana to see the lumber mill and make a direct order there. What I didn't add was that I would be able to bypass dealing with the merchants in St. Vincent. I was going to need more than a boatload of wood and I didn't see why I should pay the one hundred-percent markup to them. I think what won Ghanny over was that I was interested enough in his work that I would go all the way to Guyana to see the family lumber mill.

So we made a gentlemen's agreement and he told me the best time to come when he would be there. In no time, I was on my way to Georgetown. I had to stop over in Trinidad to change flights. Unfortunately, when I had left Bequia, I had forgotten the immunization history card a traveler had to carry in those days while out of the country. I couldn't enter the country. I was escorted like a prisoner from the plane to a crude and dirty medical facility where I was given the necessary shots, which I had to pay for, and then released. I barely made my connection to Guyana.

We landed out near the bauxite mines of Guyana. The taxi drove along the wide Demerara River leading to its delta west of the city. As I traveled all the way into the center of Georgetown, I could see Georgetown was something else. I had never seen a place like it except in old movies with Sidney Greenstreet, Humphrey Bogart, and Peter Lorre. The tall buildings, like the huge ramshackle hotel and even the cathedral, were all made of wood. Picture St. Patrick's in New York built of wood. All the buildings were mid-Victorian. I just loved it. It was hard for me to fathom all this expensive mahogany hardwood used so extravagantly. I was the type of guy who would ooh and ah over a door or headboard of African mahogany up on 83rd Street.

The place was beautiful, lush with many shades of green and every tropical flower imaginable. But Guyana was a dangerous place to be at the time, with political factions fighting for control. The unrest was similar to many countries in Africa and especially critical the week of my visit because the next week an election was to take place. That first week, the place was in turmoil with German shepherds and Doberman pinschers in every yard and all the people living behind locked wrought-iron bars.

I shouldn't generalize, I know, but it looked to me as if the English, who governed, were on the side of the Blacks while the communists, and I use the term loosely—they were more like socialists—were on the side of the East Indians, and the indigenous Amerindians were inconsequential. All I know was that the "socialistic" East Indians, with whom I happened to be doing business, treated me very hospitably.

I had been warned by the customs and immigration officials at the port of entry to stay inside and off the streets. Great, I thought. How the hell am I going to get anything accomplished? People told me I had to be careful of the "choke-and-rob" thugs roaming around Georgetown. Demoralized by poverty and lack of opportunity, they were ruthless. Most had been trained by the English in the art of man-to-man combat before the last election to subdue any disturbances during the transition of power. Now that the English faction was in and the transition completed, the young men's services were no longer needed and they'd been released, dumped back into the general population without jobs. The result was the unsafe environment on the streets of Georgetown after dark.

One night, I found myself in an unpleasant situation. I actually saw a choke-and-rob in progress from the veranda of the hotel. Just across the street from the hotel was a disco. The street was divided by a wide grassy savannah. The concierge warned hotel guests not to cross it alone, but a smartass Texan had tried and ended up losing his money, charge cards, and watch. That was all I needed to see. I never went anywhere after dark, except for the steak house in the middle of the next block. When I went there, I ran like hell. Those thick, tender steaks, the likes of which I hadn't had in over a year, were easy to take.

The bank manager in Bequia was from Georgetown and had asked me to visit his family while I was there. His wife was my bookkeeper. Before I had ever left Bequia, he advised me always, no matter how hot, to keep the windows of the car shut and the doors locked driving around Georgetown. That had been the first time I'd heard of choke-and-rob. At the time I had thought, Oh, I see, just like Harlem. It turned out to be worse, much worse. England certainly did mess up a lot around the world, didn't she?

The Mazralli brothers, who owned the lumber company, took me up in their Piper Cub. We flew up the Mazaruni River where they pointed out their timberland. I couldn't help but think what a prosperous country Guyana should be. We flew to the west up the coast over every delta almost to Venezuela, where the lumber mill was situated, and they pointed out the railway I would take to get there the next day.

The train ride from Georgetown was an experience in itself. We crossed vast deltas, bridge after bridge, and passed through one little bayou village after another. The wider stretches of the delta had to be crossed by railroad barges. The bayou villages and the swampy coastline reminded me of Louisiana only the coastline was more colossal and tropical, with even wider stretches of water to cross. On the other hand, the temples dotting the landscape were reminiscent of India.

When I jumped out of the jeep that had been sent to meet me at the end of the railroad track, I was greeted by Ghanny, a number of mill hands, and a group of attractive women in saris. I was taken to a private two-story home near the lumber mill and given a room. Later Ghanny took me through the mill and introduced me to the mill manager, whom I was to do business with. I had all my measurements—lengths, widths, and breadths or depths, and the total number of each. I sure hoped I was correct, or at least close to it. It was more than Ghanny's boat could transport at once. His boat was seaworthy but not large enough for such a big order. I hated to think what it would be like if I had to rely on Vincentian merchants for all this wood. I would have to settle for treated pitch pine like most Vincentians did, and it was inferior. Well, I was winging it and I hoped to hell God was with me.

I found some of the customs around the house strange, and the food too, but I did my best. Every night the table would be set with many place settings. The food was placed on the table, many dishes of all kinds including succulent fresh crabmeat, lamb roti, and hot curried goat. Every night looked like a feast. Then the food was covered with cloths and netting. The women told me in broken English to help myself when I was ready and not to wait for the men, as they would be back much later. Then the women dispersed, where to, I didn't know, I guess to bed. I waited for the men the first night, but when they hadn't arrived by midnight, I decided to eat alone and go to bed. I didn't know when the men came in. I assumed they were in a rum shop drinking and playing cards, dominos, or whatever Indian men gamble with. Every night they came back noisily in the wee hours, ate, and then dispersed, I knew not where. I never did see the women eat. Ghanny wasn't there—he lived in Georgetown—and only the manager and the head woman of the house spoke English. It was a lonely week but an intriguing one, with only the manager to talk to, and yet every one showed me deference.

Ghanny came out my last day there and told me about an Englishman who was a very good cabinetmaker in Georgetown. Would I be interested?

I asked, "What about all my doors, could he do them?"

"Why not?" Ghanny said. "I could ship him the wood. He could make them and then send them back to me for shipment to Bequia on the second shipment."

13 Cinnamon Buns and Silverballi

I thought of what the mill manager had told me about the pilfering on the docks and how the government did little or nothing to prevent it. This wood did not get onto the docks in Georgetown.

He explained, "When I go to St. Vincent, I just take off from up here. We are all the same up here, not to worry."

So I asked, "What about the doors in Georgetown with the Englishman?"

"Gemmie," Ghanny said, "the Englishman is a gentleman, you will see, and it is the Mozralli men who will be doing the deliveries. OK?"

"Then I will have to stay over in Georgetown and design the doors before he can make them."

"That will be good because I want you to meet my wife and children."

On the way back to Georgetown on the rickety old train, I daydreamed about the pending wood order and where it would end up and how it would look. I bought purpleheart, greenheart, and silverballi, all woods that appealed to me because of their durability and resistance to woodlice. The living room would be in purbleheart, which looked like African mahogany, the dining room in greenheart, which was like a dark blond mahogany, and the master bedroom in silverballi (the name itself was intriguing). Some of the wood was going to be humongous (4'x6'x34") and heavy as lead. The boards were so dense they would sink in the sea. How would the men manage to get those heavy beams up on those high walls once I got them home (if I got them home)? I decided I would be very Bequian about this: "Not to worry, not to hurry." They would find a way. They'd built schooners, hadn't they?

Once back at the hotel, I purchased drafting paper and other supplies and found a place to work on the design of the doors. As I sat there drawing, I could hear the loudspeaker from the election campaign and all the noise and hoopla of the rallies. I had visions of TV and newspapers back home running a little article about an American builder shot and dragged through the streets for conducting business with the communists. It was not without trepidation that I attended the dinner party where Ghanny's wife introduced me to her friend, Janet Jagan, a former Chicagoan who was wife of the Leader of the Opposition. Not only did the English dislike her but the Americans consider her persona non grata as well. The Honorable Cheddi Jagan, the previous prime minister, having lost the last election, was fighting to get back into office. He eventually did, and years later, after her husband's death in 1997, Janet Jagan became prime minister herself. I must say they were very nice people and seemed to me from my limited knowledge of the country to be doing a hell of a lot more productive and humane activities for the less fortunate than the other side.

In spite of everything, I took a day off and went to the mammoth market where I bought a lovely Indian filigree gold necklace for myself, a heavy gold-nugget watchband for Sandy that he loved and wore until he died, and a gold chain with a peace symbol for Boolu. I also found a lamp shop where I purchased sixteen English lamps that they shipped to Bequia for me.

I finished my drawings and took them to the English cabinetmaker. He was a lovely old man and willing to please. He took my drawings and said he would do his best to get them finished before Ghanny's shipping date. What else could I expect? When he finished he billed Ghanny, who paid him. The fifty-odd cabinet and room doors he made cost only US $26 each and some of them were nine feet high, three feet wide, and three and four inches thick!

Two weeks had passed, and my work here was completed.

Successfully? I wouldn't know till it all arrived on Bequia. I packed my bag and headed for home.

This Job Was Up To Sandy

When I got home, I called Sandy to give him the update on the lumber. As it turned out, the total cost of the wood on the Bequia dock was going to come in at a dollar BeeWee a running foot. At the exchange rate ten, it came to US 37½ cents. I was ecstatic.

Sandy said, "Great! See, you did it again."

"Not yet. Too soon." I said. "The wood isn't on Bequia yet. The boat could sink, you know, and then what?"

He said, "Don't tempt the fates." Then he went on. "Now, the next step we should attend to is to check on the furniture that was sent to storage and then begin thinking of the appliances we'll need."

The lawyer had told us no duty would be charged on all our personal possessions when we first came to the Island, as is the case for Nationals if they've been out of the country for a certain length of time. So this exemption covered everything we had or would need in the house. When I was in Guyana, Sandy had been out with Paul shopping up a storm. They went to Sloan's on Fifth Avenue of all places for garden furniture, but then that was Sandy. He got the latest caloric stove with a top oven, a refrigerator, a clothes washer and dryer, a water pump, and a hot-water heater. He also picked up some power tools: electric saw, drill, rooter, and sander.

When he told me, I was amazed. "Sandy, you impress me! You've never shopped so much in your life and probably never will again!"

I could see we were really on our way now. When all this stuff would arrive was still another matter, and when we would get hooked up to electricity was anybody's guess. But when it happened, we would be home free.

"Sandy," I said, "I'll have to find a place to keep all these things until the house is ready for them. Maybe Joan's old empty shop up on the road will hold them. I'll check with her. Golly, Sandy, I can't believe you did all that. You really surprise me. I'm so proud of you."

"OK, OK, just get back to work. You have a lot of work still ahead of you."

"OK, OK, hang up now."

"No, you hang up."

"I'm paying on this end. Love ya," I added.

14 Coming Together

Sandy's Social Life

Sandy was back in the wind, sleet, and snow-swept canyons of New York to begin the winter semester. With his new apartment at 440 East 57th Street and Paul's place just around the corner, the two of them were able to see a lot of each other. Paul loved to cook and invited Sandy for dinner along with old friends. He would get Stella Adler and her cousin Pearlie to come over. Harold Clurman, Dorothy Patten, Bobby Lewis, Beanie Barker, Ruth Nelson, Virginia Farmer, Luther Adler, and Paul's friend, English actor John Gielgud, were some of the old crowd invited over. Vivian Matalon and English actor friend Alec McCowen, Kim Hunter, and Robert Emmett were also regular guests. Sandy appreciated these dinner parties, and they kept him from feeling lonely. Many ex-students as well would stop by for a talk or advice, Ken Cory, Jon Voight, and Bill Alderson among them. Elizabeth Wilson and Kathleen Nolan both had apartments only a block away, and they stopped by for an occasional chat. Dick Dunn, a daytime TV producer-director and former student, lived down the street on Sutton Place. It was the wonderful location of Sandy's apartment that kept him and his friends coming and going and allowed him a rich and supportive social life. Since he hated to be alone, it was a great, soothing place for him and Nora to be, except for the time a drive-by shooter happened to put two bullet holes in the plate glass doors of his building. At the time New York wasn't the safest place in the world to be, no matter where you lived.

Stones

On Bequia I busied myself with the foundations waiting to be dug, ordering cement, sand, water, and stone, stone, and more stone. The cement was in St. Vincent, the sand was on the beach, and water was in a tank down the road at David's place, the house Japheth had just completed.

Now about the stones! By mid-summer the walls were going up. I needed stones and I didn't get them from the quarry. Why not? I asked myself that questions many, many times after my decision not to use quarry stone. I had come up with the smart idea that I didn't want cut stone, I wanted full, round fieldstone. These stones are found in unaltered form lying on the ground individually. Most of them are back up in the bush, spewed up from the belly of volcanoes before the age of reason. My workers, three women and two men, offered to get them for me. What they didn't tell me was that they had to crawl up in under the mosquito-infested bushes, find the stones, and pile them up in heaps for Henry to cart away in his truck. The day I went, out of pure curiosity, to see the job they were doing, I was covered in mosquitoes and ended up with bites all over me.

When I got out of the bush, I asked, "Don't the mosquitoes bother you?"

Their answer was "Yeah, they do."

"So why didn't you tell me? I have to do something about this! And I will," I said as I left.

I went to the Harbour and bought liberal amounts of insect and bug spray. I brought it back to the group and told them to tell me when they needed more. They couldn't have been more pleased if I had given them a three-day week. The whole incident embarrassed me greatly. I later asked them how it was going and they said, "Oh, Mr. Jimmy, just fine please. So easy to fix, and to think they never told me. I thought of one of Sandy's lessons: "Never assume anything."

The stones were found on an undeveloped piece of property in Gellizeau belonging to the Ollivierre family who lived out there. Dolly Ollivierre had arranged with Japheth to let us take the stones for a price based on so much per truckload.

One day Japheth told me, "Dolly is driving me crazy. She say's I'm cheating her but I am not. Henry keeps very good track."

"I'll take care of it, Jay."

What I didn't know, because no one ever told me, not even Japheth, was that she was the biggest "Bequia virago" in Paget Farm.

Soon afterward, I spotted her coming down the road by Kenneth's. I told Sandy I was going up to meet her and talk to her about the stone problem.

"Japheth was upset," I told her, "because you called him a thief."

"Well, he is," she replied. "Henry took out twelve loads last week, and Japheth only paid me for eleven and a half," she yelled at me in stentorian tones and by now every window or door on the street was ever so slowly opening.

"Dolly, that's because Henry only took eleven and a half."

"I counted twelve!" she yelled back at me. "I know because I see from my window and I counted Henry taking out twelve loads."

"Dolly, that's because it rained Saturday morning and they couldn't get a whole load, so Henry only picked up a half load." She was so indignant that I was becoming upset. And I went on, "Where do you come off calling him a thief? How much of this money is going over to your two sisters in St. Vincent, who own the property along with you? Should I give them a call?"

She took off down the road in a snit. She went right on selling us stones until we were finished, thank God, but didn't speak to me for three years after that. Much later, when I was doing special work with her son in school, we ran into each other at the post office. She came up to me to me and said, "Don't you speak to anyone anymore?"

I answered, "I speak to anyone who speaks to me."

"Well, I'm speaking now," said she.

"Well, that's just fine," said I. "As you can see, I'm speaking to you."

Then she said, "I want to thank you for helping my boy Eddie in school."
We then became fast friends. She was a complicated lady.

After our little confrontation over the stone, Sandy was waiting for me out on the porch.

"How much do you pay for a load of stone?" he asked.

"Fifteen dollars."

He repeated, "Fifteen dollars a truckload?"

"A load," I came back.

"Then half a load is…?" Sandy asked.

"Oh, God," I said, exasperated. "Seven-fifty… EC."

"Jimmy?"

"EC, Sandy," I reiterated.

"Do you mean to tell me you were up on that road in front of the whole village making an ass out of yourself for a meager two dollars and eighty-odd cents US?"

There are times when you lose your sense of reality and the place gets the better of you. What else can I say?

Fire! Fire! Fire! Help! Help! Help!

One afternoon, I went to town to get a pound of butter. I was in front of the police station talking to Lee Austin, Debra Wallace, and Chesly from Paget Farm. Lee was the son-in-law of Captain Thompson, the new owner of the Friendship Bay Hotel. (I have implied that the Young brothers were apparently spending their way into oblivion via their benefactor, a member of the Bush family from New England, and indeed they did it in less than four years.) Debra, the clerk-teller in Barclay's Bank, had just come off duty, and the four of us were standing there exchanging the usual niceties when an SOS came over the rather loud marine radio in the police station. The Antilles tourist ship had run aground off the north coast of Mustique.

Lee had the Captain's large motor launch, *Freedom*, at the pier, with Chesly as his crew. He said, "Let's take off and get over there right away." He was, one could say, a rather adventuresome type of guy. We all agreed and the four of us sped off as fast as Lee could make the boat skip over the oncoming swells. It was now about four o'clock and we made it in less than fifteen minutes, never mind the strain on the boat or on Debra, who was in the cabin up-chucking all the way over.

We reached the ship and circumnavigated it, noting it was a little long in the tooth as tourist ships go. We could hear the engines revving up. Obviously the crew felt they could back themselves off the reef, but although they kept up the revving for quite a while, the ship never budged. As we circled the ship, we noticed than an oil slick was building up. We were yelling up to whoever was looking down at us, trying to alert them, but our voices were being carried away on the oncoming breezes. The crew just yelled and waved back as carefree as the breeze.

We were the first boat on the scene. A few yachts were approaching in the distance. I learned later that the first decision on the part of the captain or captains (you see, there were two), was to wait for the rising tide to help lift them. They were also calling Barbados for assistance to pull them off if needed. How long it would have taken for help to arrive from there is anybody's guess.

Meanwhile, we could tell that they were having, for want of a name, a "going aground party"! Everyone had a drink in their hand, and the waiters were passing around cocktail-party food. The more we motored around, the more they waved and the more they partied. We could even hear music coming from a band! It was getting late. We expected them to be abandoning ship by now. As we continued to circle the ship, we were noticing an even greater build-up of oil all around it that was gradually drifting off with the current. The motors had shut down completely now. No one was paying any attention to us as they went on with their celebrating, except for giving us a shout and a wave or two.

We had arrived some time after 4 PM, and the ship wasn't that far from shore. Now, the seas were getting higher with the setting sun. Only about a half hour of daylight remained before nightfall. When night falls in the tropics, it happens very quickly. As we cam around the aft of the ship, we saw what looked to us like a small flickering light.

"Is that a flame?" Lee asked.

"I can't tell in this light," I answered. "The portholes are so small from here. Can you get closer?"

He did, and it was a flame. We then got a little farther out from the boat so we could yell up to the deck to warn them. Forget it—the party was going in earnest. The flames were building higher and higher.

Then the alarm to abandon ship sounded.

By the time everyone had manned the lifeboat stations, it was well after six. We would be losing the sun by six-thirty. Indeed, by the time the lifeboats were filled and in the process of being lowered, it was dark and foreboding. The sea swells were ten feet high and frightening. We were still the only boat in close proximity to the ship. Others were standing off at a safe distance. Obviously they didn't want their precious yachts messed up in all that oil slick.

As the boats were lowered, we could see a couple of them were in trouble. The crew was having difficulty keeping them in alignment from front to back. One almost toppled altogether, but they caught it just in time. As they reached the water, the boatswain unhooked the lifeboats from the cables, and the boats started bobbing about in the oil slick swells. When the passengers were told to push and pull the bar in front of each seat so they could maneuver the lifeboats away from the ship, they found that the bars were frozen in place. All the lifeboats were bobbing about helplessly.

Meanwhile the flames were now shooting high above the smoke stacks.

14 Coming Together

The lifeboat closest to us yelled for help, and Lee taxied slowly over to it in the wide swells. As we drew alongside, we could see the panic on the passengers' faces. We were bobbing up and down too, yet many attempted to board our boat. Lee sped the boat forward then around to the boat again.

"Throw us your line," he instructed. "No one gets on this boat. Just stay in your seats! Do you want to sink all of us?"

They threw us the line, a heavy, two-and-a-half-inch rope covered in slippery oil slime. The line was too big and slippery for the *Freedom*'s cleats, and the lifeboat was big and heavy. It just pulled the cleat out of the fastening bolts holding it. We were compelled to maneuver the lifeboats in to shore manually. Lee was at the controls and Debra was useless. With only Chesly and myself to hang onto the rope, we needed assistance.

Lee yelled out, "We need two strong men and that's all." Four men stood up and Lee pointed, "You and you."

Both boats were floundering about in the sea, each going in its own direction. With difficulty, we helped the two men onto our boat and all four of us grabbed hold of the rope to tow the first boat. It was all we could do to hang on to the slimy thing. Debra found some towels and dry pieces of cloth that we wrapped around the line to help secure our grip. Slowly we inched our way to the pier just across the savannah from the Cotton House. I can't tell you how the passengers disembarked, because Lee didn't wait to find out. We turned about to go after the next boat still floundering out there.

Now other boats, working boats from Paget Farm, were moving in to help. I noted no yachts came in aid, save that of Hugo Money-Coutts, the manager of the Cotton House. We grabbed hold of our second boatload and got them in to safety. We made off for the third boat, but by this time other boats were pulling the floundering lifeboats in, so Lee steered around to the other side of the ship. It looked as if the lifeboats on the side facing the open sea had floated farther away in the stronger current. I could see one being hauled in a little further west of the ship.

We could see a rather large opening in the side of the ship. It looked like a doorway with people standing in it. It was only a few feet above sea level so in spite of the flames lapping up around the smoke stacks, we went in closer. None of us thought about the heavy oil slick building up, getting thicker by the inch all around the ship now, that could burst into flames any minute with our little boat bobbing around in the middle of it. Why, the whole damned ship was in danger of blowing into smithereens in seconds. But who thinks of such things in times like these? I like to think I did, but what choice did we have? People were standing there waiting to be saved.

We pulled up closer and could see they were members of the crew. One was dressed in what looked like a nurse's uniform with makeshift bags stuffed chock-full, but full of what, I asked myself. Anyone could see that they had been running around cleaning out cash registers and jewelry stores. The only way they could get on board our boat was to jump. But before they would jump, they yelled, "Take us to Bequia!"

"This is Mustique," Lee yelled back. Bequia is seven miles from here. We'll take you in here."

Would you believe it? They wouldn't jump, not one of them. From our position on *Freedom*, we could see the flames off in the distance behind them, and it was a roaring inferno by now. Still no one jumped. You would think they were standing at a taxi stand.

At this point I saw a lifeboat drifting out with the current, heading for a large landmass, nothing less than a cluster of rocks sticking out of the water. In no time they would be smashed into splinters on the rocks. I said to Lee, "To hell with these guys. What do they think this is? Look at that lifeboat out there. Let's go!"

So we left them to their own greedy devices. I heard much later that they inflated some rubber life rafts, jumped into them, and floated westward in the strong current. They were plucked out of the dark oily sea to safety just south of Ile de Quatre by Gus Coven's yacht, which had been hovering at a safe distance. The captain, Morris Nicholson, told me. They were then carried to Bequia where they had wanted to go from the very first. Marie Kingston at the Frangipani Hotel and Tiare Austin at Friendship Hotel both told me the crew ended up in either hotel. They spent cash like drunken sailors, which most of them became before morning. Even the woman who looked like the nurse abandoning her posted ended up on Bequia along with the rest of the crew, with her little satchel of loot. What's more, the two captains split just like their crew, leaving their shipwrecked passengers wandering helplessly about on their own with only one office and the doctor to look after them.

When we reached the panic-stricken lifeboat drifting toward the rocks, I could see no member of the crew in charge. The man who did take charge was a Parisian, on vacation with his wife and children, who worked for the municipality of Paris. I learned that later because he wrote me to thank us for saving them. He got into our boat with another tall passenger, and we ever so slowly hauled the boat full of frightened survivors through the swells, which were huge by now. The line was slimy and slick with oil, and gripping the rope over every swell rubbed my hands raw. They ached with each lift. We made it to shore and safety, the last lifeboat in. The Frenchman shook my hand and said something in French as we walked toward the Cotton House.

Lee said, "You go ahead, Jimmy. We'll stay and find a mooring for *Freedom*." I looked at the once sleek and shiny motor launch, the best looking motor launch in the area at that time, and it looked as grubby as an oil-stained derelict.

As we walked along the savannah in front of the Cotton House, we could see all the passengers strung about in small clusters, some sitting on the grass, others standing. Still others were sitting on the steps leading up to the veranda of the small hotel and spilling over onto it. The Frenchman pulled out a little pad and pen and asked for my address, saying he wanted to write me

14 Coming Together

when he reached home. There were over 350 people on the passenger list. I saw no crew members tending to them. If they were there, I didn't see them. No captain was in evidence either, even though two had been on board, or so I was told. (In all fairness, maybe one was in training.) On Mustique I saw no one moving about tending to the passengers. Oh, there was one officer, the officer in charge of passengers when they were at a port of call, but I don't think Mustique was a scheduled port of call. The miracle of this whole fiasco was that no lives were lost.

Mustique had a surreal feeling to it with the survivors disheveled and stunned, and the gracious accommodating Mustique staff dressed in their formal finery in anticipation of their usual formal dinner when all of this broke loose on them. I saw the Mustique workers running about trying to be hospitable. One was mustering up milk for the little ones and hoping to hell they were going to have enough.

I went over to the home of Hugo Money-Coutts. The manager's place was to the left of the Cotton House on a small knoll next to and overlooking the north shore. Moneyy-Coutts was talking on the phone. When he hung up, he said, "This phone has been ringing off its hook! I wish someone would tend to it."

I offered, saying, "I can do that, Hugo. I'm not doing anything. Just let me wash up these sore hands of mine."

So I sat at the telephone as my contribution for the night! Calls flooded in from all over—the St. Vincent police, Barbados, France, New York. Out of St. Vincent, efforts were being made to find a boat large enough to get the survivors over to Barbados, about a hundred miles away. I got one call from Paris, and the guy on the other end said, "Dees ees zee président."

I thought, president of Paris—no, France? No, stupid, the president of the shipping company, of course. I have to admit it took a little time—I was getting tired. I told Hugo, "They want to speak to the captain."

He got the officer who came ashore with the passengers. If I had been able to speak French, I would have told that president myself, "By the way, the captain is mysteriously missing as well as all the other officers except one. Please hold and I will try to find him." But I couldn't so I didn't.

Actually, two officers came ashore, only I didn't know it at the time—the ship's doctor had come along too, minus his nurse.

I received a call telling me that the Queen Elizabeth II was in the area and coming to the rescue. She was equipped to accommodate the full complement of survivors and should be arriving between 4 and 5 AM. The plan was to take them to Barbados. The calls tapered off after that, so I left my post and made tracks for home.

I cannot remember how I got there or who took me back. Obviously, I was on overdrive. I do remember talking to Tiare at the Friendship Hotel where I came ashore and her telling me I looked like a grease monkey and asking me what I had in the mangy bag. I looked at it for the first time and said, "Ohmigod, my butter!"

Boolu, Boolu He Can Too

Boolu was a work in progress in his classes, and getting along with Winnie and Joan and her kids, but now I felt he was ready to expand his experiences. I thought the job-site would be the best place for him to start.

"Japheth," I said, "I have an idea I wish to take up with you. It's about Boolu."

"Boolu? What about Boolu?" Japheth asked.

"I want him to work here half days," I said.

"Work here? The dummy boy? Don't get me wrong, he's a nice boy. But on the job here?"

"Japheth, I know he doesn't look it, but he's the same age as Christmas," I told him. "You've got Christmas learning here on the job, and I feel Boolu could learn a lot working with the women."

Japheth said, "But what will the workers think?"

"Japheth," I said," I don't pay them to think. I pay you to think. But let me tell you, Japheth, if they want their jobs, they will think. They'll think twice and then get over it, and if they want their jobs, they'll agree with me. Japheth, I know I can handle this one. This is going to do Boolu the world of good, and—you know what—everyone else as well. Trust me."

Now I had to tell Boolu he had a job every morning and had to go to school every afternoon. I worked with him every afternoon after lunch and then he went across the street to Erne Dewer who was a former teacher out at Paget who had had quit teaching to make babies instead. She took on the job of teaching him his numbers three days a week, for a nominal fee.

Getting him to understand this new arrangement took a little time. His life was getting a little complicated, but I thought it was about time. When I took him up to the job on Monday morning, he was excited. When the workers arrived, I didn't know what they already knew. So I acted as if they didn't know anything.

"I'm asking you guys and gals to help me here with Boolu. I feel that right now he needs to be around people who treat him with kindness and understanding. He has been neglected and abused for so long and by so many, and this has to change. Not one of you would want one of yours to go through what he has had to face just to get by. Treat him like a mascot," I said.

"A mascot?" some asked.

"That's like a little helpless pet or a doll even," I explained.

I Love A Parade

One day the circus came to Bequia. It really was a circus, the arrival of Japheth and his brother Ormund Hazell in Bequia on their boat the *Rosareen*, loaded down with the goodies that Sandy, with Paul's help, had sent from New York.

14 Coming Together

All our personal effects had reached St. Vincent the day before. Although it was before the days of ship containers, there was no way the international ship was going to make its way over to Bequia. So everything had to be unloaded onto the dock in St. Vincent and reloaded onto another boat for the final lap of its journey to Bequia.

Everything had been unloaded, more truthfully dumped out, onto the pier in St. Vincent awaiting transfer to the *Rosareen*. Japheth and I had just completed the clearing of the manifest and the complicated signing of all the papers in the Customs House and were headed for the pier when I spotted all our possessions lying about helter-skelter, scattered in haphazard heaps on the pier. Then I spied a huge dark rain cloud looming over Cane Garden in the southeast and heading straight for us.

I saw Sandy's 1871 Steinway Grand lying on the pier minus its legs, completely uncovered, exposed to all the elements. I yelled out, "Ormund! Get your men to get these things into the hold quickly before that deluge reaches us. But wait, get this piano on first and get it covered with a tarpaulin before it gets ruined, if it isn't already trashed."

A couple of men just stood there staring at it, and I said in my panic, "Come one! Move your asses!"

One onlooker asked quizzically, "What is it?"

I was so upset, I said, "What difference does it make? It's a coffin for a kangaroo. Now, let's get a move on!"

When we arrived on Bequia, Cosmus decided that instead of clearing everything on the pier, he would wait until we unpacked at Joan's empty store, which was right at the roadside up the hill from the house. That would save unpacking twice. I had asked the authorities for permission to bring our personal things to Bequia in two installments, and they had given their approval. So the second load would be no problem, but this one had me sweating. I had no idea how Cosmus would handle me.

I was nervous about this inspection because we were bringing so many new appliances and all at the same time. Yet we did need them if we were going to live here. Customs could give me a tough time over duty, if they had a mind to. Duty was normally high down here in the first place. That was the way it worked, so this load could cost up plenty. The reason I was staying down here was to cut costs, and I wasn't doing too badly so far. That is, I worried—until to-

Ship Docking in Bequia

day. We had been told we could legally bring in all our personal effects duty-free, but I didn't know for sure that personal effects included brand new purchases. But I had convinced Sandy that I could cut the cost in half by being here, so I had better try.

When the boat arrived, Henry commandeered every jeep, van, truck, and pickup truck on the Island, and Japheth and he soon had them all loaded down with as much as each could carry. In order to control the group, Japheth had all in a line. He wouldn't let them take off individually, but had them move as a convoy.

I was at the site waiting for them to round the point in Friendship. I would have plenty of time to get over to the house after I saw them coming around the bend toward Lower Bay Gutter.

As they left the Harbour, everyone was standing outside their shops looking on. I was told some American shouted, "Here comes Barnum and Bailey!" and someone else yelled, "What's that? A circus parade going to Mr. Jimmy's?"

When I first saw the caravan rounding the point, I thought it looked a little overwhelming for this small Island, and for me as well. There had never been such a large movement of personal possessions all at once before. That's not to say it hasn't happened many times since, because it has. But this being the first time, the Islanders took notice, and the children followed happily along like they do at a parade back home.

When I got to Joan's, she said, "Cosmus Cozier is on the phone."

He said, "Remember, Mr. Jimmy, I didn't check out anything on the pier. I thought it would be better for both of us if I do it when you unpack at Joan's, so you won't have to unpack twice."

"Fine," I said as the trucks were pulling up along the road.

Meanwhile, all of La Pompe was gathering, and half the kids on the island were following the slow-moving convoy as if they were in a carnival road march in Trinidad. I put down the phone and went up the hill to Japheth and Henry.

Henry said, "Here it is, Mr. Jimmy."

"OK," I said. "Now let's you and Japheth get this stuff unloaded as quickly as possible. Take in the large appliances first. You can start with the refrigerator, then the stove, and then the clothes washer and water heater."

With people gathering about, I didn't want everything strung out all over the place. It would be too risky—I could lose control. So I said, "Let's check each vehicle first to see where everything is. We'll leave each driver responsible for his truck until it's unloaded. Here's the refrigerator. Put it in first, way back next to the wall, and then do the stove. Look, there's the pump and the hot water heater. Put them way in the back also."

Everything moved along smoothly. "Here, Jay," I said, "take these electrical tools and have Tutu and Earl put them in our house. We'll be needing them soon." Pointing down to the house, I said, "Come here, Boolu. Tutu, take the tools and put them in Boolu's bedroom." I felt they would be safer there; Cos-

14 Coming Together

mus could check them there later. While the drivers stood by guarding their own jeeps, I said to two more of Japheth's men, "Pick out the small odd pieces of furniture." I had them pile them in a small grouping near the door to the old store in a safe spot away from the curious crowd.

Before Cosmus came, Japheth laid and spread the rugs in front of and blocking most of the appliances. On the last two trucks were large blue and white boxes with the name "Sloan's" plastered across them. "Damn it," I said to myself, "I told Sandy to have someone scuff up the lawn furniture with dirt, and look at them." I was never going to be able to pass them off as old. I told the drivers to pile them up any which way on top of each other, and I told Christmas to keep an eye on them. It was becoming very close quarters due to the crowd. Santa Claus and the calamity of Christmas kept running through my mind.

When Cosmus showed up in his official uniform, cap and all, he said, "You know, I have to check out all this stuff."

I said, "Of course you do," pointing to the open door.

He stepped over to the well-packed garden furniture sitting outside the door all wrapped in its snappy blue and white boxes. "What's this?" he asked.

I heard myself saying, "That's our old garden furniture."

"Old?" he asked me.

"Yes," I said.

"Well, what's all this?" he asked, grabbing hold of one of the Sloan's boxes.

"Oh, Cosmus, that's Sloan's, the moving company. They do that to protect their shipments. That company is something else; you can't believe the lengths they go to. Damage suits can cost them plenty."

He never said a word, as if he didn't know. He then went over to Japheth at the doorway and looked into the house. I was concentrating so heavily on Cosmus that I was unaware of the commotion that was festering behind me over the wooden crates and boxes that had been discarded by the men unloading. The backyard was full of them by now. At this point, Joan called from the house to tell me I had a call from Captain Sergeant.

"Hello," I said.

"Mr. Jimmy, dat you? Listen, I see dem boxes go over de hill. I want ya ta save a couple a dem for me."

When I had heard who it was, I was about to tell him I needed his help. Instead I said, "Captain, if you want a couple of boxes, you had better get over here right now, because they're going fast."

Where had I heard those words before?

When I headed up the hill, the commotion had turned into an all-out brawl over the boxes. As I passed a young policeman stopping an argument, I told him, "I just got a call from your captain, and he wants you to bring him two of those boxes."

I went on up to Japheth and Cosmus who were talking to each other. Most everything had been brought into the old store except the lawn furniture, which was being stacked near the door. I walked over to tell the drivers that Henry would take care of them tomorrow. Some already had an empty box or two in their truck.

I went back to Cosmus, who said, "Here, sign this."

I did, asking, "No duty?"

"No duty. It's all your personal effects, right...? I have to get back to the office." And looking down at the commotion still raging over the empty boxes, he said, "Survival of the fittest, neh, Mr. Jimmy?" And he was off.

I didn't know if he meant the scavengers or me.

Japheth and Christmas were putting the last few pieces of furniture into the store. I was one beat foreigner as I stood there with Japheth as he locked up the place with Joan's padlock. Japheth shook my hand as he handed me the key, and said simply, "One more down."

Most of the crowd had dispersed and the rest were leaving with their boxes. Boolu, Rajje, and I headed down to our temporary digs on the point where Winnie stood on the porch, looking up the hill at us. "What's for dinner?" I cried.

Everything was stowed away safely. That's what I thought we had done, at first. But it didn't take long for me to become apprehensive. I could see the old store up on the road, but the door was on the other side. Every morning, the first thing I did when I left the house was to go up and check the lock. And every time I passed the door during the day, I would check it. The place was too vulnerable, especially after so many people had seen all that was in there, just waiting to be plucked off at the first opportunity. Whenever I heard Rajje barking, I would look out and always up at the store, and there was nothing.

Until one morning when I went to check, and it had finally happened, everything I had feared since the day Japheth had first locked it. The padlock had been broken. I opened the door and went in. Everything seemed to be in place. If anything had been taken, it wasn't much. I looked around as best I could under the circumstances. I did note one missing, very small but sweet, dining room rug that I had purchased in Portugal. It wasn't until we unpacked up at our home much later that we were aware of a missing stand from a fold-up Biedermeier tabletop. Two boxes were also missing. In one were all my scrapbooks and theatrical memorabilia from years past. In the other were lithographs of Civil War officers, both Union and Confederate, some with autographs.

Joan and Winnie felt that our next-door neighbors, men from St. Vincent, were the culprits. They were construction workers from up behind Friendship Bay Hotel living temporarily in the old rundown house that Boolu had lived under more than a year and a half ago. Sure, Joan and Winnie would think that, but who knows for sure? It could just as easily have been any one of the onlookers the day the circus came to town. One thing I am sure of, whether Bequian or Vincentian, their haul was of precious little value to them. And it could have been much more serious for us.

15 Adventures Across the Water

Sink Or Swim

Boolu Showing Off his Back Flip

On Easter Saturday afternoon that year, my friend Marie came to spend the day. We sat on the deck looking out to sea beyond Semple Key, an old whaling island out of the past. Whalers used to take their catch there to be butchered and distributed to the population. It's not used any more and there's nothing on it. A triangular reef extends from the shore to Semple Key, a distance of approximately 100 yards. The point of the triangle reaches the little island, and its twelve-yard base runs along the shore right in front of our house. At low tide, the water can be less than three feet deep.

Marie said, "Look, the tide's changing. It's the time to walk out to the island."

I told her, "I've lived here for over a year and I have never seen anyone go out there."

"Oh, come on, chicken, let's go! You can see it's shallow."

I gave in and said, "We'd better wear shoes."

She had running shoes on, and I got a pair of Sandy's heavy sandals. So with no more than a "Let's go!" we were off on our adventure.

We walked out onto the reef, Marie on the side facing into Friendship Bay, and I on her right, closer to the edge facing the open sea. More than halfway out there the water was getting deeper. I looked down at my feet and found large, round, black sea urchins of the worst kind surrounding me. I floated up off both my feet to avoid the long, spindly, prong-like spurs sticking up at me. I hadn't anticipated the current whipping in from the Atlantic across the outer edge of Hilary Point across Friendship Bay. As the tide was changing, it was rushing directly across the reef. Unfortunately for me, I was on the wrong side, the steep ocean side and just a little too close to the edge of the reef. I was swept off in an instant by the force of the oncoming current. I turned and started to swim back to the reef.

I had never had trouble swimming before. I remember stroking left, right, left, right, but I wasn't getting anywhere. I kept at it for quite a while without giving up, but I still wasn't getting any closer. The water was clear and I could see the bottom as the reef tapered downwards. I thought, if only I could get close enough to put my feet down. Where I was stroking was too deep for footing, except I was able to rest my feet on the tip of a large sea fan, and I was working hard as hell just to stay there. Marie knew I wasn't making it. I yelled, "Marie, I can't make it!"

I could hear Marie calling out now. I gave it one try but the current was pushing me away with every stroke and I got nowhere for my efforts. I had no choice. I gave it one more last-ditch effort. All I achieved was total exhaustion. My chest was pounding; it was really hurting. But the pain was minor. Much worse was that I couldn't breathe. Or I felt like I couldn't breathe, but that wasn't the case. I was gasping in all the air I could, but it didn't seem enough. My adrenalin must have been racing a mile a minute, using up my oxygen like a burning flame.

Marie was still calling out, from the safe side of the reef, near the shallow Friendship Bay side. I was being drawn toward the mouth of the next bay, La Pompe. I gave up fighting and floated on my back. I thought, take it easy, a boat will come. But there was no boat. How could there be? It was about noon and every available boat was out with the fishermen. They wouldn't be back for hours.

Winnie, who had heard the commotion up at the house, came running out with my fins. She tried to get Boolu to put them on to swim out to me. He was afraid of the sharks out there, and the fins would have been too big for him anyway. Winnie was grasping at straws as I was gasping for air. I could hear Joan yelling to Marie about a sailboat. I was thrashing about and I realized that I wasn't being carried into the small bay of La Pompe. I was passing it by. If I hadn't been so tired, I could have angled my way into La Pompe, but it was a long way in to the shore.

When I mustered up enough energy to survey my position, I could see I was heading out beyond the bluff on the far side of La Pompe and into the narrows between Bequia and the neighboring island of Petit Nevis. There the Atlantic becomes a swift current forcing its way through the pass between the next farther island, Isle a Quatre, and Bequia, then surging out into the Caribbean, and eventually flowing all the way to Venezuela. I knew now I could never make the long way into La Pompe fighting the crosscurrent.

There was no hope. I started to pray as loud as I could, making sure He heard me. "Our Father who art... Hail Mary, full of grace..." I didn't know for how long. Later Marie told me she had heard me and started praying too. As I prayed, I felt as if I were settling up, making myself ready for the final trip.

I was truly spent. I feel now that I must have been burning up even more energy in my head than in the muscles of my body. My mind was going like a house afire. Whatever came over me during my prayer I have never been sure of, but it made me turn around and start thrashing like a madman for the reef. I plowed and plowed my way through the water right up to the reef where I could see the sea bottom again. Here the current takes on more strength, where it crosses the reef and falls into the deeper water, rushing like a waterfall does on land. And here I saw out of the corner of my eye a boat off to my left. "Thank God! Thank God!" It was Pellie Cozier and little Boolu.

15 Adventures Across the Water

What happened on shore while I was out there poking away at the sea and thrashing my way from oblivion was miraculous. Joan had a younger brother whom she cared for. He was not quite all there, but harmless. He was somewhere in his thirties and, on top of everything, a hopeless alcoholic. Joan knew that all the boats on my side of the reef were off with the fishermen. But there was one small sailboat on Marie's side of the reef. It would have to be dismantled and dragged across the reef near shore to the ocean side, the deeper side where I was. This was no easy feat for two fishermen. Yet with Joan's direction and help, Pellie, little Boolu, and Marie managed to pull the boat with brute force across the shallow end to the La Pompe side where I was floundering. Pellie and Boolu got in and rowed out to me. I was so exhausted I couldn't pull myself up into the boat. The two of them literally lifted me out of the water, and I fell into it. Between Pellie and Boolu, my life was saved.

When we made it back to the deck of the house, I lay back trying to catch my breath and settle my nerves. Marie kept apologizing. I said, "I was the fool, not you. Forget it! Forget it! It's over." I didn't want to move, I just sat there. In time, Winnie got dinner and we sat down to eat.

After dinner Boolu said, "What to drink?"

Marie said, "Tea." I said simultaneously, "Coffee."

Whereupon Boolu said, "Tea and coffee."

I repeated, "I'll have coffee." At the same time, Marie said, "Coffee, Boolu, and tea."

In a short while we were served. I got my coffee. Marie asked me to taste hers, holding her cup out to me. I did. She got just what she asked for—coffee, and tea!

Soon, Marie left, along with Winnie and Boolu. I hadn't let on through dinner, but I was feeling nervous and on edge. I was frightened. When Boolu got back from taking Winnie home, I told him to stay in my room next to me. I was feeling dizzy so I took a dining room chair and put it in place of the bed stand and asked him to sit while I lay down. I was afraid of going into shock. I told him what to do if I started to shake—go over and get Joan even if it was late, late, late. I was feeling strange, very strange, and I could see by the look on Boolu's face that I was scaring him. I lay on the bed and was out before I knew it.

When I woke up, it was about 6 AM, and Boolu hadn't moved an inch. He was still sitting in the straight back chair right next to me. I told him that everything was OK and to go to bed. Actually, it was. I felt great. It was as if nothing had happened the day before, nothing at all!

It was Easter Sunday, and I was to sing at Holy Cross in Paget Farm. So I washed up, dressed, and left Boolu fast asleep in his room, recovering after his all-night vigil. I jumped into the Moke and made off for the church. I made it just in time for the 7:30 service. This time the organ didn't stick while I sang "I Know That My Redeemer Liveth" from the *Messiah*, with Mrs. Benn chording me through it as best she could.

Whenever the Semple Key misadventure came up in Sandy's presence, he would have a strong negative reaction, never wanting to hear anything about it. It was all too much for him to handle. The whole near-catastrophe had been too close for comfort.

Nora's On Her Way

Back in New York, Sandy was making ready for the big move to take place as soon as Bequia was made ready for him. The plan was for him to move into the Dover Hotel on Lexington and 57th when the one-year lease ran out at 440 East 57th. Then the second installment of furniture at 440 would be sent down to me on Bequia. Nora, our big, black, and beautiful German shepherd, would have to be sent down as well before the move to the Dover.

Nora was a big factor in alleviating Sandy's phobia of loneliness, so this move would be no small loss to him in New York. Because England, and therefore St. Vincent, had stringent quarantine laws banning entry to animals from other countries without their first being cooped up under surveillance for six months, Nora would be sent to Martinique, a French island without quarantine laws. (Now, there's one good thing about France, if you were looking to find one.) This way, Nora would be registered in the West Indies and be allowed to travel in the area legally by boat.

"How will Nora take to being a French citizen?" Sandy joked.

"Not too well, but we don't have to tell her," I replied.

"Oh, yes, we do, but we can promise her we won't ever tell anyone else, and we'll never bring up the subject unless absolutely necessary!" said Sandy.

Soon, Nora was on her way to France in the West Indies. Tiare Austin offered to take me up to Martinique in her schooner, Staffordshire, with Captain Chesly from Paget Farm. Tiare's Aunt Helen, who was visiting Bequia with Tiare's mother, came along for the ride. Tiare had some shopping to do while I picked up Nora. I would then have to smuggle her onto Bequia, and then what? Who knew?

Sandy said, "Whatever you do, don't tell her she's going to be a wetback. She's a very sensitive dog. French, and a wetback—why add insult to injury?" Sometimes his dry humor was too much.

We sailed up the Caribbean side of St. Vincent and St. Lucia to Fort-de-France, Martinique. The day before Nora was to arrive, I went to the authorities to pick up the necessary papers, and the following day I went

Nora in Bequia

out to Lamentin Airport to pick her up. Papers in hand, expecting to run into the same autocratic, burro-cratic, mumbo-jumbo I always ran into on St. Vincent, I was pleasantly surprised at their expeditious efficiency. In no time at all, I had Nora out of her shipping crate and into the back of a cab, doped up with whatever they had sedated her with in New York for the trip.

The boat was moored in the harbor. I got her on board and secured her comfortably to the mast. I took her for walks on the savanna. We waited another day for Tiare to finish her shopping. I spotted a marvelous French bakery that I insisted we load up from before heading back. We had a ball picking out all the luscious little goodies. The young local woman behind the counter couldn't have been more helpful explaining the various ingredients. What a place it was! That is, until we went up front to the cashier. Judging from the way she was ordering everyone around in an unpleasant, arrogant manner, the white French woman with her Parisian accent was obviously the proprietress. She tallied our order and then told me the total in French.

I said, "Excuse me, what is that in English, please?"

She repeated herself, still saying it in French, "$######, s'il vous plait."

I just stood there looking at her. She called the busy clerk over from behind the counter, said something to her, and then the clerk translated for me into English. I paid the woman, but I was furious. She was looking at me with so much contempt because, I must assume, I couldn't speak French, that I said, "F—you, and I bet you understand that!" and we left.

When we got outside, Tiare was as mad as I was. She said, "They take your money quick enough."

I was steaming at the insult and said, "Come on, Tiare, let's take these cream puffs and scrawl 'F—you' on her windows."

Tiare laughed and said, "No, no, we can't do that. They're too delicious. And don't forget the 'gendarmes,' isn't that what they call them?"

And we laughed all the way back to the boat burlesquing a French accent. "Zee gendarme weel get oos for sure, zo let oos get zee 'ell out of 'ere."

The trip was also memorable because of the excessive heat and the unrelentingly broiling sun. There wasn't the slightest breeze, and we had to motor most of the way down-islands. In the lee of St. Vincent, the motor conked out. We bobbed up and down in the motionless sea. The captain said, "At this rate it's going to take us days."

Nora was on her best behavior and in good spirits since she had come out of her stupor and recognized me, but the sweltering heat and excessively slow pace were wearing away at our human nerves. My main concern was Sandy. He was to meet us after dark at the bottom of Lower Bay Hill. The plan was that we would first drop off Nora in a dinghy, making her officially a wetback. Then we would round the point of Tony Gibbons Bay and go into the Harbour for inspection without her.

Sandy went over to Lower Bay and sat on Tiare's deck watching the sun go down and constantly searching the horizon for our boat. Of course, it wasn't there, for reasons unknown to Sandy. Still, he sat there till the wee hours. At 3:30 AM he felt he should get back to the house. What if something serious had happened and they were calling Joan? So a weary and worried Sandy made it over the hill to Friendship and his little blue cottage on the point where Boolu awaited him.

We didn't make it to the tip of St. Vincent till well after daybreak. The breezes were picking up, thank God, and we made it across the pass to Bequia and into Port Elizabeth Harbour, but headed over off the shore of Hamilton out of the direct view of the customs office. If the customs official came, we told Helen, Nora would hide in the john and she could go in with her and strip. Then when the officer started to open the door, she should simply show some skin and say she was dressing.

"You'll have to show enough skin to intimidate him so he'll shut the door on you," I instructed.

"Why me?" she complained.

"You have a thing about bathrooms. Aren't you the one who locked yourself in the bathroom at the hairdresser's in Fort-de-France and were in there all day before anyone knew you were missing?" I teased.

"Oh! Stop it. I couldn't speak French!" she said. "You two are never going to let me forget it." Then, seriously, she added, "What if he doesn't close the door on me?"

"Then you ask him for a date," I advised. By now Tiare was in tears of laughter.

Helen said, "Oh, you're both crazy. I was ready to do it."

The captain had left to take our passports and ship papers to the customs office, hoping the officer in charge wouldn't come out because he knew all of us. While we were sitting in the cabin laughing with Helen, the boat started to drag. All of us ran excitedly up on deck and, unbeknownst to us, so did Nora for any and all in the Harbour to see. Tiare and I settled the anchor again to the sound of car horns. Someone had told Sandy to get over to Hamilton in the Moke. Looking over at the Hamilton shoreline, we could see Sandy and Boolu in the Moke, Rootie and her two kids and Paulette in Rootie's car, "The White Queen," and Pat and Jane bringing up the rear, all honking away and waving.

"Well," I said to Tiare, "so much for the clandestine smuggling attempt."

The captain came back and said, "Everything's fine. Cosmus says 'Hi.' They didn't expect anything. They can't see us too well way back here with the other boats in front of us."

We left the boat quickly, with Nora in tow. I told Boolu to go get in front and I put Nora in back. She was all over Sandy in a flash. I turned to Rootie and said, "Please, disperse the motorcade. We don't need the publicity. We're in the process of sneaking Nora onto the Island. Thanks! Take off now, and we'll see you all later. That is, if we're not in the slammer before nightfall! If we are, please bring us dinner!"

As we neared Port Elizabeth, I told Sandy, "Take the back street and go behind Customs, up the hill and over to Joan's. Not until then will we be home free."

PS: When I was in town the very next morning, Cosmus approached me. "Mr. Jimmy."

"Yes, Coz?"

"When that dog has pups, I want one."

"You bet. You got it. You get the pick of the litter." And he sure did.

This summer my Birthday Card read:

A store-bought gift may heal a rift, if rift there be. A golden charm may ease the pain, if pain there be. But rift or pain that needs a chain of gold to assuage it, is tiny rift and petty pain. Not worth one cent, one penny spent upon it. This potent poem, this un-bought ditty says Happy Birthday in style so witty. There is no choice, say what you will!

With love and devotion to James Carville.

Sandy—Bequia, July 28, 1971—Concert Master

In September 1971, the Bequia Anglican High School opened its doors for the first time in what was formerly Mr. Blusy Simmons's Sail Loft. It was right on the beach in the Harbour over a bar known as the Step Up. The building and bar were owned by the church. It was a temporary housing, since the regular high school was being built on the Spring road over and beyond the Commons. The Harbour Primary School was down across the Commons. Up behind the primary school was the Seventh Day Secondary School overlooking the Commons toward Bequia High.

Bequia Anglican High, or BAH as it came to be known, was started by a husband and wife team from Canada, Bill and Jane Brown. Bill taught language and arts classes while Jane taught math and sciences classes. She had also been a gym teacher. (That should have been an early clue for me, but I didn't pick up on it just then.) They had come to Bequia for two years to kick off the project, starting the school with only the first form of fifty students. Sometime that first month, Bill, the principal, came to me and asked for help with a program celebrating the Harvest Festival. It was the time of year the congregation came to the church with their offering of crop donations. This custom was all part of tithing, an old practice in the church that was still carried out in Bequia, like many other ancient rituals. The celebration was similar to North American Thanksgiving or Crop Over Festival in Barbados, only it was church-oriented.

Bill wanted the school children to participate with a song but he could only find North American songs like "The horse knows the way/ to carry the sleigh/ over the white and drifting snow." I don't think so. He did find one from Hawaii, but still the words were not quite fitting. He came to me and asked what

I thought.

I said, "The Hawaiian song could work, if you just change the vegetables like eddoes, tanyas, pigeon peas, and cassava. Yes, please."

Jane laughed and asked, "Why 'yes, please'?"

I said, "Because they use the expression all the time."

Bill added, "But grammatically?"

"They will think we're making fun of them," Jane said.

"No, no," I said. "They won't think we're making fun of them. It's perfectly normal. What they're saying is 'Yes, if it pleases you.' You see, short speech—Bequia is full of it."

Bill said, "Let's do it. Even if they don't get the joke, we will." Well, they didn't and they loved it.

Then Lynn Joshua cornered me and asked me to help the churchwomen. They wanted to do something for the Harvest Festival as well. "What will you do?" I asked.

"You tell us," she said, "OK?"

We met one evening at Tantie Tiny's and worked there. Josh met me down on the road, and we walked up through the bush on a narrow sandy path. There were houses all around, but none let off much light. Here and there in the houses, a single kerosene lamp flickered on a table, but they were of little use to us out on the path so I followed Josh closely. The ladies were gathered in a room that served as a dining room on the first floor of Tantie Tiny's house. All the chairs had been taken out to make room. The table was still in the middle of the room with the ladies standing all around it in the dim light from the kerosene lantern that sat in the middle of it. Everyone was all jammed together. There wasn't enough room for the crowd that had gathered there. I could see only the outlines of variously shaped bodies, and, except for eyes and white teeth, faces were a blank. Everyone was either short and fat or tall and thin. I could make out only four women I recognized: Josh, Mrs. Benn, Tantie Tiny, and Eldica.

I had brought my pitch pipe for whatever good it would do. I was thinking a round would be good to start with. We could treat the second number antiphonally, and for the finale, I thought a couple of solo patches with the chorus chiming in and out to a big ending with everyone singing full-out would be suitably stirring.

I asked them, "Pick three hymns you would like to do, something like 'The Old Rugged Cross' or 'Nearer My God to Thee.'" At first, no one had an opinion, but after a brief pause, they all started to throw names of hymns around. Eventually Josh, in her inimitable way, got hold of the situation and gave me the name of three hymns. "Fine," I said, "Let's get to work."

I split them in three sections, high, low, and very high and light. I blew a C on the pipe and launched in. We worked for most of two hours. It was pushing nine on the clock, late for a Bequia weeknight. We covered the three hymns that night, and the day of the concert we gathered a second time. Everyone knew the hymns, so all they had to do was remember when to sing and when not to sing.

The night of the concert, the school kids sang in two parts for the first time, and the women did a bang-up job. Doing the hymns in this manner brought out different colors of sounds the likes of which they had never heard before. The women were so proud of themselves and they thought I was a genius. God forbid, one in the family was enough.

Teacher Jimmy

Soon after the concert Father Adams collared me into his office where he asked me if I could donate a little of my time to his newly founded school. Bill and Jane could use all the help they could get, and he thought a person of my background could contribute so much in whatever way I felt best. He expressed how much he would appreciate whatever little time I could manage to part with, said he was well aware of how busy I must be with our house. No money was mentioned. The word "donate" was paramount.

I said, "I suppose so. Let me think about this."

The subject of teaching had come up many times in my life, and I always emphatically rejected the idea of a real job in a regulated school system. It was close to being repulsive to me. In hindsight, I think I know why. To a person who dreamed of performing professionally—in whatever area of the performing arts whether dancing, singing, or acting, and in whatever style—any other activity was a threat to the goal. Just a nine-to-five workday was a threat. A red flag would go up. It was tough enough to develop a career in the entertainment world without getting sidetracked, hindering any progress. Money was the big snare. It was the primary problem if you weren't lucky to have it or some support until you made it. So I was ever so leery of teaching or any nine-to-five job, because they were the culprits, they were the enemy.

Yet, I was always teaching someone something. I never thought of it as teaching; I was just helping. When I was very young, I taught many neighborhood kids how to dance, apparently. More than once someone has told me I was the one who taught them to dance. But to me, I was just playing around. When I was thirteen, my dad the singer started family shows, and I was the one elected to train my seven younger siblings to perform in them. When Joan, my sister, needed help in playing an eight-year-old in her senior class play, I was the one who assisted her in finding the childish behavior in the character. The part won her the Drama Award her senior year, which put money in her pocket. As a member of Calvary Episcopal Church choir in Manhattan, I taught the singer the dance numbers in the fundraising shows.

A much more serious teaching experience in my life came about after my sister Joan's auto accident. After lying comatose for more than three months, she was left with complete amnesia, a total loss of everything she ever knew. So she needed the ultimate help. At twenty-eight, she had the rest of her life to relearn everything that could be learned, and anything else was lost forever. As life would have it, I was free at the time and able to help her with her recovery.

Here I was at it again helping Boolu with his battle for survival on Bequia. And now Father Adams's kids needed some help. Sure, why not?! When I told Sandy about the request from Father, he told me, "If you want to do it, do it. I'll back you. I'll pay your salary. It will be my contribution to the Island. At the same time you can look after my interests here as you always have. So you can have a job down here and everyone is happy."

"Not yet," I said. "I haven't talked to Adams yet." I told Father, "I'll teach at the high school, and Sandy will back the project. It will be his contribution. But only on certain conditions."

"Whose conditions, yours or Sandy's?" Father Adams asked.

"No, of course not Sandy's. Mine," I said. "Music as an elective for students in schools just doesn't cut it. My point is, how can any student be expected to intelligently elect to do or not to do something they know absolutely nothing about? That's not even considering that music can have an effect on all their other studies. Didn't Socrates say that music and art were an essential part of one's overall education?"

"That's right, Socrates, Plato, or Hercules, one of those guys like that," Father laughed. "I'm with you. So what's your plan?"

"I will have to have the students, and I mean all the students, the first year they're here. Their first year will consist of Rudiments of Music, Music Appreciation, and Chorus. With these subjects, they'll become aware of the materials of music, they'll hear fine music, and they'll make music, I hope. All three subjects will be compulsory and not electives. The electives start the second year. Then they're in a position to choose, to elect once they know what they're electing," I said.

"That sounds just fine with me," he said.

"Wait, Father," I said. "There is one more thing, and it's a stickler. About the grading of the students: I would insist that first year music courses be computed in with all other courses and averaged into the total that decides the students' standing in class. This way the arts will be on an equal footing with every other subject in school. The students won't have to wait till they reach college before they value music the same as every other subject." Father told me he was OK with these conditions and would not interfere. I must say that in the entire eight years I was there he never messed with me once and supported me in every way.

When Sandy offered to pay my salary, everything changed. Until then, I had been living my life moment-to-moment, project-to-project. I had been planning to go back to New York to look for work when I finished the house here. I always had a theater job of some sort there. Now he was making it possible for me to stay on Bequia. I chose at that point, and not before, to stay, and to try a stint at teaching.

16 Fait Accompli

Bye-Bye New York

In October '71 the lease was up at 440 East 57th Street, and the interminable wait for the short move back to the Dover Hotel across 57th was over. Sandy's elegant surroundings at 83rd Street were rented and 57th Street was gone. Nora had been sent to Bequia. Every part and parcel of our personal effects still in America was being packed and shipped to St. Vincent. The shipment wouldn't make it to Bequia till long after Christmas. The timing worked for me up on the hill in the new house. We would be well settled in by then and ready to receive it.

The two-room suite at the Dover was a far cry from what Sandy was used to. To him, the hotel was sparse and temporary by comparison, but exactly what he expected it to be as he forced himself to change his lifestyle. The worst part was missing his dog. The good thing about the Dover was that all he had to do was pack, close the door, hand the key to the desk clerk, pay his bill, and walk away. Life would now center around his soon-to-be-completed home in the tropics. New York's East Side and the Neighborhood Playhouse would no longer be home, or so he told me anyway. He was making ready for his approaching retirement in his own way. He was getting closer by the minute to his ultimate goal. In truth he wouldn't have been able to afford such a move if he hadn't been making it just now. He got a second mortgage on 83rd Street, he had the rental income from it, and he took on extra classes. Even though he was a giant in his field, the closest he ever got to Wall Street was Canal Street.

Bobble, Bobble, Boil, And Trouble

"Bobble" was a name given to an ancient practice here in the West Indies, an illegal way of trading that benefited the consumer. The buyer dealt with the merchant and, since each side the transaction was in a different jurisdiction, avoided government intervention. The practice eliminated tariffs, just and unjust alike. The boys on the job were planning a run to St. Bart's. They asked me what I needed, but I said I couldn't do that, I could get into a lot of trouble doing such a thing. They said, "Not to worry, everybody does it around here."

"Everybody?" I queried.

"Well, a lot a dem, Mr. Jimmy," one of them assured me. It was like a regular business, he explained. What a temptation it was. He went on, "So, what do you want?"

"Oh, don't get me wrong. I can't order anything, but I would accept anything as a gift, and I would be generous and very grateful," I joked. Bobble is one thing and barter is another, I mentioned.

"Well, we get booze, cigarettes, cameras, anything."

"I don't need anything now, but booze is good anytime."

He persisted. "What kind?"

"Oh, vodka, rum, wine. I could use it all." That was the extent of our talk.

Weeks passed and on a moonless night dark as pitch, I heard tap, tap, tap on the windowpane. I got up, turned on a light, and pulled back the curtain. A face stared up at me, a horrifying face, like something right out of an old pirate movie. He told me to snuff the light and come out. Out on the deck, I saw a dark figure all scrunched up as if he were hiding from someone, but no one else was there. He motioned for me to follow. He led me down through the bush under the trees and out onto the clearing on the reef where a local fishing boat had been drawn ashore. It held cases of liquor.

The leader of the group asked, "Where you want us to put dem, Mr. Jimmy?"

I said, "Up under the house beyond the deck." I had once found Boolu hiding in there and I thought it was a good place. I could put it in the house later.

When I saw the loads they were bringing in, I truly thought they were using me as a supply base. It couldn't all be for me. What do I do, I wondered, call the police? I knew in seconds they would be gone. I should have, a good citizen would have, but I didn't have a phone. What is the sense? I didn't know them. I couldn't bring this stuff into the house. So I left it there. After all, I reasoned, I have to live with these people, not the Vincentian police. All the police had ever done for me was ask for Santa's century box and our empty packing boxes.

Days passed and I got a call at Joan's from a well-known, influential woman in the Harbour saying, "I'm just calling you to tell you, they're coming over to the south side to make a bobble bust." What is it she knows that I don't know that she knows? What do I do? I knew the answer: do what anyone else around here would do. I was one of them now. So I nervously talked myself into believing that I knew from nothing.

I called Boolu, and we moved the stash down by the reef beyond the bush among the sea grass bushes. We couldn't even cover them from view so we just left them there with grass and leaves over them. They stayed there for well over a week before Boolu and I went down there one night and brought them back in under the house.

Back on the job, I guess when the all-clear went out, one of my men came by and asked if I was pleased with my gift. I asked, "All? I'm not opening a rum shop."

He answered, "All."

I asked, "How much?... That's all?" I said, astounded, and I said no more.

16 Fait Accompli

It wasn't long before Sandy arrived and we were on our way up to the house on the hill, moving in, the whole kit and caboodle. That stash of liquor lasted well over a year and all for less than US $100, not bad considering our social activities. We hosted many sit-down dinner parties accompanied by wine, Sandy drank his double vodkas at sunset, we held local rum salutes of appreciation for a job well done shared with the local workers once in awhile, and we held card parties with drinks aplenty in the living room.

Move-in Time

Once I started teaching at the school, the movement up on the job-site slowed down to a snail's pace. My best workers were milling about like they were novices. I tried to nudge them on, but nothing seemed to change. On December 15 Sandy came up to the site and saw the workers shilly-shallying around and talking to each other as if there were no tomorrow.

He took me aside and said, "What do you expect? You have a damn big crew here and if they finish the job, where are they going to find more work? Tell me, where is the next job coming from? I don't see building sites springing up around here. You're going to have to take a stand. The only way you can get this house finished is to tell them it is finished."

"OK," I said to Sandy, "We're moving in." I went over to Japheth and said, "Jay, we're moving in next week."

Japheth said, "How can you move in? It isn't finished."

"Oh, yes, it is," I insisted.

"How can it be finished? Frankly?" Jay asked.

"It's finished because we say so, frankly," I said. "No kidding, Jay, this has gone on long enough. Truth be told, it will never be finished. So there it is, Jay, the crew finishes up next week." I kept a carpenter and a plumber to finish up. I also had a tile man from St. Vincent. He was living in the galvanize shed. Bebe was his name and he was looking for a place he could afford, because we had a lot of tiling yet to do.

Construction in Bequia

I told Sandy we were moving in next week and it was going to be rough sledding. We had a few of the workers come back to help us move in. We moved in downstairs into the guest room. We had to change the building plans when Boolu came into the picture. Boolu's room, which was first designed as a garage, was transformed into a bedroom just by adding a small bath. The kitchen was finished. We connected all the appliances the week before we finally got rid of the cabinetmaker. He was excellent, but he was as slow as molasses. The inside was completed, and when we moved in, the painter was painting the outside.

Our very first night in the house was a nightmare. Boolu was bedded down in his room as we were in ours, and I was drifting off to sleep when I heard water dripping. The only effect it had on me was to hasten my descent into never-never land.

Sometime in the middle of the night, Sandy woke me up saying, "What a mess! Just look at this place." The red and black antique Persian rug was sopping wet from water running down the stone wall behind the headboard, cascading like Niagara Falls. It was running across the floor and out under the sliding doors onto the terrace.

"Ohmigod, Sandy," I said, "there must be a crack in the water tank."

"Which one?" Sandy asked. "Which one?"

"How the hell do I know? They're both overhead. Ohmigod!" I exclaimed.

I ran out of the room and upstairs, switching lights on as I went. As I entered the dining room upstairs, I could see where the water was coming from. Thank the lord it wasn't the big tank under the dining room. I could see the water was cascading down the stairs from the master bedroom and into and across the dining room where it flowed down the stairs to the living room and eventually down the wall of the guest bedroom below. It was like a river running through the house from top to bottom. Boolu's room was unaffected and he slept on totally unaware of the flooding. It wasn't a flood. This house could never be flooded—it was built on a steep hill with every floor terraced off like rice paddies. I went into the bathroom, stood up on a chair, and turned off the valve of the overhead tank hoping it would stop the water flow and praying to God it wasn't a settling crack. The water flow eventually stopped, so I knew the cause was not the tank. I went downstairs and sank back into a chair.

Sandy, standing at the door to the bath, said, "Is this the beginning?"

"I hope to God it isn't," I said.

It didn't take the plumber long to get to the bottom of our water-soaked predicament. Monday morning, the cold-water system had been turned on for us while they worked on the hot-water pipes. The plumber had disconnected or had not yet connected the hot-water pipes to the hot-water heater. The heater was next to the upper bath. The plumber had planned to finish the hot-water system on Tuesday. What he didn't know or didn't think of was that, even with the hot-water disconnected from its source, the cold water could work itself through the system by passing through the mixer at the faucet in the guest bath, then work up through the hot-water pipe to where he had stupidly left it disconnected the day before. No one had ever told him the plumber's basic rule: water seeks its own level. Do you believe it? After that night, I did.

Housewarming

The second week, we moved upstairs and we had the dining room set up. We hadn't yet touched the living room. We used it to hold all the furniture until we found a place for it. We couldn't do much with that room anyway until the second load came from New York with the living room furniture. The window treatments were not even started. In spite of all that remained to be done, we decided to hold our housewarming party on December 15, 1971. We had the kitchen, dining room, and terrace overlooking Friendship Bay in order. What more did we need? Oh, yeah, Winnie, Boolu, and drinks—we couldn't have done it without them! We set two round tables out on the terrace with linens, candles in hurricane lamps, flowers, and Sandy's mother's best dishes. It all looked out of this world, with the view of the bay and ocean beyond.

The guests arrived and we were all out on the terrace. Boolu had served drinks. The winds started up rather slowly at first, hardly noticeable. Boolu stood in the doorway and nervously, shyly, quietly announced. "Dinna is served." Over the chit-chat as they sipped their aperitifs, no one heard him; consequently they paid him no mind. So very quietly and privately, he went to each couple on the terrace and told them individually that dinner was served. He then walked back to the dining room door, turned around, and once more stated, "Dinna is served!" He looked over at me and flashed his big smile. By now he had everyone's attention, so he announced one more time. "Dinna is served!" It was a big moment for him. Everyone applauded; he all but bowed and then went back into the kitchen. Ever after at dinner parties, this phrase became his trademark.

The winds were picking up now, and Marie said, "Jimmy, you had better move inside, if my guess is right." With her experience at the hotel with dinners outside, it behooved me to heed her advice. The Christmas winds were blowing in from the north and with them came rain.

The men carried the tables laden as they were through the eight-foot opening of the pocket door into the dining room. The dinner party proceeded with the usual chatter. Winnie and Boolu busied themselves scurrying in and out of the kitchen. Everything started innocently and easily enough without disruption or spilt wine. Sure enough the rain came, but so lightly that no one noticed at first. As the animation of the conversation around the table picked up, so did the momentum of the approaching storm. We were shocked when lightning began flashing across the sky. All the walls of the house facing the ocean were glass. The three walls of the living room a few steps below us were mostly glass, taking full advantage of the breathtaking view. Because of the expansive, curtain-free windows, the elements in all their grandeur were displayed before us. The candles dancing wildly behind the glass of the hurricane lamps distracted us from our bantering and reminded us what was going on outside.

As the meal progressed, the winds were whipping up; candles were blowing out, linen was flapping. We had to close the doors even to the small kitchen terrace. The closure made serving more difficult for Winnie and Boolu since it was their route to the dining room. Through the ample plate glass, we could see lightning streaking across the sky. The banter stopped. Everyone sat there as the room lit up brighter than day, waiting for the thunder. It came with a crackling crash that vibrated the room! Now a strong wind was whipping at the windows. I sat there in the silence wondering if they would hold. We were so exposed out there on the side of the hill. As the storm got closer, the downpour intensified.

Root spoke up. "This is damn dramatic!'"

"It's exciting!" May Dale exclaimed.

Pam interjected, "So long as we don't get struck."

"Or washed off this cliff into the sea," Sandy added.

Nick said, "Who knows? This place hasn't been tested yet."

"That's right," Tiare said. "This is a first."

May's friend Ed, who was beginning to feel his oats, an effect of the freely flowing grog, said, "This is Edward R. Murrow of CBS and the *See It Now* show coming to you live from the beautiful island of Bequia: YOU ARE THERE."

Instantly another streak and flash, this time a crack of lightning right overhead. The stone walls shook. I got up and went to the kitchen to tell Winnie, who was cowering in a corner, to bring in her coconut-banana-cream pie and see who needed coffee. She sent Boolu in first, then followed. The rain was pelting down now. The dessert distracted everyone for a while, until the next big flash flared across the heavens. The chitchat stopped. We were all waiting, waiting for that crack, which came like the snapping of a whip right next to our ears. The stone walls shook again. Every time lightning flashed it was like high noon, nerve racking.

At this point, Sandy asked, "Does this place have lightning rods?" Of course it didn't.

Thank God dinner was over and it was time for people to go home. But no way was anyone about to go out in the middle of that downpour. More coffee made the rounds as did a tot of brandy here and there. The conversation started to get spooky and somehow came to center on Jean Dixon, the psychic. I think Ed knew her or had talked to

Driveway up to Bequia House

16 Fait Accompli

her, and then it went on to Ouija boards. The question went around the table as to who had ever played with one.

"You mean, whoever worked it." Sandy directed this comment to Ed.

"You want to...?" "Shall we?" The questions went around. May was all for it.

"Look, we're not going anywhere," someone affirmed as the lightning flashed. "So let's have a little fun."

And they took over the evening. As the storm raged on, Ed and May went about making a Ouija board. Ed got the lid of an old mayonnaise jar to use as a cursor, a large enough lid for everyone's fingertips to rest on. May was ripping pages out of a notebook I gave her and writing a letter or number on each piece. I collected the napkins and pulled the tablecloth off the table and gave them to Winnie. Everyone got up and Pam put the chairs around the table.

Sandy said, "Count me out," as he sat at the other table sipping a double vodka. "Nothing like a Ouija board to liven up a lightning storm," he remarked.

The Ouija board was made ready for the game. The storm was blowing overhead and everyone was gathering around the table when Winnie came out and said, "How will I get home?"

Nick said. "I'll take you, if I can use Tiare's jeep."

Tiare said, "Sure, go ahead."

Boolu came out of the kitchen, and, tired, ran down to his room in the downpour. Everyone else sat around the table except Marie, who sat with Sandy. I just worked the room. Tiare in her trailing white chiffon gown was roaming around down in the living room with the furniture piled high in the center. The windows were more like glass walls surrounding the room except for the back stone wall with the staircase leading up to the dining room. The windows were all naked, defying the pelting rain, but embracing every flash that exploded into the room. Tiare floated around, as was her wont, like a poltergeist.

Everyone at the Ouija board was well into their quest. I went into the kitchen to check out Winnie's work and filled the ice bucket, replenished the Pepsi, and opened another wine bottle. When I got back to the side table, Tiare was floating upstairs.

As she passed Sandy, she twirled and said, "This place is fabulous, I mean the whole evening." She twirled in place and said, "It was like that movie *Last Year at Marienbad*." And she disappeared up into the master bedroom.

"Who was that? Tinkerbell?" I asked. "May, you got anything yet?"

"Nope," she said. "So far there isn't a message for anyone here. No, no, no."

Ed was getting desperate. Then he asked, "Ouija board, Ouija board, is there any message for anyone, anywhere?"

I watched as the cursor slid around and stopped at Yes. There was dead silence in the room. Then flash, crack, and crash, and May asked. "Yes? Yes, who? Who is the message for? Do we know them?"

"No, May," Ed said, "only one question. Ouija Board, who is the message for?"

It almost immediately slid to the letter B, and after a moment or two to O, and around about and back to O again, and surprisingly quickly over to L and back again, and finally on to U.

At that moment, a very waterlogged Nick walked in. "What a mess out there!"

"Shush!" chorused everyone at the table.

Pam whispered, "Nick, it's Boolu."

"Oh," said Nick. "Boolu? Pam. the road is littered with boulders."

Ed asked, "May, who is Boolu?"

May answered, "He's the little fellow who just went downstairs."

Ed then said, "Come on, everybody concentrate. Let's get back to the board while it's still hot."

"Let's go," May said. "Ouija, Ouija, mighty Ouija, what is this message for Boolu?"

Ed instructed, "May, you should say 'Ouija Board, Ouija Board...'"

May said, "Excuse me, I'm not talking to any board. I'm asking Ouija himself."

"Or herself," Rootie interjected.

It started with a jolt and jerked around and jerked around sliding this way and that. In the end it spelt out K-I-L-L. "Ohmigod!" someone breathed.

"Is that it?" asked May. "Is there more?"

Then Root asked, "Mighty Ouija, mighty Ouija, kill who? Who? Boolu kill who?" In time it slowly spelled O-L-I-V.

"STOP!" May's sister screamed. May's sister Olive, who had just arrived on the Island and who had never in her life seen a Ouija board before, was all shook up.

"Let's stop, Ed," Olive's husband said.

"Oh, lord! Olive! That's your name!" Root exclaimed.

The game ended, but not the aftereffects. The rain was letting up, the storm had passed and the dinner party was over. Everyone said their thanks and goodbyes and was slowly feeling their way down the rain-sodden river of a driveway. The night was dark as pitch and no lightning now lit the way. The steep, rugged, yet-to-be-paved drive was still full of loose stones like marbles underfoot. One person was slipping this way, the other sliding that. Everyone was grabbing at and gripping hold of each other to keep from falling. They were as noisy and raucous as a bunch of rowdy "Harpies" leaving a pub after being booted out at 4 AM on a Sunday morning. They were hooting and hollering, singing and laughing as they inched their way down to the main road. I stood above hoping that once they reached the bottom, their cars didn't stall. They still had to get themselves home on this pitch-black, waterlogged night.

Tiare came floating down out of the master bedroom asking, "Where is everyone?"

"They just left, Tiare," I said.

She asked, "Who did Boolu kill anyway?"

Sandy said, "Who knows and who cares? Good night, Tiare. Watch your step going down that drive."

And "Ollivierre," an old family name on the Island, kept running through my mind.

Santa '71 Ready Or Not

"Am I doing Santa this year!? Do you think I'm a glutton for punishment?" "I damn near caused a massacre last year." "This place doesn't know the meaning of Santa." These were my retorts to the frequent question this year after last year's fiasco. I had made up my mind months ago not to repeat this dangerous community event. Imagine a place in the world where Santa Claus for the children was synonymous with danger.

It wasn't until I spoke to Mistress Tannis, who runs the Harbour dry goods store, that I took another look at the situation. She asked me if I were playing Santa this year and I said, "Miz Tannis, I would like to be able to, but the adults won't let me."

She said, "Oh, no? Why do you say that? I know they behaved badly last year, but that will not happen again. We adults never had a Santa before. We got carried away. Believe me, it won't happen again this year. The adults this year will leave Santa to the children."

"Do you really think so?" I asked.

"'I do, Mr. Jimmy. We're all looking forward to it again this year."

"Well, I'll think about it," I told her. I figured that if I were to do it again this year, the event would have to be held somewhere inside. When I inquired around, the primary school was readily offered. So I decided to do it again.

Everything was pretty much the same, including my wearing the see-through suit. When Santa and his helper got out of the dinghy on the pier, we marched over to the primary school without incident, to much joy and shouting. A big crush greeted us at the entrance. I got in with difficulty, but having a doorway was what kept the ruffians out and let only the children in. I was told that some kids still had to take that ride over the heads of the older ones crowding at the door, but the older ones did let the little ones in.

Eleanor Thompson said later, "When I saw my granddaughter Melanie flying in over the heads of the teenagers on her way in to see Santa, my heart stood still."

This year, when we had finished at the school, we took a good-size bag back to the Harbour. We buzzed around in the dinghy giving out goodies to quite a few surprised children on the yachts. We also ran into some childlike adults out there who were loads of fun, and isn't that what it's all about? For those of you who wonder whether there was a night with Miss Marie this year, the answer is no. I didn't want the kids to think that was the reason Santa came to Bequia.

Marie invited us to Christmas dinner at the Frangipani with Pat and Son Mitchell, where we had our first Bequia Christmas pudding. The traditional English pudding was an annual ritual of Son's mother. It was special and, needless to say, rich and tasty. Even though dinner was held at the hotel, we sat aside at the family table with their close friends. It gave us a feeling of inclusion that was very important to us at that point. It was heartwarming to find a spot so far away from our home that accepted us on nothing more than face value so quickly.

We also spent New Year's Eve 1971 at the Frangipani Hotel. That year's celebration became an annual event thereafter. It would always be packed shoulder to shoulder with locals, guests on the Island, and all the yacht people and their charters. Many people began to make it a point to be moored in the Harbour over the holidays. Bequia became the place to be. A steel band played through the night, and Son shot off flares at midnight. The boats joined in, turning the Harbour into a dream-like fairyland as the rosy puffs and plumes of gases spewed forth from the flares. They billowed through the swaying coconut trees and engulfed us all. It was surreal. This ritual continued through the years all the way to the millennium when they held a fireworks display over and beyond Hamilton. When the holidays were over, Sandy had to go back to New York and the Playhouse and face the slush, snow, and sleet that awaited him.

Home Alone

By mid-January of '72, the plumber had finished with his work and was gone. I had to let the carpenter go in spite of the fact that he wasn't finished. He was caught walking away from the job with lumber, not the first time he had ripped us off. He had come with a long-time reputation, but I had felt he was safe enough if I kept an eye on him. But he turned out to be too shifty even for me. The first time, a young woman came from Lower Bay Gutter and said, "I have something to show you, Mr. Jimmy. Would you please follow me?" She led me down the road to a spot just this side of the Gutter. Hidden in the grass were four pieces of 1x12x18 hardwood. "I think these are yours," she said.

"I know they're mine," I said and thanked her. "And I know who the culprit is too." I went over with Japheth to Lower Bay Gutter and looked up behind the culprit's house. We were told he already had some of my wood there. I'm afraid the word was already out. When we got there, no wood was to be found.

I still kept him on when everyone left because he was such a crackerjack carpenter, but he just could not be trusted. I never did catch him until one day Winnie called me to the little terrace in front of the kitchen that overlooks the driveway and said, "Look at that." There he was with two long pieces of 2x4

16 Fait Accompli

over his shoulder. It was thirty minutes before the end of his day and he was heading down the road on his way home.

I said to Winnie, "That's it. He's finished." So I sent him packing. Eventually no one would hire him, and I think this was a shame and a terrible waste. In fact, he had to leave for a neighboring island to find work.

Now that Boolu was in his room on the first floor, Winnie in her kitchen, I up in the master bedroom and, with the exception of Bebe, all the workers gone, the place seemed empty with just us "family" all alone. I had become so accustomed to the crowd around the place for damn well over two and a half years that I felt this aloneness was going to take some getting used to.

Carnival Time Again

Kenneth Alex from La Pompe asked me whether I was doing Carnival again this year. Carnival on Bequia was celebrated much like in other parts of the world. The previous year, Boolu, Sammy, Metrius, and I had all played Carnival. The popular Road March song in Trinidad that year was "Nasty Racon." The lyrics went. "Why do all the girls love Racon, Nasty Racon with the mackerel in his hand?" So Kenneth had decided his band would stage a take-off on the song, a shotgun wedding between Racon and his daughter.

First across the stage, down the "church aisle," had come the beautiful wedding party. The men wore white dress shirts and four-in-hand ties, the women lovely pastel gowns, and the bride, five months gone, a flowing white gown and veil. The mothers had followed dancing the cakes, an old Grenadines custom where the women swirl around balancing their tiered and decorated cakes on their heads. Then came yours truly playing Racon, being carried into the church over the heads of the bride's brothers with my dead mackerel and a bottle of rum in my hand and my bare, mud-caked bottom sticking out of the seat of my pants. Kenneth, the father of the bride, had followed with his shotgun at the ready. I was dressed in three layers of rags. I had doused myself in motor oil and rolled in powdered cement, dirt, and sand and topped it off

Jimmy as Racon

by dumping catsup, mustard, and coffee grounds over my head and face, and down over my oil-soaked rags. I had also cut the seat out of my reggae pants, exposing my bare bottom. In short, I was a sight.

After the morning's competition, our band had paraded through the streets from one hotel to the next, covering the length of the Island and ending up at dusk in Paget Farm. A hell of a time was had by all. So the next year, Boolu, Sammy, Metrius, and I were more than willing to play Carnival. Kenneth told me the theme this year was based on the story of an African tribe waging war against an Aztec group over the theft of the African princess. Kenneth declared, "I am depicting the Aztec chief I assumed because of the fancy costume the part demanded."

So I told him, "I'm playing the African witch doctor who uses magic to solve the problem."

"Great," Kenneth agreed. "Now we have to get together at my bar for rehearsals."

For my role as La Mumba, Joan made a palm-leaf skirt with arm and ankle bands. I painted my skin with a combination of coffee, coco, and Texas dirt left over from Tyrone Guthrie's production of *Pirates of Penzance*. Over the dark paint, I designed red, black, and white markings on my chest and belly. I topped it off with a big Afro wig and carried a large, colorful witch doctor's mask on a big staff. Someone yelled out, "Where did you get those big green eyes?" I had a ball and I think everyone else did, too. You better well know, La Pompe placed first both years.

The Day Of Reckoning

In the summer of '72, Verne Wallace's estate was finally probated. The land was surveyed and split up among the three women, with our section parceled out and the proceeds evenly split among them. I told Erma that the transaction was all well and good, but Sandy would still have to disabuse Doris of the notion that as the eldest she should receive the total payment. He still had to convince her to accept only one third of the total price of the property. I told Erma that when Doris had been here last, that summer of '69, Sandy had pacified her by letting her think she would get the whole kit and caboodle, which she thought she as the oldest would then parcel out to her younger sisters. He would now have to convince her otherwise. His job was cut out for him, as was mine, which was to hold off the payments to the other two sisters until Sandy got Doris's signature on the bill of sale. His task wasn't going to be easy, and Doris's refusal could throw a monkey wrench into the whole deal.

I sent the necessary papers on to Sandy for Doris's signature. Sandy went up to 110th Street and Lenox Avenue just north of Central Park and gave the papers to her so she could go over them with her lawyer. An appointment was scheduled for a meeting at her lawyer's office in Harlem. Paul also attended. Everything went well, until it came time for Doris to sign the papers. At that point, she ever so calmly said, "Of course, you will give me the total amount, and I will take care of my sisters."

Sandy was waiting for this moment. He took one deep breath, hesitated for a moment, and then said, "This paper will need their signatures as well. They will want their share before they sign." He paused and then went on, "I will be able to expedite—"

"I am the oldest and entitled to the property," Doris interrupted.

There it was, Sandy thought. Her father had died many years ago, and she hadn't paid a penny tax on the property all through the years. She hadn't even set foot on the land since she had left the Island some sixty years ago. Moreover, her dad had never left her the land in the first place.

Her lawyer now spoke up. "Doris, do you want to sell this land to Mr. Meisner?"

Sandy stopped breathing. All she had to do was say "no" and the deal was off. All that work and money would be gone for naught. And we were already living in the house. This can't be happening was racing through his mind when he heard Doris answer, "Yes, yes, I do."

"Well, sign right here," the lawyer directed as she handed Doris her pen. Doris took the pen, paused saying nothing, and then leaned over from where she sat and signed the papers. That was it. After months of waiting, the house was ours. What would have happened if Verne had lived? I think we never would have straightened out the maze, with everyone living. I later saw it happen many times, where the heirs of a property never would agree. The island of Petit Nevis was just one example. It was in and out of litigation for over thirty years and it still hasn't changed hands.

Sandy made out a check to Doris and handed it to the lawyer so she could look it over. She handed it to Doris saying, "Here. That wasn't very difficult now, was it?" What was that I said about "Fools rush in"? All things considered, we were pretty damn lucky.

Sandy picked up the signed papers, shook hands with the lawyer and Doris, and turned to Paul. He couldn't get out of that office quick enough. When he got back to Paul's, he called me in Bequia to say, "Mission accomplished." He decided to carry the papers by hand back to Bequia. Having experienced the haphazard mail system, no way was he going to entrust such important papers to them.

So Erma Wallace didn't get her much-needed money until Sandy reached Bequia in December. Winnie (Wallace) Simmons built herself a new house up on the hill behind her old one and lived there until she died. I don't know what we would have done if Doris had reneged. She was in the driver's seat and could have demanded anything. She had no idea we had gone ahead digging and building while we were waiting for probate. Well, all that was behind us now, and we could get on with our lives.

17 Bells A'ringing

Boolu's School Grows Like Topsy

My work with Boolu had suffered over the past few months. We'd been so busy with the move to the house before the holidays and then there was Santa Claus. It had been Boolu's second time as Santa's helper, and he took great pride in the job. He was right there whenever I needed him, Black Peter to my Sinterklaas, and everyone made a fuss over him. Christmas and New Year's had left little time for classes, and we had so much work to be completed around the house. When we got rid of the carpenter and the plumber, only Bebe the tile man and Boolu his helper were left.

We still had plenty of tiling to do. All the outside terraces had yet to be done. Boolu and Bebe got along like a house on fire. The friendship was an opportunity for Boolu to communicate with someone else. Bebe even took him home with him up to Fancy beyond Owia on Sandy Bay, up on the northernmost tip of St. Vincent. They would go over on Bank Holiday, which was the first Monday in August. It was Bebe's vacation and they would stay for a week or more. Boolu loved being where no one saw him as the little old "dummy-boy Boolu."

Once when Boolu was packing his little suitcase, I noticed he put in six cakes of sweet soap. "Who is all this for?" I asked.

He said, "Dat's fo de old Queen." The "old Queen" was Bebe's mother. To Boolu his soaps were the equivalent of giving the old lady perfume. I thought it a very sweet thought.

Finally, with the tiles finished and only the driveway left to do, I felt it was time to get back to Boolu's training. Around this time, Darwin Compton's father came up the drive with Darwin in tow. He asked me if I would take his son, who was deaf, and teach him like Boolu. Well, I couldn't teach him like Boolu because Boolu was, in effect, in class all the time. If he was working in the kitchen, serving in the dining room, or working with Bebe, I was always correcting and helping him with vocabulary and pronunciation. His schooling was 24-7. Whenever he misunderstood anything, I would stop and correct the problem no matter where, no matter when. Believe me, it took time, a lot of time, but it was worth it when it paid off and he understood. A sibilant consonant was extra difficult for him, but he always tried. How could I do that with Darwin? I didn't say no; I said I would look into it.

As luck would have it, for Darwin, that is, a little girl came all by herself with a note from her mother asking for help as she too was deaf. So I decided to start a class for all three. It would be a windfall for Boolu. Every morning at 10 AM, my three young scholars showed up outside the guest bedroom with notepad and pencil. We moved in a small table to sit around, and we began. Except I didn't know where to begin. So I did the obvious. I started with their first names, working with them as I had with Boolu. I knew absolutely nothing about sign language, nor did anyone else on the Island. All I could teach them was lip-reading. I felt lip-reading would help them at home communicating with the family. I was rationalizing, of course. What choice did I have? I did what I could do. All I had were numbers, letters, words, mouth and lip positions, and my knowledge of voice learned from my voice teacher, Bernard Taylor, and my speech teachers, Fanny Bradshaw and Marion Rich. They had each had their own method, and I used all three as applicable—Marion's cork between the teeth, to get the diaphragm going, Bernard's exaggerated "ee" for depth and chest vibrations, and Fanny's nasal hum for facial mask vibrations. The rest was mostly common sense.

Bequia School for Deaf

I started with Boolu's "A for Apple" book. The review proved to be good for Boolu's self-esteem. I worked for total communication while emphasizing lip-reading. Then Andy was introduced to our little group. Pat Mitchell from the Frangipani had called telling me of a boy in Paget Farm who was deaf and needed help. She warned, "He may be beyond your help. He could be autistic as well. I wish you would take the time to check him out."

"What's the harm, as long as you don't give the mother false hope. Come over any evening after four o'clock," I told her.

They arrived one evening. I guess Winnie Kidd, the mother, didn't get off work till late, and for Pat at the hotel, it wasn't any easier. Not to worry, there they were coming up the drive. Pat had told me that she had heard that the boy, as well as being deaf, was not able to relate to other people face to face. He would not make eye contact but instead would turn away, twisting to the right trying to roll up into what looked like the fetal position. When I saw him, I didn't think for a minute I was ever going to be able to help this little boy. I didn't know if I was really helping the ones I already had. I was flying blind with the plane on autopilot. Nevertheless, they were standing out on my dining room terrace, Andy clutching his mother's hand and hiding in her skirts.

We all sat around on the terrace and I got them drinks. I realized I wasn't going to get any more information just sitting there talking. I asked Mistress Kidd to bring Andy into the kitchen where I opened the refrigerator. I walked him over to it and told the mommy to leave us alone. I had to restrain him to keep him at the refrigerator as his mommy slipped out of the kitchen. I pointed to some milk. He looked at it and quickly looked away. Still holding him, I picked up a chocolate cake that my housekeeper had baked that day and put it on the table. I could see I was making progress when I got a flash of a smile out of him. I let up my hold on him and he didn't dart away. I took the milk out and topped the cake with some ice cream. I took his hand again and poured milk into a glass. I gave it to him and poured myself some. His eyes flashed back and forth, from the food to me. I paid no attention to him. I just kept getting the food prepared. I fixed ice cream and cake for us both, took it and him up to the master bedroom, and sat him at a card table where we proceeded to eat. I avoided his quick glances, which were much like Boolu's early glances. He was watching every move I made. If I ate, he ate, if I stopped, he stopped.

Pat had brought a child's educational game, the type with various shaped pegs that you hammer into the appropriate slots. I started to play with it. I intentionally made mistakes and exaggerated my reactions like Bozo the Clown. My act delighted him immensely. As I got more into the game—making mistake after mistake—I pretended not to notice him. He had finished his cake and ice cream. I was trying to get a round peg into a square slot and was acting perplexed, then determined, and lastly dejected. I then gave up and tried another piece, which also wouldn't work. Andy was watching my every move and becoming more amused every time I goofed. Once in a while I would get one in and I would all but jump for joy. He was laughing in his own inimitable way. When I asked him to try, he stopped dead. He made no movement and gave no sign of emotion. So I kept on making mistakes and started to hesitate before making a choice. By now he was into my perplexity, my inability to get it right. My heart stood still when I saw him pointing to the correct hole. He was now helping me get the right one! He was giggling and smiling now, in his oh-so-very-shy way.

We went on like this for a while. Once when he put his hand out to point to a correct hole, I put the peg into his hand and helped him put it in. His eyes lit up and he smiled. We both clapped. Once when I got it right, I overreacted with joy and pride. Then I continued with the wrong choices, and Andy pointed to the correct one. I gave him a round one, and he found the right hole. I reacted with extravagant approval and he liked that. After a few more mistakes on my part, I gave the board to him and he didn't do too badly after a fashion. He was smiling and happy, and so was I. I shook his hand, gave him a big hug, and we went down to his mother and Pat. He stiffened up a bit when he reached the terrace and went directly over to his mommy where he tried to hide behind her skirts again.

Pat went upstairs to get the toy. I excused myself and followed her up into the bedroom. I told Pat that something was causing Andy's fear and mistrust. That fright I was seeing led me to believe he was harboring something terrible. It must have happened a long time ago, and he was feeling the aftermath of it. Only the family would know for sure what it was. Later I heard stories—nothing of any consequence ever happens in Paget Farm without the whole village knowing it. Whatever happened happened. What I was concerned with was the here and now. And what was here and now was that little Andy and I had been brought together, and I was going to do whatever I could to help him as I found him. As Winnie Kidd thanked me profusely after Pat told her I would take on teaching Andy, I couldn't help but wonder what I thought I was doing, giving that woman false hope. God help me, I thought, I'm going way out on a limb with this one. On the other hand, what choice did he have? Right now there was only me, and if I didn't try to help him, then who?

Now there were four, until Father Adams called me aside and said, "I have a young fellow from Union Island who is deaf and needs help. Would you take him?"

"Sure, why not?" I said.

"I knew you would," he said, "That's why he's already here!"

I just shook my head, waved, and went about my business. I was thinking, Now we've got five. This boy was not only deaf, he had a behavior problem, attention deficit disorder or the like. What did I know about these things? The only consolation I had was that no one else around here had a notion either.

Before long the school was well underway with six students, once Mr. John, the electrician, finally talked his wife into letting their little deaf daughter come over the hill from the Harbour to our school. Mrs. John was obviously an over-protective mother who, I felt, stood in the way of her daughter's progress, making it very difficult for me. She wouldn't let the girl get fitted for a hearing aid. At first, she wouldn't even talk to me about her. The child didn't come to school much, and I felt the mother had the problem, not the girl.

We later added to the school a program for mothers of deaf infants. I used the Tracy Program for mothers, a program created by Spencer Tracy's wife to work with her little deaf baby. Thus the school was well on its way that spring. Then Pat decided she could help. She took the class in her home in the Harbour every Tuesday and Thursday at 10 AM giving me a small respite. I had to be at the high school at 11:30 AM every morning, and my last class was Choir at 4:00 PM up in the choir loft in the back of the church. We used the old pump organ there. It stuck sometimes, but we kept it humming until 6 PM most days.

Music For Bequia Anglican High

The first year, the high school was in the old Sail Loft above the Step Up Bar. There I started my first year of teaching Rudiments of Music. In England, First Form was for age ten plus, specifically ten years and six months and up, approximately equivalent to Junior High in America. I had all fifty First Form students in one class, and that first year all I had was a pitch pipe. We concentrated mostly on theory, and I saved their singing for over at the church. Junior High proved to be a good time to start the study of music. At that age, students were starting to make decisions for themselves. It was a good time to show them something new and then ask, "What do you think of it? Do you want more of it? What part do you think you would like?" These questions reflected my biggest challenge. How many would I win over? Enough, I hoped.

I was able to hold the attention of most of the class. But one boy acted as if he were in a different school entirely. If he didn't already have his head buried in a book, he would get up at the beginning of my class and go back and peruse the bookshelves to find one. He would then stroll back to his seat, never paying any mind to me. It was as if he were in a little world of his own. No one in class was fazed by his behavior, so I surmised something was wrong with him and, like everyone else, just ignored it. I let it go for weeks and it never got better, but I was getting more furious by the week. His behavior was so blatant and blunt. What was to him inconsequential was everything I was teaching!

I finally spoke to Bill, my principal, and asked, "What's Lorraine's problem? He doesn't seem to be all there."

Bill just laughed and said, "Lorraine Friday? Jimmy, he's the smartest kid in the school. From his earliest days in primary school, he has always had permission to pick up a book and read whenever he was bored."

Lorraine was so far ahead of the other students that the teachers had no other way to handle him. So that was why it didn't bother the other students in my class. Well, it bothered me. It was like a slap in the face, and I knew how I would handle it. He might be ahead of the other students in other subjects but he certainly wasn't ahead in music. I went to Father and explained what was going on in my class. I told him come midterms, if Lorraine couldn't answer the questions on the test, I would be flunking him.

Father said, "It's your class, you do what you must do."

It was true that Lorraine could go through life never giving a fig for music. So what? The world wouldn't stop. And yet why turn down a chance to find out about something you might appreciate for the rest of your life? When midterms rolled around, I made him sit down and take the test like everyone else. Let me tell you, I failed the hell out of him. He didn't know a B flat from an A sharp. By the time I was through correcting his paper, he damn well knew what an F was. I was merciless because I felt he had it coming. His low mark brought down his class standing. It was the first time in his life he came in second to Elvie Ollivierre. After that, he buckled down and became a passable music student.

Elvie was so pleased she was beside herself. She kept thanking me. "Don't thank me," I said, "I didn't do it, you did." She went on to become the first girl in the country to achieve the equivalent of an O-level in music, majoring in Percussion in the school in Canada where she finished off her training. Lorraine went on to get his doctorate in Government and Law, also in Canada. He then came back to Bequia and became our representative in Parliament.

Ears For The Deaf

School closed for the summer, but I kept the Deaf School open. I didn't want to interrupt their progress just yet. They would be getting a long leave at Christmas. That summer, Ann Schwartz, a teacher at the deaf school in Barbados, came to Bequia on a two-week vacation, staying at the Frangipani. There she heard of our efforts from Pat and Marie. Pat arranged for her to attend a class up at the house. When the class was over, we sat up on the terrace and talked over a cold drink. She offered to send me material from Barbados, flash cards and mimeograph material they used as teaching aids. I showed her my lip drawings, which I used for sound recognition in lip-reading. Now that the students had learned their numbers and letters, we were working on one-syllable words. What I relied on mostly, since we were a small group, was repeat, repeat, and more repetition.

Ann said the best thing we could do was to get them hearing aids. It would raise their hearing level about 15% from wherever it was normally. That increase would be helpful for a start and make my work easier. Now Barbados had a hearing program sponsored by England. They supplied the deaf with hearing aids and a six-month live-in training period to teach the child how to use them. Ann explained, "St. Lucia, St. Vincent, and Grenada are included, but it's up to each country to apply for each child and get them from Barbados." She suggested I submit a request in writing to the Surgeon General's office in St. Vincent (or the equivalent thereof). I did and never even got an answer. Ann went back to work in Barbados and waited to see if the officials in St. Vincent would contact her, but no request ever came from the Surgeon General's office, not even a request for further information. Ann called me from Barbados to suggest I personally call the office in St. Vincent. I called and was never put on to the Surgeon General himself; all I ever got was the usual runaround. God, how I was used to that in St. Vincent.

In desperation, I called a friend who had access to the Surgeon General's ear. I explained my predicament and asked for her advice. She said she would see what see could do herself. She was able to talk to the Medical Officer, our Surgeon General, and when she told him of the program in Barbados, he asked her, "Just where is St. Vincent going to get the money to send all the deaf children of this island to Barbados?" Upon learning we had friends of Bequia willing to pay their way, he turned a deaf ear saying, "And who is going to pay the way for all the deaf children of St. Vincent?"

Well, that was that. I was so mad, I could have spit nails. I called Ann to tell her, and she was more upset than I was, if that were possible. "To hell with him," she said, "I'll come to Bequia myself. I'll bring over a portable audiometer, hearing aids, and materials for ear molds. We'll fit up these kids ourselves with hearing aids, and you can teach them how to use them."

I thanked Ann and told her I had plenty of room, so she should let me know when she could find the time to come over and help. We'll show these bleeping bureaucrats, I thought. We'll do it without them. However, we found it wasn't going to be as easy as we had anticipated.

The first problem was power for the audiometer; our power wasn't the same as Barbados'. We had Tim Burgess duct-tape batteries together till we managed to get enough power to run the audiometer. It took two rows of twelve batteries to make it work. The next problem was making the ear molds. Ann had never been trained in making them or made one or even seen one being made. When it came time to make them, she froze.

"What are you afraid of?" I asked.

She said, "What if I can't get it out? Those tender little ears...?"

I said, "Those tender little ears? If they don't work, what good are they?" I called Boolu over and got him to understand what had to be done and that Ann was afraid to do it. Would he let me try to do it? He didn't hesitate, just looked at me and nodded his head yes. I said, "Please God, let's go."

Boolu stretched out on the bed, and I filled the wax-like molding guck into his ear canal. After it set, with a little prodding and gentle pulling, I got it out in one piece. We then proceeded to make thirteen more, one student after the other. It took us two days. When each still-soft mold was removed, we connected a plastic tube to it and looped the wire leading to the pocket batteries used at that time behind the ear. Our Bequia children now had hearing aids, no thanks to those bureaucrats over in St. Vincent, and thanks to Tim and many, many thanks to Ann Schwartz originally from Long Island.

The hearing aids made a marked difference in the classroom. They helped every one of the students and made it much easier for me. The big job ahead of me now was to get the students to realize that these little instruments were not toys and they shouldn't play with them or let anyone else play with them. One mother would take the hearing aid away from the girl when she got home. She kept it in a drawer until it was time for her to go back to class; she was so in fear of it being broken by one of her daughter's playmates. Yet I needed her to wear it all the time to get used to it.

An old fisherman saw some boys, one of whom was his grandson, taking the hearing aid from one of my students. The boys were grabbing at it, snatching it away from each other, and trying it on. After the lunch period, the fisherman went to the primary school with Darwin, the deaf boy, and told the principal what had happened. He said he had to speak to the whole student body about it.

At the next assembly, with Darwin and his grandson in tow, he mounted the small stage at the front of the large room. He grabbed his grandson's ear. "See dis?" he demanded. "Dis is an ear. You all have two and you all hear outta dem." He then let go of the ear, and the grandson stood there rubbing the pain. "You all be very lucky," he continued. "You have one on either side a your head. Dis little guy has only one ear and it's right here in his pocket." He held up the hearing aid and said, "Dis is an ear also, dis be Darwin's ear. He needs it ta hear outta, just like you hear outta your ears. It is not a playting, so leave his ear alone. He has as much right ta hear as every one a you." That said, the old fisherman helped me more than he knew, more than one can imagine.

Our Move To The Commons

At the high school, we packed it in at the old Sail Loft and made tracks for the hill along the Spring road beyond the Commons, where the sheep and goats grazed. In the new school, my music room was at the far end on the left where I taught first year Harmony to students who had picked a music elective the second year. My large Rudiments classes, where I taught all the entering students that year, were held downstairs. The Rudiments of Music was their one compulsory music course, besides first year choir whether they could sing or not. I would decide that after I worked with them.

We worked in a large open room where we would be undisturbed by the rest of the school, or so it was presented to me. Actually, it was the only place we wouldn't disrupt other classes. We started preparing the Christmas program early because we had another program to prepare for shortly after New Year's. What we lacked in ability we made up in practice since we were blessed with an abundance of time to accomplish whatever we set our minds to.

We had rhythm classes and we had vocal classes that prepared everyone for section rehearsal. The men's and women's sections each met twice a week. Full choir was held once a week or twice if needed. Our bass section was weak for the first few years. They had to grow into it, and they did. All it took was time. There were some altos as well who over time became tenors. At first we were restricted to two- and three-part pieces. I had heard about a little musical keyboard about an octave-and-a-half long that was activated by blowing through a tube and pressing a key or two. The sound was like a mouth organ or an accordion and quite true to pitch. The students learned their keys, their chords, and much of their theory on these keyboards; after all, we had no piano or even an accordion. We had about a half dozen of these keyboards, and the students would accompany the chorus with each student playing a vocal line.

Holiday Rituals

Paul came down with Sandy to spend Christmas. The plane was packed. Barbados airport was bedlam. They knew before they left Kennedy they would never make the Friendship Rose in St. Vincent. The mail and packet boat left around 12:30 PM, give or take a little—or even a lot some days. Sandy and Paul wouldn't even arrive at Arnos Vale Airport in St. Vincent until well after four. I made arrangements for them to stay at a little no-frills, laid-back hotel called the Heron not too far from the Grenadines pier. I didn't bother to go over to St. Vincent to meet them since they had each other for company. They would have talked about nothing but Neighborhood Playhouse problems anyway, which was all they ever did when they got together.

Whenever I had to meet Sandy in St. Vincent on his way down, I would make the excursion a shopping day, killing two birds with one stone. I really hated going over there with a passion and I mean with a passion put to use. I would do anything to avoid that trip, which necessitated being up at 5 AM and finished by noon. For a night person, this was asking much too much. To avoid it, I worked it out to have to go only once a month. I would get enough provisions to last for four weeks, and if they didn't, I would just make do.

St. Vincent's merchants were stuck in some old ways of merchandising. The supply ships brought whatever the captain felt he could sell, and that was it. Then, whatever the ship brought the merchants took and sold. I don't think they ever thought of ordering in advance and spacing their order to ensure a steady supply for the customer. No, it was much easier to accept whatever came in and sell it. When the merchandise was gone, it was gone, zilch, caput, nada. Of course, if there wasn't anything else, a merchant could always sell Spam.

I found out soon enough that you had to be a savvy shopper if you wanted to keep a steady flow of food in your pantry. You might be able to manage without onions, but, oh, gee, dinner was damn good when you had them. Sugar was like that, too. Most of us eat too much sugar anyway, but after a short while, food became pretty dull without it. Things like rice, flour, and powdered milk were a problem sometimes but not often, thank God. Try to cook and eat without any one of them for a long stretch, and you would soon get what I'm driving at.

I taught Winnie to cook according to my New York taste, well, to my standards at least, and they were more New York than Utica. Since my preferences were my idiosyncrasy, I felt it was my responsibility to make sure she was amply supplied. Fortunately, when I mucked up and failed to stay on top of supply and demand, Winnie would come through with something delicious anyway using her Bequia know-how. So for all these reasons, I had gone over to St. Vincent on December 1 to stock up for the approaching holidays and didn't have to make the trip over to meet the "boys" on the 17th.

December 17 was no day to be shopping in any case. All the stores would be out of everything except flypaper and glass kerosene lampshades. It was much more important to tend to my rehearsals. We finished the *Nine Lessons* and were now working on our next appearance at midnight mass. Sandy and Paul arrived at the dock in Bequia about 2 PM, and Boolu and I were there to meet them. Our Moke was too small for passengers and bags, so Parnell was there to lend a hand. Parnell Hutchins was amazing. He was always in demand somewhere, fixing a motor here and welding a part there, yet he was always there for me when I needed him. He was like another son.

Paul slept downstairs in the guest bedroom next to Boolu's room. He went about his own business painting sea- and landscapes, swimming, and sunning himself. Every day in the late afternoon, when the oppressive heat of the sun had lessened and before the sun began to set, Sandy took Nora over to Lower Bay for a dip in the sea. It was a regular daily ritual that he never missed, even when it looked like rain. Paul always went along, and Bill and Jane Brown from the high school were regulars. When I was free of rehearsal, I was always there. Boolu was never there. This was his free time, and he liked to spend it with his, by this time, many friends.

It was Sandy's and, I believe, Nora's favorite time of day. Nora was a playful dog who loved children. She was a large, solid-black shepherd whose size alone made it scary for the children to play with her, but they loved it. She had a game she would play with the children on the beach at Lower Bay. First, she would chase them as they ran hollering down the beach until she almost reached them, and they would run into the surf. Then they would chase her as she raced barking down the beach until she pranced into the surf near Sandy. This game went on until one or the other tired of the action. It was the only time I ever saw children play with a dog this way. Dogs on the Island were mainly for protection and not love and affection. If someone didn't like your dog, they just poisoned it. It happened frequently.

When we got home, I always made a beeline for the shower. I hated that feel of salt and sand. But not Sandy. He never showered after. He would say, "The French say the sea salt is good for the skin." Ah, what did they know? I would find him out on his terrace having his first drink of the day, a double

Absolut on the rocks. Then we would sit and talk. This was my favorite time of day. We never ate till after 7:30 PM so we had quite a good, long talk-time and get-together. After dinner we would sit over coffee and talk some more or go upstairs and dive into our respective books for the rest of the evening.

Every year, the Christmas program opened with the first-year students posing in a tableau of the crèche and singing two-part carols. They opened the program with "O Come, All Ye Faithful" and "O Little Town of Bethlehem." We then did the reading of the *Nine Lessons* of the Bible leading up to the Nativity. Then the choir sang two carols that were appropriate to each lesson. The lesson was read by a cross section of people representing students, teachers, parents, and public officials. We started with a first-year student and went up through Bill Brown, the principal to, lastly, Son Mitchell, our minister to St. Vincent.

Our accompaniment up until 1973 was keyboard instrumentals played by my more musical students. I would put four of these toy-like instruments together to simulate the score with each taking a voice line. They accompanied me on the "Comfort Ye," the first tenor aria in the Messiah. By 1973 we were gradually replacing the carols with chorales and the arias from the Christmas section of the Messiah ending with the "Hallelujah Chorus." It was gratifying to see the students' progress through the years.

Santa Innovates

We decided to do Santa again this year, but I made some drastic changes. For one thing, I involved more people. I also checked out the old cheesecloth suit. It was a mess, but after ripping off the old cotton trim, rinsing the suit out in cold water, and ironing it, we were able to apply new cotton trim and it looked fine again. I cleaned up my rubber boots, and, with the new wig and beard Paul had brought me, the sprucing-up made for one svelte Santa that year. I ordered some small toys by catalogue and had them sent to Sandy. He packed them in a couple of suitcases and brought them down with him when he came in December. He had quite a time convincing Customs he wasn't in the toy business, that they were toys for Santa. Violet and Ralph Wallach, a couple who came to Bequia every year, had a company in Germany that made trinkets and toys for gift shops in New England, and they brought down a suitcase full of toys for the children, too.

This year, in order to make the event more manageable, Santa was going to visit each village separately. We started at noon in Paget Farm then went on to Society Hall at Gilford's at the Gap. After that we went down into the Harbour to Saltfish Hall and over to Hamilton to St. Michael's social hall, and lastly Santa went out in a dinghy to the yachts in the bay finishing up about seven o'clock. Thank God there was a full moon. Parnell, who was now my mechanic, handled all the transport and security. The women in each village supplied the gaily frosted cakes and cupcakes for the children in their village so long as Santa could supply the poorest with eggs, which were scarce at this time of year. Each party site had formed a crew of mothers and young adults, both male and female, from that particular village. Now that the group was under control, we could have more of a party with songs and children passing candy to one another, thereby introducing a sense of giving on the part of the children as well.

Midnight Magic

Paul Morrison sent me about thirty-five altar boy cassocks and white surplices, even one for me that came all the way down to my knees and made me look very official. Now that the boys were covered, I felt I had to do something to robe the girls as well. I went to St. Vincent and found Fred Dare, who became my friend and a great helper with all the future productions that called for fabric. He was Lebanese or Syrian, I never knew for sure which. His fabric came from India and the Middle East via Trinidad, I would guess. It was as close as you could get to a mill-end shop. Since our school colors were yellow and black and the men were in black and white, I put the girls in yellow and white. I found some solid white nylon with a chiffon organza feel to it, the kind you see on curtains. Gathered liberally under a yoke across the chest and back, with inexpensive white muslin underneath, it looked very light and flowing. I found some yellow sea-island cotton with a nice sheen to serve as a high shoulder yoke with a mandarin-style collar that would match the boys' black cassock tops. When Joan and Dovey and the other mothers finished them, they looked great. Standing next to the boys with their altar-boy look, the girls looked like angels on top of a Christmas tree.

We were singing in the robes for the first time at midnight mass. The church was all lit up, and the open windows let in a slight breeze. When it came time for mass, the choir started singing over at the rectory and filed in procession on the main street along the side of the church, into the church, and up into the choir loft. They sang "Stille Nacht" in German, and for the offertory I sang "Adeste, Fidelis" backed by the choir. We sang the rest of the mass in Latin in two parts. Vi and Ralph Wallach, who were German, came up to me after mass, very emotional, and said how touching it had been for them to hear "Stille Nacht." I said, "Why not? It was written that way." We didn't have a repeat of the misbehaving F# because I told Mrs. Benn to keep her hands off it.

We all went to midnight mass, Parnell driving me on ahead and Sandy and Paul coming later. I didn't see them till after the service. Everyone seemed pleased with how it turned out. After all, it was a first. But most meaningful to me was that I could see by Sandy's behavior he was very proud. He hadn't heard my kids sing since last year – he hadn't arrived soon enough to hear the Nine Lessons. Bill and Jane told him how well it had been received. Violet couldn't stop fawning. I guessed the German really got to her.

On Christmas, Boolu went to Winnie's for dinner. Marie had again invited Sandy and me for dinner with her as Son's guests, but since we had Paul this year, we had Christmas dinner with Bill and Jane. Bill was my boss, they were Sandy's swimming companions, and he had a lot of fun with them.

Now the Frangipani, of course, was the in place to be New Year's Eve, or Old Year's Night as the Bequians put it. Everyone always dropped by the Frangi to see "What's happenin', mon?" And this Old Year's Night was even better than last, well, bigger, that was for sure. The dance pavilion was packed shoulder to shoulder. Marie said that they were full to capacity both dinner sittings. Those at the second sitting had a guaranteed seat for the rest of the evening, and she made sure we had a ringside table. In this case, it was one of the outer-ring tables near the dance area and bar. Boolu was with us, but after dinner he vanished into the crowd and we didn't see much of him from then on. Over the course of the evening, I caught glimpses of him on the dance floor with this one and that one. He was having a grand time. On the dance floor, he was in his element.

Midnight was even more magical and dramatic than the year before. At the stroke of twelve, Son set off the red flares, casting a reddish hue over everything in sight, as if we were at the rim of hell. Like last year, the yachts bobbed up and down in the bay and the tall palm trees swayed. The noise was deafening as yachts blasted their horns, firecrackers popped here and there, and off in the distance up in the hills gunfire cracked into the air. Puffs of blazing red smoke wafted up over the bay and gusts of breeze rustled the leaves. The lush fuchsia bougainvillea blossoms turned blood red. The steel band was playing "Auld Lang Syne." What more could one ask for? It wasn't Times Square but it had its own charm.

Sandy looked at me and smiled. God, how Sandy loved New Year's! For some deep emotional reason, he stopped at New Year's and took stock of his position in life. Perhaps he set his introspection by New Year's because he had no religious calendar in his life, no atonement day, and no confessional where you start over, no personal, meaningful Christmas or Easter, not even a Passover. Yet he was a deep, purposeful, emotional, understanding kind of guy who was liberal and giving, with no fear at all, and full of love for everything and all people. He only believed in truth. He had a lifelong quest for the truth, whatever that was. That is what he believed in. In his life, New Year's was the one thing he could count on as sure, steady, and as solid as concrete. He once said, "It comes and goes, just like all of us." Every New Year's Eve, no matter where he was, he called his mother. He said he never missed a year until she died.

As the rockets blasted, I kissed him on each cheek and said, "This is one thing we're sure of: we're here now. And 1973—here we come and watch us grow!"

18 Metamorphoses in the Making
Our First Big Concert

We had been rehearsing our forthcoming concert ever since the start of the winter quarter. Father Adams had arranged a prestigious formal opening of Bequia Anglican High School with dignitaries coming from all over the Windward Islands. Bequia was just a tiny little Island, so why all the fuss? The idea for a school had been Father Adams' and no one else's from the start. He had made it clear he wanted no one who belonged in school to be left out because they were unprepared, or didn't have the money, or came from a non-caring family. So when it came time for Mary Lynn Lully, our math teacher, to pick students, we didn't give them the regular entrance test. They were given a general test, and if they were not up to secondary school work, we planned to pattern the first year to the students' needs and add a year to our program.

For students who could not afford to go to school, we asked foreigners to sponsor them. Sandy sponsored a young fellow. Violet and Ralph Wallach sponsored more than one and were great boosters in getting others involved. Mary Lynn found children who couldn't live at home for various reasons: an absent father, the death of a young mother, too many children, or a large family whose father was lost at sea, even a single mother with too many children unable to care for them all. In some cases the children had been handed over, usually to a larger family who could afford to take them in and feed them. In many cases they served as "Step'n'fetch-its" for the family. If they were very young, they might be allowed to go to school but usually for only half a day. Some of these children were quite bright and should have been in school with other children their age. Some of the families were not too keen on letting them go. As the children got older, the families would sometimes keep them at home where they could be useful. When one was accepted into the high school, they were in danger of being dumped by their foster parents. In fact some were, and we had to find homes for them.

I had been appointed to the Board of Governors by Father the fall that the Bishop had come to our first meeting. The school was into its second year. At that meeting I learned the Anglican Church, just like the Catholic Church at this time, was not in the business of opening new secondary schools. The yield didn't warrant the cost; it simply wasn't financially sound. In fact, they were closing school after school because of the expense. At that first meeting, the Bishop made it clear that the school and all its responsibilities were on Father's shoulders, and he was not to look to St. Vincent for help of any kind. I remember noting how blunt he was. After listening to the Bishop, I knew this was no time to bring up the problem we teachers were having with some students, but I did anyway. When I brought up the question of uncaring families at the Board meeting, a couple of prominent members of our community were indignant, saying we were opening a Pandora's box. Often children from families with problems were sent to families in St. Vincent, and Vincentian children were sent to Bequia. Obviously, it had been going on for years. To the foreign teachers at the school, in many of its aspects it seemed like invisible child slavery. The practice was never talked about. The Board listened to me, and abruptly dropped the subject.

Mary Lynn was appalled when I relayed their response, or should I say non-response. She thought the teachers would just have to take the children in while they were still in school, and some of them did. For example, when a couple of these children graduated and went over to St. Vincent for their A levels, two of them stayed at a house rented by Sandy. So, after that Board meeting, I could see that in Father's quest to educate the Anglican children and all other children no matter their faith, he was on his own, and I was more than willing to help him.

The 1973 Synod of the Windward Islands Dioceses of the Anglican Church was to be held on Bequia. Father wanted to hold the official opening of the Bequia Anglican High School at the same time. With this arrangement, he would have all the dignitaries here for our school opening. No one ever said he wasn't manipulative. Father had finessed the grand opening for the high school with all the church and political officials of the Windward Islands to be present, and it was my job to get the kids to rise to the occasion. I was going to have to shake my tush and crack the whip to get my kids up to snuff. How was I ever going to get them jumping through hoops in time? That's just a metaphor, right? We now had two classes of fifty students, and I planned to use all of them. I sat down at the drawing board. I figured I would take a bit of everything we had ever worked on. It began to become like a Broadway opening to me and I didn't know why. They were just little kids; it was supposed to be fun. Why am I working so hard, I wondered, and why am I making them work so hard? They liked working hard for me, so I expected it. If you work hard, it's going to be better. If it's better, it's going to please you more and everyone else as well. It would also be good for their work ethic in general. And that was what it was all about.

Of this group of 100 young scholars, only five or six, and that's a generous estimate, would have gone on to higher learning if it hadn't been for Father Adams and his efforts. By higher learning, I mean junior and senior high school. These children were otherwise destined to become fishermen, sailors, yacht hands, or taxi drivers and maids, laundry workers, or salespeople at the hotels. That is, if they were bright enough to achieve such a station, without much education. I don't know about any other island around here, I'm speaking of Bequia alone. There's nothing wrong with these ways of life, but how can you compare it to the life-styles of lawyers, ministers of state, doctors, dental surgeons, nurses, architects, librarians, qualified high school teachers, owners and operators of supermarkets, and computer specialists? These are a few of the careers an education could open up for them and that they did eventually achieve because someone cared enough. I hoped I was helping by insisting on 110% of their efforts. If something was worth doing, it was worth doing better than you ever dreamed you could.

Our first contribution to the program was to sing the 9 AM mass in Latin and in two parts as the Archbishop from Guyana celebrated the mass. Between the hymns sung by the congregation, with gusto, the children sang the "Kyrie," "Gloria," "Sanctus," "Benedictus," and the "Agnus Dei" at the appropriate times throughout the mass. For the offertory, the choir sang Mozart's "Ave Verum," a little weak in the bass section, but they did their best, considering. Then I sang the "Our Father," backed by the choir. At the communion we sang the popular "Let Us Break Bread Together on Our Knees," accompanied by a small band and bass drum with Flazzo Kidd, Len Leach, and Boolu playing in the rhythm section. Well, it wasn't a Broadway opening, but it was an historical first. It was the first radio broadcast from the Island of Bequia and it was being broadcast throughout the Windward Islands. I was told that every radio on Bequia was tuned in, and the families of the children were so proud of them.

It wouldn't be Bequia if something unexpected didn't occur, and believe me it did. Father had purchased a second-hand Hammond organ from a Canadian on the Island overseeing the construction of a hotel on the top of Hilary Point. So Mrs. Benn and I didn't have to worry about a sticky F sharp any more. My Canadian friend who sold the organ to Father asked me if he could help.

"Sure," I told him. "My basses could use your help with the 'Ave Verum.' Could you accompany us?"

"Yes, sure," he said.

Well, when it came time for him to play, he froze. No organ came in. I looked at him, and he was catatonic. He couldn't read music; he only played by ear. So I reached over and sounded the keynote, and we did it a cappella. The basses had a rough time without the organ to help, but my tenors and girls carried us through. The "Aniens" started a little raggedy because that section begins with the basses, but the tenors carried it through. After all, the basses weren't even basses yet.

Next on the schedule was the school opening. Many grandiloquent speeches were given, while the choir waited downstairs dressed in new school uniforms. What I had picked to perform for this part of the ceremony was in line with what we were studying. I used songs that would depict their heritage. I believe as West Indians they were a true mixture of the old world, both African and European, and of whatever else evolved, especially by way of the Caribs on these small West Indian islands. The choir performed five songs. The first was an early European classical piece we performed in a classical style. We sang Bach's "Air for a G String," the first line translation of which is "Jesus, joy of man's desiring." The second piece was a medley of children's songs. It began with Stephen Foster's "Camp Town Races" sung between the boys and girls antiphonally. Then, in a round, we sang "Row, Row, Row Your Boat," segued into "I've Been Working on the Railroad" (working for enunciation, speed, and agility within a style of freedom and child-like abandon), and ended with "Good Night, Ladies." The third number was a West Indian song from Barbados using African rhythms. I picked an interval of a sixth for harmony, and we danced in place in the style of a carnival road march as they sang "Kill La Lay Pom Pom." The place was jumping! Even I danced as I conducted, and I still remember Sydney McIntosh calling out, "Go, Jimmy-boy, go!" The fourth song was a popular recording by a girls' school in Trinidad. We did it with a soprano soloist, Avila Ollivierre singing "Sing Out My Soul to the Lord." The last rendition was the "Desiderata." I split the speaking parts between three girls and three boys. They did the chorus in three parts, one part being a high descant giving the piece the spirit and feel of gospel singing.

Desiderata - *You are a child of the Universe / No less than the trees and the stars / You have a right to be here.*

To accompany us we had a West Indian band with Leach playing cuatro, Flazzo the guitar, and others playing local rhythm instruments. Boolu played the bongos and the conga drums. All I can say was, the kids rocked and so did the audience. Our foreign dignitaries were expansive in their appreciation. One official rose to say, "What we are witnessing here today is the birth of West Indian culture." That said it all as far as I was concerned. Son Mitchell said, "It was a humbling experience."

Country Bumpkins Persevere

The choir was on its way to St. Vincent for the second time. We had gone the previous year to attend the All-Island Inter-School Music Festival, the first time a group of children from Bequia had gone over to St. Vincent to participate in a school function. Oh, St. Vincent had held them many times before, but Bequia was never a part of them. Not that they couldn't have gone. It was just that nobody cared enough to take them.

When my students had walked out onto the stage last year, the audience laughed. My back was to them, and I envisioned a big rip in my pants. What to do? I couldn't even check it out. I just waited till the laughter subsided and went on with our required piece, "The Harbingers of Spring." Soon it was over, and so were we. The Thompsons from America, who owned a house out in Spring, had come over to hear us. They were the only ones who did. They were concerned with the laughing and mentioned it. They believed it was because of the way my children were dressed. The children were in their old bleached out, faded-into-many-shades-of-blue, primary school uniforms. They couldn't yet afford their new secondary uniforms. Their accent was different as well. They did speak and sing in a slightly different style.

"Let's face it," Tom said. "If you're from Bequia, in St. Vincent, you're different."

"I get it. We were the country bumpkins," I said. It had all been part of a learning process for me. Back in New York, I had considered myself streetwise, but down here I wasn't yet island-wise, not by any stretch of the imagination. Now we were going to the Music Festival for the second time, and we had new secondary uniforms. Maybe they wouldn't laugh.

When it came time for our competition piece, I discovered it was an accompanied piece. But no one had bothered to tell me and no one had sent us the piano music. All I had was a lead sheet for the singers. We had prepared it as an a cappella piece without the interludes. A nun offered to play for us, but I had no music to follow. Consequently, when it came time for the piano interlude, I allowed eight measures and there were sixteen. I brought the singers in early. In short, I goofed! I didn't even bother to tell the kids what happened. I only told them that why we lost had nothing to do with them.

Nevertheless, we did win a couple of prizes. The judge that year came from England and knew nothing of the politics or lack of communication in these parts. We won first place in the senior female duet category. Our soprano, Joanna Osborne, had her four front teeth missing, but she had a glorious voice. Remember, on the Island they didn't fill teeth when needed; all they did was pull teeth. If you were too poor to go to St. Vincent, only nine miles away, gaps were the result. Never mind Joanna went on to become a dental surgeon and is now working in St. Vincent with a smile that won't quit. The alto I used was Elvie Ollivierre with a voice that matched Joanna's soprano. I told Elvie to stand upstage from Joanna, forcing Joanna to look away from the audience ever so slightly so they couldn't see her handicap, and it worked. Erdly Simmons, my First Form baritone, won first place in the solo senior men's category. He sang the "Banana Boat Song," with its signature lyric "Day-O," made popular by Harry Belafonte. So we did better than the first year. And most importantly, we weren't laughed at.

Back On 83rd Street

Sandy was having landlord troubles on 83rd Street. If this account seems a little fuzzy, it's because he never confided in me on the happenings there. Everything was always "fine." I always said 83rd Street was paramount in my mind, but maybe he felt I had enough on my plate without having to deal with it, too. He never told me when anything went wrong, answering any of my inquisitive comments with an offhand remark. He was afraid to tell me the truth, that he was having trouble with the house all along. I was going to be the last to know. If I had found out, I would have gone home and done my damnedest to fix the problem at the expense of Bequia. He wanted nothing to come between my Bequia efforts and all I'd accomplished to date. So I never knew of his 83rd Street troubles.

The Lady of the Gorilla, a Miss Harriman of the Harrimans, stayed only a year or so. Miss Harriman, her gorilla plus his monstrous cage, and half the cellar doorjamb as well were all gone. They discovered the gigantic cage was too big to fit through the narrow cellar door. How they ever got it in was anybody's guess. Sandy was glad to see the back of her. The second tenants in the triplex had trouble with leaking under the terrace because they didn't trouble themselves to shovel the snow. It piled up and melted, eventually making a mess in the kitchen. Sandy got a stranger in to fix the terrace. Instead of repairing it, he destroyed it altogether. The couple upstairs split up. The husband took off leaving the wife and two girls. When their lease was up, they had to leave because they couldn't afford the place. The new tenant upstairs was a single woman, but according to Sandy, she was crazier than a loon and drove everyone around her wild. She would do anything to satisfy her insatiable craving for attention. Sandy said she was certifiable and tried to get her out, but she would not budge and went right on being difficult.

I later learned how things had gone from bad to worse, but first, to my shock, I heard he had put the house up for sale! He called to tell me what he had done. Only then did he tell me why, and I told him I would have gone back to New York in a flash, moved into the basement apartment, and taken the load and responsibility of the landlord's job off his hands. I reminded him that 83rd Street was our ace in the hole, in case anything went awry. I had designed the basement apartment with that possibility in mind. But there was no talking to him. All he lived for now was his classroom and Bequia. He was sixty-eight. All he was thinking about was his retirement. In New York he had his bridge club, he had a few former students who stopped around to go to a movie, and that was the extent of his existence, except for the Playhouse. While all this turmoil was going on in '72 and '73, he was calmly teaching future stars such as Mary Steenburgen and CBS President Leslie Moonves. Even while he was dreaming of leaving, he was turning out stars. It was no time to sell a house. The house had tripled in value, but there was no money around except oil money, and an oilman expressed interest in the house.

When Sandy called to tell me he had found a buyer, my heart stopped. When I had left for Bequia, I had been banking on 83rd Street as our little piece of security. Maybe he didn't feel that need once he had Bequia, but at this point I knew Bequia better than he and I still didn't feel that secure yet. I tried to tell him, but he turned a deaf ear. He said he was finished with being a landlord. He hated it with a passion, I could see that. He never heard me out. His accountants, Lenny and Tommy, apartment dwellers who never owned a damn thing, were of no help at all. Little did we know, or anyone else for that matter, that in three or four years the value of East Side houses was going to skyrocket into the millions. Certainly Sandy's house would have, considering the location and the shape it was in. So much for hindsight!

What Sandy said at the time was, "I am selling," and he hung up. I went out onto the upper terrace. It was all I could do to breathe. I was so upset and felt so helpless, I could not catch my breath. I began to hyperventilate. I kept walking around in circles, gasping. I felt much betrayed and alone. I felt like a fool for having let myself get into such a predicament. 83rd Street wasn't my house to keep or sell. I had always been in charge of my life until now. But I was not the type to go out on a limb either. My Dad had warned me early in our relationship to be cautious and not too gullible. I kept asking myself, was I? Was I? I realized right then, at that very moment, that no matter how close we were, we were individuals first and partners second. No one said life was easy. I am sure Sandy felt, in his old-fashioned way, that he was thinking for both of us and had my best interests at heart as well, and that he knew best. Best for whom? For me? I didn't think so. I wasn't a kid. I was forty-four years old and life in Bequia might not last forever. 83rd Street was his and always had been, but now it was gone. That is how he saw it. I had to console myself with the fact that at least Bequia was now ours.

Not long after that I started to think of my own retirement plans. I knew that what Sandy was paying me was not enough, that I had to come up with some way to start making money so I could put something away for my old age. Sixty-five was just around the corner, and gray power without money was no power.

Musical Cars

That summer of '73, Sandy began to help us out on Father's newly acquired electric organ. We were preparing songs for the Christmas program. We were replacing the carols with oratorio music. We used the Recitatives, Choruses, and Chorales from the Christmas section of Georg Friedrich Handel's *Messiah*. Boolu was now official drummer for Sports Day and led the field march with the big bass drum on loan from the Burial Society out at Paget Farm. I thought it was now time to start teaching him the kettledrum rhythms for the "Hallelujah Chorus." We set the bass drum turned on its side at a slight slant on the floor for vibration, and he played it on one side like a kettledrum. The first-year students would be doing their usual crèche tableau with their carols. But the songs accompanying the *Nine Lessons* this year would correspond with the Christmas section from the *Messiah*, finishing off with the "Hallelujah Chorus" and Boolu doing his fabulous drumroll at the end.

Now that the Bequia house was finished, the next project was to extend the driveway farther up the hill and build an extra water tank for gardening. Then we could work on landscaping. After that, we decided to stop for a while and enjoy the fruits of our past labors. While we had been racing around building the house, the little Moke had taken one hell of a beating. The condition of the roads only helped it along its way to oblivion. One day out of a clear blue sky, William Tannis offered Sandy $600 for it. Right then and there Sandy said, "Sold." We then went over to St. Vincent

Bequia Bay from House

where he bought a new English Austin Mini from Dick Gunn at Hazell's.

I asked, "Why do you need a covered car?"

Sandy said, "Because I'm tired of getting wet."

"Fair enough," I said. A few weeks later, Mac Simmons wanted to know if I would be interested in his Moke since Sandy had sold ours. "How much?" I asked.

"For next to nothing," Mac answered.

"Fine," I said. "For next to nothing, I'll buy it." And I did. When Sandy asked why I had bought Mac's Moke, I said, "Because you sold our old Moke."

Sandy said, "But—"

"No 'buts' about it. I had a Moke, I want a Moke, I need a Moke, and I got a Moke." He hadn't asked me, why should I tell him? I was learning and I was sure he would learn too because he was a fast learner.

I busied myself with my teaching projects. Sandy came down for the summer and spent his time sunning and swimming. He was getting himself in great shape. We had a number of dinner parties and many reciprocated, filling up our social calendar. Life on Bequia was everything he dreamed it would be. I was getting over the loss of 83rd Street and getting used to the idea of looking at my future differently. I was thinking of some kind of business I could get into. So much was needed here. Sandy kept remarking on my transformation. First of all, he was exceedingly pleased with and grateful for my accomplishing the entire project. And then he was amazed at how much my work with the children was changing my persona.

"You are like a silkworm that's transformed into a butterfly," Sandy commented.

"Oh, thanks for the strong compliment. First I'm a worm and now I'm a butterfly. All that's missing is my fairy wand!" I snapped.

He said, "No, I was referring to the stark contrast. You've really come into your own. You're a born teacher. I only hope you'll begin to see your own self-worth. You have so much to offer, if you could see yourself as others see you."

"This has got to be a joke. OK, what do you want?" I asked.

"Nothing. Forget it," said Sandy.

We spent a lot of time with the young teachers Father Adams brought in through Canada's CUSO, England's OVSO, and the US Peace Corps. They would come for two years; some would stay an extra year. They were young, interesting, and full of life. They added to a rather pleasant existence. In spite of how well everything turned out for us, no way was Sandy going to give up teaching. He wound up splitting his time—half on Bequia and half in New York. I could see he was going to teach until he dropped. He could never stop.

Mom And Pop Make An Appearance

That year I was honored with three very special guests, my dad, mom, and sister Joan. They arrived the second week in December. Sandy was coming down on the 17th so he would overlap with them for a few days before they went back. I went over to St. Vincent to shop for the holidays and go out to the airport to meet them. Actually, I would have two mornings to shop since we would have to stay overnight at the Heron Hotel. The night they arrived, we sat around the lobby, and the next morning I took them shopping. I arranged for the food to get to the boat in time. We went back to the hotel for the bags and made the boat by 11:30, early enough to claim seats out on the deck where they could see all the proceedings. That day we had our share of livestock—a cow, a goat, a few live chickens, and a rooster—as well as boxes, bags, and bundles. With everyone getting ready for Christmas, the hustle and bustle was extraordinary. My mom was taking it all in and having the time of her life.

By one o'clock the boat was loaded to the gunwales. We set sail a little after one. As we crossed the channel, a pod of porpoises began leaping out of the water far to our right, heading south. There must have been about twenty-six or so in tandem in a long line, one couple after the other. Dad said, "Don't tell me you arranged this?"

"Sure, I had nothing to do yesterday." It's quite a sight, but it doesn't happen often.

As we approached Bequia, the swells started picking up with the fast current near Devil's Table. The *Friendship Rose* was sailing along at quite a clip, rising and falling with every swell. Spray blew across the deck, adding to the anxiety but also giving a little relief from the heat. The tropical sun was still high in the heavens, and its rays pelted down on us. Joan wasn't fazed by any of it. She took on the air of a seasoned traveler, since this was her third trip. When we reached Bequia, the pier was jammed, as it had a way of being every time the *Friendship Rose* docked with all its goodies. "All these people aren't here for us," I said.

Pop asked, "How many would you say?"

"I'd say about two, Pop."

When the boat slid up to the pier, immediately the unloading started. Boolu and Parnell were waiting. Mom and Pop were introduced, and then we got busy unloading all our paraphernalia. We stopped to watch the deckhands unload the cow. They were having more trouble getting the cow off the boat than they had had getting her on. Just as they got her front feet onto the pier, a large motor launch farther out in the bay caused a wake that splashed up against the pier and then washed back against the boat, sweeping the boat away from the pier. In an instant, the cow was standing in the sea with her four feet flat in the sandy bottom. The water back then was as clear as drinking water, and the sight of that cow, the securing weight still around her neck, staring up at us was either tragic or hysterical.

My pop, not believing his eyes, said to me, "Is this some more of your shenanigans?"

"Oh, God, no. Who could think up such a thing?" I said. Fortunately, someone jumped in quickly and walked her to shore. The look on her face was so perplexed, not understanding what in hell had happened to her. By then everyone was hysterical.

My mom said, "Now I've seen everything!"

Joan asked, "Is the cow all right?" I assured her the cow was fine.

After all the commotion of the cow's fall, we finally got the bags and our provisions off and into a jeep. Parnell took Joan, Mom, and Pop in his Moke, and Boolu and I went in the jeep, the footman, as they are called down here, hanging off the back. When we reached home, the footman unloaded the bags and took them into the house. Then Boolu helped Winnie with her boxes of food for the month. Unloading, hauling everything up to the kitchen, and packing it away was a job in itself. I showed Mom and Pop around the first floor: Boolu's room, the baths, the guest room, and the terrace. Then I took them up around the living room terrace and into the living room, and then up to the dining room and out to the kitchen in the back. Mom then went back through the dining room to the terrace there and the great view of the ocean beyond. She sat down.

"You've got more to see," I told her.

She said, "Not today. I'll look at the rest tomorrow. Give me a chance to digest this much."

Pop spotted the wing chair in the corner of the living room and said, "I've found my spot. I'll just sit here and let the rest of the world go by, thank you."

After they freshened up and were sitting out on the terrace, Mom came into the dining room and asked, "Who's having dinner?"

"Just us," I answered.

"Just us?" she repeated. "What about Boolu?"

"Oh! He eats with Winnie in the kitchen."

"Didn't I get it right? Isn't he family now?" she asked.

"Well, yes," I said. "But— "

"'But,'" she mimicked. "But then I'll eat in the kitchen with Winnie as well."

"OK, OK. Boolu!" I called to him. "Fix another place." Winnie, having heard our conversation, was smiling from ear to ear. Boolu picked a spot on my left, where he sat for years to come. It was as if he had come of age and it was time for him to eat at the adult table, thanks to his new granny.

The next morning I heard someone in the living room. Mom and Pop were sitting on either end of the Victorian couch, their hands in their laps, looking like some gothic painting. I asked, "What's this?"

Mom asked, "What is this?" indicating the couch.

Then I asked, "What do you two think it is?"

"It looks like the couch we courted on some fifty years ago at Mrs. Proctor's."

I simply said, "'Looks like?' It is more than 'looks like,' it is like. It's identical to that one! I got it from the grandson of Mrs. Proctor's friend. They ordered identical couches as part of their trousseaux in the 1840s." Then I asked, "You mean you courted?"

18 Metamorphoses in the Making

"No," Pop said, "that was Mrs. Proctor's word for it. When I went to Proctors' to pick up your mother, if we were going out, she made me sit here on the edge of this couch and wait for your mother to come down. Then she would sit in her big winged chair and conduct an inquisitive interview. When Mom came down, she would have her sit at that other end and would continue to interrogate me as to whether my intentions were honorable."

Mrs. Proctor had brought my mom over from Ireland in 1922 to be her personal chambermaid, and she felt she was responsible for her as a surrogate mother. I guess that made Mrs. Proctor my surrogate grandmother, only I had never known it until now. I took them out to Sydney McIntosh's for a barbeque. He was a Scot, born on Bequia, but that didn't keep him from wearing the McIntosh plaid pants. Pop, noting this, sang Harry Lauder songs, and Sydney was in seventh heaven. As a newspaper photographer, Sydney had taken the first picture of Papillon in southern Trinidad after his escape from Devil's Island off the shores of French Guyana. Sydney's barbeque was a weekly affair. Its primary patrons were people from the charter yachts who ventured into the interior to the McIntosh farm out in Industry beyond Raintree.

I had Winnie invite some Bequia women over to meet my mother. Everyone came except two. I was surprised because they were the two I thought I knew and liked best, next to Winnie. Oddly enough, Winnie wasn't fazed by their absence. She explained that it had to do with false pride. Now, after many years, I think I understand what she was referring to. Simply said, I have found some Bequians could bridge the culture gap, as Boolu did beautifully, and others couldn't or didn't want to. It was like: "You on my turf if you like, but never me on your turf, because I don't like." The two women were Erma and Joan, both women I liked and appreciated. They were my friends, but friends who never entered our house despite many invitations. Before long, our invitations stopped. I didn't need to be a rocket scientist to see they drew a line, so I honored it. This situation grew out of their needs, not mine. The other women I knew as well and was proud to introduce to my mom and dad as friends. They were relationships that proved lasting to both Sandy and me.

Winnie prepared a lovely lunch and we had drinks available to satisfy everyone's taste. Winnie's only concern was what to do with Dad. I told her not to worry, that he wouldn't miss meeting the ladies. He was a man's man but just as strongly a lady's man. We used to kid Mom about the women who loved him. She would smile and say, "Just remember, he always comes home to me," and he always did.

During the lunch, Winnie came into the kitchen where Boolu and I were washing dishes and said, "You're so right! What a gentleman! He has some of them in there swooning. He's in there singing to them, and what a beautiful voice!"

"That's what my daddy does," I said. "I only wish I was half as talented as he is."

Some told Mom she reminded them of Dolly Ollivierre, that she could pass as one of her sisters over in St. Vincent. I looked at Winnie—we both knew Dolly!—and said, "Whoops." The women stayed and stayed and everyone was having a good time, including Dad. All you had to do was ask him to sing. He really was a modern-day John McCormack.

Sandy arrived on the 17th and spent a few days with my family before they left. We decided to go out for dinner to the Thursday night barbeque. The Frangi was the in place to be on Thursday nights with their steel band rocking the Harbour. We had finished dinner and were walking over toward the bar to get closer to the band so we could see some of Boolu's antics on the dance floor. Everyone else walked on ahead while I looked for an ashtray. The servers had cleaned off the tables so I couldn't find one, and the ash on the end of my cigarette was an inch long. I spotted one un-cleared table with an ashtray. By the time I reached the table, I had had a revelation. I felt like a stupid ass. Thoughts rushed through my head. What am I doing over here? Everyone is whooping it up over there having a great time, and here am I, enslaved to this damned ash. I took the damned half-finished cigarette and slammed it into the sand-filled coconut half-shell. As I heard myself saying, "That's it! I'm finished," I knew it was the last one. I had tried to quit many times before but this was it. Now, thirty-five years later, I can say it was. I was a two-pack-a-day smoker, with the stained fingertips to prove it. No one even noticed I had quit at first.

My family left on the 21st. Mom loved it here but she needed to be back by Christmas. You couldn't get my mom any farther than ten feet from the farm at that time of year, not with all her grandchildren converging on the place to celebrate the season. "If I had no grandchildren, I would be up on Mount Pleasant raising goats and making goat cheese," she said. At another time she said, "That trip over on the *Friendship Rose* was one of the most memorable days of my life. It took me back fifty years."

Postscript

On the evening of the 24th, Sandy asked, "Where's my Christmas present?"

"I already gave it to you," I replied.

"Well, where is it?"

"I gave it to you on the 20th last Thursday night at the Frangipani. Sandy, I stopped smoking and you never even noticed. Now you, with your voice and sore throat problems, should stop, not for me, but for yourself." It didn't work. He went right on smoking. I stopped, I guess, for myself.

We spent Old Year's Night at the Frangipani waiting to usher in 1974. Just "de tree a we" having dinner like the extended—or was it alternative?—family we were. Sandy got a kick out of watching Boolu operate after dinner. It was amazing watching him grow. It was already over five years. Actually, it was heartwarming.

19 The Ides Betide

Jimmy in Bequia

Sandy Joins the Music Department

Sandy went back to New York on January 6, 1974, planning to come back earlier in the spring. I put a bid on an Italian two-tiered organ that a yacht captain had for sale. I was hoping Sandy would now play for the choir. My piano playing relied on chords and the hunt-and-peck method. I began work on the Easter section of the *Messiah*. I wanted to bring some music down to Paget Farm. I hadn't been down there, with the exception of Carnival, since our first Folk Concert held in 1970 at the primary school. That had ended in a riot. I figured we should try again. So, come Easter Sunday, we were going to sing the Easter section of the *Messiah* in place of their traditional, non-musical Easter Cantata.

I had the children "robe up" in Paget Farm's Burial Society Hall up over Walter Bynoe's Bar, with Mary Lynn keeping the bedlam to a minimum. We waited while the congregation filled the church to capacity, with the children standing outside at the large open windows. Then we marched down the dusty dirt road, with Boolu in the lead banging on the big bass drum. We marched past the old cemetery with the enchanting, overgrown tombstones and graves of the distant past. Beyond it, off to the side of the road along the waterfront, stood the little old stone church. Up on the altar stood Father Adams with Sandy sitting at the organ waiting for us to march down the center aisle. Boolu, with the help of a choir member, set the bass drum on its side on a stand, so he could play it as an improvised kettledrum. Joanna Osborne, Suzanne Wallace, Eloise Simmons, Mrs. Benn's son Junior, and yours truly sang the arias. With the master at the organ, everything went along at a steady clip. It was such a joy for me to conduct with Sandy at the keyboard. He made it so easy for the kids they didn't even need me.

Everything was going fine until Boolu spotted his friend Antoinette standing at the open window. He was sidetracked by his need to show off for her. His eyes were on her more than they were on me—until her mother, Joan, sitting on the aisle in the fourth row, noticed. All of a sudden, I heard a commotion. Out of the corner of my left eye, I could see Joan grab Boolu by the arm. She was physically instructing him to keep his eyes on me and not on her daughter. The hubbub never interrupted a thing, and at least when I needed Boolu's attention, I had it.

The "Hallelujah Chorus" ended the program with Boolu finishing it off with that beautiful drumroll of his. That particular concert was so well received by the village folk, it induced in me a warm sense of giving. I got so much out of that concert personally. I wanted to say to Sandy, but I didn't, that this is not Hollywood, for here "Za gratitudine non e ram."

The Night Of The Three Moons

One night we were reclining on the lounge chairs relaxing, just gazing up at the sky, when Sandy said, "I see three moons up there tonight."

So began our unimaginably precarious roller-coaster ride! I am here to tell you the heights and depths of that ride were truly death-defying. And it lasted for twenty-three years. It was said that Montgomery Clift suffered the longest suicide in history. If so, one could say Sanford Meisner suffered the longest drawn-out natural death ever. He was so invincible he fought it off time and time again.

I asked him, "Why do you think you see three moons, because I assure you there is still only one."

He answered, "My doctor says I have cataracts and that I have to wait until they get 'ripe.' I'll get them done in the fall."

"Sure, you'll get them done in September, but then how will you teach with bandages over your eyes? I'm calling Dr. Katzen tomorrow. I can't go with you, I still have my classes, but I'll come up when you're finished. That's when you'll need me. I'll call the travel agent, get your return ticket changed, and Paul can meet you."

The next morning I called the doctor who said he would see Sandy just as soon as he got back. I thought Paul would make arrangements for him at the Dover Hotel and that I would come up when he came out of the hospital. But Paul said there was no need for me to come. As he talked, I thought, not on

19 The Ides Betide

your life am I not going to be there when he needs me. How could Paul take care of him if he was at work? I gave my students early tests because school was almost finished anyway.

The first operation went well according to Dr. Katzen. Sandy was ready to come home from the hospital after the second operation. Paul insisted we go to his house. Sandy came home with large bandages over both eyes. His surgery was pre-laser, but before long the bandages came off and his vision was in pretty good shape. He didn't really need me there at Paul's. Nor did I like being the odd man out. I decided to go back to Bequia.

When Sandy had come home from the hospital, he was still struggling with laryngitis. He had had it when he was on Bequia at Christmastime. I said, "You have to promise me you will see your throat doctor before you come back."

"Sure, sure I will," he said, but he was making light of it. I made him call the doctor for an appointment and insisted he promise to go with Paul.

With Paul's assurances, I packed my bags and hightailed it back to Bequia, believing Sandy would be close behind because of the good prognosis he was getting from his eye doctor. He was planning to be on Bequia for my birthday July 28. His throat examination showed he needed a biopsy. It was scheduled for the 16th or 17th and on the 20th he was to leave for Bequia. He said, "I'm not waiting for the results. I'll meet you in St. Vincent on Sunday the 21st and we'll celebrate on the 28th."

Saturday came and I went to St. Vincent to be there for Sandy's arrival, but on Sunday he never showed. I called Paul's and the phone was busy. I tried a few times at the airport, gave up, and went back to the Heron and kept trying, with no luck. The phone system in those days was little more than a relic. I called him from the hotel the next morning. Still no answer. It was possible Sandy would make it that day. I tried to get Paul at the school, but was told he hadn't come in yet. All they knew was that he was in the hospital with Sandy.

"Which one?" I asked.

"We don't know, but Paul said to tell you he was at the doctor's with Sandy and he"ll call tonight." So I hopped on the *Friendship Rose* for home. That Monday was the longest day of my life.

Paul called about 6:30 PM and said, "Sandy is still here. While he was packing for Bequia on Saturday, he went blind in his left eye. We've been frantic trying to find an eye doctor, which, on a weekend in the middle of summer, is impossible. But he has one now and he's being operated on tomorrow at noon. Sandy told me to tell you not to do anything. I'll call you tomorrow."

"What happened to his eye?" I asked.

"The retina detached. That damned throat doctor... I'll tell you all about it tomorrow."

What happened? During the biopsy, the throat doctor was pinching Sandy's throat. Sandy tried to tell him so, but the doctor's response was, "If you just sit still, I'll get this done." The pinching continued until he finished.

Paul said, "When Sandy came out of that office, he was as red as a beet.

When I asked him what had happened, he said, 'That doctor damn near killed me.'"

The doctor had been Sandy's doctor for years and had to have known about Sandy's recent cataract surgery. Come Saturday, the retina in his left eye had ripped. In hindsight, that was not surprising with his eyes so vulnerable. When I talked to Paul on Monday, he didn't tell me that the throat doctor had called that afternoon, saying he too had to see Sandy. When Paul told the doctor what had happened to his eye and that he was having an operation the next day at noon, the doctor told Paul to bring Sandy in to see him Tuesday morning at 8:30 AM before he went to the hospital.

Tuesday morning the doctor told Sandy he had cancer of the vocal chord. He had two treatment options: a local operation or a radical laryngectomy. Unfortunately he, the doctor, was going on vacation. He handed Sandy a list of doctors to choose from. This advice was coming from a doctor Sandy had depended on for fifteen years! The doctor's wife sent Sandy a bill for her husband's botched-up services. Needless to say, we ignored it. She was damned lucky they weren't sued, but Sandy just wasn't built that way.

Now! Tuesday afternoon, while he was on the gurney being prepped for the operation of the left eye, the retina in the right eye ripped. There Sandy lay dreading a future where he would be both mute and blind—and all this within a three-hour period. The causes were totally unrelated, according to the doctor, but then again, were they?

I couldn't believe what Paul was telling me. That day, July 23, was a day of infamy for both Sandy and me. I immediately made arrangements to leave, but this time I would be gone for an indefinite period. I spoke to Mary Lynn Lully, now our principal, and to Father Adams. They too were upset by the news about Sandy and said their prayers were with him. Mary Lynn agreed to move in with Boolu to keep an eye on him. Bill Esper, Sandy's assistant at the Playhouse, happened to be vacationing at our place with his wife Suzanne and their two children and offered their apartment on 57th Street and Second Avenue. When I reached New York, both Paul and Sandy's sister, Ruth, had him practically dead. Sandy was in the Manhattan Eye and Ear Center on East 63rd undergoing an operation on his second eye. Dr. Sudarsky found Sandy a reputable Head and Neck doctor at Memorial Sloan-Kettering Cancer Center who would be ready for Sandy the following week.

Recovery from these eye procedures back then was a slow and delicate process, but Sandy didn't have the luxury of time for either the cataract or the detached retinas. He had to plow through with all five operations. Dr. Sudarsky warned that he must not trip or fall on the journey over to Kettering because any shaking or disturbance of the eyes could be harmful.

So Monday morning August 5, Sandy, his eyes bandaged, and I cautiously left by cab for Memorial Sloan-Kettering on East 68th Street and York Avenue. When we entered Admitting, even the workers were a little taken aback by his condition. Neither Sandy nor I spoke of our circumstances. We talked

19 The Ides Betide

about everything else but. If we didn't talk about what was happening, maybe it wouldn't get any worse. It was like walking on thin ice. We were going inch by inch, moment by moment, making no pronouncements, just doing what we were told by the medical authorities. Only they could help us now.

Sloan-Kettering in 1974 was like walking into the 21st century, everything was so futuristic. I hadn't been in a hospital since '52, except for the years I spent visiting my sister during her fight back from her traumatic accident in '59. Sandy was on the 9th floor in a private room. Every two rooms had their own supply closet with everything within arm's reach. Because of Sandy's blindness, I asked for a private duty nurse. I was told the hospital was so tightly run they didn't have them, that they were equipped for any emergency. I certainly hoped so. I was apprehensive about the whole situation. The nurses' station in the middle of the floor was like a command post. It stretched across the width of the building on every floor. Everything was efficient. Unfortunately, the flow of visitors was regimented, too. Only two were allowed at a time, and the main entrance was barricaded. The regulation made it difficult for me because since Sandy wasn't used to his blindness, I wanted to be with him to help him. My continuous presence caused a visitor problem. I had to find a way to get up to the 9th floor without having to go through the barricade.

I soon discovered a way to get into the hospital through Memorial's Outpatient Department on First Avenue. Then I would work my way over to the Inpatient section and take an elevator to the 9th floor. Once in Sandy's room, I was relatively safe. This routine left the two visitor tickets for Sandy's visitors to squabble over—not my prob-bub-lem. I had Sandy's welfare to think about and that was enough for me. The visitor problem was left for Ruth and Paul to work out between them.

Both Paul and Ruth were beside themselves, and Ruth's desperate nervousness made her seem extra pushy around the nurses. Her extreme love and loyalty to Sandy made her behave like a TV Jewish mother. No matter what anyone did for him, it wasn't enough. She thought the sun rose and set around him and couldn't see why everyone else didn't understand that. She reminded me of the Jewish joke about the university student who was pushed around to his classes in a wheelchair by his mother. When asked why, since he could stand and walk perfectly well on his own, she answered proudly, "Tenks G-d, he don't hef to." When Ruth was around the nurse's station, I was so embarrassed I avoided being there. Having been around hospitals with my sister so much, I had learned that emotions run high sometimes with families as well as with patients. Most hospital workers then tend to become less helpful. When they don't perform as you would expect them to, you never demand, you finesse if you can.

That week dragged on interminably. In spite of being healthy in every other way, he was totally helpless and emotionally all bottled up, as was I. Moreover, wedged in between pillows while his eyes were healing, he couldn't move. We were both so apprehensive about a future that seemed foreboding, frightening, and unknown, with so many possibilities and perplexities that had yet to be answered. What if he should never see again? What if he was never able to speak again, and what if this cancer is the beginning of the end? Who speaks of such things? He couldn't and I wouldn't. So we spent the time in silence, and I jumped at every provocation. I was useless. All I could do was wait, and that was really all Sandy could do as well.

Not many visitors came, just Paul and Ruth and a few close family members. That was fine with me. What could talk do? It was now up to the doctors. On August 8, I wanted to see him before they took him to be prepped for the operation. For some reason the workers on the floor said nothing about my being there outside visiting hours. Maybe it was the circuitous trip I had to take, avoiding the 1st floor barricade, to get up there at that hour. More likely it was Sandy's condition. Whatever. I was there and that was all that mattered. I didn't say much, just held his hand as they wheeled him down to the 4th floor. As he went in, I told him I loved him and I would be waiting for him. He waved. I sat where families wait for the operating physician after the operation. I thought about our life together, what it was like, and wondered how this catastrophe would affect us.

I then went over to First Avenue to an Eastern European Catholic Church and lit candles and prayed. What else is there to do in times like these? When you need so much help, there is no one except Him. I went back to the waiting room and waited for Ruth. She would be the first to arrive and then Paul. Ruth kept asking the clerk at the desk if there was any news, but I knew we would hear nothing until the physician came and told us himself. I had been quietly waiting for well over a week. A few more hours wouldn't change anything. Sandy's nephew Danny and his wife Laura came, then his brother Bobby and sister-in-law Ginny from Jersey, and still no word. My family called from upstate. I told Hugh there was no word yet, I would call later.

Dr. Shapiro came down about 4:30 and said he had performed a laryngectomy. The growth was malignant and being sent to the lab for confirmation. The prognosis looked good. The cancer was contained within the larynx preventing it from spreading any further, and at present Sandy would not need radiation or chemotherapy. He was in recovery, doing well, and would soon be sent up to his room. But he would not be able to have visitors until tomorrow. He would be groggy for a few more hours.

Well, that report seemed to reassure Ruth. I had to see him and would not rest until I did. So we all said our good-byes and went our separate ways. Only I didn't go home. I went to the desk and asked for information on Mr. Meisner. I was told he was now out of recovery, in his room, on guarded status with no visitors until tomorrow. It was not yet five o'clock and the doors over at Memorial would still be open. I could get up to his room once I got in there.

I was so worried. With no private duty nurse, he wouldn't be able to find the buzzer in his condition and wouldn't be able to call out. He was totally

19 The Ides Betide

helpless, like a newborn baby. Why no private duty nurse? I couldn't understand it. He was in a private room all by himself and way down the hall from the nurses' station. I was getting more nervous by the minute. I went to Memorial and took an elevator to the 9th floor. All the office staff was going in the opposite direction on their way home and paid me no mind. I worked my way across the 9th floor to the York Avenue end of the complex. I was almost there when I ran into an area under construction. You couldn't tell which way the hall ran, or where the rooms were because there were none. The area was basically just one open space divided by heavy-duty hanging canvasses, around which work was in progress. Wires and pipes and partially built walls of cement were everywhere. I am sure the workers all left by four o'clock. It was dark with no light except a far-off window and here and there a hanging light bulb. I fumbled around to the opposite end of the room, which looked like a kitchen under construction. I found a large double door, which opened onto the 9th floor of Kettering, just two doors from Sandy's room.

I went in, and there lay Sandy, his eyes still bandaged. Tubes protruded from his body in all directions connected to plastic bags of fluids and a heart monitor machine ticking away. His throat was clear of bandages around the operation, exposing the stoma and the dark sutures. Every time he exhaled, blood spurted up through the hole in his neck like the hole in the head of a whale.

I walked over to him and said quietly, "Sandy, it's Jimmy." I took his hand, and he squeezed mine. "Well, you made it, and when you get those bandages off, everything is going to work out, thank God! I can't stay because they said you must rest and get some sleep. Take it easy, and remember, I love you. I'll be here first thing in the morning." He squeezed my hand again and I left.

I didn't want them to see me there with him, so I went into the room next door and spoke to the woman in there. She had just had a mastectomy and was leaving the next day. I told her of my concern and she said, "I understand, but don't worry. The nurses are in and out every five minutes. He's getting excellent care."

While we stood talking, I could hear two nurses in there with him that very moment. I told her, "If you hear banging during the night, please ring for a nurse because I know him and that's exactly what he will do."

She was reassuring. "I'll keep an ear out and check him every once in a while during the night."

I didn't go back into his room. Although I did feel much better after having seen him, the sight of him was a little rough to take. The blood spewing up out of that hole like a humpback whale and back down again really got to me. I couldn't get it out of my mind. I thanked my newfound friend, said I would see her in the morning before she left, and took off through the visitors' entrance.

By now it was dinnertime. Though it didn't cross my mind at the time, I make note of the fact now that there was no dinner invite from Paul that night. Just a little insight in hindsight. I didn't want to be with anyone just then anyway, I only wanted to be with Sandy, who totally occupied my thoughts. I could think of nothing else. He consumed me. I stopped at Shopwell, picked up a little something, and took it back to Bill and Suzanne's place. After dinner I felt exhausted, emotionally drained. I fell into bed and was fast asleep in minutes.

Sometime in the middle of the night, I was jolted out of my sleep, as if waking out of a shocking dream I remembered nothing of. My throat felt as raw as beefsteak. It was so sore it pained me to swallow. I gargled with warm water and salt but it did little good. I got up early, showered, shaved, dressed, and tried to have breakfast but I couldn't swallow. I was heading up to Sloan-Kettering when I realized I had to do something about this sore throat. I went to my doctor on East 30th Street who said he couldn't remember seeing a throat so raw. It was more like a child's sore throat. When I told him about the preceding day's events, he said he wasn't surprised, it was probably psychosomatic. Who knew? He numbed it some with a medical spray and gave me a bottle to take with me.

Again, I circumvented the visitors' entrance, which wouldn't be open until noon, by going in at the Memorial end. Crossing over on the 1st floor to an in-house elevator to the 9th floor, I made my way to Sandy's room. Sandy was glad to have me there. I could see he was now all bandaged up, with only the stoma opening visible and no more blood spewing out. He was breathing easily. When the nurse came in, she never said a word about visiting hours. She just gave me a pad and pencil for him, saying, "If he feels the need to write." But he would have to do it with the bandages over his eyes. She said he was doing very well, as well as could be expected, and in case he needed anything, I should just ring. When she left, the lady in the next room came in and said he had slept most of the night. The nurses had been in and out all night taking good care of him. I thanked her and said good-bye as she left for Baltimore about noon.

Ruth came in about two o'clock, and she and I did all the talking, of course. He got better day by day and was soon able to move enough to scribble a word or two on the pad. "Where are you staying?" "Vodka?" "Water?" "Where are 'LN' and Joe?" "Ruth, don't worry." " Did Bobby come?" These few notes don't seem like much now, but then they were everything to Ruth and me.

During this month, Paul received a call from Steve McQueen asking if there was anything he could do for Sandy. Paul told him Sandy was doing well and would be home soon. Still, Steve wanted to know if Sandy needed anything: "I mean money, does he need help?"

"Oh, no, he has insurance that will cover most of it."

"Well, I'm here for him if he does," Steve replied. You know, Steve McQueen was the only celebrity who came forward and asked if Sandy needed anything, I mean ever. Maybe they called the Playhouse or Paul, but Sandy didn't hear from them. He heard from Stella, and Lee's wife Anna, and Eli stopped by, but not many others. From what I heard, a lot of them had him dead. That

19 The Ides Betide

was the way of it then. Many people reacted to news of cancer fatalistically. But boy, were they wrong!

One day, an older man came by and said, "You don't know me, but I know about you and what you've been through. I had an operation like you just had, about ten years ago. I went to school and learned to speak again, not quite the same as I did, but it works for me, and I believe you can do it, too."

Sandy damn near jumped out of bed. He rose off the pillow to a sitting position. He became so full of life again after a complete month of just lying passively in his bed. Both of us were transfixed by the old fellow. I couldn't believe myself what I was hearing coming out of this gentleman's mouth. He spoke in a strange, deep, slow, halting cadence as he stepped forward and introduced himself. With no voice box, no larynx, he was making sounds, then words, and eventually sentences that made sense. He was talking! It was like a miracle.

Sandy motioned for the pad and pencil and started scribbling questions so fast and furiously I could barely decipher them. "Is this a school?" "Where is it? Here in New York?" "What is the name of this speech?" "Is there a book?" "Jimmy, write this all down."

Sandy handed me the pad and pencil and fell back onto his pillows, exhausted. No one at the hospital, no doctor, no nurse, not even a social worker, absolutely no one ever spoke of this type of communication for Sandy. We had heard of a machine you hold up to your neck while you mouth words that come out sounding like a robot, but that was all. This gentleman gave Sandy hope for a continued life. He turned out to be the contractor who was installing the kitchen that I had stumbled into the evening of Sandy's operation.

When the man left, Sandy pulled me close to the bed, took the pad and pencil in hand, and started scrawling words across the pad in spite of his blindness. "Get the book... Call the school... Get the number... Where is it?... Can I go?... When can I go?"

I could see that as far as Sandy was concerned, the eye operations, even though the bandages were not off yet, were all behind him, and the cancer business, although he was still in the hospital, was also over. He was now on to another quest and he couldn't wait to get started, the sooner the better. He would be out of the hospital by the end of the month and was going to stay at Paul's. Bill and Suzanne were back and I was moving over to Paul's to take care of Sandy. Paul wouldn't hear of Sandy's moving back to the Dover, so he had to suffer my presence. I didn't care. My concern was Sandy's wellbeing and that was all. Eventually the bandages came off and he wore dark glasses. But he still couldn't see. He could tell light from dark and make out shapes and shadows, but that was it. I had to direct him by the arm or lead him by the hand.

By the first week in September, right after Labor Day, Sandy was sitting in a classroom down on Irving Place just south of Gramercy Park in his first esophageal speech class. He was told it usually takes a year or more to learn this technique and that some never do master it. I guess that's why he was given that machine that he hated so. He called it Robby the Robot. Nevertheless, he said his first word in a month, and by November he was in his own classroom at the Playhouse. I fixed him up with an amplifier and tied a tiny microphone to his glasses that dangled next to his lips. I helped him with translation the first month, and then Bob Scott took over. His vision was improving and he could now manage by himself. It was obvious—it was time for me to return to my own life back on Bequia.

The Roller Coaster Plummets Again

I had a month to get the Christmas program in shape, so I got busy. The new Geography teacher, Jonathan, was a young gentleman from England just out of college. He had studied piano since he was just a wee tyke, but he was shy and said he only played for himself. I explained how much I needed his help and managed to persuade him. He started at first playing the simple pieces, but I ever so slowly finessed him into the more difficult numbers. I told him to just take it easy piece by piece, and before I knew it, he was doing very nicely. When the chorus was doing a piece they knew rather well, I told him he should just bang it out, wrong notes and all; at least we would be in the same key. Actually, he was much better than he gave himself credit for. His playing made it much easier for me, especially given the lack of time. Before he realized it, he was knocking off the Chorales from the *Messiah*. He actually was a godsend.

This year Paul was to bring Sandy down when the Playhouse closed for Christmas on December 15. Sandy was planning to play for the *Nine Lessons*. Frankly, I wasn't sure his eyes would be well enough. Still, last Easter when he had played, it had all gone so well that now I took a let's-wait-and-see attitude. When he sat down and started to play, I was ecstatic. So was Jonathan because he was off the hook, as it were. The students were excited to have Sandy back; he hadn't been around since Easter.

What happened during the performance was unforeseen. Not in anyone's wildest dreams could it have happened, but it did: the roller coaster took another wild dip. Toward the end of the evening, Sandy's sight started to go. Jonathan was the page-turner and even he didn't cotton on to what was happening. By the time he reached the "Hallelujah Chorus," he was blind. Still, he played on to the end, blind as a bat. Only once it was all over did he let on. Later, he had to be led to the car.

Dr. Gun-Munro was now the Surgeon General and had a home on Bequia. He happened to be an eye specialist. Sandy's retinas in both eyes had ripped again. Sandy must get back to the States as quickly as possible to get them cared for. The doctor's prognosis was that they could possibly save the right eye but the retina in the left eye had folded back on itself, like a thin onion-skin. He would probably lose the sight in that one.

Back to New York, as predicted, Dr. Sudarsky was able to save the sight in the right eye, but the left one was gone. The folded back retina had seized. There was nothing to be done. Sandy was still at Paul's when I went up in February. Would you believe it? Sandy was back at the Playhouse, teaching with the one good eye and his amplifier. He was also heading down to Irving Place for his speech classes.

My parents were celebrating their 50th anniversary on February 22. I went up for the celebration, but Sandy and I agreed it would be too much for him. He would be better off staying at Paul's and taking it easy. He could well afford to now. He had Bill Esper, Ed Moore, Bob Modica, and Bill Alderson helping at the Playhouse. Actually, he had plenty of help at the school for the most part. All he really had to do was oversee their work and keep everything on an even keel.

The Anniversary

As part of their 50th anniversary celebration, Mom and Pop were renewing their vows. They were married in St. Patrick's in Utica where all eleven of us were christened, except for Ed. The six oldest all went to school there, and I was the last to graduate. The school and the church were gone now, due to the inner city financial plight. So the Irish and the German parishes had merged and were now called St. Joseph and St. Patrick's. Three priests celebrated mass, with the grandchildren assisting as altar boys. Leo and yours truly were delegated to the choir loft as usual. The organist said he never got to play the songs we picked to sing any more. In fact he didn't get to play this huge organ very much at all. The kids, along with a couple of nuns from the school, now played for the mass with guitars, you know, folk music. All I could say to that was, "What a shame. My kids would just love this fabulous organ." There's nothing wrong with folk music but there's so much more out there.

Nora & Tom Carville's 50th

Leo sang Bach-Gounod's "Ave Maria," we both sang "Panis Angelicus" as a duet, and I then did Georges Bizet's "Agnus Dei." The organist enjoyed playing for us, an unfortunately rare treat for him. I was affected by his remarks greatly, thinking that when we change anything and attempt to modernize, we should be careful not to throw out the baby with the bath water. I thought of the three-chord folk music the organist spoke of and of the more sophisticated music of Handel, Mozart, and Bach that my kids were singing. I felt that the stronger demands were doing more to build their character than anyone could conceive. It really is simple—the more demands you make, the more you get.

After the service, a big reception took place with a sit-down dinner and dance. All fourteen of my aunts and uncles from the Old Country and many of their families as well made their appearance. With all the cousins, Dad and Mom's eleven children and their families, plus all the friends they had made over the past fifty years, you can bet it was quite a gathering. It truly was a grand affair, and no two people deserved it more. Throughout all the years I had seen and heard my father sing, many, many times, to Mom, I believe this was the first time I saw him sing to her, hand-in-hand, in public.

Needed

I returned to Paul's and checked in with Sandy who was coming along nicely. He was adjusting well at the Playhouse and teaching more and more each day. As each day went by at Paul's, it became increasingly obvious to me that I was just in the way. I knew better than to take one step into the kitchen to help because it was off limits if Paul was in the area. Not that he ever said anything. He didn't have to, you just knew by the way he jumped into action to do whatever first.

When I was deciding what to do next, Mary Lynn called to inform us that Nora was bleeding. She had been whelping, and the report was that some child from Lower Bay Gutter had hit her in the stomach with a stone causing a breach birth. Nora had been carrying only one pup and it was so large that she had had difficulty giving birth to it. The bleeding wouldn't stop. We told Mary Lynn to do whatever she had to do to get Nora help, whatever was necessary. Sandy was destroyed by the news. He wanted me down there as quickly as possible. So I took off the next day. But alas, whatever they did was not enough. Nora was dead and buried before I got there. They had waited, hoping the bleeding would stop, but it didn't. Sandy went ballistic. He felt so helpless and blamed himself for not being there when she needed help. He took the news badly, worse than his own troubles, because those he felt he could and would do something about. But Nora's state was final. It was something he had no control over and having no control was hard for a strong person like Sandy. If I had been there, I would have straightaway put her on a plane for Martinique to a veterinarian. Hindsight is no sight. There was no sense blaming someone who was doing you a favor in the first place. Now Nora was gone. She would be missed by all, even the children on the beach.

Sandy was planning to come back to Bequia as soon as he felt up to it. I went back to teaching in March. I had a lot of material to cover. The technical work was slipping, and Rudiments and Harmony classes had suffered from the lost time immensely. I had a month of work to make up in both classes. Choir wasn't affected much. I just had to pick up where I had left off. Thank God, Pat Mitchell and Kathy Meyers had thoughtfully covered my deaf school. I also relied a lot on Jonathan now. He had come a long way as an accompanist since last fall. He would help get me through the school competitions and the Easter program this year. Mary Lynn Lully was a much tougher disciplinarian than Bill, who, with Jane, had returned to Canada, and the school was running much more tightly now.

When I was in New York, I had looked for more material for my deaf kids. We had used up "A for Apple" and the simpler books like Dr. Seuss, and we needed to go further. I went up to a preschool in East Harlem and talked to the head teacher there. They used a reading program called "Let's Read" created by a couple of educators up in New Rochelle, New York. Geared to inner city children who were having trouble with Dick-and-Jane-style readers, it worked on the premise that the novice reader had no previous knowledge, that is, the child was never expected to know anything that hadn't already been taught. It began with three-letter, one-syllable words and went on from there with no pictures to assist, phonetically using words that sounded alike. I ordered a set of books from book one to book nine for each child, book nine being roughly equivalent to grade nine. My deaf kids moved slowly but what they got they understood. They seemed to be able to keep what they grasped, and I was able to build on that. When Mary Lynn saw the books, she started a program for the entering first-year students who were slow readers. When Sandy came, he took on the tougher students, the ones who needed special help. They would come to the house for special tutoring. Life during this period was pretty much routine.

One day I got a call from the Frangipani. Some people were in off a boat and were looking for me.

Rocky

They turned out to be a young couple sailing down from St. Martin, their last port of call, on a catamaran with a German shepherd. They had heard about Nora way up in the Leeward Islands and wanted to know if we were interested in mating her with their dog Rocky. With deep sadness, I had to tell them she had died just a short while ago. They invited me out to their boat to see Rocky anyway. They put me on guard, saying I should be aware that he was a highly trained watchdog. Police in Venezuela had trained him and he was a prize-winning guard dog. I decided to go and have a look. Why not?

When I saw him, I couldn't believe it. He looked so much like Nora that he could have passed as her identical twin. They had been told the same thing in St. Martin, and had got the idea of mating them. I would have liked that. They had him all chained up with a large, spiky, pinch-collar that I didn't like the looks of. They seemed to be a nice couple but just a little uptight. They kept warning me to be careful and not to forget he was an attack dog. He came over and sat right next to me. He didn't look threatening to me. The wife noticed and remarked on it, saying it wasn't like him. "We're on our way back to Venezuela and we're worried about Rocky making the trip. His black coat attracts the sun and it's burned his back. The sea isn't the best place for a black furbearing animal."

I could see that his back was a little reddish. They had been hoping that I might agree to keep Rocky with Nora long enough to mate and perhaps the burned back might heal up while he was off the boat. That wasn't going to happen now. They asked if I would be willing to take him for a while. Sandy was still in New York and wasn't expected back for another week. I told them I had to think of how Sandy would take to the idea of another dog in the house. I knew he wasn't over Nora yet, and Rocky would only be a reminder, especially since we would only have to give him up when the couple came back for him. They understood. By the time I was ready to leave, Rocky had his paws on my lap. I patted him and hugged him. He sure was a beautiful dog. Then I left for the Frangipani by dinghy.

A week later, I got a call from the young couple who owned Rocky saying they wanted to talk to me. I suggested they come out for lunch the next Tuesday and bring Rocky out to see where Nora had lived. In the meantime, I saw them once in a while in the Harbour around the Frangipani where the yacht people tie up their dinghies. They always had Rocky tethered tighter than a mountain lion. I assumed he was vicious since they thought so, but to me he didn't behave as if he were. Sandy came down on Friday, and I went over to St. Vincent to meet him, doing my usual shopping in the morning and having the boxes held overnight with the cold stuff in the freezer until the next day. Aside from looking a little tired, he was in rather good shape and he managed fairly well with the one eye. His speech was soft and halting and a little hard to decipher with other outside noises. He was using the larynx machine when he had to, and it really wasn't that bad.

Once we got home on Saturday, I unpacked everything and put it away, Sandy's clothes as well. Only later, up on his terrace over a cup of after-dinner coffee, did I tell him the Rocky story. All he said was, "Imagine that." I couldn't tell how he might feel about keeping him for a while, so I didn't pursue it. I told him they were coming up for lunch on Tuesday. Sunday and Monday were empty for him without Nora. I took him to her grave.

"Look at that," he said. Our two black cats, Dorothy and Lillian, were sitting on her grave looking out to sea. For the past two weeks, they had been spending a lot of time out there. He then asked, "Where are the flowers?"

19 The Ides Betide

I said, "You can cut some this afternoon for her." And he did.

Nora had raised Dorothy and Lillian from little black kittens. She had two because when I had got her only one, she killed it by mothering it to death. She wouldn't leave it alone. She kept cleaning and cleaning the tiny thing with her big tongue until it finally succumbed. She couldn't have been more upset with the loss if it had been one of her own pups. So the next time, I got her two, and between the two sharing her attention, they were able to survive her smothering motherly affections. She raised Dorothy and Lillian from when they were only weeks old. Down here, if you don't get the kittens away from their mother early, the tomcat comes and kills them.

When Nora died, they were very affected by her loss. They would go and sit on her grave by the hour. From the day Nora died, they would never allow another dog near our property. They would fluff up, screech wildly like a Halloween cat, and attack any dog whether big or small. This behavior was so unlike them. They had always been docile and genteel. Marie's dog Tamarind was a recipient of this treatment when Marie and Nolly came to dinner one night. They got up as far as the dining room terrace before the cats both descended on Tamarind. Nolly interfered and they went at him. Tamarind took off and Boolu grabbed the two cats, one in each hand. They went as limp as rag dolls in his hands, and Boolu took them downstairs and locked them in his room.

Lunch preparations on Tuesday morning were interrupted several times, a common occurrence around here. I forgot completely about the cat question. Neither had I mentioned to Sandy on Saturday that the couple was bringing Rocky with them. Now here Rocky was coming, and where were the cats, and where was Boolu? Oh God, Boolu was gone for the afternoon and I didn't know where he was. But I did know one thing: I had better talk and talk fast to clueless Sandy. I came on to him like a steam-engine, and he didn't get half of it. He just said, "There's nothing you can do now, so just wait and see."

Sandy saw them first coming up the drive and said, "Jimmy, it's Nora! Look at that!" I rushed over to Sandy and watched them come up the drive, with Rocky on his notorious monstrous leash to which a long rope was attached. When our visitors reached the stairs, turned in and ascended, the cats were there. They stepped aside and let them pass, Rocky included. When the couple walked into the dining room and I was doing the introductions, Rocky was trying to get over to me, but he couldn't because of that damned chain.

I asked, "Will he run if you take the rope off?"

"Oh, I don't think so."

"I'll close the door some so he can't get out," I said. So she took off the chain, and I said, "Now that's better." The dog came right over to me. "I think he remembers me," I said.

We sat down and had lunch. Every time I went into the kitchen, Rocky followed me. We sat around the table and talked about dogs, Rocky and Nora, and cats. I told them about Dorothy and Lillian's reaction to Nora's death and their reaction to other dogs on the property since, and how they had both made an exception for Rocky. At one point, I went up to the bedroom to answer the phone, and Rocky followed me up there, too. He was sniffing all around. When he went over to the sliding glass doors, I opened one. He went out and sniffed about and in no time at all he was sitting on Nora's grave just like the cats, looking out at the sea beyond. I called Sandy to come and take a look and the others came as well. This really impressed me; to this day, I can still see him sitting there.

The afternoon progressed with small talk and civility as it has a way of doing when strangers come together. Their ride eventually came and they went back to the Harbour. That left Sandy and me with plenty to talk about, especially about Rocky and how much like Nora he was. What a shame it was, the way they treated him with that vicious collar and all that fear.

Sandy and I ran into them again after dinner at the Frangipani's Thursday night barbeque and jump-up. We sat out along the periphery of the crowd so I could hear Sandy when he talked. They sat down with us and went on and on about Nora, the house, our life up on the hill, and how much Rocky seemed to be at home there and how relaxed he was with me. They had been talking for two days straight about it. They explained how their life was on the boat. Now that Rocky was big, the boat was no longer the place for him. His black hair only attracted the sun and it burned him. They said they loved him too much to submit him to that anymore.

"There's a reason we looked you guys up, and now we know what that reason is. We've both agreed he would be much happier with you two at your place, and we would like you to take him for us."

Sandy said, "For us and not from us?"

She said, "For us. We love him very much and giving him up, believe me, is very hard for us."

"What do you say, Jimmy?" Sandy asked.

"Oh, Sandy, I say yes," I answered.

Then Sandy simply said, "OK, that's it."

Late Monday afternoon, they came with Rocky still in his collar, a big bag of dog food, and his pedigree papers. We had one final sit-down talk. There we were again around the dining room table making light talk about Rocky and Nora over drinks. They had acquired Rocky as a puppy in San Diego, and we had found Nora near Allentown, Pennsylvania. They gave us his papers, and we finally shook hands and said our good-byes. They hugged up Rocky and said their last good-bye, never to be seen again. As soon as they left and headed downstairs, I took that damned collar off for the last time. Would you believe Rocky stood their next to Sandy and me out on the little terrace in front of the kitchen watching them make their way down the hill to their ride back to the Harbour?

Rocky was so much like Nora in so many ways, only stronger, that it was as if Nora had never left. Thanks to our canine benefactors who thought enough to bring Rocky's pedigree papers before they sailed off into the sunset never to return, I noticed a familiar name. There it was—sired by Von So-and-So. I went to find Nora's papers. I was right. There in black and white was the same Von So-and-So. Nora was Rocky's aunt.

One day about a week later, the breezes were blowing up from the road. I could hear two young lads in bitter dispute over Nora's demise. One was insisting she was still alive, and the other was disputing the fact. I stepped out of the kitchen onto the little terrace with Rocky close behind me. Pointing up the hill, the first one said, "See, I told ya. She still alive."

The other replied, "Dat's not Nora. She done dead."

The first insisted, "Yeah, her is. She be de only dog like she on de Island."

And the other ended the debate with, "Take a look. Dat's not Nora, no way. See em seeds?"

Sandy's Understudy

Came Easter Sunday and Jonathan played for us, but Sandy wasn't too happy about it. That was too bad. I hated doing this to Sandy, taking his job away from him, but I wasn't taking any chances with that one eye of his. He insisted that after Easter he was going to start playing for choir again.

"As long as we have Jonathan," I countered, "let's use him some of the time to give you a break." I talked him into it by pointing out that it was good for Jonathan, he could use the practice. Sandy agreed to share the work.

Jonathan's parents came down over Easter and were there to see Jonathan playing in public. They were astonished but pleased to see him playing in front of people. After all those years of paying for all those piano lessons and all those years of study, he was still shy about his playing.

His mom said, "What you did here for Jonathan was next to a miracle. I'm grateful."

"Well, so are we," I said, "to have had him."

Sandy had gone through so much this year, and I believe his pushing ahead too quickly took a great toll on him. I felt what Sandy needed most right now was rest in the sun, whether he liked it or not. Well, he didn't like it, so he used up the time practicing his speech. He would sit in the sand on the edge of the quiet surf and speak out to the open sea as loud as he could manage. I had found another spot on Lower Bay, the calm Caribbean side of the Island, where a low reef would protect Sandy from the waves coming in. It was as calm as a lake in the Catskills, with no danger of his stoma being flooded by a flash wave, which would have been a catastrophe. The very small children of the Island came here and played safely in the sea with no surf and made friends with Sandy as well. We all called it Sandy's Reef. Any afternoon about three you could find his little white Mini just off the road next to the sea grape bushes, and there he would be sitting in the sand at the edge of the sea, doing his exercises.

20 From Webber to Mozart

Superstar In The West Indies?

Before Bill and Jane Brown had left for Canada, they had given me a recording of a new Andrew Lloyd Webber rock opera called *Jesus Christ Superstar*. Along with it came a songbook with renditions of the songs in four parts, as sung by a Canadian group. The group was currently touring Europe performing a concert version of the show not unlike the first London production. Bill and Jane thought some of the songs would be good for the choir. I loved the music instantly. Normally, I found rock music hard to take. So did Sandy, that is, until he saw *Hair*. Sandy loved *Hair*. I hated it with a passion. At the time I could have done without the Beatles as well. I did grow to appreciate them, but it was a slow growth and not until I saw how really bad rock music could get. Remember, I was a jitterbug nut from a different, earlier time, the Big Band Era of Glenn Miller. He was King, and to me he still is. I felt sorry for the kids in the '50s who missed having those bands. That period, in my opinion, was nothing but a void. Now this *Superstar* music comes along, and I can't get it out of my head.

The notion percolated in my head for months. Several aspects of these pieces attracted me. First of all, they had all four parts. Secondly, the music was popular music of the day that the kids would take to easily. Finally, all God-loving or -fearing people on the Island, including the kids, would understand the subject and need no interpretation or translation. So when I got back after Sandy's second eye operations, I embarked on *Jesus Christ Superstar*. Some of the rhythms were a little rough on Jonathan, so I held some of them off "till Sandy reach," as they say in Bequia.

Superstar turned out to be a great choice because it introduced rock music, a sound the students could relate to. It was music of their generation, music they were hearing on radio. (TV hadn't reached Bequia yet.) They took to it like ducks to water. They splashed into *Superstar* with all the gusto, vim, and vigor of a bunch of guppies—well, let's say hippies. "I Don't Know How to Love Him," "Hosanna," and "King Herod's Song" ("...walk across my swimming pool") all grabbed them musically like they had never been grabbed before. I had most every kid in school in my pocket, as it were. They all wanted to be a part of it. Even young adults who had finished with school at fifteen wanted to be a part of our group. The principal, Father, and I considered the possibility and agreed to be flexible. We called their group the Young Adult Group and integrated them into the after-school program.

When Sandy came down in May, he had some vision in only his right eye, with not one but two retinal tears in it. He found it difficult to read music at the normal distance from the piano. We built a wooden stand that rested on the piano or organ, raising the music up closer to his face. He could then read the notes without bending way over. This apparatus made it impossible for him to see his hands on the keyboard for about the distance of an octave around middle C. Still, like Stevie Wonder, he was able to work around the problem as if he were touch-typing.

When Sandy sat down and started playing this rock-style music for the first time in his life, he took to those 5/7 rhythms like duck soup. He looked like a wild, crazy hepcat at the keyboard. The kids got a big kick out of just watching him knocking off that cool stuff. The first time, all eyes were on him. When it came time for them to sing, nobody did. Sandy stopped and looked up, and the whole choir broke into applause. This was going to be one hell of a ride for all of us. Listening to Sandy being able to diversify musically no matter the style was also a lesson to them in stretching beyond their own expectations. They would learn, I hoped, to be open and ready to take whatever the big wide world presented them with.

Everything turned around. Father and I no longer had to go around picking up the boys and herding them in for rehearsal. Now they were there early waiting for us. While in New York, Sandy had asked Paul to look for the orchestration of *Jesus Christ Superstar* music at Schirmer's music store. But it hadn't yet been published. Broadway shows have to run for a certain number of performances before they can be produced at another venue. This practice helps control the purse strings of the show. However, as part of the production hoopla around the forthcoming movie based on the musical, a magazine was published with vivid color pictures of the making of the movie. In it was the complete book of the show, albeit without the music. So when Sandy went to New York for his various medical checkups, he had Paul pick up a copy.

A Little R And R

This time, the winter of '75, he didn't stay up in the States long. The doctors thought rest in the sun was best for him right now. He checked in with his speech therapist down on Irving Place who said that whatever he was doing, he should keep it up, he was coming along faster than most at the school. Months before, one night at dinner, I had seen him throw his Robby the Robot across the dining room table and down into the living room when the batteries went dead on him. Cursing, he growled, "What did I expect from anything depending on batteries?" He never picked it up again. I took it and stuck it in a drawer. He swore, "I'm going to master that damned esophageal speech if it kills me."

In nine months, he had it down pat and never looked back. His speech was now just a little slower, lower, and softer than before. Oh, of course, it was a hell of a lot deeper, with breathy gasps. Nevertheless, his class at the Playhouse went on now as usual. All he needed was the amplifier. His vision was harder for him to deal with. He found it tiring, depending on only one eye. But his hearing was getting keener by the day. He was relying on it more and more, especially in class.

When he came back to Bequia, the school term was over. He felt I needed a change of scenery, so he suggested a week or so in Martinique, reminding me, "They speak French, you know."

"I know," I replied.

He continued, "Well, it's not far and it's different, or at least the language is. Remember Vi and Ralph spent time there at the Poisson Grand on that little bay across from Fort-de-France? I remember Vi telling us about the concierge, Philippe, the guy who used to wipe his hands together as he walked away professing, 'Not my prob-bub-blem.'"

"Why not?" I said. "We could fly that little French line out of Arnos Vale. We could drink French wine and eat pate de foie gras and pastries for a week." So off we went to points north, two islands north to be exact. We sat around eating and doing little or nothing and laughing at Philippe once in a while, until we were asked to be extras in a movie.

Sandy said, "Are you kidding?"

I said, "Well, I will."

Sandy quipped as he wiped his hands together, "Not my prob-bub-blem!"

My big part was to dance around a dance floor with a group of people doing the Papillon, whatever that was. The butterfly, I guess. Sandy sat and watched and laughed. Before we left, we took a trip into the hinterland of the island to see a little museum, nothing more than a small farm house containing artifacts and papers of Napoleon's wife, Josephine. A week of France in the Caribbean was enough, and we were flying back to St. Vincent and home.

Superstar Is A Go

All the time I was away, I had kept thinking about the possibilities in that text of *Superstar* Paul had sent. We could work on it all summer and do it sometime in the fall. By the time I got back to Bequia, my daydreams of the *Superstar* production, which started out as a simple concert, had gone through several re-visionings. First, I saw it as a watered-down version of the stage show, then it became a complete production of the stage show based on the London concert, and now I was envisioning it as a full West Indian *Jesus Christ Superstar* with fifty steel pans thrown in for good luck. Now my big problem was how to present this concept to Sandy? Well, I thought, I've had crazier ideas; one more wouldn't make much difference.

Sitting out on the terrace, I said, out of a clear moonlit sky, "We have most of the *Superstar* songs and the book. So why don't we do the whole show—acting, costumes, sets and all? We don't need all the orchestration."

Holding his head with both hands, Sandy said, "Acting! Acting? Wait a minute! Wait a minute! What did you say about acting? Whatever you do, leave the acting alone. Don't even use the word. Whatever they do, they do. They're free enough already, they don't need any more. You just teach them the songs and the dancing. I assure you they'll handle the rest. And what's this, we don't have all the music? Even if you had the musical score, they wouldn't give you the rights to do it anyway."

"We don't need either the music or the rights. Who cares what happens on this little Island?"

"I know."

"We don't even have a movie house or television," I added.

"Well, that's true," Sandy said. "You have all the music you'd need right there on that record. All we have to do is match the words to the right chord on the record and then transcribe the music by picking up the chords."

"Pick up the chords off the record? How do you do that?" I asked.

"By ear. How else?"

"You can do that?" I asked.

"Why not?"

"Well, my ear isn't that good," I said.

"So I'll listen, and you write down the chords as I give them to you. You can do that, can't you?"

"Yeah, of course I can. Yeah, sure I can," I assured him.

That's how it all began. Sandy sat down at the piano and, with a pad and pencil, I began jotting down chord after chord as he called them out to me. We knew we didn't have to transcribe the whole record because we had the music to all the major songs in the four-part renditions. Still, the process was time-consuming, and we were expecting it to be a lengthy undertaking until we met a chap at the Frangipani. He was a recent graduate of a prestigious music school in Tex-

Boolu and dancers rehearse *Superstar*

as run by some Juilliard graduates. He was interested in what we were doing and offered to help. He, like Sandy, had a fabulous ear for music. He came home with us, and together they knocked out what we needed in no time at all.

Now that we had all the words and a facsimile of the score, I had to orchestrate it for the instruments we had on hand. Believe it or not, on this tiny Island we came up with two electric guitars, one electric bass, a trumpet, a flugelhorn, a saxophone, two sets of drums, and twenty steel pans from St. Vincent plus Sandy's two-tiered electric organ.

I started working with the electric guitars first, giving them their chords. I then sent out the word we were looking for dancers. Boolu was our first applicant. The Sunny Caribbee had a huge tiled veranda they let us use as a rehearsal hall since it was off-season. Over at the church, the choir was working on the main songs that involved them. Sandy and I cast our Jesus and Judas, Corny Lloyd and Flash James respectively, from the Young Adult Group. Mary Magdalene was Suzanne Wallace, a student, Pilate was Denny Wilson, a high school teacher from Union Island, and Pilate's wife was Joanna Osborne, a student. The High Priests were Andrew Tannis, Camillus Fredericks, Josiah Glynn, and Erdly Simmons, two from the Young Adults Group, a teacher, and a student respectively. Simon Zealote was a character we split between a deaf dancer and a legally blind, squint-eyed singer, Boolu and Gideon James. You see, even the handicapped were represented!

We couldn't have had a better cast. At first, we held lead rehearsals, like those for the instrumentalists, privately at the house because it was easier for Sandy and me. We were going to work on this project all summer.

Sandy's Flying Leap

One evening in early May, choir rehearsal in the Harbour was over just as the sun was setting. Sandy took off alone in his Austin Mini while I followed in my Moke with Elvie, a student, and Flash, our former Calypso King now Judas. Sandy was moving along the curving road in his white Mini, the three of "we" driving just behind, singing "Jesus Christ/ Jesus Christ/ Who are you? What have you sacrificed?..." We passed through the Gap and over onto the Friendship side of the Island. Sandy made a 90-degree turn to the right, heading directly west into Lower Bay Gutter. We too made the turn. The huge blazing sun was setting behind Lower Bay Gutter straight ahead. Everything went blank. Even with my twenty-twenty vision, I couldn't see a thing. I slowed the Moke down and when I recovered from the sudden visual shock of blazing light, Sandy was gone. Off to the left of us was a fifty-foot drop.

When Sandy had rounded the curve into the blinding light, the vision in his remaining, weakened right eye was stunned into nothingness. He felt helpless. He was so afraid of the possibility of oncoming traffic that he veered left to make room on the narrow nine-foot road. But because he hadn't compensated for the lack of vision in the left eye, he was already slightly closer to the left than he realized. The car rolled over the edge of the cliff, over and over and over.

Up ahead was David Ollivierre's house. On his porch was a group of people from Trinidad who were having a going-away party. They saw the car turn over five times as it bounced over the rocks on its way down, its doors wide open. They could see Sandy in a vivid blue shirt tossed around, flying back and forth with every roll. Some said Sandy looked as if he was half in and half out of the car. The seats went flying out and bouncing down the hill along with the car.

In one fell swoop I braked, jumped out of the Moke, and ran down the hill and onto the first large rock. I leapt to the next rock and my wooden clogs split in two, damn near sending me headlong. But I caught myself, flipped them off in opposite directions, and continued down to the Mini, which was now lying upside down, wheels still spinning. When I reached the bottom, all I could see lying about were the car cushions but no Sandy. I looked inside the car. It was completely empty, just a shell cleared of everything! No car seats, and no Sandy. I frantically looked about, but Sandy was nowhere in sight. I was pleading to myself: where, for God's sakes, could he be?

Elvie had made it down the cliff behind me and was standing over on the far side of the overturned Mini. I heard her shout out as she pointed to the car, "There him is! See him shoes?"

She was pointing to the rear window of the upturned car. There he was, like the Wicked Witch of the East from the Wizard of Oz, all you could see were his shoes. He was lying on his back with the length of the car on top of him. I was thinking, My God, how can he breathe with the weight of the car on the stoma in his neck? The next thing I realized, I was bent over him, with his body stretched out underneath me, and the car was resting on my back. Somehow I had lifted the car off him as much as I could and let it rest on my back, all the time thinking only of the stoma in his neck. It could be squeezed shut, blocking off air to his windpipe! He had dirt on his face and neck.

The next moment, Flash was at my side and, with his strong upper torso, had lifted the car enough off me to allow me to turn around. My adrenaline was really pumping. Together we shoved the car back upright onto its wheels. I also saw Elvie on my left, shoving along with us. I got quickly onto my knees and cleared the dirt from Sandy's neck and face. He opened his eyes, he was alive!

By now the men from the party had clambered down the cliff with a fold-up garden lounge chair. Several men gingerly moved him, careful to keep his neck and spine in alignment, from the ground to the lounge chair. Then they picked him up, stretched out in the chair, and worked their way up to the top of the steep cliff. All the while, I was worrying about his spine and about his one remaining eye giving up the ghost altogether.

At the top of the cliff, Henry Nichols was waiting with his truck. They slid

Sandy, still in the chair, into the back of the pick-up and took off for our house on the other side of the Gutter. A group of men followed behind. At the top of the drive, they lifted him in the chair out of the truck and into the house, and up into his bedroom. Then they carefully moved him onto his bed, trying not to cause any more damage than he had already incurred at the accident site. Before long Dr. Gun-Munro showed up and examined him as best he could without disturbing him. When he had finished, he had Winnie pack pillows around him to steady him in place. He told me he couldn't say much yet. Sandy was conscious and breathing normally. His eye was so far intact, but he was badly bruised on the back of his neck. The doctor said this was the difficult spot. He shouldn't be moved for any reason just yet, not even to go to the bathroom.

When the good doctor left, the women from down the road came by to see how he was doing. When I told Sandy, he said, "Let them come in and see for themselves. If you don't, they'll have me dead by morning."

The women stood around talking to each other, some encouraging Sandy. When Mallet, the albino from Lower Bay Gutter, came up into the bedroom from the dining room, she saw Sandy on his back with me sitting on my bed. She threw herself down at the top of the staircase. Clasping her hands in prayer and then covering her face with both hands, she bawled, "Thank God, thank God. Oh, God, I thought it was Jimmy."

The women looked at her in disgust, and Erene said, "Will someone get that woman out of here?" In due time they were all gone, and Winnie, Boolu, and I were left alone with him.

The next morning, a yacht captain came in with a doctor from Paris who examined Sandy and said we should put him in traction right away. If he were to snap his spine, he could be paralyzed from the neck down. The doctor said, "We need to steady him in traction in a plaster cast for a couple of weeks. We could lay him in one of the lounges from the terrace and hook him up to the stone wall here in the bedroom. Then his spine will heal and strengthen by itself."

The next day, I relayed this advice to Dr. Gun-Munro. "Let's wait and see," he said. I never did hear from the Parisian doctor again anyway. Dr. Gun-Munro skipped a couple of days and came back on the fifth day. "It looks to me," he said, "like that bruise on the neck is shrinking. It has shrunk a little off to the right."

He also found five bumps on Sandy's head that attested to the alleged five rollovers. After a week and a half with Winnie, Boolu, and me tending to absolutely every need, he was still packed with pillows. He was moved only as gently and as little as possible. His eye was still a worry.

One day Doc came in and said, "I'm not certain, but there is a strong possibility that the main damage is a little off to the right. It may not be threatening to the spinal cord after all. Sandy, you could begin to move about some. I could very slowly and gently move your head. If the pain should start to increase, I would stop. Now, I'm leaving this decision entirely up to you." I thought to myself, this could be a disaster! Doc went on, "If you don't feel any more pain than you already have, then you're out of the woods."

I remember thinking, Ohmigod! If it is his spinal cord, and that turning snaps it, he will be paralyzed from the neck down. I kept saying to myself, say no, Sandy, say no. Sandy shot one sharp look at me and quietly said, "OK. Let's do it, Doc."

Dr. Gun-Munro said, "OK, Sandy. Very slowly. Jimmy, help me."

I was shaky, fearing that if I touched him with my unsteady hands, I'd snap his neck myself. But I was too embarrassed not to help. So we helped sit him up on the side of the bed. Then I got away as fast as I could. It was one of the longest moments I could ever recall. Doc, with his expert touch, completed his experiment. With gentle, minuscule manipulations, he ever so slowly and gingerly moved Sandy's head to the left and then to the right. When Sandy felt no increased pain, the doctor said, "That's it, Sandy. It's not right on the cord. It's off to the right. A few more weeks of rest and as little movement as possible will make all the difference. Then you will need X-rays, of course."

When it came time, we went to St. Vincent for the X-rays, then made arrangements with the airlines. We had to get back to New York for a thorough examination. We were grateful the eye had held together. The lumps on his head eventually disappeared. The bruise on his neck was barely visible. The only thing wrong with him was a dislocated collarbone. He went to his grave twenty-two years later with that dislocated collarbone.

Medical consultations over, Sandy said, "Well, Jimmy, what do you say we head back to *Jesus Christ Superstar*?"

I said, "If you feel ready, fine."

Paul said, "Not until the final demonstration at the Playhouse and the graduation dinner at the Players Club."

Robert Whitehead, President of the Board, had his wife, Zoe Caldwell, speak to the graduates about her life in the theater. I had the thrill and pleasure of sitting next to King Kong's lover and an old lover of Clifford Odets' as well—the incomparable Miss Fay Wray. It was great talking about the golden years of old Hollywood. She was now married to a doctor and living in Trump Towers.

Production Commences

By June, I had had so much time to think about *Superstar* that I knew exactly what I wanted to do and how I would handle it, number by number. I had it all cast, and I had worked out the costumes, even who would make them. I had the staging all worked out. I didn't go to see the show in New York when I was there, or even the movie for that matter, and it wasn't like me not to go.

"Oh, yeah," said Sandy, who knew me better than I knew myself. "You're just like Stella Adler's mother. In the Adlers' productions at the Yiddish Theater, she was definitely chief cook and bottle washer. She wasn't only the actress. She did everything from making the costumes to mopping the stage. You're just the same."

"No, Sandy," I said, "I didn't need to go to the show in New York. I was busy creating my own. I just wanted my production to be West Indian."

Sandy replied, "I rest my case."

When we got back, the kids were out of school and we could really concentrate on the show. Pat Mitchell and Kathy Meyers had been carrying on the deaf school. Now that I was back, Kathy would work on math, Pat on reading comprehension and writing. I then got back to lip-reading, vocabulary, and speech. It was also time to go over to Calliaqua, out beyond Arnos Vale airport, to work with the bandmaster of the steel-pan orchestra. I was given free lodging by Dave Corrigan of the Mariner's Inn while I was over there, a generous offer on his part.

The orchestra had ten players. Some played as many as four pans each, while the tenor played only one, the melody. A pan was an old oil drum, and a whole band took up quite a lot of room. The logistics of transporting them to the boat, across to Bequia, and back again were going to be complex. I would worry about that when the time came; right now they were smacking out *Superstar* on their pans and it sounded fantastic. We wound up with four musical groups to cover the score. We had the quality of the steel pans, the rock sound of the electric guitars, the regular combo sound with horns, and finally a liturgical sound from the organ. It was a cacophony of sound the likes of which Bequia had never heard before. We had a total of twenty musicians, backing a cast of seventy-five singers, dancers, and soloists.

The large cast all had to be costumed, so costuming was going to be a job in itself. I had gone over to Fred Dare in St. Vincent to purchase the material needed for costuming the various characters. Fortunately the main chorus was hippies, and that was easy since the cast were hippies already. I still had Dovey as a seamstress but I lost Joan Stowe. Her daughter, who was one of my top sopranos, left the school over some stupidity with the old principal. Nevertheless, some of the schoolteachers, now from England, pitched in and pulled the job of the costumes together. The high-priest costumes were hysterical, as they themselves were. It would be hard to single out any one of them, since each one of them in their own way was an original. Sandy had advised me in the very beginning just to leave them alone and let them do their own "ting." I did, and they sure did, and Sandy sure was right.

Jesus was as black as the ace of spades, and Mary Magdalene was as white as an Easter lily with long straight blonde hair. Jesus, played by Corny Lloyd, had a gripping, natural, earthy African quality in his voice that tore at your heart when he vocalized up and down his extended vocal range. Mary Magdalene, played by Suzanne Wallace, was a contralto, with the belting quality of rock-a-billy. Their contrast was enchanting. Judas, our calypso King of Carnival, had a powerful, free-wheeling instrument from the top to the bottom of his phenomenal vocal range. It was so free and sure, he was able to give himself over to the extreme emotional demands of the character. Our Pilate had a natural sense of pomp and authority; in a word he was the essence of the character. One might say I took the easy road and stooped to type-casting, and I guess I did, but the natural ability of these performers made it so easy for me. It left me free to concentrate on other things that needed my attention, such as the job of keeping the whole cast and crew concentrated on the moment at hand.

Superstar Boffo

I shall never forget that opening night. The jazz horn player, Shake Keane, the internationally acclaimed European recording artist from St. Vincent, started the overture off with the little solo on his flugelhorn. It was an electrifying moment. The room was packed, literally jammed to the rafters: children actually perched up on the rafters seeking a better vantage point. Others were glued to the latticework around the windowsills of the primary school. Then that chill ran through my body. I had all I could do to snap myself together. I had a job to do. The steel band segued into "Superstar," and the show began. It was a memorable moment for all who were there. What a ride we were embarking on!!

Eardley Simmons as High Priest

When the overture was finished, Sandy took over on the organ with the rock band, grinding out those 5/7-beat rhythms. When all the electrically amplified sound started, I said a quick little prayer to God to hold off trouble for two-and-a-half hours, nervous because all the floodlights on the stage, the light over my score, Sandy's light over his music, the electric organ plus three electric guitars, the two microphones and their amplification, plus a tape recorder for the sound effects of the crucifixion scene were all plugged into just one outlet. Just one outlet!—that was all this huge room had. Why, it was the only outlet in the entire building!

That afternoon I had had Chris Bowman, who was building Bob Dylan's schooner in the Harbour, make me a light board from the one outlet. I asked, "What do you think? It's only one socket, but at least it's 240 volts."

Chris answered, "Well, we'll find out, won't we?" And we did, for he stayed with us for the rest of the evening.

The show went on flawlessly, until we got to the one number that wasn't even in the Broadway show called "Could We Start Again Please." The song was written for the movie, to be sung by a sexy young woman in a pop style. I arranged the piece in close harmony a la Patty, Maxene, and LaVerne and had three of my younger looking girls, Elvie Ollivierre, Reanna Dewer, and Judy Tannis, do the number as a trio. I dressed them in primary school uniforms, with big straw hats with long ribbons trailing down their backs. One had a big lollipop, another had books on a leather strap, and the third had a rag doll hanging from her hand. In the middle of the show, they came out before the crucifixion and sang in three-parts: "Could we start again, please / I think you've made your point now / You've even gone a bit too far to get the message home..." And start again is exactly what happened. When the girls finished, the audience went wild. The trio left the stage, but the audience wouldn't stop. I couldn't go on with the show. I had to stop and bring them out again. So the three girls came back on stage to "start again, please," and sang it once more.

Another showstopper was Boolu as Simon Zealote. The dancers did a number with Boolu-as-Simon called "Simon Zealote/Poor Jerusalem" ("Christ you know I love you"). Now, Boolu couldn't sing because he was deaf as a doorknob, but he could dance the tail off a lizard. And the legally blind Gideon James had a melodious pop voice. He later went to New York, had his eyes fixed, came back to the Caribbean, and became a successful pop singer. But this night Gideon sat on a rock and sang Simon while Boolu did Simon's big number dancing in the style of a very zealous Shaker. He quivered every muscle in his body as he gyrated around the stage in front of the dancers, waving and dancing as if in a trance. I knew every eye in the house was on the crazy little boy from the bush now holding a room full of hundreds of people spellbound. The cheering was deafening. The little guy had finally arrived: he was now one of them.

"King Herod's Song," "... walk across my swimming pool," was sung by Abel (pronounced Ay-bell) Ollivierre, a handsome yachtsman from Paget Farm who had never stood on a stage before, accompanied by a group of dancers dressed as flappers from the '20s doing the Charleston with their escorts, Boolu among them. I was told all eyes were on Boolu and his straw hat. He was kicking his feet up so high he damned near lost the hat a couple of times. Another high point was our leading vocalist, the one who wound up singing at St. Patrick's Cathedral in New York City. The talented Suzanne Wallace sang, "I Don't Know How To Love Him" with all the girls of the chorus and the steel

20 From Webber to Mozart

pans and Sandy at the organ backing her up.

When Jesus mounted the high wooden cross center stage in front of the painting of Mount Calvary with the two crosses on either side, in the silence of the room all that could be heard was the agonizing sound of the mallet hitting the spike and driving it in. An anguished cry arose from the audience, the sound of a grieving mother wailing in stentorian tones, "They crucified my Corny!" No, it wasn't his mother; but it was Corny Lloyd's grandmother.

At the end of the show, when the steel band had finished the reprise of "I Don't Know How To Love Him" and "Superstar," no one got up to leave. So the band started to play again, and as many of the audience as could fit joined the cast on the stage and started singing and dancing. Others cleared the chairs from the center of the hall and changed the theater into a dance hall so more could dance.

Sandy said, as he locked up the organ, "Jimmy, they're going to go on forever."

I said, "I'm beat. We don't have to stay, and Boolu will find his own way home."

It took a while just getting out of the place and over to the Moke. We gave Winnie and her daughter Hazel a ride home. Walking across the field to the Moke, Winnie said, "You know, Jimmy, you told a whole story there tonight. It's one we all understood, and none of the actors had to say a word."

As I started up the Moke, Sandy said, "Jimmy, this one they will all remember."

The show was brought back by popular demand. The kids wanted to do it again, and people in St. Vincent and Mustique wanted to see it. If we did it near Christmas, we could get the tourist trade as well. We mounted a second performance on December 17, and if I say so myself, the whole cast was up to their original performance. The only downside of the repeat performance was that half the take at the door was ripped off by someone tending the door that night. Because of the theft, some players in the steel band felt their share wasn't high enough. It was Christmas and they didn't ask, they demanded. They hit up Sandy, as angel to the production, for $300 more. Both incidents left a bad taste for both of us, but we were determined not to let it affect us for long because the show itself left so many people with a good feeling. Wasn't that what it's all about?

Now Boolu and I moved immediately on to the next activity, Santa for the kids on the 20th.

Santa Brings On The Smiles Again

This year for the first time, the Hotel Frangipani's second dinner-sitting on Christmas Eve and Mac's Pizzeria were new stops for Santa. Both Boolu and I were going to have a couple of busy days, and I was already spent. Sandy just stood by and watched, enjoying being a bystander. Even when the teachers and some students came over to stuff the toys into the hundreds of bags in our living room, he took no part in it, just stood off at a distance and smiled. He was still recovering from his efforts at *Superstar* on the 17th. What he had done then was no easy feat. He and Elaine Ollivierre, the page-turner at the organ, kept the whole shebang together that night, pounding out the rhythm. I just stood up front in my tux, waving my hands in all directions as if I knew what I was doing and trying to look good doing it. Sandy, on the other hand, was working hard. That one weak eye didn't make it any easier. What he needed afterwards was to rest on the beach. Normally, we would be going to Sandy's Reef with Rocky in the late afternoon and playing with the kids on the beach. Sandy would sit there practicing his speech, and Rocky would run up and down playing with the children, just as Nora had. Ever since Sandy's operations, I had been afraid to let him go alone, and I think he agreed with me because he never insisted on it. Since the car crash over the cliff, he had been hesitant and careful no matter what he was doing. So, with Boolu and me busy, the next few days for him would be days at home with Rocky.

Sandy hadn't picked up a book since he had lost his sight, and he had been such an avid reader. I always hoped he would find a good book that would hold his interest, but I also knew he wouldn't read with that one bad eye. He always said it was too tiring for him. Dr. Gun-Munro gave him a rather large magnifying apparatus used by doctors when doing minute work during surgical operations. It was a magnifying glass with lights on either side underneath. I could never get him to try it. He would have to sit at a table to read the book underneath, but he never once gave it a try. It was such a marvelous gift, I was too embarrassed to tell the good doctor, and I never did. Right then Sandy would spend his time with Rocky out on the terrace in front of his bedroom working on his speech. He was an avid correspondent and out here in the daylight he read his correspondence from David Craig and Paul Morrison, who kept him abreast of happenings in the good old US of A. This was no easy exercise for him either. Often he would ask me to read for him. But now it was time for Santa and his elf to hit the highway with goodies for all the little boys and girls of the Island whether good or bad.

We made the regular trip from village to village, but this year, along with the usual Christmas songs, I thought it would be nice to tell them a story of Christmas. I picked, "Twas the Night Before Christmas," but instead of telling them the story, I decided to sing it to them. I knew an arrangement written by Fred Waring way back in the '40s. I was having as much fun singing as the kids were hearing it. We were to hit the Frangipani Hotel and Mac's Pizzeria at dinnertime on Christmas Eve. At Mac's, I climbed down out of an overhanging limb onto the terrace where they were serving, and at the hotel, I shimmied down a pole into the dining room from the overhanging veranda. I almost landed on a table and what a reaction that got! I loved it, and so did they.

Christmas day we went to the Frangipani for dinner and Boxing Day we stayed home. Sandy and I both collapsed but not the indefatigable Boolu. This kid was and still is insatiable.

Sandy Gone And Joany Back

Sandy planned to spend the winter back in New York testing out his teaching prowess after all his setbacks. He was apprehensive and anxious about his esophageal speech. He had been working so hard, spending every free minute of his time trying to perfect it. I could understand. Boolu had no trouble understanding him either, but Sandy said, "Boolu doesn't count because he lip-reads me."

"But look," I told him, "Winnie has no trouble either. You're going to do just fine once you get up there with the amplifier." I offered to go to New York to help him in the classroom.

"You have classrooms waiting for you right here, and this is where you belong."

While Sandy was packing to go up, my sister Joan was packing to come down. Sandy and I were open about Joan and the problems created by her presence in our house over any length of time because of her physical and mental handicaps. He had compassion for her and an understanding of her difficulty and he didn't mind her company in reasonable doses. But if she had had her way, she would have stayed for six months. I didn't mind if she came for two years. We grew up together, and I was the big brother figure in her life. When she had had that nightmare of an accident back in '59, I was able to be there to help her. My being there had only increased her dependence on me. She made no secret of her gratitude to me, and I admit that was easy to take. So Sandy and I had worked it out over the years. Joan would come to Bequia when he was in New York and stay until he came back. That year, he was going to see to his medical needs and speech therapy while tending to the Drama Department at the Playhouse. Then he could spend a week with Joan here before she went back home.

Joan was coming down this year by herself. She took an early flight from Syracuse and was assisted when she made her change at Kennedy. Jonathan, the owner of and an officer of Air Mustique, assured me his brother Jeremy would look after her himself in Barbados and get her over to St. Vincent. There Lou Keane, an English friend of mine, a teacher at Boys' Grammar School there, picked her up at Arnos Vale and took her home for the night. At noon the following day, she got her ensconced on the *Friendship Rose*. Boolu and I met her on the pier. She planned to stay as usual until Easter week and be at the farm by Easter Sunday.

Her accident had happened sixteen years ago. She was now forty-four and she had improved greatly. She was still a far cry from her former self. At twenty-eight she had been doing computer engineering work and serving as an analyst for the New York telephone company AT&T. Now, she still had a lot of childlike qualities and had to be watched constantly. When she was with me, I included her in everything we did. I think she realized this, and it was one reason she liked being here. She had a much more active life here with Winnie, Boolu, and me. She went swimming every day and out to dinner when we were invited. She became very much a part of our dinner parties. She was included in school activities I was connected with. Of course, she didn't attend classes, but she did sit in on rehearsals, which she loved doing. I think many people here loved her attitude and sense of humor. Whatever it was, all or part of this, she seemed to get a great kick out of being here. I felt at this time in my life it was the least I could do for a sister I loved very much. When her life as she knew it was taken from her at twenty-eight, she was my closest friend. The Joan I once knew was gone, but she was still Joan. That I had to accept, as she herself did very well.

Because of my work at both schools, I wasn't going to be able to spend as much time with Joan this year as in earlier times, but she didn't seem to mind. She just loved being here on Bequia with all the friends she had made through the years. Joan was and is an easy person to like. Bequia was such a laid-back place, many people enjoyed her company. It was easier if one had a little patience. That quality was common down here, and I was learning it by the day. It was an asset that Sandy never had a problem with in the classroom, but otherwise, look out.

I saw her at breakfast every morning, after which, twice a week, I went down to her room to teach the deaf students. Joan would spend time with the students after their class and with Kathy Meyers, the math teacher, when she came. I spent the late morning and early afternoon at the high school; Joan spent time at the house. I would go home often to pick her up and take her to choir practice. She always looked forward to that.

Competition In St. Vincent

Dancing was now part of the curriculum, once a week, and we were working on an eight-hand reel, one my family had performed at the National Irish Counties Feis (pronounced fesh) held at Fordham University in '54. When the Sunny Caribbee opened for the season, we moved from the verandah into the Town Council Hall, upstairs. A new teacher arrived from England, with her flute. She not only played for us, but she also taught Flazzo "Miss McLeod's Reel." Boolu and Leach played the bongos and a conga drum. Fred Dare supplied me with beautiful West Indian plaid. We made kilts for the men, and the women wore period dresses with long, flowing, plaid shawls.

The group was preparing for the high school dance competition being held the next month in St. Vincent. The school choir was preparing two songs to enter in the vocal categories, and my soloists were preparing too. Entering as well was a songwriter presenting a composition in the writers' competition. The adults from my *Superstar* group, not wanting to be left out, entered in the open folk category as well. Unfortunately at performance time, one of the girls in the dance group had trouble with a ballet slipper partially falling off, which detracted from the performance. These things happen.

My high school group won first place singing "Kill La Lay," and our young composer placed very well. Suzanne, who was only sixteen, entered the Adult Contralto competition because she wanted to sing "He Was Despised" from the *Messiah*. Some women were a little miffed when she walked away with first place.

When the combined group of seventy-five young people from Bequia entered on stage and kept coming and coming dressed in their colorful orange, yellow, black, and white West Indian costumes trimmed in West Indian plaid, the audience broke into applause before they ever uttered a sound. To me, they looked like so many oranges and bananas. What they really looked like were so many Carmen Mirandas and Harry Belafontes. The master of ceremonies said, "It looks like everyone on Bequia must be here tonight." They sang "Jamaica Farewell" opening with market and street cries that I wrote. There was no laughter that night. This time, St. Vincent went wild, and the ensemble did an encore. It was so gratifying to me to see our little island accepted at last.

Not long after the music festival, I got a school communiqué about the Schools' Cultural Historical competition to be held in Victoria Park, our Yankee Stadium. This event was going to be a big one, right in the center of Kingstown. I vowed this time we would show them. I felt that strong competitive spirit I had felt growing up back home amongst my brothers and sisters. Bequia had been ignored for so many years by Vincentians, it was time to turn the tables.

I told the dancers I wanted them to be better than their best. I told the amplified flute and drum band—the four of them, Hillary, Flazzo, Leach, and Boolu—to rehearse until they could play it in their sleep. The choir was to sing songs of the islands, of the Caribbean. I picked Jamaica, Trinidad, Cuba, and Barbados. We did a medley of "Jamaica Farewell," "Guantanamara" in Spanish, "Kill La Lay Pom Pom," and "Sing Out My Soul."

It was a night affair, and the weather was perfect. The Bishop let us use his house, which was just across the road from the park, to make ready in. The grandstands were full shoulder to shoulder, as were the infield and outfield. They held Carnival, political rallies, and soccer games in this venue; it couldn't be bigger for St. Vincent. We could barely make it through the crowd out to the stage in the middle of the infield.

Those beautiful, colorful West Indian costumes and the West Indian plaids of the Black Scots-Irish group were spectacular under the floodlights. To the crowd they looked like Carnival all over again. Joan didn't come. It was no place for her in her condition. Sandy was in New York. I wished he could have been there, but it wouldn't have been a place for him either. West Indians in such large numbers could be pretty rough and rugged, rowdy and raucous. When we finished, it was truly frightening. We did it again perfectly. No one had to tell us, and what a glorious feeling it was to walk away with first place once more.

Rest Time

Easter was here and so was Sandy. He didn't wait for the Playhouse closing this year. He came early, saying he had spent all winter there and that was enough; he couldn't wait to get back to Bequia. We weren't singing at Paget Farm that year. Sandy had just arrived, we had just finished with Victoria Park, and the kids needed a rest. Joan left on Friday with Jeremy seeing her through Barbados. T.P., my nephew and godson, picked her up at Kennedy and drove her back to Utica. I told her she would make it back in time to color eggs for the grandchildren with Mom.

After Victoria Park, I stopped section rehearsals. The break enabled me to take Sandy to Lower Bay now that he didn't drive any more. He spent mornings out on the terrace with Rocky.

Twice a week after school, I came home and we went to rehearsal. We were working on some Beatles songs. Paul had sent me the music to "Let It Be," "Hey Jude," and "All You Need Is Love." Then every other day and twice on weekends, weather permitting, we went to Lower Bay and sat in the surf, safely protected by Sandy's Reef. His reef was just this side of De Reef Beach Bar where everybody went late of a Sunday morning for brunch or lunch, whatever. That was a lovely summer.

When school closed in June, we had it easier than we had had it in a long, long time. "I haven't felt this laid back since I came to the Island nine years ago," I said to Sandy.

"Isn't this what we came here for?" Sandy said. He loved to sit in the gentle surf and splash salt water on himself saying, "It's medicinal." He would walk along the beach for exercise, and Rocky would follow along beside him. Rocky had served to take Sandy's mind off the loss of Nora. It was an easy thing to do. Rocky was so much like Nora it was uncanny.

Paul was coming after the summer session and would go back in September with Sandy. When Paul arrived, he handed me some classical tapes, saying, "Here's something new to listen to, if you two ever have the time,"

"Ha-ha," I said, at the same time noticing one was a recording of Mozart's *Requiem*. The soprano had been a student of my voice teacher, Bernard Taylor. As it turned out, it was a fine recording, and I found myself listening to it quite a bit during that blessedly inactive summer, the first since I had stepped foot on the Island. That piece was the very first classical piece I had been introduced to as a kid. When I was fourteen, my buddy Bobby Gottuso and I were the only boys singing in an all-male church choir, thanks to his uncle. I remember singing, "Carry Me Back to Old Virginie" in blackface in one of the minstrel shows we did. I was a tenor, my friend a bass. Bobby had a cousin who told him about a group she sang with downtown. She asked, "Why don't you two come on down and join it?"

Now this was an adult group who called themselves the Civic Chorus of Utica. They rehearsed in the Board of Education building on Elizabeth Street. Professor Alderwick of Hamilton College, a violinist, was the conductor. Bobby and I were, to begin with, just a couple of small fourteen-year-olds, but he welcomed us with open arms. Well, you can be sure I was one intimidated fourteen-year-old, but it wasn't long before I was enjoying every minute of it. That winter they were to sing Mozart's *Requiem* with the Utica Civic Orchestra at Proctor High School.

This whole happening was an eye-opener for me. I was thrust into a whole new world of classical music, such glorious music, and I had such gratification in being part of it. This experience left an indelible mark on me. I am forever grateful to Bob's cousin, for it has affected my very existence for the rest of my life. Out of those leisure moments of listening to that fabulous music, I fantasized and daydreamed. Just maybe...., why not...? of course not, silly, presumptuous, ridiculous, but then...?, there was a possibility, we did, I did, who knew? could be..., might be... were all fragments of interrupted thoughts that ran through my mind every now and again, never to materialize into a full-blown, mature idea. You know, like a thought that had a subject, a predicate, and no object.

Paul was busy every morning with his watercolors. He was painting everything in sight, even Boolu, one of whose portraits I framed. He did a wonderful moonlight scene of the dining room terrace, which I have and take great delight in.

Growing Pains

September rolled around again, and this year the high school would be opening its doors to 250 students. The school was evolving. When we had begun, all we had were the academic subjects and music. The students didn't have a choice. Now there was football, basketball, rounders, track, woodworking, home economics, and science. Elaine had an entire science lab for her students. The curriculum was normal, with electives for the students. So, in short they had choices now and choices they made. That was as it should be. I still had the first-year students, but now second year opened them up to other things.

What I saw missing in the lower grades was a strong school spirit and pride, not only in their school but in Bequia and themselves as well. Who knew what caused the apparent lack of caring? I wasn't the only one who noticed. The older ones seemed to have a persona that was developing as they grew from year to year. I was certainly glad they still had it, whatever it was! It made it so much easier for me to continue my work with them.

Sandy At Paul's Place

New York time was here, and Sandy and Paul were back at the Playhouse and the East Side. Ever since Sandy had had the car accident and the cancer operation, Paul had insisted he not go back to the Dover Hotel. It was best that Sandy stay with him. He could keep an eye on him and be there for Sandy when he was needed.

This arrangement couldn't have been better. Paul would often invite long-time friends from the past. They had visits from Harold Clurman, Bobby Lewis, Luther Adler, his sister Stella and her cousin Pearlie, Gadge Kazan, and Lehman Engel. Women such as Beanie Barker, Dorothy Patten, Ruth Nelson, Virginia Farmer from Philadelphia, who had been married to Claude Rains, were invited. Playhouse people like the president, Robert Whitehead, and his wife, Zoe Caldwell, Frances Chaney and her husband, Ring Lardner, Jr., Doris Blum, and Richard Boone also visited. Paul loved to cook and entertain and throw little soirées!

If it hadn't been for Paul, Sandy would never have seen these people at this stage of his life. He was becoming less social in his advancing years, though he had never been very social in the first place. Yet he obviously enjoyed having Paul go out of his way to bring these people together at his charmingly decorated little pad on East 59th Street.

Paul told me the Playhouse was moving along well now that Sandy was back. Both he and Oleta D'Ambry, with Sandy's blessing, were still working on a transition plan for the school since they all three were thinking more and more these days of their retirement. The president of the board along with the board didn't seem to be too sympathetic to their financial plight as far as their inevitable retirement was concerned. Something was going to have to come to a head pretty soon; none of the three was getting any younger. With the exception of this knotty question, all was very much copasetic at the school.

The Requiem Germinates

In October, I got a note with the seal of the Bishop on it from a secular church official of the Anglican hierarchy. The note informed me of the coming celebration of the 100th anniversary of the Anglican Diocese in the Windward

20 From Webber to Mozart

Islands that was to take place in St. Lucia, St. Vincent, Grenada, and Bequia in October of '77, a year away. The official was inviting the Bequia singers to partake in the celebration. As I read the note, Mozart flashed through my head, but as the better part of valor, I shoved it back into the recesses of my mind.

Shortly after, on a visit to my dentist in St. Vincent, Dr. Inniss, who played the violin, I asked if he knew any other violinists in the country. He knew of three and said there might be a few more that he didn't know of. I mentioned the Mozart idea that had been bouncing around in my mind and he said, "Count me in."

That was a start since I knew the brass section from the police band should also have a few players who might be interested. A Peace Corps worker who played the trombone was helping some of the players in the police band. Landing him would be a coup. I had Sandy who could fill out the missing instruments, such as violas, cellos, bassoons, clarinets, and whatever, on the organ when needed. By the time I got home from the dentist, I had made up my mind. I was going to try to pull off the *Requiem* for the Bishop's celebration. I wasn't about to share this outlandish idea with anyone, not yet, that is. The first thing I had to do was to get the music. I was sure Paul would come through for me. It was part of his nature to be helpful. I called Paul and told him I would appreciate his checking at Schirmer's for the orchestral score of Mozart's *Requiem*. I would also need twenty copies of the vocal line for all four voices, plus a keyboard score.

Sandy arrived for Christmas, in time for the now annual *Nine Lessons*. Jonathan was back in England, but Elaine, our math and science teacher, who came to us under the auspices of the British OVSO, was, fortunately, a musician. She was a violinist who also played piano, and she turned out to be a godsend; she was to me anyway. Sandy, with his impaired vision, relied on her for everything. All Sandy had to do was sit there and play. Elaine was always there for him when needed. She was a real trooper. When she arrived from the UK, she was Elaine Miles. She then married a local fisherman, Orbin Mitchell, and became Elaine Mitchell, but then Orbin turned out to be Orbin Ollivierre (don't ask). So, to me she is Elaine Miles Mitchell Ollivierre, which I still call her to this day. And I called her plenty back then because she, with all her own multiple obligations at the school, became my right arm.

At this time of year, Santa was on his way. Boolu and I were up to our usual bag of tricks, only this year we added a little class. We got ourselves a little guitar accompaniment for our Christmas songfest. The days of pitch, shove, and grab were over. We had evolved into a regular, civilized, give-and-take party with nothing but nice things happening. Oh, except we still had to block the door and hold the children in, to give Santa time to get to the next venue before the party crashers arrived from the last party.

Sandy arrived from New York just before Christmas. As he was unpacking, he pulled out the Mozart scores, threw them on the bed, and said, "What's the meaning of this Mozart?"

21 The Requiem

So Sandy Comes Aboard

Picking up the large orchestral score with all its instrumental parts, Sandy wanted to know, "I can understand an organ score, even the vocal scores, but what the hell are your kids going to do with this orchestral score? Have you gone mad? This stuff's not cheap."

"Sandy," I said, passing them off as nothing significant, "I need a new project for them. It's just an idea I've had percolating—"

"I see!" he interrupted. "I always wondered what you had going on up there. Listen, I could use a cup of coffee—cream, no sugar."

"No kidding, Sandy. Here's what I'd like to try," I said pleadingly, "I've been thinking about this for some time and I haven't told you. You see, Bishop

21 The Requiem

Woodroff has asked me to do something with the kids for the 100th anniversary of the Diocese of the Windward Islands. I assume he means at the cathedral."

"Well, I can understand you need to keep busy... I suppose you want me to go along for another ride?"

"Who else?"

"OK! I like Mozart. Now, tell me. The organ score and the vocal score for the kids, I get that. But an orchestral score I don't understand. Poor little old, limited-minded me, would you please give me a clue?"

"I thought we could use whatever instrumentalists we found in St. Vincent," I answered, squirming just a little, "and you could fill in on the organ for whatever instruments we didn't have."

"The organ score will have all the instruments," Sandy pointed out.

"Our organ isn't a big pipe organ, and whatever instruments we find in St. Vincent will just make it more interesting."

"Interesting?" Sandy echoed. Knowing me, he didn't need to say anything more.

That conversation over, we were off on another glorious roller-coaster ride. Throughout the trip, whenever I ran into some unsolvable difficulty, he would pull a Philippe on me. He would just smile at me, wipe his hands together, and say, "Not my prob-bub-blem."

First Hurdle

After the first of the year, I went over to St. Vincent to track down every instrumentalist I could find. I felt like a private eye. The first one I found in the magazine store she ran with her son. Mrs. Robertson was a violinist, and there weren't many string people left in the country. "There were many more back in the '30s, when they got together and played, but not anymore," she said shaking her head. I asked if she would be interested in joining a group to work on some Mozart. She replied, "I'd love to try; I'm not that good."

"Not to worry," I said.

She added, "Now there's Chick. He's a good player. You better get hold of him." I told her Dr. Inniss was already in touch with him and that I would get in touch with her when we were ready to start. Chick brought Soso, a bass fiddler.

I called Bishop Woodroff to tell him the plan. I could tell he was a little taken aback. He was a pianist himself, originally from Grenada, educated at Oxford. "Why a requiem?"

Just the way he asked, I knew my plan was in trouble. I had a feeling he was thinking more along the lines of folk-like entertainment like we had done at Victoria Park. I quickly thought, dead souls, and replied, "Your Excellency, in honor of all the souls who have died in the diocese in the past 100 years."

I could tell when I put it that way, he was all for it. I knew then I had the go-ahead needed. But he added, "We would still like the group to perform some fun West Indian music for us as well." (And "as well," we did.) Then he said, "We have George Thomas, a secular leader here in the church. Perhaps you know the name? He's the author of Ruler in Hairouna. He's a violinist and he will want to play." (And play he did, after a fashion.)

Then there was the retired school principal way up leeward in Barrouallie, who made the long trip in every week for rehearsals. He told me he sometimes had to make strings for his bow out of the inner veins of a coconut tree trunk. He explained that when you are so far from civilization, you learn to make do. I said I knew from living on Bequia. William Roberts, the trombonist from the Peace Corps, got me six men from the police band. By the end of January, I had six violins, a bass fiddle, four horns, two trombones, a flugelhorn, two flutes, three recorders, and a kettledrum player. We had no kettledrum of course, so we made one out of an oil drum with the required pitches for the *Requiem*. Sandy at the organ with his page-turner would make up for any missing instrument. The *Requiem* was written for the obsolete basset horn, for which the clarinet was now substituted. So, for instance, Sandy managed to produce the clarinet sound on the organ. I believe we ended up with more than twenty musicians. Woodwind instruments were unknown in St. Vincent except by the three children of a Pakistani man married to a member of the Gumbs family, who were studying the recorder. I included them in our little orchestra. Maggie Howard, a classmate of mine from Sandy's course back in the '60s, donated an alto recorder, which one of them played. We called our little group The Kingstown Ensemble.

When I got back to Bequia and reported my findings, Sandy said, "Not bad, but still, it's pretty sparse."

I felt if we managed twenty instrumentalists, that number would be enough with Sandy at the organ. A Mozart orchestra is small to begin with, consisting of no more than thirty members at most. "Sparse" or not, it was a start. I was sure we would pick up more members as we went along. I said to Sandy, "Now I am determined."

When I spoke to Father Adams about my plan, his advice to me was to confine my work to Bequia—reaching out to St. Vincent wasn't a wise move. He told me it was too complicated to explain. He would only say, "Listen to me, I know what I'm talking about." Well, I didn't listen.

"The Boy With The Cart"

We started right after the first of the year. We held a rehearsal every Monday night at the University Complex in Frenches. This little episode changed our lives considerably. We couldn't go over at 6 AM, hold a rehears-

21 The Requiem

al, be finished by noon, and make the *Friendship Rose* back to Bequia. These people all had jobs, so evening rehearsals were all they could manage. So Sandy and I had to look for a place to rent overnight on Mondays. We heard about a volunteer teacher who was going back to England and giving up his little two-bedroom house near the University Complex. All we would have to do was move in and pay the rent. It was perfect for us and very inexpensive. The landlord was Winnie Wallace's son. It really was a small world here.

This arrangement meant I wouldn't be free to teach at the high school on Mondays and Tuesdays any more. I would now have to double up on Wednesdays, Thursdays, and Fridays. That shift, in turn, was possible only if I made a change at the Deaf School. Fortunately, Avila Ollivierre, a student from my first year of teaching, was finishing up her O-Levels and would have time to help the deaf students. Mr. and Mrs. Jack Bachelor from Stockbridge, Massachusetts offered to pay her salary. The timing was serendipitous with the choir, too. I was no longer holding section rehearsals anyway.

So it was that 1977 embraced our household. Looking back, I think that if I had a brain it must have been scattered, as Sandy would say. When I started dreaming of the Mozart project, I never once cared a fig about all my other responsibilities and commitments. Somehow I thought, because I didn't care, that it would all fall into place for me like a jigsaw puzzle. On I went, moment to moment, pressing forward to my goal.

Come Monday mornings, we were up before the sun at 5 AM and schlepping that heavy portable organ, plus a special reading light for Sandy, down to the *Friendship Rose*. In St. Vincent a young chap met us with a cart and hauled the organ up to the University Complex. Sandy and I would go shopping for food and spend the day around the house in Frenches. We had an early evening rehearsal at which everyone seemed to enjoy themselves, though we never had a full complement. Still, enough showed up for a rehearsal, and these players all worked hard and accomplished a great deal at each rehearsal. After the session, Sandy and I walked home up the short hill to the house where I would cook dinner. Nearby was a little neighborhood restaurant, if you could call it that. It served only fried chicken-leg with rice and a little salad with a beer or Pepsi, for a buck-fifty. It didn't beat cooking, but it did beat doing dishes, so sometimes we would stop there and have dinner.

In the morning, I would go into town and shop for Bequia, then have my purchases sent off to the boat. After lunch we would walk to the harbor along Front Street to the Bequia pier with "The Boy with the Cart." I was in the first American production of the play of that name by Christopher Fry, just another little coincidence. Aboard the *Friendship Rose*, when Henry, the owner, collected the passage, he always passed us by. When I asked him one day why, he answered, "We have a contract with the government to transport the mail down islands, and all the government workers as well."

"So?" I probed.

327

"That includes teachers," he explained.

I thought it was very nice of him, though he was stretching it just a little. Sandy said to me, "Never mind. Look at it as a contribution to our efforts on the part of the *Friendship Rose*. We can use the support."

The crossing, getting everything, including that monster of an organ, off the boat and back home up the hill, was always enervating for both of us. As Tuesday afternoons on the beach had to be struck off the agenda, we had only five beach days to get us back in shape and reinvigorate us. Sandy didn't let me forget it. My answer to his complaints was, "Well, if you hadn't prevented me from building the pool before we stopped construction…"

Sandy quipped, "Pool? Fresh water? I didn't come thousands of miles out of my way for fresh water. We're here for the sea, the sea! Lest we forget."

"OK, OK, I get it," I said, "This too shall pass, and we'll have all the time in the world. Look at this period as just a little distraction."

"Distraction from what?" Sandy asked. "My sea time?"

"You are kidding, of course," I said.

"Of course, I'm kidding. Even kidding is a distraction. You will do your thing anyway. That's what I like about you," Sandy said.

We bantered back and forth like this most of the time. But we always made Tuesday afternoon's choir rehearsal at the church.

A New Teacher For The Deaf School

I had taken on Avila Ollivierre as a teacher at the Deaf School and trained her in my approach to teaching. In no time she had my exercises down pat as well as my method of lip-reading, which the students were picking up very well by this time. Her presence there enabled me to take on a heavier schedule at the high school on Wednesday, Thursday, and Friday. When school closed in June, the Bachelors arranged for Avila to attend a summer course at the State School for the Deaf in Connecticut, after which she came back to Bequia and took over my job. She also took on three new students and started another group who were growing up and had reached school-entry age. The Deaf School then moved into Gilford's Burial Society Hall behind his store over the Friendship Gap. The Canadian Mission run by Ron and June Armstrong paid the rent. The Armstrongs had both been heavily involved in helping me ever since I had started the Deaf School. The Deaf School was the forerunner of the Bequia Mission and eventually of the Sunshine School sponsored and built by Japan (for which, by the way, Boolu is now official Santa Claus).

21 The Requiem

The Sun's Over The Yardarm

After the Kingstown Ensemble program had started up, days in Bequia found us up and at it much earlier than usual. I had morning classes at school and was finished mid-afternoon. Sandy wasn't reading anymore because of his eyes, so he was left at home with little or nothing to do. He would get a ride down to the Frangipani and wait for me to come around after classes. Most expatriates and the yachting set checked out the Frangi about noon every day, to see what was happening or for nothing more than to see one another and socialize. Sandy and I would meet there, have a drink, and talk with Marie Kingston or Pat Mitchell, the women who ran the place, or with Pat's husband Son, if he was there. He was then our Member of Parliament from the Grenadines and Minister of Agriculture and was spending most of his waking hours over in St. Vincent.

Regulars like Jack Lindsay, the curmudgeon, hung out at the Frangi. The invidious Jack, drink always in hand, played the cynic, talking of Louise, the snake he had on board, which by the way, no one ever saw, not even after he died. He would blare away in objectionable language, just for the shock value. One of his favorites cracks he used to yell out to the bartender: "Harold, take your thumb out of your ass, wash it, and get me a drink." This crudeness was meant, of course, to attract attention to himself. Some said he was living on an annuity sent by his family back in Michigan just to keep him down here out of the way. He was more to be pitied than censured. He was a hopeless alcoholic. Was it any wonder he died of liver failure?

Then there was the marvelous Englishwoman Nora Birmingham with a Pepsi in her hand and her head in a Scrabble board. When she wasn't at home teaching Alex the sail maker how to read, she could be found on the Frangipani veranda, doing her thing. She had been a schoolteacher for years in Jamaica and now lived on Bequia in her retirement. Nora was the only person I know who found a way to play Scrabble with herself, legitimately, without cheating. You could run into charming Eleanor, with husband Tom Thompson, the writer from Spring, and Melanie their granddaughter, waiting for their son Michael. Not many from Spring came around at noon; they showed up in the evening for dinner. You might see the delightful Rita with her husband Sam McDowell, the artist from just this side of Paget Farm, checking some boat people out while selling his wares. Mac Simmons, since his last paramour, Mary Lynn, had left, could now be seen with Judy Armstrong talking to her sister Mary Budgell from Canada and Elaine Miles from Coventry, all three of them teachers on their lunch break. Ellen Schwartz on shore off her yacht might be doing a little shopping for herself now that all her brood had grown up and left for the States and on to other things. You rarely saw Moon Hole people, and never ran into Tom or Glady Johnston, who ran it. Ron and Stan from Friendship never made an appearance, but you might run into Father Ron or June Armstrong just past the bank out by the Step Up Bar (now called the Porthole and run by Lennox and Noelina Taylor), which was just in front of their Canadian Mission headquarters. Some of the local regulars like Nolly Simmons, Ermina Antrobus, or Kingsley King could be sitting at the bar. Paulette Dewer would show up with the New Yorkers, Rootie Derujinsky, the ex-cover girl, or Pat Field, the photographer from Friendship, and Tiare Austin might be there looking for Lee, her husband. Norma was always there on her marine radio with Arlene O'Neal the housekeeper keeping her company as she kept contact between land and sea, something we all had to do at one time or another.

When the sun crossed over the yardarm, the Frangipani was the place to meet, or find who you were looking for. If they weren't around, someone would always clue you in as to where they were, no matter where they happened to be.

Changes At The Playhouse

The doctors gave Sandy a six-month respite this time. The break not only made him feel good but it gave him more time on Bequia. The Playhouse was getting along beautifully without him, so he said, but such was not the case if you listened to Paul. William Esper was driving Oleta D'Ambry up the wall, and Paul also felt Bill was overstepping his position. Bill was usurping Sandy's position by claiming Sandy's office as his. Martin Waldron, a speech teacher, was holding class on the roof, and neighbors were complaining about the noise. Sandy said to me, "These are not my problems. I don't run the school and never did. And I am not going to fly up there and tell them how to run it now."

I'd like to know who Sandy thought he was talking to. I knew that if he hadn't been running that school up until then, then who had? Certainly it wasn't Paul, at least not Paul without Sandy. Didn't Sandy know that I knew Mrs. Morgenthau was dead? But I said nothing; Playhouse matters were definitely not my business. The plain truth was I couldn't have cared less. They didn't pay him enough for me to give a damn. He didn't need the school. In fact he would have been a hell of a lot better off without it long before.

The truth was Sandy didn't like confrontation and sidestepped it whenever he could. This was one hassle he was using his doctors' stay of grace to avoid. He said, "Paul and Oleta will have to work it out between them." When Paul called down to Sandy on the Island, not knowing what else to do about some problem or other, Sandy said, "Jimmy needs me on Bequia. If you all can't get along together, then you, Paul, should do something about it. After all, you run the school."

That was all Oleta needed to hear. She would have sent Esper packing long ago. It didn't take a rocket scientist to see that with Oleta it was personal. In her eyes, Esper wasn't Sandy Meisner. The upshot was, Esper left and Martin followed him. I know Paul blamed me for keeping Sandy on Bequia. If truth be told, the outcome was the best thing that could have happened to both Bill Esper and Martin Waldron. I have to admit that I too benefited from the whole folderol because I had Sandy here with me helping me all summer long, and there was no way I was going to discourage that. 1977 may have been a bad year for the Playhouse, but it sure was a good one for us on Bequia, until...

The Bequia Singers Take On New Life

Lots of hard work went on, and the choir was growing in size. Now some mothers wanted to join, so I included them in what I called the Not-So Young Adult Group. We were now a force seventy-five strong. Attendance was remarkable, and choir rehearsals were jammed. The choir loft couldn't hold any more. They were picking up number after number, and the Latin wasn't a problem at all. It was summertime with absolutely no distractions or abstractions either, for that matter.

Now, the orchestra was something else again, moving at a much slower pace. The few who came to every rehearsal were progressing, but the brass section just limped along. Their attendance was bad, and their reading wasn't good. I handed them over to Bill, my Peace Corps friend, and told him to take them alone. Truth was, Bill had better luck than I. Wasn't he one of them? Maybe I intimidated them or moved too fast. God knows I knew absolutely nothing about horns. My second violins were in a bad way and needed extra help, but I couldn't stop now. When Elaine, my first chair of their section, came over from Bequia when school closed, she would whip them into shape, I hoped. It was a shame she could only make it over to St. Vincent once in a while because of her commitments. The same situation held for the woodwinds. Mary Budgell, the flautist, also taught at the school and couldn't make all the rehearsals in St. Vincent either. I had my three little recorder players, but I left them to the older brother, who worked with them until I had my two flautists there to move along with them, and that wasn't until school closed either. My first violins, string bass, and organ were coming along just fine. The flugelhorn player was a professional in Europe. He could hold his own anywhere, that is, as long as he was sober. My only solace was that I knew damned well that by now my chorus wouldn't even need an orchestra. They would do fine with just the organ. So I decided to play a wait-and-see game.

Summertime & the Livin' is Easy-and Busy

It was a wonderful summer for both of us, plenty of play and parties with lots of work to balance it off. I found the expatriates who came to retire, rest, and do nothing seemed to go to seed. What I call jungle rot sets in, and all kinds of problems take over. So many couples break up, with one leaving the

Island and the other staying. Then there is the danger of the rum taking over. The drinkers tend to attract each other, and a little group is formed. They only encourage one another down the slippery slope to cirrhosis of the liver. That is, if their pocketbooks hold up that long. It is not a large group, but it is a noticeable one on such a small island. On the other hand, the expatriates who become involved and find something productive to do fare much better.

On the work front, my recalcitrant horn players were not my only problem. I had to come up with at least thirty-five to forty friends of Bequia willing to part with a US $100 each to help pay for the soloists' airfare from New York. I was not good at begging, which to me was tantamount to ass-kissing. Thank God for the Bishop, Father Adams, the Canadian Mission, and Santa's Friends, because they were the ones who came across with the donations. One even sent her check for US $100 to "Father Jim." I wanted to send it to my dad, but Sandy was willing to buy it for $200 so he could frame it. Another hundred was a temptation, but as it worked out we didn't need it.

Barbara Carville, the choir mother of Grace Episcopal Church in Utica, New York, was my sister-in-law, so she agreed to organize and get the soloists rehearsed. She took charge of the logistics. The soprano was Roseanna Giotto; the alto, Jean Engstrom; the tenor, Leo Carville, my brother; and the bass, Robert Parry, whom I had gone to school with and who had studied voice with my teacher, Bernard Taylor. Leo had studied with Bernard for a short while as well. Along with the four soloists, my niece Beth Carville, a flautist, made up the complement of visiting artists, as did a violinist, a tourist who came on her own.

Paul came down for a month. He painted up a storm, working in watercolors. He swam with Sandy in the afternoon and partied with us at night. Sandy and I went right on working on the Mozart. Came the end of August, Sandy and Paul left for New York. Sandy's doctors' appointments were a little overdue, but Sandy didn't mind. He hadn't felt so well in years. His plan was to go home with Paul, see his doctors, and then take over his position as Head of the Acting Department at the Playhouse. He would set up the classes and teachers for the coming year, take on the new students himself, and start them off on the right foot with an assistant. He was going to teach until the last week in September and travel down with the soloist contingent from New York. They were planning to be here in time for a few last-minute dress rehearsals.

Not Again

Yes, '77 was a good year, until... The end of August came and Sandy gave me a call to tell me Dr. Shapiro had found a malignant nodule on his neck. He was to be admitted to Sloan-Kettering as soon as possible for radical surgery. That was one bit of news neither of us was looking for and certainly the last

21 The Requiem

thing we expected. But here it was staring us both in the face. "Should I chuck all this and come right up?" I asked Sandy. "I could postpone our part in all this down here—"

He stopped me dead in my tracks and coolly and calmly said, "If anyone is postponing anything, it's going to me. If you think for one minute that a thing like this is going to get in our way, you're as mad as I always thought you were."

"Now look, Sandy, I can come up and be with you and when it's over I could find someone in New York to come back with me and play for us," I suggested.

He came back at me: "Now listen. I have looked at this matter of the cancer versus the Mozart from every possible angle, and this is what we are going to do. And I'm not asking you, I am telling—"

I interrupted, "Sandy, you're in no condition to be even thinking of the Mozart."

The next thing he said was, "Listen, and listen good. That nodule is small. I'll have the operation and I'll be out in a week, and afterwards I'll have most of the month to rest up. Then I'll be down and that's that. You stay there with the kids, they need you now. Paul is here, Ruth is here. Who else do I need?"

Sandy wasn't making any sense. Once he went into the hospital, I'd talk it out with Paul. Well, he went in and had radical surgery to the right side of his neck. This surgery was no small event and I knew it, I could tell from Paul's reaction. So I started making plans for an organist. I had a very close friend from Juilliard, Richard Eikenberry, who was now teaching at NYU, and just maybe he could make it down on weekends. He would have to go back and forth, but you do what you have to do and to hell with the expense. It turned out he played in a Catholic church up in Inwood on Sundays and he wouldn't be able to even consider it. He said he would check with some friends of his, that he should be able to find someone for me.

Sandy's operation went well. They were then scheduling him for extensive radiation treatments as an outpatient. He made it emphatically clear to Paul and Ruth that he was not starting his radiation until after the Mozart. Ruth went ballistic. Of course she blamed me for Sandy's crazy, unrealistic notion of putting off the radiation for as much as a day. She had Paul call me from school, where he could talk freely, and explain that Sandy wasn't in his right mind, that I shouldn't expect him on Bequia for the Mozart. Paul told me Sandy, at 120 pounds, was a shell of himself. The operation had been extensive. They had taken all the muscle from the right side of his neck, from under his jaw to his collarbone. I assured Paul I didn't expect Sandy to come and had already told him so. I also told Paul that my friend "Dick Ike" was looking for an organist to fill the bill.

Sandy called me from Paul's quite upset. "Tell Dick to forget about that organist. I'm coming down and I'm going to play. Do you think after nine months I'm going to let anyone else play for those kids?"

"I understand how you feel," I answered, "but your sister and Paul think you should stay and take that radiation as soon as possible."

"Listen, my sister and Paul are not you and me. If this is the last thing we do, we are doing it together. No one knows what this means to those kids and what it means to you and me, except you and me. I am not going to let you do it without me."

I could see how all this was affecting him, and I could also hear over the phone how difficult it was for him to express himself both physically and emotionally. His words were coming slowly and hesitantly and slurred. It hurt me just to listen to him. The last thing he said to me was, "Jimmy, the doctors have sent me home, I am not in a hospital, I am at Paul's. So why can't I be with you, where I want to be? The radiation will be there waiting for me when I get back."

"Do you think you can make it down here by yourself?" I asked.

His answer was simple: "Watch me."

I knew if his mind was made up, no one was going to stop him, neither Paul nor Ruth. And they knew him well enough to know that six of each of them couldn't stop him. So when the time came, Paul arranged for his plane tickets and they both waved him off at Kennedy. Knowing Ruth, I'm sure she must have felt she was never going to see her dear brother again.

A Shocking Sight It Was

I went over to St. Vincent to meet him coming off the plane. It was heart wrenching to see this once dapper, sprightly, full-of-life man I had lived with all these years. I could see why Ruth and Paul felt the way they did about his making the trip down. As he made his way across the airfield, he was struggling just to keep the strap of his overnight bag on his shoulder and trying at the same time to hang onto the topcoat he was dragging on the ground. I wanted to rush out to help him, but of course the area was restricted. Just then the flight attendant noticed him floundering and ran over to him, took his coat and bag in one hand, and, with her other hand, assisted him slowly across to the Customs Office. Where was the man I knew who was so full of life, love and dreams, piss and vinegar? He seemed to be only a shell of himself, with a single-minded determination, a will of iron, and a face as stern and concentrated as granite stone.

After he made his way through Customs, and that wasn't an easy feat for anyone in the best condition, he stepped out the door into the open, next to the taxi stand. He was on the arm of a Customs official, who spotted me saying, "Oh, there's Mr. Jimmy." And I saw Sandy smiling over at me. The officer continued, "Here's the old gentlemon, still in one piece." Turning to Sandy, he said, "Take it slow, mon." He was handling him like a Dresden doll. He handed me his coat and carry-on with one hand and with the other he handed me

21 The Requiem

Sandy, saying to Sandy, "Watch your step there," and then to me, "His luggage is coming right out." I thanked him.

When I hugged Sandy, I was shocked. I could feel his bones. He was so thin, and it had been little more than a month since he had gone away. Helping him into the taxi-van, I shuddered. A fear ran through me, and at that moment I knew both Ruth and Paul had been right. He shouldn't be down here at all. We were supposed to stay over at Frenches and get over to Bequia the next day, but my instincts were to get him home and into his own bed as soon as possible. The taxi driver told me the *Roseareen* was going over to Bequia later that day. I asked him to see if we could make that boat.

"Sandy," I said, "you'll sleep a lot better in your own bed."

Parnell was on the pier to meet us. I could tell from his initial reaction as well as some of the others' that they could see the drastic change Sandy had undergone in such a short time. The deterioration in his looks and manner were horrendous. DD, our housekeeper, had some chicken soup ready, and after a cigarette and a drink, he was ready for bed. As I helped him upstairs, he stopped and said, "You have no idea how good it feels to be back here with you and Boolu."

He slept the sleep of the damned that night—he was dead to the world. The trip down must have demanded every ounce of energy he had. I thought a lot that night about his actually playing for us. Even if I let him, would he be able to? I had my doubts. I thought of the organist at the cathedral and also of Pat Prescott, a piano teacher in Kingstown. They could do it, either one of them, if they would, and I never had told Dick to stop looking. I was in another wait-and-see period in my life. I had to wonder why it was I seemed to have so many of them.

In the morning, he was looking much better. He was more rested and relaxed. I had a rehearsal that afternoon, which he insisted on coming to. As we left the house, he asked, "Elaine is going to be there, isn't she? But I'm playing, right?"

All I said was, "Who else?"

The choir, when he walked in, saw how weak he looked. They just sat there quietly and did nothing until he walked over to the organ and sat down, and then they all applauded. I kept the rehearsal very simple, picking out the easier, more familiar pieces.

Toward the end of rehearsal, Sandy said, "Come on. Let's do the 'Lux Sterna.'" This section was the big, fast finish with all the runs. Sandy waded in knee deep and so did the chorus. They rocked the rafters with it, including my basses, my Achilles heel. Sandy looked up from the score when we finished and said with a big smile, "They still have it." He applauded and everyone joined in.

If I had had any doubts, and I sure did, he had just wiped them away. He was going to be able to carry this off. The most important job I had was to keep him as relaxed, peaceful, and rested as possible. Happy, joyful, and content he was, just to be back with the kids. They were all around him, curious about his operation, which he himself made little of. The experience and concept of cancer was much different down here. To people here, it was a death sentence, especially since this occurrence was the second. Truth be told, Ruth, Paul, and I didn't feel much different. We thought his chances were slim and we weren't the only ones who felt this way. But you can rest assured that Sandy didn't. Well, one could never tell what Sandy truly felt. He had such control of his behavior that what you saw was what he wanted you to see. This ability worried me most. Was he holding on with every ounce of energy he had? Then, when it was all over, would he collapse?

In spite of Paul's and Ruth's feelings, I had to think of Sandy's wishes. If he wanted to go out vital to the end, so be it. At the same time, I knew I would never forgive myself for letting him. But the plain fact was I didn't have a choice in the matter. He was doing what he wanted to do, and what's more, he was able to do it well. I truly believed the choice was his, and I decided to make it as easy and as comfortable for him as possible.

The Maestro Snaps

Everything was fine until after the soloists arrived and we were holding our soloist and orchestral rehearsal in St. Vincent. I was being very careful and listening like mad, when something went awry with the clarinets in the "Agnus Dei." Even I was having trouble with this piece, so much so that I took it in a fast six count just to keep everyone together. After all, I told myself, it wasn't written by Mozart anyway. I don't care what anyone says, that piece has a completely different feel about it from all the rest of the pieces in the *Requiem*. Mozart died before its completion, and one of his students finished it. So much for excuses, the fact was the clarinets were taking off double-time, again. Once I realized where it was coming from, I simply said, "Let's take this piece from the top once more. Remember, right or wrong, I'm taking it in a six count."

This run-through was our second. We were at the end of the rehearsal, which had gone relatively well. This time, the piece started out just fine, but when we came to the run just before Roseanna's solo, Sandy took off in three count again, consequently in double time. Whereupon, I threw my hands up in the air and blurted out, "Damn it! Sandy, the count is six, even in the runs."

He looked up at me from the score he could barely read. The score sat on the small wooden stand that raised it so he could see the notes on the page more clearly. But remember, this apparatus blocked the keyboard from his vision around middle C. Consequently he had to hunt and peck in that area like Stevie Wonder, sort of touch-me feel-me, you should excuse the expression. Yet in spite of his difficulties, as I said "Sandy!" he looked up at me smiling from ear to ear and said, "Sorry, sorry!"

"OK, OK!" I snapped back and, with an exasperated sigh, directed, "Once again."

We started and there at the back of the orchestra went Beth, my niece, walking out the back door. We were almost finished, and it had been a long, anxious rehearsal for me. Now Beth was walking out the back door! I stopped, turned to Barbara at the front door, and said, "Find out what's wrong with her."

Barbara came back and quietly explained, "She's out there crying because of the way you yelled at Sandy."

"Yelled at Sandy? Is that what I did? Well, tell her to wipe her eyes and get back into this room so we can finish this rehearsal. Yelled at Sandy? If I was yelling at anything, I was yelling at this piece and the shape it's in."

This incident brought to mind mezzo-soprano Jennie Tourel singing the "Esurientes" from Bach's Magnificat. She was having trouble with a turn in a vocal run, and Leonard Bernstein, the conductor, took the time to go over the section three times. Then he told us all, "Take five." He took Jennie to the Steinway, and went over the vocal problem with her. When they broke up and she went back to her place, he said for all of us to hear, "Take it to your teacher." He loved her; they were the best of friends. It was a joke. Besides, it could have happened to any one of us on that stage at Carnegie Hall that night. Another story, before my time, has Arturo Toscanini rehearsing a concert. This time it was soprano Helen Traubel experiencing difficulty with a spot in her aria. They had to go over it a number of times. When he was finished, Toscanini stepped down off the podium, walked over to Traubel, and grabbed her by both boobs. "If these were only brains!" he exclaimed. Then there was the one about the conductor who was having trouble with one of his female cellists. He stopped the rehearsal and snapped, "That's quite an instrument you've got there between your legs. But will you please, for Christ's sake, stop scratching it!" So the stories go.

So why was Beth out there blubbering? It does show you what a sweet, feeling kind of kid she was. I was very proud of her. She studied with a couple of the finest teachers in the country, in New York and Boston. I knew she, in first chair, would carry the wind section through.

Finessing A Performance For Bequia

In St. Vincent, billets had been arranged for the soloists. Jean and Roseanna were staying with the church organist, and Bob was staying with Arthur Connell, a member of an old island family. Leo and Barbara stayed at the vicarage with Beth. On Bequia, the soloists all stayed at Father Adams' in the parish house in the Harbour. Little Beth stayed in our guest room.

The big final dress rehearsal with organ, orchestra, soloists, and chorus was scheduled for 3 PM the last Sunday of October in St. Mary's Church on Bequia, with an open invitation to anyone who might be interested. I knew the reception wouldn't be anything like for *Superstar*, but for the students singing this work, it would be with them always. This I was sure of. With the *Friendship Rose* making the run over and back on Sundays, I had thought I could call a rehearsal on Bequia. I wanted one here for many reasons. First, the orchestra had never played the piece with the singers, and the kids needed the practice. Secondly, it was only fitting that the friends and family of the seventy-five singers get to hear them. With only twenty orchestra members, it made more sense for the players to come to Bequia. Thirdly, Sandy and I couldn't even count the number of trips we had taken over and back. Fourthly, I was really upset about this whole business of Bequia's being some never-never land, even to an otherwise reasonable person. It was high time Vincentians grew up and got over themselves... This nonsense had been going on for years.

The logistics of just getting the orchestra over the nine miles from St. Vincent to Bequia was proving Father Adam's prediction. I couldn't believe more than half had never been to Bequia before and expressed little interest in even going. George Thomas was one of the worst. I couldn't believe it. Here he was, the islands' writer, like their poor man's poet laureate, the historian of the people, and yet he had no interest in an island that was a part of his own country, only nine miles away. He couldn't have cared less, had absolutely no curiosity. A writer? I thought. Not by my definition.

The police band was playing somewhere that morning in St. Vincent. After much pleading, I got the so-called Coast Guard with their one and only boat to agree to bring them over after their morning gig and back on Sunday afternoon. I was truly grateful; it eased my mind when they agreed. Even with the *Friendship Rose* coming over on Sundays now and also making an early evening trip back to St. Vincent, I still couldn't get definite commitments from all of the orchestra members. My woodwinds were fine, and because of the Coast Guard I had the brass and horns section, but the holdout was the strings.

Nevertheless, I determined the orchestra would come to Bequia. I just announced it, with the American soloists still in the room. I simply said, after the soloists' rehearsal, "All players and soloists are expected to be over on Bequia Sunday, in time for a three o'clock performance in front of a congregation." I could feel the resistance mounting. I stated, "No discussion. The Coast Guard will pick up all the horn players after your gig, wherever it is Sunday morning, and the *Friendship Rose* will get everyone else over and back." A few started maundering amongst themselves. I reiterated, "Everyone!" I turned to the boy with the cart and told him to bring the organ up to the house in Frenches.

I left the hall immediately with Sandy on my arm, and the soloists followed. Leo, my brother asked, "What was all that about?"

"Don't ask," I replied. "You wouldn't want to know." I thought, this little episode is a taste of what Father Adams was warning me against. Is it really true? Could he be right? No, I concluded, he's just being Father Adams, giving St. Vincent a hard time. So I went ahead in my Pollyanna way. I still had a lot to learn.

21 The Requiem

Sunday arrived, and everyone surprised me by showing up, even George who came over on the police boat. The Bishop, who was a friend, must have shamed him into it. I got a kick out of his taking the police boat over, when the crossing on the *Friendship Rose* would have been much easier on him. The performance went off like clockwork and all our friends and their families were considerably impressed. During the applause I thought to myself, that's it, another first for Bequia! I was so proud of Sandy holding up the way he did, and the soloists just blended beautifully as a quartet. Everyone did a class-A job.

Oh, Ye Bishops Of Little Faith

In final preparation for the big event, Sandy and I went over to the University Complex once more that week to work with the orchestra, and we had two more rehearsals with the choir on Bequia. Saturday, we had our first and last dress rehearsal with the entire company at the cathedral. Halfway through the work, Bishop Woodroff came in with the Bishop from Chicago. Neither had heard us before.

When the Bishop in Chicago had been told we were doing the Mozart *Requiem* from Bequia, he thought, that tiny island? and disbelieved it. So when he had disembarked from the plane at Arnos Vale, he had handed a tape of the *Requiem* to Bishop Woodroff and said, "Listen to this. This is what you say they are singing on Sunday." It wasn't until they came to the dress rehearsal that they really believed it was going to be performed cover to cover. I realized they were both skeptical because the program stated: Musical renditions from the Mozart *Requiem*. Once I'd seen the program, I knew no one believed me, not even our Bishop. He may not have had faith in us before, but after that rehearsal it was another matter indeed. He said he was pleased and proud of our work.

Performance Sublime

Sunday of the big performance went so well. But mostly I was happy that the cathedral was packed, with standing room only. The Bishop had transport available from every church in the country. I'm sure most of them knew from nothing about Mozart, but it was free and transportation was provided. Plus, and a big plus it was you see, what else was there to do? The answer... nothing. So they were there, and that to me was the main thing.

What a glorious night it was for all of us! Members of the Music Society of Kingstown didn't even wait for me to leave the altar when it was over. They crowded around to thank me, some with tears of joy. It was very gratifying. When Sandy and I got outside on the street, some members of the orchestra were grouped around the hood of a car. They were listening to a tape someone had made of the performance that night, and they all seemed pleased by what they were hearing. It was another warm moment for me. Sandy, Boolu, and I stayed at the Heron Hotel while Vincentians put up everyone else, all eighty-five of us from Bequia.

On Monday morning, the next day, we were transported in school buses way out leeward to Barrouallie, where we sang and danced in our colorful West Indian costumes. We made it back to Kingstown about five o'clock, where the *Friendship Rose* awaited us at the Grenadines Pier, and we were back on Bequia just after dark, our first big performance of *Requiem* behind us.

Requiem - Jimmy Conducts, Sandy Plays

A Flea In My Ear

A few days before that performance, Wednesday or Thursday night, while I lay sleeping, a bug crawled down the canal of my right ear. Its wings fluttered desperately. It had gone down too far and couldn't return on its own. The fluttering was so loud it sounded like the engine of an old C-54 starting up. I got up and tried to dig it out with a Q-tip. After a considerable amount of time, I gave up. I could neither work it out nor squash and kill it. The nurse in the clinic the next day had no better luck. When the bug was quiet, it was all right, but when it fluttered, I couldn't hear a thing. How was I going to conduct on Saturday and Sunday if something wasn't done and done really fast? We were going over on the early boat Saturday morning for dress rehearsal, so I called ahead to Dr. Cyrus at his hospital there and explained my plight. He agreed to see me.

We all went over, singers and Sandy and Boolu and I, on the 6:30 AM boat. To this point I had told no one about the "flea in my ear." What good would it have done? One worrier was enough in this case. I took Sandy and Boolu to the Heron and told them to go ahead with breakfast. I told Sandy I was going

21 The Requiem

up to the hospital because I had a flea in my ear.

Sandy said, "You have got to be kidding. I never heard of such a thing—well, I've heard. But not for real. You know what I mean."

I said, "Sandy, it's true." And he laughed. "Sandy, I do, and it's still alive and it keeps buzzing."

Sandy was still laughing. "Well, this could only happen to you! What are you going to do?"

"I'm going to Dr. Cyrus to see if he can get it out."

I never stopped to explain it to Boolu; he had no idea what we were talking about. I told him Sandy was going to lie down, and he could go find his sister but he must be back at the hotel by noon. I left them eating their breakfast and took a taxi up to the hospital next to the botanical gardens.

Dr. Cyrus dug and dug and dug. Never mind getting it out, he couldn't even kill it. He finally got some long, skinny, copper prongs, I guess you could call them. Each had cotton on the end like a huge Q-tip. He dipped them in some kind of acidy liquid, and at last the buzzing seemed to subside, but he still couldn't get the bug out. The one bright spot was that he silenced it. I guess he killed it. But there was no way it was coming out, at least not that day anyway. To be without the buzzing was a big improvement, but I was experiencing a little hearing loss.

Sandy had rested all morning, and Boolu had gone out looking for his family around town. At noon Boolu returned and we had a little lunch before taxiing over to the cathedral for the final rehearsal.

Everything about the ear stayed the same all day Sunday, thank God, but by Monday I was hearing less and less and my ear was getting hotter by the minute. So, on Tuesday I went to the clinic in the Harbour and saw the government doctor, who stated, "Someone has been poking around in this ear, and it's badly infected." A gross understatement, I thought. He gave me some antibiotics, said to take them all week, that that should clear it up.

By the end of the week I was hearing a lot better. My hearing eventually returned, but I didn't get rid of the flea in my ear until I got back to New York in December. My New York doctor was able to flush out a decomposing flying insect with clear opaque wings still intact, measuring just under, believe it or not, an inch long. I needed that like I needed a hole in the head. When I said that to Sandy, he quipped, "Well, I know a fish that would have one 'whale' of a time without one."

Bequia Hospitality

The soloists came over to Bequia for the week between performances in St. Vincent and Grenada. They were put up in Father Adams' rectory so they could spend a week on the beach getting some sea and sun. Sandy and I were grateful to them for rendering their talents free of charge for us. They came for dinner a couple of times and we all had one hell of a time. I hadn't been together with them since the early '50s. They took island trips and went on beach picnics.

One afternoon while snorkeling out off Friendship Reef, Leo accidentally banged his knee into a rather large black sea urchin. He was in excruciating pain. When Boolu told him the only way to ease the pain was to dissolve the tendons sticking in his flesh by peeing on them, everybody thought he was joking and laughed—until Boolu obliged Leo by pissing all over his knee. Leo exclaimed, "My God, it works, it works! It must be the acid."

Cosmus Sylvester, The Boatman

The original plan had been to go to Bequia, St. Lucia, and Grenada. My singers and orchestra thought it was a great idea. I assumed the Bishop was making arrangements for transport, but he told me the week before that he had had no luck in finding anyone willing to take us. I took this to mean the tour was off, until someone mentioned Cosmus Sylvester, who was the owner of the Arlingham, an old steel-hulled cargo ship. He might take us, if asked. I said, "I'll get the Bishop to ask him."

"No, you ask him. He knows you. He don't know the Bishop." Well, I thought, everyone knows who the Bishop is, but I guess there's a difference between "knows" and "knows of," so I went with their advice.

Cosmus was raised in Grenada by his mother alone, not an unusual practice. She was of the Sylvester family. His father was an Ollivierre from Bequia. Cosmus was now living in and working out of Bequia. With just a week to go and no transportation, I had to wait for him to come home from Barbados. When he came home, I walked the beach to where he lived on Friendship. Now, I was well aware of the cost to run a rather large steel-hulled ship. Fuel wasn't cheap. Remember, I didn't have a dime to pay him for doing it. Bishops were not used to paying for things like this. The word they knew was "donation." Easy for bishops, I thought as I crossed the expanse of beach leading to Cosmus's place along the waterfront. My task turned out to be easy from the start, because someone had already told Cosmus why I was there to see him. He was the type of person who liked to be in control, so I let him take over the conversation. I just answered his questions. "What do you need?"

"A ride to Grenada for my kids."

"Who? the *Superstar* kids?"

"Yes. The Bishop has asked them down for the 100th anniversary celebration."

"To sing?"

"Yes, the Mozart *Requiem*," I said.

Now he was a sailor who had been around. He said, "I've heard some of his

21 The Requiem

music. Classical stuff, right? They can sing that stuff?"

"Yes," I said, "and more."

"I saw *Superstar*. They were great."

So now I said, "Well... now they need your help so they can get down there and do the *Requiem* for the dead souls of Grenada."

"I see," he said. "Like my mom and dad. You know, that's nice."

"Well?" I asked.

"When?" he asked.

"We would have to go down on Saturday, November 8, and come back on the 10th. Could you do this for us?" I was pleading now.

He paused, then said, "I have a trip to Barbados on the 12th, but if I turn straight around, we could make it. OK, it will be an honor for me."

On the way back to the house, I realized he had never once mentioned money or cost of fuel. He was something else. He really was a character! I could tell he felt it was a feather in his cap just to be doing it. As far as I was concerned, it truly was.

The kids were thrilled, and so was I. On Friday night the 7th, Cosmus sailed to St. Vincent, and on Saturday morning he picked up Bill from the Peace Corps, Shake Keane, the police, and the string and woodwind sections. Except George, he flew down. The pier scene in Bequia was such a beautiful sight, all the children, their satchels in tow, their families kissing, hugging, and waving them off. The big old, rusty cargo ship standing next to the tiny pier, and Cosmus Sylvester at the helm in his captain's cap, smiling from ear to ear—it is a picture so engraved in my mind that I still can recall it vividly to this day.

As Parnell drove us in the Moke out onto the pier and the crowd parted for us, Sandy said, "You did it again."

I answered, "Sandy, ohmigod, not yet! Will you look at that rust-bucket?"

"It's floating, isn't it?"

The trip was slow and hot. God, was it hot. We were sailing south the length of the Grenadines in the lee of the islands, so we got no breeze except from the forward motion of the boat. The kids were sprawled out all over the deck, sitting on the tarmac on top of the cargo hold. It was like a geography lesson for them, naming the islands as they passed each one. The orchestra, including Sandy, found a small room on the second deck with easy chairs out of the blistering sun, but with absolutely no breeze at all. I, feeling responsible for everyone even though I wasn't the captain, kept circulating, checking on everyone.

We arrived late but safe, and that was all that was important. It was an experience for the children to pass through Customs. The Bishop's assistant and the church committee were there with transportation to take everyone to their designated digs. Sandy and I were put up in a nice hotel near the cathedral with Beth, while Boolu and Parnell went with the boys from choir; that was their choice. Even Parnell had managed a spot on this trip, taking charge of the organ and our so-called kettledrum.

Sandy was none the worse for wear after the trip through the Grenadines. We were asked out that night, but we didn't accept. We just took it easy, sitting out on the veranda in the cool breeze, overlooking the Careenage, Grenada's inland harbor. It was a lovely night. For the first time we were able to talk honestly about the cancer and radiation that were staring him in the face. He was going to fly home to New York from Grenada and get started on his series right away. I would come up for the month of December.

Monday morning at the airport when I asked him if he was going to make it home all right, he said, "I got here, didn't I?"

And I said, "Always the smart-ass."

Sunday was a lovely day, and that night was magical. The choir sang even better than they had sung so far. It was the best all-round performance I had had from them to date, and the soloists and orchestra outdid themselves as well, with the exception of our one real professional. Shake had met up with some old buddies the night before and partied all night and Sunday morning as well, I think. He was still drunk, drunk as a skunk, and I didn't know it till after the concert started. Though his pitches and timing on the flugelhorn were right on, his dynamics were sometimes wanting. I never knew how he was going to play his line. What I didn't know about Shake was that he had a really serious drinking problem. All in all, his aberrations didn't mar the performance much. They weren't that bad, and everyone else made up for him. I remember asking Elaine, "What did you do to George, sit on him?" She just giggled.

The trip back on the old Arlingham was uneventful. Everyone seemed spent. I remember thinking a lot about Sandy on the way back. He had really held up very well, but I will never know what it took out of him. He would never reveal what it cost him, not to anyone. I had a talk with Captain Cosmus on our way back up islands. He couldn't put into words what it meant to him to bring these kids down from Bequia and how proud he was to be a part of what he had heard yesterday.

He said, "As I sat there, I cried, Mr. Jimmy. A big grown-up man like me and I cried, for my mom and my dad and even for these little kids. I've been out there and I've come back, and what you're doing for these kids is going to help them get out there. Believe me, yesterday was next to a miracle."

"Cosmus," I said, "that's a stretch, but thank you anyway. And I can't begin to thank you for helping us."

When we reached Bequia, Adlene, Goff Wallace's wife—they were owners of the Fig Tree—had a chicken dinner ready for all the Vincentians who were still on their way home to St. Vincent. I think Father Adams had a hand in it. The New York contingent stayed on in Bequia as Father Adams's guests a little longer, soaking up as much sun and sea as possible. And a great time was had by all.

22 Life is a Bumpy Ride

The Winter Of Our Lives

I was full of apprehension and I knew my teaching suffered. I kept thinking about Sandy and how he had looked as he boarded that plane in Grenada and the radiation he was facing. I knew I should have gone with him. I told Elaine the kids had had enough music that fall to last them for months. "I'm testing them next week for the term. You can take over the Christmas program. Do whatever you want. I'm going up to be with Sandy and won't be back till after Christmas, God willing."

I was on my way as fast as I could arrange it. I left Boolu and Iris John, a "farmed-out student," for want of a better term, who needed a home until she got through school, in the ever-reliable Elaine's care. Winnie by now had left for the States to look after her ailing half-sister. I left the Santa Claus project up to Hilary Saunders and Hodge Taylor to work out, and a workout they got, so they told me later. Nevertheless, the kids had a ball.

Once I got to New York, I went to Paul's. Sandy had already arranged to sub-lease an apartment in the Kipp's Bay Tower between First and Second Avenues on 33rd Street from an old bridge partner. Thank God he did. We didn't realize how sick and feeble Sandy would get before the treatments were over, and Paul's place would have been much too small for three then. At moments I doubted Sandy would ever make it at all.

Christmas Eve was the lowest ebb of our lives. Sandy was so frail he seemed on the verge of dying. Paul was generally good with sick people. Caring for them and waiting on them he was at his best. But Sandy, in his condition, was too much for him. Paul never came down to 33rd Street to spend an evening or just to see how Sandy was coming along. Sandy's brother Bobby never came to the apartment once, but then neither did his sister. Yet she had been at the hospital with him every day. Go figure. In truth, she was a basket case; all she wanted was to get him back into a hospital before he died on us altogether. He wasn't sick. It was the radiation that was beating him up so and destroying him. He couldn't keep a thing down, and whatever he did manage tasted like gasoline. He had wasted away before the radiation, and now the radiation looked set to finish off the job. They all loved him so much, and to see him becoming more and more emaciated was too much for them.

Although I feared losing him, I knew from the doctors we had to continue. Once the treatments were stopped, he would rally. I worried that moment might come a bit too late. He was down to 115 pounds. I didn't want to leave him for a minute, even for our everyday needs. Christmastime we were very much alone. I never asked anyone for anything. I wasn't good at that, and consequently, no one called us in return. I remember all we had in the house were two tins of Campbell's tomato soup. That was our Christmas dinner that year. We didn't even have bread in the house. On Christmas Eve we sat watching midnight mass on TV, enjoying the music from Rome. I sat there praying we would make it through. Yet as bad as it was, I had a feeling we were going to make it. I believe I picked up positive vibes from Sandy himself. He didn't speak much but when he did it was, as always, upbeat and uplifting. He had no doubts.

Our friend Jo Ynocencio came by with Jewish penicillin: a big container of chicken soup. Sandy had me play the tape recorded in Grenada of the Mozart Requiem. I think she was the only one in America who ever heard it, except of course for my buddy Dick Eikenberry and my voice teacher Bernard Taylor who asked to hear it. Yet it meant so much to us. Life is funny that way.

Winter kicked in with a vengeance after the first of the year. Once a week, we grabbed a cab and went up to Sloan-Kettering on 68th Street for Sandy's treatments. One morning we woke up to hear the icy wind blowing against the windows. The snow was swirling in all directions; it had been piling up all night. It was the kind of morning you pull the blankets up over your head, even if you're not a bear. But oh, no, it was a treatment day and you didn't miss them: each week and every treatment brought us that much closer to the end of this grueling, ghastly nightmare.

I bundled Sandy up within an inch of his life—he could barely move, let alone walk. He could ill afford a cold, and why he didn't catch one in his condition beats the hell out of me. I thought I had better call for a limo-cab, but nothing was moving. However, out the window I did see some cabs braving the elements. So I said, "Well, Sandy? Do we give it a try?"

Sandy replied, "Yes. It will be one more down, and that's what's most important to me just now." I felt the same way. So out we went.

Needless to say, every cab was full, and when one let off a fare, somebody else always beat me to it. Sandy couldn't stand up against the swirling, penetrating wind without my holding him. So I said, "Do you think you can make it over to the bus stop? The glass enclosure will be a little protection for you."

"OK," was all he said. It took a while to get there against the biting wind and the blinding snow, along the ruts in the deep snow with the slippery ice underneath. The bus enclosure wasn't much protection from the cold, the bitter wind, and the swirling snow, but it was better than nothing. I left Sandy hunched up in the corner and ran out to look down First Avenue for anything: bus, cab, whatever. There was nothing, just an occupied cab dashing past. I have no idea how long we huddled there. It seemed like forever. Then through the blinding snow, way down the avenue by Bellevue Hospital, I spotted the outline of a bus. Oh, God! The sight of it actually warmed me up a bit. I yelled, "I think I see one!"

I ran back in under the shelter, waiting for it to reach us. No one else was around. As it came closer, we both went out to meet it. It passed us right by, full to the brim, and no one got off. Two more soon came along, and again we went out into the street. They didn't stop either, and they were empty! "Where are they going?" I asked.

Sandy said, "Going to pick up people, but obviously not us."

As sure as I am alive as I write, while we stood there in the bitter freezing cold, thirteen buses passed us by, and most were empty! It was as if we were in some never-never land that wasn't connecting with reality. They were coming in tandem, two by two and empty, obviously heading off somewhere on this frostbitten, godforsaken island. I was ready to give up and hobble, slipping and sliding, back to Kipp's Bay and our cozy apartment with Sandy in tow, making sure he didn't slip, fall, and break a hip in the bargain. We were like two frozen Russians banished somewhere in the middle of Siberia, yet we were in the heart of "heartless" Manhattan. As we stepped out to head on over to the apartment and count the entire episode a dismal failure, there it was—a bus slowing down to pick us up. As I hopped up into the bus behind Sandy, the blast of warm air was as inviting as an afternoon on Friendship Beach. The doctor had never expected to see us. Sandy thawed out and was treated. We were a hell of a lot luckier going home. As we left, a cab was dropping someone off. We scurried in, and the driver jaunted down York and skirted across to Second, then slithered down to Kipp's Bay.

As I helped him into a warm bed, Sandy asked, "Now how many more?"

"One less, that's for sure. Was it worth it?"

"You bet."

One Friday afternoon when we got home from the hospital, we found yellow police tape barring the apartment door. I took Sandy in anyway and then went down to the office. The manager informed me that the rent had not been paid in months. I told him we had been paying the tenant ever since we moved in.

"Well," said the manager, "that's between you and our tenant. All I know is that the rent hasn't been paid. No one is getting in and nothing is coming out until everything is settled with the housing authorities. We're getting a court injunction on Monday morning. The lock's been changed, and that's that."

Well, I knew differently. The lock had not been changed, not yet. "Thank you for the information," I said and walked out. What was there to be said? We had been had and we were being evicted without our things. I had to move fast.

I hurried up to the apartment where Sandy was waiting for me. "What's up?" he asked.

"Has anyone been in here?" I asked. I knew we had to get out of there kit and caboodle.

"No. Why? What's going on?"

"Look, Sandy," I said, "your friend hasn't been paying the rent on this place. The courts are taking over and confiscating everything, including all our stuff. We have to shake ass and get the hell out!"

Sandy's medical paraphernalia, his medication, and all our clothes and personal effects were just sitting there. I figured I could use the elevator on the side of the building away from the building manager's office. Thank God it was a big place. Boy! I thought, I could use a "Boolu" right now. I packed everything as best I could into our suitcases, then dumped Sandy's friend's stuff out of boxes and used them to pack Sandy's machines. I held up an elevator with a heavy suitcase and piled everything in there at once. Leaving Sandy waiting in the room ready to leave, I went down. Then I stacked everything next to the outside door downstairs and went back up for Sandy. Fortunately, it was quitting time on a Friday evening by now, and the people coming and going paid little or no attention to us.

Out back at the curb, cabs were coming and going at the drop-off and loading bay. Leaving Sandy inside, I hauled everything out to the taxi stand. Then I went to the front of the line and waited for one of the large, old-fashioned cabs still in use in the city, the kind with the extra jump seats between the front and rear seats. After I'd loaded the luggage, just enough room remained for two passengers. I went back for Sandy at the door, and we were off.

"Where to?" Sandy asked.

"To the Hotel Dover up on Lexington and 57th, where else?"

Fortunately, we were able to get Sandy's old digs. We called Paul, who couldn't believe our afternoon saga, and he came across 57th Street for a late dinner at the hotel restaurant with us. Sandy had vodka and water, a smoke, and just a cup of beef broth. He was so feeble by now he looked like death warmed over. But he never complained; he just rolled with the punches.

"Well," Paul said, "that's what you get for not staying with me. I have room." But he didn't. He would have had to sleep in the living room on a couch. For Sandy, he would have done so.

That slime of a sleazeball who took our rent money had the nerve to send us a letter signed by a lawyer threatening to take us to court for breaking the sub-lease. In his dreams... Enough said.

Well, time passed and God wasn't willing, so I didn't get back to school after the holidays. First things first, I thought, and that was Sandy right now. The doctor told me, "You'll be surprised to see how fast Sandy will rally. He's a tough old bird."

"Well, he sure has the will of one," I said.

The doctor thought Sandy would be able to go home to Bequia and relax in the sunshine and exercise a bit. "A place like that will be ideal for his recovery, and he couldn't be in better hands," he said.

The eye doctor confirmed his eye was holding, thank God, and fitted him for glasses. Sandy said, "One pair for reading, another pair for the piano, and a third pair for seeing, if I only could."

What he prayed for was never to go completely blind. He feared total darkness. As it turned out, he was able to see some to the end.

Sandy's general practitioner retired, so we both got a new doctor on East 30th Street near Bellevue. He was an openly gay doctor recommended by Tommy Axt, Sandy's accountant. It was an adjustment for both of us. Acceptance in those times was complex, but we felt it was about time. What the hell! We knew there was no difference. If we didn't know, who the hell would? The question was just how good was he? That is what mattered and remained to be seen. Well, he was good enough to get that flea out of my ear.

Back To Living The Life

We reached Bequia before Easter but too late to do any Easter music. Instead we launched off into the study of the chorus score from Porgy and Bess. Why not? The students were perfect for it. They were already on a "James Island," and all the elements of that period were being lived out on Bequia at that very moment. We had a real live Sportin' Life character, a Porgy, a Bess, and, lest we forget, a Strawberry Woman. Only there wouldn't be strawberries: we would have to settle for mangoes. Like James Island, Bequia had burial societies, fishing off the Tobago Keys no different from off the Grand Banks, hurricanes—oh, yes, the hurricanes—and picnics on nearby islands like He de Quatre. What an experience this was going to be!

While browsing through Schirmer's music shop in New York, I had found some rudimentary, well-known, classical orchestrations to suit the Kingstown Ensemble. So why not a concert? I would have my work cut out for me. And if I knew Sandy—and oh, I knew Sandy—he would be close behind with a helping hand, jumping into the fray to add his efforts as well, efforts I couldn't do without.

Not Marcus Too

When we reached Bequia, we were stunned to learn we had lost our third black German shepherd. A neighbor had poisoned him. We had been gone four months, and Marcus must have been missing us more each day we were away. In his loneliness, I guess, he was venturing farther down the hill. Unfortunately, our entrance was precariously close to a neighbor who had sheep or goats, though Marcus never touched one. The neighbor was a small, mean-spirited man, and I was told he put poison out. The upshot was now Marcus was gone. At this writing, they both are, the mean-spirited man as well.

We had got Marcus from Mary Barnard who sent him over from St. Vincent when she heard Rocky had been poisoned over there at the Mariner's Inn. Rocky's story had ended when my friend David Corrigan, a Canadian, wanted to mate his bitch with Rocky. So we had taken Rocky to St. Vincent to do his duty. Dave was the manager at the Inn, and some nearby locals thought he had acquired Rocky as a night watchdog to ward off pilferers. They simply poisoned him. A dog's life wasn't valued very highly in these parts. The way some of the people lived, it wasn't any wonder. To some this may sound harsh, but life was harsh in some areas. Very, very harsh. One had to learn how to circumvent it and strive to make it better.

Porgy Aborted

Before long Sandy was back at the organ. He would never return to his formidable self and he would forevermore give an impression of frailty. He occupied most of his time working on his voice. He worked hard to get enough strength back to be heard. I had never seen anyone so determined. We found our Bess, Porgy, and Sportin' Life, and the chorus jumped into their numbers, stepping off double-time like a fast-marching band.

The goal of a certain organization in New York was to bring classical performances to the grass roots of America. The organization's efforts gave young classical performers an opportunity to bring artistic performing culture to depressed areas. The president of the organization and his assistant were on Bequia when we were presenting the Mozart and said if they could ever be of any help to just ask. When we got into *Porgy*, I asked. After all, we couldn't get any more grass-rooted than we already were—less than six square miles out in the middle of an ocean. I knew as well that one of their young artists, Clamila Dale, had recently finished a performance of *Porgy and Bess* in Texas. I went up to their offices in New York and explained what we would be doing. All we needed was permission and an orchestral score. We couldn't buy a score without permission to perform it. We would do the same as we had done with the Mozart: we would fill in missing instruments on the organ. They seemed excited by the idea and said they had connections through not only Clamila but also the conductor of the Texas production. I left pleased with the whole idea.

On Bequia, we continued working on the opera. As time passed, the chorus knew practically the whole score, Porgy and Bess each had a good handle on their parts, and I was spending a lot of time on Sportin' Life. Oh, he was talented, but he wasn't much of a worker—after all he was Sportin' Life!

When I didn't hear from New York, I sent my friend Sally Hawkins Schiffer to talk to them. More time passed and still I heard nothing. My kids were getting increasingly restless, so I asked Sally to stop in again. She obliged me and reported they were downright rude. How unlike them, I thought. Something drastic must have happened. Sally was one tough cookie, the reason I sent her in the first place. There must have been some shifting of power in the organization. I never heard from anyone, so I never found out. Consequently, I wrote the whole thing off. In hindsight I should have said to hell with it, screw them, and gone ahead with a piano and organ and done the opera anyway, as we did with *Superstar*. To this day I feel we should have. But we chucked the project.

Jesus Revived

Now at this same time, I had Cameron King from St. Vincent on my back every time he saw me. He wanted me to do a revival of *Jesus Christ Superstar* in St. Vincent. He had been my soundman for both our productions. I told him I would never dream of taking the show to St. Vincent, not unless I had him as my right-hand man and troubleshooter. Even then, there was much more to think about: the house, the tickets, the set... "No, Cameron, I don't think so," I said.

One day he called to tell me the nurses' school would bring the show over to the Lyric Movie House right in the middle of Kingstown, as a fundraiser. The hospital needed sheets and pillowcases. The nursing school would take care of the house, and he would be my technician. He assured me of both. So I said, "Let me think about it."

When I told Sandy, he said, "Are you sure you want to do this?"

"I don't know," I said. "Yes and no. I'm going to talk to the kids."

At rehearsal, I put it to them. "Now that *Porgy* has gone up in smoke, what do you think of taking a production of *Superstar* to Kingstown?" They were all for it.

I told them I would have to talk to Father Adams first. Father tried everything to dissuade me short of saying no. "If I say no, then to the children I'm the bad guy. No, I won't say no. You've got my blessing. You'll need it." The final decision was entirely up to me.

The nurses were a big plus factor, and I had Cameron at my side. Bequia deserved it, and so did the kids. Anyhow *Porgy*'s falling through had left us open, free and clear for the revival of *JCS*, full speed ahead. We had the same cast, with the exception of Mary Magdalene. Suzanne Wallace was taking off, like Sportin' Life. Remember his song, "There's a Boat Dat's Leavin' Soon for New York"? (God, how I wanted to do that show!) Suzanne was on her way to New York and her eventual gig at St. Patrick's Cathedral. But I digress. Iris John, one of our homeless students, replaced her. Iris had come a long way from the days of her childhood when she had slaved for mere subsistence. She didn't know it at the time, but she would go much further. She went on to graduate from university in Madison, Wisconsin, and became a teacher.

More Of The Same In St. Vincent

During this period, Sandy and I decided to start an interfaith chorus in St. Vincent to work on the entire Handel's *Messiah* with orchestra for the celebration coming up next year—our independence from England. So we began running back and forth on Mondays and Tuesdays again. Getting members from the various church choirs was like pulling hen's teeth. Most people liked the idea but weren't ready to commit to the Monday rehearsals. How unlike Bequia the Vincentians were, but then Bequia had taken time to get going, too. So we just plodded along. I truly thought they would come around, that, for instance, the members of the Kingstown Chorale would surely be for this particular idea. Was I ever wrong! With the exception of one or two, they were not with us, no way. I was from Bequia and not a Vincentian. Was that it? Maybe I didn't cater to the Kingstown pecking order. I couldn't have even if I were so inclined, which I wasn't, because I wouldn't have known where to begin. No matter, we kept at it all summer until Sandy left for New York. Then I went on alone until his return after which we planned to pull *Superstar* together for a December 1 performance in Kingstown.

And Back At The Playhouse

Meanwhile, in New York, the Playhouse was readying itself for its Golden Anniversary. The celebration was going to be held at the Shubert Theatre in Theatre Alley with a big bash afterward at Macy's department store. Mayor Koch declared December 3, 1978, "Sanford Meisner Day" to honor Sandy for his contribution to New York City. New York pulled out all the stops. Paul Morrison, as director of the school, was in charge, while Kent Paul, a graduate of the school, masterminded a big production at the Shubert made up of ex-students. What a glorious occasion it was. Everyone in town received an invitation, everyone, that is, but me. I hadn't gone to the two-year program at the school. I had attended the school in the graduate professional program, as many others did, but that didn't cut any ice with Paul—unless you happened to be a celebrity. Oh, they were all invited, including Jon Voight,

22 Life is a Bumpy Ride

who hadn't gone to the school either. Ha-ha! The truth was, you know, I never worried about it. I just assumed I would be there, at Sandy's side to boot. Only many years later, after Paul's death, did I read correspondence written at the time between Paul and Sandy. Then I learned the lengths Paul went to, just to keep me away. I was persona non grata. I was once told that I was referred to as "nothing more than a chorus boy," and what would I know? What they thought of me I couldn't have cared less. Star-fuckers are star-fuckers no matter where they are.

On Bequia, Sandy played the whole affair down to me. Yet I could see the affair was all about Sandy. He was the school. And if I shouldn't be at his side for this recognition of the culmination of his work, then who the hell should be? Paul? Over my dead body. Sandy damn well knew this, no matter what he told Paul. He knew me better than anyone else. It made no difference what Paul felt. I was going to be there and at his side. If, in Paul's mind, I would be out of the closet, well, that is where Sandy wanted me to be. Sorry for you, Paul—or anyone else who had a problem with it.

My old friend Bill Brown, the first principal at the Bequia school, had an interesting spin on coming out of the closet. He and Jane had since divorced and he eventually married his lover of the past fifteen years in Canada. His take on this "closet business" was clear. "You never just open the door and walk out. It's an evolving process which may take years," Bill said. "First you open it just a crack, and take a peek. Then you open it a little wider to get a better look, and, as painful as it might be, you step out, but just a little. Before you know it, there you are in all your splendor, in spite of all the pain. You're standing there for the first time in your life as you, yourself, standing there in your own shoes and no one else's. You are now, finally, at last, not that person everyone else wanted you to be." Oh, Jane, by the way, went on to find her own way, and they remained friends.

Now that I think of it, Paul Morrison couldn't even say the word "gay." He broke out in hives every time he heard it in conversation with its new connotation. He would just bristle. He once said, "I refuse to be labeled. You don't see me running around giggling all the time."

I don't think he enjoyed the closet game either. It was just that he held to that old-fashioned school of thought best summed up later by President Clinton: "Don't ask, don't tell," to which my retort is, "Why not? Why the hell not?" Things have been changing whether we like it or not. It is about time these Jesus freaks, who are anything but Christian, got over themselves.

I once said to Sandy, "You know, whatever your sexual persuasion may be—you sure are on the cusp in more ways than one—you seem to understand Paul's way of thinking, and yet you easily embrace our way of living. I guess that's what makes you special."

I remember him saying, "I am not my brother's keeper, that's all."

So the preparations for Sanford Meisner Day in New York went on, and I looked forward to attending at Sandy's side.

Revival From Hell

By November, Sandy was back from New York and banging out *Superstar* on the organ every afternoon at 4 PM up in the church choir loft. In many ways, preparation for St. Vincent was much easier. We even improved on the costumes. This time we decided to include the Kingstown Ensemble. We also had twenty-five pans in the steel orchestra, three electric guitars, and Dermot and his sax, with two complete sets of drums and drummers. The stage at the theatre was monstrously wide but, like most movie houses, not very deep. The dancers would have a time adjusting. Because of the movie schedule, we were not having a rehearsal. We were winging it. That was enough to deal with; I didn't need any more obstacles. But we were plagued with problems. Every time I was confronted with one, I was reminded of Father Adams and his warnings. I wouldn't have accepted this gig without Cameron King as troubleshooter. He had told me he would be there at my side. Yet, when we disembarked from the boat, there was no Cameron.

"Why am I not surprised, Sandy?" I asked.

"Well, we're off to a good start," Sandy replied. "Take me to the hotel and do whatever you have to. And God help you."

That's exactly what I did. But first I set up a 10 AM call for the next day for the whole company. I also told the crew to get the organ over to the theater while I got Sandy settled in. Then I had to see what the hell had happened to Mr. King.

"Don't worry about me," Sandy said.

"You just sit your ass at that organ tomorrow night. That's all I'm expecting of you." Some of the kids laughed, and we all took off.

Sandy, Boolu, and I were staying at the Heron Hotel since our place over in Frenches was a haven for the girls in the company who needed a place to stay. Iris John and Chrisenthia Leach were living there while they worked on their A levels for college entrance. When we went over on Mondays, we just doubled up. So at present the place was full of females. De tree a we marched down Front Street with our bags in a pushcart. We were leaving for New York Monday morning. The Heron was convenient, in the middle of town.

I dropped Sandy off and told him to get some rest. "Do I have another choice?" he asked.

"Stop it," I said, "Boolu will be back for lunch. I may and I may not, but I will be back for dinner and we'll have the whole evening."

"Oh, great, we can go to a dance," says he.

"Cut it out, Sandy, I'm worried," I said.

"Go," he said. "Go. Everything will work out."

Off we went, Boolu and I, to the Lyric Movie House. Cameron was waiting for me. Sheepishly, Cameron said, "I'm sorry, Jimmy, something has come up.

22 Life is a Bumpy Ride

I have to leave for Jamaica. I have to attend a meeting there tomorrow."

I was stunned. "You are sorry. Sorry you didn't tell me sooner, or what? What the hell are we going to do? You have a meeting in Jamaica and it's just now you're hearing about it? If you had at least told me yesterday, we could have canceled—God, they do it all the time around here. So you won't be here. Well, we can still cancel."

By now my whole crew was gathering around. Cameron just kept saying he was sorry and that he had seen to everything. The speakers and the mikes would be here tomorrow morning early. He had spoken to the government about the wood for the cross and stages.

"What about the tech during the show?" I asked.

"Come on, Jimmy," Andy said. "We can't cancel now. It's been all over the radio. We can do the show."

By now a few dancers were saying, "Cancel? No way."

"OK. You want to—we do it," I said, throwing up my hands and walking away from the group. When I turned around, Cameron was gone. Things started to go downhill from there. The backdrop was still being painted and wouldn't be hung until morning. The artist who executed the Calvary scene—minus the cross in the center because that one would be real—was almost finished. The stage was so shallow we had to build two raised stages on either side as we had done in Bequia. We would also have to build a bigger cross for Jesus. Cameron did say he had arranged with the Minister of Internal Affairs, I think that was his title, to supply wood for the carpenters.

It was already late in the day to get the workers in time for the show tomorrow. I had to get over to the minister's office with a couple of the boys. We had no trouble getting to him, the trouble was getting through to him. What Cameron had told him was anybody's guess. It was as if he had told the minister absolutely nothing except to expect us. I believe the minister wanted the request to come directly from me. So that's how it was. After I went through the complete explanation as to what we needed and why, without hesitation he said, "Fine." He went out into the front office and promptly returned, his hand outstretched, saying, "Everything has been arranged. Just go out to the lumberyard in the government complex and the foreman will assist you." Still shaking my hand, he calmly added, "And the cost to you is only... well, this is just a round figure, by the way—$6,000 US. Whom do you want the bill made out to?"

I was floored! I could have shot Cameron with his own gun and walked away happy. I had explained to the minister that it was for the nurses at the Government Hospital who needed sheets and pillowcases. Sheets and pillowcases for the hospital, my ass. That US $6,000 would have supplied all of Kingstown with bed linen. This joker has got to be kidding, I thought to myself. Who does he think I am? I was furious because I knew he saw me as the rich, juicy, fat-cat American, and here was his chance to milk me. I resented it immensely. The way I was feeling I could have ranted on and on. Instead I said, "Sir, I believe there has been a gross misunderstanding." Then I thought, that moocher doesn't deserve an explanation. I turned and walked out with my boys at my heels.

Outside, one of the boys asked, "What are we going to do now, Mr. Jimmy?"

"Nothing," I said. "This one is for the nurses to handle."

I called Nurse Gumbs at the nurses' school and told her about our little fiasco. I also told her that if it wasn't straightened out within an hour, we were heading back to Bequia. She was so mad she could have spit nails. She asked me to meet her at the Heron Hotel after she sorted this mess out. In about an hour, I heard her stomping up the stairs to the lobby, hotter than Hades.

Sandy observed, with a big smile on his face, "Only here in St. Vincent."

Boolu had no idea what was going on—who had time to explain? But he was used to it, and knew he would find out sooner or later. Actually, he was patient and accepting.

Nurse Gumbs declared, "Things are tough enough around here without damn fools making it worse. Get a taxi and get out to the lumberyard," she continued. "The manager out there will take care of you."

The manager was willing to help me, but he had no one to help him. They were off working at some government official's private house. After I explained the urgency, he wrote a note, saying, "Take this, the taxi driver knows where. I'll get the wood ready."

I told Andy to stay and pick out the wood. Andy Tannis knew better than anyone what we needed. He knew the size of both the stage and the cross we would require. I took off in the cab. The driver knew right where the lumberyard employees were working, and cracked ironically, "I wish I could get dem to work on my house. It be finished in a month at a ha'penny to de dollar."

With their foreman's command, after he'd read the manager's note, the men stopped work, piled into their trucks, and headed back to load the wood that Andy had laid there at the ready. We then went back to the Lyric and slammed up two crude stages and put the cross together to be laid aside out of the way of the movie screen, because tonight they were still showing a movie. The scenery would get hung first thing the next morning. Just before the house opened for the movie, we were cleaning up and clearing out. I thanked the carpenters and offered them tickets, but not one took me up on the offer. Not their "ting." The foreman said he would send two men the next morning, even if it was Sunday, to help set up the cross, and I thanked him again.

My crew was headed for who-knew-where on a Saturday night in St. Vincy. That was a rare one for them. I thanked them for a long day of hard work and said, "Don't stay out too late. It's going to be a long day tomorrow." Then I went back to the Heron and collapsed before dinner.

Boolu at this time went out to check in with his sister June. I said, "Boolu, it's an early night. Remember, they lock the door here."

As he rushed down the much too narrow hallway, I heard him say, "I know, I know." St. Vincent was an early-rising town, and the Heron Hotel was right in the middle of all its hustle and bustle. We all had an early breakfast.

"Now you have the whole day ahead of you," Sandy said. "Just take it easy."

"I'm so sorry I let myself get talked into this, by a person with no sense of responsibility to it at all. The kids, they'll do their best no matter what, I know them."

"You're right about that," Sandy agreed.

"It's all that technical shit we have to deal with. Doing it without anyone to look after things, anything could go wrong. In Bequia it was small, with only one outlet, and I still had two electricians, a light man, and a soundman, plus two wardrobe mistresses. Now they're all gone, not one of them is here. All I have is zilch, in a house my performers have never worked in before. God knows what the audience is going to be like. Sandy, this is madness."

"The audience, they're not your affair," Sandy counseled. "I mean it, don't you worry about the audience. They've just come for a good time, while you have your performers to keep control of."

"Sandy," I moaned, "there'll be over 100 up there on that stage either singing, dancing, or playing an instrument!"

"Good," said Sandy, "There'll be so much going on up there, if something does go wrong, no one's going to be the wiser. If they are, they won't give a damn. All they want is a good time. Tell the kids to have a ball. If they do that, the audience will, too. No matter what, just keep going. That's professionalism. The kids will go right along with you. They will, they will." Then he added, "Now you better get the show on the road."

We left Sandy at the hotel. At the theater, the crew was hanging the scenery. The carpenters were steadying the huge cross in the middle of the scene with heavy 6'x6' planks so they didn't have to hammer into the stage. Thank the lord these are morning people, I thought. Precious little of a stage was left once the planks were down, putting the dancers in a precarious spot. I spoke to the dance captain who reassured me, "Not to worry, we'll just dance around them."

Where? I thought, but all I said was, "Well, I won't worry," and I didn't and they did. They just grabbed their partners, found a clearing big enough, and all twelve were kicking away in time with the music with no one the wiser. Except for Boolu and his partner. They seemed to be down front and center every time. God, he was such a ham! Well, so much for the dance problem.

The next thing I was hit with was Flazzo, my all-round musician who, by the way, couldn't read a note of music. Still there wasn't an instrument he couldn't handle, be it wind, string, or keyboard. He came over to me with a piece of news. The bass on the organ wasn't very clear. If it wasn't working right, I knew damn well who the culprit was. I told him to keep his hands off the "mother" thing, and we would see if we could get it fixed, at least I hoped so.

We were going to have what I call a speed-through with Sandy and the singers. It was just a warm-up. Any instrumentalists who felt they needed it could chime in. Meanwhile, I sent teacher Josiah Glynn and Hodge Taylor to hunt down Noel Inniss, one of our violinists. He was supposed to know someone in Kingstown who knew about electric organs. An hour later I found out Noel didn't know anyone who could fix organs, but he did know someone who had one. So I told them to go find him and see if he would lend us his for the night. He wasn't home. "Forget it," I said. "We'll run with it as it is."

By now Elaine had brought Sandy over from the hotel. He was complaining because I hadn't come back for lunch. "You have got to be kidding," I retorted, and we made ready for a quick little warm-up, my speed-through.

Our boys, men I should say, set up the sound system that had arrived earlier—thank God, which I always seemed to be doing—a microphone for each side stage, one for the main stage, and one for in front of the chorus which would be singing on and off throughout the show, four microphones in all. Wide risers led up to the stage so the chorus sat right in the center below the stage. The acoustics were much better.

My recorders, with Mary Budgell the flautist, were there from the start of the run-through, but the orchestra straggled in. By the time we finished, most of the musicians had arrived and it was beginning to sound like something, even with the weak bass of the organ. It was almost five and still no sign of Noel Inniss. I thought he just might show up with a working organ, besides his own. Stranger things have happened around here, like Cosmus's freighter to Grenada. Everything wasn't always bad. But when Noel did show up, just before the dinner break, no such luck.

"OK," I called out, "take a dinner break and be back by six o'clock—real time."

Just as Sandy and I were ready to leave for dinner, one of the dancers rushed up to me all in a dither, saying, "There's no dressing room!"

I pointed to the door on the left. "Check in there."

She shook her head, saying, "No, Mr. Jimmy, that's not in there, that's out there."

I opened the door, and she was right. It opened onto an alley. "Oh, fine," I said, "no dressing room."

"No dressing room anywhere. We looked all over," said another.

"Ohmigod!" I said. "And you kids have four costume changes!"

One of the girls corrected me. "Mr. Jimmy, some of us have five."

"All right, all right already. Where's Andy?"

Someone brought him over. I told him the problem. "I know, Mr. Jimmy. I saw some old galvanized sheeting lying out back. We should be able to rig up something right outside the door using the leftover wood."

"Well, you only have an hour to do it, so let's pray it doesn't rain."

I must tell you that Andy wasn't only my chief cook and bottle washer; he was also my head high priest. Every time he played the role, he broke the house up when, in his deep vibrating basso, he told Judas, "You backed the wrong horse."

"Come on, Sandy," I said, "Let's get out of here before something else goes wrong."

"Listen, the best thing that could happen is for the roof to cave in, or better yet, a hurricane," Sandy said and then added, "I'm just kidding. Remember what I said. Take it as it comes."

As we left the theater, I said, "Where the hell is Boolu? Come on, Boolu," I called out. "Let's go eat."

A Performance To End All

When we got out of the cab back at the theater, a rather large crowd was milling about. The marquee was all lit up with "TONIGHT LIVE JESUS CHRIST SUPERSTAR." Let's hope so, I thought as I read it, sending up just a little desperate prayer: "Dear God, stay with us tonight!"

Inside the theater, the orchestra was tuning up. I told the chorus to take their places on the risers once they were in costume and the leads to wait in the wings. Sandy took his place at the organ and fiddled about setting up his score on the music stand with Elaine Olliviene as page-turner. Sitting behind me in the front row were Bequia followers. I noted we were building up a little fan club. As I stepped up onto my small podium, I looked out into the house for the first time. The place was gigantic; it held thousands. Normally a moment like that would fill me with a thrilling, joyful anticipation. Yet actually the feeling was oppressive. I felt as if I were about to be shoved off a cliff.

Curtain was seven o'clock. I turned around and looked at my watch. It was well after 7. But where were the steel drums? There was nothing but an empty space. My stomach fell, dropped right down to my shoes—mine could do that. No steel pans! Fortunately, the house was still filling up. People were taking their seats, and taking their time talking to one another. It was now close to seven-thirty. What do I do? I walked over to Chick, my first violinist, behind Sandy, and I asked, "What do we do? Should we start? Can we do it without them?"

Chick simply said, "Why not?"

"OK," I said, "let's go."

I walked back to my podium noticing the audience was extremely quiet now. They had no idea what was happening. I stepped up, turned my back to them, and picked up my baton. All of a sudden the audience began to applaud, and I thought, good God, now they're restless. Great! I was thinking, what a way to start—when out of the corner of my eye, I saw men making their way down the aisle to my right with huge oil drums on their shoulders. The steel band had arrived, and the audience went wild as the pan-men set themselves up below the stage and off to the right. Their setting-up gave me time to compose myself. They were an hour late. But right then, I sure couldn't have given a damn what had held them up; right then they were there and we could now begin.

Later we learned that on their way in from Calliaqua, their truck with all the pans had had a flat tire just the other side of Kingstown. No one had thought to come ahead to warn us. Oh, what the hell! This was St. Vincent. We just got on with it. It was the anacrusis to the whole damn fiasco.

We started off with the horn solo and then segued into the Steel Pan Band playing the overture, starting with "Jesus Christ Superstar" and "I Don't Know How to Love Him." And that did it. When they heard those pans, the audience went wild! This was their sound. We had them in the palm of our hand. Then we launched into the show. I was concerned that the singers might have trouble hearing the little organ in its present condition in such a barn of a place. Being so far away from the orchestra could throw the young inexperienced singers off their timing and some even off their pitch. Not to worry, as they say in Bequia. My concern was unwarranted. Not one of them faltered!

The first part of the show went like clockwork. But when the dancers made it out the side door to change after the "Simon Zealotes" number ("Christ you know I love you"), my heart stopped. Boolu as Simon had just finished his big spot, taking off down front as a Shaker in the middle of a religious trance with all its fervor. His antics had brought some of the audience to their feet, and he stopped the show with their cheers and whistles. Now the dancers were heading out for their first costume change, and not only could I hear the rain pouring down but I could see the deluge through the open door under the exit light. I knew that only an enclosure of galvanize with no roof overhead was out there, and it was coming down in buckets. I thought, What are they going to do out there in the alley? They'll come in soaking wet, drenched to the skin. A picture of them doing "Walk Across My Swimming Pool" looking as if they were in it instead of around it flashed across my mind.

But when they came in for their next number, they were dry as a bone. You couldn't have asked me how, for then I had no idea. At the time, I merely thought, resourceful, these kids! They had solved the dressing-in-the-rain problem one way or another. As it turned out, someone had found a room in the building across the alley, and they ran back and forth under umbrellas. By now we were really rocking. Then I noticed a Vincentian walk out onto stage left and calmly take a microphone, including the wire and the stand. My first thought was that something must be wrong with its amplification and he was going to fix the problem. Right then the dancers were doing their damnedest, dancing around the 6'x6' beams spread around the floor supporting the big cross in the center. But then I had another flash. Where were the singers on stage left going to find a microphone? They would have to share one of the remaining ones. I leaned back to Flazzo's girlfriend, Janelle, who was sitting behind me and slightly to my left, and whispered to her to go out to the front of the house, speak to the nurses at the door, and find out what the hell was happening with this guy. Oh, by the way, all this time I was simultaneously waving my arms around, trying to keep everyone together and all on the

22 Life is a Bumpy Ride

same beat. I thought, what the hell is happening here? Then the same guy reappeared, now on stage right, and repeated his performance.

Meanwhile back at the ranch, the show was still going on. The dancers danced on, and the chorus still had their mike. Then I spotted a lady in white talking to the guy, who was dismantling the mike on stage right. The conversation was hot and heavy. I could tell whatever she said to him didn't make a dent in him. He went right on dismantling it. In desperation, the nurse flung around and returned to the back of the house. Our mike-stealer went right on with his activity.

Janelle came back, working her way across the front row. When she got close to me, she whispered in my ear, "The nurses are packing up their money and leaving. Some are going back on duty."

Well, so much for the nurses. They had got their booty and they were splitting. Not one stayed to express their gratitude after the show. I don't think Nurse Gumbs was even there. At least, if she was, I never saw her. I thought of what Sandy so often said, "La gratitudine e rara." Oh, Father! I thought, you were so right! And I turned around and continued, saying to myself, we will continue for as long as possible. What else was there to do? Now there was no mike on either stage right or left. As luck would have it, he had left one mike center stage, and Joan Simmons had one with the chorus down front. He had probably been told by someone to leave a mike. Maybe he couldn't get at Joan's, or maybe it was an oversight. In any case, Joan, seeing the difficulty our soloists were having, handed her mike up to Mary Magdalene, and we finished the show with two mikes. The soloists felt quite at home because back on Bequia they had had only two mikes to work with in the first place. They already knew how to pass the mike when they were finished with it and who to and where to be to pick it up when they needed it again.

The whole final proceedings went off without a hitch. I had to cut out the thunder and lightning effects for the ten last words of Jesus. After all, I had no technician, so what choice did I have? We went directly to the Steel Band with "Jesus Christ Superstar" and the big finish. Everyone in the house was singing along because so many of them knew the music by now from listening to the records and seeing the movie. We finished to a standing ovation. While I was still on the podium, a man in the center aisle began pulling on my coattail from across the railing. It was the Anglican priest from Australia, now the pastor in Calliaqua, saying, with tears in his eyes, "Jimmy, that was beautiful, beautiful! I have never seen the likes in St. Vincent... I'll write you."

After the bows, which I do not remember, I went over to the orchestra to congratulate them all. Elaine handed me Sandy's music and all the other scores, which she had gathered up, and I gave them to Elvie to take back to Bequia. Then I shook Sandy's hand. He was beaming as he said, "See, I told you to take it as it comes."

"Whatever comes?"

"Whatever." We were leaving for New York in the morning, so I turned to

Andy and said, "The wood, and I mean all of it, has to get back to the government. That's the most important thing."

"I know, Mr. Jimmy."

"I don't give a damn about the backdrop. Do whatever you want with it."

Never Again

"As far as I am concerned, this nightmare is officially over," I whispered to Elaine and Sandy. To everyone else, I yelled out, "Great show, everybody! Merry Christmas, and we will see you after the New Year." Then I turned to Sandy. "Come on, Sandy, let's get the hell out of here and on to other things! Boolu! Don't be too late, remember they—"

"I know, dey lock da door," he finished for me.

At Arnos Vale the following morning, as we waited for our flight, Cameron spotted us and came over, smiling from ear to ear. "Hi," he said. "How do you think it went last night?"

"It went, but it went without you. You should have been there."

He didn't have a clue why I was so cold, but he must have been afraid he would slip on the ice because he quickly backed off, saying, "Oh, good, fine. Excuse me, I have to speak to that guy over there." And he retreated. I never saw or spoke to him again. I was told he unfortunately passed away very young. One could say he meant well, but that was true of a lot of people around here. Including us, I guess...

I later did learn what the commotion over the microphones was about. A dance the week before had been rained out—not uncommon down here—and they had postponed it to the following week, the very night of our show! So what, you ask? I'll tell you so what. They needed the sound system we were using for their dance that night. It was as simple as that. We had started almost an hour late and were running later than expected. The time had come for their dance and they were ready for their sound system. They came for it, decided to leave us one mike, made a mistake and left us two. So much for the reliable Cameron... But, you see, there is a God!

Later, on our return from the holidays, four letters awaited me. One was from the Australian pastor, praising Bequia and me for our efforts. Another was from a priest from Canada expressing his thanks to me for what this work was doing for the young people, and a third was from a priest on the Island of Mayreau. All were letters from clergy, with one exception, a letter from a member of a prominent family in St. Vincent, Arthur Connell. Yet there was not one word from the nurses, from Cameron, or from anyone else. So what? You can tell I enjoyed myself. Can't you? Ho-ho!

Sitting on the plane going back to New York, I was still miserable. "Oh, yes, we did it, but how? Not the way I was trained to do things," I said to Sandy. "Don't ever let me get into anything like this again. Just shoot me first!" He only laughed.

23 Exhaltation & Dejection

Sandy at Sanford Meisner Day

Sanford Meisner Day In New York

We were not staying long in the city this time, so we stayed at Paul's for the first two weeks to see doctors, planning to go upstate for Christmas and New Year's. We arrived the evening of December 2, and naturally Paul met us. He had everything ordered and laid out for us as only he could—all our formal attire and the schedule of events for the big day tomorrow. From Paul's behavior, you would never know I was persona non grata. I don't think he really blamed me for anything. He truly felt, because of the way things were, it was better for all concerned for me to remain out of sight and in the closet. I'm sure that's where he felt safest. He didn't care if everyone knew who and what he was, so long as no one spoke of it specifically. You know, "Don't ask, don't tell." I knew that feeling. One got used to it growing up, but all that shame and sham were behind me now and here we were. We were proud of who we were. But it truly made Paul nervous.

The next day we hung out at Paul's just resting up. We both needed it after St. Vincy! It was going to be one big red-letter day for Sandy—limos, flash bulbs, reporters and all, and for a man who deserved it for a change. And that's exactly how it turned out. Sandy wanted me at his side in spite of Paul and his and everyone else's hang-ups. He didn't give a damn, and I loved him all the more for it. I don't know why all the lead-up had bothered me so when not one member of Sandy's family was invited either. What was it about these theater people? They were all so insular; everything was about them.

Paul said, "The limo is waiting." He insisted Sandy arrive in style, and there we were in our best bib and tucker. Well, not ours precisely, but we looked pretty sharp in them anyway. At the Shubert Theatre in Theatre Alley I thought, it couldn't be any more Broadway than this. The paparazzi were all over the place. One photographer with a camera up to her face was singling me out for shots. What do you know, low and behold, there was Pat Field, our photographer friend from Bequia. I flashed a big smile, and she waved back and yelled, "You finally made it, ha-ha!"

"Yeah, sure," I yelled back.

People made way for us through the cheering, crushing crowd. It was Sandy's night, that was for sure. We were escorted into the theater and down to our two-on-the-aisle to a standing ovation. The stars who dared to come rushed over one by one to wish him well, that is, the ones who hadn't managed to finagle a position on stage. Then the curtain rose on the star-studded variety show created by Kent Paul, and it unfolded resplendently. On the stage were Tony Randall, Eli Wallach, Annie Jackson, Diane Keaton, Barbara Baxley, Liz Wilson, Marian Seldes, Louise Lasser, Peter Gennaro, Mark Rydell, Kathleen Nolan, Zoe Caldwell, Harold Clurman, Stella Adler, Martha Graham, Maureen Stapleton—so many Tony and Oscar winners on the stage together.

In the audience were many others too numerous to mention. And these were only the New York crowd. Hollywood was just a little too far away or the actors there just a little too busy. Not many came from Hollywood. But Mark Rydell had flown in for the occasion, and a letter of congratulations came from Grace Kelly in Monaco, which I still have. Nevertheless, there were stars aplenty and stars to spare. My old buddy from class on 23rd Street, Louise Lasser, was on stage. I didn't know how she managed to be up there, but she was there all the same. What the hell, right then she was hotter than a pistol. Do you remember Mary Hartman, Mary Hartman? So why not? Wasn't that the nature of the business? I wondered where Jon Voight and Tyne Daly were. They also went to AMDA down on 23rd Street.

Zoe Caldwell and Maureen Stapleton performed a Peter Gennaro tap routine. Maureen said, "It was like a dog walking on his hind legs. The miracle wasn't in the execution. It was in the fact he could do it at all, I mean, that I could do it at all."

Martha Graham came out, as was her wont in yards and yards of flowing chiffon covering up her terrible, painful, arthritic hands. Sitting, she spoke about Louis Horst, her accompanist, whom all the ex-students remembered, and about her working relations with Sandy, "which were not always copasetic," Sandy said. Though most of the graduates became actors, some went on to become successful dancers. One even wrote a book about her time with Les Bluebell Girls, which eventually became the popular movie *Les Girls*.

Harold Clurman pontificated over Sandy, as only Harold could do with all his knowledge of the theater, beginning with meeting Sandy at the Theater Guild back in 1925 thanks to their mutual friend Aaron Copland, of all people... I thought, and so the saga began. I mean the American theater, as we

23 Exhaltation & Dejection

know it today began with them.

Finally Stella Adler spoke of her friendship with Sandy beginning in 1929 at the forming of the Group Theatre with Lee Strasberg and Cheryl Crawford, when they had all banded together to save the American theater. Stella described their meetings where they all sat about anywhere—on the floor, on a radiator, on a coffee table, anywhere—trying to figure out the true mystery of acting. What was the key to finding the answer, the truth? "There was Sandy," Stella reminisced, "always sitting in the big, soft easy chair with his head thrown back, in his own little world. One got the feeling he had the answer. He knew even then; don't ask me where he got it. Perhaps it came to him through his music."

Stella spoke of the summer Harold took her to Paris, where she met Constantin Stanislavski and worked with him, the only American ever to do so. When she came back to New York, she related, she told Sandy everything Stanislavski had taught her. Then, pointing at Sandy, she said, "That's the man sitting over there, he's the one who understood it. He is the teacher!" The theater broke out in thunderous applause. Then she announced, "Oh, don't worry about me, I'm just a legend," and the audience broke out into even louder applause, with shrieks and whistles, and they stood up to give her a standing ovation, including Sandy, with a tear in his eye. The applause must have lasted five minutes.

Almost fifteen years later, I remember one morning about seven o'clock her daughter Ellen called and asked me to tell Sandy that Stella had died. Sandy said, "A great loss for all of us, and not just the theater." When I went out to the mailbox that very morning, there was one small envelope, a note from Stella to Sandy and me. She had written it two days before.

Stella was the memorable moment of that evening for Sandy and the high-

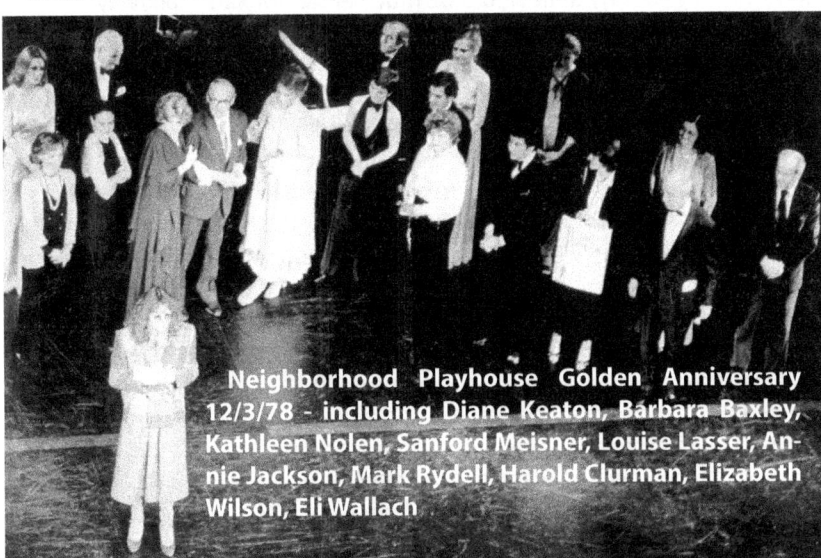

Neighborhood Playhouse Golden Anniversary 12/3/78 - including Diane Keaton, Barbara Baxley, Kathleen Nolen, Sanford Meisner, Louise Lasser, Annie Jackson, Mark Rydell, Harold Clurman, Elizabeth Wilson, Eli Wallach

light of the evening for all of us as well, which was only fitting for Stella, the Grandest Dame of them all. At the end of the show, Sandy was escorted up onto the stage. At that moment, everyone was standing, clapping and cheering, and many had tears in their eyes.

Afterward, we were whisked off in the limo to Macy's department store for a catered sit-down dinner in the Tomorrow's Man department on the 2nd floor. I remember going up the escalator in front of Kim Stanley. Just talking to her was such a thrill for me. She was one of the greatest in my book, which is small by the way. Maybe it's more accurate to say exclusive.

Sandy and I sat together and never left the table all evening, while Paul, who was also at our table, kept circulating. We didn't have to move; people kept coming over to speak to Sandy all evening long. Arthur Miller danced with Zoe Caldwell with a long-stemmed rose in his teeth, and the old character actor Jack Gilford danced around the floor with child actress Tatum O'Neal. When we left, dancers were still in full swing. On the way out, someone snapped a photo of Sandy in front of the huge Tomorrow's Man sign. That sign was like a prophecy, or a blessing. Little did we know seventy-four-year-old Sandy would have eighteen years of tomorrows.

Christmas In The Snow

Sandy saw his doctors and got an "A" clearance from all of them. He checked in at the school, and we saw our friend Jo Ynocencio and a few other close friends. Then we made ready for the trip north on Amtrak. I spent too much time in New York and the Caribbean to feel secure driving on all that ice and snow. The trip by train would be much easier for Sandy anyway.

As always my brother Ed met us at the station and drove us to the homestead up on Coupe Hill overlooking the Mohawk Valley outside Utica. Mom and Pop had moved out there in 1955 to live out their retirement years. The grandkids and great-grands and all the rest of the family were the beneficiaries. Everyone had such a great time there on the windswept, fifteen-acre farm. The winter vistas out there from any direction were fabulous. It was a real Norman Rockwell world, and no one deserved it more than those two. Pop's philosophy was live, trust in the Lord, and everything has a way of working out in the end, and they were living proof. The growing family had some rip-roaring times out there; they were varied and many.

Sandy loved being there. It was one place he could just be one of the gang and melt into the bunch like any other uncle. He thought a great deal of Mom. He said she was a very special person and enjoyed talking to her. He once said to me, "I learn more about you every time we go home," meaning Utica.

Christmas on the farm was like no other Christmas Sandy had ever known. There were the children of every age, from a baby of a few months to TP, the first-born grandchild then twenty-nine years of age. There were any number of great-grands, and, as Sandy once said, "There are always more on the way."

Christmas always began with Pop bringing in the tree with TP or Eric. Then the presents started pouring in from everywhere. They would be placed under and all around the tree to the point where we could barely get through the living room, and that's no exaggeration. Even "Santa" had to work his way into the room. There was always a Santa, done up in anything that was handy, from a red baseball suit to red long-johns. No matter the outfit, it served the purpose. Santa could be anyone from Eddy or Tommy to Leo or me. That's right, even yours truly got into the act. Everyone gave a present to everyone else—none of this name-pulling-out-of-a-hat stuff for us. Everyone, that is, except Pop. He felt this was one time of the year he would sit back in his big armchair and graciously accept each gift "Santa" handed him. After years of "Pop, shoot me here, Pop, shoot me there," why shouldn't he? He would never open any of his presents. He would just let them pile up in his lap. When the distribution was all over and nothing left under the tree, he would hightail it to his room with all his loot still wrapped in its lovely Christmas paper.

I once asked him, "Why do you do that?"

"This way I don't misplace a thing. It would be too easy to lose something in all that hodgepodge of ripped wrapping paper, abandoned toys, and whatever," he explained.

"But this way you never know who gave you what," I said.

"What difference does it make where they came from? Whatever I get, I got from all of you." You know, that's exactly the way he loved us. He loved us one and all, and that was that. A present one way or the other wasn't going to make one iota of difference.

Santa always came following breakfast, which we had right after midnight mass. When we were through eating, the mothers would wake up the little ones, wherever they were sleeping, and the festivities would begin. It would be daybreak before they ended.

Mom's House On Christmas Eve

By Jane Board Carville, December 24, 1953

Won't you come with me to Mom's house
On this Merry Christmas Eve?
You'll have such a jolly time there that you won't want to leave.
You'll see a lovely Christmas tree and presents stacked high as the sky.
And wait till you see all the fun when the paper starts to fly.
But first you'll come along with us to midnight mass we'll go,
Where we'll bump into all our friends and cheerfully say hello.
Then inside of God's house we'll ask his blessings for the poor
On their Christmas Eve and many, many more.

After mass is over, Back at Mom's house we'll all meet,
Where we'll all sit down together and our breakfast we will eat.
Now that breakfast's over the fun has just begun,
'Cause down the stairs still sleepy come the children one by one.
We even have a Santa Claus and for everyone a gift.
Just watch their eyes and faces at the presents Santa lifts.
There are toys for Dickie and Carol and gifts for Dad and Mom,
And Santa hasn't forgotten TP and Dickie John.
Soon all the gifts are passed out and everyone seems pleased
At the wonderful job that Santa's done on this Merry Christmas Eve.
Now that it's almost over, did you ever see anything better
Than a Christmas Eve at Mom's house? I doubt that you will ever.

New Years Eve

New Year's Eve was never quite as spectacular. All the adults of the family would be off somewhere celebrating. Mom and Pop would be home with many of the grands and great-grands. Granny would throw a party in front of the TV, with everyone watching the Times Square festivities. Just before midnight she would drag out every pot and pan in the kitchen and a bunch of big spoons. They would all count down to the stroke of midnight and watch the big ball fall, and everyone would bang in the New Year. Sandy and I always attended this party when we were on the farm for New Year's. Sandy was always fascinated by my mom's ability to become a child among the children and by how she connected with each one on their level. He considered it a gift and said I was lucky to have been raised by such a woman—she had so much insight. I remember responding, "Yeah, I know, just like you," and I meant it. That gift of insight is what made him the teacher he was.

One of those nights stands out as memorable. An unexpected flash blizzard dropped tons and tons of snow leaving everyone stranded until the plows could get out to clear the roads. The storm stopped as quickly as it started, leaving a light powdery snow that, though deep, was easy to walk in. The night was still, except for the distant barking of a dog. With the slightest bit of imagination, its howling could sound like Lightning of *Renfrew of the Mounties*, its wolf-like quality adding an ageless dimension to the moment. The moon was full and pale, a white orb. Not a wisp of breeze disturbed the stillness. The white birch trees stood still as stone, like thin marble pillars against the night sky. It was a magical moment, right out of a Jack London novel.

We trudged down the road past strawberry fields that, though laden with lush ripe strawberries in the heat of a summer's afternoon, now lay hushed under a thick coating of freshly fallen snow like powdered sugar. It was after midnight yet it was as bright as day. Not a soul was about nor any sign of life at all, except for a flickering light here and there in a distant farmhouse. We walked all the way down past the Bass's horse stables where Juanita and Clarence lived with their brood and almost down to Jimmy Ferguson's farm before turning back. I remember Sandy saying to me from under a heavy woolen scarf, "It's moments like these that make one want to live forever, especially if you're not alone." As he spoke, I remembered that dark foreboding night we first landed on the shores of Bequia and I prayed to myself: How much longer? Yes, dear Lord, how much time, how long?

St. Vincent Fade-Out

Well, the month went by like Superman past a speeding bullet, and we were back at Paul's en route to Bequia. Since the last bout with cancer, Sandy had been working less and less at the Playhouse. He had no intention of teaching this winter and had asked, more than once, "When are they ever going to close that school? I really believe it's time. If Paul weren't such a procrastinator… He can barely make it to and from school himself these days. Haven't you noticed how weak he's getting?" It was true. He had less energy than Sandy. He just wouldn't admit it to himself.

No sooner had we made it back to Bequia and settled in than we had to get back over to St. Vincent. The first Monday in January was our first rehearsal call of the year for the *Messiah* for Independence Day. After a month off, it was like moving in melted lead to get up at five o'clock, dress, and drag that heavy portable organ down to the car and onto the boat. I didn't know how Sandy felt and I didn't really want to know, because it must have been awful and asking would only have made it worse for both of us. Who had time for breakfast? All I focused on was getting down to the boat. After that it was routine.

We were over in St. Vincent in no time at all. I slept most of the way. At the house, we crashed and slept till almost noon. At noon I made some chicken soup—you know the kind, Mr. Campbell's out of a tin. We had no bread in the house and no milk, only some stale saltines in the bottom of a box and that was all, save some tea. The girls were still over on Bequia. Even if they had been back, the larder wouldn't have been any more accommodating. I don't know what they ate or when they ate or even if they ate at all.

I went out and shopped for dinner that night, nothing fancy, just simple but tasty. I easily got back in time to walk over to the hall, not that far away, for the Ensemble rehearsal. I knew the police wouldn't show up for the first rehearsal because Bill's Peace Corps contract was up and he was going back home to the States. There wasn't going to be a replacement for him. We were going, not expecting much, quite honestly. So I would have to muster them up myself later in the month when I had some time and more energy. Today we would be lucky if we had enough strings. Surprise! The strings were all there. In the wind section I had no one. Mary Budgell was teaching on Bequia, and the three kids were still on vacation so they wouldn't be coming. I had my first workout on the *Messiah* with my first and second strings, including Soso on bass. After all, that was all I had, so I worked with them. They were still talking about *Superstar*. It wasn't a long rehearsal because we had the chorus coming or, I hoped, at least part of it. So Sandy and I took a short break between.

A half hour passed, and Sandy said, "Are you sure they knew we were coming over today?"

"I'm positive, but I could be wrong, Sandy. I've been wrong before, you know," I said.

"You sure have," Sandy agreed jokingly.

Fifteen more minutes passed, and Charles, my number one tenor, showed up. He had been the principal over on Bequia at the Seventh Day School and was now heading one here on St. Vincent. He assured us the rehearsal had been scheduled for that evening. "Well, what wasn't scheduled was this dreary weather, and it doesn't take much to keep them home," I added.

"But every one of them?" Sandy asked. "We were supposed to begin fifteen minutes ago."

Charles expressed his disgust for their lack of commitment. Commitment was an attribute that ran scarce around here. He himself wanted to see this project work for St. Vincent. He had had his students over on Bequia doing the "Alleluia Chorus" from the *Messiah* after he heard our kids doing it.

"Well, commitment or no, this time we're waiting an hour, and if no one shows up, that's it. We are out of here. We're through trying to do something with them," I said. "Sandy, we'll go back to Bequia, and then it will be up to them to make the next move."

Charles waited along with us. When no one came, Sandy and I both expressed our regrets to the young tenor. "I'm sorry," I said. "It was nice knowing you. It's too bad we didn't find more like you over here."

Father Adams had been right about this place. So we went back to the house, had a late dinner, and left for Bequia in the morning. Sandy merely said, "You tried your damnedest. Now let go of it." On our way back on the boat, we didn't talk much. I knew we were finished over there, and it wasn't a good feeling, I can assure you.

Back on Bequia, I waited for a call from St. Vincent, from anyone, singer or instrumentalist, but nary a call came. Not a single, solitary soul wondered what had happened to us after all those trips we had taken to St. Vincent over the years. Consequently, I never called one singer over there, or any of the Ensemble either, to tell them we were finished and would not be coming over anymore. This was the way of it down here. Nothing stops; things just seem to fade away. We didn't even have the luxury of telling any of them we were through, let alone why.

23 Exhaltation & Dejection

School Sunset

The high school was now going full tilt, and I was back in the classroom. Avila had taken over the Deaf School, so my life for the most part was easier. At the end of the month, we had our usual teachers' meeting at Bequia Anglican High with the good Father presiding. This issue and that issue were taken up, the usual everyday problems that come up at any school—the John that was stopped up, the broken desk in the Science Lab, or the complaining mother threatening to pull all three of her children out of the school if this or that wasn't done... Nothing monumental was happening.

Then we turned to new business and the subject of a pending guidance counselor came up. I was shocked to hear Father Adams announce that he had already picked someone. Oh, I knew he had been pushing the idea. He had already picked out a room and had the door painted with the word COUNSELLOR across it. I had thought this meeting was called to discuss the matter and come up with some suggestions. The matter hadn't even come up at the school board yet. I knew because I was still on the board. Well, this was his baby and who the hell was I to question. But when he told us who, you could have knocked me over with the blast of a fart, that's how low the blow was. The person he picked was a known thief, and I mean a serious one. And all the kids in the high school knew the particulars of the incident. Oh, there had never been a conviction, but then there never was on this Island, except maybe for using the password on someone. (On Bequia, "fuck you" was called the password. You could be brought in front of the magistrate by anyone for uttering it to anyone.) The mother of the thief allegedly went all the way to Guyana to work Obeah on the problem, and it must have worked because there was no charge, let alone a conviction. The culprit was only fired.

When I expressed my concern to Father, he asked, "How can you besmirch someone's name like that? It's not Christian. You should be forgiving and helpful toward this person who was, after all, let go and is now jobless. Why, now [So-and-so] needs the job more than ever."

"Father," I rebutted, "this is not about being Christian or forgiving. This is about impressionable teenagers who need to be taught standards, with role models. Be Christian and forgiving if you want, go ahead and give the person a job, with my blessing for what it's worth, but not as a guidance counselor. How about out in the field with the girls' rounder team, or as the boys' soccer coach? Yeah, a sports coach, that's it, or even offer the job of janitor with Mrs. Leach for all I care."

"How can you judge this person without proof? You don't know. You weren't there," Father went on defending.

"Because I do know, because I was there at another time, another incident. When we did *Superstar*, at the end of the show the take at the door was passed to the person in question. But only half of what the gate was expected to bring in was turned in. Others knew it. Others knew what was taken in. It was about $1,400 and what we saw was closer to $700. Even I had an idea from the last show what that take should have been. Sandy had to make up the difference in the cost of the show. No, you don't, Father, not this time. Not with these kids. We have all worked too hard, too long, to come to this," I insisted.

He answered, "It's my school, I founded it, and I will run it as I see fit. The teachers don't run this school, I do."

"Maybe you forget that I'm also on the Board of Governors, and I have a vote."

"Perhaps you didn't hear me," he snapped, "I run this school."

"Well," I answered, "you go right ahead and run your school as you see fit. But you run it without me. I refuse to be a rubber stamp for anybody. Excuse me." I turned and walked out.

I never did return. To this day I haven't set foot in that school. That was the way this place worked, sunrise sunset, fade in and fade out. At first they brought another music teacher in from the Royal Academy of Music in London, but she never made it to Christmas. I was told she had a nervous breakdown and practically had to be carried off the Island in a basket. I wasn't the least bit surprised. Oh, and by the way, Father never did appoint that counselor, or any other. I've sometimes wondered whether that door with the big word COUNSELLOR across it is still there.

Shortly after Father and I aired our differences at the teachers' meeting and I was through at the school, I found myself out on the terrace with absolutely nothing to do, thinking, well that did it! I severed my last function with a purpose around here and why the hell did I do it? I was, as they used to say in the army, lower than whale shit. I couldn't even do gardening because it was the middle of the dry season. Every living thing was as thirsty as Dan the mule fighting off the devil and the blazing waste praying for the grace of a little taste of water, cool, clear water. Yeah, water, clear, blue water. The Bequia cedar trees were as yellow and lifeless as any elm, oak, ironwood, cottonwood, or hickory in the fall along the Mohawk—without the drums. All the trees were stripped of their finery. I too felt naked as a jaybird, stripped of everything I stood for, with nothing to do but stand there in the noonday sun. Not being needed by anyone, I felt a taedium vitae. I was in a bad way.

Sandy came out and sat down. "Come on, sit next to me here in the shade," he said. "You're not feeling too bright. I'm afraid you have a bad case of the malaise."

I snapped, "A bad case of the malaise! Lah-de-dah. Only if you were from Bennington would you say a thing like that."

He laughed, getting the joke. "Well, you've been nervous and jumpy as a heron on a griddle all week. Do you know what your problem is?" he ventured to ask.

"No, but I'm damn sure you're bloody well going to tell me," I snapped back

23 Exhaltation & Dejection

again.

He went on, not paying me any mind or giving me flack, "Jimmy, it's as plain as the—"

"I know, it's as plain as the nose on your face," I butted in. "What is it?"

"It's so obvious to me, but you would be the last to see and recognize it for what it is."

"So, what is it?"

"Jimmy, it's burnout. You're suffering from a classic case of burnout. You've been fighting upstream like a salmon for years now. You've been doing it ever since you got here ten years ago. It's time you let up. You were doing it even when you were in New York, and that was long before I knew you. The only difference then was they wouldn't let you swim. You know, that's what saved you. Jimmy, you don't always have to win. Now you've stopped yourself, and thank God you did. They would have chewed you up and spit you out without a second thought. They would have let you go on until you dropped... You did it for Joan, you did it for Boolu, and yes, you've done it for me. Now enough already! Thank you. Now it's time for you and me. We can go on now and enjoy ourselves until we're a hundred. I've come up with an idea. What do you say we go on a long vacation? And I mean long. Take as long as it takes, just the two of us."

"Like where?" I asked.

"Anywhere," Sandy said. "There's Europe, Italy. I would love to take you to the Italy I know. Jimmy, so much culture, it just oozes of it. Then there's Greece, the temples, the ruins, the Acropolis under a full moon. Jimmy, what about over to your family in Ireland? I would love that. That would be new for me."

"Stop! Stop it. Wait just a freakin' minute. You don't have to convince me. The way I feel just now, I'm all for it. It's just—what about this place? Boolu? Number one and number two, the... the... I can't think."

Sandy stopped me, saying, "And the cat's ass behind the moon. We just go, that's all. Everything will take care of itself, just like *Superstar* did, remember? That's it, we go."

"OK, OK. We go!"

24 Culture, Culture and more Culture

1979: Before And After The Big Trip

Once we made up our minds to visit Italy and Greece then stop in Ireland on the way home, everything at Casa Luna went full throttle, like the building of the house years before. Every conversation was geared to when, how, where, and for how long we would travel. We pulled out the old red atlas from Reader's Digest and perused all the maps. We filtered through Sandy's Guide de Bleu and Fodor's guidebook. We had a ball all winter long planning our tour. Once we settled our plans, Sandy had me contact his old travel agent in New York. He told the agent what he was to work on—the how, i.e., air travel, hotel accommodations along the way with the exception of Ireland, car rentals. All we would need in Ireland was a hotel the first night, to pick up a car rental that he would arrange for two weeks. That, with my address book, would suffice.

Sandy was planning one lollapalooza of a trip. Certainly like nothing I had ever experienced! Yet, Ireland aside, he had been to all these places before with his wives. It was obvious that he was doing this trip especially for me. When I tried to thank him, he said, "Don't thank me, I'm not doing this for you. You haven't the slightest notion of what this is going to save me."

"Save you?" I queried.

"Yep. In psychiatry bills," he said. "I did therapy for eight years, and those bills can be monstrous. This trip is going to get your head screwed on right. Truly. This trip is going to change your whole outlook on life. I saw you in Spain and I saw you in Portugal. Remember, I saw you in that old Roman ruin outside Seville. Was it Italica? Who was born there? Trajan? It's going to do you a world of good. I guarantee you will never look at things the same way again. I'm banking on it!"

We left Boolu in the house with Parnell, with our housekeeper looking after both. When we eventually got back, everything seemed to be in order. When I asked around, Rusty Ford said, "I don't want to be a busybody, but you happened to have had an Island thief living in your house when you were away."

What had happened? Parnell's little brother, "Sweetbread," got into trouble with the police. He was caught breaking into foreigners' homes, taking anything he could get his hands on—the usual radios, recorders, small TVs, anything of value that could be easily disposed of for whatever the traffic would bear. So their mother had asked Parnell to take him in and keep a short leash on him. We would never have been notified by a Bequian. You fade out, they fade in. Why, Genghis Khan could have holed up there while we were gone and we would have been the last to know. Not even Boolu would have told us.

"The fact is, you were harboring a thieving criminal," Rusty, more than a little upset, implied. Apparently his house had been given the once-over, probably more times than he was aware of.

My answer to him was, "If truth be told, I would rather have the thief coming to live in our house instead of coming to ransack it for its valuables." You protect yourself any way you can, but that disease never changes and don't ever expect it to. All you can do is to try to insulate yourself as best you can and devil take the hindmost. I really think Rusty understood. If Parnell hadn't taken Sweetbread in, I could have been next.

Leaving Our Troubles Behind

Early of a Good Friday morning in April of '79, we left Paul's place, driving up Roosevelt Drive. Coming off the Triboro Bridge into Queens, we heard on the cabby's radio, "Last night on the Island of St. Vincent in the Caribbean, the island's volcano, La Soufriere—shpt! shpt! shpt!," as we proceeded down into the tunnel under the overpass descending into Astoria. We both sat upright, all ears, but when we came out of the tunnel, the announcer was on to something else.

I turned to Sandy. "Did you hear?"
"I sure did. Hear what, what?"
"I don't know what I didn't hear," I said.
"So why ask me?" Sandy asked.
The cab driver chimed in, "Anything wrong back there? What is it?"
I started, "Last night the..." but thought better of it and just said, "Oh, no, it was nothing." I knew we would have to wait until we reached the airport to find out what had happened and the extent of it all.

But no one we spoke to at Kennedy had heard anything. When we changed planes in France, no one knew what we were talking about either. Maybe it was because we were speaking English. I tried and tried again. Sandy finally said, "Give it over and forget it."

When we reached Venice, no one knew either, and Greece wasn't any better. It wasn't until we reached Ireland two months later that the people knew what we were asking about. That made me realize just how insignificant St. Vincent was to the rest of the world. We could have called home and found out, but Sandy's attitude was, it couldn't have been much or someone would have been talking about it, so why fret it?

He said, "Trying to call Bequia from this part of the world would be a nightmare. And right now, I am so far from St. Vincent I couldn't care less. Out of sight, out of mind! After all, we don't live on St. Vincent, we live on Bequia, and they're worlds apart."

"Don't say that," I said. "Things are changing."

"Yes, well," he agreed. "But this is a three-month vacation from that place and I won't let anything muck up my plans right now, certainly not St. Vincent. That's the place I'm trying to get you away from because I believe you need it right now."

Well, no matter. As it turned out, La Soufriere had erupted and it rumbled on and off for well onto three weeks. All the Caribs from around Fancy, Sandy Bay, Owia, and Orange Hill were evacuated all the way down to Georgetown, and many were evacuated from there as well. Most of the people migrated to the Grenadines and southern St. Vincent, some never to return. Bequia schools were closed for months to house the displaced refugees. It also changed the topography of the crater somewhat, leaving a rather large exposed plug sticking out in the middle of the lake that surrounds it. The plug hadn't been there when I went up to the crater in '70.

Italy The Glorious: 1

Venice was a delight but rather cool for April. No, it was damned cold for April! We were in a hotel across from the rail station by the Grand Bridge of Sighs, a beautiful piece of architecture. But then, wasn't everything we looked at in any direction? 17th century culture was everywhere, in the bridges, the buildings, the paintings, the churches, and the museums holding the clothing of the period and the furnishings. What can I say? I went berserk, as Sandy knew I would. Then, to top it all off, there were kids, kids everywhere. What we hadn't known was that spring break in Europe took place here in Venice, just like in Fort Lauderdale, Florida in the USA. Their presence made the place vibrate with their lustful quest for the joy of life, and that is exactly what I needed. At the very moment that St. Vincent was vomiting up toxins like the toxin that had entered my life, here we were with all these lively kids full of the zest of youth, reminding me at every turn that life was a merry hayride, a sleigh ride, a Christmas in July. Life was sure worth living. It was whatever you wanted it to be. I could see it everywhere I went.

Maybe it wasn't July, it was only April, but it really did feel like Christmas. It was so cold! It didn't bother the kids any, in their sleeping bags thrown around every which way all around the rail station on the other side of the canal, but Sandy was another matter. Here he was with his stoma, his narrow bridge to life, clogging over, depriving him of the breath of life. The mucus was crusting over because of the cold, no different from ice on a river in winter. I would

24 Culture, Culture and more Culture

look at him and feel shame, because he was still getting a kick out of my take on everything I laid eyes on. I went to the apothecary and explained the problem to the druggist. He rigged me up a strong manual suction pump I could work by hand to keep Sandy's air passage clear and clean, making it so much easier for him to breathe. We had an electric one in New York for the cold weather, but it was 110 volts and we didn't need it in warm weather. We never brought it to Bequia. Who the hell knew it was going to be so cold in Italy? It could be cold in "April in Fairbanks" maybe, but never in Italy. Be that as it may, the manual pump did the job and Sandy felt fine.

He took great pleasure in observing my reactions to everything. Once he said to me, "You see, Italy is nothing like East Utica or New York's Little Italy. These people know how to live. It's a shame what money does to people, with it or without it, in America."

He just loved Italy, and I was beginning to find out why. Easter Sunday morning found us three rows from the front at High Mass in St. Mark's Cathedral on St. Mark's Square. It was all so majestic with all the pomp and glory and multitude of priests in their gorgeously woven vestments, some of white and gold and some in green and gold signifying hope, this I knew. With the choir singing gloriously overhead, it was splendor at its best. That afternoon, as we sat all bundled up fighting off the cold with a cup of hot espresso in St. Mark's Square, Sandy was reminded of one extra-hot day in August sitting there with Betty, his wife, trying to keep cool. It was siesta time and the Square was abandoned. Not a soul in sight! It was much too hot even to move.

"It felt like 110 degrees in the shade," Sandy said, "and there pranced Bea Lillie across the middle of the Square laden down with packages, her dog in tow. You couldn't dream up this happening in a 100 years. I turned to Betty and said, 'Mad dogs and Englishmen go out in the noonday sun.'"

"Sandy," I said, "she's a Canadian."

"Don't tell her that," he quipped.

Just off the Grand Canal stood the most beautiful house I had ever seen. More Ottoman-influenced than Romanesque, I would say, the Calle della Oro was built in 1422 by B. Bon and M. Raverti. It was my favorite building. It was unsurpassed by any other building I had ever seen throughout my limited travels thus far.

After Venice we were on to Florence, with much, much more culture to soak up. Sandy knew the place like the back of his hand. It was as if I had my own personal guide. I got to see twice as much as I would have without him. The first day in Florence we woke up early enough to be at the doors of the Palazzo Medici-Riccardi when they opened at 9 AM. Following a saunter down the Via de' Martelli, just a short sprint further we were standing in front of two mammoth, magnificently majestic, bronze doors of the baptistery of the Cathedral of Saint Giovanni. Saint John's is one of the oldest buildings in Florence of Romanesque structure. Many artisans contributed to its construction in the 11th century. One of the earliest contributors was A. Pisano, and even

V. Dante had a hand in it before its completion.

Continuing down the Via de' Calzaiuoli, we found a charming little cafe in the center of town across from the Piazza della Signoria where we sat outside sipping dark coffee, eating real Italian pizza, and admiring Michelangelo's divine David, created as a symbol of the Florentine Republic. We finished lunch, then meandered through the spectacular Palazzo Vecchio and finished off the day in the unusually elongated Galleria degli Uffizi.

The third day we were off to the museum of Saint Marco. Right next door was the Galleria dell' Accademia where we saw the original David. We saw so much, so fast, who could remember it all? We did save the last day for shopping on the Ponte Vecchio, a bridge the likes of which I had never seen before. The fact that it was the oldest one might have something to do with it—996 CE was a long time ago for a bridge.

We left on a train down the east side of Italy along the Adriatic to Rimini. Already there were memories, and many more left unfinished, of "Firenze," for, like "Roma," one could never be saturated; there would always be something left yet to be seen. In Rimini we had dinner with a homesick baseball player on contract in Italy. I guess he could make more money there than he could back home in Podunk. His scene was right out of an old '40s movie. He was like a down-and-out club singer stuck in some godforsaken outpost like Maracaibo, working his way back home in a rundown piano bar with the likes of Sidney Greenstreet or Sadie Thompson as bit players in his life.

We stopped in towns to see the sights along the way, taking a side trip to the principality of San Marino, a country in a country like a fetus in its mother. Then we went on down to Ancona on the sea and reminders of Mussolini's fascist socialism. There were remembrances of Hitler and the Second World War and memorials to the Italian Jews and their plight. We finished up in Brindisi where we caught a boat across the Adriatic to Greece.

Greece: The Birth Of Culture As We Know It

We sailed the canal built by Nero before Rome burned between renditions on his violin. The canal started near Corinth in the north, crossed the isthmus of the Peloponnesian Peninsula to Isthmian in the south, and emptied into the Gulf of Saronic. We then sailed across into Piraeus. Ah! Then there was Athens, the Acropolis, and my God, as luck would have it, under a full moon! Sandy said, "Words are useless. What more is there to be said? Except—oh, to be young and in love."

"Yeah, why is it wasted on old fogies like us?"

"Because it's old fogies like us who can afford it," Sandy quipped.

"Well, better late than never."

To walk where Socrates thought! I don't care if he was ugly, his soul wasn't. And Plato, though he wasn't much of a looker either, to me it was a privilege. I

24 Culture, Culture and more Culture

could identify with these men. I made a note to myself that I was one of them and I mentioned it to Sandy. "Yeah, and do you know there's a long line of you all through history?" he replied, and we laughed.

We followed this excursion by a bus tour to Corinth and all around the Peloponnesian Peninsula, stopping everywhere. From here St. Paul sent out his letters to the Phoenicians and the Corinthians. I said to Sandy, "I must say I disagree with him on a number of matters. But then, he thought the world was coming to an end. He was wrong about that, too."

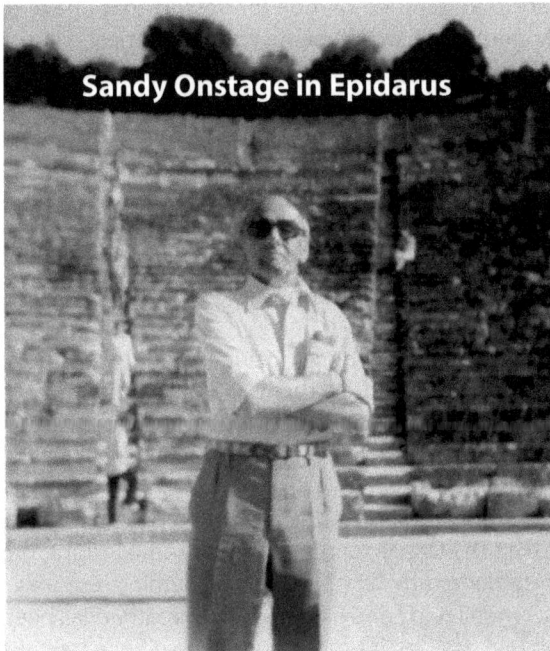

Sandy Onstage in Epidarus

"Will you let the poor man rest in peace," Sandy said. "After all, they crucified him, didn't they? And at that they did it upside down. Or was that St. Peter?"

"It was St. Peter. I think they beheaded St. Paul. No matter, they were both finished off. But he did a hell of a lot of damage, even though he did propagate the faith, before they did him in."

"Yeah, propagated it through fear," said Sandy.

"I know. To him women were an abomination, sex was dirty. What was it he preached? 'Marry and burn'? or was it, 'many or burn'? No matter, it all amounted to the same. But let's face it. The Church says he meant well—after all, they made him a saint, didn't they?—and I was taught the Church was never wrong."

We then drove to Epidaurus, site of a great Greek amphitheater. Sandy tested the acoustics by dropping coins and having me go up to the top to see if I could hear them drop. When I said yes, he asked me how many. He also checked his esophageal speech as he spoke.

"Come back and tell me what I said," he requested. "I want to see if I can still play tragedy."

So I did, and believe it or not, there he stood reciting something from Euripides' *Medea*, not that you could prove it by me. I went back down and told him what he had said: "'Would that the Argo had never winged its way to the land of Colchis, through the dark-blue...'" Well, a bit of it. OK, OK, the first few lines.

Then we skirted over and down to Sparta and the Spartans, the no-frills soldiers of Greece, a far cry from Athens and Plato. It brings to mind our very own Republicans and Democrats. How is it any different? The next stop, as we bussed farther over to the windswept foothills, was Messini. If Athens was old, this place was even further back in time and beyond. Here they entombed their dead covering their eyes with thin disks of gold, somewhat like gold leaf, I would say.

On the bus tour we were provided food as well as hotel accommodations. Sandy grouched, "If I never see another plate of moussaka, or goat cheese wrapped in grape leaves, or that damned orange for dessert that I have to peel with my teeth and fingernails, it would be just fine with me. I will not complain. I would rather go on a hunger strike." It was obvious no dietician had been involved with the planning and setting up of this tourist bus jaunt across Greece. "What's with these people?" Sandy griped. "Haven't they ever heard of variety? How about a thick strawberry milk shake or an ice cream sundae for a change?"

Our next stop was Olympia where Sandy took pictures of me standing on a winner's pedestal. I said, "This is the closest I'll ever come."

"You got that right," he replied. "Aren't you surprised you got this far? Ho-ho."

Even that long ago, the Olympic winners' booty included political positions and commercial endorsements bestowed on them and an entrée into the theater. That much hasn't changed. With pieces of dismembered statues and demolished pedestals scattered about on the ground, you could still feel the past lingering.

Lastly, we went back around to the north and over on a boat to Delphi, where I leaned over and asked the Oracle for a message or some insight into my future. I was willing to settle for any bit of advice on anything. But alas, I could not hear her answer. When I told Sandy, he said, "The weather has been bad for the past couple of days. It's possible she caught herself one hell of a severe case of laryngitis. So if I were you, I would humor her just now because you don't want her to send you away with a curse."

"Is that any worse than being sent away with a flea in my ear? Because I have already had the pleasure."

Our next jaunt was over to the Greek islands of Syros, Mykonos, Delos, Crete, and others. It was all mind-blowing to me. While on Crete, we were taken out of town to the foot of a high hill where you had to get out and walk—I should say climb—up a narrow, scraggy, winding path to the summit. "Look, Sandy, you can ride a donkey all the way..."

"You ride up, I'll walk. I'm not getting up on any ass. Living with one is rough enough," Sandy answered as he slowly made his way to the top.

There one got to savor Greece mixed with a recognizable flavor of the pharaohs of Egypt. Looking south under the gaze of the overpowering sun that poured a glistening glaze over everything, and out across the Mediterranean to Egypt not so far away, one could comprehend the fusing of one culture on the other. In the combination of breathtaking view, magnificent edifices, and offerings to the gods, one could conclude that the Deity had to have been inspired and guided by something beyond us all. The light around us was unearthly. It was to me like stepping into the unknown. All Sandy said was, "See, I told you." To others it may have been nothing more than another Greek ruin of an ancient temple high on a clear and windy hill, as they all seemed to be. Yet to me this spot was special.

When Sandy felt we had finished with the Greece experience, we sailed from Patra back to Brindisi.

To The Land Of Dram And Song: Italy 2

We rented a car and drove all the way across the boot of Italy to the west, over to Naples on the sea precariously close to Mount Vesuvius looming to the southeast. We stayed in a lovely hotel, an old mansion with marble everywhere, chock-full of Italian antiques, on beautiful Amalfi Drive overlooking Positano. Here an antique is really an antique, like the oil lamps we saw from the 1st and 2nd centuries. We went on down the coast road from Amalfi to Paestum, an early Greek settlement from the 7th century BCE, where we read on a stele of one lover's undying love for another. "You won't find many of them around now-a-day," Sandy said. It was touching and gratifying to me to think that even then... Being at Paestum again put me to thinking about cultures overlapping one another, like the fusion of cultures these days, although it seems it is happening at a much faster pace now. I believe people are finding it harder and harder to keep up, as I am.

Back up to Pompeii we went. There I discovered the richness and beauty of the colors saffron and terracotta that embellish the city. It was apparent all over, on and in so many homes. I found it both compelling and restful, like being bathed in magnificent fiery sunsets...

We headed north from Positano toward Rome on the autostrata that skirts the outer environs of Naples. Just before we reached Naples, we came upon a crossroad with a sign directing traffic left to Ercolano. "Turn here, you must see this," Sandy said.

So we took a detour to the village at the edge of the sea along the Gulf of Napoli. There we found the dig called Herculaneum. The area had been destroyed in the 2nd century at the same time as Pompeii. Due to its lesser importance, it had never been excavated to the extent of Pompeii. It was in the process of being restored the very moment we were there, and I think it must be completed by the time of this writing. It was enlightening to see the whole operation in progress.

We were in a cave along the shoreline where the populace had tried to escape the eruption of Vesuvius in boats. I had a mental flash of my fellow countrymen in St. Vincent escaping La Soufriere, pushing out from the shores of Fancy, Owia, and Sandy Bay in their families' fishing boats with the entire family and as many of their earthly belongings as they dared take lest they be swamped in high seas. I was a friend of Susan Barnard Simpson and the Barnard family—Susan's brother Martin, his wife Mary, brother John, and sister Heather—owners of Orange Hill Estates. I had spent time there when I first came to St. Vincent. Susan and family had been living at the old homestead; Martin and family had a place close by. Their father had bought a goodly portion of the eastern slope of La Soufriere back in 1906 for pennies on the dollar when it was nothing but burnt stumps after the last big eruption of 1902. Looking at the ancient site of Herculaneum, I couldn't help but stop and wonder at the similarities. That mental picture brought up another one, of Sandy and me in that little dugout with all our luggage, skirting out and around the southwestern tip of Roatan off the Bay Islands in the high seas of the western Caribbean in our haste to get Sandy back to a doctor in New York. Such predicaments we mere mortals end up in on this journey through life! I prayed for St. Vincent for what might have happened on that questionable Good Friday morning, and then quickly put it out of my mind. I didn't mention it to Sandy for he was silent and seemed to be deep in thought.

Back in the cave were some bodies entombed in their shell of hardened lava, entrapped in whatever position they were in that second more than 2000 years ago, frozen in time for posterity. So many years had passed, and they still hadn't been exhumed from their grave in the depths of the cave. We looked down from solid ground level on a two-storey house that had been partially protected from the elements. It looked to me as if the house had been torn in half. One could still see the condition it had been left in. On the second level, we could see clearly what looked like a cross or a crucifix over a table or desk. I was impressed that here at the time of the eruption in the 2nd century, a cross is in evidence. Was it just a symbol of the mode of execution of the day or had a symbol of Christ and Christendom reached the shores of the Mediterranean in Italy just south of Rome?

That stop was our last before Rome. Things had changed a little since our trip through Portugal and Spain years before, but now I was the only one who didn't know the language, unless you wanted an aria from me. I knew words but I could not read it or speak it intelligently, and that handicap made for fun because Sandy could. I say fun; in truth it was driving me wild. It was tough enough trying to get into the center of Rome not knowing how to read a sign or understanding what people were saying to me when they were giving directions—that is, if they were willing to take the time to do it in the first place. But with someone as strong-willed as Sandy interjecting his read on what may or may not be so on top of everything else, the solution to the situation at hand did not come clear. It was positively horrendous. At least years before in Portugal, neither of us had understood a thing and we had to rely on my intuition, which I felt left us none the worse for wear and was the better part of our success although it had instilled in Sandy a nervousness and uneasiness that he couldn't cope with. Still we muddled through anyway then, and we muddled through now. We navigated our way to the top of the Scalinata della Trinita dei Monti, better known as the Spanish Steps, and to this day I am not quite sure how. We stayed in a lovely hotel right at the top of the Steps.

The Eternal City

When we hit Roma, Sandy went Italian. It was as if he were a little boy exploding with explanations. "Over there at the base of the steps on the left is housed the Keats-Shelley Memorial Foundation. That's the house where Shelley lived with his friend and where he died from a heart attack, furious over a review he got from a critic for one of his works, so the story goes... And this is where Betty broke the heel off her shoe and she... The Pieta was just around... The inside of that church you won't believe... Go on, stick your hand in there..."

During this latter explanation, we were at the end of the Circus Maximus, a great cruising ground, by the way, for those of you who may be interested. We were in the portico of the Church of Saint Maria in Cosmedin (from the Greek for "lovely") built in the 6th century. Just inside the portico is the famous Bocca della Verita, or "mouth of truth," which popular tradition has it would bite off the hand of a liar. When I stuck my hand in there, Sandy asked me a question that I would rather not repeat but you can rest assured I told him the truth.

"Hey, Jimmy, that's where Tosca jumped," Sandy said. We were out in front of the Castle Saint Angelo, now a museum, which once held a prison cell. He was always pointing this way and that.

"How was her high C?" I asked.

"Great, oh, great," he joked. "It was Maria Callas, you know. Ha."

We went on like this for days having the time of our lives. We were so far away from all those petty everyday problems that didn't mean a bucket of piss when all was said and done. I had been wasting time and energy worrying and letting myself be plagued by the insignificant, small, and belittling things in my life back on Bequia. So they all were, in the grand scheme of things. I was feeling like the Roman Spring of Mrs. Stone—without the young lover. One had to get away to be made aware of such things, and Sandy knew this. Now I saw what he meant by saving money. He was something else.

Brother Ed's Polish Friends

My brother Ed and his wife Jane were active in our local Polish church in Utica. Ed donated a lot of time and effort to the school there. He helped out in the kitchen planning and producing food for the cafeteria. He was a general handyman around the school making himself useful on his off time which he enjoyed doing more than going to a ball game. That was his way.

Well, as luck would have it, Ed and Jane knew the Mother General who led a worldwide order of Polish nuns who had their motherhouse in Rome. Sister Beatrice, the former Jane Beirsinski, had been born in Utica just down the way from where we grew up. I went to school with her younger sister, Marcella Purnie. Ed and Jane insisted I stop and see her in Rome. "Give her our best wishes. I'm sure she would enjoy hearing from Utica and Lincoln Avenue."

So when we got to Rome, Sandy said, "Why don't we look the old girl up? It should be an experience. That is, if you want to?"

We looked up the address of the convent and paid her a visit without any fanfare or advance warning. We just dropped by to say hello, that was all. A nun informed us that the Mother General was in Poland and wouldn't be back for weeks. When I told her who we were, she exclaimed, "Mother of God, bless us and save us! You are Edmond's brother. I'm Sister Victoria from Connecticut, but I taught in Utica; in fact, I taught your nephew Brian. Do come in, come in! How thoughtful to drop by. How are Edmond and Jane and the children? The little one, what's her name?"

"Ann Marie," I said.

"Oh, yes, Ann Marie. A lovely little girl, such a lovely family."

In we went and sat and talked for a while. She told us they were having a first communion ceremony for a little girl who was the last girl studying at the convent school. They were closing it down due to insufficient interest and a lack of proper funding. "I feel these are bad times for the Church," she said.

I added, "These are bad time for everyone, any institution. I felt it even in the Caribbean."

"Would you two like to join us on Sunday at the communion mass and have dinner with us after?" she enquired. "We would all love to have you celebrate with us."

I looked at Sandy and he looked at me, but all I saw was a blank face. We both graciously accepted, but Sandy only after I did. When we got outside, Sandy asked, "What did we just get ourselves into?"

"I don't know," I said. "Dinner with a bunch of single virgins?"

"How can you be sure?" Sandy asked.

"Look, you could have said something. Then I could have apologized profusely," I said.

"Oh, sure, make me the heavy. Actually, this could prove interesting, just as a behavioral study. How many guys get to dine with a bevy of holy women, and that's not funny."

"So it is on for Sunday?" I asked.

"Why not? How bad could it be?" Sandy answered with another question.

You know, it wasn't bad; in fact, it was very pleasant. The communion service in a motherhouse in Rome with only one little girl did seem a bit sad. I knew the Church was in a bad way but I had no idea how bad. When I had re-

24 Culture, Culture and more Culture

ceived my first Holy Communion, insufficient funds were also a problem, and not only for the Church but for everyone else as well. Ours was a poor parish in the best of times, but it was 1934, the middle of the Depression. They were pulling down houses with the likes of us still living in them with shingles flying over our very heads and no place to go. Yet my communion class had fifty-nine of us. Funds had nothing to do with it. In 1979 religious schools were closing down all over the place, my grade school had been ripped to the ground, and in St. Vincent it wasn't any better.

When I told Sandy how sad it was and all because of money, money, money, Sandy said, "It's more than money. Cool it, kid. Remember, you're on vacation."

Well, the dinner with the "single girls"—there must have been about twenty—was very interesting and enlightening, truly pleasant. Sandy and I sat together in the middle of a long table with the acting Mother General from Connecticut opposite us. We sat eating perogies, polish kielbasa sausage, 'cabbusta,' and Polish sour-rye bread with caraway seeds. Oh, yes, and a lovely wine. There were serving nuns, and there were obvious sit-down nuns. The kitchen nuns came out to meet us. Who decides who is going to be which? Well, we never found out because we were too chicken to ask. But that was the first question Sandy asked when we got outside. One serving nun was from Texas, we knew, because she told us. While serving the perogies, she overheard that Sandy was born in Green Point, Brooklyn, and butted into the conversation. "Well, then, you must have been baptized in St. Stanislaw's."

I saw Sandy look up at her, pause, then turn to the Prioress across the table. Sister Victoria swiftly interrupted, abruptly inquiring, "Mr. Meisner, would you like some more wine?"

Then, turning back to our inquisitive Texan who was still standing there waiting for an answer, Sandy nodded his head up and down, saying "Yes," and kept nodding up and down repeating himself saying, "Yes, please." Again he turned away from the Texan, his head still bobbing up and down and said for the third time, "Yes," to Sister Victoria, while holding out his glass to her, even though his glass was still half full. If looks could kill, that look from the Prioress would have finished the yellow rose from Texas right then and there.

John Paul II, before his election to Pope, had been their chaplain at the convent. St. Stanislaw's claim to fame for them was that their chaplain had said mass there years before when he had visited America as a priest. Because St. Stanislaw's was a predominately Polish parish, he had stayed there while in New York. Anyone could see they were full of pride that one of their boys had made it.

My brother Ed also knew the highest Polish prelate in Rome under the Pope. He had met him years earlier before he became an Archbishop when he was in America and had visited Holy Trinity in Utica. So Ed had written him requesting an audience with the Pope for both Sandy and me. We were told to go to the Archbishop's offices in Rome in advance.

As in Portugal, neither of us could speak the language. All I could say was "dobrze, dobrze" and "Wise up, Sta, I'll see ya down de Uptown." But in spite of our linguistic limitations, we got our tickets, which had been set aside for us by the Archbishop. It was to be the second audience ever held outside in the grand plaza. That day was the largest gathering of the faithful held in St. Peter's Square in all the years of Christendom. Later, in the third audience that he held in the plaza, the Pope raised Ed's friend to Cardinal, but we didn't make it. We were on our way to Ireland by then. Only shortly after that, the Pope was shot there on the plaza, and the practice came to a screeching halt.

The crush of people the day we were there was maddening, but it was organized. All you had to do was follow your numbers and the color that matched your tickets. We showed our passes at every turn and eventually we were personally directed past all these people to a small group up in the front next to the dais the Pope would be sitting on. Our small group was off to the right side. Everyone in our group appeared to be Polish and most were clergy, priests and nuns. When the Pope came out, the people cheered. When he spoke, the people cheered. At the end of the ceremony, he came down off the dais with a man assisting him as he walked over to a group sitting in wheelchairs in the center where he proceeded to shake hands and bless them. With some he put his hands on their heads. He then turned to our group, which was all jostling and jockeying for a vantage point. We were in the front row, but when a nun began to edge in between Sandy and me, Sandy stepped behind me, giving her his place next to me. I looked back at him. He shook his head saying, "Fine, fine."

By now Pope John Paul was coming down our line to my right, shaking hands, blessing people, and I could hear him speaking in Polish. He took my hand in his two to shake it and found the rosaries in it—one for Mom, one for Pop, and the other for Joan. He looked at me, said nothing, just smiled, blessed the rosary beads, and went on to the nun next to me, speaking Polish to her.

When we finally got outside, away from the thousands upon thousands, as we stood there in front of the Castle Saint Angelo and Tosca's prison jump, Sandy said, "Wasn't that awesome? All these people, and the Pope is blessing your beads. Somebody is doing something right."

"Why did you move?" I asked him. "How could I tell him as an actor, which he was, that he was meeting America's finest in the business?"

"Yeah, sure you would have. Now you tell me! So... where do we go from here?"

We went to turn in our car at the airport, and going out was a hell of a lot easier than coming in. We boarded a plane for Heathrow, and after a short stay, we were on another to an airport just outside Dublin.

25 To the Land of Saints and Scholars

The Feel Of A Homecoming

I was excited. I was in Ireland, the land of family legend. We were holed up at a large, new hotel, rather ugly after the grandeur of Italy. You know, the kind that aircrews stay at. It was out of town so it could service the nearby airport. It was convenient, adequate, and sterile. Sandy said, "There's no sense in moving. We'll be renting a car and leaving for your Aunt Mary's tomorrow."

My mother's sister, whose husband was dead, lived with her son and daughter-in-law. It was a small place halfway between Dublin and Castleblayney, Monaghan, my father's home. The farm was in the middle of many more farms with no sizable town anywhere around. But the land was beautiful, rich farmland. Aunt Mary was alone so she called my cousin over to meet us. Aunt Mary wanted to hear about Utica because she had lived there when she was young. She had gone back home to Ireland just like her mother before her. I knew the man who had been planning to marry her in America, my Aunt Kathleen's brother, Mike Prendergast. Mike played the accordion for all of Dad's dances and our Irish shows as well. He was heartbroken when Aunt Mary left, but in time he married a woman named Julia and they were happy.

Aunt Mary made tea, we had sweets, and we talked and talked. She wanted to hear about everyone. We stayed talking longer than we had planned; consequently, we had to stay in a bed and breakfast in Carrickmacross, a town just east of Castleblayney, where Jack Slevin, husband of my mother's other sister Aunt Baby, came from. Aunt Mary had no place for us anyway, so it was just as well. We stopped there to overnight because, as Sandy said, "It's getting too late to barge in on your family tonight. Let's go tomorrow morning at a more civilized hour."

When we got up, we had our first traditional Irish breakfast, as the waitress called it. It consisted of a little bit of everything—that's the best way I can describe it—juice, porridge, eggs any way, bacon, sausage, and ham, with homemade brown bread, Irish soda bread with raisins and caraway seeds, topped off with a sweet roll all washed down with tea or coffee, whatever be your habit. When we were served, Sandy commented, "What's Irish about eggs and bacon? The only thing different is there's too damned much. Who eats this much ever?"

"Sandy, lest we forget, there was a time they didn't even have a potato. I think this is the equivalent of our farmers' 'hearty breakfast,' eaten after they've been up since the crack of dawn doing chores for four or five hours."

"Well then, why don't they serve it to farmers? Why us?" asked Sandy.

"Because we can afford it," I told him.

When we went outside on this lovely summer morning, we were greeted by a parade of children all dressed up in their finest white shirts and green ties, carrying the green, white, and orange flag. It reminded me of our Irish shows back home, except for the black armbands they wore in honor of the father, brother, or uncle lost in the Troubles. I thought at that moment, Oh, God! There, but for the grace of God, go I, or any one of my siblings. I heard that at that very moment there was a Hugh Carville in H-Block, the infamous prison-block of the Maze Prison where Bobby Sands would starve to death two years later. A James Carville from Mullyash Mountain in Armagh over the border from Dad's home was on the run in Mexico because he was wanted for killing a constabulary officer. Some say he didn't do it, but it happened in his home. They were out to get him, so what kind of trial would he have got?

As we watched the children board their transport, we were told they were partaking in a demonstration being held at Black Rock that afternoon. Black Rock over on Dundalk Bay, I thought, where my dad and his brothers and sisters played on the beach as children and dug for mussels and clams in the sand. These children's towns were right on the border, a fictitious border drawn by some Englishman in 1922 leaving these families with close relations on either side, just like mine had been. As a mere lad of thirteen or fourteen, my dad had smuggled guns and important information back and forth from Armagh to Monaghan over Mullyash Mountain. It didn't split a country in two then. It took a country like England to do that. They have been doing that for years, from the time of the first Elizabeth. Weren't they proud of their motto, "Divide and Conquer"? For centuries, England had been leaving despoliation everywhere she went, never having the decency to clean up her mess when it was prudent for her to leave. What a mess she left to the United Nations back in '48 when she pulled out of Palestine. As if changing the name to Israel would solve the problem and make things any better! I was seeing this very pull-out-process taking place all around us in the Caribbean. They obviously never were potty trained! Sorry, there is no delicate way to put this.

Sandy said, "We've been looking at culture for well over three months. Now here we come to witness children speaking up for theirs."

"Well put," was all I said. As I looked at those lovely children boarding the vehicles, I thought, yes, you're right, damn right. It is your affair, for there never should have been a "North" in the first place. In the south, Protestants and

25 To the Land of Saints

Catholics had been living together for years. We loaded the car and headed for Castleblayney.

Patsy's house was easy to find. As we entered town, we took a left across from the church, drove up the hill, and took a right into Patsy's place overlooking the church. Patsy was my first cousin, daughter of my father's oldest sister Annie, and she couldn't have been more hospitable. Sandy wanted to stay in a hotel, but I couldn't refuse their hospitality. It would have been an insult.

"What a mistake that would have been," Sandy agreed. "I'm damn glad we didn't. We would never have gotten to know Ireland any other way, for Ireland is its people." If you don't live and mix with them, how are you ever going to experience such hospitable, fun-loving people? They were genuinely interested in you and your affairs, and if you happened to be fun-loving too in the bargain, so much the better. Every time we turned around, we were heading for another house party at some cousin's or aunt's.

The biggest disappointment was the old homestead Lurganmore that Dad and his sisters in America, Tess, Jo, and Flo, always talked and raved about. They were like an old southern US family stuck in the north constantly reminiscing about the antebellum plantation they had to leave, never to return because it wasn't there any more. My dad knew that it wasn't what it once was and what had taken place for he had gone back with my brothers Hugh and Gerald a few years earlier. He had seen the deterioration and devastation for himself. Patsy warned me about its condition and that of the family as well. She asked me not to bring Sandy; he didn't need to see this. I couldn't have cared less whether he saw it or not, but I didn't want to embarrass her. The Carvilles were a proud bunch, a legacy of Grandmother Mary Corrigan Carville who was a proper, proud lady. Position, status, and decorum were tantamount to respectability, which was important to them, again like the old families of the American south. I explained to Sandy and he willingly stayed home.

But as it turned out, I saw precious little. Years before, half of Lurganmore had burned to the ground, and my Uncle Hugh had never attempted to restore it. He had just moved his family into the remainder of the house still standing. Gone were the Queen Anne hunt tables, the green Connemara marble fireplaces, the music room with all its furnishings and instruments. Gone too was the room my father said was always kept locked by my grandfather and only opened to visiting guests who could play. Grandfather Ned would always have the instrument there for them. Pop said his mom used to let him in when his dad was away at a fair so he could strum and fiddle, daydreaming into the future.

Every stick of antique furniture in the house was gone as far as I could see. The small section that I was led into was a sparsely furnished room in need of a polishing. We sat around a fireplace, or what was left of one for it was nothing more than a hole in the wall. Whatever had happened to the green

Connemara marble, I asked myself. Destroyed in the fire or sold? Uncle Hugh, it seemed to me, might be suffering from early signs of dementia. My dad would have said nothing "early" about it; the dementia started when he was seventeen. His clothes were disheveled and stained. He needed a shave and probably a bath as he sat there, poor fellow, asking me questions about my dad and Aunts Tessie, Josie, and Flossy who had followed my father to America. Pop always said that what had happened to the place was Uncle Hugh. Hugh was the real reason he left Ireland. As the second son, my dad would never inherit the place. He would have worked for his brother all his life, in charge of the stables. It was already happening before he left home. He never went to the fairs with their dad as Hugh did. When he was twenty-one, he could see the writing on the wall.

When he left, Old Ned said, "If you leave, never come back." He never did, leastwise not until Old Ned was dead. The rest of the family in truth wanted my dad to come back home. They always hoped he would return and save the place. Knowing him, I'm sure he could have, but alas, he never did. He made his own Lurganmore right up Coupe Hill among the lush green hills overlooking the Mohawk Valley.

My aunt served watered-down juice and sat there saying nothing, perhaps wishing we would just leave. She was no more a conversationalist than she was a housekeeper. It was pathetic. If it hadn't been for Patsy, we would have been at a total loss for words. My cousin came in looking not much different from his father. Patsy introduced us and he ran upstairs. Seconds passed and Patsy covered by speaking to my aunt about her teacher daughter, another cousin of mine, working in Belfast. My cousin, the horse trainer, came back down and headed out the door without a word. I had nothing more to say and knew I wasn't going to see what had happened to my father's home. Patsy caught on and we made our farewell. I left that house not even remembering their names, save for my father's brother Uncle Hugh. I knew they certainly didn't know mine.

Outside we passed the old wrought-iron gates, a relic of times past when they opened to a large mansion that had now just wasted away from neglect and hard times. I couldn't begin to imagine my father's heartache over the loss when he saw it. We saw what was left of the family's horse training business when I observed my cousin with his clients, a man and his wife standing next to a beautiful, rather large horse, talking over business in the middle of the road. My cousin never even looked at us as we left.

Back in the '50s, I had seen fancy horses like this in pictures hanging on a wall in an advertising office on 34th Street in New York City. Each picture had the horse's lineage and history, including their owner's and trainer's names. There, lo and behold, was my grandfather Ned's father, Carville, Sr., Esq. 1825 in the County of Monaghan. Dad once said that as a child he remembered an Ascot winner was trained at my grandfather's stables. My grandfather supplied Greece with a boatload of horses in 1914. The boat was sunk by the

25 To the Land of Saints

Germans, and Ned lost a small fortune. He supplied horses to Belgium as well during the First World War and recouped a couple of times over. That was his way; he had the Midas touch.

We turned and waved to no one in particular, because no one was looking. Patsy couldn't get me out of there quickly enough. It was a long way to come for such a disappointment. I would have liked to peruse the site as my brothers had, as one would a ruin with a member of the family who remembered it, as my dad did, that was all. Now, as time passes, such a journey isn't likely. I never even got out to Oram, the family gravesite. Patsy saw to it that I wouldn't get back that way again. So I didn't push it.

Ironically, my cousin Patsy's husband, Jack Maquilin, worked for the same man that I had once worked for. Sir Tyrone Guthrie had a jam factory and theater school at Anna-ma-Kerrig Castle in County Monaghan, not far from Blayney. Guthrie's family had an estate just outside Blayney like my dad's family. He was a little older than my father, who remembered Guthrie going off to school in England with his uncle when Dad was still young. I sang in both of Guthrie's Stratford, Ontario, productions of Gilbert and Sullivan's *Pirates of Penzance* and *H. M. S. Pinafore*. Both shows originated at Canada's Stratford. Then we played the Phoenix Theater in New York City and went on the US tour of both shows before the troupe went off to England where they played for the Queen.

I remember one day when Sir Tony put me up on the rigging in Pinafore and the boatswain, Douglas Campbell, was doing business downstage. It was during a rehearsal, and Guthrie shouted out, "Carville, don't just hang there with your Castleblayney eyes bugging out. For Christ's sake, do something." No one in the house knew what the hell he was referring to except his assistant, Jack Meriweather, and his rather tall, regal-looking, aristocratic wife, Lady Judy, who referred to herself as an import while living in Ireland. In Guthrie's production of *Pirates* the year before, I damn near beheaded Canada's Eric House with my outstretched saber when I accidentally slipped into footlights center stage at the Phoenix Theater. And now here was my cousin Jack working as Guthrie's electrician at his theater and jam factory at Castle Anna-ma-Kerrig. Small world!

Every time we turned around on our Irish journey, we were going to a party. One to remember was Patsy's. The church organist came, a Mary Foyle, with her older sister and younger brother, and she played the piano with everyone singing and dancing, except Sandy. When I sang, she told me how well she remembered my dad. "Now there was a voice. I played for him many a time. That's where he learned his music, right down there in the church," she told me, pointing as she spoke. "Now, he was a singer. He'd sing anywhere, any time. He was a real delight. We all missed him when he left."

Every time she finished a number, no matter which one, she would break into a Scott Joplin ragtime interlude, which led her into the next number as if she were playing in a piano bar or a dance hall in the Gay '90s. She played non-stop all night like the Energizer Bunny on TV. After she left, Patsy told me how old she was. No wonder the ragtime—she was ninety-six!!

Then there was the big dinner at the house of my cousin Arthur Mallon, Patsy's brother. The dining room table was immense. It could accommodate more than twenty-five people. That night we got to meet a completely different branch of the family. They were the meat-packing Mallons, Auntie Annie, my father's oldest sister's brood.

One side trip we took was over to Black Rock, a one-time summer playground for Pop and his brothers and sisters. It was their swimming spot on the Irish Sea and also a great place for seafood. They all looked forward to the jaunt across to the sea and fought to be one of the few who got to ride in Ned's new French electric car. Usually the girls got the privilege. Old Joe or Rose Fitzgerald Kennedy must have spent time there as a child because their young ones, Joe, Jack, and Bobby, also spent some summers there in the 1930s.

On the day we were there, no demonstrations took place, but we did see signs of unrest here and there. On our way home, Frankie, Patsy's youngest, was driving. We approached the lake where Hope Castle, said to be owned by the family who owned the Hope Diamond, is situated. They were no longer living there and had the castle up for sale.

"We could cross over to the North up ahead because there's no check point, and then we could go home on the north side of the lake," remarked Frankie, proposing to give us a local busman's tour of the area. So we turned right and traveled until we reached a rather large official building. Passing it, we turned left heading toward the lake where we were stopped by the Northern constabulary. What we didn't know until Frankie passed that building was that it was a large police retention barracks.

The police pulled Frankie roughly out of the car and slammed him down over the hood, and when I say slammed, I mean slammed. It was as if we were back in America and Frankie were a black in redneck country. I was in the passenger seat searching for our passports. No one had yet approached my door. I was just sitting there, passports in hand, when I realized Sandy in the back seat was being approached by an officer from the other side of the car. The officer asked for his identification. Sandy, who had already been fumbling through his wallet, handed him a card. The man took it and read it before I had a chance to turn and give Sandy his passport.

The officer handed the card back to Sandy, saying, "Oh! Ye're from New York, are ye now? Over on a wee bit of a vacation, are ye? Well, I hope ye'll be havin' a grand time of it now."

They had searched Frankie's papers and were letting him up. They told him he could get back into the car. One officer said, "Ye better get over on your own side taday, and stay there. A gentleman from the RUC was shot this mornin' outside this very banacks."

Someone then slapped the car, indicating we could go. Frankie sped off

25 To the Land of Saints

down through Crossmaglen and back around the lake. "I had the passports. What the hell did you show him, Sandy?" I asked.

"I don't know. I was so nervous I gave him the first card I could grab out of the stack in my wallet. Here, it was this one," Sandy said handing it over to me in the front seat.

"My God!" I exclaimed. "Sandy, this is your Bloomingdale's charge card."

Frankie laughed. "Whatever works!"

"Does this happen often?" I asked. "More than I care to tell you." He continued, "You see, the IRA steal cars on the free side, then go over to the North to make a hit, and then they abandon the car. This way they cannot be traced, and we who are living on both sides are caught in the middle."

I noticed the green, white, and orange flying everywhere, as if celebrating some holiday. "If we're still in the North, why are most of the houses flying the Free State flag?"

"Because they're all Catholics," Frankie said. "Some Englishman made a big mistake back in 1922 when he was scribbling that fictitious border line around here." Crossmaglen was a hotbed of terror for years. Just a little dash of a line over the town on the map in 1922 would have saved a lot of lives, bloodshed, and years of heartache.

We took another trip when we were up there, to Belfast to search for Pat Turner. She had come to Bequia for a couple of years to teach English. I had promised her we would look her up and come to see her in Ireland if ever we got around to making the trip. Well, there we were crossing the border, against everyone's better judgment. Our Belfast teaching cousin told Patsy that things were a little dicey at present, bombs going off indiscriminately here and there. I told Patsy that I had been in hot spots before. "Fine for you, but what about Sandy?" she replied.

Sandy brushed away her concern with, "My resume just might surprise you, Patsy."

And off we went. We didn't have an address, but I knew her father was principal of a Belfast public school. So our plan of action was to track him down through the Belfast Board of Education. We merely had to find Belfast and then the Board of Education building, obtain from them his address, and, through him, get Patricia's address. Now how difficult could that be?

We reached the center of Belfast after driving by the shipyards. We could see the huge steel scaffolding towering over the yards. Looking at all this industry, I could see what made Northern Ireland so important to the world but mostly to England, the beneficiary and the benefactress of all this. I thought of the *Lusitania*, the *Titanic*, all the Queens, and all those Conrad ships. Oh! All that money. Why in the world would she hand it over to the true Ireland, even though it was built on the backs of Irishmen? She was always building on the backs of someone else. I believe she fostered the religious difference to suit her own self-interest. Why wasn't there that problem in the Irish Free State? I didn't see it, if it was there. However it happened, England was now in another mess, a quagmire, and there was no foreseeable way out.

The center of town, where most of the government buildings were, was inaccessible. All the streets were cordoned off and no traffic was being allowed in; it was being routed away. Not knowing what to do, we kept on driving until we passed a school where children were being released for lunch. I called one over. He was about twelve years old and came over to the car with his two buddies. I asked if he knew where the Board of Education building was. He did. "You go down this street to the red light." He turned to his friend and asked, "How far would ye say 'tis, Jack?"

"I doon' know."

Turning to me, he said, "'Tis not far. We can show ye," he suggested.

I looked at Sandy and he just looked back, so I said, "Sure, come on, hop in."

Turning to the other two, the boy said, "Come on, let's we take a jaunt and show de gentlemen."

They piled into the back, tickled to be getting a little ride in a car. They hung over the back of our seat full of the piss and vinegar of youth, all three simultaneously directing us to our destination. After a few twists and turns, one finally directed, "No, back up, and now dis way down der."

Thank God it wasn't too far away. I thanked the boys as they jumped out, and one said, "Nuthin'," waving his hand and then said, "Pull in dat lot over der," pointing across the street. Then they all waved and were on their way.

Many empty lots blighted the landscape here and there; it looked like a bombed-out war zone. We had been told no one left a car unattended anywhere in Northern Ireland for fear of its being hijacked and used in a hit by either side. The parking lot attendant directed me to a spot. After I had parked, I turned to Sandy and asked, "Staying?" and he replied, "Staying."

As I got out of the car, the attendant approached, his AK-40, I think, slung over his shoulder. "Good day ta ye and where would ye be goin'?" he asked.

I told him and he continued, "Sorry for the intrusion, but what would be the purpose of your visit?" I told him. And he explained, "Ye can't be too careful around here these days and me not knowin' ye and all. I'm sure ye'll be understandin' my position and all."

"Yeah, sure, sure..."

"What about the other gentleman?"

"He's staying in the car." And I made tracks for the building.

When I explained who I was and who I was looking for and why, they found Pat's father's school and called it. He was on his way home so they gave me his address and said it wasn't far out the Quay road and along the bay to the north of the city.

When I got back into the car, Sandy asked me, "What is 'tweakin'?"

"'Tweakin'?" I repeated.

"'Tweakin,'" Sandy reiterated. "'Tweakin'', in Irish, what is that?"

"What...? I don't know," I told him.

"Well, that watchman came over and asked a barrage of questions."

"I know," I said. "He has nothing else to do but ask questions."

"Yeah, but," Sandy went on, "he asked me if I heard the tweakin' this morning, and I didn't know what on earth he was talking about."

Tweakin', I thought, tweaking this morning. "Oh! I know what he was saying. He was asking you if you heard the bombs, the explosions going off this morning. That must be why we couldn't get through those streets leading to the government district."

"Bombs," said Sandy. "Explosions. But 'tweakin'?"

"You see, Sandy," I went on, adding my two cents, "they've had to live with this, day in and day out, why, for years now. That's why he was making light of things. I'm sure they all do it; otherwise they would have all gone mad by now."

We had no trouble finding the house alongside the Quay. Mrs. Turner answered the doorbell and seemed pleasantly surprised to see us. We had met when she and her husband had made the trip to Bequia to visit Pat.

"How did you find us?" she asked. I explained how I'd gone to the Board of Education. "I'm surprised," she said, "that they would give it out just like that these days. Normally, they don't. You were lucky to find me home. Usually I would be working. I work in the government finance offices, but we had a bombing this morning so they let us off early today."

I looked over at Sandy to acknowledge the parking attendant's "tweakin'" and Sandy gravely shook his head. She noticed and said, "Oh, this is usual. We were still sweeping the glass from last week's bombing."

Shortly afterward, Mr. Turner came in and was also surprised. We explained we had actually come by to find out where Patricia was, because we would like to pay her a visit.

They got Pat on the phone. She told me she had married a Welshman she'd met while teaching in Wales. They were now teaching in the same school in the country northwest of Belfast. She insisted we come out for dinner. "Yes, I can't wait to see you both!"

"I'll get directions from your dad," I told her. Right after luncheon with the Turners, we left for points northwest.

The next stop on our sojourn through Ireland was "Mayo-God-help-us." Now that expression had to date back to 1848 or thereabout, from the time of the famine. A lot of that county wasn't only back and beyond, but the farmers there were primarily simple farmers. When I say "simple," I mean they farmed pitifully small farms. They were hit badly by the potato blight and what else was there? It must have been devastating.

Mayo is where my mom's family hailed from. Mom remembers when she was small the stories told by her old aunts from way back in the hills. There they drank "poteen" (pronounced puh-cheen), potato moonshine whiskey, behind Croagh Patrick. On top of the holy mountain was a shrine to the place where St. Patrick fasted for forty days. My Aunt Ann remembered crawling up a good part of it on her hands and knees, which was the custom. It was a badge of honor she carried with her for years. My mom spoke of the tales recounted to her of little girls digging for roots for a boilleen to subsist on while surviving through that blight with no help from anyone, be it local government or national or foreign. I assume it was much like Africa today.

That very experience made my grandmother Mariah save her tuppence and ha'pennies in order to get to the golden land of promise one day. Some in 1888 really believed the streets were paved in gold. She was a sweet young girl of eighteen who didn't know a soul in the New Country. For a single working girl, America was no bed of roses. She boarded an employment boat going up the Hudson and crossing the state on the Erie Canal. When she reached Utica, she was picked out of the workforce by a couple who had a farm in Kirkland, New York. She worked for them for as long as she could stand it.

One day, when the mistress and her man were making the long arduous trip into Utica in the wagon for their monthly supplies, she got permission to go along to get provisions for herself. Late that afternoon when it was time to return home, Mariah hid herself under the hay back behind the horses in the stable. After a long search, they couldn't find her. Finally, they couldn't linger any longer and still make it all the way out to Kirkland in the buggy before nightfall. So they left Utica without her.

Mariah then got a job in the cotton mills of Utica, dreaming of the day she would return home like Kathleen in the song, "I'll take you home again, Kathleen, to where your heart will feel no pain." The dream wasn't to materialize until she managed to save enough to bring three of her half-sisters over, the Jennings girls who were waiting to follow her. Once all three of her sisters were in Utica, she told them she didn't find America a land of milk and honey. She then had to muster up enough by the sweat of her brow for her fare back home all alone... So she went back to the Old Country and the home she loved. It didn't take her long to find my grandfather, Pat Devaney, and raise their family of nine in Shannagh, Turlough County, Mayo.

And that is where Sandy and I were headed. But before we made a beeline for Castlebar, we headed northwest to Donegal. My cousin Arthur Mallon had a friend, Mary Fay, who owned a hotel up there. The hotel sat near the craggy, windswept shore that had been battered by the wicked North Atlantic since the beginning of time, like in Messini on the Peloponnesian Peninsula only with more ferocity.

What an experience it was to encounter such hospitality. At an authentic Celtic caeli (a feis, a festival of dance, pronounced "fesh"), we danced until the wee hours, at least I did. They sang and I sang. They danced and I danced and danced. About midnight, Sandy leaned over to me. "Do they ever go to bed? It's a Sunday night! Don't they have to be up in the morning? Do they ever sleep?"

We were so close to the Arctic Circle, it was still daylight at 10 PM. Many of the people didn't bother to speak English at all. All the locals could speak the Gaelic. When Sandy heard it for the first time, he asked, "What is that?"

"That's Gaelic, our ancient language," I replied.

"Oh, listen to you! 'Our ancient language.' Well, speak it then."

So I did. "In ainm an Athar, agus a Mhic, agus an Spioraid Naomh,"

"What are you saying?" he asked.

"I'm just blessing myself," I said.

"Well, thank God you still can," he quipped. "My God, they still speak it."

"My mom and dad both learned their catechism in Gaelic."

"It sounds like Hebrew!" Sandy exclaimed.

"It's almost as old, if not older. And they still sing it and dance to its music and live it. Yes, Sandy, it is still very much alive and well," I went on, "at least here in this section of the country anyway. You know, the English will never wipe this out, time maybe, but never the English. For culture is something so organic it never should be wiped out any way anywhere or any how... Change, I accept that, but culture never should be forced out of existence."

At that point, Sandy said, "You're raving again. Come on, let's get back to our room and get some shut-eye."

We did have a grand time there, and when we left, Mary wouldn't accept payment. I said, "A whole weekend, and she won't take a dime, Sandy."

"A whole weekend, we don't even know her, we have never seen her before, and she won't even take a dime?! We must..."

So Sandy tried, and Mary told him, "To me, Arthur is family and Arthur is Jimmy's cousin. Now how can I take money from family? That would be bad luck! I don't need a curse around here." She added. "Next time at your place, OK?"

"OK." What else could he say or do?

We drove down through Sligo, the county of my Uncle Jerry, the Irish patriot of the old IRA. He was one of the decorated heroes of 1917. He was a bright man who had left the seminary to fight for Ireland. He would always say, "I'm from Sligo, Yeats country," and he would start reciting him. If there were ever a toast to be made, he would quote Yeats.

"What about Sean O'Casey?" Sandy asked me.

"How should I know? I guess he recited him, too."

We were now in Mayo, and Sandy said, "My, this sure is a small country, and more than 44 million in America alone. God knows how many everywhere else. Where did they all come from? They're everywhere, all over the place like hor—"

"All right, hold it," I interrupted.

"Like Holy Land Jews, I was going to say," Sandy recovered.

"Sure you were," I retorted. "But you know, Sandy, it has been said that Ireland did export people to a fault, and what it caused was a brain drain."

"A brain drain, what's that? It sounds like a disease," he quipped.

"Ha-ha-ha. It's a disease I wouldn't want."

"Don't worry, Jimmy, don't worry," Sandy said. "Not a chance... But where do they all come from?"

"Not from around here," I said. "No, sir, not from around here. There isn't a soul in sight, yet we can't be that far from Castlebar... Look! Look!" I slowed the car and pointed to a sign. We were in the middle of nowhere, no houses and no sign of life. Yet the sign indicated a little road leading off to the left and announced "Church of Ireland Turlough."

"So?" asked Sandy.

"This is my mother's area, Turlough. Shannagh, Turlough. The place is around here, Sandy."

"I don't see any Turlough around here and I don't see any Shannagh around here either. Let's get on into Castlebar and find a hotel. It's getting late."

So I started down the road again and a little farther on was a farmhouse on the right with a few cows grazing in the pasture just beyond. And then I saw it! It was an early Norman round tower the likes of which you find all around Ireland. They served as shelters from the invaders from the northern countries when they were built by the Normans. There it was! My uncle Pat talked about it all the time. It was just up the hill behind the cow pasture.

Sandy pleaded, "Jimmy, there's nothing around. There are no people, no village."

"Look," I said. "There's a road ahead on the right going up that hill." Saying no more, I turned in and drove up that hill to the top. There the road went straight ahead, but on the right was a narrow macadam road leading to the Norman tower. I stopped the car in front of the tower and we both got out and walked over to it. It was about 8:30 PM, not dark yet, but it was clouding over and beginning to sprinkle.

At the base of the tower stretched an ancient cemetery all cordoned off by a wrought-iron fence. We walked over to the large wrought-iron gate and shoved it open. We walked along the paths looking at the head stones. Sandy said, "Look—Devaney."

"Mary, Patrick, and Mariah, my granddad, grandmother, and his mom Mary my great-grandmother. This must be them. Mariah was my grandmother. This is the place, it has to be."

Sandy said, "Look, there's nothing or nobody around, so let's get to a hotel. It's drizzling."

We got back into the car, but I kept driving straight ahead. I truly felt Shannagh must be just a little farther down the road. A little way along, we passed a road on our left. Out of the corner of my eye, I saw a man in high rubber boots jaywalking across that road. I stopped and reversed into the road. The man was obviously a local farmer. He walked over and asked, "Lads, are ye lost?"

"We're looking for Shannagh," I said.

"Ye were heading straight for it down that road. Ye're Yanks, are ye now? And who would ye be lookin' for?" I told him we were looking for the Devaney place. "Oh, I worked with Martin in London," he said.

"He was killed by a lorry there," I told him.

25 To the Land of Saints

"Tragedy that, and the missis with all them childer," he sighed. "Ah, that was a number of years ago... Look, ye could go the back way. It would be much easier. Just turn yourself around and take the first road to the right. That will take ye right to the Devaney place at the bottom of the hill." He then continued along the road leading to Shannagh.

I turned the car around and took the first turn to the right. Still we saw no houses, but we kept going until we went down a short, steep hill. Then, out of nowhere appeared about ten little houses all in a row, just back a ways off the road. So I drove slowly down past them, and where the road veered to the right over a small bridge, I stopped. "Look, Sandy, that's Mickey Boyle's lake off to the left way over there."

"How do you know that?" Sandy asked.

"Because my mom has spoken of it and of Biddle who lived there. Mom remembers her being a bit simple. When she did something wrong, old Mickey would say, 'Lift your oxter, Biddle,' and she would lift up her arm and he would give her a clout with his fist under her armpit."

"Why?" asked Sandy.

"Who knew why? Maybe he felt the blow wouldn't leave any telltale signs. Mom said he wasn't quite all there either. I have to turn around. We passed the house," I said. I turned the car around, pulled up in front of a house on the right, and stopped.

"Now what are you going to do?" Sandy asked.

"Sandy, it has to be one of these houses," I said as I sat there calculating. "Look, there's still the same old cobblestone barn."

"Jimmy, it's too damn dark and it's too damn wet and worse yet, it's too damn late to be barging in on anyone who isn't expecting you. Come on, for the last time, let's go," Sandy said impatiently.

As Sandy spoke, a man crossed the road just up ahead walking toward a house. I started up the car and pulled up into his driveway. He came over. "Can I help?"

"Yes, please," I said. "We're looking for the Devaney place."

"Well, you were just parked out there in front of it. Now which one ner oo?" he asked.

"I'm Nora's boy."

"Ogh," he said, "de ginger one. She used to look after me when I was a wee bit of a lad." Later Mom told me he was one of the Welches. I thanked him and backed down to the house.

I looked at the old stone barn standing out next to the road and said to myself, that's the old barn all right. I jumped out of the car without a word. I was too excited to be thinking of Sandy. I just ran up to the house in the rain and knocked, but there was no answer. I knocked again and still no answer, yet I could hear a television blasting somewhere in the back of the house. One more stronger knock and I gave up and went back to the car thinking maybe Sandy was right. They're probably just a little leery about answering the door on such a dark rainy night, which it was by now. And yet maybe they hadn't heard the knock over that loud television. Either way, Sandy knew best, so we had better come back in the morning.

I ran back to the car and explained to Sandy who said, "Come on, let's get out of here and into a hotel." The rain was pelting down now.

"We can come back in the morning," I agreed.

Sandy in Ireland

Castlebar was only seven miles away, I knew because Mom had told me. I was in such good spirits that night on the ride into town, I started singing, "On the Road to Castlebar," that's right, "in my 'ould'-sided car." We were both having fun, I because for some reason I felt I was home, on familiar ground, and Sandy because he enjoyed seeing me this way, a far cry from how I had felt on Bequia. Sandy asked, "Are you making that up?"

"No. Pop was forever singing it when he sat behind the wheel of his car, ha-ha-ha."

Sandy sat there shaking his head. "Back there, you know, that was uncanny. You drove right up to the house, the one house in all of Ireland that your family lived in for most of a 100 years, as if someone were leading you home."

"Maybe they were," I said. "Just maybe."

It was getting pretty late and in my excitement I had completely forgotten about dinner. We found a hotel and of course we had missed dinner. But after we checked in, we were directed to a charming little pub where there was still some activity, thanks to the many late-night people in Ireland. Or was it because the days of summer were so long? In any case, we had some ham and eggs.

The following morning we contacted my aunt, Marty's widow, for she was now living here in town. Her son, my cousin Jack, and his wife and their two children were living in the old house. Well, not the exact same old house. The old thatch-roofed, white-washed cobblestone, earthen-floored cottage consisting of one room with sleeping alcoves on either side and a fireplace at either end was gone now. One end had been used for living and the other end for cooking. A half-door had opened to where the chickens, ducks, and all the other smaller animals were kept in a shed. Across the road was the big old cobblestone barn for hay, a donkey, a cart, and maybe a big fat pig in better times. Nothing but an empty shell of a barn remained. Alas, that cottage of yesteryear, that beautiful relic of the past, was gone. The thatched roof that my mother and her siblings had to keep in good condition to ward off the cold, heavy rains of winter was gone. The many trips in the donkey cart to the peat bogs to cut turf to warm up the cottage in the hearths at either end of the house were no more. All this activity was now lost in time, nothing more than a memory.

The legacy of our past had been passed down in memories like my mother's of her childhood. One memory described how she and her sister Baby were heading home with the donkey cart full of turf. Storm clouds were gathering and it was getting darker by the minute. It began to sprinkle. Thunder and lightning started off in the distance and began to approach closer and closer. As they were crossing a little brook, the two-wheeled cart stuck. Baby urged the animal on with a crack of the whip. The donkey desperately pulled. The cart, nothing more than a trap or a sulky, lurched forward unhitching the whiffletree from the donkey's harness. The two girls were pitched forward into the creek with chunks of turf piling down on top of them and Baby screaming out to the high heavens, "My God, Jesus, Mary, and Joseph and all the saints in heaven, preserve us. We've been struck!!" But the two of them sitting there in the shallow water, caked in mud and covered in turf, laughed and laughed.

The story of the unanswered knock was explained to us the next morning. Jack, my cousin, the father of the family, was away on an inter-county pub-dart competition. He was one of Mayo's champs. As Sandy put it, "That's what comes of hanging out in pubs too much. It shouldn't be a total loss." Jack's wife had gone into town to visit her brother-in-law Jim and didn't expect to be back till late, leaving orders that the kids were not to answer the door to anyone. That's why I as "anyone" had been left on the rainy doorstep in front of the existing house. The house had been built just behind the site of the old cottage just after World War II, before my grandmother Mariah died in 1954. The young boy in the house watching television that night went on to become one of Ireland's outstanding television writers and teachers, with books on the subject to his credit.

The next morning they took us up the hill behind the bush to the gap where my grandfather eked out a meager living for his brood on a tiny, barren, rocky strip of hillside not much bigger than half a city block. We went over to Knock, the shrine of St. Bridge (Brigitte).

When I pray, no matter where, I always pray especially for my sister Joan, and I had since added Sandy. I never prayed for myself. I always found it hard to do. The act of praying for oneself always felt a little self-centered, a bit selfish, and I found it rather presumptuous of me. It was hard for me to ask for help from anyone. I think I am a realist and a fatalist and I've learned to accept whatever God doles out and devil take the hindmost. In other words I live life believing in doing your best day by day and helping others, leaving the rest up to the Almighty. I got that from my mother. She was a realist. My dad, he was something else, he was a dreamer.

One morning Sandy and I were in Galway before taking off for the Ring of Kerry. It was ten o'clock with no sign of the bank's opening. I wondered whether it was an Irish holiday, so I asked a bobby I saw standing nearby. "Oh! Na, sir, not at-tall. There was a big shindig last night," he explained. "Dey'U be along in a gibbet."

"Oh, my God! We're back on Bequia!" I exclaimed. "They have a recovery day here as well."

The lakes and the many shades of green around the Ring of Kerry were beautiful. We then turned south to Kinsale where an English couple, Fred and Mary, friends of ours from Bequia, owned the hotel and lived in a lovely house overlooking the quay and the sea. Not far off-coast lay the remains of the *Lusitania*, sunk by the Germans in World War I. We talked of Bequia and the ways of the Irish and found many similar traits. Mary told of ordering a rug from Cork for the hotel. When it arrived, it was the wrong color and didn't match a thing. When she told the men they would have to take it back, they said they couldn't guarantee the right colors right away. They suggested they put this one down and she could make do until the correct one arrived. She insisted that she didn't want that color, and they assured her they would replace it. Believe it or not, six months later they came with the new rug in the correct color, put it down, and left with the now old, walked-on rug, apologizing for the delay.

I asked, "What would they do with the one they took back?"

"Don't know," Mary answered. "All I know is I wasn't charged for the use of it."

"How can they do business that way?" I asked.

Jack answered, "Beats de 'el out of me." It was a pleasant stay, and we left looking forward to seeing them on their next holiday.

In Cork at Blarney Castle after I kissed the Blarney Stone, I asked Sandy if he was going to kiss it. "Not on your life. It will be a cold day in hell before I do a thing like that," Sandy responded. "You know that the yahoos from around here—the blokes, the local yokels in the neighborhood—come up here at night and piss all over that stone, and guys like you come up in the morning and kiss it. I don't know why you Irish feel you need a Blarney Stone in the first place. You all have the gift of gab and you're all full of it... Blarney, that is, I mean blarney."

Next we were in Dublin at the old Shelbourne Hotel, chock-full of history, across from St. Stephen's Green. It wasn't much of a hotel, but the ambiance was right out of the past. Then there was O'Connell Street and I said, "You remember The Plough and the Stars?"

"Yes, of course I do, dummy. You think I only read Chekhov?" was his snippy reply.

The museum I swear had artifacts dug up in western Ireland that date back to Messini in ancient Greece by way of the Phoenicians. They were those gold leaf burial eye patches. But it's just a theory of mine. From the hotel it was just a hop, skip, and a jump to all those wonderful Georgian homes with all their famous doors. We enjoyed our visit to the legendary Abbey Theatre, with its long list of international stars. It was at the Abbey our friend, director John O'Shaughnessy, had studied and worked as a young man. Then there was Oscar Wilde's house, soon to become the flagship of the American college founded by my cousin, Donald Ross, and my kid brother, Gerald Carville, president and dean respectively of Lynn University in Boca Raton, Florida. On top of everything were the people and all my relations in and around Dublin and more parties.

Some came halfway across the island—sorry, the country—to attend the party Bernadette held for us. She was a cousin who came to America and hit it off with my mother as Sandy had. She couldn't do enough for us. Maura Brennan O'Malley, one of my cousins whom I had met in New York with her husband when he had worked as a doctor in Connecticut many years earlier, came a long way just to attend the gathering.

When it was all over and we were home, every time Sandy was asked, "What did you think of Ireland?" Sandy would answer, "You have never experienced such hospitality everywhere from everyone and especially Jimmy's relations, all 3,000."

26 For the Record

July 1979: The Big 5-0

When we hit New York, we made tracks for Utica. I couldn't wait to talk to Mom and Pop about our trip to Ireland and our encounter with the Pope thanks to Eddy and Jane. As luck would have it, my 50th birthday was just around the corner. My family planned a gathering out on the farm up on the hill and around by the creek below the small harness-racing track Pop had built. Pop's sister Auntie Jo and our IRA hero from Eamon de Valera's time, Uncle Jerry from County Sligo, came. My godparents, their son Joe, and his wife Nancy were invited. Mom was like Joe's second mother for he grew up with us, and our families were intertwined. Joe's father, my mother's brother, my godfather and uncle, was my father's best friend. When the two had come to America in 1922, they roomed at O'Hara's boarding house over in East Utica near the old Forest Park Amusement Center, a turn-of-the-century amusement park with a Ferris wheel, bumper cars, other rides, and a midway full of games of chance. From here they took the trolley all the way in on the Broad Street Line to work at the Savage Arms Rifle Factory.

One night back in '23, "me boyos," nothing more than a couple of young skins, took off and headed for Mrs. Hankinson's up on Capital Avenue knowing that all the newly arrived Irish girls would be there. When my mother from Mayo and Kate from County Cork with the girls from Mrs. Proctor's walked in, my mother spotted my dad across the room. He was a sight the likes of which she had never seen. She turned to the girls and said, "I'm going to marry that one." And the rest is history—mine as well as ten others.

More than fifty years later, Aunt Kathleen sat out in the back next to the driveway with her arms and legs crossed and a sweater over her shoulders even though it was a sweltering 28th of July. My sister Joan, Ed's Jane, and Mary Malloy sat next to her enjoying the proceedings. Mary, from County Sligo, was an old friend of my parents whose husband had died years before. She was eagerly anticipating my stories of Ireland. Marlene and Barbara were spreading out the many, much too many, bowls of salads—you name it: egg, tuna, potato, macaroni, and Mandy's new concoction. There Mandy was, directing the layout of the spread with the other two not paying her too much mind. At the far end of the table were Diane and one of hers, Karen or Kelly, with hot lasagna and a mess of Italian meatballs. She was speaking out to someone, I think it was to Tom her husband, but he was busy talking to Sandy with Fred. Leo sat there just listening.

Mom was down at the dammed-up creek with the little ones, each with their tiny fishing rod. Now and again, when they weren't looking, she would hook on a fish or two that she got out of a small Styrofoam cooler. Then they would run back toward the house yelling "Mommy, Mommy, see what I caught!"

TP, Gary, and Dickie John, football in hand, were over on the other side of the house down in the side field challenging Hughie. The smaller boys—Bobby, Bryan, Johnny, Timmy, and little Tommy—were all on Hughie's side. Uncle Pat got a big kick out of the Round Towers story as did Uncle Jerry. Aunt Kathleen asked, "Now, Jimmy, how did you manage that? Walking right up to the door like that, I mean."

Uncle Pat said, "On his own two feet, Kate. How in the world do you think he did it?... Can you imagine that?" That was his brand of humor, but she paid him no mind.

"Kate," I said, "it was like I was just drawn there."

"Jesus-Mary-and-Joseph," sighed Auntie Jo.

Kathleen said, "It's the spirits, Jimmy. God works his wonders..." And Pat just laughed that laugh of his.

Pop took out Black Beauty, hitched her to the sulky, and drove her over to the miniature racetrack for Eric, Lisa, and all the others who happened to be equestrian-inclined.

Cousins

There were girls, girls, and girls huddled here and there, sitting in the clover discussing things over, whatever cousins dare. No matter the rank and file, 'twas hesitation in their guile for it had been quite a while.

The revealing and the dealing sends them a-reeling and a-wheeling, ending up in swirl, swirl, swirl.

There were Leo's and Tom's with Ed's, Mandy's with Hugh's and Fred's, giggling here and laughing there and for whatever reason, a bonnie broad smile.

Joe and his wife Nancy had quite a talk with me about Rome and the Pope. They were impressed with the connections of Ed, an Irishman, and Jane in the Polish Catholic community.

Later in the day, Hugh's Gerry and Mom came out carrying a huge decorated birthday cake, with Gerry's Joan and Fred's Beth carrying plates, napkins, and forks. I looked at Hughie and asked, "Bahzon's Bakery?"

"No, Gerr's," he said, "and I didn't even help her this time."

Gerry chimed in saying, "Sure, you better believe it," with a big broad smile of her own.

I hugged and kissed Mom and became officially fifty. It was the big half-century mark, and I felt good, damned good. Sandy shot me a thumbs-up, and Pop shook my hand with a big hug. What more could one want or ever need? Oh, of course, they all sang "Happy Birthday." Pop also sang "Fifty Years Ago

Today I Left Old Erin's Isle" and "Phil the Fluthers Ball." Leo sang my song, "Danny Boy," as he always does, but I do add he did it very well. Beth's girl Kathy did a high-stepping reel. Fergy, a neighbor friend of Pop's from down the road, sang "When Irish Eyes..." Then the girls—Chrissie, Beth, Denise, and Janis—did their four-hand reel. After that, Eric and Janis executed a two-hand reel. Mandy and I stumbled through our old jig from the '40s. When we had finished, she said to me, "We have to stop this." I agreed it was about time. Eric then did his high-stepping jig, which I had taught him when he was about four. On second thought, he picked it up himself just watching me. I finished with a standard of mine and an old favorite of Mom's, "The Rose of Tralee."

Mary Malloy said, "All that's missing are a couple of square sets. It's not quite like the old days without them. Where's Mike with his squeeze box?" We would have stepped off doing a couple of Irish square sets if Uncle Mike had been there with his boxeen, his Irish button accordion.

Uncle Jerry said, "Things are always changing. It's a constant struggle to hang on to tradition."

Sandy said, "Tradition? You Carvilles have it all over the Jews when it comes to tradition."

One could say: A good time was had by all.

Artifacts Conjuring Up Korea

Much later that night, as we were settling in upstairs, Sandy said, "Every time I come up here to Utica, I learn something new about you. This evening your mother gave me this. It must have meant a great deal to her because she's kept it all these years. And yet today she gave it to me." He handed me a piece of aging yellow paper neatly folded up.

I knew instantly what it was. A feeling of pain engulfed me similar to what I felt when I had to write that letter. It was a letter no mother looked for nor wished to receive, yet twenty-nine years earlier, while I was deployed in Japan before the Korean War (correction, Police Action) ever began, I was forced through circumstances to sit down and write it.

A Letter To Mom

Tokyo, Japan 7th July, 1950
Dear Mom,
I think I have stalled long enough before answering your last letter. I wanted to have something definite to tell you before I wrote. So much has happened since then that everyone over here has been going around in circles.

You didn't answer some of the questions in my last letter, but it makes no difference now as so much has happened to alter my plans for the future that

I will not need the answers for some time. I had planned to leave Japan the 26th of July for discharge upon arrival in the U.S. All this was very well and good, and perhaps still might be except for a little incident that happened approximately 10:30 on the 3rd of July. I will try to relay to you the dramatic details as I remember them, surprisingly, since it all happened so fast.

Before I go on, please don't hold my decision against me. I made it myself and I am as yet not sorry. Pfc. Dilks, a buddy of mine who worked in the same office as I did, was on duty in the main Translator and Interpreter Service (TIS) headquarters office; he was on for the whole day. The Executive Commander of the outfit, a Col. Adams, called Maj. Perry, our boss, at his home and told him he needed a typist with a Top Secret Clearance in a hurry. Major Perry recommended me. Col. Adams then told Pfc. Dilks to get me down to the office right away.

When I got there, the Colonel told me to go to the conference room and he would be right in. In the meantime a draftsman came in, a young Nisei boy (Japanese-American, second generation). Col. Adams came in with a Captain and told us that this morning General Church's outfit in Seoul, Korea, had notified G-2, Army Intelligence here in Tokyo, that they needed a draftsman and a typist with G-2 clearance, and, he said in no uncertain terms, the Nisei and I were the chosen two. There was nothing we could say or do. We were to get our medical clearances, and go get all our needed shots, take out life insurance, if desired, and be packed and ready to leave for Korea by 4 AM the next morning.

I went to the dispensary and had my medical. I might add that when the nurse took my blood pressure, the needle in the glass case was moving so fast she couldn't record it. She said I was too excited. When she saw my medical reports, she said, "Nothing like going to Korea to heal up an ulcer." I had been discharged from the hospital on June 10th and sent back to my outfit on "limited duty." I had gone back for a check-up on July 2nd whereupon they had told me it was almost healed completely. I might tell you, it didn't feel so by the 4th. I had four booster shots for tetanus, cholera, typhus, and Jap-B as well as vaccine. You can imagine how I felt on the 4th. I then [July 3] went to see the chaplain. I wanted to have a talk with him before I left.

When I got back to the NYK building, the sergeant in the personnel office said I was wanted in Col. Stark's office, the CO of TIS. When I walked in all the bigwigs were there, standing around the desk. I would give anything to have had a picture of myself at that moment. I must have been as white as a sheet, and my stomach felt like a mix master. There was Col. Adams, Col. Kenny, and my boss Maj. Perry. Col. Adams did all the talking. "Carville," he said, "Major Perry informs me that you are already on orders to go home shortly. Because of this, we cannot force you to go to Korea. We have to leave it up to you to decide whether to go or to stay and leave for home and discharge on the 26th as planned." He went on to explain that the President was waiting for the UN, and hadn't made a declaration of war against North Korea as yet.

Well, they had me over a barrel. I had just finished reading in the paper that the government was making provisions for the men serving in Korea to receive benefits under the G-I Bill. That is one thing I would like very much to get in on. It wasn't like I was going to the front lines—I knew that General Church's outfit was way down south in Seoul. If the conflict lasted for a short time, I could get out on a medical and get the G-I Bill benefits. If it didn't cease shortly, I might just as well stay in a good outfit and make a few good points for myself for promotion. Over there in Korea, promotions will not be frozen like they are here because we're so top-heavy. Also, if I were to go home and be inducted again, God only knows where I would end up. Last, but not least, this is a religious war as well as a political one.

What with all these thoughts going through my head, I couldn't decide right then and there, and I knew it. So Col. Adams said I should check with personnel as to what kind of extensions I could make, and whatever I decided, to come back and tell them. The shortest extension was a year. After some reflection in my room, I went back and told them that I had decided to extend for a year and go to Korea— "Go to Korea as requested."

My Major said it was a wise choice, but, of course, he would say that. Later that day I found out that Col. Stark had given me excellent efficiency and excellent character ratings for my service record, which is quite rare for TIS. The next day I had to rush over to the enlistment office and re-enlist for another year so I could be sent to Korea. Finding the enlistment officer wasn't easy on the 4th of July. The office was closed as it always is on Independence Day, but they eventually found the officer at the Miji Park celebrations and he came in to do his job with a 'Who-the-hell-are-you-that-you-have-to-enlist-on-the-4th?'

"I'll be damned if I know," I answered. Well, I am ready to leave now and have been since the 4th. You know the old saying—hurry up and wait. They tell me there is a big backlog at Tachikawa Air Field waiting to go over in C-54s. We expected to leave about Monday. Since then, four officers and seven enlisted men, all of whom are linguists, have also been alerted.

Mom, I have just been interrupted. It is now about 10 PM. I was on duty in the Colonel's office and have just been told to report to Captain Potter. We are leaving tonight. May God bless you all, and say a few prayers for me. Mom, please don't worry, I'll be all right.

Love, Jimmie

An afterthought not sent with the letter, but which I now explained to Sandy: I later found out why they didn't just replace me with someone else. Major Perry had picked my name by mistake; he didn't know at first I was already on orders to go home and be discharged. Since General Church had asked General MacArthur during a conversation between the two for a draftsman and a typist with G-2 clearance, among others, General Mac had signed the orders for us himself. I think I wasn't simply replaced because of

26 For the Record

MacArthur's involvement: it would have meant having to acknowledge an embarrassing error at a very crucial moment. Consequently, I was probably one of the very first groups ordered by the old man at the onset of the conflict.

We hadn't been sent right away because everything was happening so fast in Korea that contact with General Church in Seoul had been cut off. Due to the change in plans, I was now sent to the front lines in Taejon, Korea, to set up a correspondence and file system for the interrogation reports for the advance outfit until it could be built up. The unit consisted of a colonel, a captain, two lieutenants, seven enlisted translators, and yours truly, a lowly Pfc. I was sent "TDY," temporary duty, with the Advanced Allied Translator and Interpreter Service because I was already on orders signed by the old man himself to go to Korea. I later worked as secretary to General Dean, a West Point linguist who had been stationed in Okinawa. He was flown in to take over command of the Advanced Allied Translator and Interpreter Service in Korea.

A sidelight: General Church and his men of the headquarters office of the Korean Military Advisory Group in Seoul, where I was to be sent on the 4th of July, were all annihilated. We were informed of their fate when we reached Taejon, Korea, with the 24th Division. Here, the 24th was pretty much slaughtered too, and General Dean, Commander of the 24th Division, was captured while leading a Tank Division in a delaying action fighting for time to evacuate the airfield and retreat. He was the first American general ever taken prisoner by a foreign country. It happened the very day our little unit from TIS left Taejon in three jeeps with a footlocker containing our correspondence, captured documents, and interrogation reports. After the war, my uncle Pat gleefully noted that in all my letters home I had never used the word "retreat." I always said we "moved south this morning," as if we were on a vacation.

We headed for Taegu where we were to set up operations in the police station. We waited there for the advancing American 8th Army. On our way south, we had passed an advanced echelon of the 8th on their way to the battlefields in the north. They were very young, inexperienced, and frightened as hell as they trudged past us. They were well aware of the ten-to-one odds they were facing. It was a segregated black unit even though President Truman had desegregated the Armed Services in 1948. General MacArthur still wasn't taking orders from Washington, at least not yet. After all, he was the Supreme Commander, although not for long. He underestimated the power and strength of that little haberdasher from Missouri. As we passed each other, my unit and those young innocent men no older than myself, I couldn't help but wonder how many of them wouldn't be making it back home to the ones waiting for them.

At the time, I didn't know how close I was to not making it home myself. Just north of Taegu was an unmarked, complicated, deceptive junction, and our navigator suggested we veer left. Left felt like East, which seemed correct. But after many miles and most of the morning, one of the Weapons Specialists of our little group, who was sitting next to me in the back of the jeep, asked me, "If we're supposed to be going south, where should the sun in the heavens be?"

After a slight moment I said, "Just up ahead and a little to our left?"

"Then, pray God, why the hell is it just behind us and a little to our right?" he asked. "It's been like that all morning!"

"You mean—" but I hesitated at the thought: we're going north?"

"Stop!" He yelled out to the jeep up front and repeated it a couple of times. We were in the middle of our three-jeep convoy. We all stopped and the officers had a conference and decided we had better turn around immediately. At the time there was no front line and no one knew where the North Korean forces were or even where ours were for that matter. All we knew was we were supposed to be going south and we weren't so we better get to it pronto.

The trailers were unhitched, and the drivers proceeded to turn the jeeps around on the narrow, single-lane, dirt road which rose about five feet above rice paddies on either side. The men managed the turnaround by heading down the slope just enough to make the turn without plunging headlong into the muddy rice paddy. One dumb-ass officer stayed in his seat next to the driver. When the driver did an abrupt stop to avoid slipping into the paddy, the officer was thrown forward into the windshield and broke some ribs. This little mishap resulted in his getting back to Tokyo even before the war started. I wouldn't be a bit surprised if he got a Purple Heart in the bargain.

The drivers having, with difficulty, turned the jeeps around, we hooked up the trailers and then we were off, headed, we hoped, for Taegu. We made it before dark, settled in, and had a bit of K-ration. I got a soybean Popsicle from a street vendor for a couple of cigarettes.

Our 8th Army was advancing just to the west of Taegu that night, and we could hear artillery mortar blasting off north of the city. Word had it that some heavy-duty enemy Russian tanks were headed for Taegu, coming down from Sangiu on that narrow dirt lane through the miles of rice paddies that we had traversed that very morning. An encounter with them could have been it, we would have been finished, finito. What ran through my head was fate, fate, fate.

A Korean lieutenant, a lawyer who had been on duty at the Pentagon in Washington, was now connected with us in Taegu. He had been assigned to our outfit because of his linguistic abilities. I couldn't believe his antics that night when the heavy mortar started up. He was scared shitless but, unlike the rest of us, he couldn't keep himself from showing it. He was sweating profusely and moving nervously to and fro without purpose. I wondered what happened to all that OCS training. I was still just a young kid from upstate New York, but I was beginning to realize that it took all kinds.

Back To Reality

Now a quarter century later Sandy and I were moving on... Down out of the forest pine needle where the murmuring hemlocks and pines entwine and livestock in the Adirondacks flock amid boulders and rocks dropped helter-skelter in the ice age. Down into the blistering, sweltering cement slabs of the city. For the heat of July from that sun in the sky, one has to control a nice rage.

"Cool it," Sandy said.

All I could say was, "The heat on Bequia, thirteen degrees from the Equator, could never, would never, match this! I don't ever remember New York like this."

"You've been away too long."

"Well, I'm ready to go back," I said.

"We will, we will," he promised, "just as soon as I see all my doctors." He was given a good bill of health by one and all and told to continue whatever he was doing, save smoking. I knew he would never quit, no matter how much they preached at him.

Back on Bequia one could still feel the aftermath of the volcanic eruption, though it had been over four months since the disaster. The fine gray ash like human cremains got into everything. It brought back memories of the digs at Herculaneum in Italy, and they weren't very pleasant. Stories were everywhere. Boolu told of sitting on the front steps and seeing the massive mushroom cloud rise up into the stratosphere carrying ash as far away as Barbados, a hundred miles off to the east. He told of cleaning out gutters and plugging up waterspouts to keep the water in the cisterns pure and safe for drinking. He said, "Lancy helped me." Yes, the infamous Lancy Ollivierre of the discarded-shoes-and-red-ants episode so many moons ago. Those days were behind Boolu now, and he held no grudge or malice toward anyone.

Boolu told us tales of all the Carib refugees from St. Vincent living in the Harbour holed up in the school. Some were still on Bequia; they hadn't gone home yet. Others, due to the trauma, were not planning to go back at all; they were going to attempt to start a new life here. Boolu knew a lot of these people and their families from his many summer vacations up in Sandy Bay, the center of Carib country on the northern tip of St. Vincent.

It felt good to be home after such a long time. I hadn't been away from Bequia for an extended period in over twelve years. We were so busy on our trip, it was so full of activity, that neither of us realized how much we missed Boolu and Bequia. It took a time away to make us aware just how much of a home we had here.

The Playhouse Attempts Advance Work

But Sandy couldn't settle in for long: it was almost time for the Playhouse to resume. They were still depending on him. I wondered just how sick and feeble he had to become before they let go. In all honesty, I also knew that he wasn't letting go either. Now he was waiting for a call from Kent Paul, who was waiting for a call from Sydney Pollack about Sydney's directing a film shoot of Sandy's classes. It looked as if the project were about to begin. So Sandy would be leaving any minute for New York, pending the call.

For the past few years, Paul had been trying to get a third-year program started at the school. But he couldn't get the government's help, or anyone else's for that matter. Bill Esper had been named the president of another project, a graduate program development project called the Neighborhood Playhouse Repertory Theater. But at that time, even with many graduates behind the idea, it never got off the ground, except for the organizing of it and lots of talk. Because he left the school, Bill had eventually handed over the reins to Kent Paul just before the school's Golden Anniversary.

Soon after the anniversary, Sandy and I heard that Kent had plans to do a production of *The Days Between* by Robert Anderson. Kent picked the play, cast it, and directed it. Kathleen Nolan was the female lead. She had attended the school but never graduated; nor were the male and female character leads Playhouse people. "Hey, wait a minute. What's wrong with this picture?" I said to Sandy.

Sandy's only response was, "Sit back and shut up."

It was a subdued, ineffectual performance. I know, I was there. Sandy never said a word. Many of the bona fide graduates were disappointed, disillusioned, and discouraged. None of this seemed to dissuade or discourage Kent, because, with his assistant Robert Scott, he launched into his next project still under the umbrella of the Neighborhood Playhouse Repertory Theater.

Taping Sandy's Classes

Kent came up with the idea of filming Sandy's classes with Sydney Pollack as the director, with Paul's blessing. But of course he would need Sandy's permission. Sandy had first been presented with this idea before we took off on our trip, and he was dead set against it.

When I asked him why, he said, "You don't learn to act by reading or looking at something. That's impossible. You learn to act by doing, and preferably on a stage and in front of an audience. All I can do is give you exercises to help you when you're having trouble doing it. I don't teach you how to act, acting does that. It's just like singing: no one can give you a voice. Either you have the talent or you don't. Remember Margaret Truman? Even Helen Traubel couldn't do anything for her, and Helen was even a Democrat! She might as well have been at one of her favorite ball games. Remember, acting is in the doing."

"So why do you have a class?" I asked.

His answer to that was, "I told you, just to help novices with the materials they will need along the way. And it's all individual, everyone's needs are different. We are not machines, not robots, Jimmy."

"OK, OK, but what about posterity?"

He looked at me and asked, "Posterity? What's posterity got to do with me?"

I knew he couldn't care less. I disagreed with him intensely on this subject. I felt there ought to be a book, and why not a movie? What about all the actors who would come after Sanford Meisner? They should be able to learn all they could about the man who gave so much to their profession. His intellectual contribution to the art of acting was staggering not to mention his insight into life in general. I knew I had to work on him to get him to come around. I also knew that if anyone could convince him, it would be he himself, with my encouragement.

Idle conversation while we were on the trip often wafted toward this unresolved subject. By the time we were back in New York, he had come to his senses, at least that's how I thought of it. Sandy said he would go along with the idea, providing I went with him and worked alongside him on this project as we had on Bequia.

I balked. "But what about Bequia? I just pack up and go back to New York?"

"Just for the shooting of the project," he said. "How long can it take? You have nothing to do on Bequia now anyway. You quit the high school, and Avila has the deaf school, so come up and help me."

I thought of Kent and said, "We'll see." I knew Kent wanted no part of me, but I did feel strongly that this project was one Sandy should do, so I relented. "If you say so." But I didn't expect much.

As it turned out, Kent had been doing his homework. He had the class of recent graduates all chosen and ready to start whenever Sydney was free of commitments in Hollywood. Kent called Sandy in Bequia to say Sydney would be in New York the last week in August with a couple of weeks he could spare. He would start the shooting then.

We hadn't even settled in yet. Not knowing the movie business, I said, "Sandy how much can they shoot in a week? I have so much to tend to down here. You go up and do whatever you have to do, and I'll stay here. You'll have Paul to help you, if you stay at Paul's, and I can get things sorted out down here. You'll be able to come back for a month before the Playhouse starts."

I was surprised when he came back and told me that Sydney had shot the complete first year's work. I couldn't believe he was able to cover all those exercises in two weeks. I knew Sydney was good, but then I didn't know the movie business. Sandy said they couldn't have done any more even if Sydney had had the time because Kent had run out of money and would need time to raise more. Jack Lord had donated $15,000, but no one else's contribution came anywhere near that. Suzanne Pleshette, even with all her TV shows, couldn't help because she was working on her apartment complex. That was the case with most of the graduate actors, no matter how many movies or TV shows they did or how much they were making, their reaction was pretty much the same: zilch.

When Kent told me how tough it was to raise funds from actors, I could only think, millions for defense but not one cent for tribute. Did an actor say that? Later in the year I was told Shari Lewis was able to wheedle, finagle, or whatever another $15,000 from the National Endowment for the Arts. And why wouldn't she? Wasn't Shari's little Lamb Chop born in Sandy's classroom as one of Shari's independent activities? With that added help, Kent was able to complete the shooting the following summer.

At Loose Ends

For me, there were no more classes at school, no more trips to St. Vincent, no more orchestra, and no more choir rehearsals over there. Most of the students we had worked with had graduated by then. They had been the bulk of the choir and they were now on to bigger and better things, I hoped. Some went to England or Canada and most went to the USofA. One even went to Cuba to continue her studies in medicine on scholarship. The rest were over in St. Vincent continuing their studies, be they in nursing, teaching, or business-secretarial school. Some went into the police force and onward into the police band. I also noticed a number of dance and rock bands springing up here and there. Gideon James, with his eyes now fixed, was back from America and over in Barbados working as a pop singer. It seemed as if Boolu was the only one from the group who was stuck on Bequia, and he only wanted to go to Hollywood and become a "Star Boy," a sheriff in a western. Nolly Simmons always said we should shoot a Mango Western here on Bequia with Boolu as the two-gun-toting lawman.

Sandy was back for Christmas and New Year's of '80 and that winter he didn't rush back to the Playhouse. His practice, since his last bout with cancer, was to start the students off in the fall term and finish them off in the spring. He felt it was about time his assistants took over.

Book Projects Kaput

We spent most of the winter talking of Kent's project and also a new one stalled in the fall. Kent was trying to get Sandy to cotton on to the idea of working on a book on acting. Sandy had given up on that idea after spending three months in Puerto Rico in the summer of 1964 working on just such a project, which he had concluded was futile. A few years later, Joyce Henry, an ex-student who was then an English professor at a college in Pennsylvania, had presented him with the idea of her doing a book. He had said, "No way. You don't read a book about acting and learn how to act." She had written a couple of books, as English professors often do, but nevertheless Sandy was saying no. I felt he was right about the reason.

But if he didn't write a book, others would. It was another manifestation of the integrity that had kept him from being another Strasberg or Stella Adler, or even Uta Hagen. Most people outside the industry didn't know who he was. He once asked me, "Jimmy, it seems to me anyone who washes up on the shores of Bequia from Trinidad, Guyana, or any other backwater place knows who Strasberg is. Why is that?"

"TV, magazines, and newspaper articles. You know that," I answered. "How else would they know him, ya blithering, senseless schmuck?" I used to lose my patience. For such a brilliant man, sometimes he seemed so naive. "They don't know who the hell you are because you are the Greta Garbo of acting teachers. You enjoy your anonymity. 'Vhy, you vant to be ahlone,' you enjoy it, it's your nature. If you let Joyce write this book for no other reason than to get your name out there, it could be beneficial to aspiring young actors who know nothing about the business. I didn't know who the blazes you were until I'd been in the business almost ten years. I thought Meisner was an architect in Palm Beach, Florida!" I was raving on as I so often do. "Why don't you look at the book not as a How-to book but rather as a How-I-did-it book? Sandy, people should know."

"OK, OK. Stop it already. I'm sorry I asked."

Well, he did come around to this way of thinking, after a fashion, and he gave Joyce Henry permission to write the book, making her one happy English professor. She set to work on the book, pronto. In no time at all, she had reams, but when Sandy read the first draft, he was very disappointed. He said it read as if she had dashed it off one morning on her way to work. Within three months or thereabout, the book was finished. Sandy read it and described it as drivel, or something like that, and I read it and said it was garbage. It was so un-Sandy! He had so much class, and the book was trash, cheap and tawdry. She had already sent it to Random House, which was accepting it and ready to publish. Fortunately, Sandy had the right of refusal. The only problem was the publishers had paid up-front money to the professor and Sandy was going to have to make good those monies. Sandy said, "I have to stop this book whatever it costs me." And he did.

Now here was Kent trying to get Sandy to attempt once more to portray his classes in writing. In a weak moment, Sandy let Kent talk him into letting Ms. Rue Drew write his book. She was helping Kent on the documentary. She seemed bright enough and certainly eager enough. She had had sessions with Stella Adler and worked with Lee Strasberg for a while but never finished with either. That should have sent up a red flag. But what the heck, she was working with Kent, so Sandy gave her the green light. She would do three chapters on spec, and the agent would then get them to the publisher. This time Sandy had enough sense to hire a book agent named Connie Clausen, a former student.

So now, the documentary and the book were both under way again, and we were in the middle of making plans to leave for New York for an extended stay. What the hell, I thought, I have nothing to do around here except keep an eye on Boolu. But Boolu had grown up and didn't need my eye any more, a fact he made me aware of in no uncertain terms. Naturally, Paul—who else?—met us at the airport. We were going to Paul's but only for a short stay. As it happened, Kent had an investor friend who was getting married and moving out of his East 58th Street apartment into a larger one. He left it to Sandy, kit and caboodle, just as it was with everything in it. He was starting out afresh, as it were, farther up on the East Side. The building was and still is called the Picasso. We planned to move in by the end of the week.

On Bequia we had moved Boolu out of his small 9′x12′ bedroom into the larger guest bedroom and made a small kitchen for him in his old bedroom. We put in a small table and two chairs, a little fridge, and a small four-burner stove and oven. The stove was not an American one; it was a small foreign make you see in third world countries that we had brought over from the house we had rented in Frenches along with the little fridge. Parnell was moving in to keep him company. We had no idea when we would be back. We were leaving on Sunday, March 2.

Saturday, the boys went into town and purchased a twenty-five-pound bottle of propane for the stove, which West Indians hook up to the stove right there in the kitchen. Sunday we locked up and made our way across the channel to St. Vincent and Arnos Vale airport, not knowing how long the separation would be.

27 A Near-Death Experience

Now Boolu Get Hit With A Bundle Of Bricks

It was only Tuesday, and back on Bequia Parnell got up, had breakfast, and went off for the day to his job fixing sick automobiles. Boolu on the other hand had nothing to do, so he decided to go up Monkey Hill and watch whales for the day. Whale-watching was one of Boolu's favorite pastimes. Boys would go up to the top of the highest hill and scan the horizon for whales, ensuring for themselves a piece of the whale if and when one were caught. The whalers were at sea in the little whaleboat, but the scope of their horizon was much more limited than that of the boys on the hill. When the watchers spotted a whale, they would contact the six men in the boat by flashing them with the reflection of the sun from a mirror, then direct them to the whale. This practice increased the whalers' odds. Boolu wanted to become a member of the crew in the worst way, and many years later Balem Olliviene did offer him a spot, but I thought better of it. I knew that because of his hearing loss it could prove dangerous.

That day, he later recounted to us, he quit for the day about 2:30 in the afternoon since the whalers always headed for home about three. When he reached the house, he decided to lie down for a while. Lying on the bed, he detected a faint smell of gas. He got up and went into the kitchen to check out the stove. He lit a match over one of the jets on the stovetop and nothing happened. So he leaned over to check out the oven below. No one had ever told him, or me either, or any other Vincentian who happened to have a gas bottle in their kitchen, that propane gas is heavy and doesn't float away. What it does is settle where it is, especially in a completely closed-up area. For the most part, the gas in Boolu's kitchen was not escaping but lingering on the floor about the room just high enough to catch Boolu's flame when he bent down to check the oven jets. This time the match ignited the propane causing an explosion of massive white light that rocked Friendship valley.

Anything that was animal or vegetable standing in line with that white light, be it human, dog or bush or tree, was instantly burned. It was like the principle of an atomic explosion. Anything outside the white light was spared. For instance, only the top half of the Norfolk pine burned, but I should say disintegrated. Marcus's tail was in the line of light even though he was outdoors, and that burned. Otherwise he was spared.

Absolutely nothing ignited, only smoldered or melted. The white light with its tremendous heat only lasted for an instant not burning anything that took a little time to ignite and burst into flame. Wood, hard plastic, wool, and cotton went unscathed. But anything synthetic, like nylon, the curtains, and Boolu's synthetic pants, melted. His pants melted on his skin. He was wearing a Greek wool fisherman's hat that didn't burn and protected his hair and his head. He also had on cotton underwear and a cotton tank top, thank God, which protected his torso. The tank top was left as intact as it had been. It had had a hole in it with runs like in a woman's nylon stocking. The single layer of cotton weave protected Boolu's skin under the tank top except for beneath the little hole and between each and every thread of the runs. In other words, anything in shadow at the instant of the flash was preserved. Unfortunately, anything that wasn't, like all of Boolu's exposed skin and the skin that the synthetic material melted on, was burned and destroyed deeply.

The door that Boolu had opened and the open windows enabled the white flash to escape instantly like electricity seeking the path of least resistance. As powerful as the explosion was, the exit path must have protected everything in the room strong enough not to burn in that split second. The foundation and walls of the house were saved from being blown to smithereens in all directions.

Boolu was knocked off his feet, and the doors were slammed shut. When he came to and got up, he couldn't open the door at first because he could not manipulate his fingers around the knob. With both hands he managed to get the inside door open and went into the shower. There he engaged the cold-water faucet by squeezing his hands together. His fingers were useless, all burnt and splayed and curled back on themselves.

How long he stood there under the cold shower no one knows. Lancy, who was down the road a ways, came running. When he got to the bottom of the drive, he saw Boolu making his way down the steep hill with his arms outstretched, the burnt flesh hanging off them. He was walking like a sleepwalker with his legs apart, swaying from side to side. Lancy said he looked like a jumbie (Bequia's word for zombie).

Mary Wallace and Teresa Housen, our next-door neighbors from either side, were at the bottom of the drive by then as well. At that point the school bus came along, loaded with children from Southside. Mary and Teresa stopped the bus and had the children file off. Somehow Monkey, the driver, managed to turn the bus around right there on the spot—the road at that time was no more than nine feet wide with a steep drop on one side and a steep hill on the other. He used what he could of our steep drive. Glenroy Adams, one of my old students, rode into town with Boolu to the clinic, holding him as best he could as the bus careened around the many twists and turns over the rugged

27 A Near-Death Experience

road the mile and a half to the Harbour.

The doctor hooked him up to insulin and began to cut the clothes off him, including what he could of the melted pants. They tell me they could not find a yacht to take Boolu to St. Vincent. I have to add here that I found that hard to believe and I still do. In all my years there on that Island, I had never seen that Harbour boat-less, and I mean never in all my forty-plus years.

Parnell went to get Wayne Gooding who took Boolu over to St. Vincent in his small outboard fishing boat. It was a windy March day with the usual high seas of that time of year. The little open boat churned its way up and over the swells across the nine-mile channel of open seas that separates the Atlantic from the Caribbean, with Parnell bracing Boolu from behind and a nurse holding up the saline solution in her hand.

An ambulance was waiting at the pier to fetch him off to the General Hospital, a hospital at the time with too many patients and not enough staff. In fact it was egregiously under-staffed and wanting in almost every up-to-date piece of equipment that was essential. June, his sister, was told of the catastrophe and immediately high-tailed it over from the other side of town to the hospital. The scene she described to me at the hospital was right out of that old movie of Olivia de Havilland's, The Snake Pit. I damned well knew what that place was like because of the one I had worked in back in '48.

June related, "They had him in an open ward, with too many patients for me to put an accurate number on." There were fifteen, seventeen, something like that. I don't know, I wasn't there, but suffice it to say too many, since one would have been too many in his condition. His sister told me the other patients crowded around just to get a better look, making it difficult for her to get up next to him. There Boolu lay with no one tending to him.

In spite of his pain he was conscious and asked her to please take off his hearing aids and ear molds. There must have been swelling there by now and they were hurting him. So with her non-sterile fingers, she took them out of his ears. His right ear was badly damaged and burned for it had been right down next to the heart of the explosion. This I know because she gave the melted plastic to me later. All I could think was, what the hell kind of an admission examination did they do, if they did any at all? There he lay an hour after being admitted, and his hearing aids and molds were still in his ears.

I asked her, "Did you speak to a doctor?"

"I never saw one," she replied, "and I was there until they came and took him away. I didn't know where he went, nor did anyone else."

I did speak to a nurse months later about his treatment at the General. She said there was nothing they could have done, they couldn't handle a patient in his condition back then. At that time they wouldn't even have had the gauze for the bandages. "Well, what about the doctors? Why were no doctors there?" I asked.

Her answer to that was, "Because of the shift change. They were going off duty and the night staff was coming on. That's our busiest time. There was nothing we could have done for him anyway. He was beyond our help."

I was furious! "Nothing except dump him into the middle of a bunch of sick patients! You couldn't clean out an old water closet so he could be kept away from the other patients and contamination?" I didn't even wait for an answer. They were ready to let Boolu slip down the tubes without even giving it a try. I just walked away, all the time thinking, Thank God for Marie Kingston's presence of mind. She was the one who saved his life.

We'll Smile Tomorrow

I will never forget the 4th of March, 1980. That day the phone rang while I was in the kitchen in the late afternoon, about 4:45. It was our third day in New York. I heard Paul's voice from the other room. "Jimmy, it's Marie. Something has happened to Boolu," he said, holding the phone out to me as I hurried into the room.

"Marie?"

"Jimmy," she said, "it's Boolu. He's been burned... badly burned... They've taken him over to St. Vincent. I don't know much, but you had better get down here as quick as you can."

As shocked as I was, I asked, "What was it? How—?"

"Jimmy," she interrupted, "they tell me it was a propane explosion. Come quick, quick as you can. I called Son," she said. He was still our Member of Parliament and she worked for him. "He's going to have him moved from the General Hospital up to Dr. Cyrus's."

Son had told them at Dr. Cyrus's to go down to the General Hospital. "Just go on in there with your litter, a stretcher, whatever, and pick him up. Take him out and bring him up to Dr. Cyrus's." That's exactly what they did and why poor June didn't know what the hell was happening. Dr. Cyrus's was a private hospital where he would get much better care. "Oh, God, Marie, thanks for calling. I'll get there. I'll get there tomorrow somehow. Thanks again," I said and hung up.

Sandy was stunned. He just stared at me helplessly. Paul had the telephone book out, looking up the airlines. "Here's the number. 800-733-3000."

I dialed it and got right through. I explained the emergency, that my son had just been badly burned in an explosion in the Caribbean. A supervisor got on the wire and said, "Just come tomorrow. We'll list you as an emergency and put you in a jump seat if we have to. Now what's the name?" I told him and that was that.

Dinner that night was a dud. In fact I don't even remember what was said. I packed that night, was up at five, and flew out of Kennedy by nine on my way to Barbados. There I caught the first flight to St. Vincent and was at Boolu's bedside exactly 24 hours after the explosion rocked Friendship valley. He was conscious and his body, as much as I could see of it, was wrapped in gauze from around his ears and under his chin right down to his finger tips, which seemed to be all curled up in the wrong direction. His face, which was not bandaged, looked like crisp black charcoal. It was like a child's black mask from China with a little slit for a mouth exposing his very white teeth. His features were mutated. His facial features were not pronounced but almost flat with little definition. Arched braces under the sheet kept the bedcover off and away from his body.

He was awake and aware of who I was. I could tell he was trying to tell me it was not his fault. It took everything I had to pacify him, to assure him that I knew it wasn't his fault. I told him I would be right by his side, that everything was going to be OK. I told him Jesus was with him, to talk to Him just like he always did.

I hadn't talked to anyone yet. I had no idea what his true condition was. I sure was afraid to find out. The doctor came to speak to me, and at first glance I could see it wasn't Dr. Cyrus. Dr. Cyrus was off the island at a conference in London. He hadn't accepted any patients into the hospital for the time he would be away and had a doctor come from St. Lucia to handle any emergency. Consequently, the hospital was empty with only Boolu to care for. We received a lot of attention that afternoon. They turned the hospital into a burn unit with Boolu the only patient.

The doctor told me Boolu was severely burned over 40% of his body. They were deep third degree burns. A call had gone out for blood. "Right now we're watching his breathing. That's what's crucial at the moment. Later he may lose his right arm—it's been very badly damaged and may be beyond repair. The fingers on his left hand look bad, but we may be able to save some. His vital organs have not been damaged and I believe that's what is sustaining him. But he's losing too much blood because of the loss of so much skin, and we're just waiting for a return on that call we put out this morning. The most important things at present are the risk of infection and his breathing. We may have to do a tracheotomy on him if the breathing becomes much more labored, but that would be just one more onslaught his body could well do without. That's why we're holding off."

I knew what the good doctor was talking about: Joan and Sandy had both had to have tracheotomies. What they do is create an air passage into the lungs by making a hole in the neck and inserting a tube into the lungs for the air to pass through. An intervention like that was bad enough in any condition, but it could be critical with Boolu barely hanging on to life.

I went back into the room as the nurses prepared for the "trach" operation. They let me into the room only because they knew he could slip away at any moment. I stood back off in a corner out of the way. I beseeched God, Jesus, Mary, and Joseph as well as every saint and soul in heaven to help him. I knew deep down that they all knew, as I did, that Boolu above all didn't deserve this.

The doctor came in and told the nurses that before they took him to the OR he wanted to examine him once more. I went and stood in the hall. After a time he came out and said, "I do believe the swelling in his neck is subsiding. He is getting more oxygen with every intake. I'm going to hold off and check in a few more hours."

I had not looked into where I would stay the night. I would have to look for a place nearby so I could walk to and fro. I would be here quite a while—that is, if we were lucky. It was getting late, but with the possibility of an operation that night I wouldn't be going anywhere. I told the nurse on the desk I would hunker down on the chair in Boolu's room for the night. So she had the janitor bring in a larger chair. By nine o'clock Boolu's breathing was much easier. The doctor decided against a tracheotomy and called off the OR preparations. "Let's see if he can get some sleep."

Everyone went home except for the night nurse at the desk. We were the only three in the hospital that night. The Head Nurse, Dr. Cyrus's wife, was next door in their home. I heard her tell the nurse to call her at any hour if he should take a turn for the worse. Throughout the night, I heard the nurse pass in and out while I sat mesmerized in the chair. By now Boolu must have been exhausted. It was almost thirty-two hours since the accident, and he hadn't had a wink of sleep. But now that he wasn't fighting for breath anymore, he must have been able to let go a bit because he fell into a deep sleep. I kept getting up every now and again just to check his breathing. I was so helpless. What else was there for me to do?

Ever so slowly, the silent night slipped by with the rasp of his breathing sounding in my ears. As long as I could hear that, I knew he was still alive. Shortly after daybreak, I heard rustlings of the mattress. I went over to him and he was awake. I remember reassuring him, and his soulful, doleful eyes looking up at me. That is about all I do remember for most of that day.

This was the third day, the one the doctor had said was crucial. He and the nurses scurried in and out all day while I huddled in a corner out of the way. A door in the room led out onto a veranda. I used it intermittently all day so that they were free to do whatever nurses and doctors do. Yet I felt close enough to feel as if I were there at Boolu's side. I knew being there was just as important for him as it was to me. He needed to know that he wasn't going through this horror alone, like he had had to do in his earlier life. I had no idea what degree of pain he was in. It was now forty-eight hours since the accident. It must have been lessening some, or so it seemed. Perhaps it was like when his grandmother used to beat him: after a while, when he could take no more, he would go numb. Maybe it was like that after a spell. The mind can take it no longer and shuts down the feeling senses. I certainly hoped so.

That afternoon he dozed off, and I felt it was a good time to find a nearby guesthouse or rooming house. Mrs. Cyrus, the Head Nurse, thought the closest was Carrie Painter's and gave me directions. It wasn't far, but I called a cab. I wasn't about to schlep my bag, no way, not the way I was feeling. We drove over the back way a short distance to Mrs. Painter's just behind St. Martin's

27 A Near-Death Experience

Boys School, the school being just up the road between the two cathedrals.

Painters' was on the back road leading in front of the Botanical Gardens, and up to the hospital on the main leeward road. Carrie's place was clean, reasonable, and adequate, with three meals a day, and that was all I was looking for. Plus it had the added feature of being within walking distance of the hospital. Carrie already knew about Boolu's accident and that I was the teacher from Bequia who had that boy, the unfortunate dummy boy. Well, that seemed to me to be close enough, except that unfortunate boy was now twenty-four years old. I settled in and, before I headed back, told her I planned to be there for dinner at 6:30. This way I would be with Boolu for his dinner, whatever that would be, and still be back to spend the evening with him until he fell asleep.

When I got back, he was awake and the nurse told me they were preparing him something to eat. That was good news to me. You hang onto every little thread. Dinner consisted of juices and broth through a straw and I think Jell-O. As he was eating, he tried to smile and I told him not to. I could see it hurt him to do it, so I said something stupid and useless like, "Just lie there. You'll get all well again, and we'll smile tomorrow."

Before the doctor left for the night, he told me things would look much different the next day. Much different, I thought, what is that supposed to mean? I wanted to hear the words "better tomorrow." The doctor never mentioned Boolu's arm and his fingers; I was too chicken to bring them up, still praying. I must have felt, foolishly, that not talking about it would make it go away! Mrs. Cyrus told me Dr. Cyrus was cutting his stay in London short and would be returning tomorrow evening. He would be at the hospital Saturday morning. I prayed most of that night that the St. Lucian doctor would hold off on the arm until Dr. Cyrus arrived. Just maybe... and that was as far as I could go.

Friday came and went and Boolu still had his right arm. He was looking just a little stronger; at least, that's what I wanted to see. Saturday morning Dr. Cyrus came in and had Boolu taken to the triage room where he gave him a complete examination. It seemed to take hours. When it was over, he took me into his office and asked how this had all happened. The upshot was that Boolu was in a very bad way. Now the big problem was blood plasma because with so much skin tissue missing, he was losing so much blood through his arms, chest, and legs. The medical team could do only so much with the wrappings. The other important factor was infection. They had to do everything they could to keep him from becoming infected. Dr. Cyrus felt if all went well they might be able to save the arm; at least he was going to try. All the time I was saying to myself, Thank God, thank God. Dear God, intercede please.

"I should tell you," the doctor said, "all his vital organs are unimpaired and in good working condition, including his lungs. Let's hope his heart holds out. Oh, and by the way, what is your blood type?"

"B-positive," I answered.

"Boolu's is O. We're sending out another call for blood on Monday. We'll need every bit of blood we can get. I'm doing an operation on a Bequia fellow next week and his type is B-positive. We could use a donation. Will you?" he asked.

"Of course," I said, and did.

That afternoon Bishop Woodroff came by. He told me they would be praying for Boolu at the cathedral at all the masses the next day. He asked where I was staying. I told him at Carrie Painter's, and he said I needn't, that I shouldn't be alone at a time like this, that he and Evelyn had plenty of room. I told him I didn't want to be putting anyone out. He insisted I wouldn't be. "So please do stay." So I did, not having any idea how long Boolu's recovery was going to take.

On Sunday I went to mass and received the Eucharist. I prayed like I hadn't prayed since 1974 for Sandy and 1959 for my sister Joan. I had kept in touch with Sandy all week. He was looking into getting an emergency airplane to go down, pick Boolu up, and bring him to the Burn Unit at New York Hospital. The only problem with the plan was that by the time it was initiated it was too late for a burn as bad as this one. It would have to have been done within twenty-four hours and no more.

The New York doctors at the Burn Unit, after several discussions with Dr. Cyrus on Saturday and Monday, decided it would be far too risky to move Boolu by air just now. Because he had so much exposed raw flesh, they would have to wait for some healing to take place before subjecting him to the air pressure in a small plane. So on Monday the painful healing process began. Dr. Cyrus was planning to do "postage-stamp grafting" with what was left of the healthy skin from other sections of Boolu's body. He would cut the good skin into long narrow strips, snipping them up into small stamp-size pieces, and apply them to the raw burnt sections of his neck, shoulders, upper chest, both arms, hands, fingers, and from the groin down the front of his legs to his ankles. Then the process would be much like squares of sod or clumps of grass, which grow and spread out across the gaps between them, filling in with luscious green grass. We have all seen it happen 100 times, only this time it wasn't grass. It would be our Boolie-boy's skin that was expected to grow together. God help us. Nor were we talking about a small patch of skin here; it involved the whole front of his body except for his lower torso. It was going to be such a major undertaking. They wouldn't be able to start until the thirteenth day after the accident, I guess to build up Boolu to enable him to withstand the assault on his system.

He got through the next week relatively well. They now had his arms held up in the air on pulleys. A practical nurse or aide, who unfortunately thought she was doing Boolu some good, was working his twisted fingers back and forth, telling him, even though he couldn't hear a word of what she was saying, to move them back and forth no matter how much it hurt. At that moment Dr. Cyrus walked in. Seeing what she was doing, he flew into a rage,

27 A Near-Death Experience

lacing into her like there was no tomorrow, asking her what in the world she thought she was doing as he rushed her out of the room, muttering something about miserable arthritis in his old age and apologizing to me at the same time for the outburst. It gave me an insight into his strict, stern, high standards that I must say at the time I was grateful for.

As the medical team made ready for the big day on the 17th, the call went out for more blood. The turnout was impressive. I was told little old ladies came to donate all the way down from Sandy Bay twenty-three miles to the north across river beds and over rough terrain. To say the whole country was praying for him would not be an overstatement. Every pastor in every church had their followers, their parishioners, or their flock praying every Sunday. Priests and ministers were always stopping by to pray with him. The hard crusty mask on Boolu's face was coming off little by little with Dr. Cyrus's help. Every time he took him to triage for evaluation, it looked a little better. When I say better, I have to qualify that. When the black charcoal mask came off, it took the skin pigment with it and left Boolu's face as white as a sheet, like the color of an albino's. He looked almost as bad as Michael Jackson. Fearing how this might upset him, we covered up the big mirror in his room. I used a rather large piece of muslin sent to him from Bequia with many signatures and messages of condolence written all over it. It looked quite decorative up over the minor above the dresser—until shortly after the aide came in to clean the room. In the process of cleaning, she took the cloth down, not using her God-given wits to think why it was up there in the first place. When I came back from lunch, a nurse told me Boolu had seen his face. "Oh, lord, how did he take it?" I asked.

"Go in and find out," she said smiling.

I walked into the room. They had him sitting up in his chair. His eyes were dancing and in spite of the pain he was trying to smile. I said nothing, and after a pause, he said, "Well?"

I still didn't know what to say. This was his first moment of joy, so all I said was, "Well?"

Then he said it. "Jimmy, I'm white."

He was waiting for a reaction from me, a sign of approval, and by God I didn't know what to say or do. For once in my life I was stumped for words. How do you explain all the complexities of skin pigment to a person like Boolu, all the complications of being white or black or even in between? I felt I should offer some explanation, be of some assistance in helping him to grasp the reality of what had happened. Then there was the question of whether he would always look like this. To me he looked hideous but he was alive and to me that was paramount. To him he was now white and that seemed paramount to him.

At that moment, Son Mitchell, our MP, walked in to pay him a visit, and Boolu greeted him with as big a smile as he could with his tight facial muscles. "Son, see, me white," he said. Son just laughed and humored him, and I could see then that was the way to handle this problem just now. It was no time for serious race relations.

The 17th of March came and the morning was spent preparing for the operation. Everyone in the hospital was involved. With the exception of the outpatient clinic, only one other patient was in the hospital, from Mt. Pleasant, Bequia, he had fallen out of a tree and broken some bones, but that was all. Dr. Cyrus still seemed to be focusing and concentrating on saving Boolu. Well, that's how it looked to me.

At one o'clock Boolu had been prepped and I wished him well. "Jesus is with you. You just hang in there." And off he went on the gurney.

The day was endless. I sat and waited, I walked and waited, I hung over the balustrade and waited. I tried to read but I couldn't concentrate. I somehow knew that what Dr. Cyrus was doing was a very serious undertaking. I had picked that up from his behavior earlier through all the preparations.

There was no one else to talk to. Everyone was in the OR, with the exception of the woman in the lab and an aide tending to the other patient who was about ready to go home. The handyman and cook came around once in a while but neither knew what to say. Sometime after three, a nurse came out of the OR and went into the lab. The lab technician had already gone home earlier. Then the door of the operating room opened again, and another nurse called out, "What's keeping you?" This piqued my interest.

The first nurse answered her saying, "I can't find his blood, and So-and-so has gone home." I didn't catch her name.

The second nurse then went into the lab and I heard her ask, "What's that?"

The other said, "It looks like his, but this blood has not been marked. She [meaning the lab technician] has forgotten to 'mark' the blood with his blood."

"Well, we're just going to have to use it as it is anyway. Bring it quickly."

They both disappeared into the OR. What the hell this was all about I had no idea. "Marked the blood" and "the lab technician forgot to"? It scared the bejeezus out of me. It was one more thing to worry about.

The day continued to pass at a snail's pace. Eventually the cook fed the other patient, cleaned up, and left. The aide and the handyman stayed on. They must be working overtime, I thought.

The night nurse had just arrived, the aide had gone home, and it was after 10 PM when the operating room door opened. Mrs. Cyrus came out first, then the handyman and a male aide carrying Boolu in a large collapsible stretcher, and then the other nurses came to help move him onto his bed. No one said a word to me; at least that's how I remember it. The operating room nurses couldn't get out of the room quickly enough. The doctor left without a word. Mrs. Cyrus said the night nurse would be at the desk. In all fairness to them, they all looked beat and bedraggled. But what about the post-op care? Was there to be none? Well, there was none. After more than nine hours on an operating table, Boolu was left there in the room all alone with only me.

I too was spent, and frightened at what I saw. I was afraid to verbalize what

27 A Near-Death Experience

I saw, I was afraid to ask about what I saw. In fact, I didn't want anyone to tell me what I thought I saw, what had happened, and what condition he was really in. I was afraid to hear. Had they given up? They must have, but I didn't know for sure. Had they done everything possible? I was sure they had. Was he already dead? I didn't know one way or the other. Maybe they didn't either, or maybe they were waiting to tell me in the morning. If that were so, why wouldn't someone tell me then and there? I never got an explanation for any of that behavior. It was as if I were non-existent.

There we were, good old wonderful Boolu and me. There was no recognizable breathing, no movement in his chest, no sound of air at his nostrils. As closely as I looked and listened, nothing: he was as still as stone. I was afraid to touch him. He was not white any longer; he was ashen green, the color of death. Oh, God! Did I pray? I sat and prayed, I walked in circles and prayed, I rocked back and forth and prayed, and I cried and cried, stopping all dried up and then crying some more, beseeching, beseeching and pleading. No one this close to me had ever died before. Joan had come as close as you can get, but she'd made it. Sandy had had some hard times but not like this.

Many months after this traumatic night, Boolu related to me what he had experienced that day. You must bear in mind as I unfold this story that Boolu, being illiterate, had never read a book save his schoolbooks. Bequia had no television as yet; he could not hear the radio, except the beat of music. What he was telling me was coming from him, unadulterated. "Dat day at Dr Cyrus's, I float quite up to de ceiling and I look down. Dere were two a me. I was on de table down dere and de nurses all round. Den I go quite up tru de roof. I could see de sky and de stars and feel de wind on my body, and I went quite up ta Jesus. He was standin' dere wit people all in white, and Mary be wit him too. Dey have long clothes quite down ta de floor, like yours, Jimmy." (I used to wear caftans around the house in those days.) "Jimmy," Boolu went on, "Jesus, He put up his hand like dis and he say, 'Go back.'"

"Why would he do that?" I asked.

"Because, He say, 'Go back, dere's no room,'" Boolu answered. "I just lay back and go quite down tru de roof."

I once asked him half-heartedly later what Jesus looked like, and without hesitating for a second, he candidly said, "You, Jimmy, he look jus like you." Oh, well, I had a beard and long hair and wore those caftans quite down to de floor sometimes, but that's what I get for asking.

Sometime during the night I must have dozed off. I was exhausted. I don't know how long I slept. I was awakened by the loud noise of metal banging. It was Boolu's wrought-iron bed bouncing on the marble-like terrazzo flooring. He seemed to be having convulsions like an epileptic. I went to the nurse at the front desk. I knew she heard the noise, but she never left the desk. She said there was nothing she could do until morning. I just couldn't cotton on to this fatalistic approach that seemed so prevalent. I had had enough past experience in the West Indies to be well aware of it. I couldn't see how anyone could be accepting when it was a loved one; I certainly couldn't.

I went back to the room and all I could do was watch as he shook and shook. I thought he was going to have heart failure. Or if he didn't, I sure was. All I could do was stand there and watch, keeping him from bouncing against the bed rails. He just shivered and shook. It went on endlessly. I have no idea how long it was, I was out of my senses by then. The noise was maddening. Then, as the light of a new day came slowly creeping over the windowsill, he subsided just as quickly as he had started. He then lay there calmly, cool as a cucumber, peacefully breathing like a newborn baby. I could actually see the life flowing back into his body. As the blood began to pump through him, the ashen green of his face was taking on a new glow, albeit it still had that albino white of the day before. But to me it was beautiful. Life is beautiful no matter what color. Boy, did I know that then. He opened his eyes and looked up at me and smiled. Oh, God, what a moment. The transfiguration was immediate. He was totally awake, clear minded as if nothing had happened at all.

I heard the cook in the kitchen making kitchen sounds. She came into the room to see how he was, asked if he was hungry, and he nodded yes. She had been a classmate of his sister June and had known Boolu from the time he was a little boy in St. Vincent. She brought him some tea and a small bowl of something that looked like cream of wheat and she fed him. When he finished, he wanted more tea and she brought him another cup. I have to say I don't know where my brains were. I must have been euphoric, out of this world with ecstasy just to see him living and eating like this. It never occurred to me to ask if she should be feeding him so soon after what he had been through. Well, right or wrong, he upchucked it all. So she cleaned him and the mess up before Mrs. Cyrus came in. No matter, he was in good spirits as if he had slept the sleep of the just. When the doctor came in, he looked pleased as well as seeming proud of Boolu. He said something to the effect of "Now we have work to do."

By noon I was seeing double and was told to go get some sleep. I went to the Woodroffs' and the three of us had lunch. Excusing myself, I left Evelyn and the Bishop and crawled into an ever-so-inviting bed.

By Easter Saturday my days with Boolu at the hospital had assumed a routine. I would get up, have breakfast with the Woodroffs, and then hike up to the hospital. The walk wasn't much farther than the one from Carrie's hotel had been. About noon I would go over to Carrie's place for lunch, returning to spend the afternoon with Boolu. I would be back at Carrie's at 6 PM for dinner and then back to Boolu until he fell asleep.

One night when I came back from dinner, he was fidgeting. Up across his arm and over his shoulder were big black ants heading for his exposed, much damaged ear. They were marching in a long line, a line that wound from the lovely tropical garden since Boolu was on the ground floor. They had marched in through the door across the floor to the leg of the bed and up along the side of the bed and across his body up to his neck. I had got there just in time.

27 A Near-Death Experience

What could one do? These were the tropics.

How can one speak of strain around a person going through what Boolu was going through? So I didn't, but the ordeal was taking its toll on me as well. That night when I reached home about 11 PM, I was in the bathroom getting ready for bed. The last thing I remember I was sitting on the John. The next thing I knew I woke up lying on the floor, my head resting on the little cement step-over into the shower. It was 6:30 in the morning. I didn't tell anyone. I wanted no one worrying about me on top of Boolu's problems. I went to Easter mass and said nothing and then went on up to Boolu. On Monday I did go to Cyrus's clinic and describe what had happened. He checked my vitals and said apparently everything was just fine. Later, many years later, at a veterans' hospital, I was told I had had a mini-stroke. My only reaction to that was that it was a warning, a small price to pay.

The next project in the medical regime was to get Boolu to heal. The hope was that the little stamp-size pieces of skin grafted to his red, raw, meat-like flesh would hold and take root. After a week or so, Dr. Cyrus said it looked like over 90% of the grafting was taking hold and with that amount he was more than pleased. The next step was to fill a tub to the top with salt water and sit Boolu in it up to his neck. This he would have to do not only once, not twice, but every day twice a day until he healed. It was excruciatingly painful. If you have any doubt, just throw a little salt on an open cut and magnify that by your legs, your arms and hands, your upper chest, shoulders, and neck. It is unimaginable, isn't it? But he did it. He would cry out in agony, but the nurses had to turn a deaf ear to his cries as they held him down in the saltwater. I remember seeing him being aided by two nurses on either side holding him by the waist to keep him from falling over as he inched his way down the corridor to the bath. He would be clothed in nothing but his hospital gown, the kind with the slit up the back. One could see the outline of his bones down his spine like a person being led to the gas chamber in Auschwitz or Buchenwald. Poor Boolu, in his feeble condition, was subjected to that torture twice daily for well over two and a half months. I wonder if at times he felt like he'd rather die.

At the end of May, Dr. Cyrus told me he could not get enough salt in the water to heal him. The last resort was to put Boolu into the sea. I mentioned the boat people and their problems with staph infection from the warm waters in this area. He said he was perfectly aware of that danger but what other choice was there? His plan was to let me take him home to Bequia. I was to take him into the sea up to his neck every morning and afternoon for approximately ten minutes. What I had to do twice a day, before wrapping him in gauze after his sea bath, was to check very closely over his whole body for any signs of infection.

"I am sure you will recognize it when you see it growing," Dr. Cyrus assured me. "They would appear as dark red patches growing out from the center. In other words, look for white puss or any changes in color." After each bathing and inspection, I was then to wrap him in gauze to prevent weeping of the greenish ooze that permeated areas of his body.

My response to all this was, "Me?"

"Who else?" he replied. Of course, he was right. Who else, indeed?

I told the Bishop and Evelyn we would be leaving, taking Boolu home. I couldn't thank them enough for their kind and generous hospitality. Up at the hospital we dressed Boolu in baggy pants over the bandages, and I put one of my XXX-size short-sleeved shirts on over his arms. After tearful good-byes from the staff and an "I'll-be-seeing-you-back-here-very-soon" from Dr. Cyrus, de tree a we, Sandy, Boolu, and I, took off in a cab for the Customs and Immigration Office. All tree a we were there this time because Sandy had arrived that month and was staying with me at the Bishop's.

Even though Boolu looked like a walking zombie, we took him straight into the immigration offices because it seemed the best way to deal with West Indian bureaucrats. Let them see for themselves so they would cut through the red tape. I told them Boolu had just been released from Cyrus's hospital. They knew who he was anyway. The crowds were gathering outside on Front Street just to get a good look.

I said, "Boolu will need a medical visa to go to America as soon as possible. We have doctors waiting for him at the New York Burn Center. Dr. Cyrus will sign the necessary release papers when you have them ready." I told them I hoped the paperwork could be done as soon as possible. I emphasized the urgency of the matter, being well aware of their natural pace. I had no idea when Boolu would be able to go, but at least when he was able, he would not have to wait for his papers. It worked, because the next time I took Boolu in to see Cyrus, they had all the necessary papers ready for me. All I had to do was purchase the airline ticket. When we got off the boat in Bequia, the crowds gathered just as they had in St. Vincent.

When we got home, we took it easy for the rest of the day and started on our ghastly routine the next day. Every morning and afternoon just the two of us, Boolu and I, went down to Lower Bay where there was no surf. We took our slow and easy walk into the salty, stinging sea. Everyone on and around Lower Bay said they got to the point where they knew when to expect the cries and just stood and waited for them to stop. It is amazing what we can all get used to.

The bandaging was a problem for me because I had only enough gauze for two separate complete wrappings. So when I took them off, Daphne washed them and hung them out to dry making sure a sudden rain didn't soak them again. I was nervous that I might not notice an infection in time, should one occur. It was hard to tell because so much of his body was still very red, but I looked and looked and didn't seem to find anything that looked very different. I tried to comfort myself constantly with the doctor's words of confidence: "I'm sure you will recognize infection when you see it growing." I never did see any infection, and in spite of that warm sea full of all kinds of organisms, he never did get infected. In fact one of the miracles in all this trauma was that from the first day of the burn Boolu never got infected. You go figure.

After a few weeks, I let him go down on the road, all covered up, of course. But his pale white face was still visible. One afternoon he was out in front of Kenneth's rum shop when Elvie and Avila's brother Ronnie approached him, three sheets to the wind, and laughed at him. The boys at the bar told me Boolu took his best fist, his left one—besides, he is a lefty anyway—and belted him one. He let Ronnie have it right on the button and sent him flying flat on his ass in the middle of the road with everyone cheering from behind the chicken-wired windows of the bar. That night his hand started swelling and I had to take him over to Dr. Cyrus the next morning. He had broken some small bones in his hand. Cyrus said he understood what Boolu had done but that he had better hold off for a while until he got stronger. Then home we went with one more bandage to care for – and Boolu's papers for America.

The Medical Visa That Changed Boolu's Life

It was July 5 and the awaited day had arrived. All tree a we were on an American 757 winging its way to Kennedy International. Sandy was relieved. "Who could have known how long that was going to take?"

"And how tough it was going to be?" I added.

Islands like this might be exotic, alluring, sexy, romantic, and dramatic. But practical? Not in a pinch and that was understating it. Yet we had had twelve wonderful, complicated, excruciatingly painful, and delightfully happy years there. Isn't that living life to the fullest? I'm reminded of Agnes Gooch in the musical *Mame* being encouraged by Mame to go out and take a slice out of life, just go out there and live life to the fullest. Well, a consequence always follows as Ms. Gooch well found out nine months later.

We were still going to get out there and take a slice out of life, and I knew we still had a heap of livin' to do. Right now we might be down but we were not out. As rough as it was for Boolu, he was tickled he was going to New York with all its wonders awaiting him.

We settled in at the Picasso on East 58th Street. Little did any of us know that it was going to be Boolu's permanent home for the next thirteen years. For now, our number one priority was getting Boolu up to the Burn Center on York and 68th Streets. The doctor who had talked to Dr. Cyrus over the phone took his case and said a few other doctors were also volunteering their time and expertise. The consensus after their thorough examination was that Boolu didn't need to be hospitalized any longer; he was to be treated as an out-patient. The doctor had one question for me: when did this accident occur? To my response of the 4th of March, the doctor shook his head saying, "Over four months and he is still not healed? Do you know up here, with the application of Silvadine, he would have healed in a month?"

Silvadine was an ointment that was spread thinly over the burned flesh twice daily. I could not help but think of those painful saltwater baths that could have been avoided for want of a little white ointment. In the midst of it all, I had once spoken to Dr. Cyrus about vitamin E. I asked him if it would be of any help in the healing process. "But of course," he replied, "but we don't have any." When I asked why, he said it was too expensive. I then went to three chemists in town before I found some. I'm sure if I had known about Silvadine, they would not have had it in their shops either, but Sandy could have sent it down and saved from pain not only Boolu but all of us who had to deal with those horrendous salt baths.

Boolu was enrolled in physical therapy and occupational therapy to get him to use his hands and fingers again. He worked in wood like boys in manual training workshop in school. He made little shelves, stools, and animals, all of which were helpful not only for his physical rehabilitation but also for his self-esteem. Though Boolu was now twenty-four years of age, he was still innocent. His naiveté added to his overall charm. He would bring home the little items he made to Sandy and me, full of pride. A far cry, I thought, from the salt baths.

By the first of August he was healed enough to be fitted for a rubber suit, something like Ace compression stockings only tighter and stronger. The suit came in two parts, the top half being like a long-sleeved T-shirt, the bottom half like women's panty hose reaching down to the ankles but with no feet. Completing the get-up was a pair of gloves that left the ends of the fingers exposed, like the gloves one used to see Diane Keaton wear. I guess she cut the fingers out of her gloves just to be different, but for Boolu it was practical—it helped him with his grip. I would have to peel the suit off him like a banana skin, only not as easily, put on a new one, which was even more difficult, and wash out the used one so it would be dry by morning, repeating the process daily. He had to wear that suit just short of a year. The purpose of the suit was to keep that purply proud flesh from growing into massive lumpy growths here and there all over his body. I could see in time the effect. It kept the proud flesh flat and close to his body like skin so it wouldn't be so obtrusive.

The problem with this cure was not only the troublesome and time-consuming fitting on and peeling off of the suit and the wearing of it night and day, but also the incessant itching that came with it, in his case everywhere except his head. Sandy and I could hear him all night twisting and turning, trying to get comfortable, scratching and itching till it drove us almost mad. It was incessant, and we were helpless. Though Boolu never spoke of it, the itching lasted long after the suit came off; he itched for years afterward, so many years I don't know when it actually stopped. Ever so slowly, it faded away. Years later I met a nurse tending to Boolu in California who had also been burned as a little girl in Mexico from scalding hot water. She told me the worst part of it all had been the incessant itching that lasted for years. I

27 A Near-Death Experience

told her Boolu knew exactly what she was talking about. She added no one except someone like him could. I had seen she had much compassion for him and now I knew why.

On top of all this, he was scheduled for painful steroid shots around his neck and face to reduce the proud flesh growing where the suit could not reach. The shots would save him from having to wear a facial mask. I used to sit in the waiting room and cringe every time he went in for his shots, until one day a little boy of about five who had been badly burned came in with his mother. I watched him get up like a little man and walk into the doctor's consultation room for his excruciatingly painful shots. It made it a little easier to accept and respect Boolu's position. Things can always be worse. There but for the grace of God... But Boolu wasn't quite finished yet. Now he was ready for plastic surgery on his right ear, neck, and lower right jaw. I used to laugh every time he was asked about it, or told someone of the coming operation. He always referred to it as his "plastic jersey." I wished that's all it were.

While he was undergoing his surgery, a nurse came out of the OR and asked if Julian were from St. Vincent. Learning he was, she said she was from Bequia. I then told her he was also from Bequia and asked her if she knew Frazeen Reno. "Of course," she said. "She lived over in Belmont."

"That's her grandson Boolu in there," I told her.

She asked how the accident had happened and observed that he was lucky to have lived at all. She introduced herself as Miss Barber. She had a house over on Tony Gibbons.

"Oh, yes," I responded, "it's now called Princess Margaret."

"I'm just across the road from Ross Lulley's place," she continued.

"I know where," I said and asked, "Are you related to Aggie Barber?"

"She's my niece," she said. "And I had better get back in there," she added as she turned toward the OR.

28 The Wonders of New York

Boolu Plunges In

All tree a we were now pounding the pavement up and down First and Second Avenues. Boolu was head up to 68th to the New York Burn Center and Sandy down to 54th to the Playhouse. I was bouncing back and forth between the two, with our home base, on 58th between Third and Second, as well as Paul's, on 59th and First, strategically located in the middle. If Boolu's treatments hadn't been put into motion simultaneously with the shooting of Sandy's tapes, I would have been able to concentrate on Boolu's recovery, as I should. Now I was going to have to juggle the two.

Boolu took to New York like a beaver in a mountain stream. Indeed, he was becoming a real eager beaver, piling up information like logs, one on top of the other. New York was so full of everything; there was so much to learn. The bridge to this new world he found himself facing was enormous. Beavers build dams, but Boolu had bridges to build, and cross, and many of them.

First he learned to navigate the trip to the Burn Center by bus from 57th Street up York Avenue. Once there, he was faced with the doors, corridors, and hallways of the hospital and then its banks of elevators, floor upon floor, up to more corridors and hallways to the Burn Unit. At first it seemed endless and insurmountable. But once there his rehabilitation took on a brand new pace.

The jaunt across 58th Street to Shopwell for the week's groceries was another challenge. In no time, he knew the names of every doorman and cook in every restaurant along 58th Street. On sweltering late afternoons, they would be standing at the open side door to the kitchen, catching a bit of fresh air. He would stop and socialize, and before long everyone in the neighborhood knew him.

The second week Boolu was in New York, my brother Leo was in town. He asked Boolu if he wanted to go shopping with him at Bloomingdale's. On the way home afterward, they stopped at a curbside hotdog stand and Leo said, "Boolu, how about a hotdog?"

"Sure," Boolu said.

Leo then asked, "What do you want on yours?"

And the Hotdog Lady said, "He wants ketchup and onions. What do you want?"

When Leo got back to the apartment, he said to me, "Jimmy, you don't have to concern yourself about Boolu making out in this town. He's already got it by the tail. Do you know every doorman on the block knows him?"

It was true, he was so happy and alert he wasn't missing a trick. He already knew how to get up to the Burn Center and taken the elevator to his treatment room. He was equally at home in the supermarket; he would be shopping himself before long.

Now that Boolu could make it to his treatments alone, I had more time on my hands to help Sandy with the taping project, the reason we had come back to New York in the first place, leaving Boolu on Bequia. I couldn't help thinking that if it hadn't been for the damn taping, the true catalyst of Boolu's mishap, we wouldn't be in such a god-awful mess.

An Unpleasant Surprise

Filming activity picked up again, and from the start I realized I was completely excluded from the conversations. I told Sandy to speak to Kent and find out what my job was on this venture. "After all," I said, "you wouldn't be doing this if I hadn't agreed to come up with you to help. So here I am. Now where and how do I help? Will you speak to Kent?"

Well, he must have said something because a day or two later, the would-be author, Ms. Rue Drew, who was also serving as Kent's "gofer," took me to one side. It was she who had schmoozed Kent into speaking to Sandy about giving her the green light to write his book. She stood there, checking off notes on her clipboard, as she said, "Oh, by the way, Jimmy, your job is to get Sandy to and from the shootings."

I was flabbergasted, speechless. I just turned without a word and walked away. I believe I would have gone ballistic if I had confronted her. If Kent had said this to me, it would have been different—he was the boss. But coming from a flunky, and one I didn't have a good feeling about in the first place, it rankled.

I knew Sandy was headed for trouble the first day I had laid eyes on the woman and took a reading of her. Boy, I spotted that one's number right off. I remember thinking, thank God Sandy's got a book agent. He's going to need one. From the outset I kept my distance, for fear of doing or saying something to her I would later be sorry for. You can't call people names and I don't intend to now. I just waited until I got Sandy alone, and then I went ballistic.

Now I have already said that Sandy was helpless when it came to confrontation. He was absolutely no good at it. I knew he wouldn't lift a finger on my behalf, no matter what we had previously agreed on. As far as he was concerned, this project was Kent's and he wouldn't interfere. Knowing all this, I said, "You said all that stuff on Bequia just to get me up here. Well, I didn't leave everything on Bequia to be your taxi driver. No way, not on your life! You don't give a damn what I do up here just so long as I'm up here with you. In five minutes I'd be packing my bag for Bequia if it wasn't for Boolu and his burn troubles. You go do your tapes. I thought you didn't want to do them without me. Well, that's what you're going to be doing; I wouldn't go near that place with a ten-foot pole." The place happened to be way downtown at Joe Papp's Public Theater below Cooper Union just south of East 8th Street. "I don't care if you have to crawl back and forth on your hands and knees, that's your problem."

I don't know how he did get down and back. I think Bob Scott took him, I wasn't sure. And to think I had talked him into this! If it hadn't been for this project, Boolu wouldn't have been burned because there wouldn't have been a kitchen let alone a stove for him to contend with. Somber and sober, yes, that was the atmosphere that permeated the apartment that week. Boolu didn't know what to make of it. I busied myself attending to Boolu's needs most of the week. Sandy and I spoke only when absolutely necessary. He knew me and was careful about what to speak about. I never mentioned the shooting of the film, and he never brought it up. Some week that was!

That is until Friday when he came home early. After asking where Boolu was—I told him he was still at his therapy—he nonchalantly announced, "Monday, I want you to come to the shoot and do a Spoon River."

"You're crazy. I haven't worked in fourteen, fifteen years. Why do you want me now?" I wondered. That's him, I thought. He knew I had been slighted and was insulted by the whole affair, and this was his way of trying to make amends. I knew they were shooting the last of the tapes the next week, finishing off with Sandy's last exercise, the Spoon River Anthologies, using experienced actors instead of students. They had Frances Sternhagen, Kathleen Nolan, and Barbara Baxley with Biff McGuire, Fred Karamen, and Keir Dullea.

Sandy said, "Look, Jimmy, Keir has a flying phobia, and now with the air traffic controllers' strike, there's no way he'll make it. All flights coast to coast will be in one hell of a mess and that'll just exacerbate Keir's problem. He was already petrified just thinking about making the flight from Hollywood. No way will he be here by Monday. I need you to step in. You have all weekend to prepare."

"Sandy, thanks," I said, "but New York is full of actors. You don't need me. I couldn't do it anyway. I haven't acted in years. You're fifteen years too late."

"Oh, sure you have. You're acting all the time." He went on. "Look, Jimmy, it's true I don't need you, but I want you and you can do this. I'll have you do Walter Simmons, the watchmaker down at the square. Come on, don't let them get to you, don't take them on so. I want you with me." Handing me the little book, he said, "Here, go on. Get to work." And he went into his bedroom.

I simply took the book, worked on it, and faced Sydney Pollack on Monday morning. Not a word was said, or an eyebrow arched. I thought, that's the power of Sandy, and it gave me a subdued inner pleasure, even though I was as rusty as hell. In truth I was awful. With no film experience I came across on camera like Ethel Merman. Experience was the necessary ingredient for the proper execution for this particular exercise, and I didn't have a ghost of a chance. On Friday Sydney called it a wrap, and we all went our separate ways, leaving Kent Paul to muster up enough funding to edit and finish the project. Unfortunately, the editing for such a large project in those days was going to cost a bundle, and Kent was never going to get sufficient funding from actors to complete the project, no matter how successful they were and no matter how much money they made.

"I Love New York Tity!"

When we brought Boolu to New York, I thought it was going to be rough on him. You see, at the age of twelve, when he had come to live with us on Bequia, he was given his freedom to come and go as he pleased without explanation. He had his work around the house to do as well as his classes to attend, but his free time was his to do with as he wished. Who he spent his time with was his business. Normally he spent it with other West Indians in the community. He knew everyone and everyone knew him. I never interfered. On Bequia, he was used to having the run of the place, the openness, the fresh air, the ocean. Now here in New York, he would be cooped up in a small apartment, stuck with two old fogies who didn't think like he did, let alone talk like he did. But then, who the hell did anything like he did? No way was I going to take that freedom and independence away from him at twenty-four just because he was in New York City.

Boolu in NYC

In no time at all, he was bussing up and down the East Side from 14th Street to 89th Street, on the West Side from SoHo up to 57th Street, and up Broadway to 146th Street in West Harlem. He even took an unscheduled and unexpected trip to Presbyterian Hospital all by himself. Grocery stores, department stores, pizza parlors, discos, movie houses, and even porno houses were in his realm of activity. I mustn't leave out the ballpark under the 59th Street Bridge, and Central Park with all its activities. Never mind how he looked! His physical condition didn't squelch or crush his curious quest for the new and unimaginable experiences awaiting him around every corner. He was insatiable; his life was a candy store, an ice-cream parlor, a toy store like F.A.O. Schwarz's just down the street. He loved the zoo, but most of all he loved New York, and every once in a while, like the TV ad, he would exclaim "I LOVE NEW YORK!" It took him all of two days to find the West Indian radio station out of Brooklyn. Anywhere and everywhere in New York that summer, he was a wunderkind in a kindergarten. The city was an eye-opener for him. He had been to the States once before when he was seventeen, to upstate New York with my mom and dad, whom he called Granny and Pap-Pap. (He called his own grandmother on Bequia, "Mommy.") To him the lifestyle in the country was a world apart from that in the city. Once, at a party in a penthouse apartment on the Upper West Side, he took me out on the terrace, pointed across the Hudson River to New Jersey, and said, "See, Jimmy, dat's American over dere and dis here is New York Tity." While I was trying to explain America to him, Suzanne Shepherd, the hostess, interrupted us, saying, "Jimmy, leave the kid alone. He's got it right. He has great instincts."

No matter how good his instincts were, he was having trouble with the new vocabulary he was being bombarded with. The new language of the apartment house, the department stores—like Alexander's, Bloomingdale's, and Woolworths—Shopwell with all that food, plus the nightlife—movies, discos, and restaurants—was mounting every day, volumes of it. I was doubtful he was capable of comprehending half of it.

These words a'bending
for to fit,
such as unspoken
the essential token
in the slit
of the mighty turnstile
we pass by.

The passage right in daily life
was an endless flight,
be it now or later,
from the perambulator.
That's right
into
words, words, words
such as
escalator, elevator, incubator, incinerator.

"What?" Boolu says, I say, "In-cin-er-a-tor, for to burn the garbage."
"Oh!" Boolu says, "Now I tee. De garbage burn, out in de hall's garbage drop."
"That's right, don't stop. 'Incinerator.'"

There was uptown, downtown, crosstown, and with a transfer you can detour all around, rebound, and come back around. As well as with a soundtrack

28 The Wonders of New York

and a six-pack, a horse and hack could bring you back. Without a bit of a fuss, there was always the bus.

Ah, the buses! He even learned to get about the city by himself by bus. I would take him first and mark out sites he could depend on. He got lost only once while riding the bus but managed to find his way home without a fuss. It was on a trip up to Harlem.

I had taken him there once to visit the Leach family from Bequia who had children his age he knew back on the Island. They lived up on 146th Street and Broadway. This trip would be his second and he was going all alone. I gave him a note to show the bus driver, and instructions.

"You take the M4. You get it on Madison and 57th Street. You remember where that is, don't you?"

"No," Boolu said.

"Boolu, you do, too. You know, just past the red disco on 58th Street," I told him.

"De red disco, yeah, yeah. I know. At dat stor on de corner where dey have de ladies' dance clothes in de window."

"Yes, that's the corner. You just turn there and go down to 57th Street, OK? Now sit right up front, across from the driver, and he will let you off at 145th. All you'll have to do is cross Broadway and go up to the Leaches' building, like I showed you."

As he headed for the door, Sandy interjected, "Now be sure you show the note to the driver."

Boolu said impatiently, "OK, OK, I know, I know."

Sandy had been sitting on the sofa taking in the whole scene and as the door shut behind Boolu, he said, "God help him. He'll get up there in Harlem, get lost, and we'll never see him again."

"Sandy!" I said, "For godsakes, I'm worried enough as it without you adding to it."

As it turned out, he got to Madison and 57th Street all right and took the M4 bus with no trouble. He was just a little too proud to show the note to the driver, though. He thought he could manage it by himself. It was quite a trip up Madison to 110th Street, then across to Riverside, up to 125th, then back east to Broadway, and on Broadway north to Inwood. By 145th Street, with all the bus's twists and turns, Boolu must have miscalculated and gone right past his stop. Soon he realized the numbers were getting higher, or he sensed he was in strange territory, so he leaned over and asked the driver, "Does dis bus go backward?"

The bus driver shot Boolu a quick glance. Can't you imagine his answer? "Listen, buddy, I have enough trouble going forward in this town."

Later, at home, when he was telling me what happened, I asked, "What did you do?"

"I got off at de next stop," he simply said.

"Where were you, for godsakes? What was the number on the street?"

"I don't know de number but I was by de hospital."

"How did you know you were at the hospital?"

"Because de women, you know, comin' and goin' in der white dresses."

Sandy chimed in with, "Good lord! Jimmy, that had to be way up at Presbyterian."

"So what did you do then?" I asked.

"Well, I say ta myself, 'You got a long walk ahead of ya now, Boolu mon.' And I walk all de way back till I fine de Leaches' house."

I turned to Sandy and said, "I know a lot of people who wouldn't be able to do what he did."

And Sandy said, "I know one person who wouldn't."

So, yes, only once did he get lost, not counting the day he got lost with Cora, an eighteen-year-old from Bequia who didn't know New York any better than Boolu did. His head was in a whirl over this girl. Their adventure took place during the Labor Day celebrations in Brooklyn for all West Indian Island people, wherever they were from. We all started off from Utica Avenue early in the day when about a dozen of us Bequians met to go and jump-up all day in the Carnival-like atmosphere. Those two kids strode off and got separated from us. All afternoon her aunt and I walked up and down Eastern Parkway in a sea of Afro, cornrows, and Jheri curls looking for them. Her aunt said, "Here we are worrying ourselves sick and we're not even their parents. I bet they're not giving us a second thought." By seven o'clock we had been to two police stations. After all, a girl who didn't know the country along with Boolu who was deaf and illiterate gave us a great deal of concern. We walked the length of the celebrations back and forth all day, only to find them back home. It was infuriating.

When we got back to the house about 8 PM that night, I asked Boolu how he had got lost. He replied, "No, mon, we didn't get lost. You did. We stayed right wit de band and we wine, wine, wine all day."

I couldn't help but smile at the image of Boolu happily "winding" his hips as they danced along following the band, but I went on with my interrogation. "Weren't you scared?"

"No, Donald see we and bring we back."

I could have strangled both of them that night.

Boolu adapted to other aspects of urban life, too. He couldn't read except for two- or three- or four-letter words and simple sentences. He could count and add amounts very little, but still he managed even shopping bills. He did most of our grocery shopping at Shopwell at 57th and 1st. To him it was a spree and not a curse; he called it "Shoppie" from the first. How did he do it? I think he marked everything in his head; his memory for some things was phenomenal. Things like packaging held meaning. For instance, I would say, "get tartar sauce" and he would come home with sandwich spread. God knows they looked the same and could be used instead. Eventually, it wasn't always a guess; he saw the difference: one was T, the other was S. He would have made out better using the kanji symbols of Japanese and Chinese pictograms. At first I gave him notes, but he wasn't using them. Although he knew all the clerks in the store and most of their names, he never asked for help when he was hopelessly stuck.

Well, whatever he didn't comprehend didn't stop him from going about making a friend. Alexandria, the young woman in the locksmith shop who made his key, was one. All the doormen on the street knew him, too, because he stopped and talked to everyone, as best he could. They understood enough to know that he was friendly and that he wished them all well. He would go through the same old routine every time, to anyone who would listen, and most did. His approach was so simple, straightforward, and charming: "My name is Boolu, I come from Bequia."

"Where?" they would ask.

"Over by Barbados. I got burned and Sandy bring me… Jimmy teach me…" and on he went.

One day I was telling him to watch the traffic both ways when crossing the street. "Why?" he asked. "It only run one way."

Another time I said, "Make sure you stop on the red and walk on the green."

"Na," he said. "You stop on de red, and you wak on de white."

"On the white!" I exclaimed. "You walk on the green, Boolu."

"It's white, I tell ya, mon."

"Green," I insisted.

"OK, OK, I show ya. Just wait, and I show ya tomorrow."

Sure enough, when he pointed to the sign "Walk," it was white. It was obvious I had been away from the city too long.

He was always so literal, so straightforward.

An Eerie Night In Tenafly

It was getting chillier, and Carol had walked over to the open window to close it a little. Everything in view gave off the tawniest hue that night in Tenafly. The air was clear and crisp. The leaves were crunchy on the trees, scratching and scraping together, nudged back and forth by the biting breeze until they wore themselves out and broke loose. Then they scurried off restlessly to the ground, only to be caught up in the arms of that breeze swishing and swigging, swashing and swagging as it twisted and scampered along with them. Leaves loping along, eloping two by two sometimes as if they were lovers racing into the night together, only to be spurned and jilted, dropped and dumped dejected onto the ground. There they lay, groveling rejects, exhausted, listless, lifeless, one on top of the other, covering the lawn like a shifting blanket of shimmering golden copper coins, glistening in the eerie glow of the street light down at the edge of the road.

What a night, Carol thought.

The bedroom TV was blasting out the eleven o'clock news but no one was listening to it. Jamie and Carrie were asleep in their rooms. Jim was in the bathroom. Carol had just laid out her things for the morning. On the news, Tony Randall was speaking. "He may not be the most well known acting teacher, but he is without a doubt one of the greatest," came blasting out of the idiot box.

Carol let out one shriek. "Jim!"

"What's that?" he said.

Carol yelled excitedly, "Quick! Come quick, it's the news."

"So what's happened? Have the Martians landed?"

"Shush," she interrupted him. "Be quiet, Jim! I can't hear what they're saying. Come on quick. It's Sandy."

"Sandy?" he asked as he walked to the door of the bathroom with a towel over his face, drying it with both hands.

Glancing back and forth from the TV to the bathroom door, to Jim and back to the TV again, she said, "My god, Jim! Will you look? They're not going to give him a half hour show—it's just a news bite, not This is Your Life. What did they say? Oh, it's his birthday. Jim, they're celebrating Sandy's birthday."

"Shush," Jim said, wiping his hands with the towel. "How can anybody hear, with you carrying on so? That's not Sandy, it's Jimmy. God, has he gotten fat. He sure looks like Santa Claus."

"What is this?" Carol was all agog. She was used to hearing people talk of Sandy and what a great teacher he was. More and more of his successful students were appearing on talk shows, and Sandy's name was always coming up. Hardly a month or so went by that she didn't hear, see, or read in some magazine about him. Now there was Boolu on the screen, sitting by, just listening. "Boolu on television! I can't believe it," said Carol.

"You can tell he was burned, Carol, look," said Jim.

"Yeah," Carol replied. "His color is much lighter, too. But look at that smile."

"I thought he was half deaf," Jim continued.

"I've never seen him so dressed up. Little 'dummy-boy' Boolu makes national television. Do you think Sandy told them, Jim? I mean to put him on, I mean the cameraman?" she asked.

Jim shrugged and said, "Nah, nobody tells those cameramen anything. They're always looking for something interesting and unusual to shoot. That's their job."

"Well, let's go to bed," she said as the segment ended. She pulled the coverlet off the bed. Jim was already in it.

"How long ago was it when we went to visit Jimmy on Bequia? Six or seven years?" he asked.

"How about eight or nine?" she answered.

"Eight or nine? Turn off the light in the bathroom," he continued.

"Why didn't you turn off the light in the bathroom? You were the last one in there... How old do you think Jamie is anyway?" she asked him.

"He's nine, but what's that got to do with the light in the bathroom? I left it lit because you'll be in and out of there at least three more times before you're done."

Carol sat on the bed and said, "My God, Jim, we went to Bequia before Jamie was born. And Boolu was just a skinny little kid just learning to talk. I remember he tried to tell me one night in the kitchen, 'Boolu do de kisshes.' When I told you what he said, you said, 'The what? Kittens?' And Jimmy said, 'No, the kind that break when you drop them.' And then we heard a crash from the kitchen! Jimmy, shrugging his shoulders said, 'Right on cue,' and got up and went into the kitchen to ask Boolu, 'What...?' Boolu said, 'Ump, kish ump,' and Jimmy said, 'No, Boolu, no jump. Boolu drop. Boolu drop. Say "Boolu duh-ro-,"' repeating, '"duh-ro-puh."' I'll never forget it. Boolu breaks a dish, and Jimmy's out there giving a speech lesson."

"Yeah," Jim said, "and I remember Boolu standing there trying to say the words correctly... Come, Carol, get that light. Let's get some sleep."

Crossing the room to the bath, she asked, "Do you remember he wouldn't go to the village with us? Jimmy told us it was because Boolu didn't want us to see the Harbour folk making fun of him. Do you know we were the first people who didn't know him as a 'dummy-boy from the bush'?"

"That's true," Jim said. "I always thought there was a story there."

Coming back from the bath, Carol said, tugging at her hair to get it in place for the night, "Do you remember he'd say 'Boolu pum, and Boolu pum'?"

"Pump what? Hey, turn off that light," he said, as he turned over to face the wall.

"I'll get it, I'm not done yet. Pump the water. Don't you remember the water in the over-head tank for the sink and the shower?"

"And the toilet, thank God. Good night!" Jim added.

Walking back from the bath for the last time, she added, "It's a crime about that burn. As if he didn't have enough on his plate already." Then she finally turned off the light and said, "I think that kid has done such a great job. GOOD NIGHT!"

Happy Birthday, Sandy

Earlier that evening had been the time, and the place, a sumptuous townhouse much like Sandy's 83rd Street home on the Upper East Side. It was the Beadleston Gallery on East 91st Street. The owner had offered the premises gratis to the Neighborhood Playhouse Repertory Company for the evening. The Company was honoring Sanford Meisner for his 75th birthday. Actually Sandy was into his 76th year. Not his 76th birthday as Sandy emphatically pointed out. They celebrated Sandy as one of the founding members of the Group Theater, a member until its demise in 1941, as a teacher at the Playhouse for so many years—forty-six to be exact—and as an actor who had played in so many Broadway plays over the years since his beginning in 1924.

You couldn't pay me to make up the guest list. After all, you could only invite so many. But who?

Jack Lord and his wife Marie were there from Hawaii, and Luther Adler traveled from his home in Pennsylvania. A goodly number of Sandy's former students were working in Flick-Land, but Hollywood was just a little far for most, thank God. Otherwise the house couldn't have accommodated the crowd. Besides Luther from the good old Group days, Bobby Lewis, Margaret (Beanie) Baker, Ruth Nelson, Dorothy Patten, and Elia Kazan came. "Gadge" spoke of Sandy's abounding energy and intense integrity. Congratulations came from Lee Strasberg and his wife Anna, who was a former student of Sandy's. Herbert Berghof, whom Sandy had worked with at the Playhouse when Berghof first immigrated and whom Sandy had got his first job in this country, along with his wife Uta Hagen, whom Sandy had directed along with her first husband, José Ferrer, up in Nyack, New York, sent congratulations and regrets along with two dozen of the most beautiful long-stemmed roses. Flowers aplenty came from Hollywood, as did heartwarming telegrams: the little Mercury man with winged helmet and heels was busy that night. Tony Randall served as major domo. Jack Lord spoke of how he had gone to Sandy, a hulk of a sailor, a merchant marine, and Sandy had given him direction and purpose and a refinement through exposure to culture—all those things that make for a bigger and better life. Stella Alder, George Grizzard, Elizabeth Wilson, Jo Van Fleet, Eli Wallach and his wife Annie Jackson, Barbara Baxley, Marian Seldes, Tammy Grimes, Diane Keaton, and many, many other New Yorkers were there.

Though it was Sandy's party, and fancy people—yes, I guess you could call them that—came from far and near, no matter. No way was Boolu ever going to be convinced that it wasn't all about him. Wasn't he being brought there by Sandy himself? He really thought that made him number one. There was no changing that. It was his night, as far as he was concerned anyway. He was to be formally addressed as Julian Martin. Turning to look up at me before we left the apartment, he said, "I not Boolu, tonight I be Julian."

He was technically Sandy's ward, for Sandy had sponsored his entry into the US for medical treatment at the Burn Center. He'd been in the States only three months and still had a long way to go, according to Dr. Herndon, his primary care doctor. He'd undergone many operations and still needed many others. Sandy's birthday party was to be his first social function in New York. Would he be ready for it? I well remember the day he punched that fool out on the road in front of Kenneth's rum shop in La Pompe, sending him flat on his ass and breaking some bones in his own fist into the bargain. But both Sandy and I felt he had to start sometime, so why not now, where he could get lost in the crowd with so many people and not be noticed too much.

What was more, this party was going to be Paul's last social function. He was barely able to walk up the stairs to a seat. He managed to get through the evening by keeping a low profile.

28 The Wonders of New York

On the other hand, Boolu was in rare form. No matter how he looked, it didn't bother him. He was on top of the world this night. Yet I was worried. He was 85% deaf and would have to lip-read like mad. He would have trouble with his hearing aids picking up so much interference, all the various noises and conversations intermingling at once with so many people in such a small space. Not to worry indeed. Unfortunately the color of his black skin had not come back to his face yet. In fact it was still quite white. I didn't and don't like referring to Boolu and his color like this. When it came to Boolu, I was color-blind.

I was sure deep down Boolu had hidden feelings of his own. He came from a society where sometimes prejudice played no part; at other times every shade of complexion had its hidden meaning, depending on the situation and the people involved. It was complicated and subtle. Boolu always thought of himself as brown and not colored, much less black, and what did he know from Afro-Americans? He didn't even know about Africa yet. He was a true Creole as many Bequians were. But just now, his lips were pale pink and not that soft brownish-red they once were. They had been burned so deep the scabs crusted over and fell off eight times. To this day, they are so sensitive he can't touch them with salt. His fingers were actually white and twisted out of shape, due to the burn, and he had all he could do to hold a glass. He wore Helanca-type stretch gloves with the fingertips cut out so he could grip better. No one would see the stretch Helanca-type body suit he was wearing under his fancy outfit. It must have been as uncomfortable as hell, itching to high heaven.

All this gave him a somewhat strange appearance, but he didn't feel strange, no, not for a minute. In fact he felt great. He'd never felt more excited in his whole life. Here he was in New York "Tity," in this big fancy house. In Boolu's own words, all dressed up in "flash" with fancy fine people that he "teed" on the "televisa" back on Bequia at Joan Stowe's house and at Kenneth's rum shop. The first thing he asked was, "Where are Kojak and Wonder Woman?"

Boolu

Tony Randall had just arrived and the TV cameras, CBS, NBC, and Channel 7, all of them, were lined up on the stairs. As Tony walked up to Sandy to greet him, Boolu spotted him from the dining room off the hall. Drink in hand like an old pro, he walked up to Tony while everyone else was holding back because of the TV cameras. "I know you," he said. "I teed you on de televisa."

With Boolu's faulty diction and his overall appearance, God knows what Tony thought. He looked at Boolu, gave him a broad smile, and said, "You do, you have, how nice and how do you do?" and shot Sandy one glance. It was one of Tony's specials. Sandy tried to explain the moment away as best he could. He wasn't the least bit nonplussed by it at all; actually he was rather amused. I intervened and had Boolu step back with me and Jack Lord's wife. We stood there on the sidelines while the media interviewed Jack, Tony, and Sandy. Marie Lord, Jack's ever-adoring wife, had watched Boolu's antics with Tony. She was rather amused as well and a little later, when she was introduced to him, said, "Well, Julian, you certainly must know my husband, Jack. See him standing over there next to Sandy?"

Boolu took one long look at the tall, handsome, impeccably dressed man in a dark suit standing by Sandy and said, "No, I ant neva teed dat man."

Marie said in what seemed like a slightly crushed tone, "You don't know Jack...? Hawaii Five-O?"

Boolu, straightforward and blunt, answered, "No."

I butted in to explain we didn't have TV on the Island and Boolu's TV watching had just started here in New York in July. They hadn't been showing any reruns of Hawaii Five-O this summer so Boolu had never seen the series.

"Is that so?" she said. "But they show it all over the world."

"I know," I said, "but there's very little TV where we are and most of it has been from the BBC. It's rapidly in the process of changing to more US shows now." To soften the blow, I told her Boolu had been watching Tony all summer in The Odd Couple.

As we went upstairs, I told Sandy of our little encounter with Marie Lord. He laughed. "That's no surprise coming from a woman who practically helps her husband on with his socks every morning. Why, she idolizes him. She thinks the sun rises and sets on him."

As for Boolu, I thought, OK, buddy, I had better keep a close eye on you, before you and that mouth of yours get us into real hot water.

Well, I was wrong. He did quite well for himself. He was so confident and poised that he was able to mingle just like anyone else. Only once did I think it prudent to interrupt a conversation he was having with an actor I did not know. It was getting a little too complicated. So I had him follow me downstairs to the bar. As I was working my way across the room with him at my heels jabbing me in the back, he spoke up. "Look," he said.

"Look at what?" I said, not paying him much mind.

There was another poke. "Look, Jimmy," he said again. "Look at dat funny Afro."

I stopped dead and turned around. "Where? Who?"

"Over dere," he said, pointing out into the garden.

I knocked his arm down and said, "Don't point. That's not nice. Ohmygod, that's not Afro that's... that's Diane Keaton."

Boolu stated, "Well, she need an Afro-pick to scuff it up from de back."

"Well, what do you want to do? Give her yours?" I asked him then and added, "She doesn't need no Afro-pick because it's not no Afro, nor does she want no Afro... I think." She did have her hair all frizzed up within an inch of its life.

28 The Wonders of New York

"Boolu, come on and help me with the drinks."

As I reached the counter where the drinks were, I turned around to see if he was still with me. He had also turned around and was heading in the opposite direction. I caught him by the tail of his coat. "Now where are ya heading?" I asked.

"To de kitchen to get dat lady an ashtry," he replied, pointing at Maureen Stapleton.

"Don't point," I said again, glancing across the room at Maureen. In truth, she needed an ashtray as she stood there talking to Sandy's cousin Bobby Fisher and Mara Safransky with her arm outstretched, cupped palm up as if she were begging for alms for the love of Allah. I watched her as she stood there talking. She had a cigarette in one hand, and every few drags, with much aplomb she would flick the ash into her palm. After a short while, she looked around once more and then expectorated into her hand. My first thought was, my God, she's burnt herself with a real hot ash! I thought I'd be gallant and offer my hanky. When I got there she was grinding out the lit butt in the spittle in her hand. She gave me a blank look and shrugged her shoulders.

"Where did you learn that?" I asked.

"In the army," she quipped. "What can you do when there's no ashtray?"

"Try the carpet. They say it's good for Kerman rugs," I said.

"Come on. No, it's not. What do you take me for? A slob I'm not," she said, fumbling in her purse with the other hand. By the time I remembered why I had gone over there in the first place and reached for my hanky, she already had a Kleenex out. With one grand quick gesture, she scooped up the whole shebang in one fell swoop leaving her hand as clean as a whistle. She held her outstretched hand and said, "See, just like new."

"Well, that is easier on the Orientals," I said. "Now, what are you going to do with it?"

"Nothing very dramatic. I'll just put it in my purse," she said as good old step and fetch it Boolu arrived with an ashtray. How and where he got it was anybody's guess.

"Just in time, thank you," said Maureen as she dumped the sooty Kleenex into the ashtray instead of her purse. "Now isn't he handy. Is he expensive?" she asked.

I don't know if Maureen knew who Boolu was or if she thought he was working the place as a butler. Not that it made any difference to him, or Maureen either.

"Jimmy," Maureen went on, "I wonder how our old friend Lyle Bosley's doing?"

It was a little private joke between us two former Upstaters. Lyle had been a commentator, an anchorman on WKTV in upstate New York. The world could be coming apart at the seems; just the minimal amount of time would be devoted to national and international news, not much more than fifteen minutes. Then good old Lyle would step out and carry on interminably about some bloke in New York Mills or down in Frankfort who damn near choked to death when he managed to get his tie caught in a garbage disposal. Bosley would go on for almost an hour reporting on inconsequential happenings in and around the area.

Maureen said, "I keep looking for your brother to reappear. What's that one's name, the political activist who comes on sometimes? Tommy?"

"Yes, Tommy. He's always been controversial."

When she was up at her summer place on Great Sagondaga Lake, she would wait all day for the Utica Evening News. She said she thought it was the funniest show on television. The show was so insular it was hysterical. Maybe it was the long, cold, damp winters. You felt as if you were within the boundaries of Alaska or somewhere off in the Arctic waste of Siberia.

Next I spotted the Blue-Jean Queen of the TV ads, Gloria Vanderbilt, with one of her young sons who was now thinking of studying with Sandy. Gloria had studied in the same class as Oona O'Neill Chaplin and Carol Saroyan, and Sandy had directed Gloria in a play at City Center.

Stella Adler arrived and worked her way across the crowded room to Sandy. She looked as if she were head and shoulders over many in the room. She was tall to begin with and she was obviously having a big hair day. It stuck out like a beacon, all done up like TV's Fran Fine's mother, Renée Taylor. The look guaranteed her a grand entrance. Why, it was more than that—it was a showstopper, which was exactly what she wanted it to be.

Of course, many former students were invited, too many to mention. As the party progressed, much small talk and smaller talk and more small talk went on. Before long the working actors had to head out in order to make half-hour. Elizabeth Wilson, who was playing in *Morning at Seven*, was at the top of the stairs giving Sandy a good-bye kiss and telling him Vivian Matalon was sorry he couldn't be there; he was out of town directing *Brigadoon*. Tammy Grimes, who was in *Forty-Second Street*, was standing by talking to Jack and Marie who were also cutting out. They wanted to have dinner before catching some theater while they were in town. Then there was Susan Kellerman, who happened to be in Mike Nichol's play, and Sandy Faison, who was in *Annie*.

Not long after that, the place started to thin out. A small group of us were going over to Rue Drew's place on Third Avenue for a late supper and to catch the eleven o'clock news. After supper, the TV was turned on and sure enough Sandy's party was covered. First Tony and Jack talked to Sandy, then, as the commentator talked, the camera panned the crowd zeroing in on the swells sitting around Sandy—Gloria, Kazan, Maureen, Stella, Gwen, Gregory, Luther, Eli, and Annie. The commentator went on about the celebration of the New York acting teacher's 76th year and for some unknown reason just before the end of the news bite, the camera zoomed in on and passed me on its way over to Boolu who was sitting next to me bigger than life, smiling from ear to ear. We all broke up and just about died laughing at Boolu sitting there looking like the cat that ate the canary. He clapped his hands on top of his head and said, "Oh, life! Boolu on de televisa. Jeezu-laud have merty!"

29 Blow by Blow

Sandy Teaching with Headset

Where Is That Book?

That fall of '80, the first three chapters of Rue's book about Sandy should have been showing up at Connie Clausen's, Sandy's book agent. But there was no sign of them, not even so much as a phone call from Rue. Nor was she answering any of Connie's office calls. Connie advised Sandy to send her a registered letter requesting them, and I did. Well, there was not a word from her, and the registered letter was returned unopened. Connie told Sandy, "As far as her contract is concerned, that's it. She has just broken it. Go find someone else to help you with the book, Sandy." That was exactly what he did.

Boy, did I ever have a bead on that one! I had that lady's number from the start. As far as I was concerned, Sandy was lucky as hell he got out of that mess rather lightly. It could have been another expensive quagmire.

I felt it was Sandy's mild-mannered, easygoing ways that got him entangled in these episodes. His anything-to-avoid-a-confrontation personality is what attracted vultures like these. Avaricious, ravenous, soul-sucking opportunists pounce on guys like Sandy. Paul must have recognized this weakness in Sandy years ago, and I'm sure it was exactly this kind of exploitation Paul was afraid of in my case. I think, from a few of our talks in the waning years of his life, Paul realized before he died that he was wrong in his first assessment of me. I certainly hoped so.

Paul's Slow And Painful Passing

Ever since the Playhouse had started its summer session, Paul had been getting weaker by the week, and I'm not making a play on words. The doctor couldn't come up with a diagnosis, only a regimen of rest and relaxation. Paul had planned to go to England after the summer session and come hell or high water, no matter what the doctors said, he was hell-bent on going. Sandy felt he was too weak to make the trip, especially all by himself, and all the more since London was having one hell of a miserably cold, damp, and foggy summer. Nevertheless, he took off, looking forward to the shows in the West End. Wherever he went and whomever he saw, I never knew, but I am sure he connected with old friends like Sir John Gielgud, Alec McCowen, and a couple of Martha Graham dancers teaching over there. He loved England dearly and deeply, as the saying goes. He had a similar love affair with Tokyo back in the mid-sixties when he was sent with Harold Clurman to tech a production of Eugene O'Neill's *Desire Under the Elms*.

After he got back from England in September, Paul couldn't make it on his own, that was plain. Sandy suggested a needy actor move in with him, one of his actor friends who had been taking care of Tennessee Williams over at the Elysée Hotel. The actor had had a falling out with Tennessee, not surprising with Tennessee's excessive drinking. So he moved in with Paul to nurse him through his final days.

Paul was back in the hospital before Thanksgiving. This time anyone could see he wasn't getting out. He was a small man to begin with but now he didn't have anything left to fight back with. He was failing and failing fast, with still no definite diagnosis. At first they thought it was pneumonia and then tuberculosis, but they couldn't find an antidote that would work. So they called it atypical, whatever that meant.

He was wasting away from lack of nutrition. In no time he was just a shell of himself. He became delirious and incoherent due to lack of oxygen. His suffering was hard for Sandy to witness. Paul's was a hard long drawn-out passing. By Christmas, Oleta D'Ambry, the finance administrator at the school, had passed away from bone cancer. Days later, on the 29th of December, Paul succumbed.

Two doctors asked Sandy and me to meet with them at New York Hospital to discuss Paul's death. They couldn't find its exact cause and they asked us about his eating habits. They said the symptoms were like anorexia. Where did he eat? Did he keep food in the house? Did he ever sit and eat with his us? Was he obsessive over his weight? He did have a small paunch. Was he cutting his intake because of it? If he was, we never noticed. Sandy said, "If it was like that, it's a hell of a thing to die for. No, that can't be so."

29 Blow by Blow

Sandy Is Left With The School And A Secretary

Sandy was facing the new year of '81 at the Playhouse without the school director or a finance administrator. The only ones left to run the school were Lydia Saunders, the secretary, and himself. I quickly offered my services but Sandy said, "No way, this is my problem and I'll take care of things without your help. I don't want you going anywhere near that place."

I said, "Fine, you take care of it. I'll take care of Boolu. And since I won't be going back to Bequia for a while, I'll sign up with an agent and go back to work."

He had his reasons, and I could respect that. It wasn't that he didn't want me at the Playhouse helping him, and I would have loved to be of some help; it was more that Sandy was still dreaming of the day he would retire. My being there would only implicate our lives in the school that much more. Deep down he was shaken that Paul and Oleta had left him to decide the fate of the school and his retirement all alone. He had always expected to have their help in that matter, and now he was by himself and didn't know what the hell to do about the problem. So he did nothing.

Because of the Playhouse and the Burn Center, I knew I was going to have to stay in the city. So I went back to making the rounds looking for jobs. I signed up with the Funny Face Agency for print and the Cunningham Agency for commercials. You see, Sandy had been right. I was now in my fifties, and I had become a character actor just like that. I didn't even have to work at it. I got calls for everything from a chef to a junk dealer. I wasn't doing badly but now that I wasn't twenty anymore, I found the schlepping around town in the middle of winter a little daunting. It wasn't a sleigh ride, that's for sure. De tree a we muddled through that winter, just plodding along moment to moment, day after day.

Sandy spent much more time with Lydia at the school, and Boolu was his usual self, having a lot of work done at the Center, plastic jersey as he called it. And me? Well, I worried a lot because Sandy was making no plans to close the school. Now I thought there was a reason to close it, with Oleta and Paul gone. The talk was only of who the Board were going to get to take over the school. They had talked this way after Sandy's first bout with cancer. Then they had brought in Richard Boone as a possible replacement, but he didn't work out. After that Paul had thought for the first time of closing the school completely until he and Oleta got so sick and it never was brought up again at the Board meetings. It was obvious to me that the Board, with the exception of Sandy, Paul, and Oleta, didn't want the school closed, ever. Nothing was being done to make changes at the school. There wasn't even talk about it after all that had happened I knew I was going to have to start thinking seriously of our future financial security, "ours" meaning Sandy's, Boolu's, and mine, in toto.

Lydia hired Beverly Sugarman to work with her. Sandy, with Robert Whitehead, the president of the Board, set about looking for a director. The discussions went on and on, but no name came up. They were settling on no one, and Sandy kept on running the school all alone. Until Paul's death, he had never had this job; he was only the head of the acting department. He seemed to be handling the job very well for someone as naïve as he was supposed to be. Why wasn't I surprised? I'll tell you why. For years Paul had never done a thing without checking with Sandy first and getting his stamp of approval. And what was my problem with that? Sandy had actually been running the school for years but never getting recognition for it. Actually, based on the remuneration Sandy got for all he did for that school, it had to be a labor of love. He once told me he did it because he did love it, and I said, "What's to love about making other people millionaires?"

His answer: "That's not what it's about for me."

"So be it" was all I could say to that. So I kept my distance.

Spring '81—Sandy Is Hit With A Bundle Of Bricks

I had just gotten in from the photographic printers where I'd been ordering more 8"x10" glossy print photos for my agent. Depending on 8"x10" glossies was a sure sign someone hadn't made it yet because once you did, you didn't need them anymore. It was about 4:30. Boolu was at the Center, and Sandy was at school, or so I assumed. As I threw my coat over the back of a chair, I noticed the flashing light of the answering machine. To me that meant only one thing: the possibility of a call from my agent, until I found out otherwise, of course. This call was one of those otherwise messages. Boy, was it ever. It was Lydia Saunders calling me from Bellevue Hospital to tell me Sandy had been hit by a van on his way to school. He was in a bad way, and I should get to the Emergency Room ASAP.

I flew out of the house, into cab, and down to 30th and First Avenue. Lydia was waiting for me in the hallway. "He's down at the far end. Just go in there," she said, pointing to the Emergency Room. "They'll let you in. He's way back in the corner on the right."

He wasn't in a bed, he was on a steel slab with gutters on the edge, for the blood to drain off, I guessed. He was alone. They had him in a hospital gown secured at the neck. But they hadn't cleaned him up yet, and he was spotted in blood from head to foot. Somehow, he was secured to the tabletop; I don't quite remember how. He had to be because I do remember he was delirious and writhing about, moving his arm and right leg. The left leg seemed to be smashed at the hip for there was more blood and damage in that area. The back of his head looked bad, too. I was sure they had checked his vital signs—they had to have when he first came in and they had undressed him and hooked him up to a monitor. Now they were looking after other patients. I noticed as I came in that although it was only a little after 5, they were al-

29 Blow by Blow

ready getting backed up. They had patients on beds in the halls with police officers standing around them.

I had seen this sight once before, thirteen years earlier when an ex-student of Sandy's came pounding on the door after midnight one night. He was a down-and-out artist and had become a hopeless alcoholic. He said, "I have no one in the world to help me, no one cares enough. I have no friends left. Sandy, please help me."

Sandy turned to me and asked, "What do we do?"

I could see he had soiled himself and wasn't making much sense other than that he needed help. God knows how long he'd been on this binge and he now needed institutional help. I asked him if he had ever been in any of the Armed Services. He had, so I told Sandy we should take him to the Veterans Hospital on 24th Street. We let him in, I cleaned him up a bit, and we got dressed and found a cab. When we got there, we were turned away because the policy was not to take vets solely because they had a drinking problem. They told us to go to Bellevue.

What we encountered when we got there was unbelievable! Late on a Saturday night, it couldn't have been worse. It was jammed with shootings, cop fights and more cops, serious highway accidents with troopers, and dope, dope, dope. I knew a hopeless alcoholic would never be taken care of under these conditions. So I talked to an aide who suggested we take him up to the Harlem Hospital above 96th Street and York Avenue. There we managed to get him admitted.

Well, Bellevue this particular evening wasn't that bad yet, but I could see the workers revving up for the worst. You never knew at a place like this. A young doctor came over to me and asked who I was. I told him I was his friend and care-provider, that I lived with him, that he had a sister out in Queens. "Good, the doctor said, "you can stay in here with him while we check some of these other patients. His is mostly bone damage, his vitals are holding. We're keeping an eye on him in that office over there. We'll be back pronto to care for him. Stay with him."

Lydia came in and asked what was happening. I updated her and she asked what I was going to do. "First, I'm calling his doctor," I said. "His office is less than a block away, around the corner on 30th Street. I'm staying the night. I'll call a friend to look after Boolu. Could you call his sister in Queens and tell her? I'll be here and I'll for her tomorrow. She's in the book—Nat Post out on Yellowstone. Don't tell her how bad he is. If I know her, she'll be calling the hospital anyway and they won't tell her much either. She will only upset herself, no matter what you tell her."

I called our doctor to tell him where Sandy was. I told him he looked pretty much beat up with bones broken. The doctor was seeing patients and would be over when he was finished. He hung up after bolstering me with, "That's the best Trauma Center you could ask for. He's in excellent hands."

I then called Rusty Ford and asked if he would see to Boolu. "Of course," he said. "You just take care of Sandy."

"I will. I'll be staying the night, Rusty. You tell Boolu, OK?"

When I got back, they were working on him. Scrubbing him down. Now I knew why they had him on that steel slab. They just scrubbed him and washed it down that drain as if he were a slab of meat on a butcher shop's steel counter. They dressed his wounds, bandaged him up, put a clean hospital gown on him, and moved across the aisle to the bed in the far left corner. I am sure he didn't feel a hell of a lot better, but he did look better and seemed to me to be more comfortable. They must have given him something, because he was falling off to sleep.

Bill Alderson, one of his teachers, came to spend some time with him, giving me a little time to make a few phone calls. He reported that Sandy was intermittently raving incoherent thoughts about John Houseman.

Friday night at the Bellevue Trauma Center—I had no idea what an education I was about to receive. At one point, I went to sit in the admitting area. It encompassed everything from the dregs of society to horrifying fatal accidents, and it all happened weekend after weekend. It was like a war zone. And here was Sandy smack-dab in the middle of it all.

The following morning I phoned home. Rusty was there and said I had a call from Rosie Edelman, our friend from Los Angeles, who was in town. When I called and gave her the news, she wanted to know what in the world Sandy was doing in Bellevue, a county hospital.

I explained, "Because this is where they took him."

"No, no, no. You have got to get him the best!"

"Rosie, I'm waiting for his doctor to come." He hadn't shown up yet. "I want to talk to him first."

"Listen to me. I'm calling my mother in Beverly Hills. She knows the best in this town; she's had to use them herself. No, you talk to her first."

"OK, give me her number," I said, thinking I would talk to Sandy's doctor first and then decide what to do.

Sandy was still extremely disoriented. They were keeping him in the Trauma Center until he was out of danger. The attending doctor said he couldn't be in a better place. I waited for our own doctor, but he never showed even though he was less than a city block away. I couldn't believe it. I couldn't get through to him. I could only leave a message. He was not only Sandy's doctor but Boolu's and mine as well.

I slept at home Saturday night. Sunday I called our doctor, and again got the message service. I was fit to be tied. When I got to the hospital on Sunday, Sandy wasn't any better mentally as far as I could see. No matter, in the afternoon they moved him upstairs.

Upstairs, we were in another world. Down in the Trauma Center, everyone, no matter how much work they were faced with, had had things moving like a well-oiled machine. They were top-notch. Upstairs the nurses, when you saw a nurse, seemed to be more fluent in Spanish than English. It was a four-bed room; the other patients were Hispanic. Two televisions on two separate stations blasted away in Spanish. Then added to all the loud jabber over the TV was the Puerto Rican Spanish of the patients and their guests, which to me seemed louder and faster and a lot harsher on the ears than any Castilian Spanish I had ever heard in Spain.

When Sandy's sister Ruth showed up, she said, "We'll have to do something. With all that's going on in here, he's going to think he's in Mexico. Talk about adding to the confusion of a patient in his condition!"

I told her I had requested a private room, but the head nurse, when I finally found her had said, "This is County."

"Well, I guess there's no private duty either?" I probed.

"You got that right," she returned.

"But a patient in his condition—"

She cut me off, stating again, "This is County."

Could I have been rubbing her the wrong way? I well could have been. I knew I had to do something, and fast. Ruth was beside herself. I remember saying, "Don't worry. If I have to carry him out of here myself, he is not staying in that room."

On top of everything else, they had him in canvas restraints. The more he felt restricted, the more in his confusion he ranted and raved. I felt the noise was unfair to the other patients, yet no one seemed to care.

I had been told down in Trauma that he would be operated on Wednesday. When I'd heard about this, I had questioned why so long, but now that we were up on the ward, I felt better about it—it gave me time to get him out of there. I called Rosie's mother, Rita, in California.

"Rosie called me and explained," she said. "Look, I tried to get in touch with Dr. Sculco at the Hospital for Special Surgery where I had my operations. He's great and he has a flawless reputation, but he wasn't home. I should be able to get him in the morning; at least I know I can get to his secretary in the morning. Will you be at home? I can get back to you early tomorrow after I speak to someone."

I went home that night, talked to Boolu some, and went to bed thinking of Rita's call and what I would have to do after she called the next day. I was roused early by the ringing of the phone. It was Bellevue calling for Mr. Meisner's sister's telephone number."

"Why do you need his sister's number?"

"He's been scheduled for an operation today, and we need her consent," the voice said.

"I was told they were planning the operation for Wednesday. I'll be right down," I said.

"But we need the consent," she repeated.

And I repeated, "I'll be right down," and hung up.

I called Sandy's doctor again but all I got was the service, which informed me, "He is on a two-week vacation as of today."

"A what?" I said and hung up.

Then the doctor from Bellevue called telling me he had to have the consent for Mr. Meisner.

"What's the rush?" I asked. "I was told they were operating on Wednesday."

"Well, I found space today. If we don't move now, I don't know how long the wait will be," he said.

I thought that sounded fishy, and he sounded very young to my ear. I said, "Doctor, I'll be down at Ward 10W in a half hour," and I hung up.

Then the phone rang again and it was Rita. She still hadn't been able to reach anyone. "The office wasn't open yet, and God only knows where Dr. Sculco is." After I told her that Bellevue wanted to operate that day, she said, "Fine, but with whom? We don't even know this doctor or anything about him. Look, call an ambulance and go down there and get him out of that place, I'll call Special Surgery when Sculco's offices open and I'll get him accepted. If for any reason there's a snag or a delay, you can have the ambulance drive him around in Central Park all day until I do."

I then called the hospital. I wanted to make sure Sandy was still on the ward before I sent the ambulance. When I told the operator I needed to be connected to Sanford Meisner on 10W, she said, "Oh, he doesn't have a phone."

"Please connect me with one of the other patients."

"We are not permitted to do that," she said and cut me off.

Now what? I thought. Let's see. There's got to be a Gonzales or a Rodriguez in that room. So I called back and asked for Mr. Gonzales in 10W. When the operator said, "Sorry, there is no Gonzales there," I quickly came back, "Oh, excuse me, I'm very sorry. I meant Rodriguez." "Thank you," she said and connected us.

Thank you, Lord, there is a God, I thought, hoping to hell Mr. Rodriguez understood English.

"Excuse me, but I am the fellow, the man, who was there yesterday in the plaid, the red, shirt with the old man who was tied down."

"Jes," he said.

"Is he still there?"

"Jes," he answered.

"Is he all right?" I was saying anything, trying to be polite and not rude or abrupt.

"Ees sleebing."

"Thank you, thank you very much. I'm coming right down," I babbled.

I then called a private ambulance company, told them there was a Sanford Meisner in Ward 10W at Bellevue County who needed to be transferred to the Hospital for Special Surgery in care of Dr. Sculco. I added, "Please wait an hour to give me time to get down there, so I can arrange his release." I hung up and flew out of the apartment.

When I reached Bellevue and entered 10W, Sandy's bed was empty. I panicked and asked Mr. Rodriguez, "What happened to him?"

29 Blow by Blow

"They came and they take heem," he said.

"Did they take him to OR—Operating—or to the ambulance?" I foolishly asked in my desperation. How the hell would he know?

"Jes, they wheel heem out," was all he could say.

I thought, of course. We're on the 10th floor. If they were the ambulance people so much for "Please wait an hour," but I thought I had better check. With no nurse around, as usual, I went out to the nurses' station. There was no one around. A patient is gone and no one seems to care. How could they take him out of here without a release? Easy, I thought, just take him. I found a pay phone and called the ambulance company. They confirmed they had sent an ambulance forty-five minutes ago that was already on its way to Special Surgery with the Sculco patient.

They had come and Sandy was gone! Well, there was no sense in hanging around here. I'll come back for his personal things tomorrow, I thought to myself, and made a beeline to Special Surgery to get him admitted, that is, if Rita had managed to do her job. I prayed she'd been able to reach someone and if she had, I hoped against all hope there was room. I had visions of the two of us circling around Central Park all day in an ambulance.

I expected to find Sandy in a hallway waiting for me, with the drivers cussing me to hell and back for keeping them waiting. When I finally made it up the East Side to York and 71st, I found no ambulance, no driver, no aide, and worst of all, no Sandy! My heart dropped. What could have happened? Did they go to the wrong hospital? Did they have to go back to Bellevue? Where the hell were they?

I found Admitting and asked after Sanford Meisner. "He has already been admitted," the clerk said, adding, "and he was lucky because a bed came available just minutes before he arrived. But we still need his insurance and credit card numbers."

"I can get them. They're still down at Bellevue. But who signed him in?"

"He did."

Of course, why not? I thought. Then I heard a woman talking in the next booth. "I just cleared a bed for Dr. Sculco's patient, a Mr. Meisner. He's a Bellevue transfer and he should be coming in soon."

My clerk leaned over and said, "He's already in it. This is Mr. Carville, his friend."

"Oh, good," the woman said coming over to our booth. "I'm Dr. Sculco's secretary and I'll need his papers, health insurance and whatever. He is... let's see... up in 612." As we walked along the hall, she told me the doctor wasn't in yet. "It's a special day for him. Last night his wife had a baby girl, so he's a little late this morning. But that's understandable, wouldn't you say? It's a first for him."

All's well that ends well, I thought. But a badly beaten-up sevnty-six-year-old was still lying up there. I finished telling the doctor's secretary what little I knew of the accident, and then went up to see Sandy.

There he was in the last room on the left. It was a private room and two nurses were working on him. This is more like it, I thought. He was no longer in restraints, he was much calmer, and he knew me. Such an improvement over his raving condition back at 10 West, Bellevue!

Dr. Sculco came in, with much fanfare from the nurses for the new daddy. He did an immediate examination. After the X-rays, they scheduled the operation for Wednesday. "The sooner the better," said the doctor.

The morning of the operation, the telephone rang. It was our doctor from 30th Street, asking what had happened to Sandy. I was livid. I had called him on Friday, it was now Wednesday, and he was calling to find out what had happened to Sandy?

I said, "Your service told me on Monday you were on vacation."

"Well, I am, but I didn't leave town."

"Where were you?" I asked.

"I told you that he was in good hands, that he couldn't be in a better place."

"Well, he is. He's up in the Hospital for Special Surgery," I said.

"How did you manage that transfer?" he asked.

"We have friends in Beverly Hills," I told him.

"Well, that's how some people do it."

"Thank God we are 'some people,'" I said and hung up. He was never to be seen again. Another doctor down the drain.

It was a nine-hour operation. Sandy's hip had been wrenched and needed alignment; his femur received spiral fracture, broken in eleven places into disks like so many checkers from a checker game; and there was a break across his upper shinbone. As well, a serious head concussion was causing some trauma. Dr. Sculco said, "The operation was tedious. Each little checker-like disk had to be screwed and bolted one on top of the other onto a long, steel, semicircular rod running the length of his femur. His bone was so hard and dense, and that was to Sandy's benefit, but it has left my knuckles raw. See these little red calluses?"

Each disk was bolted to the rod with a screw an inch and a half long. The doctor said, "He is one tough old bird!" I told him I had heard that before.

The physical damage to Sandy's body healed quickly, but the mental comeback was much slower, which saddened me and depressed him greatly. However, in less than two and a half weeks, he was inching down the hall on a walker on his way home. As he passed the nurses' station, they all applauded. When I asked the head nurse why the applause, she explained, "Because even with all the athletes we care for, we don't see this often. He isn't supposed to be able to do this, certainly not this soon, not a man of his age with such serious injuries."

Months later, because of the arraignment, he had to live through that horrific afternoon for the second time. The accident happened just after 3 PM as he was on his way to his 4:00 class. He was across the street from the High

29 Blow by Blow

School of Art and Design at 57th. When the light changed, Sandy stepped off the curb and proceeded across the street with everyone else, for there was a group. The other side of the street had a large group of students ready to cross as well, since school had just let out. A van came barreling down Second Avenue and made an abrupt right turn, speeding up to beat the approaching pedestrians in the crosswalk. The young high school students saw him coming and jumped out of his way. Unfortunately, being blind in his left eye, Sandy didn't see the van in time to jump like all the rest. He received the full impact of the speeding vehicle and was thrown thirty feet along 57th Street. The van kept accelerating across to the red light on Third Avenue, where onlookers yelled at him to back up. Later in the police report, we noted the police never wrote up the fact that the driver had left the scene and had to be yelled back to the site.

The driver was the owner of a delivery business, a company somewhere out in New Jersey. He was supposed to have been out making deliveries. The investigation showed he had not made one delivery that day. Before the arraignment, he died of liver failure. He was an alcoholic but the policeman had never even checked him for DUI. All he had done was write up a report and send him on his way. That was a hell of a lot easier than doing his job. What the heck, it was just another accident in Manhattan. There had been no attempt to get a witness, and even the traffic patrol assigned to that corner until 6 PM was missing from the police report. We had zilch to fight this case, thanks to Patrolman Caruso. To add to our dilemma, the court wouldn't be too hard on a grieving widow, according to our lawyer.

At one point we went to Payne Whitney Psychiatric Institute next to New York Hospital for psychological testing. I was aware that Sandy wanted to speak to no one about the testing, not even to me. I honored his wish and never spoke of it. His mental capacity had slowed down considerably. His IQ had dropped down to eighty-eight, which for Sandy, if he had known, would have been devastating. But I never told him how low it had got and he never knew.

Nothing is more debilitating and depressing that something you cannot talk about orshare with anyone. I knew from my youth what that kind of suppression was like. Now here we were, being presented with another kind of embarrassment to deal with. I only hoped and prayed his intelligence would return. Thankfully it did, taking its own good time.

He had to undergo another complete examination with the insurance company doctor. I was amazed by that doctor's reaction. He was visibly shocked by Sandy's condition and couldn't get him out of his office quickly enough. This doctor had never seen Sandy before. One must remember all the physical deformities that Sandy had incurred to date. He was just barely getting by, using up every ounce of his energy to keep going. When the insurance company saw the brain scans, they tried to blame the mental condition on heavy drinking, implying that he could have been drinking that day. We both knew

Sandy never drank before a class, but how do you prove that? It seemed Sandy had to do all the proving; the dead alcoholic driver had to prove nothing. How could he? He was dead. Forget about what he died from; remember the poor widow. I can tell you I was one wild Irishman. I went ape-shit. Sandy had all he could to keep me civil. In the end the lawyers suggested Sandy settle out of court. The insurance company didn't want to go to court, and of course it went against Sandy's nature to contest it, so he settled without a fight.

The lawyer said that in cases like this, value seems to decrease with age. After all, Sandy wasn't twenty-six, he was seventy-six, and to the judiciary his brain or leg wouldn't have been worth as much.

Once it was all over, he felt a hell of a lot better. He didn't like dwelling on what had happened to him. He just wanted to get on with his life. He wanted a director for the school and he wanted to get back to Bequia. However, a trip to Bequia in his present condition was impossible, and Boolu couldn't go either because of his treatment regimen. So Bequia was out of the question. In truth, I couldn't have handled Sandy on Bequia in his condition.

Lydia, with her new assistant, was holding the school together as best she could. Sandy was in no condition to go anywhere near the place. I was amazed that all his supposed admirers and well-wishers never came near him. I think that the scuttlebutt about town had it that he was already half dead. I felt it was just as well: what they didn't really know was nobody's business. Although Sandy just wanted to get back to business as usual, I knew he was going to have to do it slowly. He needed time to mend, and the fewer people who knew right now the better. This was going to be our little secret.

My approach was to keep a low profile. I wanted to see if he would heal and come back to his usual self.

Summer '82—De Tree a We Back on Bequia

The Playhouse closed after the spring graduation at the Players Club. Lydia was taking over the school for the summer, and Sandy was coming to Bequia with Boolu and me for a well-deserved rest. It felt so good to be back. We had been away such a long time that I had my work cut out for me. Boolu had improved so much that he was able to work right along with me.

One of the first big jobs was in the master bedroom. When Sandy had walked over to his bed, his foot had sunk right through one of the six-inch floorboards, the bottom of which had been eaten out by wood lice. When Boolu came into the room, he said he could smell wood lice.

"I'm sure you can," I said. "Sandy just went through the floor."

When Parnell came over, even before he entered the dining room, he said, "I can smell wood lice. Can't you smell them? Where are they?"

"No, I can't with my infected sinuses, and Sandy can't either. He doesn't breathe through his nose because of his trach."

Boolu said, "Dey're up in de bedroom. I can smell dem, Parnell, and Sandy

29 Blow by Blow

fell tru de floor. We got to clean dem out."

Parnell went to the bedroom, opened the trap door in the floor, and went down to take a look.

He came up and asked, "Who's been watching this house anyway? These bugs have been here for months."

Five huge nests had settled in, one in each corner and one in the center. Obviously, our housekeeper had not been up in this room in months because if she had been, she would have fallen through the floor herself. We had been away for over a year and a half, and she was paid every month to watch over the place herself. Well, we were damn lucky we didn't stay away any longer because if we had, we would have come back to a heap of stones, thanks to DD. Needless to say, she got her walking papers that day. You can rest assured I was a hell of a lot more particular who I employed around the house after that.

We pulled out all the infected wood and had it replaced with greenheart, which was impervious to wood lice, as hard a wood as you could find. It was so dense it was like steel and had the look of dark-blond mahogany.

Sandy sat on the terrace soaking up the sun and having a grand time doing it. It didn't take Boolu long to check in with all his friends and fall back into his old routine of family-hopping. Everyone was impressed with his progress. Sandy, Boolu, and I easily found ourselves back in the social whirl of beach and dinner parties, and they were swimmingly delightful after that strenuous, stressful siege in New York City. Our entertaining candles and dinner spreads were back in vogue. Both Sandy and Boolu were in the best of spirits, and I was back in the swing of things, in my usual position as major domo.

All things considered, that summer on Bequia was everything we ever dreamed of—the beach parties, the Thursday night steel-band jump-ups at the Frangipani, and the congenial soirées about the Island. We held little musical gatherings in our living room on a Sunday evening. The light social gatherings demanded little of Sandy and relieved him of any mental stress, thus giving him time to proceed and progress at his own pace. It was the retirement Sandy had looked forward to.

Sandy and the Board had decided on the future director of the school. He was presently directing a summer stock company in western Canada and would be ready to take over the reins of the school in November. Harold Baldridge was a graduate of the Playhouse and had worked closely with Paul on school productions since his graduation. He above anyone knew the workings of the organization and had similar cultural tastes and abilities to Paul. Paul had had Broadway credits as a set designer, a costume designer, and a lighting designer, and Harold had worked under Paul's tutelage for years. As Sandy said, "So why not Harold?"

Once the director's position had been filled, Sandy could relax and enjoy what was left of the summer. But I had a problem now.

When I had called the airlines to check our return flights, I was told Boolu would have to apply for a regular visa because the one he had had was an emergency permit that wasn't valid anymore. He would have to apply like anyone else. When I told the immigration office that he was still under doctors' care, they wanted to know why he wasn't still there. I explained that the doctors had advised he come home for a while, that the sun would help his skin pigment and improve the skin tone. They said that was fine for his skin, but—and they were very sorry—he would still have to reapply.

Over at the American consulate in Barbados, Boolu would not have a shot in hell of getting a visa with no job, no bank account, no family—neither mother, wife, nor children—to come home to. No one gets out on a visitor visa unless the powers-that-be feel there is sufficient reason for the applicant to come back home voluntarily. A completely new biography would first have to be created, invented, fudged, and finagled. Whatever I had to do to get him back to his doctors was going to be done. He only had Sandy and me to rely on.

I was sure Father Adams would help if he could, but I knew he would be totally powerless with the bureaucrats in Barbados. They couldn't have cared less. So let's see. I had a school of sorts, had had for over ten years, people worked at my school, and Boolu worked around the place. God knows, I wasn't lying. So what if his pay was deferred? So was everyone else's. That was between us.

I fixed a real nice letterhead, which I had never needed before but there's always a first time for everything. The bureaucrats in Barbados could tell from his record that Boolu had been to the States twice before and promptly returned without incident. He would have that in his favor. I sent the letter of request for a visa on the deaf school's new stationery. I stated that as a former graduate of our school, he had been working for us for the past six years. We were giving him a six-month sabbatical so that he could continue skin treatment at a burn center and undergo a new advanced hearing exam. Sanford Meisner was sponsoring him, and he would be staying with him at his home in New York City. I stressed as the Director of the School that he had his job waiting for him when he returned. I also stuck in Sandy's bank statement. We sweated it out for over two months. Finally the approval arrived and they gave him a six-month visa.

All too soon, our idyllic summer came to a close.

Contemplating Boolu's Future

Sandy, in a much improved mental state, was back at the Playhouse making ready for Harold's arrival in November, and Boolu was up at the Center getting much needed but painful steroid shots on his face to soften and shrink the purplish proud flesh that rose up from the scars of his burn. I went to buy two more rubber stretch suits but was told he didn't have to wear

29 Blow by Blow

them any longer, thank God. I thought the itching would let up without them but I was wrong. All it did was make it easier to scratch.

With Sandy busy at the school orienting Harold, and Boolu working away at his physical therapy, I had time to think of Boolu and his future. It was something I hadn't thought too much about, as far as the two countries were concerned, if I ever thought about it at all. Boolu would live in Bequia. But now I had to consider that. Here he was in America needing medical treatment, and what about the possibility of a proper education? What do we do to keep him in the States? Then there was the problem of Sandy's shuttling back and forth. It seemed that's what I would be doing now, too. What do we do with Boolu in the interim? All these unanswered questions were nagging at my wellbeing. I knew it was time to see an immigration lawyer.

I found one on the south side of Bryant Park between Sixth and Fifty Avenues. Picture this: Boolu and I alone in an elevator in a rather old skyscraper, on our way up to the twenty-something floor, and the elevator stops between floors. It had never happened to me before in all my life. I don't think I ever even thought about it happening to me, and I knew Boolu never had; he'd only been riding them for a year and a half. I rang the emergency bell. They took their own good time getting to us. It had looked like an old, lonesome building to me in the first place. They huffed and they puffed, either above or below us, I wasn't sure, but eventually I heard banging on the side of the elevator and a voice telling me to push up on the wooden side panel. As I pushed, the voice on the other side called out a warning, "Look out! Step back and let it drop." As the man shoved it in, it fell to the floor of our elevator. The man was standing in the elevator next to ours with its panel open. First he guided Boolu through the panel of our elevator into the opened panel of his elevator. Boolu was thin so he negotiated the space between the elevators rather easily. I told him not to look down. For me it was a little more difficult since those panels were not wide. With my paunch I had to squeeze out and then squeeze into the next elevator. You can bet your bottom dollar I didn't look down either. Nor did I take a breath of relief until that new elevator started its ascent. Boolu took the whole episode in stride. What was this little mishap compared to what he had been through?

The slot we were stuck in twenty-odd floors above the ground was nothing compared to the many slots we could get stuck in that prohibited Boolu from permanent entry into the country. Number one, he was above fourteen of age and would have to meet all the adult requirements for a green card. Those requirements were many, and they were beyond a guy like Boolu.

"Oh, Mr. Carville, there is nothing to worry about," said the lawyer. "It doesn't matter if he isn't eligible. We can keep him in the country for fifty years through litigation. You know, by fighting it in the courts."

I looked straight into the ravenous eyes of that lawyer. I couldn't verbalize what was racing through my head: "You bloodsucking SOB. On whose salary are we going to do this?"

By we, I meant Sandy and me. We had had Boolu in our care since he was twelve-and-a-half. If we had applied before Boolu was fourteen, we would have faced no problem at all. America would have welcomed him with open arms as it did all the children from Southeast Asia. My mother had written of this inequity years ago.

What I did say was, "We're going to have to sit on this one sir, at least for a while. I'll get back to you." Like hell, I thought.

I took Boolu by the elbow and quickly led him out of the office before the SOB started charging us by the minute. Now I knew that no lawyer or court was going to solve our dilemma. We were being forced to mount this obstacle head on and legitimately. Boolu was going to have to face this challenge on his own, with our help. And damn it, we would beat it, de tree a we.

That day marked the begging of a trip we three were to set for on, like the scarecrow, the tin man, and the lion without Dorothy or Toto or the yellow brick road to goad us. It turned out to be a twisting maze that somehow, even at the start, we all three never doubted for an instant would end successfully. The Elysian Fields and horn of plenty of the United States of America were just out there awaiting Boolu. Like Tomino in Mozart's *Magic Flute*, Boolu was going to be required to walk through the tests of the elements of wind, water, and fire that were to be his initiation. It was a quest and a test that would last more than twenty years.

New Year's In New York

With Sandy so busy at the school and Boolu still occupied with his treatments at the Center, Christmas, like last year, was going to be spent right here at home on 58th Street. We weren't making a big deal of it. New Year's on the other hand was the biggest day of the year for Sandy. We had been invited to Natalie Harley's. She had been born in France of Russian parents who escaped the communists. Her father had been the procurer for the Ballet Russe Company and had had some affiliation with the Moscow Art Theatre between 1914 and the early '20s when he finally left Russia for Paris. He was able to finagle the family's emigration because of his Lithuanian birth. Natalie and her husband owned the House of Harley, a perfume packaging business for both French and American companies. She had recently lost her husband and many years earlier had lost her oldest daughter, Tamara, in a car accident while she was away at college. Her younger daughter, Tanya, had just finished studying with Sandy. Natalie wanted to introduce Sandy to her father, Mr. Abram Raphalovik Hourvitch. Sandy was looking forward to the meeting.

Other White Russians were going to be there as well. The Russian ballet dancer Rudolf Nureyev was going to be there. Natalie was much like a surrogate mother to him. Tanya told us her mother lived to cook and was a marvelous Franco-Russian cook. I just knew it was going to be a marvelously unusual evening. As it turned out, it really was.

Boolu was going to spend the night at the 58th Street disco; he had been hanging out there on the weekends since October. By 10:30 we were dressed and heading out. We didn't have far to go, only up Madison a short way. Boolu was nowhere near ready. "Boolu, if you don't leave now, you'll never get in," I admonished. "If you don't get in, what will you do? Hear me?"

Sandy and I went down to the street and couldn't find an empty cab in sight. The buses were still running so we decided to walk over to Madison and catch a bus at 57th Street. As we passed Boolu's disco on 58th Street, we could see couples and small groups standing in a line that wrapped around the block. As we waited for a bus on the corner, I said to Sandy, "Look at that line. Half of these kids already in line won't even make it inside tonight. That place must already be packed. Boolu'll never get in."

"Well, that's Boolu for ya," was all Sandy said.

"I know, but it still makes me feel bad to think he'll be out on the street all alone. It's going to be bitchy cold. He should have come along with us."

"Look, he's twenty-five and old enough to know what he wants," said Sandy.

I still felt bad for him. What did he know? It was New Year's. It was bound to be different tonight.

Our bus came and we got on with still no sign of Boolu. We rang in the New Year in an old-world atmosphere right out of pre-war Russia or Paris, a long time past, a culture alien to America. Natalie's Russian and Parisian food was excellent, as was her guest list. As we rang in the New Year, I thought of Boolu out in the street all alone. I shivered in spite of the heat from the flames filtering through the embers in the fireplace. The fireplace was crowned with flickering candles swathed in pine sprigs fanning out across the marble mantelpiece in front of a magnificent mirror that reflected the candlelight and the splendid chandelier. The Yuletide fragrance of pine needles permeated the room like a forest of fir trees. The elegance of the antique French provincial surroundings was so civilized in my estimation that I thought, what a wonderful way to start off the New Year. I hoped it was a good omen.

Leave It To The Doorman

When we got home, Boolu wasn't in yet.

"Sandy, where could he be?"

"Jimmy, it's New Year's. He's having a good time. Good night."

Well, I thought, if he were out on the street, he would be in by now. So I turned in, too.

When I got up late on January 1, Boolu was safely asleep in his room. I felt relieved. When he finally got up, I said, "Judging from the time you got in, you must have had one hell of a good time."

"Mon, I did, I really did."

"How could you, out in all that cold? And all by yourself? What kind of a time could you be having?" I asked, adding, "You couldn't have gotten into the club last night. The line was wrapped all around the block."

"Jimmy, I don't stand in no line. I know de doorman."

Now, why didn't I think of that? It would have saved me a lot of concern and made my New Year's a little more carefree.

I should have known. Since October he had been taking tapes he had brought from St. Vincent to the disco. They contained calypso and hot reggae music, which was just becoming the rage at the time. Plus, I already told you about his relationships with doormen. Sandy said, "You see? When are you going to stop treating him like a baby? He has more on the ball than you give him credit for."

Now It Was Ruth

In the middle of everything, we had got word from Ruth that she had been diagnosed with lung cancer. This news was horrendous for both sister and brother, but it did serve to take Sandy's concern off his own recovery and transfer it to Ruth.

Settling on a director for the Playhouse, as he and Robert Whitehead had just done, was the best thing that could have happened. It was a big burden off Sandy. In November, Harold Baldridge had taken over the helm; it was just in time, and Sandy worked with him. The Playhouse managed to get through the year without incident; Sandy's teachers were carrying the Acting Department without Sandy quite well. The smooth operation gave Sandy time. He was improving by the day.

On the other hand, Ruth was worsening by the month. She had been admitted to Sloan-Kettering. God knows we knew that place all too well. Eventually she was moved to a hospice where she passed away June 9, 1983. She was buried in Salem, New York, near her daughter Ellen's home. Of Sandy's family, only his younger brother Bob and Bob's children, Sandy's nephew Danny and two nieces Carol and Elizabeth, and Ruth's daughter, Ellen Wetherell, remained. Ruth was a big loss for him. Their relationship was much the same as my sister Joan's and mine.

Boolu's Disco Years

Boolu didn't need to make that trip up to the Burn Center any more. He was now well adjusted to the city and its transportation system. He had checked out several discos. First, before the women took it over, was Chippendale's near the 59th Street Bridge. Then came the Underground on 17th Street and another on 57th Street near Madison, a gay disco. He finally settled on the 58th Street disco between Lexington and Madison. It was in the neighborhood and he could easily walk to and from home. Once he was banned for a month from 58th Street because he asked the wrong girl to dance. Her boyfriend picked a fight with him. Boolu fought back and they were both kicked out. It was no big thing. Sandy and I never knew about it until I noticed he wasn't going to 58th anymore. He sheepishly confessed he'd been banned for a month for fighting. All I said was, "Well, what do you expect?" He was going to have to learn the hard way.

One day Boolu, Sandy, and I were dining in an Italian restaurant on Third Avenue. I noticed two other diners, well-dressed younger men, who seemed to be talking about us. When they had paid their bill, they walked over to our table. My first thought was that one of them must have been a student of Sandy's. One said, "How're ya doin', Boolu? Who are your friends?"

Boolu stood up to shake their hands and said, "Dese are my friends, Sandy and Jimmy. I live with dem."

The other man said, "How do you do?" They both shook our hands said, "Pleased to meet you. Boolu is a good friend of ours. We're the owners of Disco 58. He's quite a guy, isn't he? And a hell of a dancer. We'll see ya Friday, Boolu." And they went on about their business.

Boolu was now filling his days cleaning apartments for friends of ours who were in need of a housecleaner they could trust. He went to a different place each day. He went to a law office on 38th Street in the Murray Hill district, a TV commercial studio on 17th Street, a photographer's studio on Third Avenue in Murray Hill, and a penthouse apartment around the corner on 55th Street and First Avenue. He had no trouble getting around. He found it easy now. He took much pride in telling everyone he was now a janitor. He loved that word!

Once, the people upstairs from the lawyer's office asked Boolu to feed their cats while they were away. They gave him keys to let himself in. Not being too clear about the alarm system, he set it off and the police came running. He explained he was trying to get in to feed the cats for his friends.

"Sure," they said. "Who are you? Where are you from? Where do you live?" They were bombarding him with questions.

"My name Boolu. I live with Sandy and Jimmy," Boolu nervously blurted out.

"Where?" they asked.

"On 58th Street," Boolu answered.

"Well, where are you from?" was the next question.

"My mother lives in Texas," was his reply, a very smart answer, I thought.

They went on questioning. "What are you doing in New York?"

"I go to school," said Boolu. That seemed to pacify them and they took down our telephone number. They then helped him with the door, went in with him, and checked as he fed the cats. This encounter was the first time Boolu had been confronted by the law. He was scared as hell that he might be sent back to Bequia. I have to admit I too was concerned because of the green card dilemma. In order to stay, he had to have one. The cost of using lawyers to secure one was prohibitive. I had to find a scholastic method to qualify him for his green card.

Another Uphill Battle For Boolu

I had heard via the Bequia grapevine that Boolu's mother had married an American in Trinidad, moved to Dallas, Texas, and once there, divorced him. No flies on her! She may have been incapable of mothering her children when they needed her, leaving all ten farmed out around the Windward Islands, but she damned sure was capable of caring for good old reliable Nola. She was now in the process of scraping them up like so many chips on a poker table here in the US of A. Even so, she wasn't the only winner because in the end her children reaped the benefits, too. My feelings toward her, no matter what they were, were irrelevant. If Boolu could also be helped by her, then why not? All her children were in America now except two, one in St. Vincent and the youngest in Trinidad.

If she, as his mother, requested an application for him from Immigration, he was entitled to enter the country, providing he could pass the immigrant exam and not be classified as disabled. If she agreed, then Boolu had one tough job ahead of him, but I felt it was worth a try. After many phone calls and a few letters, she agreed to apply for him if I were willing to take on the responsibility for him once he got his green card.

I then went to another New York immigration lawyer for advice because of Boolu's limitations. As it happened, their offices were in the same building I had come to in 1948, fresh out of high school to study at the Alvienie Academy: 1780 Broadway and 57th Street. Boy, did that take me back in time. I was starting out in this town then, and now here was Boolu starting out on his fight for acceptance into a new life, in the very same building.

Winnie said, "Good, Jimmy. It's a sign. It's an omen!"

"And a good one, I hope," said I.

What I found out from the lawyer wasn't good. He informed me of a Jewish couple living and working here in New York who was having trouble getting their deaf son into the country. He was an Israeli college graduate with degrees in Science, and yet when he had been interviewed at the American Consulate, he had had trouble communicating because he was deaf and his first language was Hebrew. He didn't know sign nor could he lip-read in English so he had had trouble understanding the English of the American clerk. What's more, he didn't have a job to go back to in Israel. The clerk had said he would be a handicap risk, and his application for a visa was refused. Now his parents were fighting through lawyers for his admittance.

"Thanks," I said. "I needed this little story."

The lawyer responded, "I tell you this to give you some idea of what he's facing. Because of his deafness, it won't be easy."

Now I was certain Boolu needed more training in language.

Educating Boolu

I took Boolu to an institute for the deaf on 26th Street, hoping they could help him. I paid several hundred dollars to have him tested and categorized. They told me he was profoundly deaf, something I already knew, but they had no program for him. There was no placing him anywhere. In the end, I didn't know what I had paid for.

I was furious. I took the yellow pages and looked up every institute and school for the deaf. I found seventeen listed and called each and every one. Every one of them had some reason why Boolu didn't meet their prerequisites, most often his age. Too old at twenty-five! When he was thirteen, they said he was too old to learn to talk, that his left-brain had probably atrophied. And yet he did learn to talk. Now, at twenty-five, you couldn't shut him up. No, he was not too old.

I called Hunter College and asked for the Special Education Department where I spoke to the second in-charge, a Ms. Kate Garnett. She made an appointment with me. When I explained Boolu's predicament, she was truly, visibly upset. "This really bothers me," she said. "Why and how can anyone put an age limit on learning? Categorize it, yes; age-group it, yes. But never an age limit on learning." She said she had an idea she had been bouncing around in her head that she would like to get implemented at Hunter, but she still had to present it to the Board of Governors. It was now September. She said to come back to see her in January.

By Christmas of '83 Sandy still wasn't ready to leave town, and Boolu could not leave the country because if he did, he couldn't get back in. So New Year's we went to Natalie's again, and this time Boolu came, too. He looked great in his light beige raw-silk suit surrounded by old-world European splendor. He was now a far cry from the bush and backwater of Bequia's ravines. Now he made a pleasing appearance and quite a splash as well. He was becoming comfortable in his own skin, such as it was, at ease with people and with conversation that was within his limitations. Most people were understanding and didn't mind.

January rolled around, time to see Professor Garnett at Hunter. She was at the 26th Street campus just below Bellevue. I took Boolu with me this time. I still hadn't found a place for him. But she hadn't made any headway either with the powers that be. I introduced Boolu to her and she spoke with him for quite a while. I could see she was getting a big kick out of his social antics. Boolu was turning on the charm as he has a way of doing, especially with women. She took one long look at him and said, "I don't know what it is about this guy, but I know now I have to do something about this idea of mine, right now—I'm not waiting for any Board."

There is no doubt that Boolu was a charmer. It's his nature! As she was telling us that she hadn't been able to sell her idea to the school but that she planned to bring it up again over the summer, and perhaps... She stopped and said, "The program I have in mind is for the graduate students working on their Masters' here to take one student and work with him or her privately for a year. It would become part of the school's curriculum. I'll take Boolu and teach him privately from now until September in a pilot program. Then I will have something concrete to show the Board when I present my project in September."

Within a week Boolu was working privately with Kate at the downtown campus. Kate was promoted to the head professorship position of the Special Education Department. In September the school embarked on the new project as part of the curriculum. Every Masters' student in the department was given a student to work with privately. The students mostly came from local high schools. Some were physically or developmentally disabled. Others were foreign students with English as their second language, and that was holding them back. Eventually the program moved to the uptown campus on East 66th Street. Boolu stayed and worked in the program for the next twelve years.

30 Boo, He, and Me Full Tilt

1984—Boolu On His Own

Because Boolu needed to be in New York to work on his language skills at Hunter College, Sandy and I had to make it possible for him to live at 210 East 58th Street while we were on Bequia. While we were making plans, he was actually looking forward to it.

An officer in the bank agreed to help him with his banking transactions. The Shopwell manager was also willing to help with his grocery needs. Rusty Ford, for whom Boolu worked under the table on West 17th, and Pat Field, our friend from Bequia who was now down on East 23rd, were both going to keep any eye on him. He was able to fill out his weekends with disco visits and trips to Winnie's out in Queens. He even braved the subway alone all the way to Brooklyn where his sister Sherry Reno lived on Jefferson Avenue. There he checked in on his many friends from home who lived in the area. With school, work, and his weekend socializing, he was kept pretty busy.

For the first time in fourteen years, Boolu would not be in Bequia with us, and his absence threw everything off kilter a bit more than it already was. The fledgling had flown the nest. It was as normal as blueberry pie, yet it didn't seem quite right somehow. We had no idea how much a part of our lives he had become and, yes, damned straight, how much we had grown to depend on him. He was always there. We now both knew the true, magnanimous meaning of the phrase, "step and fetch it": it was anything but demeaning and insignificant. He had developed into a vital part of our lives in the running and working of this establishment called home. In truth, he was our emissary between the two cultures here on the Island. Mr. Will, our gardener, and Parnell both seemed lost around the place without him. He had an uncanny gift for remembering where everything was squirreled away, no matter how long ago, no matter how small, even the most insignificant document or tiniest needle. It was as if he had a photograph in his mind of right where it was nesting. Even the cook missed him.

We were all just going to have to tough it out without him, for no way could he show up until he had a green card. He had too many strikes against him as far as immigration was concerned. Now was not the time for him to leave the country. He couldn't jeopardize the slim chance he had of becoming an American like us.

I was hoping Kate and her students would help prepare him. They tested him within an inch of his life. Kate even sent him up to the Cornell Brain Research Center on York Avenue and 70th Street, a neighborhood he and Sandy were both well familiar with. Cornell's test showed atrophy had not set into the left-brain, not that it couldn't start to any day. For people like Boolu, who effectively had no linguistic exposure or experience from birth, atrophy has been known to occur over time. I was told that after twelve or thirteen years it could be too late to correct, and it had been well over twelve years already.

Why atrophy had not set in with Boolu was anybody's guess. I suspect Boolu's childhood made-up language might have played a part in keeping his left-brain clear. He used made-up words like "imprim," "digina batati," and "halipoco." Those syllables seemed to me to be pure nonsense sounds, but could have been mispronounced words. There were many that he incorrectly heard due to his profound deafness. In fact to this day he mispronounces words, which I then correct.

I did wonder all along whether atrophy might explain Boolu's apparent slow progress in other areas than vocabulary (which was phenomenal). Back in school my other students moved along at a much better rate in reading comprehension, math, and time sequence comprehension. And these were areas Boolu needed to pass immigration tests! Atrophy or no atrophy, he was still going to have to face Immigration, sooner or later. Sandy and I were grateful that Professor Garnett had agreed to try to help Boolu.

It didn't take them long to discover Boolu had multiple learning disabilities. So other problems needed addressing, even though he was coping rather well with his deafness. The nun who was head of the Deaf Department at Hunter College said, "For all intents and purposes, Boolu doesn't behave as if he were deaf."

Although signing was beyond him, his lip-reading was so keen he didn't have a communication problem. He could even lip-read a lot of television. I used to have to tell him to please turn it up so I could hear it. He would quip, "What's de matta? You deaf?"

"Never mind, smart ass, just turn it up so I can hear it."

Communication Breakdown

Sandy and I were looking forward to finally getting back after a two-year hiatus jam-packed with vibrating emotional roller-coaster rides that had demanded our total concentration. Many issues had been left unresolved, suspended in air like the parachute ride on Coney Island. How were we ever going to unwind? We were as tight and stiff as an overwound alarm clock, too seized up to ring.

That summer of '84 on Bequia, Sandy and I started off on the wrong foot. First of all Sandy was in such a weakened state that he was reduced to dependency on a walker to navigate about the house. Long walks were out of the question. In our house he was confined to two floors connected by a nine-step staircase that he could no longer manage without assistance. This restriction he was not going to accept from the day he arrived. While Daphne and I were in the kitchen making dinner, our first in two years, he got the notion to come down to join us. He must have thought that if he hung onto the balustrade with his left hand, he could make it down the nine steps holding the folded-up walker in his right. What we heard in the kitchen was one loud crash as the walker fell out of his hand and bounced, turning over, slipping and sliding down the stairs into the dining room, then one thud after the other as he tumbled down on top of it. He landed on top of the walker sprawled out face down on the dining room floor. We rushed into the dining room. Miraculously, he was unscathed. Daphne was full of compassion, sympathy, and concern. I was concerned all right and even compassionate, but sympathetic? I don't think so after the scare he had just given us. We sat him up on a chair, and I laced into him for being so stupid. "You could have broken the other hip," I ranted on. Daphne told me to go lightly, and went back to her work.

So began the worst nightmare we ever put ourselves through. That unforgettable Christmas of '77 had been pretty horrendous, with the nightmare of the radiation. But then at least we were facing the fight together, and it bonded us even closer. This experience was to become entirely different, completely out of our control.

Sandy had thought once we got back to Bequia everything was going to be as it had been. Well, it wasn't, for a multitude of reasons. He was the weakest he had ever been since that nightmare Christmas. He had been improving both physically and mentally, though ever so slowly. His memory was giving him trouble, and his forgetfulness didn't set too well with his attitude. His patience grew shorter and shorter. Because Boolu wasn't with us just when we needed him most, I had only Daphne's help. All this put him in the worst of moods, and did nothing to improve mine.

Sitting in the sun on the terrace was easy enough for him. And in spite of his condition, I was able to get him down to the beach to "Sandy's Reef." We did have friends in to help break the boredom because with little or nothing to do, it was the pits just getting along. There was no way around it. We were constantly bickering over any unpredicted predicament, or the slightest detail no matter how insignificant. All our troubling unfinished business in New York—Boolu left to live on his own for the first time, the book left hanging, the Playhouse left to wing it on its own—kept creeping up in conversations. It was an endless barrage of ugliness and it went on and on. Yet all the time he was getting stronger and stronger. And so were the arguments. Yes, arguments were what they were. I call a spade a spade. At times all I wanted to do was pack up and run. But of course I didn't.

Our financial situation was shaky. No, scary. We had left New York without a positive notion as to Sandy's future pension from the school, should he have to or choose to stop work. His professional classes had already come to a screeching halt because of the accident. It was then that I first became aware of the meager return he was getting from the Playhouse in the first place. For a man of his stature, it was nothing more than an honorarium, but all a non-profit organization could afford—or at least that's what I was told. In his present condition, he had no idea of the larger picture, such as what we could be facing in the long run. He had made no private arrangement for security in his old age. Before we had left New York, we had agreed that he should invest all he got from the accident settlement, whatever that was. Yet at the end of each month, we spent a week bickering over money. He didn't want to let go of what he had had under control all his life. He had never had to look to anyone for financial help or support and he wasn't about to give over easily now. In New York I had spoken to his accountants, but they were absolutely no help; they were bookkeeper accountants. Sandy's future security didn't seem to be a priority for them. Boolu and I were not their concern at all. From the bookkeepers' perspective, everything was copasetic as long as they had enough money to pay the bills. I felt otherwise! What he had wasn't going to last very long. That the futures of three of us had to be considered seemed beyond his understanding. He truly felt in his confused state that we had nothing to worry about. As he once put it, "Haven't I always handled it?"

I remember one week that summer when bills were due. Because of my concern and the way I was acting, he wouldn't even let me look at the list of bills or the checkbook. I went bonkers, ballistic, and brutish. I was seeing purple. I picked him up out of the chair by both biceps, shook the hell out of him, and threw him on the bed. I didn't want to hurt him, but at the same time I wanted to split him in two. Where was his concern for us, Boolu and me, that is? What was fair was fair. Yet because of his condition, we seemed to be going down the tubes. As I saw him lying out on the bed, I thought of the stories I had heard of grown-up children beating up their helpless parents and I was devastated. If the authorities or any outsider had witnessed that scene, they would have had me put behind bars. There was the person I loved more than anyone in the world laying on the bed looking up at me. He was helpless and petrified, and I was shaking like mad with rage, and we couldn't communicate. I just turned and walked away. I went out to the drive, got in the car, and drove to Hilary overlooking the sea where I sat and fumed...

Later that night, Daphne was in the kitchen preparing dinner, none the wiser, though then again maybe she was. I'd been around long enough to realize that house staff knows full well what's going on. I also knew it took two to fight, and Sandy wasn't a fighter. Strong-minded, pig-headed, stubborn, and stern he could be, but only when he felt he was right. Oh, I could say because his mental state was what it was, that his wits were a little foggy, that this time he was wrong.

Well, he wasn't wrong. It was his money. He made it and what he did with it was his business. If he didn't see things as I did, well, that was my problem. My security and Boolu's were my problem. If I had to go back to New York, find work, and take care of Boolu, I just would.

30 Boo, He, and Me Full Tilt

We had been through so much together; whatever we were bombarded with we had faced together, trusting and depending on each for the better of all tree a we. Now here we were confronted with the root of all evil. And why should I be surprised? Yes, it was the demon of all demons and it was destroying us. I was helpless. In the end, I concluded that what everyone needs is more sense than dollars and cents, and that was the end of the bickering for me. I couldn't hold him responsible for what was happening. He was trying to hang onto the man he once was. I could be fatalistic and chalk it up to life, you know, the age-old expression "such is life," but there was no solace in that. So whenever I felt our conversation bordering on money, I changed the topic or I walked away. That would have been his way of handling it, anyway. The last month on Bequia we were getting along much better. Our relationship seemed like old times, except it wasn't because I wasn't being truthful. This wasn't the time for truth. He had to get well and he needed his total concentration for that task.

He was making headway: he was now on his feet with the help of a cane and could make it up and down stairs without assistance. He was becoming much livelier and a hell of a lot quicker mentally. He truly was making his way back to his old self.

At our last dinner together that summer, I told him I wasn't planning to come back to Bequia with him. "I have to take care of myself, which means getting a job when I get back. What you do is up to you. I have to look out for myself, and Boolu if necessary. God willin', we still have another twenty-five years to think about, at least!" I exclaimed.

He went on about all sorts of things, how when he was dead everything would be ours. I interrupted him. "Who knows how long you will live, or how long Boolu or I will, for that matter? Money should be based on life not death. I need this problem solved now, not when you're dead. I have to know now. I need to know where I'm going. I thought we were a team. Your way of thinking is back in the dark ages. We should be sharing everything, the good and the bad. You need to start to share with us right now, for richer or poorer, corny as it sounds.

"Sandy," I went on, "the past few months have been the darkest nightmare I can remember living through. I will never set foot on this Island again while you're on it. I don't want to dissolve all those magnificent memories I've made here with you."

"But this place is ours," Sandy said.

"That's right," I said, "and you can just let me know when you plan to be here and I will come when you aren't here, like a time-share. I'm not kidding. I don't feel you're thinking enough about your future, let alone Boolu's and mine."

I think he could tell I was dead serious for the first time. A quiet, dark, and thoughtful Sandy left for New York the next morning. I left with him, resolved.

Changing Times

We had made this trip back to New York from Barbados many times since 1968. The big difference on this trip, for Sandy anyway, was that in all those years, this arrival would be the first that solid, reliable Paul, his old friend from the Theatre Guild days some fifty-seven years ago, would not be meeting him. When he asked who was meeting us, I told him no one. I could see the loss on Sandy's face. It was another reminder of the absence of his lifelong friend and companion, which perhaps triggered a reminder of where he was in life. I wouldn't know, but death, the grim reaper, is always a good eye-opener into insight.

In the past few years, things had been changing for us faster than we could keep up with them. To recapitulate a bit: it started with Boolu's burns and rehabilitation; then the losses of Paul, Oleta D'Ambry, and his sister Ruth; added to which, Sandy's having to take over the school single-handedly; and then the interruption of the 57th Street accident, which had necessitated the rehabilitation of both his physical and mental injuries and brought a total halt to his teaching. With the loss of Sandy's professional classes and the need to find classes for Boolu, everything had been changing and whirling around faster than a hurricane.

Boolu was out there working five days a week now. He even landed a TV athletic shoe commercial in which he did Michael Jackson's Moonwalk. Boolu had it down pat, I might add. "It's who you know in this business," I told him, since he had landed the job at Rusty's TV commercial company, where he worked regularly as a janitor.

Now that I was back, I had to shake "ma rass" and get busy working again. I was hoping I might bag a show; I didn't care if I had to go out of town. Boolu and Sandy were capable of looking after themselves. I just had to get started again.

I started working out with my old vocal coach and accompanist, Charlie Kingsford. We had not worked together in almost twenty years. I told Sandy, "Now I can go out and do all the 'old fart parts.'" He didn't think it was funny.

Boolu Acts in a Commercial

He wasn't getting much of a charge out of being back at school these days either. He missed the camaraderie he had shared with Paul. He had been very much part of running the school, which he truly enjoyed. He just wanted Harold to take over the responsibility, the complete running of the school, by himself. He felt it was time he let go. After all, he was teaching only part-time now. It was time for his trained teachers to begin to take over. But the changeover left Sandy with an empty space in his heart, and neither Boolu nor I could fill it.

Boolu was excitedly going about his new life at Hunter and happily working five days a week. I went about doing exactly what I had said I was going to do—getting out there to get a job wherever possible. I don't know what Sandy thought because he wasn't a talker. I was the talker, but I wasn't doing much of that just then.

Sandy Finally Catches The Ball And Runs With It

I noted Sandy had been taking frequent trips over to his accountants alone, without me. He would have a student take him over to their office from school. Whatever they were hashing out I wasn't privy to, but the upshot that one day out of a clear blue sky he announced, "I want you here Friday afternoon. A broker from E.F. Hutton is coming over to discuss our financial future."

"Our future?" I said.

"Yes, stupid. Just be here."

Sandy had spoken to Lenny and Tommy, his accountants, and they had found a broker from E.F. Hutton. Barry Vener cottoned on to our particular problems and had a great deal of advice for us, all objective and full of common sense. Sandy admitted to Barry that he was getting too tired, and really was weary of the responsibilities. Barry asked if there was anyone he trusted more than Jimmy: if he couldn't hand over the financial reins to me, who else was there? Sandy told Barry that he had already handed over the care of his life to me for more than ten years. Barry had some staunch advice and laid out a clear, concise, sensible, secure, and conservative approach for us to follow. I then asked, "So, what does this make me? The financial officer of the company?"

Sandy replied, "You got that right. And I'm still the president of this mangy company, and don't you forget it. I'm the boss."

"Oh, I believe it, all right. You is de boss-mon, sah, I know dat, ho-ho." And we three shook hands on it.

Feeling good about all that had been arranged, set about our daily activities with a more positive outlook, Boolu included, for he was somehow always keenly aware of what was going on.

1985—A Way Out Of Our Dilemma

About this time, Elizabeth Wilson, our friend and one of Sandy's students from the class of '41, spoke to me about Bequia. At first I thought she was talking about master classes, but she said, "I was thinking in terms of a place for a vacation. But if classes are a possibility, that's a better idea. Wouldn't that be great?"

Kathleen Nolan was another actress who spoke to me about the possibility. Robert De Niro first came to Bequia to go yachting. When he heard Sandy was on the Island, he spoke to Judy Kwaloff, the yachting lady, and he asked her about the possibility of his coming down to work with Sandy. He even called and spoke to Sandy. Sandy told De Niro he didn't need to work with him, that he already knew how to act, and very well indeed, he added. I still feel De Niro would have liked working with Sandy anyway. How unlike Strasberg this approach was. Lee attracted every successful actor he could get his hands on while Sandy was only interested in novices who needed his help.

>I don't remember the when, why, or wherefore
>because it was then that I did restore
>
>every ounce of resource within me
>to sail our ship within the lee,
>
>out of the swarms
>of life's unpredictable storms.
>
>This meant I had a hell of a job to do,
>and I wouldn't quit till I was through.
>
>The Neighborhood Playhouse wasn't the answer,
>but if he wanted to stay, it wasn't a cancer.
>
>To him it had always meant quite a bit,
>he had a strong loyalty always toward it.
>
>That would work out just fine with me.
>That would be of some help, you see.
>
>Now this notion of Sandy on Bequia with actors
>germinated, and I was exploring all factors.
>
>Liz, Robert, and Kathleen had started the notion.
>I believed we had promise out there in the ocean.
>
>I first called the airlines to bicker and barter.
>There were group fares and combos and also Mark Carter.
>
>The Mustique Air agent said it's cheaper to charter.
>Now there was a sweet fare for us, as a starter.

I checked with a hotel that sprang up on the bay,
got a special rate as it was a long stay.

The time was off-season—the difference was great.
The basic cost was a deal, I hoped not too late.

I proudly presented possibilities quite endless.
Said Sandy, "Values and reputation I really must stress.

"So, to all your speculations I add reservations.
And be aware I'll insist on my own stipulations."

What were his stipulations? Above all, he would not have a master class. As he explained, "They're not much more than a scene-study group and don't demand an acting teacher. If the classes are doing scenes, they should already know how to act, even if they don't have the talent for it. What a scene-study class needs is a director. I'm not interested in being a director to would-be actors. At the Playhouse I teach acting exercises to give the student an awareness of how to approach acting, how to go about working on acting. That is what I would consent to do on Bequia. I would be doing what I do best—teaching and working with beginners."

Sandy truly felt a two-year course with him was all one needed. After that, the actor needs nothing more than his or her natural innate talent combined with the luck of being born with body parts that are in demand in the market. These attributes would give them a chance to obtain experience in front of an audience and work under a good director to develop into an actor, a profession Sandy believed took twenty years to perfect. So he told me to give up on the idea of stars, even though they were the ones who could afford such a project. In stars he wasn't interested. "If you can find enough beginners, I will be more than willing to get them started on the right foot," he stressed.

So I suggested a one-month intensive program covering the first three months of his two-year program. If afterward they were still interested and he felt the student would benefit from the rest of his two-year, private, professional program at the Playhouse in New York, then they would be accepted into a professional class. Economically, the cost of the one-month intensive was not only cheaper than the cost of a three-month professional program in New York, it also demanded less time. It was a far better deal than he had ever offered before.

Once I got the green light, I was off and running. We had no office; I worked from the apartment on East 58th Street. The first issue was the name. Sandy said, "That's easy. Who started it?"

"Well, we did," I said.

"So..." Sandy said, "The Meisner Carville School of Acting, because that's what it is."

Golly, I liked the sound of that. We were now officially partners.

We advertised in the trade papers and at colleges, and the mail poured in. Sandy went over the letters, deciding whom he would interview in the city. Then it wasn't long before applications started coming in from England, Germany, Hong Kong, and Alaska. We even had an application from a Russian in Paris. By 1991 we had had representation from all five continents, even Africa and Australia, on little old Bequia only one mile wide and just over six miles long in the middle of the ocean. I remember Sandy once asking me, "Jimmy, who's the Garbo of acting teachers now?"

Sandy went over the letters from the foreign applicants, too, and chose these students without an interview. His criteria were their life experience and their reason for applying in the first place. His decisions were based on his own educated guesses. Their acting experience was inconsequential, except for expressing their seriousness and attitude. He always assumed the applicant didn't know how to act because if they did, they had no business wasting his time and their own, something he found an awful lot of actors do until it's too late to start a career. At this stage in his life, he would rather be sunning himself out on his terrace.

I costed out airfare and hotel rates (with two meals a day) and came up with a fee of $1,250 for the whole shebang, classes included. After all, it was 1985.

When I told an agent the cost, he asked, "Can I go? I wouldn't be able to find a vacation in the tropics at that price!"

But Sandy was worried about the young actor who was just getting by as a waitress or bartender. I told him not to worry about bartenders: they do damn well. One young Canadian actress came for an interview. Sandy knew she was working as a waitress and he wanted her in his class. "She will never be able to afford it," he fretted. When he called her in and told her he would accept her, he asked if she could afford it.

She replied, "Oh, I'll afford it somehow."

Sandy inquired, "Will your family help?"

"Oh, no," she said, "but I'll get it, Mr. Meisner. Don't you worry."

In three months she was in his office with the fee. "I juggled two waitress jobs. I knew I could do it."

When she left, Sandy said, "Now there's an actress. Give me the ones who have to be, not the ones who want to be."

Even today, every now and then I see our little Canadian friend, Annie Grindlay on TV.

That May of '85 we were packing for Bequia once more. "Sandy, we're making ready for a new chapter," I said. "I think we've found our niche."

I did wish Boolu were going to be with us that summer. He would have had a good time with the students. He could have been my number one helper, too, and I feared I was going to need one. But no such luck. I missed him more than ever. I only hoped he wasn't too lonely there all by himself, but then he had his friends in Brooklyn and Queens. "He's very resourceful," Sandy pointed out. "Remember, he is twenty-nine years old. He isn't a helpless baby anymore. I'll bet he's glad to see the back of us."

Sandy had his students picked for the summer—enough for two full classes—and ready to go even before the final demonstrations at the Playhouse. Sandy's attendance at the graduation dinner held at the Players Club down on the Corner of Gramercy Park South and Irving Place was his lasts obligation to the school for the term.

We met the first class at Kennedy Airport at 7:00 one summer morning. It was an outwardly exuberant and excited group who met at the American Airlines departure lounge that day. It was a sure bet that they were all inwardly apprehensive, as were both Sandy and I. All of us were traveling in uncharted waters.

I knew my responsibilities as head of the school were going to be nothing like Paul's had been. I was well aware that I was going to have to be chief cook and bottle washer and then some. After all, they were not just coming to class. In truth they were coming to live with us on a rock in the middle of the ocean. I kept thinking of Murphy's Law, you know, anything that can go wrong will go wrong, God forbid. That "God forbid" part I added. At least when I was at the school in Harlem, I had had Dorothy Mainer to help me, and God knows she was a pistol when it came to managing those kids. All we had going for us was hope. We were all winging it. The only certainty in this whole venture was the three hours with Sandy in the morning classes. I trusted that Sandy could handle his additional daily, informal cocktail hour lectures ending with a question and answer period. It was all the everyday living problems that would come up that I would be the one to calculate and sum up. When I was growing up, my mom was the one who kept everything on an even keel. She never suffered whiners nor was she taken in by a trumped-up deal. That I took after her was no secret. It was going to be hard for me to hold my tongue.

> Sometimes whining can have a legitimate cause,
> so I was forced to purposely pause.
>
> Being diplomatic and sugarcoated
> wasn't my natural bent, I noted.
>
> Blunt? Yes. Stern? Yes.
> Quick and short-fused? I guess.
>
> One might even say a little sarcastic now and again.
> This was going to be a challenge for me to the end.
>
> That's right, a difficult one for me to fight
> but damned good for me, I might

learn a bit no matter how slow.
To be frank, it helped watching how the money did grow.

When we reached St. Vincent and we all filed through Customs, there was Charlie, my taxi man, with the vans lined up outside. The footmen were at the ready to take the students' luggage and load it into the corresponding van, while I yelled, "Keep an eye on your bags, and I don't mean your lady friends. That's right, stay with them."

Everyone hopped in and we headed up and over the twisting road from Arnos Vale to Grenadine Pier in Kingstown. We took a steel-hulled cargo ship to Bequia, where Parnell had pickup trucks waiting on the pier. Some stumbled off the boat with a severe bout of seasickness. It's a short trip but at times it can be a rough one. As many times as Sandy and I crossed over and back, we never had a problem with it.

I asked Sandy, "How are we ever going to tell them that it's usually a hell of a lot rougher going back? With the crosswinds, and the currents running at a slight angle in the opposite direction, on an empty stomach, at 6 AM?"

"Don't tell them," Sandy advised. "Let them cross that bridge when they come to it."

"Very funny, Sandy—bridge."

They piled into the pickups and crossed over Friendship gap to the Bequia Beach Hotel that nestled on the flat, right on the beach at the foot of the steep hill below our house.

Akuyoe Graham, Alias Charlotte

Thursday at 7:30 o'clock in the morning on May 28 we gathered at JFK. We came by bus, by cab, by train, private car, and limousine. Excitement had kept me awake all night and so for the first time in my life I was early for an appointment. Fun began by trying to guess who the other Meisner-ites were. Actually it was quite easy. Travelers going to the Caribbean are surely acquainted with the tremendous amount of foodstuffs and other packages that friends and relatives take back to their families. Well, we Meisner-ites for one thing were traveling very light in comparison and then too, young actors tend to adopt a certain look of bewilderment, hunger, curiosity, and a swagger in the walk. After a 2 ½-hour delay both off and on the plane, we were off. Four hours later we landed in Barbados where we were divided into two groups of ten and whisked off in small propeller planes to St. Vincent. Upon arrival in St. Vincent, we are counted by James Carville, Mr. Meisner's assistant. Confirmation. The adventure has truly begun. There was further division of the group as we were carted into aged pickup vans and bumped along dusty, narrow, un-leveled mountainous roads to the harbor. These clanking vehicles are the buses and taxis of our new homeland. At the harbor, wearing our hearts on our sleeves, we take a fishing boat to the bigger motorboat, which had been specially chartered to take us finally to Bequia. Already this trip was a lot more than we'd bargained for. Several of the group were beginning to show signs of wear and tear. 18 young actors had thrown all care and worries to the wind and were bound, by land, air, and sea, to participate in a training workshop conducted by the master himself, Sanford Meisner. Bumping along again in pitch-blackness our travel-weary bodies are shaken and revitalized as we descend 106 concrete steps to our final destination, the Bequia Beach Club, which we affectionately came to call the BBC.

A number drawn from Jimmy's hand proved to be the most democratic way of choosing up roommates—two in each spacious apartment. I certainly was not expecting such luxurious digs, and right on the beach too! We had a cocktail welcome at the bar and then a tingling sensation went through all of us with the announcement of Mr. Meisner's arrival. Beaming with relief, he shook each person's hand and immediately his strength and unassuming spirit made me feel warm inside. Well fed and exhausted, we bid each other adieu and went to bed. The noisy chatter of crickets and the crashing of restless waves upon the sand was the bedtime rhapsody that first night, which eventually lulled each bright-eyed soul to sleep.

A dip in the pool, running on the beach, by 8 AM the camp was astir with its zealous hungry members. Breakfast was wolfed down and then we were off. School was to start promptly at 10 AM. Up the 106 steps accompanied by the glaring sun was a chore—never mind jogging. I was no fool. Climbing the steps to class would be plenty of exercise, for me.

Classes were held in Mr. Meisner's Spanish-style home—the Casa Luna, a beautiful spacious house atop a mountain. One would think the classes had been in mind when the house was built fifteen years ago. The split-level guest bedroom we used was perfect. Furnished and equipped with spotlight, this room was better suited for our purposes than most studios in the city acting schools.

Although anxiety and nervous jitters had us all gripped in fear, the overwhelming energy of the group was most definitely positive. Then we heard light footsteps and spied Mr. Meisner coming down the stairs cane in hand. It was a sight, which would become familiar and dear to us.

We got down to business right away. Time is precious and as I was soon to learn, Mr. Meisner didn't believe in wasting any of it. We went straight to the task at hand. The building of technique for the actor, with the premise that acting is the ability to live truthfully under imaginary circumstances; we started working on the repetition exercises which Mr. Meisner had composed. We progressed from mechanical repetition through improvisations and eventually into scene work. These exercises were designed to train the actor's instrument. We were working to develop truthful human use of ourselves. Our emotions and imaginations were challenged through the daily practice of the improvisations. As Meisner pointed out, these exercises were to acting what scales are to music.

Emphasis being on living truthfully from moment to unanticipated moment: responding impulsively to what exists and adjusting to the other fellow. We were aiming for spontaneity in our work so that exercises and scenes presented would be a "truthful extract" of life, so that we'd have the ability to live truthfully on the highest optics of the Theater.

We had 6 classes a week from 10 AM to 1 PM lunch immediately following. Prepared by Mr. Carville, Daphne and Rosalie, the cooks, lunch was served on the 2nd-floor terrace overlooking the ocean down at the bay. The setting looked much like a Parisian café on the Riviera with a world of difference of course being in food prices. At "Jimmy's & Daphne's Place" we could eat all kinds of cold or hot sandwiches and burgers from the grill including old favorites like peanut butter and jelly sandwiches (my personal favorite) or fresh fruit and vegetable salads and soups also cool Island drinks and Mr. Jimmy's magnificent Rum Punch and nothing for more than a dollar or two. The cost of the airfare, lodgings at the luxurious BBC and breakfast and dinner eliminated any reservations we had about getting our money's worth immediately on the first day.

For one month we had an opportunity to come to the center, work diligently on our craft without any commercial pressure or interference from family and friends. Inspiration came not only from our teacher and members of the group, but from the Island itself. It paints a picture of daytime with bright blue skies, tempestuous waves on seductive beaches; sweet mangoes; rum punch; fresh fish; hand-crafted sailboats; pesky mosquitoes; giant land crabs; palm trees; coconut; goats and sheep; proud roosters; baby bats; cool breezy evenings under twinkling stars at night, with Black people, White people, Indian & Spanish people and the Rasta men—yes, all Bequians are indelible in my mind. It is their rhythm tempered by a lingering carnival spirit and the slow drag of the reggae beat, wonders of nature that give Bequia its unspoiled individual beauty. This was home for one month. I was personally overcome by Bequia because it reminded me strongly of my native home—Ghana, West Africa. The Black Bequians were obviously of African descent because of physiognomy and gait. A barefoot woman with a basket balanced on her head and a baby on her back was instant déjà vu. It was a sort of homecoming.

Group discussions gave us an awareness of the need to be well-rounded human beings. To know the world we live in, to experience different cultures, to explore other art forms and also to enjoy the work and the process.

The beauty of the technique is in its simplicity and clarity. The beauty in Mr. Meisner's teaching is in his ability to meet each student as the individual he or she is. I felt as though I were in a private class. No comparisons were made between any of us. Problems facing any one individual were really a problem we all had to watch out for. Compliments were also particularized. Each "Instrument" in the workshop was different with her or her own unique talent. Certainly we faced difficulties. There were times when the group was just absolutely unbearable! Twenty-four hours daily with the same group of people is trying on any stamina. But always what brought us back to center was to focus on the work at hand, and the chance we had to really mark our lives with an historical, riveting experience. We didn't have time to indulge in our personal neuroses. NYC was waiting to cater to those needs. We all felt very fortunate for the opportunity. As if studying with a great teacher on a paradise island were not enough—genuine friendships were made. People fell in love.

It's over now. The "courageous 18" has disbanded. We'll try to keep in touch but it will be very difficult in our hurry-scurry lives. Most of us will be competing against each other. But I know the memory of the sweet days on the Island of the Clouds will stay with me forever. Since our return, most of us are anxious to put our inspiration and positive energy to good use. Simply we want to live! When the pain that all too often accompanies this life in the Theater comes, I know that the strength and love that I discovered in the magical month of June 1985 will somehow be stimulated and help me to recover.

'Charlotte'

The First Bequia Class

The Meisner Carville School Of Acting

Classes started after breakfast with the students trudging up the hill for the 10:00 class with Sandy. Daphne, with the new helper Rosalie Ollivierre, was making ready the menu for lunch. During the class break, I would post the luncheon menu, and the students would fill out an order slip for lunch. We then had an hour and a half to put their orders together. That's right, we turned the kitchen into a short-order luncheonette. When the morning classes were over at 1 PM, the students came upstairs to the dining-room terrace for lunch.

We held the class in the same room that had once been the Deaf School. Now, it had been transformed for the actors with room on one side for the students and Sandy, and with the rest of the room, which was raised up a step, set up to accommodate exercises and scenes. A door led to the bath and the outside, which served as a place to prepare. I rigged Sandy up with a loudspeaker with a small mic that dangled from the temple of his glasses. After a brief adjustment, the class had no problem hearing and understanding him.

We were at last on our way, hoping we would fulfill the students' expectations while improving our financial security down the line when we had them back in New York as well. If we didn't, no one else was going to, God knew. It made it easier for me knowing that teaching acting was what Sandy enjoyed doing more than breathing, not an exaggeration because teaching was living for him. So I vowed I was going to concentrate my efforts 100% on being his backup for as long as he needed me. At times he wanted to know why I didn't teach. I honestly felt it was a far, far better thing I did keeping him in the driver's seat. I truly felt no one alive could steer that ship on a truer course. Little did I know at the time that the job I took on was going to last another ten years. He was truly invincible. I knew some wondered how he could possibly teach as he did. He was so old and feeble. Oh, I could name them and most of you would know their names, but why bother? They never stopped by to find out how he was doing. All you had to do was speak to any of those Bequia students. Sandy kept working on his teaching technique to the end of his days, and they were the beneficiaries.

We would start the session with a little pep talk, a get-acquainted talk, rules-of-the-hotel talk, rules-of-the-house talk, class-regulations talk, and lastly a Bequia-geographic and economic talk including the social mores of the Island. This introduction ended with my saying, "Any questions or complaints, I will be at your disposal upstairs before class or after, but never during class. That is Sandy's time; you are my responsibility the rest of the time."

Thus we proceeded with first one, then the second group with only a few minor hiccups. You know, the usual: this one sleeping with that one, with the other one objecting; this one smoking grass with that one in their room; another one hiding under a bed in another room; or a girl throwing some boy's tape recorder into the ocean because he had set it up under her bed. Oh, yes, I had to be on my toes. I found myself saying things like: "So she is having an affair with her. You got a problem with that? You jealous?" or "What do you mean you want her to pay for your tape recorder? It was new? It was your own foolish fault. The recorder had no business under her bed, and it sure as hell didn't walk under there on its own. It got a little help from someone! I'm positive of that. And I'm surprised that's not all she did." Or, "Listen, Heather, I don't care who it is. You're the manager, and if their pot-smoking is causing them to be

Sandy Toasts his Acting Class

breaking glasses, you just charge them. Don't wait. After all, you are running a business." I had to be chief cook, cashier, consultant, coach, confessor, criminal detective, judge, and jury. The buck stopped here with me, and I loved every minute of it.

On the 28th of July, just a few days before the end of the second group, the kids gave a party at the hotel. It was my birthday. They had a big birthday cake made by Rosalie all nicely decorated, candles and all. It was a warm, friendly finish to the final week. The four weeks had flown by all too fast, with many emotional peaks and valleys. To see a big ex-football player trudging down the drive with tears in his eyes was not unusual. In spite of the emotional ups and downs, not one in the group was ready to leave. Unfortunately, even the best of times must come to an end.

It came none too soon for Sandy and me. We were ready for a vacation. Within days, we were flying south over the southern Caribbean to Caracas.

Venezuela, Ready Or Not

As I lay back in the taxi catching my second breath after the flight to Caracas, it hit me. I suddenly realized that I should have gone to the Venezuelan Consul General's office in St. Vincent to apply for a visa. We had left in such a hurry I had never given it a second thought. Second thought? Americans never need anything more than a passport or driver's license to get about in the Caribbean, so I had never given it even a fleeting first thought, until we were fleeing that airport. Now it was dawning on me that we were the ones the officials had been yelling at in Spanish across that crowd as we all headed for the baggage area after having our passports stamped. They must have been immigration officials, had to be because of the way they were set up with their papers on an inconspicuous table and a few officers standing around it in a passageway. When we ignored them, they must have figured we were Venezuelans, and simply gone back to waiting for more travelers to come through. As fate would have it, for the first time ever, our bag had come first out of the chute. I had grabbed it and we had headed directly outside and into the waiting taxi. We had never cleared and departed an airport so quickly. If we had been caught, we could have been thrown into prison. What a hell of a vacation that would have been. Now here we were in Venezuela for three weeks, without permission. We were illegal, wetbacks, yes, undocumented like Nora on Bequia and Boolu back in the good old US of A. I never let on to Sandy that I had done such a stupid thing.

We spent a few days in Caracas at their number one posh hotel. It was so cheap—the exchange was nineteen to one in our favor. We ate at some exquisite restaurants. It was such an experience, just pampering ourselves. I felt we deserved it. Well, I could honestly say Sandy deserved it. We then went up to Merida, a little university town at the base of the northern Andes where the locals came to escape the incessantly hot muggy days of August, to frolic in the cool mountain breezes. There we took a ride up the mountainside on the longest funicular in the world. In fact it was two connected together and it transported people to the top of the Andes 18,947 feet above sea level. First we had to rent gloves, hat, and jacket.

When we went through the gate to board the tram to the top of the Sierra Nevada Santa Marta, the ticket man stopped Sandy and said, "He is too old to go up."

Sandy replied, pointing at me, "If he goes, I go."

We rose up the mountain in two installments. The temperature at Merida was 85 degrees Fahrenheit when we left, and at the top of the Andes it was 7 degrees below zero, with deep snow piled up all around. Here I was in Venezuela in the middle of August right next to the Equator, frolicking and sliding around in the snow. Sandy was having a grand time talking to some college students from Maracaibo. He was the only elderly person up there, and I was the one having a tough time breathing. They had oxygen tanks for little children, who needed it because of their tiny lungs. Big fat people were having a time of it breathing as well. I felt like a big blimp. Going up and down stairs was difficult. The step never seemed to be where it was supposed to be, as if I were out on a boat in rough seas. I was having a swell time, giddy and lightheaded as well. Then we flew from 7 degrees below zero down to the beach where it was 111 degrees on the Caribbean Sea for a week.

Our next trip we flew up the Orinoco into the jungle and over to Canaima on a tributary of the Rio Carom where it was 120 degrees and humid. There we spent some time with the South American Indians. We stayed at a little hotel, something like a commune or an Israeli kibbutz. The place was full of Europeans and South Americans, but only one other American. Asian and North American tourists were as scarce as hen's teeth in this country, though I don't know why. It was so full of so many interesting things and all so exotic in what was offered the tourist. Sandy kept asking, "And it's all so inexpensive, so where are the tourists?" We talked with our fellow travelers as well as the locals from nearby villages. We bought native trinkets and local jewelry that was much like that of the Native Americans of Arizona and New Mexico only different in style and execution, cruder and simpler but charming.

I went swimming in the Orinoco River. We were assured that piranhas were no threat, that our activity in the water would scare them away. Besides, they were not in this area. I wasn't totally convinced. I remained apprehensive. I didn't stay in the water long, but long enough to say I swam in the Orinoco.

Sandy enjoyed the jungle immensely. The Indian villages didn't require much

Sandy & Jimmy in the Snowy Andes

walking, and the boat rides were easy on him as well. I must say they were not easy on me. The dugouts didn't look too sturdy to me and their narrowness concerned me. I felt one false move could capsize them, yet Sandy insisted on going on every river trip. Sandy with his stoma, that hole in his neck—one dip would have made him one dead duck.

We took a flight up the same tributary to the Salto Angel, Angel Falls, the highest falls in the world. When the huge plane banked sharply to give us a better look, we damn near died of fright. This was no small plane, with six seats across and jet engines. We heard later that there had been a crash, and no wonder. On our way back to the rather large but crude airfield, we saw here and there smaller aircraft that had crashed and were lying in rubble in underbrush, amidst the lush, deep green foliage of the jungle.

One afternoon we jaunted off in a beautiful limousine into the hills outside Caracas, to a German settlement. Germans had immigrated to Venezuela many years ago, and their descendants were living just as their ancestors had lived in the Black Forest back home. You would swear you were visiting a German hamlet in the hills beyond Baden Baden not far from Stuttgart with dark beer, cheeses, wiener schnitzel "mit Sauerkraut und Schnapps," not to mention German being spoken everywhere. Such a pleasant surprise, that was.

Before we left, we purchased some gold pieces I still wear. We hadn't had a time like that in many years. The three weeks seemed to be over before they began, and we were back at the airport with nothing more than our ticket home and our passports to help us exit. Sandy didn't have to know my concern about our lack of visas: there was no incident. As we sat at the terminal watching tourists, Sandy asked once more, "Where are the Americans?"

"I don't see any cameras from Tokyo either," I remarked.

"Don't worry," Sandy said. "Wait until everyone cottons on to the exchange rate. They'll all be down here pronto."

We had a stopover in Grenada. It was a chance to hole up at Betsy Frisbee's a friend from Bequia who was now living there. She had wanted to retire on Bequia, but the government had given her a hard time, I think because she was a single woman. It looked to me that it was just a way for the machos to flex their muscle in a matriarchal society. It was enjoyable spending time with her, hashing over all the fun we had had back in the '70s. She'd been a great Santa's helper every Christmas.

Sandy and I went back to Bequia to close up the house for the winter months. We would be in the city, with Sandy teaching regular classes at the Playhouse where his new batch of Bequia students would also be studying in his private professional class. As well he would train a few new apprentices in his teaching program. At 110 East 58th, Boolu was a welcome sight. Anyone could see he was quite at home busily making friends as he went about building a new life for himself that had yet to adopt him. I went back to the Funny Face agency and picked up where I had left off, one of the good things about being in such a racket.

31 One Thing Leads to Another

Summer Of '86—Restless Spirit

By January applications were coming in for the next Bequia summer season. Before I knew it, I was up to my ears in preparations. This time we were planning the same two, month-long sessions of beginning students and another month for the second year students out of the professional class at Playhouse who were, of course, Bequia graduates. It would be a larger class than usual because it was made up of the two classes from the previous summer. The larger class size presented me with a new logistical problem in Bequia. The hotel could handle only twenty students, so I was compelled to find another residence for the overflow. I found a house at the bottom of our drive across the road. The location could not have been better, and it had a complete apartment on the first floor with another on the second, so a flat for the women upstairs and one for the men downstairs. This setup was perfect for protection purposes. Lovely actresses have a way of attracting attention from unsavory blokes with nothing better to do than lie about counting coconuts and leering at unsuspecting sexy women. The women couldn't help that; that was just the way our actresses came.

After the introductory welcome, I opened the floor to questions. I noticed a little reaction in the back of the room, nothing more than a little unrest between two men. So I asked whether they had a question. One fellow said, "No." But I could plainly see some disagreement. They were two of the fellows renting the house down the road. I remembered one as a pain in the ass from last year, what I would call a whiner. Putting him the house went against my better judgment, but I did it because he was so strapped for cash. He wasn't the type who could be left to his own devices and I should have put him in the hotel where he would have been coddled. If they were having trouble down at the house at the bottom of the hill, I didn't have many options because at present there was no other place they could afford. Oh, well, my mistake.

"OK, fellow, speak up," I said, thinking, here we go again. He's going to be a pain in the butt all month. That's what I get for being an old softy. "Come on, will you tell us what's bugging you?"

"Well," he said hesitantly, "it's that house down there. It's hot, very hot. It was so hot we couldn't sleep."

I appealed to the men who were down there with him. "Was it? Speak up."

Finally, the other fellow spoke up, "Yes, Jimmy, it was hot, damn hot." I was thinking, if this doesn't work out, where the hell will I put them? He went on, "But it's OK, we'll make out."

31 One Thing Leads to Another

I think he was thinking about the money they were saving by being there. I said, "But it wasn't hot last night. The breezes were cool. Charlotte, how was it upstairs?"

"Jimmy, I don't get it. It was cool upstairs. We closed our shutters. The breezes were blowing things off the table."

"How was it at the hotel last night?" I asked, and all agreed it had been pleasantly cool. "Well, I'm stumped," I told them. This discrepancy was perplexing.

Then one of the boys from the house said, "Tell him the other stuff."

He picked up, "Jimmy, it's weird down there. It started off calm, cool, quiet, and pleasant. Then as we got ready for bed, all of a sudden things started to happen. First, the kitchen door starting banging back and forth furiously. Then ants started coming out of every crack imaginable. They were in both the kitchen and the bedroom. They were covering the floor. We had nothing to spray them with, so we took a brood and swept them out the door. We latched the door, and it was sweltering inside. So we opened the top half and tied it back hoping to let in some air. Then a black cat splayed itself across the closed bedroom window, like a Halloween cat, with all four legs stretched out in four directions and its fur on end, all fluffed up. It was screeching like a cat in heat. One of the boys knocked at the window, and it flew off the sill. A little later it appeared over the half door, just its head showing, hanging on with its two front paws, the claws buried in the wood. It looked like 'Kilroy was here' from World War II, if any of you remember him. Someone knocked it away with a broom and closed the top half again, and the heat built up." He continued, "Jimmy, it was spooky. I don't get bothered by much nonsense, but last night even got to me."

I had no answer for them. I said, "We will tend to the matter after lunch." And I went upstairs to Daphne and Rosalie.

Up in the kitchen, I told the women what had happened last night at Olivette's house. Rosalie stood there, dumbfounded, her mouth wide open, her eyes popping. Then Daphne said to her, "Why are you so surprised?" and turned to me and said, "Jimmy, do you know what happened last night?... The virago from Paget Farm died."

"So, what's that got to do with it?" I asked.

"Jimmy, she had been living there for the past six months, until she went into the hospital, Jimmy, her restless spirit was on its way home."

She was an impossible woman in life; I knew. I had had my run-in with her. She seemed to have a split personality, viragos can be difficult people. Daphne told me that for the past year and half she had been fighting cancer. When it became difficult for her to get to appointments in the Harbour, she had moved into the basement to be closer to her doctor. When finally, as she came closer to death, when she had to be in the hospital, she became impossible to handle. Gossip had it that nurses refused to care for her because of the deplorable language. She drove one of her sons away from her bedside with her antics as she lay dying. The truth of all this "milly-milly" would be difficult to document. No doubt she had a troubled passing, and coupled with the prevalent belief on the Island of the power of jumbies, soucoryants, and Obeah, the definite consensus would be that she had become one of the restless spirits on Bequia. These were spirits not ready for heaven or hell and therefore unable to go to their rest. Could she really be a restless spirit? Who knew? Some would say yes, others would say no. All that mattered to me was that I had a few freaked-out students with no other place to go. I had to do something and I had to do it fast.

At lunch, I explained to the boys what had happened last night. I had an idea I wanted to try. I asked them if they would humor me for just one more night, and they agreed. I took down from the dining room wall the old crucifix that we had come across while renovating East 83rd. It had been rolled up in an 1866 Salt Lake City newspaper along with two medicine bottles dated January 1866 from a defunct apothecary store on the corner of Lexington Avenue and 86th Street. It had been hidden in a rafter in the cellar when the 83rd Street brownstone was constructed in 1866. The crucifix had been made in France with the ancient skull and crossbones prevalent at the time of the Spanish Inquisition, the use of which had later been banned at the Council of Trent. It had been around awhile. I also found some prayers, as close to the subject as I could find in a Sunday missal.

I took the boys with me and went down to the room and prayed. I thought, if the place needed prayers, why not provide them? The boys laughed, and Marty said, "What are doing? An exorcism?"

I said, "I don't know what I'm doing. Just stay the night and find out."

Well, the ending of this tale is short. Marty reported that that night things subsided a great deal. But it took a few days before everything settled down and returned to normal. The boys stayed and everything was cool and quite copacetic after that. They couldn't get over it. I told them we never knew when we were going to celebrate Halloween around here. On All Souls' and All Saints' Days, we burn candles all night over all the graves down here and spend all night with the spirits. Now he knew why.

Picasso Boolu And His "Riding Shoes"

In September back in New York, Boolu was successfully holding down the fort. I can't tell you what a pleasure it was for de tree a wee to be back together. Boolu was happy as a June bug up at Hunter with Kate and her crew. Home from the park one lovely Indian summer afternoon, he announced, "Hey, Jimmy, can I have riding shoes?"

Riding shoes, I thought. He must have seen the likes of Jacqueline Kennedy and her crowd prancing along the bridle path and figured if he had some he could also prance along the East Side swells. After all, he knew how to ride Black Beauty out on Pap Pap's farm.

"Boolu," I said, "if there's one thing you don't need in this town, it's riding boots."

At dinner that night he brought up the idea of boots again. Only this time he asked Sandy. "Sandy," he says, "can I have riding shoes?"

Sandy repeated, "Riding shoes? Where does he get this stuff? Does he want them just to make flash? As it is, he already looks like Superfly every time he sets foot out the door. Or does he really think he can go riding in the park with the rest of the social set? Jimmy, tell him he lives on the Upper East Side all right, but that's all. He doesn't get all the perks that go with it just because he lives here... Why don't you give him the boots Dick Dunn gave you? You don't wear them, they don't fit you."

I said, "You're right about that. They're a half size too big, but I still can't even get them on because of my 'Doc Blanchard calves'—they're too thick for the boots."

The next afternoon Boolu started up at me again about the riding shoes. Halfheartedly, I went into the closet and pulled out the boots, dropped them on the floor in front of him, and said, "There. Now you got riding boots, but I sure as hell don't know what you're going to do with them."

"I don't want dem," he said, walking over to the window and pointing out at the sidewalk. "See? Riding shoes."

I went over to take a look. Sure enough, riding shoes. Four kids roller-skating back and forth. He got his "riding shoes" for Christmas.

A Christmas Gift With Clout

Just before Christmas Boolu received notice from the federal government that he would be informed of the time, date, and place of his Green Card interview approximately three months or "there-about." Sandy said, "Knowing the government, it will more likely be 'there-about,'" Very vague!

I figured that should bring us to March or even May and we should be in New York. But maybe not—we could well be in Bequia. I called Rusty and explained my dilemma. He offered to accompany Boolu if we were out of the country.

I spoke to his immigration lawyer, who confirmed that "Because Boolu is deaf, someone had better go along with him. They're tough on the handicapped. There is always the danger of their becoming a liability to the state because of their existing condition, and one has to prove that will never be." He reminded me of the Israeli couple's dilemma, which still hadn't been settled.

This problem was much the same as what Boolu had faced in Barbados the second time he applied, when I had written the mock letter. America was paranoid about people with disabilities becoming a burden on the state. They discriminated against the disabled by not even giving them a chance. How could we prove that Boolu could hold a job if he could not get one in the first place without a Social Security Card? How could he get a Social Security Card without a Green Card? It was a real catch-22. Rusty offered to employ him legally as a janitor if they would let him, but without a Social Security Card it was impossible.

The Social Security office for our district was just down the street on 58th and Third Avenue. One day I got the notion to take Boolu by the hand and march him there to try to explain our quandary. So over we went. We trudged up the stairs to the second floor, took a ticket, and sat and waited. Eventually, a lovely looking black woman came over to us to ask, "Can I help you?" I gave her our ticket and she directed us into her office.

I had heard somewhere that Social Security numbers were sometimes given out without a Green Card under certain directives. I was well aware that Boolu didn't fall into one of the necessary categories. Nevertheless, I explained how Boolu was deaf and had been studying at Hunter College in a special education program since 1983, how he had been brought to the US on a medical visa because of severe burns, which had been treated at the New York Burn Center. I added that he had been offered a job here in Manhattan as a janitor, but he couldn't accept it because he had no Social Security number although he was scheduled for a Green Card interview in March. I handed her the letter.

The officer had Boolu sit next to her at her desk and proceeded to talk directly to him, asking him questions. I didn't interfere, leaving it totally up to him. After a while, she paused and looked over at me. "Once he gets his Green Card," she said, "he can get his SS number. Under certain restrictions, we can give out a Social Security number without a Green Card, but he..." She paused again and looked at Boolu. Then she said, "What the heck! You'll be getting your Green Card in less than three months anyway. Here, give me your passport."

She proceeded to fill out the application, taking down all the information. "You'll get it officially in the mail." Handing the papers to Boolu, she said, "Here it is." She took another short pause, then, smiling, addressed me. "Go over to 57th Street and Fifth Avenue and look up." Turning to Boolu, she simply said, "Good luck."

Boolu and I both thanked her and we were out of there. We trudged across 58th Street with a sharp westerly wind nipping at our faces as large snowflakes soft and powdery met us head on, making it impossible to see oncoming pedestrians. They were faceless, squishing along in the slush with their heads buried in their Christmas bundles. It was the fifteenth of December and all New York was out shopping with a vengeance. We turned down Fifth Avenue to 57th Street, and there hanging high in the center of the intersection was a huge, white, glistening snowflake. She was telling us it was the season; it was her way of giving Boolu a little Christmas gift. Some Christmas gift! Little did she know the ammunition she had given us to use on the Green Card people, if we had to. Rusty could now immediately employ him, so Boolu would now be able to prove he could work and take care of himself: the government need not fear he would be a liability.

When Sandy came home and heard the story, he said, "Boolu, me boyo, you're ready to take them on now. Go to it!"—and, turning to me, "What a relief!"

La-La Land, Here We Come

That Christmas we stayed in the US. After all Boolu couldn't go to Bequia anyway. We decided to stay in town and planned a little trip to Los Angeles, just the two of us, for the first of the year ('87).

The closest I had ever gotten to LA was Pasadena back in '49 when I was in the army, when I was routed north to Stockton after a cross-country trip from Chicago on the Southern Santa Fe. Sandy had spent time there back in '47 or '48 with Betty and again at 20th Century-Fox in '59. An old friend from their radio days back in the '30s had been bugging him for years to come out. He was now living in Malibu after a successful radio career, but had suffered making the change to movies. Thank God he had had enough sense to invest after the Crash of '29; consequently, he wasn't doing badly clipping his coupons. He was a warm person who, I could see, held Sandy in high esteem. His wife was another kettle of fish. It was as if we were her husband's guests, not hers. Maybe she just couldn't cotton to the notion of two grown-up men living together—we just bothered her a bit too much, perhaps. It was the kind of situation that I didn't like being in, that I was careful never to put myself in. When Sandy's old friend and bridge partner from New York, Dick Dunn, asked us to spend some time with him at his home in Beverly Hills, we took him up on the invite. In truth, we jumped at the offer. He was one swell guy.

Rita Edelman, Rosie's mother, gave Sandy a big splash, one whale of a party, inviting Sandy's friends from his days at 20th Century-Fox. We met Bob Carnegie and his wife Maxine of Playhouse West and were invited above and beyond the Hollywood sign to the new home of Natalie Harley's daughter, Tanya, and her recently acquired husband, TV director Reza Badiyi. All in all, we had a very hospitable time.

Though he met many of his old-time successful students at Rita's, I noticed no invitations were extended to Sandy from any of them. I remembered hearing tales of Sandy's 20th Century-Fox days. These people had been actors just starting out, and Sandy and Betty's home on Londonderry Drive up above the Strip had been a real hangout for many of them. Sandy had held a bash every Sunday at poolside, and they were all there. In those days they weren't anybody yet and in Hollywood that meant not successful. I guess now they didn't have the time for Sandy. He wasn't Hollywood now. Sandy was the type of man who never gave it a second thought. He couldn't care less, but it was hard for me to fathom. I was used to hearing them carry on about how much Sandy meant to them, how they owed him so much for what he had given them. Well, you couldn't prove it by me, not from where I sat.

I left Hollywood with mixed feelings, while Sandy had none: New York was his town. I liked the weather and the lifestyle: everyone lived in their own house, moved about in their very own car. Nonetheless we were winging it back to New York and the responsibilities that awaited us.

Busy, Busy, Busy

I was beginning to get print work, Boolu had his janitorial work down pat, and Sandy with his new loudspeaker and mic dangling from the temple of his eyeglasses was finding teaching a lot easier. We were all three gunning with both barrels. Sandy was back at work teaching his professional class of students made up from the Meisner Carville School from Bequia, while I was assisting. He was also working with ex-students who were interested in becoming teachers.

This season was turning into a relatively lucrative year for me. Things seemed to be looking up when I even landed a commercial! Rusty called me on the phone. As president of the company that had used Boolu for the soft running shoe commercial, he had a commercial for me, if I liked cheese, a commercial for a new cheese produced in Pennsylvania and test-distributed throughout the Northeast. The commercial would be aired in that location only and featured me as the cheese taster. Health regulations forced me to shave my beard but allowed me to keep my mustache. I was to be the spokesperson, and as it worked out, they put a caricature of my face on the package, like Aunt Jemima. I had a cousin in Syracuse who told me she had been shopping one day in the supermarket and there I was in the dairy section, staring up at her like Elsie, the Borden's cow.

I felt this was finally it, the end of our money problems. I was going to be another Phil Rizutto or, as Rusty put it, "Yeah, another Palmolive 'Madge the Manicurist.'" I later learned the commercial had been a real success within the industry, a big boost for the TV production company. But unfortunately for me, the cheese was lousy; the cheese company went bust, and I got zilch. If that wasn't the story of my career, what was?

Summer of '87—Looking Forward To Spoon River

March came and went with no notice from the Green Card office. In May, Sandy and I went off to Bequia with a new group, leaving this crucial bit of business to Boolu, Rusty, and the immigration lawyer. It was all unnerving. But you can't speed up the bureaucracy.

This third summer we decided to add another month to the course, to delve into Sandy's Spoon River exercise with the students who had completed his two-year program where it was the last exercise he taught. It's purpose was to strengthen and deepen one's emotion, to help the actor sustain that single emotion, "deepening and sustaining a single emotion" being the operative words. In truth, Sandy never expected much in the way of results from the younger students with this exercise because it demanded emotional maturity. It came with experiences out there on the firing line working. In other words, it is an ability that comes with practice, assuming the actor is talented in the first place. So now that he had older, more mature students at the Bequia school, Sandy felt they might be emotionally more open to the exercise, it still being only a peek into the future of the demands of the craft. It was just one more step on that twenty-year trek to becoming an accomplished actor.

A Time Of Reckoning

In June, Boolu's notice finally came. He was to go to the Federal Building across the street from the courthouse in lower Manhattan, just north of City Hall. He was advised to arrive early. Rusty was ready with his proof of employment, if needed, his Social Security card, and copies of paychecks in hand.

When the caseworker called out his name and went over to him, she told both the lawyer and Rusty that this was one interview Boolu was required to take alone. The lawyer persisted. She took Boolu by the arm with one big fat hand, for she was enormous, and simply said "Sorry" as she led him into her little cubical.

The lawyer leaned over to Rusty and said, as she closed the door to her little cell behind her, "Poor boy. She looks like one mean machine."

Rusty and the lawyer sat outside with all the other applicants. As the questioning continued behind the closed door, hers was the only voice they could hear. They were able to follow every one of her inquiries and she seemed to be using a directive tone. She was checking and cross-checking. She seem to be grilling him actually hollering at the poor boy in a voice as stern as a drill sergeant's. They couldn't hear one word out of Boolu. Rusty could see the little old ladies awaiting their turn stiffen up and begin to squirm in their seats. If they had been scared or nervous before, they were now just downright petrified! Rusty thought, my God! Boolu's got himself a barracuda. He's going to crack for sure.

After a good twenty to twenty-five minutes of this interrogation, the door swung open and there was Boolu engulfed by this huge woman, her arm slung over his shoulder. She was smiling from ear to ear as she led him over to Rusty and the lawyer. Through her broad smile, she announced, "Well, we made it, we did. He's a very bright young man." Turning to Boolu, she said, "Congratulations, Julian. Welcome to America." And she walked back to pick up the papers for the next applicant.

Comprehension dawning, Rusty said to the lawyer, "She was pulling for him every inch of the way! She was only yelling at him so he wouldn't misunderstand a single question and give a wrong answer. But she sure had me sweating bullets."

Rusty and Boolu said their goodbyes to the lawyer and went out to celebrate. Boolu was legal now and could come and go as he wished. He was now truly a free man, and what a relief it was for all of us.

What Happened to Phil

The summer of '87, we lost a student. On an island less than five square miles, still we lost a student. Phil Forman was a mild-mannered chap, bright, well spoken, and somewhat shy. The day he was missing was the day he was scheduled to work on his first scene, which was supposed to be memorized and off-book. He had last been seen in Kenneth's rum shop, drunker than a skunk. The other students checked every inch of the Island that afternoon, to no avail. The next day there was still no Phil. All the boatmen were checked, but nothing indicated he had left the Island. When I heard that, I was worried.

He showed up at the hotel in the evening two days later. It unfolded that, petrified of Sandy, he had got loaded, meandered out beyond Spring at the far end of the Industry—as a boy Boolu used to find scorpions and fuzzy little black tarantulas there—and had hung out there over the weekend. In class, they had reached the point where he was expected to stand up in front of everyone and demonstrate his mettle to Sandy. He froze. Little had Sandy known he had problems, real problems.

In spite of what happened, first thing Monday morning Sandy had him get up and he very gingerly finessed the last week's exercise out of the boy before continuing with the next segment in training. Some of the students later told me that the way Sandy handled the lad was magnificent. One young woman said that Sandy had had them sitting on the edges of their seats. It was as if Sandy were playing him like a Stradivarius. It was a lesson in itself.

Later, when Sandy learned that Phil's mother was a psychiatrist and his father a righteous evangelical-type preacher, he said, "No wonder the poor lad has problems. This is going to be a real challenge for him."

We knew Phil had already studied with Stella. But, he explained, he had never got up and worked in front of the class. When asked how long he had spent in the class he replied, "Three years. I used to walk her dogs."

Sandy told me, "So much for integrity. She should have paid him to be there. What did the poor boy think? It was going to rub off just being around her?" Sandy couldn't believe it: three years, and he had never been asked up to work! All I can say is, by the end of the month he was working for Sandy like had never worked before, and I am here to tell you Sandy never had a more grateful student.

31 One Thing Leads to Another

Sandy Buckles

It was the last week in August the third year of our Bequia school when Sandy was hit again with a ton of bricks. The feeling had come over him all of a sudden. He complained about a lack of energy. He was having difficulty breathing, too. "I think I'm coming down with the flu," he said.

I had been too busy to notice. With only a couple of class days left, he managed to get through. Monday we all left for New York together. It wasn't until we started down the steps toward the garage that it was apparent he was going to need assistance. At that instant, a dreadful wave of fear engulfed me. I remembered once how Tiare and her husband Lee had been seriously poisoned. They had a doctor waiting for them at the airport in Barbados ready to rush them to the hospital once they got there. But it had been too difficult to appear perfectly well until they could get on the plane in St. Vincent. That St. Vincent wasn't equipped to care for them was inconsequential. In the end, a pilot aware of her plight offered to fly her over without clearance.

Knowing these risks, at the airport in St. Vincent we herded Sandy into the center of the group. The biggest and strongest gripped him under the arm and literally carried him out onto the tarmac and up into the plane with no one the wiser. The plane back to New York was quite empty so we were able to flip up the armrest and stretch him out across three seats so he might catch some shut-eye. At one point, one of the older flight attendants took me aside and said, "That man is very sick. What is it?"

"I think it's the flu," I answered.

"That looks like pneumonia to me."

"I'm getting him back to his doctors," I explained.

"With all the help you have, you won't need us," she said, "except for a wheelchair. I'll tell them to have one waiting."

I thanked her.

I got him home in a taxi, very late, and when I put him to bed, he crashed. In the morning, his doctor said, "Bring him in this afternoon." After a thorough examination, he said, "He has pneumonia. We'd better get him over to New York Hospital immediately. I'll call ahead."

The hospital was just one block away. When we got downstairs, I couldn't get a taxi to stop. Finally I said, "Let's walk slowly down the street to York. It's not far."

Sandy was getting weaker with every step. We managed to get to the center entrance, but he literally couldn't take another step. We sat on the wall in front of the library. Try to get help on the streets of New York when you need it! Forget it. The Admitting Office was one block to the right. A woman stopped, said she was a doctor, and asked if we needed help. "Yes, we need a wheelchair," I said. "I'm trying to get him to Admitting." She never came back. She did send an ambulance but by the time it came I had Sandy at the entrance, asking for a wheelchair. Then the paramedics came in asking all kinds of questions. By now he was having trouble breathing. They sat him in a chair and started yelling at him, asking him his name over and over. Who was I? And was I family?

What was it with these people? What's with this blood relation thing? I could never understand it. A spouse was never a blood relation. Was I family? Who is family? I finally told them he was my father.

They took him and sat him on a couch, yelling at him to keep him conscious because he was fading away. Here we were in the middle of a hospital and yet there was no wheelchair to be had. Eventually they got a gurney, took him to the emergency room, and hooked him up to some oxygen. Shortly afterward, a doctor came out and said, "He's not your father."

"So what!" I retorted. I was furious.

Eventually Sandy was moved to a private room. He slipped in and out of consciousness the first couple of days and then was out of it for almost two weeks, completely unconscious. The doctor stated that it was obvious he had been abusing himself with heavy drinking and smoking over many years so that now at his age, with all that he had already been through, it was impossible for his immune system to kick in. They couldn't give him enough antibiotics or right ones at least. The pneumonia, they said, might be atypical. His vital signs were holding, but he was too weak to come to.

I thought I was going to lose it completely. I don't know what I would have done without Boolu at that time, just to have someone to talk to. Paul was gone, Ruth was gone, and I practically lived at the hospital. Almost no one stopped by, except for Harold Baldridge who stopped once, and Donna Gatsparo, a student from Bequia. Did people not know, or did they think he was half dead again, so why bother? Who the hell knew? All I knew was that we were pretty much alone, and I wasn't one for reaching out. I just sat and waited, day after day.

After almost two weeks, when he finally came to, the first thing he said to me was, "I'm not drinking or smoking anymore." How the hell did he know? You know, from that day on he never smoked or drank a drop for the rest of his life.

I said to him, "What some people have to go through to learn a lesson."

Upon discharge, he was in no shape to start off the season at Playhouse. They would be kicking off the year without him. I could also tell from the physical shape he was in that he was in no condition to brave out the winter in New York City. We had a second-year class from Bequia waiting to begin at the school as well. When Bob Carnegie called from Hollywood to see how Sandy was doing, I told him he was getting better, but I felt he was in no shape to spend another winter in the city. Bob matter-of-factly said, "Why don't you come out here? Sandy could teach at Playhouse West."

When I presented the idea to Sandy, I couldn't tell if he thought it had merit. He himself may have felt he couldn't get through another winter in the city.

Yet he wasn't up to making monumental decisions.

I figured we could hold the classes for the Bequia students out there in LA from November through April. He could then start the students off at the Neighborhood Playhouse next September and check out his teachers and the students at the end of the school year the following May. This arrangement was forcing the teachers at Playhouse to take over and finessing him at eighty-two, into semi-retiring. It was much better for them and for Harold than his quitting completely. I don't believe he would have done it any other way. This solution was fine with me; it was what I had wanted him to do all along.

1987 - Semi-Retirement from the Playhouse

Boolu didn't take too kindly to our move early in November. I hoped I had convinced him of the need for it based on Sandy's health, and I hoped he understood. Confucius says, "If you don't understand, stand under." And I say, "Devil take the hindmost."

The LA students who had been planning to come to New York were delighted, although some east coast students were not happy about the move. Most changed their plans and moved out with us. We had room at Playhouse West to increase the class size to include a section for writers, directors, and producers who were interested in observing Sandy at work. He would spend some time with them after class answering their questions.

A by-product of this move was an improvement in our financial situation even though Sandy took a 50% cut in his Neighborhood Playhouse salary. Without the Playhouse eating up his time, we could handle three groups of students at the LA school. It was a pleasant surprise to both of us, despite the skimpy salary that Bob Carnegie offered.

Our winter clothes we left in New York, which heartened Boolu—it meant we weren't leaving altogether. All we took to LA were our summer clothes and plenty of apprehension because we hadn't had time to prepare. If we were going to begin classes on time to satisfy the awaiting students, we had to get cracking! Just weeks before Sandy had been in a coma. Now there we were moving across the country to start a new school and begin in new life.

All Paul's furniture and books had been stored away in my brothers Hugh's attic for the past seven years. A friend offered to take a U-Haul truck upstate and cart the goods across country for us before he started work at the Playhouse in New York that year.

We were taking Maxine and Bob at their word, and let the chips fall where they may. Because of Maxine, where they fell was more satisfactory, pleasing, and pleasant than anyone could ever have imagined. We stayed at Dick Dunn's while Maxine and I went about shopping for furniture, food, and house supplies, filling the little bungalow that Maxine found for us on Bellingham Avenue in Studio City. The house came equipped with a beautiful pool and Jacuzzi. It was lovely. I found one of the most luxurious, hedonistic, and sensual pastimes in life is to pamper oneself soaking in a hot tub out under the stars looking at the snowcapped mountains in the distance, a pastime in which, I might add, I indulged myself night after night. Sandy soaked in the tub during the day although he had to be careful because of his stoma. It was soothing and therapeutic for him and extremely beneficial for his muscle tone. We found LA an energizing and uplifting way of life, and the classes just flowed along.

Yet Another Hospital Visit

Just as we were settling in to the new house and at the school, where we were only into the third week of classes, Sandy developed a pain in his lower abdomen. His doctor said he had ruptured an old hernia. He also wanted to ready him for an overdue prostate operation. Dr. Sugarman arranged for double operations at Cedars Sinai Hospital on the morning of the last Wednesday in November. Two doctors performed the surgeries back to back. Two operating rooms, one across the hall from the other, were readied. When the first operation finished, they just rolled Sandy across the hall where the next team was waiting. Sandy taught class on Monday, was prepped in the hospital on Tuesday, underwent the surgeries on Wednesday, was recovering on Thursday, and was on his feet on Friday. When he left the hospital Monday morning, he insisted on going to class Monday afternoon.

"What?" was all I said.

"What," he asked me, "would I be doing at home?"

"You would be taking it easy sitting on the couch."

"Give me a pillow and I could be sitting in my class," he replied, and he was off again with me dragging behind. He missed only three classes the week of the operations.

A Stitch in Time

Boolu had come out from New York so we could all be together. He had planned to go back the following Sunday. He talked all week about going to Disneyland. I said, "No way, next time."

Sandy said, "Why not?"

"I'll tell you why not," I said.

"What's the problem? I'm feeling fine and I would be in a wheelchair anyway."

Saturday morning we were heading south on the 405 on our way to Anaheim. Once there we discovered that people in wheelchairs were not required to stand in the long lines to board the rides. All they had to do was enter at the exits and get on the next vehicle escorted by two others. What a bonanza. We dashed from ride to ride, with Boolu pushing the wheelchair of course, de tree a we having the time of our lives. We rushed along, never looking at where we were particularly, just following the exits signs. We darted into one exit where an attendant helped Sandy into a car with Boolu sitting between his legs. I climbed into the car behind and we inched up ahead to let the waiting crowd board. Only when we started up, heading into the steel girders, did I realize we were on the Space Mountain or the Matterhorn, a wild rollercoaster-type ride. My heart sank. All I could think of was stitches, not only the stiches in Sandy's prostate that he was sitting on, but the ones for his hernia that Boolu was being pushed up against due to the centrifugal force. I thought, Ohmigod, it's only been ten days. He's going to be ruined. I hollered out to Boolu to hold himself forward and not lean into Sandy, but I remembered he couldn't hear, the other couldn't speak, it was hopeless. I felt helpless as we crashed, smashed, dashed, and bashed from side to side and up and down and all around. I thought the ride would never end; it was the longest amusement park ride I had ever taken. I had visions in my head of taking Sandy into Cedars Sinai with a busted ruptured hernia, bleeding from a split prostate, and me wondering, worried and embarrassed as hell, how in the heaven I would ever explain without sounding like a complete jackass.

When it was finally over and we were easing Sandy into the wheelchair, I asked if he was alright. He looked up at me a bit puzzled and said, "Sure. Why not? Wasn't that great? Better than Coney Island when I was a kid."

"Did Boolu scrunch up against you?" I asked.

"No, no. He held himself forward; I would have stopped him if he had. You're such a worrier," he replied making light of it.

I made damned sure I was a hell of a lot more cautious after that. He may have felt fine, but it was many weeks before I felt it was truly behind us. I didn't tell anyone for years how stupid I had been letting such a thing happen. It could have had serious consequences!

32 Reaping the Rewards

The Seed is Planted

Sandy flourished under the pleasant California sunshine with the pleasing soft breezes caressing him every day. It was more therapeutic for him than any medicine could ever be. He was teaching under ideal conditions and he had a crackerjack class making it more delightful for him. The lifestyle was easier on him with no running after taxis and everything just steps away. Our social life was more active than New York. It was much the same as on Bequia. We visited back and forth with dinner dates in the homes of Shari Lewis, Rosie and Rita Edelman, Dick Dunn, the Carnegies, and David Craig and Nancy Walker. The move might have seemed rash and spur of the moment with little or no planning. In truth, it was one of the wisest moves we ever made. We were now living in three places. Sandy used to get a kick out of telling people we were "tri-coastal." I felt bad for Boolu, but under the circumstances we had no choice. What kind of life would he have had out in Los Angeles? After all, he was thirty-one years old. It was about time he was cut loose, as much as he could be.

We advertised for the Bequia summer school of '88, interviewing in LA and leaving openings for New York where we interviewed at the Neighborhood Playhouse the first week in May. Sandy was back there, teaching the *Spoon River* exercise to the graduating students, the last exercise he taught in his two-year program. He attended the final demonstration and the graduation banquet, fulfilling his semi-retirement obligations, while I kicked it with Boolu for a couple of weeks.

While we were at a dinner party in New York, an ex-student of Sandy's raved about a trip she had taken up the Nile. She captivated her listeners with descriptive and dramatic detail of her sojourn. Sandy was spellbound by her performance. He enjoyed listening as much as she enjoyed telling it and being the center of attention throughout the evening—quite a feat for anyone at a New York East Side dinner party.

I started thinking about Sandy and what he was getting out of all our jumping around. I was doing whatever I could to make it possible for him to continue what he enjoyed most, as long as it was feasible for all concerned. I truly felt his method of teaching acting, as compiled in his book, Sanford Meisner *On Acting*, was a complete, clear, and understandable approach to realistic acting, that is, to "living truthfully under imaginary circumstances." My own mother could understand the book. It was the culmination of sixty years' work. I felt if I kept him going for as long as he wanted to and certainly as

32 Reaping the Rewards

long as he was able, then the Approach, supported by the book and his tapes, might just spill over into the 21st century for future students of acting. God knows there wasn't much realistic acting in demand or being demonstrated in the industry. But just maybe, if students do what Sandy always asked them—"Never forget what the theater could be"...So you can see I had my work cut out for me.

The proceeds of all this effort were being sent to Barry on Wall Street. But for whose benefit? Certainly not Sandy's. It was going to Boolu's and my retirement down the line. Once Sandy was gone, the two of us would be getting zilch from the Neighborhood Playhouse. Even now Sandy wasn't doing much better from them. Forget the US government and any benefit from Sandy's pension. This wasn't Canadia. As far as the US government was concerned, I was a non-entity in this relationship. So Sandy was making provisions for Boolu and me and reaping none of the benefits of his work.

I approached Sandy with this inequity and asked what we could do about the problem.

"Nothing," he said. "It isn't a problem, unless you make it a problem."

"No, no," I said, "this isn't fair. The way it is, we're working for only Boolu and me. Look, I've been thinking—"

"At your age, why start now?"

"Sandy, no kidding," I said. "I have an idea. This summer, we're taking only two groups. This gives us a month and a half to do nothing. On the other hand, we could take a trip if you have a mind to. What about the Nile? You seemed to be so interested the other night at dinner."

He answered me half-heartedly, "Sure, why not?" I would like to do all the important rivers of the world. When I was younger, my wives preferred places like London, Paris, and Rome."

"So why not?" I said. "We could go in August."

"So let's do it. Call my old travel agent; his office should still be on Fifth Avenue. What about going to Israel while we're over there? Stella was always at me, asking, 'What kind of Jew are you?' So what if we can, why not?"

Before we left for Bequia, I did get on to the agent and one day Sandy picked up two books at Doubleday's on Fifth Avenue, one on traveling in Israel, the other covering Egypt. "If we're going to do this," he said, "let's do it right."

On Bequia that summer of '88, when the students were not around we did nothing but plan the trip. One of the first things we discovered was that, because of the political climate, we could not book air travel from New York to Israel and then directly on to Egypt and back to New York. Neither could we book Egypt to Israel. The agent came up with the idea of flying Sinai Airlines, which flew from Cairo to Saudi Arabia with a stopover in Tel Aviv. First we booked a flight on Moroccan Airlines, changing in Morocco for Cairo. After a week there we would board Sinai Air for Tel Aviv, with tickets back to Cairo in two weeks. Then for another week, we would explore the overflowing antiquity of Egypt in Alexandria and El Giza, returning to Morocco via Moroccan Air for another week before finally winging our way back to New York from Casablanca, five weeks after we'd left. That was some itinerary, a week in Egypt, two in Israel, back to Egypt for another week, ending up with a week in Morocco—over a month in three wonderful countries with similarities, yet still as different as day and night. What an education it would turn out to be, and choked-full of serendipity.

The first thing we were going to have to get was a wheelchair. Sandy was dead set against it. He was managing well with his cane, but it would be totally inadequate on the heavy-duty sightseeing spree we were contemplating. "Sorry, Sandy. No wheelchair, no trip. We can't do without one," I insisted. So we hightailed it up to Second Avenue and 72nd Street to a hospital supply store. I wasn't about to put him in it just then. I folded it up, and with Sandy on one arm and the chair dangling from the other, I tried to hail a taxi. One after another cabbies just sped on past with their overhead lights on, I could tell it was useless, so I unfolded the chair and said, "Sit!"

"No."

"Come on, sit down," I insisted. "Can't you see? How else are you going to get home?"

Grudgingly, he sat down, and we sailed down Second Avenue from 72nd Street, stopping at the lights when necessary, and in a jiffy we were gliding down the ramp to the entrance of the Picasso at 210 East 58th Street. "That was terrific!" Sandy said, and for the next nine years he never balked at riding in a wheelchair.

Bequia Class of '88 Celebrates Jimmy's Birthday

32 Reaping the Rewards

Egypt—Into the Sands of Time

From the start, the trip on Moroccan Air was full of surprises. Though we flew coach, we were given first-class treatment all the way across the Atlantic to Morocco. The meal everyone was served was first class, napkins, drinks, silver and all. We stayed overnight in Casablanca and continued on to Cairo the next day.

From the airport in Cairo, we drove to the Nile River and boarded a medium-sized steel-hull ship that would sail us upriver, stopping at archaeological sites along the way. We hit every one on each side of the river, up as far as Luxor. We had a private cabin. It was the middle of the off-season when temperatures would reach triple digits, so the ship was half empty with about seventy-five passengers. All were European with the exception of two other Americans, both unmarried high school teachers from the mid-west.

At one site we got off and rode buses deeper into the desert. With difficulty, I was able to push Sandy over the hard-dirt, gravel-covered path quite a way into the desert. When the sand got too deep to push the chair any farther, I took Sandy with one arm and the wheelchair in the other, slipping my arm under the folded-up seat. And we

Sandy & Jimmy in Egypt

trudged along, bringing up the rear. In spite of this handicap, I managed to get him to each spot. At one site we went underground to see thousands of ibises mummified centuries ago from a time before the Greeks. Schlepping farther on, we arrived at one house in the middle of nowhere where we saw an ancient mummified woman under glass, with a tale likening her story to Romeo and Juliet's. The trek back seemed to take twice as long, and the heat of the day never let up.

Back on ship, as we sat out on the deck after dinner, a breeze started up. Sandy asked, "Can you please fetch my sweater?"

"Are you kidding?" I queried.

"No," he said. "Don't you feel the breeze?"

So I went to get it. As I passed the temperature gauge on the way to our cabin, I noticed it hovered around 118 degrees. As I laid the sweater over his shoulders, I thought again how frail he was becoming.

The maître d' of the dining room was a Bedouin, originally from the desert. Aren't they all? His father was now living in Alexandria. He was giving us extra special care, and I didn't know what the attraction was. I thought of Gide's play The Immoralist. After all this was Egypt. He was tall and attractive and seemed quite intelligent, but that didn't explain the attraction, not by a long shot. At dinner one night he asked if Sandy were the Sanford Meisner of the Group Theatre in America. When I told him Sandy was none other, he was impressed. The man was well versed in our theater—his brother was a well-known actor in Cairo—and was impressed that Sandy had become a teacher. Sandy in turn was impressed by the man's knowledge and couldn't believe how far-reaching the effort of theater can be.

The next stop upriver was the beautiful—well, if not beautiful, certainly sexy—Cleopatra's house. She was descended from a Greek family living in Egypt. The home had a lot of stairs, but Sandy went along anyway. Upstairs on the second floor in what would be her bedroom, the ceiling was stained black from a fire, but one could make out carvings in the ceiling around the circumference of the room, figures of the Zodiac as we know them today.

When we reached Luxor, we took a plane to where in 1257 BC Pharaoh Ramses II had had two temples carved out of solid rock on the west bank of the Nile in the land of the Nubians, known today as Abu Simbel. We arrived at the rear of the site, which looked like a huge building with no windows. It had been transported in space to save it for posterity from the rising waters of Lake Nasser, which had been created when the Russians built the desperately needed dam at Aswan. It was quite a long way from the bus to the front of the site, and I thanked the Lord we had the wheelchair. The crowd was being led off to the right in order to get around the construction to the other side. A small door led into the center of the building. Instead of following the crowd, I opened the door and pushed Sandy through. We were inside under the colossus. All the steel scaffolding holding up the fake hillside was exposed from underneath. It was like being under the bleachers at some huge astrodome in New Orleans or Houston. We could see how the Russians had constructed it high above the water level. I pushed Sandy across to another small door on the other side. When I opened it, lo and behold we were standing at the foot of one of the giant figures looking out across the artificial lake at Abu Simbel. All the other visitors stood there gawking up at us 'neath the beautiful, awesome Colossus. Fortunately I was able to wheel Sandy down off the edifice and out into the crowd admiring this magnificent, artistic relic of antiquity. The day was bright and clear without a cloud in the sky, and the sun had that same magical force it had had

Sandy in Egypt

32 Reaping the Rewards

one day almost ten years before on a mountaintop in Crete. What a powerful experience it was to crawl out from underneath that colossal structure, turn around, and be transported back in time to the days of the pharaohs.

We were then driven over to the dam, but compared to the Hoover Dam it was just another dam.

That evening we settled into a hotel in Luxor planning to make the trip across the Nile to the Valley of the Kings. There again, I was pushing Sandy around over well-trodden sand that, being a little gravelly, added to my difficulty. The tour guide came over to me and said, pointing to the wheelchair, "We don't get many of those around here." Nevertheless we made it to the tombs.

Sandy and I slowly descended the long stairway into the tomb of the pharaoh—the pharaoh Hollywood's Yul Brynner played in the moves who ruled at the time of the Exodus and the parting of the Red Sea for the Jews. Sandy commented, "If this guy had got his hands on those Jews then, I wouldn't be here today." We then went down into the tomb of Tutankhamen. It was full of color and interesting artifacts, all very enlightening. Luxor's antiquity was more than magnificent; it also had an eerie spiritual pull we both sensed.

Our last stop in the Valley of the Dead was over at Queen Hatshepsut's tomb where not too long before some tourists had been shot up by terrorists. In hindsight, I believe this event was a harbinger of things to come.

The experience of the Valley of the Dead was overpowering. It transported us so far back in time that present surroundings took second place. The hotel we stayed in, though beautiful, has dimmed in my memory, although I do remember seeing it later in an Agatha Christie movie.

Having stuffed our minds with oodles of antiquated treasures and enchanting visions of the past, we flew to Cairo and pampered ourselves at a posh hotel in the center of town. From there, we set about exploring Cairo. Strolling along its open markets, Sandy in his wheelchair, we found movement difficult with all the rushing and crushing pedestrians. But it was lively and exciting. Cairo, so full of life, was a welcome change after so much death and grave-gawking among the antiquities down south in the upper Nile. (That doesn't sound right but it is. Remember, the Nile flows north.)

Taxi drivers kept waving at us. "I wonder if they would be waving at you if they knew you were Jewish," I remarked to Sandy.

"What do you want me to do? Wear a yarmulke?" he replied.

Actually, I thought they were waving at us because of the wheelchair and were angling for a fare. But, alas, I was wrong. At a stoplight one driver pulled up, waved, and said in accented English, "I like your beard." Then he called me Allah or something like that. I did have a full head of hair and a full, disheveled beard.

Sandy said, "You see. You're the one who's passing."

We were having one hell of a time in Cairo; it was like a Middle Eastern banquet, something unusual for both of us. We loved the lovely, luxurious, balmy evenings on the expanse of the hotel terrace, with the men milling around

Sandy & Jimmy in Egypt

walking and talking in their long, cool-looking white robes. Not many women appeared, mind you, but the ratio was quite the same as in the corner bars back home, the only difference I could see being that back home men would have had their eyes glued to a television sports game. We preferred being here in an atmosphere of intelligent conversation. Neither one of us had ever been spectator barflies.

The days passed all too quickly and we were swooping across the Sinai Peninsula in an Air Sinai jet to Tel Aviv.

"Jerusalem, Jerusalem! See What the Lord Maketh"

When we arrived at the airport, the luggage inspector took hours, yet no one complained. These were serious times, people were dying, and everyone appreciated the thoroughness no matter how long it took. We arrived at the King David Hotel in time for me to take a dip in the eastern tip of the Mediterranean. The sea was just across the main drag from the hotel, which overlooked an expansive sandy beach. The water was cool and soothing, and I swam out beyond the man-made jetties that ran parallel to the shore, I think to lessen the offshore tides and currents before they hit the sandy beach. I had never seen this type of aquatic construction before.

Back at the room as I dressed for dinner, I could see Sandy was upset. "Don't you feel well?" I asked him.

"No, no, I'm fine. I feel fine," was his reply.

I noticed at dinner he didn't eat and asked again, "What is it?"

Again he said, "Nothin'. I don't know. It's nothing, nothing really."

After dinner we went right to the room and he started readying himself for bed. I had thought I would give him a stroll along the waterfront, but it was obvious to me he was upset, so I pulled out a book and started to read. Eventually I turned out the lights and went to bed myself. I knew he wasn't sleeping. He was up and down and into the bathroom three times. So I got up, turned on the light, and asked once more, "What is it? I can see you're troubled."

"That's just it," he said. "Yes, there is something wrong, but I don't know what it is, Jimmy. I'm nervous. It's this place!"

"What!" I said. "This is the number one hotel in Tel Aviv."

"It's not the hotel. It's Israel! I don't know why. I'm just nervous and restless. Let's go home, let's go back to New York. Come on, let's get out," he was pleading.

"OK, but let's try to get some sleep now," I said. "We'll figure this out in the morning."

In the morning, I said nothing until we were at breakfast. Then I said, "Look, Sandy, I can't imagine what's wrong if you don't know. But listen, we haven't even seen Jerusalem yet. If this place is bothering you, we will get out, we will leave right away. But please let's just go to Jerusalem before we leave. If you're still bothered, then we'll go right back to New York." I continued, "It isn't your health, is it? Because if it is, we can go right away."

"No, it's not my health, it's just this place," he said.

We went upstairs, packed, and then checked out. We went outside to the curb. I had never checked how to get to Jerusalem and I had no idea how far it was. I could see Sandy was having trouble breathing. So I asked again, "Are you sure you're not coming down with something?"

He was short with me now, and said, "I told you I'm fine! I'm just nervous as hell!"

I hailed the first taxi I saw and asked, "Can you take us to Jerusalem?"

"Sure. Hop in," the driver replied in a thick German accent.

"Ohmigod! Now we got a German," Sandy said in his paranoia.

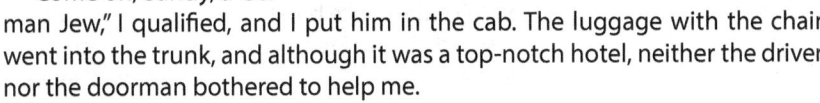
Sandy in Jerusalem

"Come on, Sandy, a German Jew," I qualified, and I put him in the cab. The luggage with the chair went into the trunk, and although it was a top-notch hotel, neither the driver nor the doorman bothered to help me.

Sandy and I didn't talk. I just let him sit back and relax, and he seemed to be calming down. It wasn't too long a trip to Jerusalem. We had reservations at the King David. Our room was spacious and comfortable with two large windows overlooking the Gold Dome of the Rock, a magnificent postcard view. Lunch downstairs was all kosher. When Sandy told the waiter he didn't eat kosher, the waiter replied, "That's all we have. This is a kosher restaurant."

Sandy looked at me and said, "Come on, let's get out of here. This is what's bothering me. In Israel you're a Jew even if you're not. You have no choice. I'm being smothered."

"But you're a Jew, Sandy," I said.

"Not this kind," he snapped.

We went out to the reception area where everyone was standing around, sitting around, walking around this way and that. Most were Chassidim. Even I could tell by the way they were dressed. There were decorative menorahs and Stars of David all over the place. Sandy hadn't been brought up around

Orthodox Jews. This, I thought, is what's bothering him. I remember Sandy joking with me, telling me he had never been inside a synagogue. At the time, I had thought he was pulling my leg. But as I thought about it, over the past twenty-four years neither of us had ever been inside a synagogue of any kind, much less an Orthodox one, not even when his mother died—except for Maimonides' little old synagogue in Cordoba, probably the only one in all of Spain left standing after the Inquisition. This strange lapse is what I believed Stella Adler was getting at when she had once asked him, "What kind of Jew are you?" I knew the answer to that question. It was simple: he was a secular Jew, not a religious one.

I knew Jerusalem was an international city, so at the desk I picked up an English language newspaper and browsed through the adverts for hotels. I found one called the American Colony. I just had a hunch by the name that it probably wasn't Jewish or, more importantly, that it was less likely to be Orthodox. We hadn't even unpacked yet, so we called the front desk to tell them we were checking out and to please send a bellhop.

The cab skirted around the walled city to the North Gate, turned left and north up the Damascus road for merely three blocks, and there it was—a charming mid-sized hotel. The building had been created by a small group of evangelical Christians who came to Jerusalem around the time of the First World War to live a simple farming life near the Holy Places. It was later bought by a Middle Easterner, a merchant who ran it as a hostel, Its décor was Middle-Eastern with carpets on the walls, palm trees, potted palms, and cauldrons made of ceramic and brass. We were escorted to a lovely room with tiled floor and oriental rugs. There was no sign of religion, not anyone's, just a pure feeling of the Middle East.

By now were starving. We hadn't eaten since breakfast. We were led out to a lovely cloistered garden and had a delicious French-style lunch of fresh salad, ham, and three kinds of cheeses with French bread and butter as well as wine for me and for Sandy a Turkish coffee and cream. He looked across the table at me and said, "You know, I believe I'm feeling better already."

He didn't like being pigeonholed just because he was born of Jewish parents. He was an individual first, an American second of Jewish parents, and that was as far as it went. I knew he was a complicated man. He abhorred the idea of any group, no matter who they were, forcing anything, be it religion, politics, even lifestyle, on any other person. The religious right and the "Reverend" Jerry Falwells of the world were his nightmare. Sandy truly felt they were a genuine threat to America and its freedoms. He was a liberal in the truest sense of the word.

"Well," I said, "I hope we can relax and enjoy ourselves now."

We were near the Damascus Gate, the north entrance to the Walled City. I was able to push Sandy in the wheelchair without difficulty, and we went over after our late lunch to meander around. We were just allowing ourselves to slip back in time—to the times of the Crusades, the Knights Templar and their quest for the Holy Grail, the disastrous Children's Crusades, the Omars, the Caliphs, the Turks, the Greek and the Russian Orthodox, as well as the Armenians and the Coptics of Egypt, and of course all the way up to modern-day Palestinians, Zionists, and liberal Jews. What a conglomeration it was. To me it was intoxicating!

It was getting late. We had only had time to cover some of the northwest Christian Quarter. At dinner, which wasn't kosher, thank God, we discovered that the international press people gravitated to this hotel. For us this added a certain charm.

The following day was the day to follow the Via Dolorosa. On Fridays, priests of the Catholic Church do the fourteen stations of the cross as they follow the route Jesus took carrying the cross on that tragically sorrowful day of infamy like no other over 2000 years ago. To be on time, we had time, we had lunch early. The tour started out in front of the Convent of St. Anne in the far eastern Moslem quarter of the Walled City. No sooner had it started than the Moslems started broadcasting their ear-shattering call to prayer from the nearby rooftops so loudly no one could hear the prayers of the priest at each station. Not until we got farther into the Christian Quarter did they fade out. I asked if the Moslems made that noise every week and was told they sure did. Sandy remarked, "So much for getting along with one another."

The procession ended up at the Cathedral of the Holy Sepulchre. The original church had been created by the efforts and funds of the Emperor Constantine's mother, Helena, and built over the alleged place of Jesus's burial. Helena's influence probably also brought the Emperor Constantine around enough to permit the drafting of the Nicene Creed at the Council of Nicaea from 320-25 CE. After all his debaucheries and killings, perhaps he felt the need for a little repentance and pathway to salvation. The tomb of Jesus was way down many, many steps into the bowels of the cathedral, for the cathedral had been built, destroyed, and rebuilt over the site of the tomb many, many times. We could see the levels as we descended.

vWe descended slowly, with me carrying the wheelchair. When we reached the bottom, Sandy was able to sit in the chair and rest. I went into the tomb, but Sandy didn't. He neither needed nor wanted to. I found it interesting to see all the various Christian religious sects from all over the world getting along. There were Greek Orthodox, Russian Orthodox, Armenian and Latvian Orthodox, and Christians from Lebanon. There were Syrian, Coptics from Egypt, Anglicans from England, Romans, and Evangelists from everywhere imaginable in the world. It gave one a little hope, but I was skeptical. Were they really getting along? I had to ask myself that question, for periodically discord broke out amongst them, or so I have been told. Even they, with all their religion and love, find it hard to get along together. If it couldn't work here, where in heaven's name will it ever work?

I knew that priests of the Eastern Maronite Rite marry even though they swear allegiance to Rome and the Pope. I have something to say about:

Rome, where do you come off saying it's Ok for them to marry but not for all priests? When it pleases you?

The following day, the Sabbath, we went to the Wailing Wall. As with the Christians in their northwest district, one could see at the Wall all various Hebraic sects from the diaspora, from the Chassidim to the Ashkenazim from all over the world, from the Brooklyn Orthodox to the Beverly Hills Reform and across our country and around the world, all trying to get along in harmony not unlike the pervious day at the Cathedral of the Holy Sepulchre. I was sure their success rate was no different.

Sandy said, "I want to go in. Do you?"

"Why shouldn't I? I believe in the Old Testament."

So I pushed him up to the Wall, but he insisted on standing to pray. He was a believer more than most, but religions bothered him. And did I understand that. "All religions," he once said, "were man-made and therefore not flawless or infallible, even though they think they are. The Old Testament, that black book the Bible, and Koran were all written by men, and as few as they were, they couldn't agree either. So I'll just tend to my own belief, if you don't mind, and I'll leave you to yours."

Just to touch the huge stones of the foundation of the Old Temple of King Solomon still in place after 2000 years was another experience to remember, like meeting the Pope. That Moslems had built their mosque on top just didn't seem right somehow.

The third day we went topside to the mosque, took off our shoes, and stood at the back. I was thinking all the while, what is wrong with this picture? There we were standing in the back of this mosque in our stocking feet, Sandy a Jew and me a Christian, standing where even their wives and their daughters were not allowed. The mosque was full of men hunched over on their knees, their foreheads touching the ground. Such devotion, I remember thinking. But I didn't pray, and I know Sandy didn't. After all, we didn't know Arabic.

We then went over to the Dome of the Rock. Now this was the place, if one had any belief at all, that should bring everyone together, all the believers of the world, be they Moslem, Jewish, or Christian, including all the various sects of each, for Abraham and Sarah were the father and mother of them all.

I said to Sandy, "If the human race is ever going to get together and unite, this is the place right here in Judah where it's going to happen."

"Aren't you getting a little philosophical for an actor?" Sandy deadpanned.

"Come on, let's go over to the East Gate," I said.

The East Gate was where, according to the story I learned, Jesus triumphantly entered the Holy City on Palm Sunday, riding on an ass. According to the "good book," this is the gate he will come through at the Second Coming. I was told it hadn't been opened in 800 years. When I told Sandy, he said, "Forget it. We won't be here."

"Y'never know, y'never know," I quipped.

I rolled Sandy out the Northeast Gate near the Convent of St. Anne. I felt

32 Reaping the Rewards

that, if my sense of direction was right, we should veer to the left and keep going in that direction to get back to the hotel. After we had rolled along for a couple of blocks, I noticed we had seen no tourists since we had left the Walled City, only a Palestinian here and there. And why not? We were now well into their district. I found myself quickening my step. We turned into a shopping area but no one was shopping or walking about. The shops were closed, locked up tighter than a drum. The vegetable stand was open, but neither customer nor proprietor was to be seen. Now I was concerned. I started pushing faster. I was positive from the position of the sun that I was heading in the right direction. All I had to do was veer left. Still there wasn't a soul in sight, no people anywhere. With the wheelchair and the way we were dressed, we sure as hell didn't look Palestinian, Syrian, or Jordanian. We could have been shot right then and there.

I took a sharp left off the deserted main market area. The side street led us smack into the main road to Damascus. Along the street were taxicabs and vans all in a row. The American Colony was just one block farther on. We scurried along the side of the road past the vehicles to the hotel. When we reached the driveway, some staff members were standing behind the gate. One on them said, "What are you doing out in all this?"

"All what?" I asked.

"The demonstration. There's been a walkout, and all Palestinians closed their businesses in support of the protest," the desk clerk explained.

"Protest over what?" I asked.

Someone said, "Some action on the part of the government. It's a demonstration against the government."

Their response was obviously a put-off, with the assumption that as a foreigner I wouldn't be interested. Glad to be in the confines of the hotel, we just turned and went to our room. I never did find out what that demonstration was all about. I'll tell you one thing. After that day, I became very aware of where we were. It brought me to my senses. After all we were Americans, and one of us was a Jew.

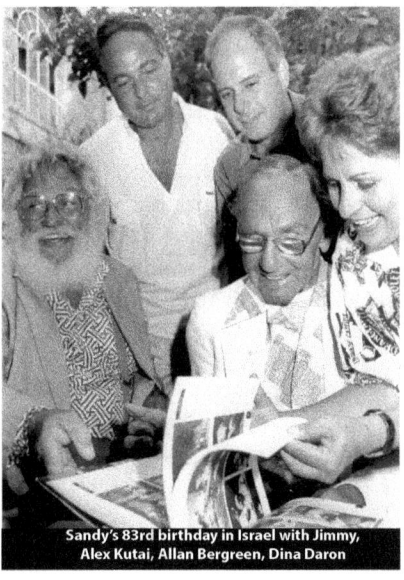

Sandy's 83rd birthday in Israel with Jimmy, Alex Kutai, Allan Bergreen, Dina Daron

The following day the demonstration was over, and we strolled the southwestern quarter, which seemed to be primarily Jewish, ending up at the Jaffa Gate. We saw stairs leading up to the top of the wall that circumvented the city. I suggested, "Why don't we go up and reconnoiter? We could get a better idea of the layout of the Old City from up there." And up we went. The top of the wall was only wide enough to walk single file, so I walked ahead carrying the wheelchair with Sandy following closely behind hanging on to my shirt. We ever so slowly took a lovely walk overlooking the Christian Quarter leading toward the Damascus Gate. We were all alone! No soldiers, no guards. But it was a lovely day and we were having a grand time, until...

...We reached the Damascus Gate and couldn't get down off the wall. The way was blocked by an enclosed turnstile that the wheelchair could not have fit through. It was only large enough for one person to pass through, and on top of that it was locked. It was a security contraption, the kind found in isolated sections of New York subway stations. There was no one around. We couldn't turn back: it would have been too far for Sandy. So we yelled and hollered, hoping to attract attention. A little boy came up, took a quick look, and ran back down. Shortly afterward, two Israeli soldiers came up the stairs, shook their heads in disbelief, and unlocked the gate for us. But the chair wouldn't fit through. They led us down the stairs to a large room with a mammoth high ceiling off to the right of the Damascus Gate along the outer wall. One soldier told us in broken English to wait there while they went back to dismantle the chair. From what I could make out, the room we were left in looked like an old grain-and-feed room dating back to the time of the Roman occupation. It was in the middle of a restoration.

"Sandy," I asked, "what if they hand us the wheelchair in pieces?"

"Well, if they do, who can we blame? I'll just check if off to another day of traveling with you."

"Oh, sure, blame me," I said.

"Who else?" returned Sandy.

It took quite a while before the soldiers came back, with the chair in one piece. If they had not had it intact, I don't know what we would have done.

Our next adventure was a bus trip to Abraham's wife Sarah's place. I guess you would call it a shrine. There, many young men, I think from the Chassidic sect, black books in hand, wearing black hats, long coats, sidelocks, and of course their phylacteries, were praying and davening. Again, I was struck by such devotion in their bobbing back and forth. It was quite a sight to see them. I realized for the first time the validity and true meaning behind the idea that Jews and Moslems are cousins. There was no doubt about it. So what the hell is all the fighting about?

Then on we went to Bethlehem. It was a little risky as it was a Palestinian stronghold, a real hotbed where sporadic incidents occurred. We both went down to where the crypt of the baby Jesus was venerated. The size and opulence of the cathedral-like structure in which the crypt was housed were a far cry from the cold little manger in a field where it was claimed he was born.

Back at the American Colony, some of Sandy's Israeli former students from Tel Aviv and Haifa, as well as a writer from Tel Aviv were joining us for dinner to celebrate Sandy's 83rd birthday. The writer was a former Russian. She had come to interview Sandy for one of the Tel Aviv newspapers. One young

32 Reaping the Rewards

woman who came from kibbutz was leaving in three weeks for the Neighborhood Playhouse. What a wonderful evening was had by all. It proved enlightening for me because some were liberal Jews much like Sandy. They sympathized with Sandy's initial reaction and reasons we didn't stay at the King David Hotel.

A lengthy feature article about Sandy appeared in the Sunday magazine section of the Tel Aviv newspaper shorty after.

We took one little trip just outside Jerusalem, to the Protestant Evangelicals' version of the tomb of Jesus. Without meaning to sound partisan, I'd have to say that after the Via Dolorosa walk and the Cathedral of the Holy Sepulchre, this site was pathetic and truly unnecessary. The only thing it offered was a truer picture of what the tomb of Joseph of Arimathea, who offered it for Jesus's body, must have looked like. As a child I had always pictured the stone sealing the entrance to the tomb, which caused the two Marys to worry about how they would roll it away, as big, three-dimensional, and round. Now I realized it must have been shaped like a big disk that rolled back and forth from left to right, like a wheel in a deep rut. When I told Sandy, he said, "You see. This little side trip shouldn't be a total loss. You learned something."

Our time was getting short so we took one long trip from the Dead Sea along the West Bank near Jordan. The day before in Jericho on a tour bus like ours, an American mother and her daughter had been killed. We continued to Nazareth. The area was primarily Palestinian Moslems but the tourists were mostly Christians, a combination that lessened the tension somewhat. We visited the Shrine of St. Joseph dating back to the first century Common Era. Tradition holds that this shrine sits on the site of Joseph's workshop and of the Holy Family's home. The site was way down deep below ground level and observable through bars. Above this site was the Church of St. Joseph's Carpentry, tended to and cared for by priests, brothers, and monks. The service was truly inspiring sung by all-male voices with a firm, deep, earthy quality.

In total contrast was the light-floating quality of the nuns' voices in the Virgin's church across the way. The Church of the Annunciation was by far the largest in the area, incorporating remains of earlier churches from the Byzantine and Crusade periods. The airy, fluid, and ethereal mass with all the nuns raising their voices in praise was breathtaking, unearthly, and inspiring. The church had a roped-off area so tourists would not disrupt the services. This practice made sense to me until a nun saw Sandy in the wheelchair, lifted the rope so he could get closer, then whisked the chair right up into the congregation. I bided my time until all were up to receive the Eucharist. In the movement of people I was able to approach and unobtrusively steer him back behind the ropes.

Sandy said, "What is this, a conspiracy? I thought they were going to make me a 'Catlick' again. These guys don't give up."

"And this from a guy who says he has never been in a synagogue. Maybe someone is trying to tell you something, ho-ho!"

Afterwards I took a dip in the River Jordan as Sandy watched me. It was surprisingly small and insignificant looking, by the way. We then wanted to go to Cana not that far from Nazareth where Jesus turned water into wine at the Wedding of Cana, according to the "good book." But Cana is across the border in Lebanon and, we were told, inundated with Hezbollah, a branch of the Shiite sect, so a visit there was out of the question. So we went to Lake Tiberius, more widely know as the Sea of Galilee, where we were to take a trip on a rather large ship to the village St. Peter supposedly came from. We were about to set sail when the thought occurred to me that we had no idea how much walking was required on the other end. So I told the captain I was going back to the bus to get Sandy's wheelchair. When I disembarked, I told the tour guide, who was going to make a phone call, where I was going, and we both took off. When I got back to the pier, the boat had left. The tour guide was in charge of the trip and the captain had left her behind as well.

I was beginning to notice that some of these Israelis could be abrupt, quick, officious, and unsympathetic. My reading was that many had a problem. Simplistically speaking, many were overqualified for their jobs and, with a glass ceiling they could see up through but couldn't get up beyond, frustration ran supreme. This of course was just my assessment based on nothing more than my observation of the taxi driver and the doorman at the King David. The lack of concern, of willingness to please, and of any desire to be helpful would never have occurred at the Waldorf Astoria or the Plaza in New York.

I started to yell and holler, to no avail. I was getting frustrated and I yelled some more. The tour guide said, "I'm getting the bus driver to take us up."

Some fishermen were sitting around the pier watching, getting a kick out of it all. One said, "Why don't you just walk out there? You did it once before, ha-ha."

"Yeah," I said, "but that was before I had holes in my feet."

Well, they got a greater kick out of that one, much more than I did.

Then, what do you know? While they were laughing, the big boat started turning around to head back to the pier. "Now that's a miracle if ever I saw one," said one as they all continued to laugh.

The tour guide came back when she saw the boat turn around. "Who do you know to make him do a thing like that?" she asked.

I wanted to tell her Sandy, but I didn't. We both boarded, and the ship quickly took off again with an upset captain madder than a wet hen because he had been forced to turn back. I went inside and sat down next to a very upset, nervous, but more outraged than nervous, Sandy. His face was redder than a beet.

"That damned fool wasn't going back for you," Sandy related. "What the hell would I do if something went wrong up there next to the Golan Heights with all those damned Syrians looking over at us and me without my American passport?"

"You're right, I've got them," I said.

He said as he quieted down, "What in the hell is wrong with these people?"

When we reached our destination, I was damned glad we had the wheelchair. The distance from the pier to the earliest known Roman temple in Israel required quite a lot of walking.

On the bus on the way back, we skirted the panhandle along the Sea of Galilee, where the guide pointed out the site of the Sermon on the Mount, you remember, the story of the loaves and fishes.

Time to Turn Back

The next stop was Alexandria. We landed at Cairo International and took a limo to a hotel across from the King Farouk's lavish castle, sorry, palace.

At the hotel, I was handed a telegram. What a surprise! A telegram for me in Alexandria. And I thought the worst. I saw it was from Tom Thompson, our friend in Bequia who had written a book about Bequia. He was asking me to appear on The Regis Philbin Show, which was doing an episode on expatriates. Would I appear on the show in October? Sandy said, "Look at that. You've finally got a title—an X-patriot. I wonder if the show is going to be X-rated as well? Knowing what I know about you, it probably should be, ho-ho."

Being the ham I was, I was looking forward to it.

We went behind the King's castle-palace and saw the waterway where he must have caught his last water-taxi as he left the country for Italy after the coup. We visited the first Coptic church in Egypt, which was in disrepair. It had been built over the spot where Jesus, Mary, and Joseph are supposed to have stayed on their escape out of Judah on an ass. Sandy commented, "If anyone deserved heaven, it should be that ass, considering the grueling trip he had to make."

We stayed in Alexandria only a few days because we had Morocco waiting in the wings.

Bergman-Bogart Country

I have a warm spot for Morocco. It was so bright, windswept, and clean. At least the part we saw was. The sky was the bluest and the sun so golden. Everything was spacious. We never made it to Tangier, although we really wanted to. We just didn't have the time. But the rest of Morocco, the southern part, was unforgettable. The desert and the coast along the Atlantic Ocean as well as the lovely green mountains north of Marrakech that are constantly kissed by the soft breezes of the desert swooping across northern Africa instilled in me the romantic's wish to repeat the experience over and over. The populace was mostly Moslem. To me, generally speaking, they seemed like the best kind—in a word, liberal. In the Jewish section of one town, the officials had kept intact the empty houses owned by Jews who had left for Israel in case they should change their minds and decide to return. The homes were considered still theirs, for how long I wasn't sure. Morocco was also the only Moslem country in the Middle East that accepted Jews as citizens. On learning this, Sandy said, "Well, that's a start."

We stayed at one of Winston Churchill's favorite hotels. Marrakech's fabulous medina with all its haggling over prices was to me like being down on Delaney Street on the Lower East Side buying material and mill-ends at some street stall. I got the biggest kick out it. Sandy just laughed at me, saying, "I prefer Saks and Bergdorf's any day, where everything has a price tag."

"Yeah, and you pay the price," I shot back.

After marketing, we walked out into the plaza where other vendors were still selling their wares, spread out on the ground open

Sandy in Morocco

to the elements. Unwittingly we strolled right into the cobras there in front of us. One was swaying back and forth with a dazed look in its eyes a little to our left within two feet of us. Fifteen to twenty of them swayed about the plaza with their snake charmers and a pail of water beside them. I couldn't move the wheelchair forward, or more correctly I wouldn't move forward. An American behind me said, "It's all right. They're mesmerized. They're stunned in that cool water."

As I inched back, I replied, "I don't know if the water is cool or not."

Maybe they were stunned, numbed, and in a trance of some sort, and maybe they weren't. What a scary sight it was as we skirted the plaza watching people walk right through the area among those sickly looking cobras swaying back and worth.

Sandy wearing fez

We took a bus trip up into the mountains to Fez where I took a picture of Sandy having dinner wearing a fez. Now that was an accidental, transcendental, occidental, oriental shot if ever there was one. So was the restaurant. We also had fun, or rather I did, dickering and haggling for a couple of beautiful, original, handmade Burberry rugs. I had them shipped home to California directly from the shop. We ended the trip at Rabat, the capital, back on the coast and had a few sumptuous French-Moroccan dinners there before heading for home.

But the trip wasn't over yet. We left Casablanca, Bogie-Bergman country, and Morocco for New York on Moroccan Air with one of the king's daughters aboard. We were quite a way out over the Atlantic when the seat belt sign went on and the captain announced that we were having technical difficulties.

An Inconvenient Little Detour

It was the middle of the night. The plane would be making an emergency landing on Santa Maria in the Azores. The descent started, but we didn't land. We were told the plane couldn't land there, that we would be flying on to Sao Miguel, a larger island. Then we began to feel the unsteadiness of the plane.

I turned to Sandy. "Hello?"

Sandy advised, "Just hang on and pray."

The plane was moving in a weird unstable way. We sat nervously as it bobbled its way to the next island, where we landed.

Because the plane's stabilizer would have to be replaced and they were sending to Portugal for it, we were faced with a delay. For how long, no could say. We were instructed to leave our carry-on luggage behind and disembark. I took all Sandy's medicine. As we were disembarking, I insisted on their getting Sandy's wheelchair. Thank God. Off in the distance was a large empty hangar to which we were led. It had very few chairs, but Sandy had his wheelchair. It was beginning to get cool and Sandy started to shiver. He was also so tired he couldn't hold himself up in the chair. I looked around. Off to the side of the way, I found a small, empty room. It was getting cooler by the minute. I picked up a discarded newspaper, a rather large one, and laid some of it out on the floor. I laid Sandy out on it, put a small carry-on under his head, and packed the rest of the newspaper under, over, and around him to insulate him as best I could. I spoke to a flight attendant about pillows and blankets on the plane. She hemmed and hawed until a few more Moroccan men started angrily demand in Arabic-Moroccan. Then some of the flight stewards went out for them. It was a huge plane close to 300 passengers, including mothers with little children. I managed to get two blankets and a pillow.

I had no sooner settled Sandy when a strange man rushed into the room. It frightened the shit out of me at first as we were quite a distance from the others who were out in the huge open hangar and I didn't know what to expect. I guess it was the abruptness of his entrance. He got down on his knees and started banging his head on the floor, praying to Allah.

After he left, as Sandy drifted off, another man came in. He asked in English if we were American, and, on learning we were, said, "Well, come, follow me." I got Sandy up off the floor and put him in his chair. Outside was a group of Americans boarding a bus. I asked the man leading us, who was also American, where he was taking us. "They can't get the part they need in Portugal," he explained. "They have to wait for it to come from France so it will take much longer. We're taking you to where you can get some breakfast." And that was all he said.

As we got on the bus, my mind started racing. Why just Americans? If this is the Azores, was this a hijacking? I was thinking of the princess and wondering what was happening to her. Maybe they're trying to save us from a hijacking. I had these thoughts but I didn't share them with Sandy. He was just barely making it.

It was much colder now. As we approached a barbed wire enclosure, my heart stopped. Thank God Sandy was out of it and didn't notice. I could tell from the bulletin board that we were on an American army base. At least it was heated.

The leader, whoever he was, went off to find the kitchen. I found a couch that I laid Sandy out on. The man returned to report the kitchen wasn't open yet and no one was around. I guess he had forgotten it was Sunday.

Then came a call from the airport that we should get back. The bus left us off at the passenger terminal at the opposite end of the hangar from where the others were waiting. Everyone started trudging along the side of the building on the tarmac. It was freezing cold now and no one had heavy coats. It had still been summer in Morocco so no one was prepared for the cold.

I spotted an entrance at the near end. Why walk outside in this bitter cold? I went over and tried the door. It was open but led only to an elevator leading to the second and top floor. We got on. Although the entrance hall had had lights on, in the elevator when the door closed it was pitched black. We had no illumination, not even Sandy's Dunhill cigarette lighter anymore. I fiddled around with the buttons and the elevator took us up to the second floor. We exited the elevator into what was obviously a passenger lounge, but it too was in darkness wit not a soul around. No windows faced the outside but it made no difference since it was still dark out. The only light came from small, dull fire exit lights here and there.

I felt our way down the elongated building, pushing Sandy in the chair. At least it wasn't cold. When we reached the far end where the plane's passengers were waiting on the first floor of the hangar, I found an escalator but it wasn't running. I took Sandy out of the chair, walked him down, and went back to pick up the wheelchair. I brought it down only to find that the door to the room where the passengers had waited was locked. I banged on the door furiously, but no one heard me because no one was there. They had already left!

On the other side of the little hall we were in was a door to the outside. It was locked too. Now I panicked! Fortunately, this outside door was glass, and as I banged to attract attention, someone outside saw me and had a guard come over to unlock the door. Most of the passengers had already boarded the plane way out on the field, so Sandy and I calming brought up the rear. Calmly! I use the word loosely. It took me time to collect my wits, and no wonder!

33 Life is Sweet

An Unexpected Guest

Back at the Picasso, Boolu was in the best of shape. His spirits were high as he had a nice little life going for himself within his limitations. By now there was no denying he had problems and would always have difficulty. The education he was getting at Hunter and his going it alone at 58th Street were based on the hope that he would develop his abilities to their fullest. What more could we expect?

About this time Michael Locassio, a former student of Sandy's, dropped by. He had been a director of sorts and was now back living in New York after a ten- to fifteen-year stint in San Miguel, Mexico. He very generously brought us each back a pair of lovely Mexican fire opal cuff links. We exchanged stories of the saga of the adjusting one had to go through just to settle in again. When the subject of Boolu came up, he was most interested and impressed. He spoke of a group of young men who met once a week down on 17th Street north of Union Square and wondered if Boolu would be interested in joining the group.

Funny, I thought, that he should mention 17th Street. Five years earlier, I had taken Boolu down to 17th Street just off Park Avenue, where a group of slightly disabled young people met. He had wanted no part of it. I told him he might meet a girlfriend there, but he was adamant. He protested with deep emotion that those people were "retarded" and some were sick. "I am not sick, I am strong," he insisted. When I persisted, suggesting that he might meet a nice deaf girl, he responded, "Why? I'm not deaf. I can speak and I can hear." By "hear" he meant lip-read and understand. He went on, "I don't have to wiggle my fingers and wave my hands." That was true, I had to admit. Still he reiterated emphatically, I'm not deaf. I don't be like dem." No matter how much I preached, he wouldn't listen nor would he go near the place. So what could I do with an attitude like his? Obviously he only wanted to be with so-called "normal" people. He wasn't interested in people with a problem for he truly felt he didn't have any.

I asked Michael who these young people were. He explained that they were mostly disadvantaged young people from around the boroughs and that his church had a bandmaster who met with them once a week. They came to play in a brass band, a drum and bugle corps.

"But Boolu couldn't do that. He's deaf."

To which Michael replied, "Didn't you say he plays the drums?"

"I did, but I did the teaching. No, he couldn't do that," I reiterated.

Michael then said, "Well, let him come anyway. He can hang out with the boys. They have other activities as well. And if he likes to drum, well, he could jam once in a while, when time permits."

So I agreed to let him go. Well, he went with Michael one evening and he loved it. He began to look forward to each meeting. He wound up making a few friends into the bargain.

We were making ready for Bequia one day when Boolu piped up, "Can I have a snare drum?"

"Why," I asked.

"Because de man said I can play in de band if I have a drum."

I hedged with, "We'll see, we'll see."

I called Michael to tell him what Boolu had said. The following week he called. "We have to talk."

Apparently, one of the drummers had been acting up. I don't know what it was—fighting, tardiness, or discipline. The boy had been tossed out, dropped from the band. When I asked Boolu about it later, he said, "Yeah, he was kicked ta de curb back ta Jersey."

Michael informed me that the bandmaster had said he could really use Boolu because when Boolu played he played with assuredness and authority. He was not afraid to hit those skins, and the other kids could use a little more of that. Boolu's instinct was that of a leader and not a follower, and the bandmaster felt he could teach him because of his fantastic memory for rhythm. Then Michael added, "What I have to talk to you about is the trip to Hawaii. This spring the corps is competing in an international competition being held in Hawaii. Would Boolu be able to go?

Boolu would be expected to buy his drum and pay half the fare. His uniform, one of those high-plumed, brass-buttoned, straps-crisscrossing-the-chest affairs, would be supplied by the church.

"Would you let him come?" Michael asked.

"Would you be going?" I asked.

"Yes," he said, "I'm going as one of the chaperones."

"Would you look after him? After all, he is special and would demand special looking after. He's naïve in many ways."

"You know I will," was his reassuring reply.

All Sandy said, shaking his head was, "Hawaii? That kid never ceases to amaze me."

Expatriate, That's Me

I made ready for my three minutes of fame on the Regis Show. I had no misapprehensions as to why I was there. It certainly wasn't because of what I had done, it wasn't about me. Tom was there to sell his book. After watching the show the week before, I could see people like me were asked onto the show to give Regis something to work off, like Kathie Lee herself, especially if we were not celebrities. What we might have to say wasn't significant. That was my opinion, take it or leave it. I made up my mind that if I wanted to say anything at all, I had better say it fast and all at once. Stopping would only give Regis a chance to cut in with his shtick. So I rushed through my reasons for going to Bequia and my reasons for staying—basically the need to be needed—not giving him an opening to butt in. His only comment was something like, "Boy, you can really talk." What I should have asked was, "Isn't this a talk show?" Alas, I didn't. Well, for what it was worth, Kathie Lee thought I was cute. So much for my three minutes of fame!

Sandy was back at the Playhouse getting it in shape before he handed it over to his teachers to take over for the rest of the season. We were falling into a routine, and before we had time to turn around, we were packing for California. Boolu knew he would be coming out in two months for Christmas and New Year's and it seemed to me he was looking forward to it. He loved traveling. You would think with his limitations he would be scared to death, but he wasn't. Remember, the first time he traveled to America from Bequia when he was only seventeen, he did it all alone. No, you could say whatever you wanted about him, but one thing you had to admit—he sure had chutzpah. I was glad he did and I was sure that it helped him a lot, many times in many ways.

We finally had our lives back together, and it was making for the betterment of all tree a we at last. We were now solely and completely benefiting from the fruits of our labors. It had taken us almost ten years to do it, but at last it was happening. Sandy was now working not only for himself but for his family, as it were, and as it should be. He was no longer carrying a staff of teachers along on his name and not being properly compensated for it because the school, with its non-profit status, couldn't afford to pay him. The Meisner Carville School of Acting had moved up the street to the Actors' Workout Studio on Lankershim Boulevard in North Hollywood, where the students came to finish their training after their stint on Bequia.

Nature Boy Connects

Everyone was bustling around. I am sure they were with Christmas approaching although you couldn't prove it by us. Living in the San Fernando Valley, as we were at the time, was not like living in Manhattan where the hustle and bustle of the holidays were ubiquitous. Now that's what Christmas had been for us. We were used to hustle and bustle. But out here in Studio City, it was just one more quiet, sunny day after another. We had one invitation from Rosie for the evening of the 24th and, aside from a dinner party at Tanya and Reza's during the holiday week, that was it. If it hadn't been for Boolu's coming out of the holidays, it would have been business as usual. But that was OK with us. We planned to take Boolu to San Diego and make a quick trip to Tijuana, Mexico.

The free time over the holiday was going to be rest time for Sandy. He wasn't getting any younger, even if he would be the last to admit it despite what he had been through. He was now well over eighty-three and needed to start slowing down. I knew I had my job cut out for me. I would get him to class when he wanted to teach but he would just have to start taking it easier now.

Boolu arrived in time for Rosie's party and Tanya's dinner. The day after Tanya's dinner, we took off for San Diego, staying at a hotel in the Old Town. We went to the zoo the next day, leisurely rode around the park, and enjoyed watching Boolu have the time of his life. When he saw animals out of the savannah-like range that he had never seen before, he informed us, "See, it's just like Africa."

The following afternoon we went to Sea World. I had no idea how expansive it was. We were never going to be able to cover everything. The first exhibit inside the front gate was a rather large pool full of very active dolphins swimming back and forth. You could purchase a container of small life sprat or sardines to feed them. They would swim up to the edge of the pool and open their mouths to catch the little fish the spectators threw. Naturally Boolu had to do it. So he gleefully got his bucket of fish, which he called "small-fry," and the first one he threw, the dolphin caught in its mouth and flung back at Boolu. Boolu caught it in his bucket and threw another one. The dolphin flung it back again. As I live and breathe, Boolu and the dolphin were playing catch. He then repeated it with another dolphin, or maybe it was the same one, I couldn't tell. It happened twice. After that a dolphin just caught the little fish and swam off. Boolu didn't seem nonplussed in the least: doesn't everyone play catch with fish?

Further into the park was a large tank with a gallery for onlookers. The tank held two large walruses, one male, the other female, of course. From a walkway under the gallery, you could look through little portholes and observe the walruses from below. The walkway was full of people waiting their turn to look through the portholes, and there was Boolu tapping on the glass with his Afro comb. He had brought the big male down to his porthole. All you could see from our end was his huge eye looking through at Boolu. After a short while the female swam down and nudged the big male aside so she could get a look at Boolu. The observers up top wondered what the walruses were doing. One guy said to his wife, "Will you take a look at that?" and turned to me to ask, "Does that guy work here?" "No," I said, and Sandy added, "No, he doesn't but he should."

We then walked along a path that led into an enclosed theater that was open but empty save for a man and a little girl down front looking into a large, 10-foot high by 25-foot long water tank. Swimming back and forth up at the top of the tank were six or seven black and white, small but heft porpoises. I pushed Sandy halfway down the aisle while Boolu went down front. Again he took out his Afro comb and started talking to the porpoises as he tapped on the glass. The group kept swimming back and forth except for one who dove down and nosed Boolu through the glass, his tail held perpendicular in the water. Boolu motioned with both hands in a circular movement, and the porpoise, his head still down and his tail pointing straight up to the surface, started rotating. Then another porpoise dove down and nudged the first one to one side as the female walrus in the other tank had done. The first porpoise swam back up to the others, and Boolu got the second one rotating as well. I said, "Come on, Boolu. It's getting late."

The man with the little girl had started up the aisle. When I spoke to Boolu, he asked me, "Can you see what he has them doing?"

"Yeah," I said.

"Well, he's good," the man said, walking on up the aisle with his little girl.

I looked back at Boolu. He had stepped back from the tank and, talking to the porpoise, he waved. While still hanging perpendicular in the water, his tail straight above his head, believe it or not—we were there and we saw it—the porpoise began waving his tail back and forth at Boolu.

"He's a real nature boy," I said to Sandy.

It was getting close to closing time and we had quite a walk ahead of us just to get to the gate. We started trudging along the path that circumvented the huge lagoon. The lagoon was part of the park that, at its far end, extended out next to the ocean. Boolu spotted a dolphin or a porpoise in the lagoon. It was too far out to be certain which, and too far out for it to hear Boolu. Yet Boolu ran down the grassy knoll to the wrought-iron fence that encompassed the lagoon, yelling "Flipper, Flipper." Instantly, from the far end of the lagoon, this fish came leaping out of the water all the way in to where Boolu was standing at the fence, as if to greet Boolu as an old friend. I could see now that it was a dolphin. It was leaping almost as high as the fence where Boolu stood talking to him, in his innocent simple way as one talks to an adorable little baby or puppy dog. I hated to break up this little love-fest but we were this short of being thrown out, and we had to move on.

Don't Drink the Water

The next day we left the Mercedes in the parking lot at the Mexican border and went through Customs. We took a taxi to a rather large hotel near the border. Clustered there were the hospital and drug stores. Sandy remarked, "What is this, a tribute to our US medical system?"

"Well, they obviously aren't catering to Mexicans," I observed.

The large hotel was sparsely furnished. Actually it was cold and bare, and you could have called it ugly and only utilitarian. The dining room lived up to the décor. The food was unmemorable, and we didn't drink the water. Sandy said, "See I told you." He hadn't wanted to come in the first place. Mexico never held any fascination for him. He would say the food could kill you, look what it did to Montgomery Clift. He was referring to Montezuma's Revenge, which Monty had a touch of for most of his life after catching it during a trip there with Lehman Engel. Nevertheless, Sandy had finally agreed to come with us because I wanted to see Tijuana, having heard about it and knowing it was so close.

We had dinner that night in Tijuana, and one night was enough. Sandy was right. It was so cheap and tawdry. We walked up and down the business district just watching the tourists. Boolu's one and only comment was, "Dis place is worse dan St. Vincy."

New Year's of '89 was spent quietly at home on Bellingham just de tree a we. Six days later Boolu was back on 58th Street going about his business and being sorely missed by both of us.

Life in the Valley is Comfortable

California was much easier than we ever imagined it would be. No more running after taxis in the rain, no more pushing shopping carts around supermarkets the size of a postage stamp, no more schlepping shopping bags full of heavy groceries across town for three or four blocks for want of a cab, no more waiting in cabs trying to get across town in rush hour. Now our car was in the drive, ready to spin off down the street to work in less than ten minutes. The bank, supermarkets, shopping malls, Costco, and Home Depot, and oh, yes, even K-Mart were all within fifteen minutes and all with accommodating parking lots. We were living in our own house with a pool and Jacuzzi in the back yard, and that has gravy. It all came as a revelation to me. I hadn't experienced this convenient way of life since Utica.

We were invited out to dinner, and since I love to cook we reciprocated frequently. We spent evenings with newfound friends like Rosie, a former student whom Sandy adopted like a daughter, and her mother Rita Edelman and her friends Morey and Kay Amsterdam and Patty Andrews and her husband Wally Weschler. Old friends from New York like Dick Dunn and Michael Greene, the agents; David Craig, the singing coach, and his wife Nancy Walker; Arthur Seidelman, the director; Richard Alfieri, a writer; and Maxine Carnegie and Jeff Goldblum, were also now living and working out in film-land.

Now that Sandy was living in La-La Land, I noticed that, even though we had a full social life, there was an obvious lack of phone calls from his supposedly ever-adoring, loving, and appreciative former and now successful students living and working out there of whom there was a multitude. Never once did one of them ever call, and when I say "never once," I mean "never once," not even to find out how his health was doing. Forget ever coming around to visit him. Oh, Mark Rydell came once. Luckily Sandy was a man who never did ex-

Sandy & Jimmy with Jeff Goldblum

pect much from any of them, although once later in life he did tell me that this callous indifference was his biggest disappointment in life. He singled out Sydney Pollack in particular, saying, "Personally, I thought he was a friend." Oh, there were others, many others, but why take the time to even mention them now? That was the nature of the business. Actually it was the nature of Hollywood itself. I could see where one could get lost in oblivion out here.

Be that as it may have been, our life in California, and I say California and not Hollywood because we were a million miles from Hollywood, was full of fun and work. It was all so much better for Sandy than plodding it out in New York. We were out there where the weather suited our clothes.

Yet all along Boolu was still plugging away at it in New York, now all by himself at the Picasso on East 58th Street. His departure date for Hawaii was approaching and he was full of anticipation. But Sandy and I would be down in Bequia by the time the day arrived.

Time flies. We were already collecting our brood for the Bequia school and on our way black to the Neighborhood Playhouse and Boolu. Carl Johnson, who had just finished his second year, was coming back this summer to assist Sandy. We took only two classes in '89, forcing Sandy to ease up a bit. When he complained, I said, "Look, this gives you some free time in August and Sep-

Chef Jimmy

tember. You can go somewhere else again this year."

He replied jokingly, "Yeah, sure. Now that we're experienced, we can sail up the Amazon."

The Band Comes Home a Winner

No sooner were we ensconced in our fifth summer of classes than Boolu was winging it across the wide Pacific to Hawaii. Michael had assured me before he left that he would take care of everything. When I worried that Boolu had a foreign passport, Michael had to remind me that Hawaii was the fifty-first state. No matter, both Sandy and I were just a little apprehensive about the whole affair. Yet we couldn't help feeling happy for Boolu. The occasion turned out to be an International Arts Festival sponsored by the Buddhists, a faith of which Michael Locassio was now an active and devout member.

When Sandy and I finally got back late that summer of '89, Boolu was full of stories about his experiences. The first thing he related was that the New York Brass Band had won first place. He also mentioned the long, long trip on the plane—"Jimmy, it was over ten hours all round de world"—and how he had fallen asleep and dreamed. He described the tall buildings right on the beach. "I tell ya, mon, it was like New York and Bequia put together." They had all toured the Pearl Harbour site and he was full of stories of the "Japs" and World War II in 1941 and the sailors still entombed in the sunken ships below. He spoke of the band marching through the streets of Waikiki and all the people watching. I'm sure he loved that, the old show-off. He told how in the big athletic stadium, they filled the field and made long, rolling waves with material of blue and white across the field. He had really had a grand time and only felt bad that he had forgotten to take Jack Lord's telephone number. "Maybe I coulda been a cop in Hawaii Five-O," he lamented.

"Yeah, sure," I said. "And then on to Hollywood."

"Yeah, of course, why not?" was his artless reply.

Sandy simply said, "Jimmy, I tell you, you've created a monster."

When I asked Boolu what song they had played, he couldn't tell me. He explained, "It go like dis," and with his two forefingers he drummed it out on the dining room table. "Trrrrrrrrum tum tum, trrrrrrrum tum tum," then a pause… and "Tum tum ta tum tum, tata ta ta ta ta tum." I started singing "The Stars and Stripes Forever," and he said from ear to ear, "Dat's it, mon, dat's it, Jimmy."

At which Sandy chimed in, "That's some communication you two got going there. That's even better than semaphore."

34 On the Road Again

Brazil—"We Stood beneath an Amber Moon"

By 1989, summer school on the morning side of the hill had become routine. Sandy knew how to pace himself, and I could get a handle on whatever came up. It was a pretty uneventful season with no suicides or murders, and that was remarkable considering what Sandy put the student-actors through. Marty Barter came back to assist Sandy for the first session, and Carl Johnson for the second.

One afternoon we were sitting around on Sandy's veranda. (Only with TV's The Golden Girls did I learn to call it a "lanai.")  The two of us were discussing this and that when our carpenter, Christmas Marshall, came over to the house from the construction site, a garage he was building over the recently built water tank. Yes, Christmas was his name, and why not? He was born on Christmas Day and christened Noel, so they called him Christmas. That needed little figuring. He told us the greenheart from Guyana was scarce these days. If we insisted on hardwood, it would have to come from Brazil.

"Because of wood lice," I reasoned, "what choice do we have if we're going to use wood? So what's the difficulty? Sandy has said he wants to go up the Amazon anyway now that he's done the Nile." Turning to Sandy, I continued, "What do you say, Dr. Livingstone, are you ready to go again?"

"You bet I am, anytime."

"Listen, Christmas, go with the Brazilian," I instructed. "Isn't it just as dense?"

"Well, it's wood lice-proof," answered Christmas.

"So, it's Brazil," I agreed.

And Sandy joked, "And away we go."

"I'm not talking to you, Stanley," I said. That's what Paul always called him. "I'm talking to Christmas."

After Christmas left, I asked Sandy, "Do you really want to go to Brazil?"

"Well, we have August and September. I'd like to go somewhere," said Sandy.

"But how would we get there from here? Swim? It would be impossible," I said.

"But after all this work, we deserve a vacation," he said. And that was the end of the conversation.

The following week I phoned the airline in Barbados and learned of a flight once a week to Manaus, an old rubber-producing town. Manaus was way up the Amazon River where the Brown and Black Amazons merge before the river plunges with all its might and fury through the jungles of northern Brazil to the sea. The Brown River originates in the southeastern foothills of Peru, and the Black originates in the north, in Venezuela. Manaus was a teeming metropolis established in the 1800s. It even had its own opera house where international stars such as Enrico Caruso sang.

It should prove a fun a trip, I thought, but had to admit to myself—though I wouldn't to "Himself"—that Sandy wasn't getting any younger. He was becoming needier by the day, not that he demanded anything, but in truth his safety would be in some peril. Should we take such an adventure? He was not getting any easier for me to handle, and I would have to be on watch constantly. I got the brilliant idea of asking Marty to come with us to Brazil to help me, but he had to get back to New York pronto because of some financial obligations. So I asked Carl, who seemed delighted to accompany us.

We planned to leave for Barbados immediately after the second session to catch that weekly flight to Manaus, flying back to Barbados on the 31st of August, Sandy's 84th birthday.

We landed alongside the banks of the Black Amazon, the branch from the northern source. The town was high above the high-water mark of the bank of the river, which rises twenty to thirty feet as the deluge of rain beats down through the wet season. We were surprised to see this thriving town with all its tall office buildings and teeming crowds of people hustling and bustling about, shopping in supermarkets and department stores. Many were selling their wares out in the open under the torrid, oppressive heat of the equatorial noonday sun. Yet we were in the middle of thick tropical jungle that stretched out as far as they eye could see in every direction.

We taxied to the largest hotel in the center of town and settled in. After a rest, we took Sandy for a ride in his wheelchair along the riverbank before dinner. To beat the heat, we planned to ramble about town early in the AM, have long lunches in the shade, then crash during siesta time in the heat of the day. We would venture out again in late afternoon and the cool of the evenings. Every day would be topped off with late leisurely dining somewhere about town.

We planned to take various boat rides up the Black and Brown Rivers. Anticipating excursions up tributaries deep into the jungle, we decided to go shopping for appropriate attire. The morning after arrival, we headed for one of the big department stores. As I wheeled Sandy through the men's department, down the corridor past the underwear, pants, and suits to the men's shirts, we could have been in any large department store anywhere in North America. We bought shirts, pants, and jungle shoes. I told Sandy that in his

34 On the Road Again

gear I couldn't tell whether he was Mr. Stanley or "Dr. Livingstone, I presume." He retorted, "You've got that wrong. You don't even have the right continent."

We first took a day-trip up the Black Amazon into a tributary, where Sandy fingered a huge porcupine on one of the rest stops, I inspected my first armadillo, and Carl fooled around with a huge constrictor.

The next day we went to the local zoo where wild animals surrounded us as we strolled around.

"Well, these can't eat us," Sandy remarked.

"I'm not so sure," I said. "Look at those flimsy cages and fences supposedly holding back all those wildcats, the cheetah and the cougars. Our dog Nora could break out in minutes."

I had never seen a zoo like it. It was so unkempt, and the safety factor seemed nonexistent. "Let's get out of here," I said. "We'll be much safer in the jungle."

The following day, we took off up the Black Amazon toward Venezuela. It was just a day-trip back into tributaries and backwaters. I had Sandy sitting in front of me in this scary, long, but oh-so-very-narrow dugout so that I could keep an eye and an ever-ready hand on him. I was always mindful of the consequences of a mishap because of his stoma, not that I could have helped or changed anything. Anyhow, all my concern and attention were focused there. I was so centered on Sandy that I wasn't paying any mind to some locals on the little wooden wharf we pulled up to. A few well-wishers were milling about making ready to greet us. Carl, our beloved snake charmer and prankster, was sitting behind us in the boat. Unbeknownst to me, he had an Amerindian approach me from behind and drape a huge boa constrictor over my shoulders and around my neck.

My aversion to snakes of any kind is a deeply embedded phobia. They instantly repulse me. With the shock of the boa on me, I damn near jumped out of the dugout taking Sandy with me. I had never in my life touched one, let alone had one draped over me, and I mean never. I must say the sensation was a letdown, well, a surprise anyway. It was not the least bit slimy; it was dry like a pair of snakeskin shoes. It was a wonder my yell didn't startle the snake and make the big mother tighten up and wrap me to kingdom come. Nothing like being hugged to death in the middle of the Amazon jungle by a beautiful, sloe-eyed, forked-tongued serpent!

By the time I was getting over than unexpected episode, there sat Sandy with a full-size sloth in his lap. It was as big as a ten-year-old child! Sandy was petting and talking baby talk to it. I yelled back to Carl, "Hey, Carl, now I've seen everything. I wonder if he could teach him to act?"

Carl replied, "He probably could. But slowly, ever so slowly."

The next day we moseyed about town, taking in the sites and roaming around the Grand Old Opera House, which, since it was off-season, was closed up tighter than a drum. We couldn't get inside to even take a look.

The fourth day we took off up the Brown River on a three-day outing where we would stay at a little lodge. As we left Manaus, we were all three in grand spirits, ready for an adventure in the depths of the Amazon jungle. A walking trip through the jungle was on our itinerary to acquaint us with the flora and fauna and the various medicinal trees and plants. Sandy planned to sit out this part of the tour back at the hostel. The tour would include other activities such as watching the piranhas gather at dusk and hunting—well, looking for—alligators, but from a distance, of course. We were looking forward to a great time.

    The boat, about the same vintage as Bogart's "African Queen," had an adequate galley and dining room. The upper deck was large enough for all to find a spot in the shade or to bask in the blistering sun, if one had a mind to brave the heat of the tropical sun, and some did, including Sandy. We were a complement of about twenty-five in all, most from Canada. We three were the only Americans. The excursion to the lodge was an all-day affair that included a sumptuous fish dinner served family-style in the dining room. We cruised down the Black Amazon, around the point, and up the Brown River, stopping along the way at an old rubber plantation, an old trading post, and another godforsaken zoo. This one was private like the ones along roadsides out west in American connected to gas stations, or more like the ones along the byways of the Florida Everglades where you can find snake farms, bird sanctuaries, and other collections of indigenous wildlife like alligators. This zoo had all three, including creepy crawlies, but under the worst conditions. I found it all depressing. They would have been better off back in the jungle.

    The camaraderie on the boat was jovial. Everyone was friendly, and so far I was feeling laid back and relaxed. That is, until I spotted our digs for the next three days. I was instantly overwhelmed with anxiety. The accommodation was crude with the barest of essentials, but bearable; after all this was the jungle. It wasn't the roughness that worried me. What really got to me was the safety factor.

    It wasn't built on land; it was built on huge tree trunks secured together as a raft, a floating wharf, and it was moored just offshore, enabling the buildings to rise and fall with the extreme water level changes between wet and dry seasons. They could never have built on land even if they had wanted to around there, because of the topography. It was hard to differentiate between river, swamp, and land in this area.

    It seemed to me like a rocking canoe that could easily slip out of control. This was no place for Sandy no matter how good a time he was having. Number one: his vision was poor. Number two: he needed help to walk on his own under the best of conditions. Here he couldn't navigate about on his own as there was no guardrail around the place to keep people from stumbling headlong into the river. I had my job cut out for me for the next three days. I wasn't going to be able to leave his side for an instant. It was going to be like walking across a rope-bridge with a small recalcitrant child. One false move and catastrophe awaited.

34 On the Road Again

We had really been looking forward to it, in excited anticipation like a couple of eager river rats, at least until I saw it for the first time. Sandy and Carl were having the time of their lives. Neither had ever seen such a place before. I didn't feel I needed to see it, not with the likes of someone in Sandy's condition. To tell the truth, I was scared and mad as hell at myself for not asking more questions up front. I thought, here I am, doing it again. I couldn't help but ask myself what it was about our relationship that kept getting us into these life-threatening situations. Was it a death wish, god forbid, or was it just plain stupidity on my part? Or was it a quest for life? Who the hell knew? I like to think the latter. Nevertheless, I made a mental note to be more careful.

As we disembarked, I asked myself, what is it? I wouldn't have a notion as to what you would call it. The lodge consisted of two large, single-story buildings next to each other connected by a rickety wooden bridge held together with leather straps of some kind. Everything was movable. One building consisted of the main lounge, dining room, and kitchen while the other across the bridge floating on its own set of logs held the sleeping quarters. We were led across the rickety bridge to our rooms immediately. The outside communal bath was along an open wooden walkway with no guardrail or protection from the river below. It was very precarious. The john was like an old backhouse of earlier times, open to the river below. The sleeping room was a bare, unpainted room of two-by-fours holding up the clapboards. It was Camp Triangle on Lake Mernain all over again, where I'd been with the YMCA as a kid in '38.

In the Brown River accommodations, four bunks, with mosquito netting (thank God), a solitary chair, and a small table made up the furnishings. Oh, yes, and one small sink in the corner. But no bath or toilet to match; they were down the walkway to the back of the building.

Sandy asked, "Where's the john?"

"Out back," I replied, "where you just hold your ass over a hole, smiling at the splashing waves of the Amazon below you, hoping all the while the piranhas don't jump too high."

We settled in and went to the dining room for supper, where we dined on fish broth, peasant bread, and tea or coffee. Then everyone hit the sack. It had been a long day. I heard the owner-manager saying something offhand to the cook at one point about the generator holding up, that he had been working on it all day. I thought to myself, Great! No generators, no light. I sure hoped they had a good supply of candles. A corner store was not an option.

The next morning, bright and early, the walk through the jungle was out of the question for Sandy. I told Carl to go without us, that I was staying with Sandy.

"Not on your life," Sandy said. "You go along. I can stay by myself."

"No, you can't. It's too dangerous around here. You could so easily fall in at every turn."

"I'll stay in the room, and if I need to go somewhere, I'll call for help," Sandy insisted. "Look, I can sit right in front of the cabin on that bench at the end of the building. I can watch fish jump if I get bored."

"Fine. How are you going to get there?" I asked.

"I'll stay close to the wall," he assured me. "After all, the walkway is four feet wide."

"Well, you can't go over that bridge to the next house alone, no way," I insisted. "I don't know, I really don't, Sandy."

"Will you just go? Go! Go have a good time, both of you. I'll do just fine."

Carl said, "Jimmy, you worry too much. He'll be OK."

I did want to go, but I didn't want to leave him. I was talked into it and I went. But it was against my better judgment and I might just as well have stayed for I didn't have a moment's peace. All I did all day was think of Sandy back at that nightmare of a place, and accident waiting to happen.

When we got back, he was in the lounge playing cards with one of the help. I was one relieved traveler.

"How did you get over here?" I asked.

He pointed across the table. "He brought me. But I walked across the bridge myself when I came to lunch."

"You see, Carl," I said, just a little worked up. "I can't trust him. He could have tripped and fallen in."

The question about the piranha excursion the next evening came up. I could see they were going in narrow dugouts, so I told Carl Sandy wasn't getting in one of those, especially not at night. "You go along without us and enjoy yourself. I'm not leaving him alone again."

So Carl went along with the group, and we stayed at the lodge alone. At dusk we took a walk around to the back of the building, staying as close to the wall as possible on that four-foot walkway without a guardrail. There was room for both of us to walk along, gingerly. We couldn't have gotten any closer to the jungle without stepping off into the swamp. The sky was beginning to darken and all I could think of was Longfellow. "Between the dark and the daylight,/When the night is beginning to lower,/Comes a pause in the day's occupations..."

"That's right," Sandy said. "'Comes a pause in the day's occupations' for every one of us—if we have enough sense to stop and partake of it by just listening. Listen to those sounds, will ya?"

The Screech

Like that of a banshee
from some exotic bird
calling out to its herd
for its he or she.

"Probably a macaw,
the most beautiful bird

34 On the Road Again

I ever saw," says Sandy.

"Maybe it's a toucan,
who can say?"
"You can and I can,"
says Smarty, "any day."
The squeals and yips of the monkey
swinging from branch to branch,
high up in the jungle's canopy
and it no happenchance.

Gliding from span to span
like the Flying Wallendas,
just because they can.

You could hear creatures brawling,
slithering and crawling
in or out of the water,
perhaps for the slaughter,

Or in search of a safe place,
not wanting to lose face.
Their own, all alone, that's right.
No fear, that's clear, to light for the night.

That could be a capybara
it's the biggest rat on terra
firma, or just "offa,"
just like the one in that show
we saw back at the shack.

"He can swim, y'know,
so ya better stand back
or he'll snack," says he.
"Ha-ha-ha," says me.

Then came the squawk
of a hawk,
looking for one last stalk.

    The combined noises created a cacophony of sound that instilled a kind of primordial fear, yet on another level their fusion segued into a cantus firmus of Evensong, just a song at twilight, just before the dark night.
    "It's an ode to the heavens above, an expression of love at the close of the

day," I said.

"And then what?" asked Sandy. "When it all subsides to a swoon, that's when the 'nocturnes' quietly come to spoon by the light of the moon?"

"Very funny, Sandy," I retorted. "No! Listen some more. It's a symphony like none you've ever heard before."

We stood there for a moment listening, watching, and waiting as the night crept over our universe and we heard the very last sound of the jungle subside to a whisper unrehearsed.

We had turned and started to walk back down the walk when Sandy spotted a door with a crescent moon cut-out on it. It was obviously a privy, an outhouse, a backhouse, and Sandy had to go, so he turned to it. He grabbed at the door, but it didn't budge, it was stuck. He must have pulled on it a little harder in desperation, as one does in such situations. The door swung open and simultaneously broke loose from its hinges, falling across the walkway. A good part of the door was now hanging out over the water. The force of his pull on the door and its sudden swoop as it shot out and past him threw off Sandy's already shaky balance. He fell over the door, which was teetering on its way into the river. His weight would finish the job.

I couldn't believe what was happening. I must have instantly made a grab for him because I caught him by his shirt, which held, thank god! I quickly swung him back toward the wall of the building. He landed on his hands and knees on the walkway in front of the now wide-open privy, with me leaning over him. The john door was still lying across of the walkway, much of it hanging over the swiftly flowing Amazon. Even one good look at it would have caused it to topple. I lifted him to his feet. "Sandy, you don't want to come any closer to the piranhas than that!"

Death by piranha didn't even take into consideration his stoma, that hole in his throat through which he breathed. It would have been instant death by drowning, piranhas or no piranhas.

"Thank god we're going back tomorrow. We can't stay here one more day. Do you still have to go to the john?" I asked.

"God, no!" he said. "I just had the piss scared out of me."

And we ever so slowly made our way back to the front of the building. We sat on the bench and watched the mighty river flow by out there and flow around us and under us as we waited for the piranha-watchers to come back from their moonlight excursion on the river.

The boat trip back was relaxing and safe, barring being top-sided. Yes, capsized by a giant condor. We crossed the Amazon where the Brown River and the Black River converge, a weird sight to behold, that huge river half brown and half black. It didn't mix or merge for a mile or more but divided right down the middle like some highway back home with a right and left lane and no white center line.

Heading back just east of Manaus and downriver a bit, the captain said we could dive or jump in to take a little swim in the river of rivers since the cur-

34 On the Road Again

rent wasn't too fast there. By now, I have to admit, I was spent. The trip had been too wearing on my nerves, and I was physically and mentally exhausted. What would I have told everyone back home? That the piranhas ate Sandy? No, it was all too much for me, so when Carl asked, "Are you game?" I replied, "No, if it's all the same to you. No, you go ahead and have a go at it. I'm going to sit this one out." At another time I would have been the first one in, like up the Orinoco years before.

Back in Manaus, I went about trying to book our next excursion. After many inquiries, including even quizzing the concierge, I found no one seemed to know what was happening, much less where it was happening. Obviously Manaus was not the typical tourist town, not yet anyway. It was mostly peopled by Brazilians going about their business. In Barbados I hadn't been able to get any information about excursions on the river, but I had thought that once we reached Manaus we would have no trouble finding transport. Forget it. It didn't exist, or at least so it seemed at first.

The tourist office proved more helpful. Apparently the transport shipping line ran two ships along the Amazon. One was for local indigenous travel between villages all along the river. Passengers supplied their own food and a hammock that could be hung from the ceiling on any of three decks. The other was a first-class ship with staterooms and cabins for tourists, serving three meals a day. The local ship had open booking on the day of travel; the first-class ship was booked out of Rio and Sao Paulo. It was more than likely all booked up since it was summer and the dry season, making it high season. The agent checked for us, calling Sao Paulo, and was told space for two in a cabin was available because of a last-minute cancellation.

Carl said, "Sandy, you two take it. I can go on the local ship. In fact, I would rather—it should prove to be interesting and an adventure. I'd enjoy going native."

So that was it. The ships were leaving the next afternoon so Carl had to go buy a hammock and whatever food he was going to need for the next five or six days.

The following day we checked out of the hotel at noon and were on our way. The two ships left together, the first-class ship leaving first, and the second-, third-, or fourth-class, whatever it was, following. Standing on the pier waiting to board our respective ships gave Sandy a chance to use one of his favorite malapropisms. As we were boarding, he turned to Carl and said, "We'll go first and then you can precede us."

We made many stops as we sailed down river, and I believe Carl's ship put in to a few more. When we made village stops, the boats tied up together, and we could yell back and forth to each other. As far as I could see, Carl was doing just fine even though the two ships were like night and day. Though Carl's ship looked just like ours on the outside, the inside was pretty and left to its own devices, one could say. Still Carl's spirits were quite high and he looked as if he were enjoying himself. But it would have been no place for Sandy. He couldn't have gotten into a hammock, much less slept in one.

Talk about rest, relaxation, and recuperation. It was just the ticket for both of us. We had a lovely quiet cabin, and the food was not bad. Serving was cafeteria-style and had a kibbutz-like feel to it, very egalitarian. The boat overall was absent of class bullshit; everyone was friendly, like one big family. There were middle-aged business couples, small student groups, and entire families, all mostly from Rio and Sao Paulo. We were the only Americans on board. There was only one problem. Neither Sandy nor I could speak Portuguese, and not many, in fact very few, of the others spoke English. So in more ways than one, we were the odd couple, you might say. The exception was one other couple from Sao Paulo. He was an American artist who had lived in Spain and married a Brazilian woman from Sao Paulo. They were now living in Sao Paul and were on their summer vacation as, it seemed, was everyone else on the ship. They provided us with someone to talk to over dinner, and up on deck. We became fast friends as the wife spoke English as well.

The jungle on both sides was impressive all the way down. It was one thick wall of lush green tropical overgrowth all the way to the ocean. When we reached the mouth of the river we sailed a little farther along away from Belem to a small village that was a beach resort of sorts. A large park ran along a very large sandy beach. It looked like a recreation area under development that hadn't yet caught on with the public. Few people, except our people from the boat, were there. We spent the whole day on the beach. I went in swimming, leaving Sandy sitting in a covered band shell, the old Victorian, John Philip Sousa kind of bandstand. It was well Sandy did because we had a short, heavy downpour and he didn't get soaked. Sandy, and consequently I, didn't get around much that day because the area was so spread out and was no place for a wheelchair. The day wasn't comfortable for us in particular. We just had to take our time and walk slowly with Sandy on one of my arms and the chair folded up in the other. The food wasn't appetizing that day either. It was what I would call a Brazilian barbecue cookout, and the fare was something neither Sandy nor I recognized. I guess you could call it Brazilian country cuisine.

That evening we boarded the ship again, and headed back to Belem where we waited for Carl at the prearranged hotel. When he arrived one day late, he was full of stories of his experience. Carl's trip was worlds apart from ours. He was able to buy local food cooked over coals in little iron pots from private vendors.

"Tasty?" I asked.

"Well…" he responded after a pause, "in its own way, yes, you could say that, after a fashion. The whole boat and its ambiance were very… 'aromatic,' you might say. But still, in spite of that, it was quite enjoyable." It had been a very different experience for him. When I asked him how he made out with the language, he said, "I didn't." But I knew he could speak a little Spanish. All in all, he had found it all interesting and enlightening.

34 On the Road Again

It was now the 29th of August so we had only one day to cover Belem. Of course it wasn't enough time.

Our plane left Belem in the early morning of the 31st on such a clear day you could see forever. The flight over the jungle was as the river excursion had been, if not more so. We landed just outside Manaus later that morning. It was Sandy's 84th birthday and we had a birthday lunch at a posh hotel near the airport. I found a jeweler and bought Sandy two emeralds, which I had planned to do all along if I happened to stumble across what I called a deal. As if I would know a deal if I hit it head on! When I gave them to him, he was moved but asked, "What do I do with them?"

"I don't know. A ring, a bracelet?" I said, adding, "I know it's not an emerald-studded gown, but it was the best I could do." You see, in class when he was trying to get the women to prepare themselves more deeply emotionally, he would always use the emerald gown, a gown embossed with emeralds, as a stimulus to jar and raise their imaginative minds above the pedestrian, mundane, everyday emotions of their lives. Sometimes it worked, sometime it didn't, depending on the woman and her innate talent. So that's why emeralds. Oh, I also acquired a little ruby for myself. And why not? It was my birthstone. When would I ever get another chance to buy one so near the source, as it were?

After lunch we boarded a plane back to Barbados. The following morning Carl was scheduled to fly on to LA, and we were gong to Bequia for two more weeks. Since we were all staying in the same hotel that night, we decided to celebrate Sandy's birthday again.

"How many eighty-four-year-olds celebrate their birthday in the southern hemisphere and the northern hemisphere all on the same Day?" I asked.

Carl asked, "How many eighty-four-year-olds get a chance to celebrate twice?"

Sandy quipped, "How many get a chance to celebrate at all? Only the ones lucky enough to still be around, as I happen to be, and to be a member of the jet set, as I obviously am. Next year, it's Istanbul, no, Constantinople."

Hamming it up on the Amazon

Boolu's Plot Thickens

We were falling into a routine: winter in LA, summer on Bequia, and autumn in New York where Sandy still started up the Playhouse classes.

Being in New York present us the opportunity to spend some "quality time" with Boolu. He was still going up to Kate Garnett's at Hunter readying himself for his next big test.

Kate had informed us that this one was going to be much tougher, since the information asked would no longer be about him. The test would be centered on America and the consequences of being an American.

"It will be more like a Civics test," she said, "questions about America and the Constitution. It will be a test of his knowledge of the government and how it works. They will be more abstract, questions about things outside himself, beyond his realm of experience that he will have to memorize and remember."

Along with his classes at Hunter, he was working five days a week. He had to please five different employers. Sandy once said, "I wouldn't wish that situation on anyone. One employer was one too many for me to handle."

Boolu went to a different workplace very day and did heavy-duty cleaning. He called himself a janitor and he loved saying the word, "ajanitor, ajanitor." He didn't work for the money, for it was pittance. It was more like on-the-job training to help in his development and advancement. His employers all understood his limitations and difficulties and were willing to cope, overlook, and work around them because of his good qualities, mainly his honesty and his willingness to please. Both qualities were rare in the city. The employers all gave him the keys to their places, in total trust. That told me much as to what they thought of him. He had all his keys on one big key ring. I said to Sandy, "Just look at him. He looks like he's the keeper of the keys in a state hospital or the county jail." Any employer had to come equipped with the patience of a teacher, have an understanding of his limitations, and be willing to take the time to help him along. A few were willing and that was all he needed. Yet there were some who just couldn't cope with it or didn't have the patience. Still others for whom he worked just didn't comprehend he had a disability. He did such a good job of covering it up.

One fine spring day, a Saturday, a real-estate lawyer took Boolu to help him open up his summerhouse on Green Lake out in the hinterlands of New Jersey. Boolu hadn't been in New York a year yet and he had never told Mr. Major that he couldn't read. I don't believe he ever told anyone he couldn't read. That day he never even told me where he was going. He just said Mr. Major had asked him to come in to work, he had something special for him to do, and off he went.

About 5:30 that evening, he was overdue. About 6 PM I picked up the phone and called the house. The son, Tony, answered.

I asked him, "Do you know where Boolu is?"

"No."

"He was supposed to be there working with your father all day."

"My father isn't even here," Tony said. "He's out at the summer home on the lake in New Jersey opening it up for the season."

"Well, I believe Boolu is out there with him. Do you know when they're expected home?"

"He's not expected home until Monday," Tony said. "Let me call him and I'll see what's up."

In a short while he called back. "My dad put Boolu on a bus back to New York from Green Lake just minutes to five."

"Tony," I asked, "will that bus be coming in over at the Port Authority Terminal?"

"Yeah," he replied, "over on Eighth Avenue."

"My God," I said. "Tony, he's never been in the Port Authority. Why, he's never been past Fifth Avenue!"

Tony didn't have an answer to that. There was just silence.

I thanked him and said, "I had better get over there." There was no sense blaming anyone. Neither of them knew Boolu couldn't read. This was my problem now.

When I hung up, Sandy said, "What good is that going to do you? The bus will be in long before you get there, and you'll never be able to find him in that huge place with all those people. Just call the police."

"I know this is a job for the cops, but for some reason I want to give it a little more time," I said.

"Why?" Sandy asked.

"I don't know. God, I don't know," I said. I was nervous, plenty nervous. I kept wondering what Boolu was thinking. He must be petrified. It had been after six when I hung up with Tony, and after a long harangue with Sandy about what to do and when to do it, it was now minutes to seven. As Sandy and I sat at the dining room table deliberating over our predicament, we heard a key in the lock. The door opened and there stood Boolu. Such relief!

Sandy just stared. I was full of questions. "Where were you?... How did you get home?... Why didn't you tell me?... What's wrong with that man?... You can have gotten lost." Finally I asked, "How did you get here?" That question I waited for an answer to.

"I took de bus," he simply said.

"How did you get here from the bus?" I probed.

"I took de subway," he answered matter of factly.

"The subway?" I repeated. "What subway? Which one?" I went on raving. "How did you know—?"

Sandy interrupted. "What difference does it make? He's here now and he's safe. Who cares how he did it? He did it. Leave him alone. You're only frightening him. Come on, Boolu, sit down. Did you eat?"

What had happened was when he reached the end of the line in the Port

Authority, he got off and found his way out onto Eighth Avenue. There he spied the subway station on the Eighth Avenue Line. Beginner's luck must have guided him down to the right platform. Yet he might have recognized "Uptown," "Downtown"; he had been doing that for a while, only over on the Lexington Line.

I asked, "How did you know which train to take?"

"Dat's easy, mon. 'B' for Brooklyn and 'Q' for Queens."

I guessed that gave him the clue as to which direction to go. Then Sandy piped up. "What about 'B' for Bronx?"

Anyhow at 42nd Street and Eighth Avenue, he somehow managed to board the "E" train headed for Queens.

"How did you know where to get off?" I asked.

"Dat's easy too, mon. I get off at de orange poles."

At that time the 53rd Street station was in the process of an overall paint job, and the orange paint was the rustproof primer used on the subway station columns before the final coat of dark olive-green. Boolu knew that station and he knew it was our station because he had gotten off there many times before on his way to and from work. So he got off. The weird part of the story was that Boolu acted as if it were all natural, all in a day's work, and he couldn't comprehend what all my fussing was about.

Sandy just sat there shaking his head as he muttered, "Orange paint?"

Boolu always took things as they came and worked it out as best he could, never fretting or fussing, just trusting. Sandy said, "Thank god he has someone upstairs looking out for him who really cares." He added, "Boolu is slowly putting his world together and learning how to cope and live within it his way, and you, Jimmy, have to give him time and scope to acquire a presence of mind to achieve it. I'd say that yours is a difficult but imperative job—to let him grow. But, oh! It's going to be so rewarding. You just don't realize."

Mellowing out in La-La Land

When we got back to LA, we knew we were going to have to rearrange the furniture and get the house back into shape the way we had left it. We had sublet the previous year and when we got back, all the pictures had been taken down and put away in a closet and the furniture had been rearranged somewhat. That was to be expected when you hand your home over to someone else. It was only natural that they make it their own. It was well worth it, a small price to pay for the return it was affording us.

Remember, we had been concentrating on retirement, and our retirement depended on the rental in a way. Sandy was getting his Social Security and his Playhouse check, which wasn't a fat lot, and both would be discontinued, if and when. So the fruits of our efforts were sent directly to Barry Vener in New York City to do the best for us on Wall Street. I had only ten or fifteen years left to make up for lost time, wasted time, one could say. When I was young, who thought about old age? I was invincible, especially in my particular line of pursuit. In my endeavor we were all going to live forever, we were going to lasso the moon. Who thought of such things as retirement? I was throwing the dice for the big gamble. I was going for broke as it were, all the time knowing, correction, all the time wishing and hoping I was going to cash in sooner or later. Well, truth be told, some never do. Why, many, nay, most never do, and then what? Catastrophe! Why, New York is just full of crumbled and shambled dreams and broken hearts. I was going for broke one more time when Sandy and I crossed paths, and the rest was history.

So now I was trying to make up for lost time. I couldn't nor could Boolu cash in on Sandy's security. The government wouldn't let us anyway. Boolu didn't qualify, and I was of the wrong gender. We had to start afresh. Which is why we were subleasing every summer for six months. It was a big contribution.

The previous year we had rented to Bob, of Bob and Ray, the popular radio comedy team of the '40s and '50s. His son was starring in a TV series and he had brought his dad out to act in it. The Elliotts came out to LA early and used our place as an interim stopover while they found something more permanent. This year we had rented to an English character actress who was trying her hand at TV over here in La-La Land. She managed a few spots on a couple of series. She loved the house, especially the morning dip in the pool and the fabulous Jacuzzi that had had me hooked, too. Sandy just loved sitting out back smelling the roses. Such roses out here.

In our lifestyle, it didn't take long to settle in. It was just one settling in after another.

Sandy in Rose Garden

Richard Dunn, the agent, stopped by after tennis before we even had time to unpack. We saw more of David Craig and Nancy Walker and Rita Edelman. Richard Alfieri, the writer of Uta Hagen's last play, *Six Dance Lessons*, and Arthur Seidelman, the award-winning TV director of *Hill Street Blues*, came around. Arthur was full of stories of his latest trip to Bangkok. It had been quite an experience for him.

All the while I was making ready for our school opening on November 15. Sandy was in good spirits and much better health than the year before. Now that he had mastered the esophageal speech pattern again for the third time, and now that his eye was holding pretty steady, his teaching had taken off in leaps and bounds. The students were older than most of the Playhouse students, their age range being from twenty-five to thirty-five, so they were more mature and understood the work better. In turn Sandy found teaching them that much easier and more enjoyable. This phase of his teaching was, after all, for him since he enjoyed doing it so much.

When older former students dropped by, as one did once in a while, they noticed how mellow and easygoing Sandy had become, not like the stern and serious days of the '40s and '50s. Fright in the classroom was diminished. There was no more "Sandy, the god" or "Sandy, the killer." Sandy said it was much better for the creative process. He was now just wonderful old Sandy.

Perhaps it had evolved out of Bequia's question and answer sessions held every evening in conjunction with the cocktail hour and my rum punches. Sandy had said, "This would not work with younger students. The misfortune of it all is that these students on Bequia are past their prime and the industry won't be interested in them, especially Hollywood. They're looking for the nineteen- and twenty-year-olds."

"Well," I told Sandy, "they'll make better teachers and better whatever-their-fates-may-be."

Whatever it was, we both looked forward to classes. Now everything seemed much easier and more relaxed, and I think it had an effect on everyone concerned. Sandy once said, "What was needed in the earlier classes was more love."

I think that's what was making the difference in class these days.

The Book Is Finally Born

Kent Paul had produced *Sanford Meisner: The American Theatre's Best Kept Secret*. Executive producer Sydney Pollack had got Columbia Pictures to back the project. Directed, shot, and edited by Nick Doob and released in 1985, *Best Kept Secret* had been screened at a Los Angeles film festival where it won first place in the Documentary Class. It was now awaiting broadcast over PBS in the American Masters series.

American Masters had already aired *Broadway's Dreamers: The Legacy of the Group Theatre*, produced and narrated by Joanne Woodward and featuring Sandy, Stella Adler, Harold Clurman, Lee Strasberg, and the rest. As well they had aired both *Harold Clurman: A Life of Theater* and *Stella Adler: Awake and Dream*. They planned to air Sandy's while celebrating his 85th birthday in late August of 1990.

Sandy's book, *Sanford Meisner: On Acting*, had just been released, and it was the bestseller of the Christmas season in the Theater Section that year, outselling Strasberg's 1983 book by far.

Meisner: On Acting had turned out brilliantly after difficult beginnings. Sandy had tried his hand at it and given up. Then came the professor whose work Sandy rejected. In a third attempt, agent Connie Clausen had had to drop

Rue Drew from the project to meet her contract obligations. Kent Paul then came up with a new collaborator in Dennis Longwell who had been a college friend of Kent's at Yale. Dennis had also studied with Sandy. This time the collaboration worked.

Dennis sat it on class and followed it through its paces, writing and working with Sandy simultaneously. Sandy, after what he had been through until now with so-called authors, was not about to take any chances. As it turned out, he needn't have been concerned because Dennis hit the mark. Nevertheless, as the work progressed—and I don't know whether Dennis knew it or not; knowing Sandy most likely not—Sandy would come home where we would sit over the dining room table while he read it to me, having me play the Devil's Advocate. He asked me to pick it apart for continuity and clarity from a layman's point of view, well, my point of view. Then he would go over it again, for whatever my input was worth. Who knew? He would then take his suggestions back to Dennis and they jointly came up with the book as it now stands.

What I think, and again for what it's worth, is that it turned out to be the be-all and end-all, because of its clarity. Even my mother could understand and follow it, she who knew nothing about acting and had no real interest in the process. Her acquaintance with drama was limited to seeing her husband in Father Lawler's productions of melodramas like *There's Gold in Them Thar Hills* in the '20s and being forced to partake in Dad's productions now and again. (She would proudly tell you, after the fact, about playing General Grant's wife to Dad's Grant in 1948.) To her, acting was just fun, child's play. Yet even she said, "It's a book for everyone" and she wasn't the first non-actor to say so. And she must have been right because here it is more than twenty years later and sales are still increasing. Sandy's book has been translated into four languages and is still being sold all around the world, as far away as India where it didn't need to be translated. I know because Boolu and I get the royalty breakdowns from Random House.

Without any reliance on a publicist, Sandy's classes were becoming every more popular with each passing year. This happy state of affairs gave me even greater incentive to keep him going as long as he wished to step into a classroom.

Someone down on Bequia once asked me, "Why don't you teach acting, Jimmy?"

And my answer to that was, "I should teach acting when the Master is still around and able?"

35 The Sun Rises in the Far East

1990—Last Trip, First Class

With life easy now for the first time in ten years, time flew by, and before we knew it, we were back on Bequia. Sandy had been taken with Arthur's stories of his Bangkok trip. He had all kinds of questions about the Far East. He was amazed at how little he knew about that part of the world.

I had been to Hawaii and many of the South Pacific Islands, including Wake, Guam, Okinawa, and the Philippines and I had spent military duty in Japan and Korea. In fact, I had been on my way to Bangkok in June of 1950 when the Korean conflict broken out. I was up in the hills of Baguio, then a mountain village right in the middle of the Huck communist skirmishes erupting just north of Manila. My friend Pat Paterson from the 7th Cavalry stationed north of Tokyo and I had had to cut our travels short and return to Tokyo to report immediately for duty.

The start of our trip from Tokyo to Manila on our way to Bangkok had been disturbing, too. We had traveled "MATS," Military Air Transport Services on a C54 out of Tachikawa Air Base. Out over the middle of the China Sea, the far right engine had caught fire forcing an emergency landing on Okinawa. There we were held up at the airport for hours while they fiddled with the problem. After a long wait and no information, we got a call to board a plane. You can imagine my chagrin when I realized that we had allowed ourselves to board the same plane. I made a squeamish remark to my traveling companion.

When we finally arrived in Manila and disembarked, we were told the plane was making a turnaround, heading right back to Tachikawa Air Base. Making ready to board the returning plane were mostly military personnel and their dependants. Along with the wives and children was one Army general. As we were crossing the tarmac on our way to the terminal, the general stopped me. "Yo, soldier, would you happen to have any occupation scrip for these pesos?"

"Yes, sir," I said, taking out my wallet. We made the exchange—my Far East military scrip for his Filipino pesos. He introduced himself and we had a slight conversation as to my duties at G2 and TIS, the Translator and Interpreter Service in the NYK building. We discussed the building's location along the Imperial Moat that surrounded the palace grounds and the palace, and across the street from the old Kijo building just down the street from the RTO, Tokyo's central railroad station. He knew the building and had been there once or twice. He told me he was with G4. It was just small talk as we made the transaction. I saluted and continued down the gangway and that was that.

That was that, until Pat and I reached Baguio and our R and R (Rest and Recuperation) Center. Baguio was situated quite a distance north of Manila high up in the Huck communist-infested mountains. In spite of that, we periodically took trips down to the sea for a swim in the Lingayen Gulf. One day we came back to discover that a MATS plane had crashed in the mountains just west of Tokyo. When we got the Stars and Stripes, our Armed Forced newspaper, and we read the report of the crash, we froze. It was our turnaround flight. There it was in bold print: the general's name, the commander of G4. Everyone died in the crash, all those lovely children and their moms. What a shock to Pat and me. My God! We had just gotten off that plane a few days before and while we didn't know exactly why it had crashed later that same day, let's just say we were not surprised.

A little postscript to this story. I had left my raincoat on the plane. The coat had my serial number on it. If by happenchance they should retrieve it in the wreckage, who knew what the repercussions might be? One would have to say it was a slim chance, that's true, but I thought it prudent to call my mother anyway to tell her what had happened to cover my bases. It was all confusing to her. So I tried to simplify it for her.

"Oh! I see," she said uncertainly when I finished.

Did she? I could just imagine her pondering. But at least she knew I was alive.

So because of my ramblings around the Far East, Sandy was forever asking me questions, questions I had no idea of the answers to. One late afternoon in May of '90, as we were sitting together staring out ever Friendship Bay, I asked, "So what's the sudden interest in the Far East?"

"I don't know," Sandy replied. "It's just that I know so little about it while I've been all over Europe. Except Germany, a place I could never and would never set foot. I've been all around the Mediterranean, and now even the Caribbean, the Nile, and the Amazon. I don't know. Arthur has piqued my interest.

"Is it all these sex stories he's come back with?"

"No, no," he protested. "It's the Far East in general. It's the oriental mind that intrigues me. Now that has me fascinated."

"Is that so?" I asked a little skeptically and continued. "Do you really want to go? We have the whole month of August."

Directly Sandy said, "Let's go. Why not?" He paused. "It will be rough on you without someone along to help you."

"I don't care," I said. "If you want to go, we go. I'll manage it."

And that was that. After that afternoon out there on our terrace, we were on our way.

I called Arthur for the name and number of the agent he had used. First the agent wanted to know if we wanted the sex package. "The what?" I said. He then went on in great detail about the big tourist attractions in Thailand for both straights and gays. They offered hotels, nightclubs, and spas based on sexual orientation. I must have been spending too much time on Bequia, for I wasn't quite up to all this sex-in-your-face approach. I remember wondering if this was what Sandy meant by oriental mind-set? I certainly hoped not. I told the agent we were going there to see the historical aspects of the country, what was left of Siam, you know, The King and I, the palaces, the monasteries, the religious points of interest, places like the Golden Triangle, and all the way up to Laos and Burma. Not the beaches—. Sandy interjected, "A little side trip into the seedy side of the place wouldn't kill us. It could prove interesting, from an observer's point of view, that is."

I wanted to do this trip up brown because it could be Sandy's last. So I told the agent not to spare the expense and to book us into the best hotels. So the agent worked out an itinerary that covered Bangkok and all the way up to the Laotian and Burmese borders. We had a lot of time so we could go to Singapore, then on to Hong Kong and into China. When I told Sandy my plan, he said, "Why the hell not? Let's go for it."

And go for broke we did, that August of '90.

Bangkok

When Bequia classes were over, we were on our way. After a few days in Hawaii and some unforeseen flight delays, we finally landed in Bangkok. By the time we reached the Oriental Hotel, after having disembarked, gone through Customs, and taxied into town, it was late. The huge hotel was jammed to the max; consequently, we were diverted to the old annex, just next door. We were led down a beautifully appointed passageway flanked by luxurious boutiques and then booked into the original hotel. The original Oriental was made famous by writers of earlier times writing about Siam and the king and the Second World War. It was a hangout for journalists, as the American Colony outside Jerusalem on the road to Damascus had been or as the Algonquin Round Table had been for New York writers back in the thirties. The original Oriental was much more interesting than the new section. It reeked of history and it was intimate and private and more to our liking. In the new hotel, you would never know the old building still existed. We had a two-room suite on two levels. The bedroom and bath were on the upper level, and a curved, wrought-iron and marble staircase led down to the sitting room, which was highlighted by a magnificent white marble fireplace. The room was all finished in carved teak and white marble, with lovely antique furniture.

When he saw the room, Sandy said, "You might get this at the Waldorf Astoria, but I doubt it."

It was late and we were starved. I had brought along two cases of a liquid nourishment called Jevity for Sandy. We could both have had one but I didn't want to risk running out. So I called room service for myself. The person said it was so late that everything was closed up but he could get some spring rolls

35 The Sun Rises in the Far East

and tea. Even though I didn't know a spring roll from a jellyroll, I still said fine, whatever.

When the food arrived, I said to Sandy, "Well, they're just egg rolls, only a little longer—and a lot thinner."

"Well, just eat more, Mr. Goldstone," said Sandy, quoting Momma Rose in *Gypsy*.

They were delicious. I said to Sandy, "If these are any sign, this trip's going to be one damned good one, and we are going to have the time of our lives."

The next day we took it easy. We did explore the environs of the hotel and strolled over to the river, the Mae Nam Chao Phraya, and back, with Sandy in the wheelchair. He couldn't have done it any other way.

Since it was our first real night in the Far East and with so many eating establishments in the hotel, we decided to celebrate, go for broke, and treat ourselves to the exclusive rooftop restaurant. It was a five-star affair. We got dressed in our best traveling bib-and-tucker and took the elevator up. As we stepped out onto the top floor, glimmering gold and shining brass with accents of carved teak were everywhere. The dining room was hushed and dimly lit. Out of the huge bay windows, the view down the river was spectacular with Bangkok all alight on either bank. I decided to save the local tasting for later and ordered western, for I knew they would be good at it. Sandy at first didn't order anything. I had purposely held off the Jevity till after his dinner so he could have an appetite. But he insisted, and all I could talk him into was some chilled vichyssoise. His lack of appetite should have alerted me, but sorry to say at the time it just didn't.

The next day we planned to get a vehicle and just ride around to check out the lay of the land. One of the best was by gasoline-powered rickshaw, a three-wheeled contraption with the driver sitting up front at the handlebars like on a bicycle and us sitting in back over the two rear wheels under a canopy of sorts. We were even able to take the wheelchair along by clipping it onto the back which had a space allotted for parcels. I wouldn't have gone if we had had to leave the wheelchair behind. I had vowed never to part from it for a second, except for plane travel. The chair and the Jevity were Sandy's lifeline. Without them we were helpless.

Once the chair was mounted and Sandy was ensconced in the chariot, I got in on the other side and we were off. Sandy had never been in anything like this in his life, while I had ridden in many in Tokyo, except they had been man-powered like a bicycle and without the overhead covering. I told Sandy rickshaws had really come up in the world of transport since I had ridden in them.

Sandy joked back, "Yeah, I wonder whatever happened to San Pan, the rickshaw man? I'm sure he's still running around somewhere in Shanghai."

I told our driver we wanted to cover as much as possible of the city on this side of the river, and that we had all day. We were out for fun and it was fun we had. The driver first took us up the main commercial street away from the river to the entrance of the beautiful public Lumpini Park, their answer to Central Park. He drove us all around it, and then down back through the business district pointing out the nightclubs and sex palaces.

As we passed, I said, "Sandy, is that what we came here for?"

He just said, "Drive on, MacDuff."

The driver then took us quite a ways out to a more residential district, to a government-approved commercial Expo Center. It was a showplace for products produced in Thailand, with government-approved price tags, everything from gems to carved teak. With many brass plates and bowls all carved, polished, and shiny, and jewelry, and painted silk screens, and silk clothing for both men and women, it was like an oriental Walmart. We looked at their display of precious gems to check out the prices. We found no deep red rubies, and the emeralds were also pale, not the lush deep emerald green we had found in Brazil. Generally, the prices seemed high. We did no shopping, never having intended to in the first place.

By the time we got back to the hotel, it was late and we went up to the room and crashed.

The next day we strolled up the street to the men's garment district. The stores were regular haberdashery shops, but they also made bespoke shirts, jackets and suits to order. We found a shop we liked and were each measured for a silk sports jacket. Sandy also picked out a piece of lovely, cream-colored, lightweight wool with a thin, pale blue checkered strip running through it. Very elegant! He ordered a three-piece suit that I quickly labeled his ice-cream suit. We also picked out a few silk prints and had shirts made. The salesman said everything would be ready before we left for Singapore. This experience was fun and a bit unusual for both of us. Sandy hadn't shopped since before his cancer in '73, and I hadn't since I'd gone to Bequia in '68. Clothing was one thing you needed little of on the Island. When you did need something, there was always a lady handy to run you up whatever on her Singer. But silks and luscious wools were out of the question.

Sandy & Jimmy in Thailand

Our next adventure was a boat trip through the waterways of Bangkok, off the left bank of the river. This area was Thailand's answer to Venice, with people living in homes all along the river banks, some quite impoverished and others elegant and opulent, with their pagoda-shaped roofs of orange and green tile slanting up at the ends like wings of a dove. The waterways ran in a grid formation, some narrow, others quite wide, with an oriental arched bridge once in a while, and the only means of getting around was by boat. Ferryboats carried people back and forth across to their daily jobs on the commercial side of the river running through Bangkok. The ferries loaded with people scurried back and for much like the Staten Island ferry in New York City.

On day five we sailed up the Mae Nam Chao Phraya on the Oriental Queen II to visit the Bang Pa-In Summer Palace and the palace and temples of Ayutthaya. This boat was a much larger boat, about the size of the Staten Island ferry only a little longer and thinner. At noon an oriental banquet was served, consisting of many Thai dishes, which Sandy declined, but I had his Jevity at the ready. The Royal Palace was first used as a summer retreat by Ayutthaya rulers in the 17th century. It was not until the reigns of Rama V and Rama VI in the late 19th century and as late as the 20th that the existing buildings were constructed, about the time of Anna and the King of Siam made famous by the book and the musical. The surrounding palaces are a good example of Thailand's fondness for adaptation. Besides Thai, building styles were a charming mixture of classical Greek, Roman, Victorian, and even an Imperial palace of old Peking built with materials shipped from China. The conglomerate styles fitted my taste to a "T," for together they gave the impression of some ancient land, which it was, all very Siamese and steeped in history as well as luxury.

There was so much to see. Yet I was able to wheel Sandy around leisurely at our own pace. We both wore short-sleeved shirts, Sandy's a bright solid "Sandy" Claus red and mine a solid Kelly green, that we had bought at Tannis's store in the Harbour back on Bequia for three bucks apiece before we left. We fit right in with all the brightly colored buildings of orange, green and red. We were able to cover everything. The lounge chair on the deck felt good as we sailed back down the Mae Nam Chao Phraya to Bangkok.

We then took a bus trip to the town of Chiang Mai on the river named Mae Nam Ping and booked into a government-approved hotel, the Wat Para Parownai—for only three days, thank god. The place was ugly and the food was lousy to this uneducated westerner's taste. The huge outdoor market was fun to meander through. I bought a pair of sandals that lasted forever. We then decided to press our luck and go out one night to a club. We had several to choose from and selected the Black Cat Club for no special reason.

The Black Cat

The cab driver insisted on waiting for us. We were led into an alcove big enough for one party, overlooking a stage. A lovely shy waitress with an extremely subservient manner ceremoniously waited on us. Sitting on cushions on a rice-mat floor, we were served our non-alcoholic drinks and the Far East equivalent of snacks on a low, oriental, lacquered teak table. Sandy had not been drinking since that dreadful bout of pneumonia back in '87, and I never was a drinker in the first place. I never felt intimidated about not drinking no matter where I was, gin mill, bar, or nightclub.

After the waitress had backed her way out and we sat sipping our Madame Gin Sling's answer to a Shirley Temple, in came two young "skins." The boys didn't look more than thirteen or fourteen. They too seemed shy, and the first to speak had trouble just saying, "Goot revinning." The second just giggled and said, "We sit, no?" I was taken aback at first, not expecting this, and quickly said, "No? No. I mean, I mean sure, sit." Well, they were cute in their oriental way. They plopped themselves onto the rice-mat on either side of Sandy. Looking at me, the first one said, "He ees baley old genterman. Yes?"

"Yes," I said, "he is very old."

Then the second one interjected, "Data ees baley goot. Yes?"

Sandy looked at me. "What do we do? Offer them a drink?"

"Yes," I said, "but I don't think it's a drink they're looking for."

We all looked at each other and they both giggled. Eventually the lights went out in the house and came up on the stage illuminating a winter scene of a single log cabin on the banks of a frozen river, an elaborate Siamese production of what bore a resemblance to Uncle Tom's Cabin. "Sandy, look! It's 'The Rittle House of Runcle Thomas'!" It didn't take long for my keen eye to adjust to what was a drag rendition of the now famous work from The King and I. Run, Little Eva, run! And did he ever. With all the femininity he could muster and the charms of a coquette, he pulled it off. Artistically speaking, it wasn't a bad production, with everyone in the cast playing it to the hilt.

I shot a few sidelong glances at Sandy. The boys were snuggled up against him and paying him all the deference and attention one could ever ask for. In his nervousness, Sandy gestured, inquiring whether they wanted a drink. They accepted with a simple gesture and a giggle. Uncle Tom ended, and the show continued with what looked to me like twin Siamese dancers doing an intricate foot-and-hand dance with complicated finger movements.

In no time at all, Little Eva had taken off his costume and makeup. Now in his street clothes, he came into our alcove and introduced himself. Naturally his English was accented but not too bad at that. When I asked him to join us, there was another round of drinks. The boy between him and Sandy slithered out of the way, leaving space for the "Star" to sit next to Sandy. I couldn't help but think, my, but this sure is Sandy's night.

The show was over by now. Sandy, no longer as nervous, was asking our Star questions about himself, which were readily and pleasantly answered. Two more young men came in and joined the group. Sandy and the Star were the center of attention as they carried on a conversation, with the boys and me just observing, except for my interjecting a translation for Sandy when needed. The Star had been working there since he was thirteen, and it was there that he had learned what English he knew. All the boys came from poor farms in the nearby countryside, and they all sent every penny they could spare home to their families who depended on them for survival. The Star had dreams of one day making it to America.

What kept running through my mind was the question of AIDS, how it was eating up whole communities in Africa, yes, and now even in America. What these unfortunate boys had to look forward to in a country so freely oriented to sexual permissiveness was staggering. The prevailing abject poverty only encouraged such perversion. In these times this act of purveyance was much more pernicious than they ever could have imagined.

I am sure sex was the motivating factor from the beginning of that evening, but they politely waited for the sexual intentions, advances, foreplay, and innuendos to generate from us. When none were forthcoming, the evening progressed into one of generational tribute to an unusual, "ageable" man of eighty-five being inquisitive about them. He could have been the grandfather they revered highly, as was their custom. All five of them were hanging on Sandy's every question and utterance, giggling and laughing and enjoying every minute, as Sandy was as well. I was impressed by the give and take.

We finally called it a night and paid our bill and the cover charge. Back in the cab, Sandy said, "They were really so young. Were they actually what I think—?"

"You bet," I interrupted. "It was a cathouse. Wasn't the name of the place a clue, the 'Black Cat Club'?"

"What a shame."

All Points North

The following morning, we packed and boarded a bus for the town of Chiang Rai and a brand new hotel that wouldn't be officially open until the approaching Christmas season. The same group who owned the Oriental in Bangkok had just had it built. It just had to be something else. With its mammoth size and all its twists and turns, its multi-tiered, dove-winged roofs, a pool that went on forever, and its multiple clover-like inlets and curves, it didn't disappoint. The place screamed for huge numbers of guests to fill it, but the management must have known what they were doing. We never saw a guest except in the dining room, and then just a handful. But there was staff all over the place. Then again, the official opening was another six months away.

We used the place as a home base from which to visit the various points of interest throughout northern Thailand.

The first excursion we took was off to the elephant logging camp. We arrived late and had to sit right up front with Sandy in his wheelchair. We were right in the middle of all the bustle of these gigantic beings. The elephants running this way and that were like so many dancers in a corps de ballet. The worrisome part was no one was leading them; they were on their own. Only every now and again would they get a prod here and there from a guide in a bright red shirt. To see them carrying logs this way and that, stacking them in orderly heaps, and doing it all on their own was quite a sight.

Sandy observed, "An elephant up on his hind legs is very fun to see—so long as you're not right under them, as we seem to be."

The elephants played drums and danced, and we saw them washing themselves in the river, again all by themselves.

Our next trip was to the beautiful orchid and butterfly farms. Both were a kaleidoscope, a fantastic maze of color. Butterflies were dipped in gold to make delicate brooches. When I asked how they could do that to a living thing, the workers told me they weren't living, they were dead. "How long do you think a butterfly lives?" they asked. I didn't know so I shut up and bought one for my sister Joan.

Our longest trip from the hotel was all the way up to the northern border and the Golden Triangle. I must say we kept our eyes peeled, scrutinizing everyone's movements, yet we saw no evidence of trafficking. When I mentioned this to Sandy, he joked, "What's the matter? You disappointed?"

We saw some oriental-style boats, long and extra narrow, pulled up on the bank of the Mekong River. "Sandy, do we dare ask if we can go for a jaunt?"

"We came this far, didn't we? Why not?"

"Well, they're so narrow. They look precarious, even worse than the ones in South American and more delicate."

"Look out there. I don't see any of them tipping over," Sandy replied.

So off we went, sailing rather gingerly across the wide river to Laos where we pulled up to a dock alongside a larger boat. I don't know how seaworthy it was; it was in worse shape than the "African Queen," though larger. Our boatman took us close enough to look into the portholes. We could see it filling up with people, men, women, and children in little clusters.

"Where are they going? Where are they headed?" I asked our boatman.

He simply answered, "To freedom…"

"On that?" Sandy asked.

"All the way through Cambodia and Vietnam, down through the delta to the open sea," I said, adding, "May God go with them."

We then quickly turned and headed farther upriver. As we did, a larger boat came speeding downriver, leaving in its wake huge swells. Our man stopped and waited for them to subside as we swayed from side to side. Both Sandy and I were clutching onto the boat for dear life. All I could think was, Jimmy, ya done it again. God! I need my head examined.

The boatman then took us through some swamps and pointed to Burma. Sandy teased, "Jimmy, I'm sure you can get your fix up in there."

"Thanks, but no thanks," I answered. And then we were on our way downriver again to Thailand.

That afternoon we boarded a bus that drove to the small town of Fang. I loved that name. Sandy asked, "Did Phyllis Diller's husband come from here?"

Leaving Fang we went on to a border town next to Burma (now called

35 The Sun Rises in the Far East

Myanmar) where we took a room for the night in a small hotel. We ate locally. We had to. With all my years in the Far East, I hadn't cottoned to their food, but what choice did we have?

The next morning we crossed a wide bridge over a deep crevice. A small river cut its way through the gorge with houses clinging to either side. One side was Burma—correction, Myanmar—the other, Thailand. People were hustling across the bridge to and from Namaklwe in Burma—sorry, Myanmar. I pushed Sandy in his chair along with everyone else. When we reached the other side, the barricades were opened up to let the pedestrian traffic through, so we went right along with the flow. But unlike in Venezuela, two official soldier-like characters came running after us. I stopped on command and just played dumb. They took us to the sentry house. When they found out we were Americans, they were angrier and more upset, they were downright ugly. We were marched right back through the barricade.

As I pushed Sandy back over the bridge, he said, "I've been thrown out of better places. But one of these days you're going to get us locked up for sure."

In the middle of the bridge, a young fellow approached me and offhandedly, through the side of the mouth, said, "Chick-a-let?"

I said, "What?"

He repeated, "Chick-a-let? You want chick-a-lets? You buy?"

Sandy asked, "What does he want?"

"He wants to know if I want any gum," I said.

"Gum...? Is he crazy?" asked Sandy.

The young chap kept repeating, "Chick-a-let, chick-a-let" while pantomiming the act of smoking.

And I finally got it. "No, no thanks."

"You need dope-smoky, no?" he persisted.

Emphatically, I said, "No!" I turned to Sandy. "My God! Right out here in the open, at high noon in front of all these people, he's soliciting us!"

"Ask him if he can take us to an opium den."

"Yeah, sure. And I can leave you there," I said and continued along with the flow of people.

The next day we were taken first to a village of Tibetans who had come down from the high mountains but were still living as they had back home in Tibet. The next village also had foreigners living as they had in their own country, as workers in brass. Many women were wearing brass rings around their necks as was their custom from childhood. The many rings circled their necks from under their chins down to the top of the breastplate and shoulders, stretching their necks, over the years, to phenomenal lengths like the lip-stretchers of Africa. Both villages were pandering their trinkets and souvenirs along the unpaved, dusty, red clay roads. I could just imagine what a mess it must be in the monsoon season and how unbearable it must be in the frosty, frozen days of winter.

Elephant Walk

One day a tour guide took us in his van to beautiful, bountiful botanical gardens up in the mountains. There, he said, we could have lunch at a lodge and saunter through the gardens perusing all the labels on the profusely growing flora. When we got there, the lodge was closed for repair. Only the flowers were there, and that wouldn't have been half bad, but the gardens were mostly on the side of a hill too steep to push a wheelchair. So his day shouldn't be a total loss, the driver showed us a path we could stroll along without the chair. He would pick us up at the other end. So off we went, Sandy clutching my arm. Before long the path got steeper, and still we trudged along. It got steeper still. We happened on an arbor where we could sit and rest out of the noonday sun. At least it was beautiful all around us.

Sandy said, "Come on. He's going to wonder what happened to us."

"If he's there at all."

"Jimmy, don't even think that! We haven't seen a living person anywhere around here all morning."

"Look, Sandy, he's either there or he's not. Either way I'm taking it easy, and you have to, too." I was mad as hell at the driver for getting us out here like this.

So we just moseyed along continuing up that hill flanked by all the flora of the Far East. When we got to the top, the driver was there all right. We were both panting for breath. I could tell from his behavior that he was well aware of his boo-boo; he was full of solicitude and apologizing all over the place. But we were still at that driver's mercy. To make up for the morning's loss, he offered to take us for an elephant ride.

"An elephant ride, here in the jungle?" I asked.

"Yes, right here on the Burmese border with a Burmese elephant driver sitting up front on the elephant's neck guiding it," he explained.

Sandy said, "Well, an elephant ride beats walking up Kilimanjaro."

I looked at him. "You mean that? You want to ride an elephant?"

"Why not? You ever ride one?" he asked me.

"Of course I did, when I was a clown with Ringling Brothers, Barnum and Bailey... Where the hell would I ride an elephant?" At the time I had a mental picture of us sitting in one of those elephant-grass baskets you see in pictures of India with a Maharajah in them.

Sandy said, "It'll be like riding ponies in Central Park. What harm can it be? It's that or back to the hotel. Let's do it."

I agreed.

Our driver said, "I'll have to drive on to the next town, and make a call ahead to the elephant people. Then I'll take you right into the jungle where you catch the ride on this end."

That should have been a clue, but dumb-dumb here didn't pick up on it. After he'd arranged things, we continued along a winding road up hills through the thick underbrush of the lush green jungle and came to a stop on the top of a hill. No one was around, not even a house, only a bamboo platform up off the ground as high as an elephant's eye, with rickety stairs leading up to it. The driver directed us up the stairs and said the elephant would be showing up shortly; everything had been arranged. He would drive on ahead with the wheelchair and meet us at the other end. By the time we reached the top of the stairs, the driver was already off in his van, even before the elephant arrived.

Standing there on top of the rickety platform, Sandy joked, "What time's the next elephant?"

"God, Sandy, that reminds me of when the tenor Lauritz Melchior was singing in *Lohengrin* at the Met. When it came time for the swan to show up and carry him off, its mechanism broke down and it didn't make the cue. Melchior stopped singing, stepped down to the footlights, and, speaking out to the audience, said, 'What time does the next swan leave?'"

"Well, the driver said the elephant would be showing up shortly. I hope he didn't mean all alone," was Sandy's squeamish reply.

Here we go again, I thought. Just then I spotted the elephant coming through the thicket of jungle. A party of Frenchmen on two elephants unloaded onto our platform. One elephant took off while the other elephant waited for us to mount, which was all well and good except there was no basket of elephant grass for us to step into. All the elephant was equipped with was a slab of wood across his back for us to sit on. The slab was secured by a girdle around his stomach. A single two-by-four ran across the back of the slab serving as a back rest, and on either side an arm rest, secured at each corner of the slab by four short vertical two-by-fours. As we stepped across the elephant and sat on the board, only a loosely swinging rope protected us in front. There we sat, Sandy to my right, with our backs up against the wooden bar in the back and nothing but that swaying rope to hang on to. As for our feet, they could do nothing but dangle in space.

The driver sitting on the elephant's neck in front of us with his brass prod was a lovely looking young Burmese chap. He was dressed in a beautiful red and multi-colored striped shirt, minus the turban, speaking unintelligible English at us. I thought, just through the bush to the other platform and we will be out of this precarious position and down off this docile, colossal creature. So I said to Sandy, "Hang on, this can't last forever." I had the camera dangling from my neck, and I found myself holding Sandy's cane. How the hell I got it beats the crap out of me. It should have been back in the van with the taxi-driver. Oh well, it was too late the, so I laid it across the wooden bar in the back and held it in my right hand with that arm around Sandy.

We weren't ten feet into the jungle brush when the elephant took a lurch forward going down on his knees. I started to slip forward off the board.

"God, Sandy, hang on! Grab the bar with both hands!" I yelled. I couldn't hold him any longer because I had that damn cane in that hand. Then the elephant lurched again. I started to slip some more and gripped a little tighter with my left hand onto the bar on my left.

"Damn it, Sandy. I'm so big I'm slipping."

"Hold yourself as I'm doing," Sandy instructed.

"How, for christ's sake?" I pleaded.

"With your feet behind his ear," he said calmly. "That will secure you."

So I tried and tried, but I couldn't get either foot up that high. The board we were sitting on, flat on the elephant's back, was at the same level as his ear. I was too damned fat to get my feet up that high as Sandy was able to do. All I could do then was hang there with my feet dangling in midair and hold on to the bar with both hands for dear life.

I could tell by now that the elephant was not going down on his knees but heading down a very, very steep hill, so steep that he could not have done it if he hadn't had deep holes to step into up to his knees. The holes were in two parallel rows the width of his body apart. They didn't line up side by side but were offset from each other. The distance between one hole and the next was the length of his stride. The elephant started out sinking his right front foot into the second hole on the right, leaving a hole behind for his right rear foot, which he then inserted in the hole. Swaying to the right, he swung his left front foot half a stride ahead of his right front foot into a hole on the left, leaving an empty hole behind for his left rear foot. Once his left rear foot was inserted, he swayed to the left and moved his right foot forward into the next hole, freeing up a hole for his right rear foot. Then swaying to the right he repeated the operation. And over and over one foot at a time, lurching and swaying, we slowly descended the never-ending hill. This footwork held him back from tumbling over on top of himself straight down to the bottom.

Sandy on Elephant

There we were, Sandy bracing himself on an elephant's ear and me dangling in space like a helpless rag doll. All I could say was, "Good God, Sandy! Oh, God, Sandy! For God's sake, hang on, Sandy!"

We were slipping by the inch, or at least I was, with every goddamned lurch of that pachyderm's body. The elephant's head and the beautiful Burmese boy were directly below us now. It was steeper than any ski slope. I could see the double lane of holes down the hill ahead of us as if so many telephone poles had been yanked clean out of their foundations. The gaping holes in the clay-like soil must have been made during the monsoon season.

"Holy shit!" I said. Sandy, if we slip and fall into one of those holes and this elephant continues down the hill in spite of us, we'll be squished into pancakes. They'll be sending us back to Hollywood in two film cans!"

Believe it or not, the trip continued, uphill and down some more hills, through rivers, even stopping to let the elephant drink. He squatted down on his belly so I could take a badly needed break. But Sandy didn't move. He said he was fine where he was, perched on that elephant's ear.

It was well over an hour and a half before we reached a clearing in the jungle. I could see a platform up ahead and our driver standing near his van. I said to Sandy, "I can't wait to get my hands on that dumb son-of-a-bitch. They're going to be locking me up, but I don't care because I am going to knock his block off."

By the time we reached the platform and dismounted, I could see his shit-eating grin smiling up at us. When we got to the ground, I said to Sandy, "I am livid. I'm going to wipe that smile off his face." And I turned to face our simple-minded driver. As I did, I felt Sandy's hand on my shoulder.

"No, Jimmy, don't do that. Thank him. It was the most exhilarating thing I've ever done in my life."

Seedy Sex

The last day in the north country at the big hotel, we were ready for a sumptuous dinner. I should really say I was, because I noticed again Sandy wasn't eating much, implying to me his Jevity and soup were all he wanted. He never did eat much as it was. After all, according to the label on the can, he was getting more than his daily nutritional requirements.

The bus trip back to Bangkok was uneventful, but the subtropical brush was abundant, and we passed some of the most breathtaking scenery imaginable.

At the haberdasher back in Bangkok, we tried on our duds. They fit us to a "T."

That night, our last night in Thailand, I said to Sandy, "Come on. What do you say we do a bit of the seedy side this evening?"

Sandy deadpanned, "I thought you would never ask."

After dinner we took a cab to the red-light district, but I had a feeling that district was all over Bangkok. The driver took us to a well-known, rather popular nightclub, according to him anyway. Inside was a long bar jammed with people, so we sat along the wall. The stage was in the center of the room with the brass stripper poles running floor to ceiling in the middle. The clientele was mostly men, with a smattering of couples here and there. To my jaundiced eye, most of the men at the bar were gay. I have to admit I had never been to a place like this and neither had Sandy, but I did have a notion of what to expect. I had been to Dirty Dick's, a straight club in Barbados, once many years ago. As the girls—yes, I guess even goy-girls now, with all the changes today—came out and did their thing, stripping while hanging on to a brass pole, I could not see one iota of difference. Who knew whether it was a gay or straight performer? You couldn't prove either by me. Their gyrations and antics were identical, had to be. Had to be, that is, until the Star came out with a very close friend, at least I hoped he was, and they simulated sex together. No, simulate isn't the right word for it. Their act was the forerunner of a reality show, right there on the stage.

Sandy asked, "How many times a night does he get to do that?"

"Who the hell knows?" I answered, and that was that. Oh, I should mention they were damn good at it. At this point I turned to Sandy. "If they start any of that lap-dance stuff, I'm out of here."

"Come on," Sandy said. "Let's get out of here anyway. Where can they go from here?"

So we took off and headed back to the hotel for we had an early flight ahead of us. The next day we were headed south across Malaysia.

Singapore

This flight was a first for us with Singapore Air. The minute they spotted Sandy's wheelchair, we were handled with kid gloves. We were booked first class. Remember, I had told that agent back in LA number one all the way. Singapore Air was not as luxurious as Cathay Pacific had been coming over, but just as special was far as the treatment went. Sandy took to it. Who wouldn't? He was used to it from his earlier days with his wives, when he had spent every penny he had on them. They went first class all the way on their European trans-Atlantic crossings every summer on the Leonardo Da Vinci, the Andrea Doria, and the like. Oh, we had our sparse times financially getting to where we were because of it. But by this time in his life he had nothing to save for, and I was seeing to it that he enjoyed himself to the fullest from here on out. No one had concentrated and worked more diligently and selflessly throughout his life than he had. The flight attendants doted on him, and he enjoyed it. Maybe it was because of his age, but so what? It was most pleasant. It did me good to see him enjoy himself so after all the suffering he had been through to get to this point in his life.

We flew the length of Malaysia from Bangkok to Singapore. Sandy asked,

35 The Sun Rises in the Far East

"Are we not stopping in Malaysia?" When I said no, he said, "OK. Next time." And I said, "Sure, you bet."

The Shangri-La Hotel in Singapore had the most spectacular lobby, the likes of which I had never seen before, with breathtaking chandeliers and a pool surrounded by dense tropical growth. The pool was like a set right out of the forties movies of Dorothy Lamour or Johnny Weissmuller or Esther Williams. I made quick use of it as the weather was hot, damn hot. Sandy didn't seem to mind the heat. In fact, he relished it.

Singapore was so clean and seemed so law-abiding. Sandy explained, "Why wouldn't it be? In many ways it's as close as you're going to get to a Gestapo state and the Nazis without a Hitler. So you'd better mind your Ps and Qs. This is not Thailand. Law and order are on the front burner here."

There was a lot to the place I did like. The stores were stocked with everything imaginable and reasonable as well. Everything was so orderly, including the traffic. One felt safe to walk anywhere anytime, with the police force very visible. We were told they could be stern, strict, and the consequences strong over the slightest infraction.

Sandy warned me, "Don't spit or pee in the street."

"Why would I want to?" I asked. Oh, I am sure they probably were censorious and stringent as well, and could maybe even be quite stentorian about it all. It's one way to keep a populace under control. Their crime rate was the lowest in the region, but their methods sure stifle freedom.

But all this had nothing to do with us. We were not there to break any of their laws. We were there just to look and have a good time, which we did. The by-product of all the repression was that we felt safe, and were safe, doing it.

We took the cable car from the mountain top over the Singapore Strait and across to the island off the coast where the Japanese interned captives in their concentration camp during the Second World War. The view from the cable car of the city to our left, the bay underneath, and the island up ahead was spectacular. The day was glorious, clear and balmy. On the island was a wax museum of the atrocities, the torture, and also the various stages of the signing of the peace treaty with Japan. It was most impressive and so vivid one could not come away

Birthday Dinner at Shangri-La

without being affected and touched.

One day we stopped in at the government gem display. Sandy found two more emeralds that matched in color and size the two we had bought in Brazil. They came from Colombia. Sandy planned to add them to his collection. I asked about rubies and learned they had a few from Brazil, so I made a purchase also. Sandy said, "This is fun. I've never bought any jewelry like this. I always went to a family member like my uncle Dave or my brother-in-law Nat in the jewelry business."

One night at the Shangri-La Hotel, a notice appeared under our door telling us Sandy's show, *The American Theater's Best Kept Secret*, was being aired in conjunction with his 85th birthday. The hotel wanted to know if we would accept dinner on them on the 31st at any one of their restaurants. We accepted, choosing their most prestigious restaurant. They gave us both gifts of lovely ivory chopsticks with jade-green holders, and presented Sandy with a three-tiered Dutch chocolate-mousse-filled cake with Happy Birthday on top. They also took our picture and presented it to us the next day.

I asked Sandy, "Is this the way celebrities are treated wherever they go?"

"Well, you couldn't prove it by me," Sandy said, "but I'll tell you one thing for sure. I could very easily get used to it."

Hong Kong

At our next stop, our first reaction was, Wow! What a place! Hong Kong was like New York: you name it and it was there, and I mean everything. We stayed right across from the waterfront in the Mandarin Hotel. We roamed around, sandy in his wheelchair, with masses of people hustling and bustling all around us. I had only seen crowds move like this up and down Fifth Avenue on Manhattan Island the week before Christmas or down on Wall Street at lunch hour.

I wheeled Sandy in to the environs behind the Mandarin. With the chair, we kept getting in the way of oncoming pedestrians, but I didn't give a damn. We just stopped and waited for them to continue around us in whatever direction they were scurrying. When vendors were spreading out their wares wherever they pleased, why should we be concerned or intimidated blocking traffic? Believe me, we weren't. I wheeled Sandy everywhere possible.

One day we boarded a trolley going across the bridge to the island where we took a cable car up the side of the hill. It was almost as steep as the Andes in Venezuela, close to perpendicular. It was an experience to shoot up past the extremely tall skyscrapers all jammed together like in New York around Wall Street. Except here, they were all recently built. Such ingenuity I never expected to see.

We had lunch at the top among the low flying clouds and it brought back memories of Sandy's friend Jennifer Jones and William Holden and the lyrics

35 The Sun Rises in the Far East

from the title song of their movie, Love Is a Many Splendored Thing: "Once on a high and windy hill..."

We were snapping pictures like the Japanese tourists who were all over the place. Afterward, we took a bus down the winding road to the sea. Once there, we walked along the beach, with me carrying the chair, to a rather large pier with a big Buddha at its entrance. It was a comical Buddha, painted in realistic colors. Sandy went up to it and start rubbing its big, bare belly.

"Why are you doing that?" I asked.

"Doesn't everyone?" he replied.

"Sure, if you want to get pregnant. Isn't that the fertility god?"

"Well, it's too late now!" he told me, slapping his hands together.

The harbor on this side of the island was crammed with all kinds of oriental-looking sea craft, from cargo boats to sampans. We took a boat ride around the harbor amongst the various types of vessels from seagoing to houseboats with families living on them. Boats were all lashed together so one could walk from boat to boat all the way to a pier. We found a boat schedule with listings for the country of Macao only an hour away on the south coast of China to the west of Hong Kong. We stood there pondering, Should we or shouldn't we? We both wanted to go badly, stay overnight, and come back the next day. We almost gave in, but didn't. To this day I must say I am sorry as hell we didn't just jump at the chance and go for it. At the time, I was positive we couldn't. We didn't have our passports with us, unless we wanted to see if we could pull off another Venezuela. Knowing what I know of Macao, it sure wasn't like Burma or Singapore, and maybe we could have bribed our way.

At that time, Sandy had a student from Hong Kong by the name of Elizabeth Sung. Elizabeth arranged for her sister Margaret Au-Yeung Ying to give us a call at the hotel. Margaret invited us to a food-tasting dinner. It was a special night, feature many historic and exotic, traditional, medicinal, and erotic foods of the Orient, all prepared by a leading Hong Kong Cordon Bleu chef who searched the recesses of his mind to come up with the rarest dishes imaginable. It was all very exclusive, catering mostly to professionals like doctors, lawyers, business executives, academics, and artists, all of whom belonged to a group equivalent to our Sierra Club in America. However, with only one rather large round table, this group was much smaller and a hell of a lot more exclusive. They met once a month and did something that would be of interest to them. They even went so far as to go off on trips together, back into rarely traveled areas of China.

It was such a shame because all this goût raffiné was wasted on Sandy and me. We had no business being there. First of all, it was expensive. It was also unfortunate that Sandy couldn't eat anything in the first place, much less duck's feet, shark fins, and snake soup, to mention only a few of the dishes. Most of the fare, even if I could have pronounced the names, I wouldn't have known what it was, and I couldn't have cared less. Here, Sandy and I were hoi polloi and, in our limited, plebeian and bourgeois way, we were, I have to say, out of our element. We didn't have one memorable tasty morsel all evening. Of course everyone carried on all evening in Chinese, and why not? That's exactly what they were.

At one point when all the accolades were being heaped on our illustrious chef, Sandy quietly asked, "How do we get out of here?"

"Faint," I replied tersely. I was feeling like a fish out of water. Before I began to get jumpy, Sandy started to cough. Margaret showed great concern, and I seized the moment by telling her he sometimes had slight spasms and I was dreadfully sorry but I should get him back to the hotel. She understood. We thanked her and made a graceful retreat, well as graceful as can be under the circumstances. I hoped we didn't stick out too much. I think everyone else was having too grand a time to take note of us.

Once outside, Sandy asked, "When do we eat?"

"What happened to your cough?" I inquired.

"What cough?" he replied.

We had brunch the following morning with Fredric Mao, a former student whom Elizabeth had alerted to look us up at the hotel. He was now teaching acting at the HK Performing Arts Centre, Chinese Drama Division, and was resident director at the Repertory Theatre in Hong Kong. He was delirious when Sandy told him he had a book out about his Technique. Freddie couldn't wait to get it, feeling that it would be beneficial for his students. He would have liked Sandy to come to the school, but it was closed until later in the month. Regardless, he was delighted to spend this limited amount of time with his teacher.

The Awakening Red Giant

Some of the folks at the banquet in Hong Kong cast a jaundiced eye on our next escapade. Everyone told us that if we must go to mainland China to make sure we left all our jewelry and most of our cash back at the hotel. Most people were fearful and apprehensive about that giant to the north. This was 1990, only seven years before changes, to put it mildly, were to be made around there. The apprehension was beginning o rub off on us, so we took their advice, leaving all our valuables behind and taking only a limited number of travelers' checks when we left for the train headed north into China.

The apprehension of our banquet colleagues on our account were unfounded, unwarranted, groundless. At the border into China, where we had to go through Customs before reboarding the train, endless lines of mostly Asians were being checked and searched. When a Customs clerk saw our passports, we were pulled out of line and directed up front to the first-class Pullman car, as they toted our luggage along with us. Our luggage was never examined! It was just stowed in our overhead compartment, and we were welcomed to the Republic of China.

35 The Sun Rises in the Far East

As we settled into our seats for the first phase of our journey, Sandy said, "This is easier than crossing from Jersey into the city on the George Washington Bridge."

"What was all that paranoia on the part of our intimidators back in Hong Kong about anyway?" I asked.

In due time we were rollicking along in tune with the rhythm of the rails headed for the very capitalistic town, for a communistic country, called Kwangchow, capital of the province of Guangdong in southeast China. We stayed at a five-star hotel, and a fine hotel it was. How unlike the stories we had heard about the hotels of communist Moscow.

When we went down to breakfast in the morning, we were directed to a rather large banquet hall with a breakfast buffet that ran the length of the room. It reminded me of a Sunday brunch at the Four Seasons in Beverly Hills or any other posh hotel in America or Europe, except by comparison this one was mammoth in size. Many people were breaking fast that morning, but the crowd was dwarfed in such a large room. There were as many Caucasians as Asians and most were businessmen. Most of the Caucasians looked and sounded as if they were Europeans. I noted few Americans, if any, besides us.

I had never seen such a layout of food. I sat Sandy at a table and went to check out the display. I made a point of looking to see if they had forgotten anything. I detected no oversight.

When I got back, I asked him, "What would you like? You can have whatever your heart desires." True to form, all he wanted was coffee. I said, "You can have eggs Benedict, Florentine, whatever. You should be able to handle that."

"No, just coffee."

I insisted, saying, "I'm bringing you a poached egg. That Jevity isn't enough."

"OK," he said.

Sandy had his poached egg and ate it all. I took my time and I had a ball for the rest of our stay at that hotel.

We stayed only three days and then on the fourth boarded that great red iron rooster for Shanghai. The first night, we had a four-seat compartment and took the two bottom beds. We were served tea and hot water. I had brought instant coffee and food to eat as well as Jevity for Sandy. His wheelchair fit folded up at the bottom of his bed next to our private john. The compartment was comfortable. We watched the passing landscape out our ample window. It stretched out as far as the eye could see, turning into oriental watercolors as varied as the changing topography of the land.

Two young men joined us in our room and took the two top bunks. They were out of the compartment most of the time. At night they came back to sleep. It was obvious they had been drinking for they were as loquacious as a couple of schoolgirls. With their constant giggling, they reminded me of Gilbert and Sullivan's "Three Little Maids from School."

Sandy asked, "Could we have a couple of swigs of that stuff? It sounds like good stuff."

After an hour, this incessant jabber in Chinese, Cantonese, or whatever became more than I could take. They were set to keep it up all night. So I stood up between the beds. They stopped talking and just stared at me.

"Look," I said, pointing to Sandy and speaking in English, what else? "How do you expect that old man to get any rest with you two jabbering away all night?" Putting my finger to my lips, I added, "Please."

They stared at each other across the aisle, and I slipped back under into my bed. Believe it or not, there wasn't another peep out of them all night. In the early morning, they left the compartment without making a sound. They merely made a polite gesture to me as they left. Sandy looked over at me and said, "Good riddance."

We now had the compartment all to ourselves the rest of the way up to Shanghai, and Sandy liked it that way.

I was curious about the rest of the train's accommodations and ventured out alone. I made my way down the length of the train expecting to be stopped at any moment. Two soldiers approached me from behind at one point and grabbed the rather heavy sliding door in front of me. My heart stopped. I was still intimidated by this communist thing. They merely smiled and directed me through first. At the far end of the train, I came to what were obviously the cheaper seats. The berths were just thin slabs constructed of caning, which flipped out from the wall on two chains like a bunk in a jail cell. They were stacked in tiers three beds high with no curtains. Consequently the passengers had no privacy. They were sitting around everywhere. Little stoves supplied heated water every so many feet, and the people were eating, eating, eating food they had brought, as we had. The train had no dining car.

Now everything seemed much easier and more relaxed, and I think it had an effect on everyone concerned. Sandy once said, "What was needed in the earlier classes was more love."

Destination Shanghai

We eventually rolled into Shanghai station after traveling up the entire eastern coastline of China. We did not pass in view of the China Sea but over many wide riverbeds that empty into it. A porter took our small amount of luggage and helped us into a cab, telling the driver in Chinese to take us to the Oriental Hotel. The Oriental was a top-notch luxury hotel, and we were up on the umpteenth floor.

Sandy commented, "I'm getting tired of all these hotels. They're all the same. Give me the Frangipani back on Bequia with its cold water any day."

Out the window another building just as high as this one, if not higher, was going up across the street. You could see the wide Po River off in the distance and construction sites clear out across the flat horizon.

That first afternoon we got a call from Henry O/Xi Reng Jiang, a Chinese actor teaching in Shanghai's Children's Theatre Company School. He had been to America and played in *The Last Emperor*, which, he told us, had been filmed somewhere in the American Midwest. His English was impeccable. He had been to Hong Kong many times and knew Elizabeth Sung and his sister well. Elizabeth's sister had contacted him to tell him of our arrival. We had dinner together that night.

He invited us to his humble home, where he introduced us to an opera singer friend of his. She was tall, for a Chinese, not fat but zaftig nonetheless. She naturally had those high cheekbones, like Joany Sutherland's. So if she had a voice at all, she looked as if she could pack a wallop. She asked if I would mail a large, rather heavy, brown envelope addressed to UCLA, Los Angeles. She was applying for admission, and my mailing it from the states would expedite it for her. I said, "Fine, no problem," and added, "I would be glad to help. My pleasure."

When we left them, Sandy asked, "How do you know you aren't getting into some clandestine espionage thing? I'm sure they're not too easy on mules."

"What do you think it is? Opium? Come on, Sandy, the lady is a singer."

"All the same, she should have showed you what was in that envelope. After all this isn't Oshkosh, Wisconsin."

"Well, it's too late," I answered.

"No, it's not. Open it up. If it is what she says, what's the harm?" Sandy insisted.

So I agreed. We opened it and found it was what she had said it was. So much for paranoia.

Xi Reng invited Sandy to come to the school the next day to see a demonstration by the students. We both went eagerly. We met the director and a few of the other teachers, none of whom had a command of English as our newfound friend had. We sat in raised seats as the students came out en masse and stood in a semi-circle, while two actors stepped front and center and went through their paces. The teachers all sat saying nothing, just observing. Once in a while a student stepped out and started to pantomime brushing his teeth. Another one washed his hands and face with no water, soap, or towel. Another fixed his hair in the mirror, with neither comb nor mirror. It went on like this, all demonstrating something and no one ever saying anything. Not that it would have made one damn bit of difference to us. I couldn't help but think of Marcel Marceau. Wouldn't he just love this. Sandy leaned over to me and simply said, "Archaic." Our friend, who was sitting just behind us, asked me, "What did Mr. Meisner say?"

I told Sandy, "He wants to know what you just said."

"So tell him."

I did and Xi Reng said, "I knew it, I knew it."

Sandy later told me it was early Stanislavski, about 1902. You could call it early sense-memory.

We met with the director and his teachers later and not much was said. In fact Sandy said nothing, just shook hands and nodded. The director seemed aloof and his teachers were like doting stooges. I don't know if the director knew who Sandy was, or if he even cared. I could tell Sandy sure didn't.

When we finally got outside with our friend, Sandy said, "Pathetic." He turned to me and asked, "What were Eli and Annie carrying on about when they came back from here."

The actor asked if Sandy had a book or any material he might read. Sandy said, "I'll have Elizabeth back in LA send you my book and a copy of The American Theater's Best Kept Secret, whereupon Xi Reng expressed his gratitude and we parted and went our separate ways.

One day we visited an ancient walled-in-home right in the middle of the city. In the center of its gardens was an ancient stage where we had our picture taken on the lip of stage centre, à la Judy Garland at the Palace, only this stage had been built in this 16th century, Shakespeare's time.

Another day we took a boat ride down the Po, now called the Huang Po, I believe. We went on into the Da Yunhe (a canal) and up to the Chang Jiang River, which was once called the Yangtze. The name changes and everything about China seemed confusing to me. The country was so full of contradictions. It was apparently so poor and yet so rich in potential. Industry and commerce were everywhere in Shanghai. It was bursting at the seams. Sandy observed, "America had better look out. It's obvious the great giant of the Orient is finally awakening. Everything is in a state of flux, readying itself for the big change."

In hindsight, was Sandy right or what?

The boat was about half the size of the Staten Island ferry and there were few tourists. I think the tourist season was about over. On deck we sat at a table at the edge of the restaurant area. The waitress came over and asked, in clear English, if we would like anything. We said no thanks. With no one else around, she came over to talk, asking us if we were Americans, saying she loved America. Later she came back over with two cups of steaming hot tea, saying, "It is cold today, very gray," as she put the cups on the table. "My gift to you, thank you." And a little later she came with some ice cream on a stick, again saying, "My gift, please." Later, when I went to pay, she still insisted, "No, please. You very nice gentermen, you American."

We thanked her, and later Sandy remarked, "That doesn't happen very often, now does it?"

On the way home, I spotted a jewelry shop in the lobby of an old run-down hotel. I had to have a look. One lovely ring the proprietor seemed to be giving away for the asking. When I said as much to Sandy, he said, "So ask."

"No, Sandy. I couldn't get it anyway. We have very few travelers' checks left."

"That's what you get for listening to foreigners back in Hong Kong," Sandy chided.

The last day in Shanghai we went to a government trade sale. What a mistake that was. We were still using travelers' checks, not having cottoned to charge cards yet. All those beautiful handmade rugs and breathtaking fur-

35 The Sun Rises in the Far East

niture just waiting for us to ship home. No place on earth had we ever been where such bargains could be had. I said to Sandy, "Come on, let's get out of here. It hurts too much."

That night for dinner at the hotel we had our actor friend Xi Reng over to say goodbye. I noticed Sandy was still not eating. I was beginning to worry in earnest, and after dinner when we were alone, I said so. Something was wrong, and I felt it had become radically wrong. I realized right then and there I had to get him back to New York as quickly as possible. This problem had been coming on for well over three weeks now. I knew it was best to say nothing more. My job now was just to get him back to New York into the hands of his doctor, and as fast as possible.

Sandy & Jimmy in Shanghai

36 Ups and Downs

September 1990: Strike Three

We left China by air for Hong Kong with the same ease with which we had entered. After spending one night in Hong Kong so we could collect our things, we winged our way across the wide Pacific on Cathay Air to LAX. I waited until we got home before broaching the subject of Sandy's not eating again, and it was then that he told me the truth. He wasn't able to swallow any solid foods at all. He had been depending solely on the Jevity and soups. Of course, that diet wasn't good enough; Jevity was only a supplement. Something must be wrong. I called Dr. Spiro at Sloan-Kettering in New York. Although he was in Israel, his office said Sandy should come in immediately. One day back and we were packing again.

We had dinner with Dick Dunn and others the night before we left. The conversation was light and mostly centered on our escapades in the Far East. Kettering and the cancer scare were soft-pedaled that night. Though everyone was aware we were leaving in the morning, no one was more consumed with what lay ahead than I. What if we had delayed too long and it was too late? Did I not see it coming because I didn't want to face it? Did I put the damned trip before Sandy's safety? All these answerless thoughts had me so preoccupied that I don't even remember what was discussed that night. Somehow we muddled through, as people have a way of doing.

At Sloan-Kettering Dr. Jatin P. Shah, a rather tall young man from India, examined Sandy. After the exam and all the tests, he informed us both together there in his office that Sandy had cancer of the esophagus and would need a rather extensive operation. We could wait for another week or so for Dr. Spiro to return or we could do it immediately, a decision that was entirely up to Sandy. I wasn't going to influence him one way or the other. Nonetheless, it was hard for me to just sit there. I couldn't help but think of all the time we had lost. I knew we shouldn't wait around while his doctor gallivanted in Israel. Inside I was screaming, "Now, right now, immediately, and not a moment longer!" Maybe my guilt was eating at me for having let it go on so long.

I don't know what Sandy was thinking, but maybe it was similar. Looking over at me, he asked, "If I don't wait, who would do the operation?" Then to Dr. Shah he asked, "Would you be the operating surgeon?"

The good doctor said, "Yes, I could do it immediately."

Sandy's simple answer was, "Do it," and that was that.

He was admitted that afternoon and preparations began. He was all set for the operation in two days when Dr. Spiro showed up unexpectedly early and asked Sandy if he wanted to cancel the Thursday operation so he himself could do it the following week.

Sandy said, "No, now that everything is set to go, we'll go." As far as he was concerned, the sooner the better. I got the feeling Dr. Spiro wasn't too happy about Sandy's show of loyalty.

To Sandy this wasn't about loyalty, it was about life and breath, specifically his. And a bird in the hand was worth two in Israel. Right then, Dr. Jatin P. Shah was that bird for Sandy, and time was precious. I noticed that Sandy had only one visit from Spiro after the operation, and he never saw him again. So much for his loyalty, I thought.

Dr. Shah took me aside. "Since his esophagus will have to be removed, I would like to make him a new one from the flesh of his right chest." Bluntly and simply, "A slab like this," he said, picking up a sheet of typing paper and rolling it up to make a narrow tube. He would stitch it up and attach one end of the tube to the base of Sandy's tongue, the other end to the opening into his stomach.

"Do you think this is the best and safest way to handle it?" I asked.

"Well, he is a bit old for whatever we do, but I get the impression he is ready for whatever has to be done. That zest for life is in his favor."

I, as his power of attorney, said, "Go ahead. Tell him, but please spare him the gory details. Just tell him you have to remove his esophagus and you will be making him a new one from his chest. That's gory enough. If he has any objections, he'll tell you quick enough."

When I came in that afternoon, Sandy was all talk. "Do you know what they want to do?" he asked. "They want to make an esophagus out of my chest. Did they tell you?"

I just answered, "Yes."

"Did you tell them no? Because they came in here and asked me," Sandy said.

"So, what did you tell them?" I asked.

"I told them to do whatever they have to do, Jimmy. They're the doctors. They're the directors of this show, and you just leave them to it. It's my life you're playing around with, you know."

"Sandy, I didn't tell them no," I replied but I don't think he even heard me.

Then he asked, "Did they tell you how they do it?"

"Yes," I said.

"So tell me," he insisted, and I did. That was Sandy. Just pay and leave it up to the professionals, whatever it was.

When he woke up from this operation, unlike the first time at least he could see. This bout with cancer was his third, none of them related except for the area they occurred in, and he was becoming an old hand at it. All the nurses on the floor knew him and admired his spirit.

When he recovered enough to make the trip, they took him down to the assembly room, which was as large as any Broadway theatre, for a briefing and, I guess, consultation. All the doctors on staff were there and, judging from the number, many from other staffs around the city. The chief surgeon and Dr. Jatin P. Shah were on stage with Sandy. They and the other doctors discussed his procedure and the prognosis and observed Sandy's recovery thus far. I got the impression from all this fuss that Sandy's latest brush was newsworthy back then.

Transcontinental Convalescence

By October Sandy was home on 58th Street making trips in his wheelchair to the school, just to show his face. He was also going up to the hospital to speech classes. He had to learn to speak all over again—for the fourth time—and in little time he was making inroads. The removal of his esophagus and the muscles from his right chest weakened him somewhat, making it more difficult to muster up the strength to perform the esophageal speech pattern. The muscles he needed on the outside for the speech maneuver were now serving as his esophagus. Still, he managed sound and it was improving each day.

When the question of class in LA came up, he said, "What's the matter? Don't you think I'll be ready by November? I do."

"I don't," I replied bluntly.

He broached the subject to his speech teacher at Kettering who said, "It's entirely up to you. You know how to do it. It's the dynamics and your strength that need building up."

"There's nothing like my classes to do that," Sandy stated.

So I said, "OK. But we wait until the end of November, to give you a little more time." We would be flying off to North Hollywood and the Lankershim Boulevard school on the 15th of November.

Meanwhile back at the Playhouse, Sandy felt it was time for him to retire officially although it would take another year before all the pieces were in place. Then a meager pension plan was set up. He had already earned and deserved it many times over fifty-one years of undying loyalty and service. Sandy was in no physical shape to argue, nor did he have the inclination to. And who was I to argue?

After that monumental trip to the Far East and the unforeseen trials and tribulations that befell us in New York, when we finally reached Studio City, we felt like the spy who came in from the cold. We were finally back on our own familiar terra firma, safe and sound from all the acerbating, exasperating, even suffocating problems of life out in limbo. For a short time even annihilation had been a possibility, for Sandy at least. Our cozy little cottage was all we needed to rejuvenate and prepare Sandy for his 57th year of teaching. From New York I had notified both classes of the three-week delay in school opening this year. Everyone waited and no one complained. Classes started out a little softer than usual. I boosted the speaker to its max and everyone just concentrated a little harder at first. I stayed on top of whatever translation was needed as it came up. In no time he was back to the old Sandy, and enjoying it more than ever.

We stayed put for the holidays, and Boolu came out to join us for the celebrations. We went to Rosie's Christmas Eve. The usual suspects—Morey Amsterdam and his lovely wife, Kay, Patty Andrews and Wally Weschler, and my old New York agency's owner, Bill Cunningham, a longtime friend and agent of Rosie's—were all there. Rosie's sister had her friends as well. There was quite a crowd. Wally played, Patty sang, and then we all sang. Sandy sat next to Rita and had a ball. I could easily see the transformation from September, only three months before.

Me in a Movie?

One night just before Christmas, we were celebrating the holiday season with a few friends over dinner in the Polo Lounge at the Beverly Hills Hotel on Sunset Boulevard. Arthur Seidelman leaned over to Sandy and asked, pointing at me, "Would he be interested in doing a movie?"

I could hear Sandy's raspy reply. "What about me?"

To which Arthur answered, "Next time, Sandy, next time."

Sandy said, "I don't know. Hadn't you better ask him?"

So he did, and I responded, "I thought you'd never ask."

Arthur giggled but I didn't know why. It was no joke; I meant it. He had seen me act years ago when he was starting out as a director as he sat in on my classes with Sandy. No matter, he finally did. Now all I had to do was show him I could. Even at that, he qualified his offer with, "They were planning on a semi-name, but he can't make it. So I'll arrange an audition for you with Eddie Murphy's people over at Paramount."

Eddie was the producer, Arthur was directing, and the story, entitled The Kid Who Loved Christmas, was written by W. Mark McClafferty and Clint Smith. Later I got the call from Arthur telling me the audition was all set for the next Saturday morning at Paramount. As I sped down the 101 that morning to my very first movie audition, Grace Kelly's screen test for Alfred Hitchcock came to mind. It had been shot around the time I was starting out and was the only one I had ever seen. I couldn't help but wonder: What if something like this had happened to me then, at that early stage of my career? What kind of life would I have had? How would it have turned out? I was now sixty-one. What difference did it make now? It was forty years too late. What had Sandy's assessment been all those many years ago? I wouldn't work until I was fifty? Well, he was wrong; he was eleven years off. That is, if I got this damn job in the first place. And always the unanswerable question festered in the back of my mind. Wasn't I good enough?

No matter what Sandy told me, I had doubts. It was no different even with some of his successful actors. Even Eli Wallach, with all his experience and exposure, when he was around Sandy, I could tell from his actions that he forever needed that reassurance. It was insatiable. And dear, dear Elizabeth Wilson, my lovely friend, was no different from Eli. It was an unending quest for assurance, never to be fulfilled. So as I took the exit ramp, I said to myself I guess I did because I got the job. They first asked me to tell them a little bit about myself. Well, first of all the character in the movie was Santa Claus so I told them I had been playing Santa for years, ever since 1970, for a bunch of little West Indian kids on a tropical island in the middle of the Caribbean. I told them I used to put on my red cheesecloth suit, that I had been the first see-through Santa of the '70s. That busted them up. Then I said I hadn't always looked like Santa, "I just grew-some" over the years. I felt as if I had them because in truth I did look like Santa now.

They handed me the script, and my little client, whom I was to play off, turned out to be a big fat black lady. I remembered Sandy saying, "Just work off the script." They thanked me and I left. I don't remember seeing Arthur there, but I no sooner got home and took off my coat than he called to tell me I had the part.

Right after New Year's, Boolu left for New York and we took off for Chicago. Boy! Was Boolu's nose out of joint! He couldn't fathom why I was doing Santa all alone. Hadn't he been my helper for the past twenty years? Finally we get a chance to be in a movie, and he's being sent back to the Picasso!

They were shooting in Marshall Field's department store while the Christmas decorations were still up. I took Sandy with me. We were put up in a lovely hotel. My first shot was at Marshall Field's with children lining up to sit on Santa's knee and talk to him while this little fellow is trying to jump the queue. I said to myself, forget this nonsense and get on with it; just go in there and give them hell.

Sandy sat in an alcove out of sight. When I finished with the shoot, I went out to find him talking to George and Val Rothschild. Val, as a graduate of the Playhouse, was now the Midwest's representative for the school. She had forfeited her acting career when she became the wife of George Rothschild. George had played a central figure after the Second World War as legal advisor for the Marshall Plan in Washington. He later moved to Chicago where he served on the bench for a number of years, becoming one of Chicago's outstanding and respected Circuit Court judges. They had heard we were in town and had taken time out of their busy day to stop around and see us. We all went out later to one of their favorite eateries and had a sumptuous meal.

The following day the shoot was taking place in a small Marshall Field's locker room. Sandy sat right where Arthur wanted him – up front just next to him and to the right of the camera. A sound mixer kept asking, "What's that noise I'm hearing?" No one knew where it was coming from, no one, that is, except me, but I wasn't about to speak up—like Philippe in Martinique, "Not my prob-bub-blem." The noise was coming from Sandy's stoma, a sound I was more familiar with than my own name.

At one point during a break, I said to Sandy, "I feel as if I'm not doing anything."

"Thank God, you don't have to do anything," Sandy answered. "You already are Santa Claus. Don't muck it up. Just be."

Gee, I thought, this is damned easy. What a way to earn a living.

Meanwhile back at the set, they were having trouble replacing Eddie Murphy in a little vignette. Apparently Eddie had a more pressing or engaging commitment that kept him from his little part at the end of the movie. He was to play the Angel Gabriel or Michael the Archangel, one of those guys who comes to earth as a taxi driver and saves the day. I called it the miracle in the Loop. They had tried to get Arsenio Hall, but he was busy with his TV Show. Then Michael Jackson's name was being kicked around, but the part must have been too small for him to bother with. Then, since the part could just as easily have been played by a woman, they got around to considering Whoopi Goldberg. When the powers-that-be back at Paramount saw the rushes of my scenes, they notified the production group in Chicago that they already had their Angel-Taxi Driver—in Santa. By this time I had already finished shooting and was home in Studio City. I got a call from Arthur telling me they wanted me back. I couldn't take Sandy this time because school was in session. So his former student and our travelling companion, Carl Johnson, stayed with him, and I made tracks for Chicago once again. It did change the story line just a tad, but they didn't have to change a line. The boy's line to me was, "You know, you look just like—" and I, as the taxi driver, stop him. You see, who the child saw could have been anyone, a known comic or even Santa himself. Some said it made more sense.

Since I was in Chicago alone with a weekend off, I thought it a good time to shoot up to Milwaukee to see my old friends from the Fred Miller Theatre days of the late '50s. Dardy Bauch and Susan Weber were still in town. I stayed with Dardy, her three kids, naturally, having long since flown the coop. We had a grand time reminiscing over a lovely brunch. Dardy said, "It isn't often an old gypsy comes back to check up on the ones they left behind."

On the last day of my shooting, as I was leaving the set, the writer came over to my trailer and said he wanted to thank me for making such a contribution to the story. Well, for an actor to hear that, what more did one have to hear? Oh, by the way, in the cast credits I got top billing over all the stars since credits were listed in alphabetical order. It didn't mean much in the grand scheme of things, but you can bet it sure did mean a hell of a lot to a sixty-one-year-old novice.

Moving the Bequia School to LA

That year, 1991, we decided to close the Bequia school. I felt it was getting to be too much for Sandy. Besides, each year the price was rising, and not because of Sandy. Every year airfares and hotel rates would go up. Even the prices of fruits and vegetables in the Harbour were hiked up just a little every year. In 1985, it had cost the students $1250 but by 1991 it was up to $2100.

So Sandy said, "That's it, finito. Acting students don't have that kind of money, and we aren't making anything out of the deal anyway. Why don't we do the school right here? There are actors all over the place here."

"Fine," I said, and then asked, "but when will we ever get to Bequia?"

"We can do just one month of intensive daily work in June and pick up the ones who are still interested in the full program in November. That will be our first-year group," Sandy suggested.

That arrangement gave us four solid months in Bequia, not including Christmas and New Year's. We started making plans and got the word out. To my surprise, students still applied from England, Hong Kong, Alaska, and Australia. I said to Sandy, "So much for poor actors who can't afford it."

"So much for the Garbo of acting teachers," was his retort.

I added, "Some actors are so egotistical, as if they're God's gift to the universe, that they expect it for nothing."

"That's true," Sandy agreed. "Actors are a breed apart. But bring them on. I can handle any one of them!"

I truly believed he could. When it came to actors, there were no flies on Sandy. Dr. Shah had contacted a doctor at St. Vincent Hospital in LA to look after Sandy, and we made monthly visits into town for check-ups. But he certainly wasn't the doctor that Jatin seemed to be. For some, if they were not your doctor, they had damned little time for compassion and understanding. They were like Phillippe back on Martinique with his slapping hands and "not my prob-bub-blem" attitude. There was a time when that type of doctor was rare, but today I fear they are becoming the norm and it's the compassionate doctors who are rare. I think it's a by-product of our society today... The three patients I have cared for—Sandy, Boolu, my sister Joan—and myself have all had long medical histories. Yet, of all the doctors who have tended to any of us over the years, I can come up with only twelve caring ones. A raft of others, well over forty, we could have done without. Twelve out of about fifty-two, I'm afraid that isn't a very healthy ratio. What is happening in this country?

Nor do I believe the humanitarian deterioration is confined to the medical profession. But what to do? I, for sure as hell, have no answer. I will tell you one damn thing. I'll always put my friends' needs and my own first and devil take the hindmost. If you don't take care of "Watachi," no one else is going to do it for you.

Sandy was living on liquids, soft foods, and the Jevity beverage. This diet kept him healthy. I don't know how satisfying it was, but I will tell you one thing—he never complained.

My Family's First Reunion

Classes progressed and come June '91 we had the first set of new students in the intensive class in Los Angeles. Since Easter, due to his diet Sandy had been having minor problems with digestion and periodic bouts of difficulty in swallowing. The decline was gradual, not even noticeable at first. The doctor at St. Vincent's Hospital in LA had him examined, not even bothering to do it himself, and sent us home with little satisfaction or assurance. When this intensive class was finished we were going home to the family reunion over the Fourth of July.

We didn't bother to say good-bye to our nonchalant doctor. We took off for Sloan-Kettering and Dr. Shah in New York, and the LA doctor was never seen again. From LAX we flew east to an air hub in Pennsylvania and transferred to Syracuse where my brother Ed picked us up. Rusty Ford put Boolu on an Amtrak train at Perm Station for Utica hoping he would remember Albany, Schenectady, Amsterdam, and then Utica where he should get off. He did. He went out to the street and grabbed a cab for Shaw Street, where he remembered which house to get off at. Thank God the street was only two blocks long.

We stayed at the Holiday Inn on Burrstone Road with the out-of-towners. De tree a we bunked up in a large room with two queen-size beds, overlooking the gateway to the Adirondacks. We had a view from the southwest elbow of Utica across the beautiful Mohawk Valley to the north country as we waited for what Mom called "The Grand Union."

It was the Carville clan's first reunion, and, little did we know, Dad's last. It was held up on Paris Hill in Sherrill Brook Park on New Paris Road beyond New Hartford overlooking the lush green hills of home. The site was up above the bend of the Mohawk Valley where Utica is situated and where the Mohawk River veers northwest to Rome and the Delta Dam and where the Genesee Indian Trail, now Route 5, leads off to the southwest on its way to Syracuse.

All the grandchildren were there, all thirty-six counting Boolu. Ball games were played. Ed and Mark, Beth's husband, tended the bar and grill while Mandy and the sisters-in-law tended to the food. What seemed like hoards of small great-grandchildren swung in swings and slid down shooter chutes, while others played group games led by Mandy's daughter, Chrissie. Fred's daughter, Beth, organized the Irish dancing and songfest. It was interesting to me to see the second generation handing down the various songs and dances to the third generation, as we had done to them. I could see that it touched my dad deeply, that it warmed the cockles of his heart as they say back in the Old Country, just to see the great-grandchildren stepping out as his children had done when we were kids back in the '30s.

Sandy asked, "When did we see all this last? Was it back in '79? And they're still going at it, only now there are tons more of them!"

Boolu was having the time of his life. He loved a fete no matter where it was. It was a great turnout, the biggest ever. Mom couldn't have been more pleased. All she ever wanted in life was that we stay together as a family. When I mentioned that to Sandy, he said, "Well, this has got to be a red-letter day in her life."

An Easy Fix

When we reached New York after the reunion, we went right to Sloan-Kettering and Dr. Shah. I told Sandy Bequia was out of the picture until this matter of his swallowing was faced. All I could think of was more cancer but I said nothing. I worried about the strong possibility we had waited too long in the first place back in '90. By now we knew the big secret with cancer was early detection. The big question in my mind was: Did we goof?

To my relief, Dr. Shah reassured us there was no recurrence. The esophageal tube he had made for Sandy was caving in on itself periodically and causing a blockage. He ordered a bed for the next day and was waiting and ready for Sandy that morning. He rectified the problem by inserting a flexible plastic tube the length of the esophagus inside the collapsing flesh tube. The tube was held in place by a strong black thread fastened to the top of the plastic tube and running up the back wall of Sandy's throat on through his nasal passage where it was tied to the base of his right nostril. If one looked closely enough, one could see it. Thus the passageway would be kept open. Well, all I could say for it was that it worked, and Sandy was eating again.

Boolu held 58th Street together, cooking for me while I spent every minute with Sandy in the hospital. It was wonderful being together again but all too short. Sandy's operation wasn't a complicated procedure and he was out and ready for Bequia in a flash. We had planned to get there in time to celebrate my birthday on July 28. We were able to stay in Bequia for only a little more than a week because we were expected in Washington for a big four-day do. Then we would finally return to Bequia with nothing to do but be with each other.

37 Bonbons

The Big Washington Surprise

T he previous winter, Dick Dunn had approached us with an idea one of his acting clients had come up with. Tim Wead revered Sandy and his work. His brother Doug happened to be the writer of Man of Integrity, a book about George Bush, Sr. He had also been active in Washington for the past ten years or more working, among other things, with Pat Boone, who had studied with Sandy, and the Washington Humanitarian Awards Committee. Tim wanted to know if Sandy would give him permission to present his name to his brother Doug and to Pat Boone in Washington. Sandy's reaction to all this was a simple, "Why?"

"Come on, Sandy," Dick said, "you're always doing things for people. Why not you? I told Tim all the things you're doing in Bequia and all about your work up in Harlem when it was burning."

Sandy looked at me, and one look told him I agreed with Dick. "Dick is right," I said. "Why not you?"

Sandy knew me well enough to know that if Dick had me on his side, what choice did he have? He knew he wouldn't have a moment's peace if he didn't go along with it. I knew how Sandy felt about Washington and its self-serving politicians. To them Sandy was a nobody, but the powers that be were well aware that Sandy's draw was powerful. With Sandy's patronage, the Eye Center at Duke University had attracted celebrities from Broadway to Hollywood. The Washington people, I am sure, knew they could fill the place with names if Sandy were involved. They were just using him. That was the way these things worked. So what? I thought.

The long and short of it all was Sandy agreed to go along with it, for what it was worth. That summer I was contacted by the Washington committee wanting me to arrange a few letters from influential Vincentians. I also sent along a complete list of Sandy's philanthropic contributions over the years. I listed everything starting with Harlem and continuing with the Deaf School held in his home for eight years that had developed into the Sunshine School for all handicapped children of the Island, with its beautiful building donated by Japan. On the list I included his teaching the slow students at the high school and playing the organ for the Music Department. He was also sponsoring poor students and making contributions to the students' fund. He had paid my salary and the total expense of the Music Department for ten years. Aside from Bequia, during his months in America, Mort and Sydelle Engel, fund-raisers for Dr. Robert Machemer and his Duke University Eye Center, had Sandy serve for five years as the celebrity fund-raiser at their annual art auctions. Sandy had also adopted a foster child, an abandoned twelve-year-old deaf mute. And, lest it be forgotten, I also mentioned the multitude of actors he had helped over the years.

His Excellency, Bishop Woodroff, then Archbishop of the Windward Islands, and the Right Honourable James F. Mitchell, then Prime Minister of St. Vincent and the Grenadines, both wrote inspiring letters. The following is the Bishop's glowing tribute to Sandy:

The Most Rev. G.C.M. Woodroff, K.B.E.D.D.M.A.

Murray's Road St. Vincent, W. I.

Mr. President, Honorary Co-Chairmen, Members of the Washington Charity Awards Dinner,

I am very honoured, and I count it a priceless privilege, to have been asked to write in support of the award which is to be bestowed upon Mr. Meisner, the Presidential Public Service Award, in recognition of the work with the disabled and the establishment of an acting school in Harlem, New York. The successes and the attainments of his pupils and protégés are testimony enough of the painstaking work of the man, and painstaking is a very relevant word in this context. Mr. Meisner has lived long with pain and physical suffering. Through it all he has been able to rise up and through and above much painful discomfort, which would have made many a lesser man to say, "I can do no more." Not so for him. He has in spite of gnawing illness and protracted pain continued with his work of assisting the well and the strong, as well as the weak and the disabled, so that all that come within his orbit left him feeling better and more fitted and able to measure up to the challenges which would face them upon their individual life's way. Let us take Boolu (a nick-name), born 30 years ago, a child born in the most arduous of circumstances of a mother who 'labored' over 72 hours. This inevitably left 'Boolu' somewhat disabled. He was taken in by Mr. Meisner as an almost completely deaf mute. Meisner's knowledge and experience gained in Harlem were immediately brought to bear upon 'Boolu.' The success of the earnest work on the growing young boy and man was so impressively successful that many other cases on the tiny Islands of the Grenadines were brought to the home of this pioneering man and as a result his name is now a household word on the island. To meet 'Boolu' and to 'speak' with 'Boolu' will provide sufficient testimony to support this award to Mr. Meisner. And Mr. President, this is one young man who truly knows the meaning of 'Read my lips.'

In tiny Bequia, Mr. Meisner, with the assistance of Mr. Jimmy Carville and their unique talents, took over the music department of the newly established school and in a matter of months they produced *Jesus Christ Superstar*, which I had the privilege of seeing in London and on 'screen.' That performance in Bequia... should I just simply say measured up very creditably. After I had seen this performance, I asked them what they thought they could do to celebrate the Centennial of the Dioceses of the Windward Islands in 1977. Within a few hours they offered to do a rendition of Mozart's *Requiem*. In a country with no orchestra at all and no professional singers, this seemed quite impossible. And yet with the *Jesus Christ Superstar* chorus as a base and with the odd violinist taken from here and there and members of the Police Brass Band together with Mr. Meisner on a small electronic organ, the KINGSTOWN Orchestral Ensemble was formed with Jimmy Carville conducting. We and our guests in the celebration of the Centennial in our Cathedral had a most memorable, stimulating, and uplifting experience. The work was well and beautifully performed not only at home but on other islands of the Grenadines and as far away as Grenada. Bearing testimony to Mr. Meisner's true worth and when I further hear and read he is to be numbered among such greats, it makes me glad to know that I am among these who know him and admire him and bless GOD for his life and work among us.

Retired Archbishop of the West Indies and
Bishop of the Windward Islands.
28 June 1991

Eventually, the official letter came informing Sandy that he was the recipient of the Presidential Public Service Award being presented at the White House in July. They enumerated the other awards being presented at the same time such as the Senatorial Award, the Congressional Award, the Judicial and whatnot awards. The list went on and on. They were not leaving anyone or anything out. It read like the Academy Awards of Philanthropy, as if philanthropy permeated this grand land of ours. This awards practice had been going on since the Reagan years. It was obvious to anyone who cared to scrutinize all the hoopla that it played right into the Republican's notion of self-help and less government "interference." What none of them knew was that Sandy was doing what he felt governments should be doing in the first place. Since they weren't, someone had to do it.

I couldn't help but think, wouldn't it be wonderful if everyone were like Sandy, including governments? What a wonderful world this would be. As far as I was concerned, it wasn't about ideology. It was about Sandy's being appreciated for the man he was.

Apparently the awards presentation was the largest social function held in the Capitol in those years, second only to a presidential inauguration. Our tickets arrived from Washington, and we packed for the quick four-day sojourn. But we were minus evening clothes. Fortunately, Boolu was coming down from New York, and with the help of Pat Field, Boolu got outfitted around the corner on Third Avenue and 56th Street. We sent our measurements to Pat as well, and she and Boolu brought our duds down to Washington when they came.

At the time, Pat Field was putting together a documentary treatment on Boolu and she asked me to try to get permission for her to shoot Boolu through this whole process from his point of view. The committee got back to me and asked if she would come and shoot the whole process for them. She was more than willing to do so. Boolu, Pat, and the evening clothes flew down to Dulles Airport and stayed at our hotel with us.

Sandy, Boolu, Mary Steenburgen, Robert Duvall

The first night, July 29, was a cocktail party. It was small and exclusive, but Boolu worked that joint like a pro. He knew a lot of the actors' faces from TV, and he wasn't shy about going up to them and telling them so. Even I didn't know half the names, like Mike Talbott from Miami Vice who was one of Boolu's heroes. Bobby Duvall and Johnny Cash were there, a bonanza to Boolu. He walked right up to them, and God knows what he said to them. They all took the time to talk to him. Once I spotted him talking to one of the little old rich ladies who was there because of her generosity.

At one point, Boolu walked up to Sandy and me with a tall, lusciously beautiful black woman and said, "These are my friends, Sandy and Jimmy." Altovise politely introduced herself. She was none other than Mrs. Sammy Davis, Jr., herself. Sandy talked a bit to her about Sammy for he knew him and had once had him speak to the students at the Playhouse.

The next day, thanks to Bill Anton, Mrs. John Sununu hosted a luncheon at his Anton 1201 Club. Pat Boone, co-founder of the Washington Charity Awards Dinner, was master of ceremonies. He introduced Christopher Lloyd, a former student of Sandy's, who sang Sandy's praises. That evening was the big bash, a dinner and auction emceed by Doug Wead at the Washington Hilton Hotel where the ten honorees had their various awards bestowed on them.

Sandy's was the Presidential Public Service Award. As far as I could tell with my plebeian eye, everyone in Washington was there. Boolu sat with Dick Dunn and Rosemary Edelman and Tim Wead and his wife at a table down front right below the dais, where all the swells were sitting so they would be seen. Oliver North was sitting up there bigger than life. His presence didn't make Sandy's Hollywood liberal friends, especially Diane Ladd, any too happy. We were sitting up stage center with the lovely Gwen Verdon. Various well-known people spoke of the recipients and their contributions to the humanities. Then Coretta Scott King, last year's Humanitarian of the Year, presented to Mrs. Altovise Davis, Sammy's widow, a posthumous award for Sammy. Then Mary Steenburgen spoke of Sandy's work in

Sandy, Boolu, Jamie Brown (*Sister 2 Sister* mag) & Jimmy

Harlem and at Duke University and his contribution to the American theater and the film industry. After Mary, Bobby Duvall spoke of all Sandy's work on Bequia and at the end he briefly told Boolu's story, recounting how Sandy had taken Boolu into his home. Bobby had Boolu stand up to take a bow.

Finally, the surprise of the evening for us occurred. Doug Wead announced that each year at the Washington Charity Awards Dinner, an individual is honored from either the public or private sector for his or her outstanding charitable work. He proclaimed the recipient of the Presidential Public Service Award, Sanford Meisner, as this year's recipient of the 1991 Humanitarian of the Year! "The Washington Charity Awards Committee is proud to bestow on you the title '1991 Humanitarian of the Year.' With the acceptance of this award you will be joining a long list of other outstanding Americans..." The list consisted of luminaries such as Bob Hope, Candy Lightner, and Coretta Scott King, along with three past Presidents and five First Ladies. In that group were President Gerald Ford, President Jimmy Carter, President Ronald Reagan, and their wives, Betty Ford, Rosalyn Carter, and Nancy Reagan, as well as Lady Bird Johnson and Barbara Bush.

What a surprise that award was! Neither of us had any idea. No one knew in advance except the committee, just like the Academy Awards in Hollywood. The name was announced and there was Johnny Cash with the award in his hand and June Carter Cash next to him at the mike. They both turned around, looking up at us on the stage.

Sandy turned to me and asked, "What do I do?"

"You go down and get it."

"Not without you."

"Come on, let me help you." And down we went to the center podium where Mary Steenburgen, Bobby Duvall, and June Carter were standing behind the mike, with Johnny holding out the award to Sandy.

Sandy said, quietly but clearly into the mike, "This is the first time in my life I am…" he paused "…I have stage fright. Thank you, thank you very much."

When Boolu saw Johnny hand Sandy the award, he jumped from his seat down on the main floor. Dick Dunn grabbed at his coattail to stop him, but Booly broke free and made a beeline for the stage. When he reached Sandy, you could hear June over the mike say, "Give him a hug, Boolu." Both embraced and kissed, and everyone in the banquet hall, all of whom had been applauding until now, went wild. Tears aplenty were shed. What a night!

Boolu subsequently experienced his own little fifteen minutes of fame. At the end of the festivities, a dazzlingly lovely young woman, bedecked in sparkling jewels, came up to him and asked him to sign her program. She introduced herself as Jamie Brown, publisher of the Washington-based magazine Sister 2 Sister, which covered national Black news. She asked Boolu if he would pose for the magazine with her. Boolu asked, "De tree a we?" And we did. In the article, she wrote:

Julian could neither speak nor hear when Sandy found him. Julian is from the West Indies. Now Julian talks and writes and everything's in good working order, including his glands. As he and I talked, he made sure I knew he was single… and a real Mr. Fresh-hips, he was!

The next morning we were herded into limos and driven to the White House. There we had our credentials checked before being directed to the Indian Room in the Old Executive Office Building just to the right of the White House and across the street. We had breakfast in those beautiful, famous chambers after which we were taken to the briefing room. I got a kick out of Boolu managing the first seat in the front row. We all sat and listened for about an hour to the rather good-looking young Senator from Buffalo, Jack Kemp, and some of his Republican rhetoric, which certainly didn't take Sandy and me by surprise, and then we all dispersed.

At this point a White House staffer, a lovely young lady, a forerunner of Monica Lewinsky one might say, invited Sandy, Boolu, and me to follow her. Out of the Old Executive Office Building and back across the street, she led us… It was a roundabout way down to the lower level of the White House from the outside. We were told we would get to meet the President shortly. Time passed and no President. The staffer came back to explain he had been unexpectedly held up—he was off his schedule because some dignitary from Africa was late.

More time passed and she returned a second time. She was terribly sorry, but the

Roddy McDowell, Sandy, Mary Steenburgen in Indian Room

President was running late now and would unfortunately have to cancel. She then added, "The dining room is open. Would you join Senator Kemp and some other senators for lunch?" That was fine by us. We never did get to meet Bush Sr.

We had been told that some of our morning party would be escorted through the open section of the White House that afternoon. Later they arrived, Pat and some of Sandy's actor friends and others. We met them in the main entrance hall.

Pat said, "My God! What happened to you three? We all thought you were lost somewhere in the archives of that labyrinthine old building." It was a huge barn of a place from another time though the brass was still highly polished and the white marble was spic and span. Long corridors led to other corridors.

"No," I told Pat. "The Secret Service did a check on us and found out we were liberals."

The minute Boolu walked into the Lincoln Room, leading the group, he approached the famous painting on the wall, exclaiming, "I knowed him! I teed him in Disneyland." Everyone broke up. Pat kept filming him as he roamed around the place on through the Yellow Room. She got some great shots of de tree a we as we left the White House and strolled down the walk to the north gate, with Boolu saying, "Now Boolu's been to de White House wit my bran new teet." Pat had taken him to the dentist just before they had left New York for Washington.

It was four o'clock as we checked out at the gate where the limo was waiting to swish us off to the hotel. I remember telling Sandy I could easily get used to these limos. "Well, who couldn't or wouldn't?" Sandy said.

Bone Idyll on Bequia

Pat, Boolu, Sandy, and I parted company the next morning; they back to New York and we on down to Bequia. It was August 1, 1991, as I settled in my seat on the junket to Barbados next to the "American Humanitarian of the Year." I must say I was pleased and proud as a peacock to be sitting next to him.

"Now that wasn't half bad, was it?" I asked.

He grudgingly admitted, "No, it wasn't, it was nice."

"Well, I know it wasn't an Academy Award but—"

He interrupted me, "Are you for real? Have you gone completely bonkers? Why, Jimmy, this beats that hands down. An Academy Award could never mean this. This is in a totally different league. I'm still overwhelmed, and, I must tell ya, more than a bit perplexed by it all." Our life together on Bequia turned out to be nothing like in '84 when we damned near killed each other. We were both older and wiser, I hoped. Sandy was eighty-six, and I was sixty-two and ready to try on the yoke of retirement.

We embarked on the task of building up Sandy's strength and getting a little more meat on his bones. I had time to cook and messed around in the kitchen with our new cook Aggie Barber now and again. I loved cooking and had spent a lot of time cracking open Fannie Farmer for everyday cuisine and Larousse Gastronomique on special occasions. Except on Bequia in the summer, special occasions were few and far between.

I also started a 9'x12' solid, off-white rug using a bargello stitch and copying patterns from a pillow and multiplying them many times over. Years before, in the seventies, Sandy and I had both done needlework. He did most of it sitting around waiting for me as I worked with the kids at the school. Sandy's efforts had come to a screeching halt when his eyesight faltered. Rosie Grier, the football great, used to do his needlework at Moon Hole on Bequia, but he's gone now—from Bequia that is.

That summer, I had plenty to keep me busy. Sandy would sit out on the terrace and kibitz with me while my hands stayed busy. What we had both gained by now was peace of mind, and what a gift that was. Mom and Pop had it. I remember them vividly out there on the farm. Now, like my parents, Sandy and I could just sit and enjoy each other's presence. One could say we had arrived. When you are in a state of nirvana, time flies. That's not a cliché, it really does. And this summer, it did.

Tri-coastal

In the fall, we left Bequia again early enough to have time with Boolu and take him on another trip to Utica before we went back to the Coast. Pop was really getting up there. He hadn't been looking that good at the reunion, so we felt it behooved us to spend a little time with the family whenever possible. When we arrived everyone was full of the news of Washington. They had all seen it on CNN and were so pleased for and proud of Sandy. I could not come home enough as far as Joany was concerned. I knew she missed our days together down on Bequia as much as I did. Boolu loved being up there with all the cousins whom he called his white family. He had met and gotten to know them all over the years, since his first visit in '73 when he was seventeen. Sandy could sit and talk with my mother by the hour. They enjoyed each other's company. All in all it was a pleasant trip, but it came time to drop Boolu off in New York and hightail it back to Studio City and the classes.

"That's right," Sandy said. "Somebody has to pay the piper."

"Very funny, very funny," I said. "You stop teaching and we all go to the poor house."

School was spinning along like a top, Sandy, energy up and at it, relentlessly teaching nonstop. It went smooth and breezy though with speech somewhat wheezy, I stayed by to clarify so nothing need impede, and it went easy.

His days they were of rest and of caution, 'neath the glorious sun all awash in. Out back he reclined mid roses entwined, and these, the days also mine, we got lost in. Still frail and physically weak, his mind secure never scattered. Sitting so quiet and meek, he was saving for class where it mattered. While there he would peak so strong it was sleek. What a sneak!

That Christmas of '91, Sandy was in no condition to go to Bequia. No quick-down-and-turn-around, if he were going to continue teaching as he wanted to. He had to pace himself. Boolu was missing us and wanted us to come back to cold New York, but New York was even more out of the question. Instead, we could stay right in LA and have Boolu come out again. That was the plan, until brother Leo called and invited us down to Houston to spend Christmas with him and Barbara and the family. We had been hanging around the house and going back and forth to class. The class and the backyard were all Sandy could handle. Yet Houston sounded inviting to both of us. But getting on and off planes at the height of the season was just as bad as going to Bequia.

So Sandy said, "If you drive, all I would have to do is sit in the front seat."

"Sandy!" I said, "Oh, sure. That's all the way across the southwest. I haven't driven that far since I went to Gadsden, Alabama, to drive my old girlfriend Sarah Harbin's car back to New York because her father wouldn't let her do it all alone. That was back in '53 when I didn't even have a license. That was a long time ago."

"No matter. I'll be riding shotgun," quipped Sandy.

"So you mean it? Do you feel up to it? We could have Booly fly to Houston," I went on.

"He'd get a kick out of seeing Leo and spending time with Eric and Gary. God, I hope I'm up to it."

"I can do that, you know. Ride shotgun, I mean. You'll have to give the car a good going over at the garage," Sandy continued, "and have all the tires checked."

"You know," I said, "it's this diesel thing. Not every gas station has it. We'd be in a hell of a fix if we ran dry out there in the open west in the middle of winter."

Sandy thought differently. "Out there on the highway, with all that truck traffic, those gas stations will all have diesel. Just don't let it run low—you stop every 400 miles."

Boolu went ape when we phoned to tell him, speaking through his sister Sherry. I went to the AAA, got some maps, and had a route plan made up. We were taking the Interstate 10 all the way. I picked Sedona as our first overnighter.

The Red Red Rocks of Sedona

Sedona had its own particular western charm, not so much cowboy as earlier, ancient, and Indian. As we neared the town, colossal red rock mountains appeared all around, big and overwhelming. "This is so beautiful. And it's better than a museum. At least I can see them," Sandy remarked.

Yes, I thought, Sandy's museum days are over, as well as his reading and TV watching. He would just sit in front of the set with his eyes closed resting them and listening as one did to a radio. Remember, for vision he had only one eye, and you couldn't call it a good one. He had a touch of glaucoma now as well as the two scars from the torn retina repairs. Along with all that, he had always been nearsighted. One could say in spite of his retinal tears, with students he could induce tears. Only I and his eye doctor knew he had problems. And Sandy and I never discussed it, not even when he knocked something over.

"How do you handle the poor vision in class?" I asked him once.

"Oh," he said, "I know I don't see half of what happens in class, but let me tell you, my hearing has become so acute that I can tell where the student is emotionally by the sound of their voice and what they say and how they say it. It seems even clearer to me now. What I saw in class before was a bit of a distraction, I think. And since sound cannot be so easily disguised... Does that make sense?" Whatever the case, sense or not, he was calling the shots right on in class, and the students were the first to recognize it.

In Sedona, we stayed in a lovely cabin with a fireplace next to a babbling brook. Sandy said, "Too bad we weren't getting married. This would make an ideal honeymoon suite."

The restaurant was famous for its cuisine, and dinner was fabulous. Well, for me it was. Sandy always had to be cautious. The next morning we drove around the beautiful environs of Sedona. Million dollar homes aplenty were scattered about. In every direction, the vistas were breathtaking, even for Sandy with his bad eye. At one point we were driving up the side of a cliff on an old dirt road. Before we realized it, we were in snow here and there, and in more the higher we went. To add to my problem, the road was getting narrower and narrower. Still more worrisome, I didn't have snow tires. Between bated breaths I spotted a small indentation in the side of the cliff.

"I might turn around here. That is, if I don't get stuck in the snow or a soft shoulder." Then I added, "Forget that, it's too cold for a soft anything."

Sandy joked, "That's quite a statement. I wouldn't be too sure about that."

I stopped the car, left it in gear, and went out to test the snow in the indentation. Thanks for small favors, it wasn't deep, just a light cover. I got back in and inched up ahead just enough to be able to back in. Now I had to make the turn sharp enough to head back. No way. I couldn't do it in one try. The car was a big four-door sedan. I was grateful the clay ground was hard. In fact it was solid rock, and I was able to turn around in two tries. Once I had made it, I started laughing.

"What's wrong with you?" Sandy asked.

"Sandy, we're always getting ourselves into these predicaments."

"Not me, kiddo. I'm just along for the ride," he retorted.

37 Bonbons

"Well," I lobbed back, "if we went over, we would both go over."

"Oh, will ya shut up and get us down off here?"

I looked down across a clearing to our right. A rather large crowd was mingling around a big open fire-pit. Now, I knew this place was compared to the Bermuda Triangle with all its mysterious magnetic pulls. Why, the ancients had been coming here for eons to hold powwow—like gatherings because of its spiritual power. Could this gathering have anything to do with that, I wondered. I stopped the car.

"Now what?" asked Sandy.

"I'll be just a minute. Keep the door closed." Without waiting for an answer, I took off down through the gutter out onto the flat where I had spotted the people. A sizable crowd was gathering. As I was the last to arrive, I asked the first person I came to, "What's up?"

"We're gathering like the Indians used to, to invoke the spirits," she explained.

One man stood in the center with a woman near the charcoal ashes of the fire. He was speaking out, asking everyone to form a large circle around the sacred spot and join hands. Everyone did, including me. Then he asked, "As we progress around the circle counterclockwise, speak out your name and tell us where you're from."

Now, there I was standing in the circle with everyone else, with my full white beard and long, curly white hair, wearing my leather taxicab jacket, a red and white silk scarf unfurling and twisting in the breeze. It was December 22, don't forget. One by one around the large circle, everyone called out their names.

When they got to me, I said, "I'm Santa Claus, old Saint Nick, and I'm from the North Pole. I just stopped by to wish you all, each and every one of you, a merry, merry Christmas. I'm sorry I won't be able to stay. I have a couple of very busy days ahead of me. Merry Christmas!" I yelled as I took off across the flat.

I could hear them yelling back "Merry Christmas, Santa," amid whistles and cheers as I made my way through the thicket and down into the gutter out of sight.

When I got back to the car and took off, Sandy asked, "What was that all about?"

"You wouldn't believe me if I told you."

"Try me," he insisted. When I finally did, he said, "I think you are certifiable."

That night, after another memorable dinner, for me anyway, we went to the shopping mall. It was heavily designed to create a Mexican-southwest ambiance. With all the Christmas decorations and the Latinos in their native dress dancing and singing carols in Spanish, it couldn't have been more festive. We ran into some of the mountain people who all greeted me with a hearty, "Hello, Santa!"

Sandy said, "This is worse than Bequia. I can't escape it."

Along the Rio Grande

We were up early and on to the outskirts of Phoenix, Arizona, where I got a speeding ticket attempting to pass a truck. At one gas station outside El Paso, I went into the convenience store to buy some snacks and drinks and inadvertently left my card case on the counter. We drove on to Van Horn in Texas, the first fair-sized town after El Paso on the Rio Grande, where we were staying overnight and where I discovered my card case was missing. I immediately went to the police to report it. I could stop my charge cards, but driving without a license was another matter. In recounting what had happened, I couldn't even tell them the name of the little town except that it was near an army base.

"Your name Carville?" the police officer asked.

"Yes."

"You're from Los Angeles with a California license, but you used to have a New York one once, right? We just got a brand new scanner, a tracker, so we know all about you. The police in Sierra Blanca just called us and told us they have your cards. We'll have them here for you tomorrow morning."

"Thank you. Thank you a hell of a lot!"

"Don't mention it, buddy. See ya. Merry Christmas!" he said, waving as we walked out the door.

"The luck of the Irish," Sandy muttered.

The next day we drove on through Lyndon B. Johnson country and headed to Austin, which we took time to drive around. We had an early lunch and gassed up before shooting southeast to Houston. We made Houston in time to get to the airport for Boolu, but Leo insisted we catch a few zzzz's and went to pick up Boolu himself instead. He said he wanted us both in good shape for the festivities that night.

The whole family gathered there for Christmas Eve, all four children and their families, plus the Andrews family, Barbara's mom, dad, and sister. It was great seeing the whole Houston contingent after such a long hiatus. After Christmas we went on to Galveston and stayed in a condo situated right on the beach owned by a friend of Leo's. It would have been more fun if it hadn't been so cold and damp, but we bundled up and walked along the seawall anyway.

Carville, New Orleans, and Bayous of Louisiana

After a few days' rest, we repacked the car and de tree a we took off for Carville, Louisiana, just thirty miles south of Baton Rouge on the banks of the old Mississippi. We went to the National Leper Colony, which had been established in a lovely antebellum mansion on a riverside plantation after the Civil War. We inquired about the Carvilles and were told one of the aunts lived just

37 Bonbons

down the road. But no one was home when we got there.

The town consisted of one small grocery store. There they told me James Carville's mother (James Carville of the Clinton years in Washington) lived a few miles farther along. I wish I could have taken the time to find her. We still had to get on into New Orleans and find a hotel, so we just pushed on. We drove down through the French Quarter right in the middle of the holiday season and we found a room in the first hotel we stopped at, a nice hotel right on Bourbon Street. They parked our car for us, and we settled in. We didn't do much and we hadn't planned to, just roamed about and did a little people-watching. We found a couple of good restaurants, including Brennan's, which both Sandy and I had been to before. Sandy was a good sport about it. He would always say, "I'm just along for the ride" and find something he could manage to eat.

I had been to New Orleans many times in the '50s and early-60s with my theatrical road trips. It hadn't changed much. I looked at this trip as part of Booly's education. He was enjoying every minute of it. We walked all around, taking our time of course, into St. Louis Cathedral and across Jackson Square to the trolley ride, a first for Boolu and a trip down memory lane for Sandy and me. My first trolley ride had been down Lenox Ave in 1934.

Sandy said, "I don't remember my first, but my last was across 42nd Street before they tore up the tracks."

We didn't do anything spectacular, but it was an activity as a family and that was good for de tree a we.

I decided to head back to Galveston via the scenic route through some of the bayou country along the coast. The first part of the trip went fine, but as we went through miles of bull rushes where towns became fewer and farther between, it became a little too isolated for comfort. At one point I felt I needed to get a better lay of the land, the maps not proving of much use to us anymore. We pulled up to a gas station, a store-and-bar combo. When I got out of the car, I noticed a couple of skinheads dressed in military gear staring into the windows of the Mercedes at Black Boolu and Meisner in the front seat. Instantly, I realized we could be in trouble. Farther on was a pickup truck and as I passed it by, I noticed four more skinheads. I kept heading for the store and as I gazed into the window of the bar, I could see that the clientele in there didn't look any different.

This was no place for the likes of us. We were in the middle of white supremacy country. I just knew it. Though they were Cajun, they were not the type we should be messing with. Why, if we got pulled over for the slightest infraction, we would be—there was no other way to say it—in deep shit! What a bonanza we would be for them. It would be like hitting three cherries on a slot machine: one black, one Jew, and one gay.

When I reached the door of the store, I stopped, turned around, and headed straight back to the car. I got in without a word, turned on the ignition, and drove away, not farther down the coast—we might have wound up in a cul-de-sac down there—but inland.

Up the road, after checking the rearview mirror many times for anyone following us, I said, "We damn near walked into a hornet's nest back there."

Skidding Eyes

I turned left on I-10 heading west on a more heavily traveled road that led to the high bridge connecting Louisiana and Texas. As we crossed the bridge, we spotted two signs, one to Houston and the other to Galveston. I thought Galveston would be more direct and quicker, which it was but… What a "but" it turned out to be! It was getting late, and it was dark and clouding over. Again the road was sparsely traveled, well, at that time of day it was. Sandy said, "What! Doesn't anyone travel at night around here?"

The road was wide; it was a freeway with no cars. I was going along at quite a clip, which was my wont, until a huge roadblock sprang up without warning. Obviously I had missed the advance warnings. I veered to the left onto some makeshift road, careening too far off to the right and skidding off the shoulder. I managed to keep the car upright and steer back onto the road. I stopped the car, shook up.

"What's the hurry, Speedy Gonzalez?" Sandy wisecracked.

He wasn't a backseat driver, not ever. (I couldn't say the same for Boolu. He could drive any driver nuts with his "Red light stop, green light go," and the one that really got to me, "Yellow slow down. Dat's a red light. Jimmy, you went tru a red light.") What the boys didn't know, and I didn't tell them, was that my eyes were giving me trouble. The reason we had that little mishap was I didn't see it coming. I was going too fast and my vision was bouncing up and down like a TV picture with the vertical gone haywire. It was also really dark. You can bet I slowed down to a snail's pace after that scare. But at the time, I figured I must just be tired and had better take it easy.

The road was desolate, but every now and again we would come upon a humongous oil refinery, every one of them lit up like a Christmas tree although no people appeared to be around. It started to drizzle. Inching along in this godforsaken landscape, I thought, what more can happen? Then I spotted a light, an open gas station with a little store, thank God. We filled the gas tank; Sandy had been right about most gas stations on the open road around here being diesel-ready. We got some munchies and a microwave soup for Sandy. The attendant told us the road led right to the ferry to Galveston across the bay and that the ferry ran all night. With the condition my eyes were in, it wasn't easy, but we did eventually make our way through town to the ferry. What a welcome sight for sore eyes, or should I say slippery eyes? I was so tired. I was one weary, relieved traveler!

After waving goodbye to the Carville family in Houston, Sandy and I took off for Dallas. We were going back on I-40, the northern route through Albuquerque. Leo would take Boolu up to Dallas to visit with his sisters and mother and then see him off on the plane for Kennedy. We hit cold weather up on 40 and had difficulty starting in the mornings. I didn't like cold weather but I didn't know diesel-driven Mercedes didn't like it either. Our points needed cleaning, aligning, or whatever, and, we were told, in this weather we needed a little electric heater. It fit under the hood and could be plugged in if the car were to be out all night and not in a heated garage. We picked a motel where we could drive the car up next to the room and run the extension cord through a crack in the window to an outlet inside. It worked. As a matter a fact the whole damn car behaved a hell of a lot better from then on.

After that everything went fine until we reached Albuquerque and turned north up the I-25, the Turquoise Trail to Mount Taylor and Santa Fe. We were en route to see the "Miraculous Stair Case" at the Loretto Chapel and to pay a surprise visit to Molly Burk, my old friend from Bequia, who was now living up there, painting up a storm. It started snowing heavily and me with no snow tires and no snow-driving experience and my eyes acting up a little. I did the only thing I could do, save stop altogether. I did an about-turn and went back down to Albuquerque, forced to bypass Molly and my spiritual staircase.

We forged on west through Apache Country, then hooked a left onto 117, the Black Canyon Freeway heading south to Phoenix, hoping to get out of snow country. I remember going down a slippery hill so steep that it had run-offs for trucks should they experience brake trouble. I had seen them before but never until that day was I glad to see them. Believe you me, I was all set to use one if we had to. At the bottom of the hill was the turnoff to Sedona. We had never expected to be back so soon, but we stayed at the same fine "honeymoon" hotel again. The following morning we drove toward Phoenix and caught the 110 West to LA, crossing over the Colorado River and into California at Blythe. My eyes were behaving themselves, and with no snow down here, I was tempted to hit ninety miles an hour every now and again. A big Mercedes can do that without letting you feel it.

Everything was uneventful until we reached the outskirts of LA, and I mean way out near the I-15 leading north to Barstow and Big Bear at San Bernardino. Here the traffic started to back up, crawling more slowly than a snail's pace. It was stop and start, or crawl and creep, with Sandy asleep all the way into Glendale. That was tiring. But, I repeat, the eyes held up. "Danks, God."

As we drove into the driveway on Bellingham, I asked Sandy, "Well, how was that, me bronco? You must be pretty enervated?"

"Not so, me bucko. It was invigorating, very invigorating."

38 Hanging by a Thread

1992: Stars in my Eyes, and not Because of the Movies

One evening shortly after the holiday break, we rushed home after class at 6 PM so I could prepare a little dinner party. There would be four of us: Arthur Seidelman, Richard Alfieri, Sandy, and me; and that was it. I was fixing a vegetarian meal for the guests for they were strict vegetarians, which I certainly wasn't. Anything but that. I loved food, especially French cuisine, too much. With all the marvelous foods God gave us, I could never understand vegetarians. I lived to eat while Sandy couldn't eat to live, if you catch my drift. My attitude to food was: you want to lose weight, eat less; you want to feel healthy, don't overdo. I did overdo sometimes. I think it had to do with so many years of starving myself, of not being able to eat in order to stay svelte for the stage. So now that I could eat, I did. If I even walked through a kitchen, I put on weight, as did so many of my siblings.

That evening I was fixing a meal I wasn't used to, and my heart wasn't in it, while preparing a special one for Sandy and a regular one for myself. There I was after a full day, having rushed home, standing over a hot stove. Don't get me wrong, I loved cooking. The three meals had to be ready in no more than an hour. LA was an early town and Arthur and Richard were coming at 6:30. I found my eyes flipping again as they had on the trip in Texas. They wouldn't stop. It was the weirdest feeling putting food on the table while trying to carry on a conversation with the others. Actually, I didn't try. Richard lit the candles for me—there was no way I could.

After I got everyone seated, I let them do all the talking. I don't know what we talked about because I was too distracted by everything jumping up and down. I was consumed by the fear that I would knock something over, or that one of them would notice my eyes flip. I don't believe either happened. It couldn't have, because I would have remembered that.

What an evening it was, and to top it off, Arthur was there to ask me if I was up to another movie. All the more reason they shouldn't notice my eye problem. To my mind, I was only having difficulty because I was trying to do too much and I wasn't getting any younger. I did push myself at times when it was something I loved. Not that that happened too often. Usually I could be laid back with the best of them, or should I say the laziest? Well, eyes flipping or not, there it was after a lifetime of preparing and waiting—my third movie.

I left Sandy with Carl Johnson again and flew out of Burbank, script in hand, up to Sacramento, where I was hustled off to Grass Valley. They were shooting *Rescue Me* near the old Sutter's Mill where gold was discovered back in 1848. Yes, I know the rush was in '49. The film was to be shot in the old Holbrook Hotel constructed back in 1851 and still in operation. I was to play Hector, the owner of the hotel or the manager. My scenes were with Ty Hardin and John Miranda, and we played them as hicks, hill folk. The leads were Michael Dudikoff and Stephen Dorff, a former Brat Pack kid. I believe the movie catered to a teen demographic. Nevertheless, the three old farts' scenes got mentioned in the reviews.

While I was shooting, I got a call from Mary Steenburgen whose boyfriend between husbands was the writer of *Far and Away*. Mary arranged an interview and an audition for me through him. When I read the script, I could see vividly that the part of Nicole Kidman's father was a ringer for my horse-breeder grandfather, Ned Carville, right down to all the events depicted in the movie, fire and all. It was a slice of life taken right out of his. I was so excited, I sat down and memorized the complete part, brogue and all. That part was easy since it was my father's. But when I told Kathleen Nolan about my upcoming audition, she said forget it. Ron Howard, the director, was in New York looking for TV stars. And that is exactly what he did. Maybe that was his first mistake. He should have been looking for actors. In any case, I went in and gave it my best shot for the casting director, and that was that—until a year later. We were interviewing for class on Riverside Drive in Valley Village, and a young woman came in.

I introduced Sandy and was about to introduce myself when she said, "I know you. That girl who just left said that you auditioned for her best friend for Far and Away. According to her, of all the Hollywood people she saw, you gave one hell of an audition."

Yet I never even got to see Howard, let alone audition for him. So go figure. Why, that's an easy one. I wasn't a TV name. But the best part was—it didn't matter to me anymore.

Time Passes, and so did Sandy's Black String

Winter passed, spring came, and summer was approaching. In southern California, if it weren't for the huge, luscious, succulent, mouthwatering strawberries in the markets screaming for mounds of whipped cream, you wouldn't even notice the change in the weather. It was the last week of our Intensive Class at school. Soon we'd be heading back to Bequia. I sat one morning over coffee and a brioche staring into Sandy's face, thinking of nothing in particular. And there it wasn't. Sandy's unobtrusive little black string, which for the past year had hugged the base of his nostril like a pirate's nose-ring but much, much less detectable, was gone.

"Sandy," I said, "your tube."

"What about my tube?"

"It's gone, it isn't there."

"What do you mean, it's gone? Where is it?"

"I don't know where the hell it is," I answered nervously. "What I mean is, the string around your nose is gone."

Sandy, feeling around his nostrils with his fingers, asked, "What does that mean?"

"I don't know, Sandy. It means we have to tear ass back to New York 'cause we are not going to that quack at St. Vincent Hospital again. Why, he won't even know what the hell we're talking about," I said, getting all worked up.

"Now wait just a minute. I feel fine. And besides, school's not over yet. We still have a couple of days left. We finish and then we go. It may be nothing," he concluded calmly.

Class was over on Tuesday, June 22, and we were in New York late on Wednesday evening, June 23. The next morning I took him to the outpatients' clinic and explained what had happened. A string missing from a patient's nose couldn't be too critical at a world-renowned cancer center. So we just waited our turn. I had been so busy the past couple of days I hadn't noticed Sandy's quick deterioration. At Sloan-Kettering I was still distracted. Sandy was in his wheelchair not making it any easier for me. I had to pester them for any little attention. After much waiting around, we were looked after.

They took him for X-rays and we waited for the results. Finally we were told there was no tube in his stomach. I told them there had to be, his doctor had put one into his esophagus, and that was how he swallowed. The doctor insisted he knew the history, but no matter, there wasn't any tube.

Really looking critically at Sandy for the first time in days, I could see he was failing and failing fast. I asked the doctor, "What should I do?"

He said, "His vitals are normal, and he has no tube in his stomach. I suggest you go home and call Dr. Shah in the morning. I am sending our findings over to his office."

It was getting late in the day but I knew the doctor's office was still open. I wheeled Sandy through the back ways, remembering them from '74 some eighteen years before. Things hadn't changed that much. It wasn't difficult for us to get over to Dr. Shah's office, where I explained Sandy's predicament to his nurse. She advised, "It's his operating day. Best to go home and come in tomorrow."

I was totally helpless. There was nothing to do but go home. The entrance to the clinic opened onto the middle of the block between First Avenue and York Avenue. Few cabs passed by but even those driving by with their overhead lights on didn't stop. It was the end of the day and they were going off duty. I was used to that. So I pushed Sandy up to First Avenue where there would be more cabs.

When I got there, I could see he was really in a bad way. He was in no condition to take home. What could I do for him there? I was desperate as all get-out, but I was also becoming madder than hell. Here we were, surrounded by hospitals, seven to be exact, from 64th up York to 71st Street. I could even name them for you. Sandy just sat there saying nothing, just looking up at me miserably, with pleading eyes.

I said to him, "To hell with the cab. I'm taking you up to Dr. Perrone."

Sandy's private physician was just up the avenue on 70th Street, so I pushed him up the street to his office. Fortunately for us, Dr. Perrone was still in his office. I don't even want to think what would have happened if he hadn't been there. I explained everything to the good doctor from the time I spotted the missing string to my encounter at Kettering, where they had determined the tube was not in his stomach and sent us home.

"Look at him, doctor. Something is radically wrong. He needs help."

Dr. Perrone examined him and decreed, "He should be admitted. I'm calling New York Hospital. You've got the wheelchair, and it's only a block away on York Avenue. You go on ahead and take him to the Emergency entrance, and I'll be right along behind."

And off we went. It was all downhill and we were there in no time. I was still at the desk when Dr. Perrone came up behind me. "That can wait," he said. "Bring him right in." An attendant put Sandy up on a gurney and wheeled him away. The doctor turned to me. "Go around to the waiting room. I'll get back to you later. I believe he's having a heart attack."

That was all I needed to hear. I have no idea how long I waited, but Dr. Perrone did come to tell me Sandy was stabilized and that he was resting, that I would be able to go up to his room. When I broached the subject of the tube, all he said was, "Let's get him through this. They have him on a monitor," and he left.

I got the feeling even he wasn't taking my tube story seriously. I went up to Sandy's floor and found he was sleeping, so I didn't wake him. I just sat there and waited. I was worried, angry, concerned, and furious because I felt so ineffectual, helpless, and useless. So many unanswered questions churned in my mind. Did he really pass the tube without knowing it? If it was still inside him, was that causing the heart attack? What to do? He was sleeping and they had him on a monitor. So that night when they put me out, I uneasily went home to Boolu who prepared me some scrambled eggs and toast.

Friday morning I overslept. I reached Sandy's room about noon to find him just lying there awake. He still seemed weak. I noticed his breakfast tray off to one side, untouched, and his lunch was on his bed stand, also untouched. He was noncommittal when I asked how he was.

"You're not eating," I said. "Come on, you have to get something into you.

You're not even getting Jevity here. Try some of this Jell-O." But he wouldn't, so I got the milk and tried to force him this time.

Sandy cut the matter short. "I can't," he said.

Talking to the nurse about a plastic tube that wasn't there would be futile. If they did anything at all, it would be just what the out-clinic at Sloan-Kettering had done, and we would be back to square one. Here I was between two hospitals kitty-corner from each other and I did not have the power to bring them together for Sandy's welfare. The only hope I had was to get to Dr. Shah. He at least would know what I was talking about while Sandy lay there starving to death. I don't remember if Sandy was getting any IV; all I remember is seeing him getting weaker by the day.

I got on the hallway payphone to Shah's nurse, the one I had talked with the day before, and explained where Sandy was and what had happened. She told me she would get on to Dr. Shah. She seemed to be the only one who understood our predicament, but I never did get a call back from her. When I tried to reach her a second time, she had gone for the weekend.

If only I could get the doctors to talk to each other, but that was beyond any realm of possibility. So all I wanted to do was get him out of this hospital and over into the one I felt could properly care for him. I missed Dr. Perrone Saturday morning. If he made an appearance at all, I wouldn't know. According to the head nurse, the results of Sandy's heart test were good and Dr. Perrone had said if they held up, he might be released on Sunday. Mind you, Sandy still wasn't eating anything.

I sat there all day Saturday and Sunday morning seeing no one and talking to no one, just waiting to get Sandy out of there. By Sunday I had stopped trying to get something into him. It was useless. He just couldn't swallow, and I just didn't want to get into this problem with the hospital staff. God knows what they would do. I wanted to get him into Dr. Shah's hands. He knew how and what to do.

Finally the stars were with us. Sunday afternoon, the head nurse came in and said Sandy could leave. I never was so glad to get a sick man out of a hospital in my life. He was so weak, yet to them, for all intents and purposes, he was not sick, he was not diseased. Weak as he was, I took him home. I was happy that I would get him to Dr. Shah in the morning. Sandy felt more relieved also.

Monday morning and mission accomplished. Dr. Shah examined him and found the tube had neither passed nor got stuck in his stomach, but had lodged in the artificial esophagus, blocking the entrance to his stomach. Consequently Sandy hadn't been able to eat in days and was indeed slowly starving. This blockage explained why he was getting so weak; perhaps it was why the heart was acting up. Furthermore it was why the tube didn't show up in the stomach. The medical people would have known he hadn't passed it if they had thought to X-ray the esophagus because they would have found it, as Dr. Shah did.

38 Hanging by a Thread

For Sandy Things Would Never be the Same

I looked at Dr. Shah and asked, "Now what?"

"I will admit him today because we have to get it out. Then we'll decide what to do."

After the extraction of the tube, the upper digestive tract was rendered useless. Based on his findings, Shah told me, "Sandy will now have to be fed through his stomach wall, using a stomach peg, a gastrostomy tube. We need to do an operation. I only hope his strength is up to it. Sandy will then be using a G-tube for the rest of his life."

One might say because they went down his throat after the missing tube and disrupted his artificial esophagus, the throat had been messed up pretty badly, but much wasn't said about that. Sandy's physical condition was a problem. He was weak from lack of nourishment and his advanced age—he was now eighty-seven—wasn't helping. Shah wasn't sure he could withstand the operation right now, but to wait would only exacerbate the problem and make his chances worse.

"So! Where's the dilemma? Just tell him. I know what his answer is going to be," I said.

He told Sandy and Sandy said, "So what do you want from me? I've got a choice? Do it!" After Shah left, Sandy said to me, "They do it and it could be bad; wait and it could be worse; don't do it and that's that. Jimmy, there's no rainbow at the end of this one."

I can't explain it. Perhaps it was his frailty. Whatever it was, this particular "operation- wait" was unbearable, the worst ever. I had seen Sandy through so many life-threatening procedures. Perhaps we had been up to the well just one time too many to expect a reprieve. But I prayed and asked anyway. How many times is too many? I went to my little church around the corner, lit candles, and asked one more time. Well, we were given the time. He made it through, weak, but he was still with us.

When we got him home, they sent me a nurse to help us make the adjustment. Sandy would wake up during the night disoriented and pull at the feeding tube. One night he succeeded in pulling it out altogether. I taped up the hole and though it was after 11 PM, I dressed him and took him in a cab up to Kettering's Urgent Care Unit. They accepted him because he was one of their patients. I knew nothing then of the legal mumbo jumbo pertaining to the difference between urgency and emergency. Regardless, we were told to sit and wait in the outer room. By 2 AM I told Boolu to go home and get some sleep. He had to go to work in the morning. Sandy and I sat and waited and waited. Sandy was still in his wheelchair nodding, dozing in and out of sleep, when the nurse came out.

"I'm sorry for the delay, but we don't have a doctor here at night," she explained. "The night duty doctor from upstairs comes down when needed but he must have a handful tonight."

"Couldn't Mr. Meisner lie down until he comes?" I asked.

"Oh, yes, right in here," she said. I had to ask, I thought to myself.

The doctor didn't get to us until about 5 AM, full of apologies for the long delay. "It's bedlam up there tonight. Added to that, we were short-staffed," he said as he took Sandy into a little room.

I went in with him; I wanted to see how this procedure worked. First he sterilized the flexible rubber tube and took a long thin metal rod and inserted it into the tube to make it rigid. Then he coated the tube with gel and started to gingerly insert it into the stoma. The hole had begun to close up bit by bit. I thought to myself, is it any wonder? It's going on six hours since it was pulled out. The doctor was having difficulty getting it to slide in. After a couple of tries, he admitted he had never inserted one before. He called to the nurse, but she was of no help, never having inserted one before either. He eventually managed it, and the nurse finished the job, applying the dressings around it. Finally, in daylight, we headed home.

When I unloaded the previous night's saga onto our home-care nurse that day, she simply said, "Why, if I had been here, I could have inserted it immediately before it began to seize up." She was from France and considered that Americans make too much hocus-pocus of everything. She explained to me how it was done. "It's best you put it back in right away."

It wasn't a week before it happened again in the middle of the night. I wasn't about to put us both through that Urgency Room fiasco again. I cleaned off the tube, sterilized it, and poked around in the kitchen for something to hold the flimsy rubber tube taut. I came up with a barbeque skewer, you know, for shish kebab. I sterilized it over the gas jets and it served the purpose as well as the one the doctor had used. I coated the rubber tube with water-based K-Y jelly. It was the weirdest sensation inserting this skewer into Sandy's stomach. I felt as if I were stabbing him right in the solar plexus. It is amazing what you can do when no other sensible recourse presents itself and nothing stands between you and the solution.

When we went in for his first monthly checkup for the gastro tube with the surgeon in charge of follow-up, I told him about Sandy's pulling out the tube. He asked me, "Where did you go to get it cared for?"

Well, he damned near had conniptions when I told him I had taken care of it. When I answered, "No" to his question as to whether I was a doctor, he carried on as if I had committed the unforgivable sin. I was about to explain the all-night vigil we'd had to endure the first time, then thought better of it. This guy had a territorial problem, so I said nothing and he eventually subsided.

While Sandy was in the examining room, I told one of the nurses about that first night and what a constant battle it still was to keep him from pulling it out. She asked, "What does he have, one of those brown rubber tubes?"

"Yes," I answered. She must have been on my side after that outlandish scene with the doctor, or she knew he was a pompous ass just based on his everyday behavior.

In any case, she said what Sandy needed was a G-tube. "It has a balloon that inflates once it's inside the stomach wall, after it's inserted through the stoma. If he pulls on it, the balloon stops it from coming out, plus it hurts. It'll cure him of that habit fast."

After Sandy came out, she took us over to the supply room and found us two of them. "When Mr. Meisner pulls out the rubber one next time, just insert this one instead. Just read the instructions on the box." That did the trick, and we never went back to that doctor again.

Thank God for Ambulance Drivers

We got through July and most of August. Then one night he woke me up bleeding profusely from his throat. I took him into the bathroom, sat him at the sink, and told him not to move, that I was calling an ambulance. I called 911 and then rang up the doctor on call at Sloan-Kettering, explaining Dr. Shah's plastic tube extraction from his esophagus and the hemorrhaging from his throat. The doctor told me to bring Sandy right in to the Urgency Room. He would come down. "When you arrive," he said, "I'll be there."

Two policemen arrived first, then two paramedics who both went into the bathroom and started working on Sandy. One came out and asked what had happened. I explained and he replied, "Once we stabilize him, we'll take him down to Bellevue."

"He's a patient at Kettering. I've already called them and they said we should bring him in. The doctor is waiting for him there. They know what's wrong with him," I said.

"But we can't take him there," he said.

"Why?" I asked. "They have all his records up there. They know why he's bleeding, and besides, it's closer than Bellevue. And the doctor is waiting."

"You don't understand," he said. "We have rules. We have to bring him to an Emergency Room, and they don't have one up there."

In desperation I said, "I can get the doctor on the phone and he will tell you."

To that he responded, "Sorry," and went back into the bathroom with his colleague.

Floods of memories invaded me of that nightmare of a weekend at Bellevue back in '82 eleven years before. The two cops stood there mesmerized by my antics, saying nothing, just staring at me as if I were a maniac. In the meantime the ambulance driver had come in and was roaming around the living room looking at this picture and that around the room until he spotted a framed pay sheet from the Group Theatre with all the actors' names and salaries.

After the paramedic had gone back into the bathroom, he came over to me and asked, "Who is this guy anyway?"

"He's Sanford Meisner," I said.

"That's Mr. Meisner in there? What's wrong?" he asked.

"He's hemorrhaging."

"Wow, he's one of the greatest! I know. I'm an actor. What's the problem with the hospitals?" he asked.

And I told him. The paramedics had him on a gurney ready to leave. As the paramedics were putting Sandy in the back, I walked behind waiting to clamber in with him. The actor-driver tapped me on the shoulder. "Come on, sit in the front with me." As he stuck the key into the ignition, he asked, "Now, where is this hospital?"

"It's not far, just up First Avenue," I said.

"Now, they really are expecting and waiting for him?" he asked.

"Yes. I just arranged it with the night-duty doctor," I answered.

"OK, let's go. Show me the way. I've never gone there before."

We shot up First Avenue and turned right onto 68th. We took another right onto York, passing the main entrance, and turned right onto 67th. I could see the Urgency Clinic was shut up tighter than a drum. My heart sank, but I made no comment to the driver. I just said, "Continue around the block once more to York and the front entrance."

We pulled up to the main entrance and avoided going through the main lobby by going in through the ground floor directly to the cellar and all the way over to the Memorial wing and the outpatient section of the hospital. I knew how because I had used it a couple of times to sneak in back in the '70s. Later I thought it strange that the paramedics never said a word when they unloaded him at Kettering. They took him through the cellar to the Urgency Room and signed him over to the night nurse. Not to worry, I had him where I wanted him. They managed to stop the hemorrhaging and in the morning they moved him up to the head-and-neck department on the ninth floor. All this excitement took place over the weekend.

On Tuesday evening, as I sat there with Boolu, the bleeding started up again. All I could think was, my God, they must have really messed his throat up good getting that damned tube out of him. Hindsight, I know, but maybe they should have gone after it from the outside, through an incision in his throat. But what did I know? It was after visiting hours and Boolu was beat. He had worked all day. I had no sooner told him to go home and get some sleep, he had work tomorrow and I was staying the night, when the bleeding started up again, ever so slowly. It wasn't noticeable at first. As the night progressed, it became worse. He was regurgitating a substantial amount of blood. He was getting a blood transfusion, but nevertheless it looked to me as if he were losing it a lot faster than he was receiving it.

At one point the doctor, not Dr. Shah, came to me and asked, "Does he have any family nearby? It doesn't look good. He hasn't much time left. They should get in here right away, if they can."

I went out into the hall to the payphone and called Bobby, his brother, in New Jersey. When I told him, he hemmed and hawed. I felt he was way out in

38 Hanging by a Thread

New Jersey and if Sandy wasn't going to make it, then it would be over before he got here anyway. Besides, I was in no mood or condition to hang on to the phone continuing a discussion as to whether he should come or not. I said, "It's entirely up to you, Bobby," and I hung up.

I then called Danny, Bobby's son. He lived nearby up on the East Side. He said he and Laura would be right over. I met them in the hall and told them what to expect. "By the way," I added, "I have discussed nothing with him as to the gravity of his condition, couldn't have even if I wanted to. He's just in there, fighting for every breath. He has no idea what time it is, so tell him you were at the theater and thought you would stop by on your way home."

There were two nurses at the head of the bed, one on either side. Both were scooping up the blood with a suction tube into steel, kidney-shaped spit basins, each taking a turn. Sandy was still lucid and alert. We stood at the foot of the bed with the two nurses doing their job at the head of the bed. We were just making small talk when Sandy motioned for me to come closer. Now, he couldn't make sound but I could read his lips. "I know what you are trying to do," he mouthed. He made it clear he wasn't ready for any deathbed scene with the family staring on at the foot of the bed. After a while Danny and Laura said their goodbyes, saying they would check with the hospital in the morning, and left. The nurses continued with what seemed like an endless undertaking.

Shortly after Danny and Laura left, the doctor called me into the hall. "I estimate he has about a half hour left. The records state you are his power of attorney. We need to know, do you want to put him on life support? If you do, we have to make ready."

I thought for the first time in our relationship, WOW! This is it! I knew he didn't want to be put on life support, but I still wasn't ready to let go either. Let me tell you, needless to say, no one needs a situation like this. What to do? The doctor went into Sandy's room, I knew to give me time to think.

When he came out, I asked him, "If I have the power to put him on life support, do I have the power to say when it's over? In plain English, do I have the power to pull the plug? I know he doesn't want to be on life support." I was getting a little angry now. I didn't want to be in this position.

"Yes, here there is no fuss. It will be your call," The doctor replied.

"Well... yes... Go ahead, make your preparations."

An hour passed and Sandy was still in his room and still quite lucid. In another half hour, the bleeding was subsiding. I do believe I was praying faster than the bleeding. By 6:30 that morning, the bleeding had stopped and the nurses were cleaning him up, trying to make him a little more comfortable, if comfort is possible as you fight for your life. At the 7 AM shift change, the night staff left and the day staff came on. And Sandy went on.

About ten o'clock, one of the nurses approached me in the hall. "I don't believe that man in there," she said. "When I came on this morning, he was the color of death. Come, take a look at him now. Even his color has changed." To

Sandy she said, "How are you doing, Mr. Meisner? Looks like you're going to hang around a little longer. You gave them all a run for their money last night," as she fluffed up his pillow. As she walked out of the room, to me she said, "You see miracles around here every once in a while, but this one is one for the books," and off she went. It sure was, I thought. The wonders of healing!

Within a week and a half, I had him home and in my lap, as it were. No nurse this time. I had Boolu, and he was phenomenal. He knew what I was thinking half the time, and seemed to know what had to be done.

To Recapitulate

The way I looked at things then? Sandy had been down many times before; this was just one more time. As I sat there exhausted on our living room couch with him resting in the bedroom and Boolu off shopping, I started to daydream. My mind floated back through time and space to June of '74, to that "night of the three moons" out on the terrace and the rush back to New York.

I allowed myself to muse, meandering onward in time to the cataract operations on the 12th and 19th of June, then on to July 18 and the brutal biopsy that resulted in the loss of vision in his left eye, and on to the infamous day of July 24. I remembered how he had been told at 8:30 AM that day he would lose his vocal chords, nay his whole larynx, and then around noon he went blind in the right eye so that he was rendered totally blind as well as speechless in less than four hours. This catastrophe necessitated retina operations in both eyes, after which he was rushed over to Sloan-Kettering still blind in both eyes to have his complete larynx removed. For weeks afterward, he was speechless and sightless.

Then, after suffering through and surviving all this trauma, just three months later on December 22 at the Christmas pageant on Bequia, accompanying the choir on the organ with the "Hallelujah Chorus," he lost vision in both eyes again, nevertheless managing to finish the program, unbeknownst to anyone blind as a bat. Then came January '75 back in New York at the Manhattan Eye and Ear, where they were able to save sight in only his right eye with its two retinal tears and, by then, a touch of glaucoma as well. In May of that year, blinded by the setting sun in that weak eye, he veered off the cliff and catapulted fifty feet over the rocks tumbling over and over five times. He was left with a possible neck fracture and a dislocated collarbone, not to minimize the five superficial bumps on his head, one for each rollover. And I still wondered how in the hell I had lifted that car off him to release the pressure so he could breathe through his tracheal stoma.

And after all that, cancer hit him a second time in '77 which led to the dreadful radiation reaction that left him physically devastated over Christmas. While fighting back from all of that, and tending to the problems of Boolu's burn as well as coping with the deaths of Paul Morrison, Oleta D'Ambry, and

38 Hanging by a Thread

his sister Ruth in '82 and '83, Sandy was clobbered once again, struck by the speeding van that threw him thirty feet down 57th Street. His hip and femur were smashed into smithereens, his leg broken in twelve places, and he was left senseless for months. In '87 he lay in a coma for two weeks with atypical pneumonia and we fled New York for the last time because of the inclement weather. In less than three months out in LA, he was bombarded once again with not one but two operations, performed back-to-back at Cedars-Sinai, for his hernia and prostate.

With all this adversity behind him, after only a short reprieve, in September of '90 he came down with cancer for the third time. This bout necessitated the fabrication of an esophagus from his own flesh, the muscles lifted from his right chest. That operation had to be corrected by a plastic liner-tube in '91, only to have it literally ripped out of his throat in '92 causing extensive hemorrhaging. Additionally, he was given a stomach peg, a gastrostomy tube to be fed through, which meant no more eating. Yet here he was after extensive hemorrhaging, resting on that bed in there, still ready to trudge up to a speech lesson at Kettering.

Boolu came in then, knocking me out of my reverie, to say, "Isn't you guys lef yet? Sandy gonna be late fo his teacher."

"We have an hour, Boolu. We'll make it," I said as I pulled myself together. "Get his heavy coat out of the closet. It looks chilly out there today."

Now that he was getting a little stronger, Sandy had resumed working with the speech teacher at Kettering as follow-up therapy, and believe it or not, sound was coming back. No one had a better command of the technical workings of the esophageal speech pattern than Sandy. No matter how weak he was, he managed to be audible. But as well as his speech was coming along, for the fifth time, every couple of weeks I would sense him stammering for a short spell, a day or two. He just could not verbalize as well.

One day I saw him faltering on his walker and I didn't want to face what I feared it could be. When he stumbled one night going into the bathroom and hit his head on a floor-length mirror, cracking it, the mirror that is, I couldn't ignore it any longer. I was afraid my hunches were right. I took him up to the Urgency Room at Kettering. Their findings were what I feared. It appeared he was now experiencing silent strokes or minor heart failure. Was it any wonder? This time they didn't send him up to his familiar 9th floor. No, he was moved to a section of the hospital we had never been in before. Late that night three young doctors, a woman and two men, came to examine him. They could have been interns, they may have been too young to be doctors, or I was just getting too old. Whatever they were, they examined and examined, tested and tested, mostly his physical reactions. From my amateur assessment of their arcane praxis, I figured out they were checking primarily his neurological behavior. They never spoke to me of their findings or of their diagnoses. All they did was ask me his age and how long his behavior had been like this. After nigh onto an hour of their prodding, poking, twisting, and lifting, having jabbed notes onto their clipboards and ended with a good ten-minute huddle, they turned to me from across the room and thanked me, although I don't know what they were thanking me for. The woman went back, thanked Sandy while adjusting his pillow, said good night, and all three left the room, never to be seen again.

We never saw Dr. Shah, but Sandy was clearer-headed in the morning and he was released. The head nurse told me he must have suffered a mild silent stroke. Mild stroke, indeed, I stewed to myself. No matter, we were sent on our merry way with not so much as a how-do-you-do?—or a what-for-George?—and with absolutely no advice as to what to do about the problem. This was an easy one to figure out. It was another case of not-my-prob-bub-blem.

Sandy was at the wrong hospital for what was wrong with him. Sorry, my mistake. He continued at Kettering working with the speech therapist on and off through September. Amid general improvement, he was having what looked to me, and to the therapist as well, like a little neurological setback every now and again. Finally, for the first time after all these years of fighting just to keep him in a classroom where he wanted to be, I was ready to accept the fact and admit what Jesus once said, "'Tis finished, Lord."

Sandy & Jimmy

39 Bodies in Motion

"Time to go" Like Joey in 'The Most Happy Fella'

hy hang around this town any longer? It was obvious to me we had to vacate this adverse, avaricious, and ravenous city. I notified all the students in California waiting for Sandy's return that at present everything was at a standstill. I went over to our rental agent and gave a month's notice on 58th Street. New York was an expensive place to live, especially if you weren't on the take, or at least if you weren't working anymore. If we were finished at Kettering, and it sure looked as if we were, we didn't need to hang around any longer.

I needed help with this move. Marty Barter was now teaching at the Playhouse and I knew he was not too happy there without Sandy. He might be just the one to save the day. In an instant, he offered to help in our move out to LA in whatever way he could. His fiancée Jill was all for the move as well. All her family was there and moreover she was an actor who wanted to finish her training with Sandy, in Los Angeles. They moved out ahead and found an apartment and one for us as well in Valley Village on Riverside Drive. We had to give up that charming little house with all its amenities to cut expenses. Retirement has a way of doing that to one or two or, as in our case, three. All the decisions and moves were made even faster than in '87.

The only big dilemma in this total upheaval was Boolu. He had jobs in New York; he had friends now in all four boroughs. What would he do in California for friends or a job? He was now thirty-seven years old. It wouldn't be right to rip him out of the environs with which he was now familiar and could cope. Fortunately, his sister Sherry and her partner, Elmo "Big Jim" Chandler, owned a brownstone on Jefferson over in Brooklyn and rented out apartments. They seemed glad to rent out their first floor front to us. It couldn't have been better. The area was full of his Vincentian and Bequian friends. The plan was for him to subway into Manhattan each day to his jobs. At the time, he seemed to accept the move as we did. It was unavoidable and necessary.

Ian McRae, a teacher at the Playhouse formerly from the Bequia School, helped Boolu with his move to Brooklyn. Ian loaded his truck with what furniture Boolu could use, and we sent the rest by transcontinental movers out to Villa Fontaine on Riverside Drive. The last thing Sandy and I did together in the city, on the afternoon of the day before we left, was stroll through Central Park. I pushed Sandy in his wheelchair around the little lake directly across from the Plaza Hotel. We watched the ducks and geese. I wondered how many of them would be packing up and taking off before the north winds started to blow. We ventured further in, to the Wollman Memorial Ice Rink, abandoned at this time of year. Our visit was before it had been revitalized by the construction of a brand new version of it. We sat on a bench gazing at the 59th Street skyline and the Essex House sign and the top of the infamous Leona Helmsley's Palace to the left.

Sandy reminisced: "You know, I used to love having lunch with Peggy, my first wife, at that restaurant on the corner of Sixth—or was it Seventh Avenue?—and 59th. Do you know I had an apartment in a building on the west end of 59th, looking up through the park just this side of Columbus Circle?"

"God! That must have been in better days," I said.

"It was, I was on Broadway then," said he.

"I'm sure it paid a hell of a lot better than the Playhouse," was my caustic reply.

"Hey, don't knock it. It was a living."

"Can you imagine what that place must cost today?" I asked.

"Forget it, that was another time."

"I remember going to Rumplemeyer's on 59th on a Sunday afternoon for an ice-cream sundae," I said.

"You did that? Peggy and I went there, too," said Sandy.

The sky was clear, the sun was shining, and it was a warm day for November as we sat there watching the sun rise high in the sky, ever so slowly arching its way over that familiar New York skyline. Each building of unbending steel imprisoned in cold, hard, unyielding concrete, limiting its gracefulness as it stretched straight up to its maximum capability, seemed to be trying to touch the sun. We too sat there basking in its warmth as the little yellow orb flitted its way across the heavens. We sat there and reminisced about our days in this town.

"See those rocks over there?" I asked. "Every day in the summer of '48, a group of us bought our lunch around the corner in that deli on Seventh Avenue and ate it sitting on top of that high rock over there. That was when I first came to this town to attend the Alvienie Academy."

Sandy said, "Many a time in the summer of '38, Peggy and I took our evening walk through here. You know, we lived in this park back then."

"Well, you wouldn't and couldn't nowadays." After a long pause I asked, "Sandy, are you going to miss this place?"

"Why yes, yes, of course, and so will you. But time has a way of changing everything. We have changed. Shakespeare put it most succinctly in *As You Like It* with his 'seven ages' of man. 'At first, the infant,/ Muling and puking in the nurse's arms...'"

"I know," I said. "I know Act II Scene vii. 'The sixth age shifts/ Into the lean and slipper'd pantaloon,/ With spectacles on nose, and pouch on side;/ ...Last scene of all,/ That ends this strange eventful history,/ Is second childishness, and mere oblivion;/ Sans teeth, sans eyes, sans taste, sans everything.' Is that where we are?" I asked.

"It looks that way. Well, the 'sans' part has my number written all over it, I would say. But I don't remember any mention of a wheelchair back then," said Sandy.

"Sandy, you still 'cans hear,' so hear this," I said. "Lest we forget, we still have Bequia, man. So, come on, let's blow this town." We sauntered through that beautiful square and landmark of times past, the monument to the soldiers and sailors of 1917 in front of the Plaza Hotel, and back across 58th Street to the Picasso, one last time.

Within a month, de tree a we vacated 58th Street for Brooklyn and points west of the Mississippi. When Marty and Jill had found us an apartment in Valley Village, they had had students help them move all our things from Bellingham Avenue in Studio City into our new apartment at the Villa Fontaine, even before Sandy and I got there. When we got to California and found all the students helping us, I felt like Stella Adler with all her dog walkers. I only hoped we had been teaching them something. (Not to imply that she didn't. Sandy always felt Stella had value and something unique to give in her own inimitable way.)

The Best Laid Plans of Mice and Me

By the beginning of November, time to start classes, we had just arrived in LA and needed time to settle in. I had planned for Marty to take over the classes, with Sandy just observing and kibitzing now and again as he would with a student teacher. He always worked with an assistant anyway, and I was always there to translate when necessary. Regardless, I felt he needed a little more time to adjust to the new digs; after all he wasn't the man he once was. He had been called up to the plate too many times, and the old stamina was just a little harder to come by. So the opening was put off until the end of the month.

I set everything up before classes began and explained it all to Sandy. He knew he could take it easy as the students understood about his condition and why I had brought Marty out. Yet once the class began, Sandy didn't give Marty the time of day. He sailed right into the first two students. I thought it must be taking a hell of a lot out of him, but who could stop him? He was like that little steam engine that said, "I think I can, I think I can." He snapped back like a rubber band. "Get out of the way, man. I know I can." There we were, off and running for the umpteenth time. My job was going to be to keep him rested and ready for the onslaught in the classroom, for the work was demanding for any man, never mind a man in his condition.

His friend David Craig told us about Nancy Walker's oncologist since we were in the market for one. No way were we going back to the doctor at St. Vincent's Hospital or to the one in New York either. Dr. Avrum Bluming was head of Tarzana Hospital just ten minutes away (under the best traffic conditions, say 11:30 at night). When the freeways were jammed, we could take an alternate quick route in the Valley through the Sepulveda Basin.

About this time, Sandy developed an enormous edema all through his right arm, which frightened the hell out of me. Apparently this swelling occurs in some cancer patients when the cancer is in or around the breast and neck area. Nothing could be done for Sandy's arm except to wrap it in an Ace bandage, and that was only a temporary treatment for cosmetic effect, an approach helpful to women going out in an evening gown. A man could wear long sleeves and a jacket to cover it. Sometimes it was tough getting Sandy's jacket over it.

To Sandy, this development was nothing, just one more thing to deal with. He wanted to go down to Bequia for the holidays. "Look," he said, "I sit on a plane for a day and I get to lie out on a beach for three weeks. What do you think?"

"I think not. What do you think the doctor is going to say about that?" I asked.

"Look," he shot back, "it beats running around to Christmas parties greeting people I can't talk to and looking at food I can't eat. All I have, and all I want now, is that classroom and Bequia."

It was easy to see he was absolutely right. He didn't care what the doctor said and why should I, if this was what he wanted? When he told Dr. Avrum, he apparently wasn't shocked. He only asked, "What about the supplement?"

"We can bring a case or two like we did in China," I started to explain.

Sandy interrupted, "What about all those soups they know how to make on Bequia?"

The doctor understood and said, "Well, good. Happy holidays! Make an appointment at the desk for the middle of January."

De Tree a We Back on Bequia Again

Boolu, now in possession of a green card, could leave the US for the first time in a dozen years, ever since 1981. We felt it would be a good thing for him to get down to Bequia. However, we couldn't get him a flight out of New York so late in the season, so his sister June took him out to Kennedy to stand by and hope for a cancellation. It was worth a try. Boolu was all revved up to play the returning hero, the prodigal son or whatever, now that he was a grown-up man living on his own and working in New York City. We were proud as hell and eager for all to see his accomplishments. As it turned out, as a single, he did manage to snare a seat.

In LA, I had gotten on the phone immediately with the airlines. If Sandy and I had been in New York, it would have been impossible—flights to Barbados would have been booked since September. LAX was another matter. We found a night flight to Miami, then one down to Barbados in the morning. In Barbados, Jeremy Palmer, brother of Jonathan, the owner of Mustique Air, which now flew to our very own new James Mitchell Airport on Bequia, met us and personally helped Sandy with the transfer. Sandy alerted Jeremy that

Boolu might be coming through and asked him to keep an eye out for him on American Airlines from Kennedy in the next couple of days.

"Boolu-mon may be comin' through?" He repeated it as if he hadn't heard correctly.

"You bet I'll keep an eye out. Wow, mon, Boolu-mon comin' through!" he exclaimed in disbelief. They had known each other as boys on Bequia.

"That's one little worry we can set aside," Sandy remarked.

"I'm sure he'll be on the lookout," I agreed.

The gathering this season was particularly important for our little family unit. I believe we all needed the reassurance that, with all that had happened this past fall, we were still like the Three Musketeers—all for one and one for all. Sandy was dealing with the rapid change in his wellbeing; Boolu was coping with having had his secure home ripped out from under him and being dropped all alone into an apartment in Brooklyn; and I was questioning my ability to keep us all afloat under the circumstances. Everything had taken on an air of flux. Bequia was the only unchanging factor in our lives just then. It was the place for us to be. It was always a congenial, loving place for us. Forget the coconut-heads, for although we had our share of them to deal with, they were minor. Everyone on the Island knew practically everyone else. It was as close as you could get to one of Hillary Clinton's global villages. But Bequia went one step further. We were a global family. The island became such out of necessity, having to rely on each other because for years there was no government people could truly depend on.

We arrived too late to do anything about Santa this year, leaving more than one disappointed little boy and girl. But that was beyond our fixing. We celebrated Christmas Eve at home, just de tree a we. That's what we needed just now. Christmas dinner we had at the Frangipani with Marie and Lou Keane, and of course Boolu had Boxing Day with Parnell at Sinclair Simmons' with his four daughters, Verneth, Shelley, April, and Donnet. Sandy spent many days lolling about in the sun and splashing in the sea. Driving home from the beach one afternoon in our Moke, he remarked, "Just like old times." I thought to myself, I wish they were, but I said nothing. He was obviously enjoying himself, and that was important. His demands were little more than nothing now. One day slid into the next.

Old Year's Night was approaching, and the question was what to do? I put it to Sandy and he said, "We do what we always do. It isn't Old Year's Night if it isn't the Frangipani."

"Don't you think it can get pretty raucous down there at midnight?" I questioned.

"Sometimes, Jimmy, it's hard to take you seriously. We will, all three of us, have dinner. You book the last sitting, get a table near the action across from the bar, and I'll have a seat for the rest of the festivities. Boolu can take off after dinner and do whatever the hell the boy wants."

This is exactly what we all did. There was no Lou or Marie that night as they were too busy working and controlling the crowd, well, as much as possible. Old Year's Night was always a mob scene because every festivity-loving creature on the Island—locals, tourists, and yachtsmen alike—converged and congregated there just before the stroke of twelve, just like in Times Square. Then Son Mitchell and all the yachtsmen in the Harbour shot off their red flares, and a thousand and one roman candles lit up the bay. The coconut trees and swaying palms lining the seashore were silhouetted through the billowing, swirling, all-encompassing clouds of red, and the pinkish puffs of smoke engulfed the merrymakers as well. The entire tropical scene turned into what seemed like the very edge of Dante's inferno. The only thing missing was the heat, and judging from some of the hot numbers standing around me, I wasn't so sure of that.

Wherever Boolu went after dinner, he was back at our side at the stroke of midnight. Maybe Sandy was right. Here it was 1993 and it really did feel like old times. That is, until shortly after New Year's. One evening I noticed Sandy was behaving peculiarly, not like himself at all. His behavior reminded me of his condition after the hemorrhaging, his temporary lack of lucidity. He turned in early that night. I thought he slept the night through but in the morning he was even worse. I had all I could do to get him dressed, down into the Moke, and to the government doctor at her clinic about 7 AM. I steered the Moke with one hand, keeping Sandy from falling out altogether with the other as we veered around the sharp curves. I realized I should have awakened Boolu; I could have used his assistance. Sandy didn't have the strength to sit up on his own.

I had to literally drag him into the clinic. The doctor, who lived upstairs, poked her head out the window to say she was having breakfast and would be down shortly. When she arrived, in her own good time, we laid Sandy out on the examining table. She then took me into the office, leaving him alone in the examining room. She proceeded to conduct a question-and-answer period before even looking at him. You know, the usual: what's his name, his nationality, my name, and my relationship to him. After a barrage of similarly innocuous, unrelated, and irrelevant inquiries, she asked, "Does he want to die here or in America?"

I knew Sandy could hear every word she said. His hearing had become phenomenal. "Well," I told her, "why don't you ask him?" I was furious at such a stupid question.

She got up to wash her hands, and I went into the examining room. Sandy said to me, "What difference does it make to me where the hell I die?"

"Forget it, Sandy, forget it," I just said.

After the exam she suggested I take him over to the Bequia Clinic. It was too inept in every way to be called a hospital, but for want of anything better, it served as one. Back in '68 there had not even been a doctor.

I drove him the short distance to the clinic in my Moke. The sign over the entrance rather appropriately read "The Bequia Casualty Clinic." When she arrived a little later, the doctor hooked him up, with nurse Reanna's assistance, to a large oxygen tank, the kind they use to blow up balloons at a parade. Reanna Dewer was one of my former students, one of my "Could we start again?" singers who stopped the *Superstar* show.

The good doctor (I'm being kind) said, "Sandy needs medicine that both my clinic and this clinic are out of." That came as no surprise to me. "Could you go over to the pharmacist and see if they should happen to have it?"

She scribbled the prescription on a piece of paper, and I was off to the drug store on Front Street, which wasn't open yet. Someone got the owner who opened up and found the medicine requested. I paid him and ran back to the clinic. The doctor wasn't there.

Reanna said, "She went back to her house." I took one look at Sandy, who was much more lucid now. There he lay, stretched out on the bed with a humongous oxygen tank at his bedside and a facemask over his nose and mouth that were not doing him a farthing-in-hell's worth of good.

Irritated, I said to Reanna, "Who did this?"

"She did."

"The man breathes through the stoma in his neck! Was she absolutely blind? No one could be that stupid. Or could she? Turn off that damn tank!" I took the mask off Sandy and asked him how he felt.

"I'm feeling much better."

"No thanks to her," I said.

"Get me out of here," was all Sandy requested.

"I sure will, before she does you in completely." I turned to Reanna and told her to put the tank away. It might just as well be in the broom closet for all the good it was doing Sandy. "Look at him," I said. "He's much better. I'm taking him home." What else was there to do? "If he's going to die down here, at least he's going to be in his own bed."

"Oh, shut up, Jimmy!" Sandy said. "Take me home. Good-bye, Reanna, it was nice seeing you. How's your mommy by the way?... Give her my best."

I slowly put him into the Moke and drove him back over the winding road to our home up on the hill, with just one more doctor never to be seen again.

A Long Trip back to the Valley of San Fernando

Jimmy Price always checked in with us over the holidays wherever we were. This particular year he was surprised to hear we had moved out of the Picasso and out to California for good. He offered, "Now that you're homeless in the city, when you're passing through, you should feel free to stay with me at my place. I realize it isn't the fashionable East Side, but you won't get a nosebleed slumming it up on the Upper West Side, I can assure you of that. In fact it's become very trendy in its own right. It will give us a chance to catch up. And what an honor for me to be able to just sit and talk with Sandy again."

De tree a we flew home together. Seats were easy to come by after the 6th of January, when the usual lull in traffic occurs after the holidays before the winter tourist season kicks in. Big Jim met Boolu at Kennedy, and Sandy and I took a cab into Manhattan, up to Jimmy's place. It was a heartwarming visit for all of us, with Jimmy bringing us up to date on his and John Grabowski's studio and we in turn talking about our operations. We were having a busman's holiday.

I felt the cold winter, and for Sandy it was even colder. With the exception of going out to dinner in the neighborhood, we went absolutely nowhere. The day we left, Jimmy had an early call, so he gave me a key and told us to lock up and leave the key with his neighbor downstairs. The limo arrived and I dragged the luggage to the curb. While the driver stacked it in the trunk, I took Sandy out of the wheelchair and had him hang onto a tree while I folded it up for the driver. But when I turned around for Sandy, he was down on his hands and knees. It had snowed the night before, and he had slipped on the snow at the base of the tree.

I picked him up and put him in the back of the limo as he was saying, "I'm fine, I'm fine. I just slipped."

"Newark," I directed the driver. I sat back in the cab, looked over at Sandy, and saw blood running down his face. Fortunately, I had his medical kit in the back seat with me. I always carried gauze bandage, tape, scissors, and paper towels plus all his medicines. I always needed gauze at the ready to dress his stomach stoma. He was bleeding like a stuck pig. His head must have scraped the tree on the way down as he slipped. I dabbed his forehead with gauze. As far as I could see, it was a good-sized wound but superficial. I was having trouble getting the bleeding to stop. It wouldn't coagulate. He was on blood thinners that were, I knew, making him bleed even more. There we were, racing through the Holland Tunnel with me making like a paramedic in the back of an ambulance. By the time we reached the air terminal, I had him all bandaged up. He looked like the drummer boy in the Spirit of '76.

I was happy I had him in the wheelchair. If they gave me any flack about his getting on the plane in such a condition, I was prepared to tell them he was just coming home from a hospital operation. We got on without difficulty – think the wheelchair helped. He really looked as if he were in a bad way. He slept most of the way across the country.

At the baggage carrousel in LAX, I noticed he seemed to be a little confused, not clear-headed. I spotted Lee Remick with her family and hoped she didn't recognize Sandy. He was in no condition to be meeting or chatting it up with anyone. I hurriedly hailed a cab, put him in back, folded up the wheelchair, and stowed it in the trunk with the big bag. I put another bag in the front seat and stuffed the last one alongside me in the back. Then I collapsed next to Sandy and we sat there wordless until we pulled up in front of the Villa Fontaine in Valley Village.

I wheeled him into our apartment and went back down to the lobby to drag up the bags. I didn't even bother with the mail. I just straightaway wheeled Sandy down to the garage, unlocked the car, put him in his seat, and stuffed the chair into yet another trunk. I shot over Riverside Drive just past Coldwater and three blocks down to the local emergency clinic. There they examined him, discovering his very low pulse, and immediately put him on oxygen. Since they were affiliated, they notified Sandy's doctor who had Sandy moved in an ambulance to his hospital in Tarzana.

When I walked in the following morning, he was sitting up bright as a penny. It was obvious that lack of oxygen was the culprit and may have been all along. Dr. Bluming prescribed an oxygen tank for him. So we had a tank carrier fitted to the wheelchair, and of course the little mask was secured around his neck, fitting unobtrusively over his stoma at the base of his neck. Well, the arrangement was not as obtrusive as tubes up his nose would have been or a mask over his nose and mouth. This apparatus certainly wasn't going to hinder his teaching ability either, and if it kept his mind clear, well that was all the better.

Sandy's only comment through all this latest trouble, as he straightened up in the wheelchair and I rolled him out of Tarzana with the little mask over his stoma, was, "Just one more thing."

The oxygen was an improvement: it kept him clearheaded, and he only had to use it when he was active. All this affected me somewhat as well. It added to my lifting and hauling. When anyone mentioned it to me, I just said what Sandy had said, "Just one more thing." The important thing was the oxygen made him more lucid, and it made his work in class as well as my job in class a hell of a lot easier. And he never missed a class. He was ready on the 15th of January with his oxygen tank hooked onto his chair.

In class it all went well.
In spite of the fact he fell,
our Sanford never wavered
and his wit the whole class savored.

Not a single student spoiler,
he was one hot double boiler.
On all burners, he did swell,
bubbling over down in hell.

The performance thrilled them all.
Like the Bequia "irie" call.
Dat oxygen—
kissmarass!—
made de class a gas!

If the school were going to expand, we were going to have to move to make room for Marty's classes. We soon found a place to rent only three blocks up the road on Vineland and renovated it to suit our needs, putting in a stage, an office, a preparation room, and still having a more than ample classroom. We got word of a medical clinic on the south side going belly-up as many were in those days. We became scavengers. We picked up chairs, two couches (one a convertible), two desks, a number of small tables, and a computer. It was enough to get started with. Sandy needed the school three hours a day, four days a week. The rest of the time was Marty's or the students'.

The apartment felt a little confining after the house in Bellingham but what to do about it? I'll tell you what we did: we went out more. As well as the old crowd, we now had Marty and Jill to go out with. Sandy wasn't bothered by Jill's antics and her hyper, zealous, over-the-top enthusiasm. He didn't take her too seriously. He knew how to handle her.

My Flipping Eyes

I remember three hair-raising, nerve-shattering outings that left me in a shambles both nights. The first was one night after class, when we drove over to Pasadena, an area that was completely unfamiliar to me, to hear Patty Andrews and her accompanist-arranger husband, Wally Weschler, in concert. It was a wonderful walk down memory lane for both of us, with "Don't Sit under the Apple Tree," "Boogie Woogie Bugle Boy," and the like.

Unfortunately as we got up to leave, my eyes started acting up. They felt like they were jumping out of their sockets. I couldn't find our car in the parking lot. Thank God we had the wheelchair: it gave me something to hang on to keep from falling over. I didn't find the car till half the parking lot cleared out. I then managed to get out onto the street and headed in the right direction for the freeway west. But the glare of the headlights from the oncoming cars was blinding me so badly I missed our turn-off and found myself floundering in the local streets on the far side of the freeway.

All Sandy said was, "What the hell are you doing?"

"I've never been around here before," I replied. "A person can make a wrong turn, y'know."

I never said a word about my eyes. He would only worry and I was doing enough worrying for the two of us. I was going as carefully as I could. What else was there, the police? I was perfectly aware of what could happen, what would happen, if they got involved. Life as we knew it in California would be physically impossible without a license as one couldn't live here without a car. Our way of life would stop dead. So I just inched cautiously along. Luckily, I found the freeway entrance and took off, keeping over to the right. The lights from the oncoming traffic didn't bother me there: they were too far over to the left to be in my vision. All the red taillights up ahead didn't glare so much. Driving without passing any other cars and keeping a safe distance behind the car ahead, I eventually reached the 101 and our turnoff at Laurel Canyon. Once on the surface streets of Studio City, I was OK because I knew the area.

The second nerve-wracking outing was again one night after class, when

39 Bodies in Motion

Arthur Seidelman asked us to attend an opera he was directing down in Costa Mesa. The plan was for John Miranda, my newfound actor-friend from *Rescue Me*, to drive to the school, leave his car in the parking lot, and go down to Costa Mesa in our car with us. That was my first mistake.

Everything went fine until the party afterward (where we met Jane Withers, by the way, the '30s child actress who was the antithesis of Shirley Temple's sweet image). At the party, I felt the eyes beginning to act up again. I just hoped they wouldn't get any worse as we took off for home. However, Costa Mesa was much farther from home than Pasadena, and the problem wasn't letting up. I used the same driving technique as I had the last time, keeping over to the right, following the red lights, and making sure I didn't drive too close. The longer I drove, the more my eyes jumped.

Poor John was left to his own devices. He was a talker so I let him carry on the conversation while I concentrated on my driving. I wasn't much help with only an occasional "yes," "you bet," or "I should say so," while Sandy, due to his condition, was absolutely no help at all. He could have been fast asleep. We plowed along inch by inch. I thought we would never reach the Vineland turnoff into North Hollywood. We finally did, and the rest was a breeze.

Later, after I had got Sandy to bed, I sat by myself in the living room pondering my condition seriously for the first time. Tonight had been the fourth recurrence since New Year's of '91 in Texas. I was beginning to accept the fact that the condition could be more than just being tired or overextended, and I knew I had better take it up with the doctors at the VA.

Alas, I didn't until after the third hair-raising episode, the night we took the trip down to Compton, south of LA. That night Johnny and June Carter Cash were in town touring with their band. They had extended an invitation for us to come down, catch the show, and come back to meet with them and some of their family afterward, along with Rosie Edelman and Jane Seymour, two other friends of theirs. Sandy liked Johnny and June and considered Johnny a real talent.

So that night after class, we shot down the freeway to Compton, no problem. After the get-together backstage, while I was putting Sandy, the wheelchair, and all his paraphernalia into the car, the "feelings" started to come over me again. I started the car, backed it up a bit—and backed into Johnny's bus. The damn "feelings" made me overshoot the distance. I got out, looked at his bus, and saw no sign of damage to the bus or our car. I wasn't going that fast, thank God.

It had started to rain, and by the time I hit the freeway it was coming down in buckets, a real deluge. It happened to be the first big rain of the season. The pavement was as slick as ice with all the oil build-up coating the surface after such a long dry spell. Well, that was my theory anyway. Again I kept to the far right away from the line of advancing traffic. The traffic hurtling past us, at what I thought was ridiculous speed in this torrential downpour, was drowning our car with heavy sprays of water every time they streaked by. The experience was maddening. I was in a hell of a predicament. If I went too fast on this sheet of slippery pavement, I could misjudge and be forced to brake and slide, God knew where, out of my lane into oncoming traffic from behind. Yet if I went too slowly, I could cause a pile-up of vehicles approaching from behind. I myself, in regular weather, suffered slowpokes on the freeway badly. Fortunately, the visibility was so bad that in spite of those horses' asses speeding under such conditions, plenty were slowing it up like me in the slow right lane. So it was possible for me to ease my way along. All I can say is it was one long, slow, nerve-racking drive back to the Laurel Canyon turnoff. This trip really shook me up. Now I was certain I had a problem that needed looking into.

Well, the VA had doctors examine me at Sepulveda, West Los Angeles, Mount Olive, and even Sherman Oaks, and still they had no answer. My friend Rita Edelman insisted I go up to her doctor at the Parkinson's Institute at Sunnyvale near San Luis Obispo. When I told her I had no medical insurance, that I was a Vet, she said, "Who's talking about insurance? I'm saying we have to find out what your problem is. Come on. You go up with me." Friends like that are rare.

I had three MRIs, even one of those types that slice like cheese through the brain. It took hours to do, and the process damn near drove me out of my claustrophobic mind. In the end, they didn't know any more about what causes this "paroxysmal ataxia of the brain with sporadic vertical nystagmus" in my eyes than I did. Worst of all, they couldn't come up with a medication that would ease it. What I did about the problem was to learn to suffer through it and get on with my life. It took a few years, but in time the symptoms vanished as mysteriously as they had appeared. Sandy had been plodding along facing one medical mishap like this after another for years.

A Short Upheaval

At Villa Fontaine, our building manager was moving on and up to a better place to manage, leaving a two-bedroom apartment available on the first floor rear overlooking the garden. The apartment had a small porch off the dining room and it was on the side street with less noise. Thinking about Boolu and his visits out here, we felt it a good idea to take it when the old manager gave us first dibs on it. Right across the hall from our new front door was a cute little sauna that no one in the building ever used. I think most tenants didn't even know it was there, as we hadn't until we moved down. It was as if with the new apartment I had my very own sauna.

The Intensive Class that year started off with a bang. For the most part as a group they were bright, adaptable, and eager and willing to work hard. For his part, Sandy, in spite of the oxygen or because of it, was in his best form in years. Just having the one class to concentrate on and getting to see them every day seemed to take him back to the feeling of better years. He was reconciled to his limitations. All that mattered to him now was the Technique and staying well enough to continue teaching it. It was his sole remaining purpose in life.

40 All Shook Up

1993: Pop is Failing

Another season and it was time to stop and make ready for our trip back east. We were planning a trip to Utica to see Pop. For him it was the worst of times. He had reached the point of needing constant care, and Mom had reached her limit even with my sister-in-law Jane's help. Being a heavy man, he was hard for both to lift and it was quite a job for the two of them even to shift him. Mom and Pop were celebrating their 69th year of marriage, and putting him into a home was impossible for her to bear. But now the time had come; there was no other recourse.

In this time of need, we all gathered together, all my sisters and brothers and I, to be there for Mom. Sandy's class was scrubbed. We made our way to the Pennsylvania air hub and the jaunt up to Syracuse where Ed awaited us. It was never a bother for him to do a pick-up; he was always there at the ready. Pop was taking everything in stride, as he always did in life – that was his way. With vocal cords still as clear as crystal, he sang for the nuns and brought warmth to everyone. Why, he even won an amateur contest there at the age of ninety-three.

Sandy didn't say much, in his usual non-committal way. Perhaps Pop's condition was a cruel reminder of where he was in life. He suffered more physical setbacks than Pop and was much weaker by far. After a week we said our good-byes—it wasn't easy—and off we went. We were stopping in New York, but since Jimmy P. was on vacation, we were going to a hotel. The prospect seemed strange after so many years as residents.

However, Elizabeth Wilson found out. "I won't be around. You can stay at my place," she offered. "It's not so far from the Picasso. You'll feel right at home in the old neighborhood."

And that was what we did. It was a lovely apartment and a pleasant stay. We could look out her windows and see past the 59th Street Bridge and farther up to Kettering, reviving old memories of a more emotional time. I had planned to take Sandy to Dr. Shah, but after viewing the place from afar through Elizabeth's window, I thought, what for? That was all behind us now. Dr. Avrum Bluming, of whom we were fond, was his doctor now. I felt it was time for us to move on. So we did—right on down to Bequia.

But not before seeing Boolu, and attending a little gathering, a summer cookout up on Kathleen Nolan's turf. It was held in her rooftop garden outside her penthouse apartment on 55th Street. Well, it wasn't an apartment. It was a complete two-storey house right on top of the building, with a view encompassing the full 360 degrees as far as you could see. She had invited ex-students and some of Sandy's favorite cronies. Boolu carried on as if he were the maître d'. He felt quite at home there. He'd been working for Kathleen for over ten years. He now had jobs and his own boat to row. The tables had turned. New York had become his town, and we were the visitors now.

The Might-as-Wells

Bequia went well to begin with. I busied myself finishing off building a garage. The cistern had been built earlier with the intention that it would serve as foundation for a garage. But once it was done, we figured we could build a nice rental house over the tank and build a garage as well. On a steep hill, space was at a premium, so the garage ended up next to the water tank. That was how things grew and took hold around there. We called it "the might-as-wells," the thinking being that if we're doing this much, then we might as well go further and do that, too. We had learned it thoroughly up on 83rd thirty years before and we were still at it. I found many down in the Caribbean who were smitten with the same malady. It raised the price of everything you looked at and everything you did.

Christmas Marshall was now the carpenter, jack-of-all-trades, and total fix-it man for the Bequia Inn, where all Sandy's students had stayed for the past ten years, just below our place. Christmas would come up after work to help me with whatever needed to be done. He didn't just work for us—we were friends. He had been with us from the beginning, for over twenty-five years. He grew up with us, like Parnell and Boolu. Good old reliable Will was there, too. One day I couldn't find Mr. Will. He had been cutting bush around the other side of the hill. It was about 11:30 AM, and at noon he always stopped for lunch. But there he was coming down the road and up the drive. He had gone down the road and around the bend to Kenneth's shop for cigarettes. I was thinking he could damn well have waited until noon.

I shouted, "Where the hell have you been?"

He merely inquired, "Mr. Jimmy, how long have I worked for you?" It had been over twenty-five years.

"That's telling ya," Sandy said. "You were completely out of line."

Did I feel dumb. "You're right," I said. "I'm sorry, you're absolutely right." I turned and went back about my business.

These men were the core of the people we depended on. The distaff side was another matter. The women in our household came and went like the plague. I never suffered a slacker or a petty-toter. Over the years there were a slew of housekeepers. On the other hand, Winnie Dewer was with us almost ten years. She raised Boolu and took care of us until her cancer. She was very much a part of our family. She became Winnie Carville, my wife, a marriage of convenience that lasted another ten years. We eventually divorced in the late '80s. We have a wonderful one now, Petronella no less, Petronella Barber, but we call her Nella.

… … ## A Shock in the Night

Sandy sat around sunning himself, observing my antics, taking infrequent trips to De Reef. I had brought the empty oxygen tank with us and had it filled for Sandy as Dr. Avrum had suggested. But Sandy most of the time seemed clearheaded enough to me. So I never bothered to hook him up to the tank. Then, in the wee hours of October 4, 1993, I was awakened by a loud thump. Sandy lay sprawled out over the couch at the foot of my bed, struggling to get up. It was still dark, and he had gone to the John using his cane instead of his walker, not bothering to put on a light. Did he stumble into the couch or was it a lack of oxygen? Who knew? At that moment, who cared? I jumped out of bed and picked him up by the armpits. He couldn't steady his feet under himself. I looked and saw his right leg was all askew. I lifted him up, dragged him over to my bed, and laid him out on his back. There wasn't a sound out of him through it all.

The Island had come up in the world medically since the old days. Changes were being made, and made fast. I phoned for our brand new ambulance. It arrived in no time with the stretcher. The doctor at the clinic—we had a real doctor now—said, "His hip is broken. I'll fix a splint, but he'll have to go to St. Vincent."

At the General Hospital he wound up in the men's ward, a rather large one, but fortunately his bed was down at the end next to the window. Several doctors looked at him. They all came to the same conclusion: none of them felt qualified to work on him, mostly because of his general physical condition and his advanced age (eighty-eight at the time). They didn't want to take the risk, and that was just fine with me. They told me he would have to be sent to a specialist in Barbados. They would improve on the splint and put him in a long leg brace for transport, and I should make arrangements. One doctor did say the quicker the better and advised me to get the required medical clearance from the hospital administration.

I called Aggie, our housekeeper, and told her to pack our clothes and give them to Parnell with my briefcase containing our passports and papers. "Have him bring them right over to the hospital. And don't forget Sandy's medicine bag and his Jevity. We're going over to Barbados."

I knew I wouldn't be able to feed Sandy till Parnell arrived on the early afternoon boat. I had already called Jonathan Palmer of Mustique Air and told him we would need a charter to Barbados. He said he would be ready and waiting. The specialist in Barbados had been notified by a member of the St. Vincent medical staff. He would be waiting to receive Sandy and would operate first thing the next day.

We were all set to go. I had fed Sandy and had everything ready, and the staff had him all set. I had already heard from Jonathan, asking when we would be bringing Sandy out to the airport, but I had to tell him I would call him back.

I thought I had all my bases covered—until I walked into the administration office again. When I had first gone to the discharge office earlier that afternoon, I had immediately realized I was dealing with another self-important civil servant like the one I had encountered at the Housing Authority so many years before. Now I confronted this up-tight, officious, self-important bureaucrat for the second time that day. She would be nothing more than a flunkie anywhere else, if she were lucky. A wave of recollection took me back to '69 to that dumb building bureaucrat and her 275-cent stamp. This one had not one bit of the official paper work started, telling me she was waiting to hear from all the doctors to see if Sandy really had to go.

I didn't get it; it was no skin off her nose. Obviously you don't get sent by Vincentian doctors to Barbados willy-nilly—the cost to St. Vincent would be a deterrent. But we weren't asking St. Vincent for a dime, or Barbados either. Sandy would be paying his way no matter where or when. I didn't know what the hell this officiousness had to do with us. All I knew was Sandy had to get to Barbados and pronto. He was in pain, and this nitwit was farting around playing petty power games.

I knew if I stayed around her much longer waiting for her to move, I would blow up. Pictures of grabbing the pen out of her hand, hitting her over the head with a blunt object, and then signing the papers myself invaded my mind. An act like that wouldn't have helped my cause any, to say the least. It came down to the fact that this little paper-pusher really had the power to keep him in the country. I recalled Tiare and her husband, Lee, and their little poison episode at Arnos Vale Airport those many years ago and the difficulty she had had getting over to Barbados in a hurry. She had wound up taking off on the lam thanks to a compassionate pilot.

I walked back to Sandy on the ward, passing three doctors standing outside the office in the hallway just talking. One stopped me as I passed, "You still here?"

When I got back to the room, it was well after four o'clock. Jeremy Palmer was there from the airport asking, "What's the holdup?" I told him about the bitch in the office. "Come on. We can just take him. Jonathan has the plane waiting."

"Wait," I said. "I'll go back one more time. I don't need any more trouble." I went back to her office. The doctor who was in there had told her to fill out the papers, that we should go. That was all I needed to hear. I still had our passports. I went back to Jeremy. "Come on. Let's get the hell out of here."

A ward attendant helped me move Sandy onto a gurney, and we rolled him out back to the ambulance and took off for the airport. Jeremy told the driver not to stop at customs but to drive right out to the plane because they were all ready to take off. Now not only was Sandy running away from the hospital without his clearance, we were both leaving St. Vincent without clearance as well, like Tiare and Lee so many years before. We were skipping the country thanks to that efficient lady at the hospital. God, where were her priorities?

Never mind, I wondered, where was her heart?

They had taken the seats out of the plane to make room for the stretcher. Jonathan had already cleared the tower for take-off, and as passengers we were included, I imagined. If not, tough luck. In minutes we were airborne in the dark, skirting over the pitch-black sea. I was kneeling over Sandy in the stretcher on the floor of the plane. It was much like the Holland Tunnel run, only this time I was an air-evac paramedic. I was so preoccupied down there on the floor that I never did notice my very close friend Brigitte Anderson sitting behind Jonathan and Jeremy with Jason at her side. She didn't even interrupt to say hello. It was no time for niceties, and she had enough sense to leave us alone in these trying times. When I learned later they had been on the plane, why would I be surprised? They were always flying off somewhere.

When we landed on Barbados, Jonathan had arranged for an ambulance to deliver us to Queen Elizabeth Hospital. Despite our late arrival, the doctor came in to examine Sandy and said, "I'll just take X-rays tomorrow. He can rest and we'll perform the operation on Wednesday." This delay, I thought, is thanks to that procrastinating witch back on St. Vincent.

I hadn't had a bite to eat all day, from the moment Sandy's fall awoke me. I could have grabbed a snack on the boat—they served breakfast—but Sandy, with the nurse, had been put in a little room in front of where the cars roll in on the lower deck. I didn't want to leave him to go up to the restaurant on the upper deck. Besides, I didn't want to eat, I didn't feel like food. Later, at the hospital in St. Vincent, I had had no time to eat. By noon all I wanted to do was feed Sandy and get the hell out of the country. By the time we got to the hospital in Barbados, everything was closed.

I stayed with Sandy in his private room that night. I remember a nurse giving me a cup of coffee. I know I gave him his Jevity, and I believe I ate most of his breakfast in the morning. When he went down for X-rays that day, I went out and found a restaurant. I had to eat. When I got back, he was in his room. They must have had him doped up because he wasn't complaining of the pain. He dozed in and out all afternoon. The hospital rooms were big for just one person, the halls were long and wide, and there didn't seem to be many patients or visitors around, at least in this wing of the hospital. It was like a huge empty vault. The big old sprawling building was from another time, mid-Victorian would be my guess.

Since it was a private room, I decided to stay the night once again. Sleeping in the chair was pretty comfortable—this time it was a roomy one. The following day Sandy went down to be prepped or whatever. I was on overdrive by now. It was going to be a long day, so I took the time to go out and find something to eat.

When I came back, he was in never-never land. The doctor came in later and said, "He held up quite well for an ageable man in his condition. He broke his hip, but it was at the joint and his bones are strong, so the pin should hold. He'll probably sleep the night. I'll be in early in the morning." And away he went. Well, he did sleep the night, and I stayed with him. Like Boolu in St. Vincent, he was not on a monitor, and that was one good reason not to leave the room. Anyway, I wasn't about to, not that night.

When morning arrived bringing the doctor, Sandy was still out of it. The doctor checked his vitals, but all he said before he left was, "Operations like this are hard for patients of his age. So let's give him some more time."

I was becoming used to this West Indian fatalistic approach by now. I hadn't worried so much the day before. I had had a hunch he would make it, no matter that all those doctors in St. Vincent wouldn't touch him with a ten-foot pole. But now that he wasn't coming out of it, I began to fret. I was helpless to do anything, again like that horrifying night with Boolu at Dr. Cyrus's. The nurses were in and out all day checking him, but no one said anything. Knowing West Indians as I do, I was well aware that if they had nothing to say, they said nothing.

The doctor came in again about three and checked him out. All he said was, "He's still hanging in there. He apparently has a lot of fight left in him. His vital signs are still good." And he left again.

I didn't leave that day. I just stayed, ate his food, and prayed. He never budged all day. It reminded me of the coma episode at New York Hospital in '87 when he had had the bout of atypical pneumonia. He was breathing steadily, but that was all.

About midnight he started to stir, and I started talking to him. By daybreak he was really coming out of it. Daybreak to me in any hospital, whether it be there, St. Vincent, New York, or California, or even my night shift at the Utica State Hospital way back in '48 always brought with it a sense of renewed life. Always, just as the sunlight creeps in and over the windowsill touching everything in its path, ever so slowly that warm yellow light inches its way from its netherworld into the marrow of our bones, encompassing everyone and everything. I saw it bring new life to my sister Joan, to Boolu, and now, thank God, to Sandy. He was wide-awake, without a clue as to what had happened to him.

The doctor came in all smiles; the nurses had told him. He spoke to Sandy, explaining a bit about the technicalities of what he had done, basically describing the pin he had put in and Sandy's hard healthy bone. Later in the morning, the nutritionist came in and we talked about his G-tube, the reason for it and what brand of liquid nourishment he was given. In the afternoon the physical therapist came in with a walker, all ready to get him up and onto his feet. I doubted that the doctor had talked to her at all. Nevertheless I could see she was hell-bent on doing her thing, and I certainly wasn't going to be able to stop her. Though determined, she was nice, and cute into the bargain, so I went along with it, making damn sure Sandy didn't fall by standing right behind him to catch him when he did. True, I thought, the operation was Wednesday, but still, he had just woken up that morning. Yet she had him sitting up on the edge of the bed. I saw her do a double take when she saw the

G-tube. I don't believe she even knew he had one. She pulled the walker over to him and had him stand, and after a pause asked him to step out gripping the walker. As he stepped away from the bed, I slipped in right behind him. I just knew he was going to fall, and after three steps he caved in. I got him under the arms and dragged him back to the bed.

All I said was, "He's still pretty weak, and the anesthesia knocked him for quite a loop." I could sense her changing her demeanor.

"Well, I'll be in tomorrow," she said, "and we'll have a little workout then."

That evening I moved into a rooming house that a nurse on the floor put me onto just out back and across the street from the hospital. It was none too soon; I was in dire need of a shower and a change of clothes. The rooming house was a private family home in a little local house of little tiny rooms with oversize furniture. It was difficult to move around in. My room had a double bed and a small closet—I had to go sideways to get in and out. The proprietors catered to families of patients from St. Vincent and St. Lucia. They knew the Leach family from Bequia who had stayed there.

Saturday morning our cute little therapist showed up with pen, clipboard, and paper, ready to get to work. We were more successful this time, I felt because we took our time. First we sat him up on the side of the bed and eventually and slowly got him on his feet and then went step by step. Soon he was making it over to the doorway and back, with me right behind him. By Sunday afternoon, he was out in the hall. We kept that up all week, and on Thursday the doctor said he could go home on Friday.

Maybe the doctor thought so, but I wasn't so sure. That trip to St. Vincent and Bequia was still pretty rough even for the most able. So it was my intention to find a little place on the beach here in Barbados to give him time to recuperate. My other, ulterior motive was to keep him near the doctor a little longer in case any unforeseen complication developed. I didn't want another international incident with St. Vincent.

Shaken to the Core

Most hotels were closed this time of year. I managed to find the Regency Cove, which although closed had a little efficiency unit they would rent us by the week. I don't remember the town, but it was on the main road to the airport and just across the road from the beach.

We left the hospital for the apartment on Friday. I could wheel him around the area in his chair. Saturday morning I had a big load of wash to do. It had been almost two weeks and I needed to wash clothes. I also had to buy towels, washcloths, food, Kleenex, and things. The store was a block away and the Laundromat two blocks down the road. The big problem was what to do with Sandy? He didn't want to go. So I said, "Stay in bed and don't answer the door."

"No," he said, "I'll just sit in the wheelchair."

I was leaving with a pillowcase full of dirty clothes, and as I looked back at him, it occurred to me: "What if you should fall asleep? You would tumble out of the chair and hurt yourself."

"So tie me in, so I can't slip."

I had seen my mother tie some of my small brothers and sisters in a highchair many times. Not really thinking it through, I got one of my neckties, secured him to the chair under his arms, and left.

I went to the Laundromat first, put the clothes in, and then went to the store. I returned to the Laundromat and was waiting for the clothes to dry, sitting there impatiently, when I started to get anxious about the possibility of something happening back at the apartment. "What if..." thoughts kept invading my mind. What if a fire broke out and someone were trying to get in to rescue Sandy? What would Sandy do? Never mind Sandy! What would the authorities do to me for leaving him like that? In America, they would have me up for abuse in a shot.

I grabbed the groceries and the stuff I had bought for Sandy in the corner dry-goods store. Leaving the clothes in the dryer, I double-timed it back the two blocks to the apartment. When I opened the door, there he was, sitting as if nothing had happened, because nothing had happened, much to my relief. I untied him and put him in bed, where he should have been in the first place. Later I ran back for the laundry, on the double again.

That night I took him across the street to a nice restaurant. He was on nourishment so it didn't matter. After I got him back to the room I started thinking, what we were doing. There were just the two of us, and he shouldn't be left alone, couldn't be left alone. Yet here we were in a strange country where we didn't know one solitary person save Jeremy at the airport. This wasn't a well thought-out program. Monday I would have to find a nurse for respite care.

Sunday was pleasant. We went across to the beach pavilion, where quite a bunch of Bajans were eating and swimming. On the beach, we had, correction, I had a leisurely lunch and Sandy watched the bathers coming and going. God, I thought, he couldn't even eat an ice cream cone. That night after his feeding, he hit the sack early, exhausted after our outing on the beach. He was fast asleep and I was reading when the phone rang. It was my brother Fred calling to tell me Dad had passed away. It was the wee hours of the morning. Fred knew Sandy's situation, that he had just come out of the hospital. He remained noncommittal as to what I should do, merely saying, "I felt you should know, that's all."

I thanked him, hung up, and just sat there thinking of Dad. Damn it, I thought, I can't wake Sandy up. If we're moving out tomorrow, he'll need his rest. I immediately set about packing and getting everything ready to move. In the morning at 7:00 o'clock, I called the airlines. Because it was a death in the family, they got us on an American flight for Kennedy around 4 PM. Then I called to reserve a rental car at the airport.

40 All Shook Up

Next I got Pat Field on the phone and asked her to get to Boolu somehow, call his sister Sherry if she hadn't already gone off to work. It was just after seven. "However you have to do it, please get to him. Tell him Pap-Pap has died and he should pack a bag with a dark suit and be ready to leave Jefferson Avenue about 11 PM tonight. We'll be coming by in a car." If anyone could or even would get this done, I knew Pat was the one.

When Sandy woke up, I told him. "Your poor mom. Can we make it? When's the funeral?"

I told him we would make it, that we had a flight out. I fed him and checked out at the office, called a cab for pickup at 2 PM. I didn't want to cut it too close. While unpacking the cab at the airport, I realized we had left the walker behind. The driver offered to go back for it. The time came to go into the waiting lounge and still no cab, so we kissed the walker goodbye and went in. Just as boarding was announced, I heard someone yelling at the customs check-in counter. It was the driver with the walker.

Sandy slept on the plane; he could sleep anywhere. I thought I would as well. I hadn't slept all night, hadn't even gone to bed. Alas, I was too hyped up. Thoughts of Pop and my childhood filled my mind. I had wanted to be so much closer to my dad, but how could I? Religious people seem to have no place in their hearts for the likes of me, and Pop was from the old school. From people like them, all people like me could ever hope for was just a little understanding. I knew I had let him down with the priesthood stuff, but that would have been wrong, oh so wrong, for me. All I could do was emulate him, endeavor to continue what he lived for, and that was to sing. I thought of the play, *I Never Sang for My Father*. There I sat in my sorrow hoping I had sung for my dad. I wanted to believe, based on some of our talks, though they were few and far between, that toward the end he really did understand me and my peculiar predicament, because to him that's all it must have been. I remembered one balmy afternoon in August sitting out back at the farm just passing the hour. I was twenty-nine at the time, and it was when my friend and ex-lover Dick was having marital troubles with Heidi.

Out of a clear blue sky, Pop said, "Just because all your brothers are married, don't think that solves all their problems. And don't think you have to go out and do the same thing, because your problems are not theirs. Their problems are not all solved by a long shot. In fact, they're just beginning. You just continue what you're doing. It will work out for you with those fancy people down there, you just wait and see."

"You mean do my own thing?" I joked.

"Whatever you call it. You just wait." And he slapped me on the knee and got up to go feed the horses. That was probably the closest, most intimate moment Pop and I ever shared.

When the plane landed at Kennedy, disembarking was a hassle with Sandy in the wheelchair, plus the walker, our two carry-on bags, and the briefcase to cope with. Then leaving the baggage area with all the rest of our baggage as well was so traumatic that to this day I do not recall one bit of it. How we reached the Kinney car rental place was anybody's guess, but we did and they had our car ready for us.

Getting to Boolu in Brooklyn at 11:30 PM was another kettle offish. I had only ever been there once, by subway. How the hell was I ever going to find it from Kennedy without a map? The car rental office was no help at all. I figured if I stumbled onto Atlantic Avenue, I could take it into the heart of Brooklyn, and once there someone could direct us. That is, if we were lucky enough to find someone who would stop to talk at that hour. We could just as easily be ripped off. Though the prospects didn't look good, I hung onto the hope someone might just help us. All the time I was quietly praying, pleading to God above that this night above all my eyes would hold up.

We did stumble onto Atlantic, a rather large, well-lit avenue. As we proceeded down into the heart of Brooklyn, my eyes started to go. Fortunately, the traffic was light because I needed to slow down at every big intersection to read the street signs. Sandy was absolutely no help, of course; all he could give me was encouragement.

Atlantic Avenue seemed endless. My eyes fluttered and faltered and the street went on and on. It was torture! I had had no idea how big Brooklyn was. It dwarfed Manhattan. As we finally neared the center of town, I sensed it. I must have recognized the names of some of the more familiar streets. There was Nostrum—Boolu's subway stop! I started trying to read every street sign but I kept missing some because my eyes were flipping now, making it difficult.

I was beginning to fear I had unwittingly passed it when, lo and behold, there it was: Jefferson Avenue. We turned right on Jefferson and within two blocks we were there. I cruised down the whole block but I couldn't make out the house numbers. I stopped the car, double-parking it, and got out. I had passed the house. But I spotted Boolu sitting out on the stoop with his suitcase at his side.

He climbed into the back seat saying, "I sorry. I sorry... Poor Pap-Pap..."

"Did you bring your dark suit?" I asked.

"Yes, I bring de black one."

"Boolu, you don't have a black suit."

"Yes, I do," he came back, "my duck-dee-doe."

"Oh, no!" I said sharply. "Not your tux!"

Sandy intervened. "Forget it, and lay off him. It's not important."

You see, back on Bequia, old gentlemen of any importance still dragged out their formal attire when attending a funeral; that is, if they happened to be fortunate enough to be the proud owner of such. Some still wore black bowlers.

My next big job was to get over to and through Manhattan and up to the Expressway. I knew with my eyes it wasn't going to be easy. I thought it best to take the Brooklyn-Queens Expressway up to Astoria, then the Triborough

Bridge, cutting out Manhattan entirely, and then go over into the Bronx. From there, it would be familiar territory for me. Our first hurdle was getting to the Triborough Bridge with no one to help. Boolu couldn't read and Sandy couldn't see and by now I was already feeling blotto. Well, through much stress and strain we did it and finally got to the good old Major Deegan Expressway. From there I knew my way.

It was late and the traffic was slight. It was now just a matter of endurance. We stopped just beyond Schenectady for a bite to eat and a little rest for me, which I sorely needed. Sandy needed nourishment so we taped his feeding bag up on the wall. He sat with us, being fed while we ate cheeseburgers. I'm sure we were an unusual sight to all who were there that night, but I didn't give a damn. Sandy was hungry and I was tired.

We were all a bit rejuvenated for the last lap home. We passed Mohawk and Ilion—and then ran into thick fog. With my eyes, that could have spelled disaster. They were diffusing the light enough without the fog adding to the nebulousness. I could see to make my way, but I was afraid of driving too slowly and getting plowed into from the rear. I managed to get behind a big well-lit truck that wasn't going too fast either. I maneuvered along with him until we reached our turnoff at Exit 31 in Utica. I was a shattered wreck all right, but otherwise none the worse for wear. We drove up the arterial to the Radisson Hotel and checked in about 5 AM.

I put Sandy to bed, Boolu crashed, and I took a well-earned hot shower and then crashed myself. We slept till about noon. Boolu had already taken off with someone, Eric or Gary or maybe my brother Ed who was always working at or arranging something. If work needed to be done, Boolu would gravitate there, making himself useful. For his part, Ed would be just the one to find Boolu something to do.

I fed Sandy, dressed him, and made myself presentable. We went out, and I had brunch, then stayed in the room until it was time to go to the wake.

Dad's Wake

At the funeral parlor, Sandy sat up front in his wheelchair next to Joan who sat next to Mom at the end of the front row. When I first went in and knelt at Pop's coffin, I broke up. Mom was at my side in a flash and embraced me from behind, then knelt next to me holding my hand, and though nothing was said, I knew she knew. "Now you know, Pop, now you know for sure" kept running through my thoughts. I had never cried for my father and now I broke. At last it was over.

Then we, as the children, all stood in a line. Someone gave each of us a green ribbon to wear, making it easy for the mourners to know who we were. There were nineteen of us and most people there hadn't seen us in years.

Dad had left a number of descendants counting everyone in the immediate family, in-laws and out-laws, and my extended family. Only a granddaughter and a son-in-law had predeceased him: with the exception of Sherry Carville and Ronald Babitz, we were all very much alive and well.

The wake started in earnest about 6 PM and went on all evening. About halfway through I asked Sandy, "How are you holding up? Do you want to turn in?"

"Why? Are you tired?" he responded. And he stayed to the end with the rest of us, both nights. He was very much a part of the family and he knew and felt it.

We didn't leave until after ten. Some ate early and others went out and grabbed a bite, but I didn't because Sandy didn't need to eat. We let Boolu fend for himself.

The following night was a repeat of the first. Among the mourners were teachers, politicos, clergy, and more teachers as well as all his and our friends from as far back as the '30s up on City Street. Pop was a simple man who was well loved and didn't have an enemy in the world, nary a one, with the possible exception of old Dan Rude, and Dad got the better of him in the end. That was a long story, and in any case he too had already made an exit. Pop had one sister who was still living in Florida. I was told she couldn't make it because she had broken her hip a little over a month ago.

"A month ago?" I repeated. "Sandy broke his hip in the middle of the Caribbean a little over a week ago and he's sitting up there in the front row." I knew my aunt and I knew her well. Dad was her big brother whom she thought the world of, but she couldn't have got there by herself any more than Sandy could have on his own.

The church service befitted Dad's religious belief and his loyalty to it, his unbending faith and devotion. Three priests celebrated solemn high mass, and the sanctuary was full of clergy, a number of whom spoke, as did my brother Jerry. Leo sang. I would like to have as well, but I knew it would be too emotional for me. I doubted I could manage it even if I had been asked. When the bagpipes skirled, I crumbled!

After the burial the family all gathered at Mandy's oldest girl Chrissie's place. We all reminisced as Sandy sat with Mom and her sister, my aunt Baby, taking it all in. We ate, we drank, we sang, we danced, and we told funny stories. Baby had come all the way up from East Orange, New Jersey, on a bus, all by herself.

"Had to," she said. Never mind she was eighty-eight. "Your dad was such a wonderful man. We all did love him so. And I am having the time of my life! Nora," she said turning to Mom, "It's like Tommy is still here. It's like he never left. And those kids are somethin' else."

I heard Mom say, "He is, and I hope he always will be. Baby, this is what I pray for, that they always stay together like this." Honestly, a truly good time was had by all.

Regrouping

It had only been days since we had taken that grueling trip up from Barbados, just a little too soon to be out on the road again. Mom and Joan were not going right back home, but would stay with John and Mandy in Rome to give them time to adjust. I wanted to spend time with Mom just now as well.

Mandy said to me, "We have room. Why don't you guys come up as well and take a little rest before you head back. Jimmy, I know you could use it. You look like hell. We have a hospital bed. We can put it up in the living room so Sandy won't have to climb the stairs. There's plenty of room in there, and anyway we live in the family room in the back."

"Mandy, I'm going to take you up on that invitation. It's too soon to start dragging Sandy back to the city."

It worked out perfectly for all of us, and Boolu got to spend some time with his cousin, their son Gregory. We all just sat around and talked about anything and everything for the next few days. All I wanted to do was get home to Valley Village and collapse. I was sure Sandy felt the same. En route through New York, I didn't want to bother any of our friends with a short intrusion of nothing more than an in-and-out stay. So I called Kent Paul who arranged for a room at a moderately priced hotel on West 57th Street. I found it a weird feeling, staying in a hotel in New York City. I had only stayed in one once back in '45 when I came to town with my father's friend Dave Cahill to help him off on a Cunard Liner back home to Ireland. Oh, yes, and one other time when I was in the Army in '48 and passing through town, I stayed at the 23rd Street YMCA.

Sandy remarked on the strangeness, too. "I can't ever remember staying overnight in a hotel in the city, except when I was living in one."

"Sandy," I said, "we're already interlopers. We've only been gone a year, and yet, after living here for what seems like a lifetime, it's already behind us."

A lot had happened since Sandy's trip from the John on his cane in the wee hours of that October morning. It was one of the longest trips he ever made. Well, the trip was over and he was home in LA, with the help of a walker this time. He used the walker around the house; we took the wheelchair when we were out. We left the walker behind because I felt the chair was enough for me to handle when we were schlepping around town.

When we had reached Utica, I had called off the class openings. They would have to be postponed indefinitely, if they would ever open I thought at the time. Maybe after the first of the year. Even that wasn't definite. I couldn't close up the school just now; that was the last thing Sandy wanted me to do. But Sandy's job at the time was to get his strength back. It had all taken one hell of a swipe at him.

Thanksgiving Stew

About the middle of November, his blood pressure was dropping. When his pulse hit fifty-five Dr. Avium told me I had better get him into a hospital. He was admitted over Thanksgiving, and as usual I was spending every minute with him. Whenever his vital signs dropped, he would become extremely agitated and difficult to handle, ranting and raving much like he had behaved at Bellevue after the van accident. Paul Morrison had behaved this way during his last days, and you can bet I was fretting. I would come early in the morning and leave about 11:30 PM after Sandy had settled.

On Thanksgiving Day, Dr. Avrum came in and said, "Jim, what are you doing for dinner?"

"Nothing."

"Yes, you are. You're having dinner with my family. Sandy will do just fine with the nurses," he said.

So I went and met his wonderful family—his beautiful wife and children, his mother-in-law, the grandfather, and his lovely sister, Rebecca Bell. It was a typical Norman Rockwell celebration in an impeccably appointed home on a hillside like ours, only with a modern motif. I was having a grand time with all these hospitable people whom I had just met, but alas, dinner was soon over and it was time for me to get back to reality and Sandy.

When I got back to his room, I was surprised to see the door shut. As I walked in, the sight that befell me was unbelievable. Two nurses were down on their hands and knees, one on each side of the bed, wiping blood up off the floor. The sheets and blanket were rolled up in one big ball on the bed. Sandy, wearing the typical hospital gown with the slit up the back, was sitting on the marble floor on his bare butt, his back up against the wall. He was still attached to the monitor, but his IV was ripped out and his catheter bag had spilt on the floor mixing with the blood from the transfusion bag. The older nurse stood up and started to explain what had happened.

I cut her off. "There's no need to explain to me. I know what's happened. Let's get him up off the floor and into that chair, and then we can clean up this mess." And we all did. The nurses took out the soiled linen and together they made the bed. They cleaned him up and put him back into bed and finished mopping up the rest of the floor.

Later they came back in and proceeded to hook him back up to everything. They had to reconnect the blood transfusion, catheter, and IV, and adjust the monitor. When they finished, the head nurse checked him out more thoroughly. He seemed to be unscathed. The younger nurse said to me, "My, you were so cool. I can't get over you."

"Oh," I said, "it's not me. It's him. He's already done this a few times before, which is why I feel I have to keep a close eye on him."

By the time the nurses were finished and finally left the room, they were exhausted. Sandy had done this once at the Hospital for Special Surgery after the van accident. He had been so rough on the nurses there that they used to roll his bed out into the hall right in front of the nurses' desk each night, so they could keep an eye on him. While at Kettering, on the day after his esophagus operation, they had found him walking down the hall dragging behind him the monitor box on one side and the pole with the medicine, the IV, and the blood transfusion on the other, all still hooked up to him. He was barely over the effects of the anesthetic. And there had been all those G-tubes he had pulled out on me. So you can see why this episode was no surprise to me. Whenever I had left him in this condition over the years, I always feared what I might be confronted with when I got back. Once, during that first operation at Kettering, when he was blind and couldn't talk because of the laryngectomy, he kept banging on the side of his bed. The nurses had him write, and he kept blindly scribbling my name. It was 4 AM but they called me anyway.

"Should I come up?"

"No. Let us put you on his phone and see if you might be able to quiet him down." It settled him a bit. In times like this he wasn't easy; he had a will of iron, which I was well aware of.

That little episode passed as did so many of the others. Once back home again, we spent our days on our little side porch over Radcliffe Street, with Sandy on oxygen most of the time.

41 Shaken and Stirred

A Long Overdue Recognition

Every two weeks I took Sandy in to see Dr. Avrum who was keeping a close eye on him. One day he told Sandy, "Every now and again the Cancer Hope Foundation celebrates an outstanding individual who has demonstrated excellence in his or her chosen field while battling the trials and tribulations of cancer. With your permission, I would like to submit your name as a possible candidate."

"Why me?" Sandy asked.

"That's self-evident," the doctor replied.

"When?"

"Sometime next fall."

Sandy thanked him, saying simply, "If you want." And that was that.

Christmas was bearing down on us and it was going to be celebrated at Rosie's. She always liked it when we didn't go to Bequia and were able to come to her place. We were a part of her extended family now. My only worry was how to get Sandy up that steep stone staircase outside her second-floor flat. It was an unnecessary worry. When we got there, he mounted it slowly, bit by bit, in his own time, under his own steam. After the first of the year, Sandy started to get bored and wanted to start school again. I asked him if he thought he could handle it.

"Why not? I don't teach with my legs, and my speech is fine, or as well as can be expected. We have the oxygen for support. So let's get crackin.'"

I thought to myself, if we can crack at all – we'll be lucky if we don't crack up into the bargain. I had another thought. Sandy might die with his boots on. Then I thought, oh, why the hell not?

Sandy started his 60th year of teaching on the 6th of January. Off and running again, although I wondered how long he could keep it up this time.

Dr. Avrum was not as optimistic and told me he was worried. The danger that Sandy wouldn't be with us in the fall was also on his mind. He suggested moving the date for the Cancer Hope Foundation Awards Gala to March. I thought Sandy would want to be the last one to hear this. He never was told why the date was moved up.

Sing-Along Came Along, and Why Not?

Surprisingly, the classes moved along at a clip. I would give Sandy oxygen as much as possible, though he wouldn't use it in class. He made me leave the chair and the oxygen bottle outside the classroom. With Sandy's speech holding up, I had little to do and I was getting bored. Amity Janow, a former student of Sandy's still active around the place, told me about a wonderful voice teacher, who, by the way, had also studied with Sandy back in the '60s. In those days, the class was taught on 56th Street at the old studio I had designed and set up for Sandy next door to Patelson's Music House. It was up over the Laundromat on the second floor just behind Wynn Handman's studio. Wynn was Sandy's teaching assistant in the '40s.

Apparently Seth Riggs, the voice teacher, had been doing very well for himself teaching the superstars in La-la land. The list was long with luminaries such as Michael Jackson, Carol Lawrence, and Faye Dunaway. Bette Midler wouldn't study with him, I was told, because he was too expensive. When I heard the cost, I had to agree with her. But Amity kept insisting he was so good. And I wouldn't work with anyone I felt wasn't top of the line anyway. She told me Seth thought the world of Sandy and that he knew me. She was sure he would work out some deal with me if I really wanted to work with him.

Even though I had been away from it for some time, when I found out Seth himself had studied with my teacher's old buddy, Dolph Swing, my interest deepened. Both my teacher, Bernard Taylor, and Dolph had taught at Juilliard when I was there. So I called Seth, we worked out a satisfactory fee, and I started workouts. My class was scheduled just before Sandy's class, so Sandy would come with me. Afterwards, we would hightail it over to the acting class. Sandy was getting as big a kick out of it as I was. I must say Seth lined my voice up pretty quickly after so many dormant years. This was really a happy time for both Sandy and me.

Then it happened! We were jolted out of our sleep at minutes to 4 AM to a pitch-black night. There it was again—the house was shaking to its very foundations!

1/17/94: The Earth Rolls and the House Succumbs

"It's an earthquake!" I yelled as I jumped out of bed. You couldn't see your hand in front of your face in the pitch black. I pulled Sandy out of bed and slid him across to the closet doorway, setting him on the floor in the threshold. I remembered being told that the threshold of a doorway was a safer place to be, if you couldn't be outside. I heard the pipes in the bathroom break and water started spilling into the bedroom. I was trying to remember where I had put the flashlight, and I couldn't for the life of me come up with it. My mind was shattered and scattered.

The phone rang and I cracked my shinbone on something as I stumbled over to find it. I managed to follow the wire to it. My sister Anita was on the line from Connecticut where she had heard the news over the TV while having breakfast. I told her we were OK and asked her to call Mom and please tell the others.

Crawling back to Sandy, I heard voices outside as I passed the bedroom window. I stood up to look out. All I could see were a few flashes from what must have been flashlights. I yelled out but got no answer. The window was jammed, useless. The bedroom was too far in from the street, so I slithered back to Sandy. I knew I could do nothing until daybreak. Even if I had been able to find his wheelchair, under the circumstances it would have been useless.

I said to him, "We're just going to sit here and weather out the aftershocks. No way will we get out of here until daybreak."

"Where's the flashlight?" Sandy asked.

"I wish the hell I knew. I felt under the bed stand, but it wasn't there."

So there we sat, water rising inch by inch, and as uncomfortable as it was, it didn't bother me. I knew it had to run off somewhere sooner or later. We weren't in the cellar. When I explained to Sandy, he said, "Not yet." He'd hit on what I was worried about most—that one of these aftershocks would finish off the building completely.

As daylight broke through the window, I could see that all the Sheetrock walls had buckled in on us. About then I heard banging on the front door. I crawled out of the bedroom under the Sheetrock and through it on my hands and knees, shouting, "We're in here and need help!"

The answer I got was the most welcome sound I could ever have asked for. It was Marty's voice saying, "The door is jammed but we'll get it. I got Kirk with me."

I crawled back to Sandy in the bedroom sitting in six inches of water. "It's Marty and Kirk Woller. They're going to get us out of here."

I pulled Sandy up off the floor, sat him on the bed, and started undressing him to get him out of his wet clothes. It was getting lighter now. I found his shorts, socks, and T-shirt. Marty and Kirk had broken their way through and made their way to the bedroom. Then everything started shaking again.

"Come on!" Kirk barked. "We have to get out of here!"

I grabbed Sandy's long terrycloth robe from the closet and there it was, the damn flashlight, on a shelf right over Sandy's head all the while. So much for earthquake readiness. I put the robe on him, saying to Marty, "The chair is useless. You two will have to drag him out. I'll fold it up and drag it out behind you somehow."

Kirk had pushed back the Sheetrock to make way for us. Once we made it into the hall, I said to Marty, "Take Sandy down to the end of the hall. The door on the left is a fire exit to the street, if you can get it open. Here's the chair. Come right back. There are some things I must bring."

Shafts of daybreak were peeking down through the trees, shedding a modicum of energetic light into the apartment, light so sparse I could barely see all the damage. Everything in the room had tumbled over on itself, including the TV and the bookcases. The kitchen cupboards were wide open and cleaned of every dish and glass, all of them smashed on the kitchen floor. The sliding glass doors in the dining room, the ones leading to the porch overlooking Radcliffe Street, were shattered.

I gathered up Sandy's medical supplies, the bandages, Kleenex, his empty oxygen tanks, and Jevity, piling them near the door, then turned around to collect a blanket and some towels. Kirk came back to help. It wasn't an easy task getting through the hallway with its caved-in walls. "Come on, Jimmy," Kirk said, urging me on.

"Kirk, Sandy can't go without these."

Then Kirk looked over at the gaping hole in the dining room doors. "God! Jimmy, you're going to have looters."

I thought, you're damned right. "Tell Marty to wrap Sandy in this blanket and leave him on the stoop—he'll be all right by himself—and tell him to get back in here." I went into the living room, stepping over and around the broken furniture, picking up the paintings that had fallen with the caved-in Sheetrock walls.

Marty was back at the door. As I handed some of the paintings to him, he looked at me quizzically. "Paintings?"

"Marty, don't ask. They're Chagalls! We'll keep them in the car. Here are the keys. You go see if the car will still start and if we can get it out of the damn garage. If we can't, what else can we do? Put the Chagalls in the back of the car anyway. And tell Kirk to come back in."

I went back and got a couple more paintings for Kirk. At the door I turned around and took one last look. The only thing left standing was the refrigerator, which had danced its way into the middle of the kitchen. Looking into the living room one more time, I realized I was wrong: the fireplace was still intact. There on the mantle were four pieces of Paul Morrison's rare, 17th century, black and white Italian porcelain. They were the only things left on the mantelpiece; everything else had crashed to the floor. I can still see that unbelievable sight. The last thing I did was to go over and pick them up, one by one, and put them on the floor in a closet. As I was making my way out to leave for the last time, I heard a crash and turned to look behind me. The lovely Adams fireplace mantle lay on the floor in smithereens. Go figure. Was it Paul? Why not? He must have loved those Italian pieces.

The car was still in working order. Marty got it out and put Sandy into it. Kirk explained they would go back to Jill's and bring back some plywood to block up those smashed glass doors.

"Good," I said. "Here's the key."

"What for?" Kirk asked. "The door is smashed in, remember?"

Marty said, "You better give us the key. We'll see what we can do." Then he instructed me to go to some large supermarket and stock up on water. "We don't know how long this siege is going to last, so you better get your water first before it's all gone. We got some at Ralph's earlier. Once you get the water and Sandy's oxygen, you can come back to our place. All we have are broken dishes, and we do have Jill's friend with us, but we'll make room."

"I'm sure if Bob and Maxine Carnegie weathered it safely we can stay with them. Theirs is a big house. Thanks for the offer, but you guys have done enough. We couldn't have done it without you two. Thanks a million," I said as I started the car.

They hightailed it down Riverside to Laurel Canyon, and I figured I'd better head to a supermarket off the beaten track. I knew of one in a business district beyond Vineland. The traffic lights were out of commission and cars were piling up at every intersection, with everyone crossing gingerly to avoid a collision. When we finally got there, my hunch turned out to be right. Not too many people had arrived yet and there was still bottled water left. I picked up four gallons, completely forgetting to buy food. Since we were near the school, I told Sandy I had better check it out. Fortunately, it was a new building and for the most part unscathed with only minor damage. Just four blocks farther on Lankershim, the brick facades of the building fronts had crumbled and tumbled into the street. It was an older section of town with buildings that were not up to modern-day building code.

Now it was time to get the oxygen. A card attached to the tanks had two addresses, one up north in Canoga Park beyond Northridge, an area that should probably be avoided, and the other miles away, south of LA, somewhere off the Golden State 5 between Compton and Anaheim. If the traffic around us was any sign of what it would be like making our way down there, we would be at it for days. Worst of all, I had no idea of where it would be once we got there. It was a hell of a lot closer to Canoga Park, my way up there I knew, and I knew the area. If I stayed south of Northridge on Victory Boulevard and veered around the earthquake center, then turned north to Canoga Park once I passed Northridge, I figured we should make out all right. Oh, I knew it was going to be touch and go all the way.

Along the way toward the center of the quake, people were milling about in little family-like groups—in open fields around churches and schools, on football fields and baseball diamonds, and in public parks. The FEMA people (the Federal Emergency staff) were already setting up outdoor stations, putting up tents and tables. Lines were beginning to form. Claims would have to be made, forms filled out, and questionnaires answered. In some lines people were waiting for water or food and, at one spot, blankets. Some people were staking out an area for their family or a neighborhood group, while others were pitching tents. People were obviously afraid of a large aftershock and were planning to spend the night out in the open. I had never seen the likes of this in America, or anywhere else for that matter.

When we passed Northridge, we veered north to Canoga Park. We got there to find the place open. It wasn't until that moment that I realized I hadn't given one fig of thought to the possibility it wouldn't be. They took our empty tanks and gave us three full ones. Who knew when they would be delivering again?

Now that we had our water and our gas, the next job would be to find a place to stay. I had assumed Bob and Maxine Carnegie. We were now on the

41 Shaken and Stirred

far side of Northridge and we had to go around again to get back. I thought, as my curiosity was getting the better of me, we could cut right through Northridge. We had papers now to prove where we were and where we lived, which was directly ahead through Northridge. So why not try? All they could do was make us detour around it. So I said to Sandy, "You know, things like this only happen once in a lifetime. What do you say we go back right through the center. What can they do?"

"I haven't anything better to do," said Sandy wryly.

"Very funny," said I.

Accepting the inevitable is the easiest thing to do when nothing under the sun can be done to change it. We were used to rolling with the punches and seeing things through, whatever the outcome. With nothing more than a let's-go-see from me, we were off. Driving down Roscoe as we neared the center of the quake, we saw buildings in shambles here and there. People looked dazed, befuddled, and nervous. Fire fighters and police officers, fire engines and patrol cars, scurried about. Hordes of photographers were snapping everything in sight. After a slight detour in the village of Reseda, we were right back on Roscoe where the area around Northridge Hospital was a hub of activity. I had once taken Sandy there when Dr. Avrum had sent him for some check-up. Perhaps it was nothing more than a stress test though God knows his life was enough of a stress test.

We were now approaching Balboa Boulevard and leaving the distressed area. I noted as we passed the end of the airfield that no planes were taking off or landing as yet. We turned onto the 405 and made our way to Bob and Maxine's. Sandy was still in his bathrobe, and neither of us had eaten anything since the day before. As we drove into their driveway and shut off the engine, Bob was headed out the front door and at Sandy's window before I could even get out of the car. Maxine came out and up to my window. We passed pleasantries, you might say, and Maxine told us they were OK and had been restacking books. I told them we had been hit pretty badly, that we must have been on a fault or the building code was not up to standard, maybe a little bit of both. I said something to the effect that there was no way we could sleep there that night. They could see Sandy was still in his night-clothes, and I told them we had just got back from getting oxygen. To my shock, no invitation was forthcoming from them, not even to come in for a spell or a have-you-eaten? This from the couple who had been so helpful when we first moved out to LA!

I had Sandy's food with me, but I needed a place to feed him. When Bob suggested there must be a hotel in the area, I said, "I'm sure there is. We had better go find one before they're full."

Needless to say, of all that had happened that day, this treatment was the biggest shock to me. I was livid. This man had been sitting in on Sandy's classes, every one of them, four times a week, and taking copious notes for the past seven years, and I repeat seven years, compliments of Sandy's graciousness and generosity.

"Cool it, Jimmy, there must be a reason." Sandy said.

"I damn sure don't know what it is! I'll tell you what I damn sure do know—I know the value of what you've freely given him, Sandy. After all you've done for him over the past seven years, making all your classes available to him because you considered him a friend! A friend like that you don't need. I can't believe what just happened."

"Jimmy, forget it. I'll handle this. And don't you ever say another word."

Much to my surprise, I never did say another word. The only way I could handle it was to put it out of my head completely as if it had never happened. Until almost two years later when I did sit down with Maxine. She was going on her usual tirade about the difficulties in her marriage. I then told her how deeply hurt I had been over it all. I told her then that I now knew the true deep meaning of "There was no room at the inn." But even then she never told me why we were not invited in and offered their hospitality.

When we left their place, we went directly to Marty's, where I fed Sandy and he got a chance to lie down while I figured out what I was going to do next with no home to go to. While we were there, two more strays came in, friends of Jill's from New York expecting to be put up. Jill kept saying something to the effect that, "We'll make room. Marty, Sandy can have our room with the bath... Come on, we're all Gypsies. We can do it."

"I'm sure we are," I said, "and I'm sure we can. But there is no need. We can go to a hotel."

Not long afterward, Marty got a call from Dick Dunn saying he couldn't reach Sandy. Marty explained we were there. I got on the wire and told him Sandy was taking a nap, described a bit of our day, and mentioned that we were going to a hotel.

"Oh, no, you're not," Dick protested. "You're staying with me until it all blows over. You know I have enough room."

I ate with the kids and later woke Sandy up and took him just as he was, still in his robe, over the hill to Doheny Drive and Dick's high-rise. It was better that I wait to go back to the apartment until the next morning, when I could see, to pick up what we would need for the near future. What was going to happen beyond that was anybody's guess. At least for now, we were welcomed with a warm, friendly, generous gesture. The icing on the cake, if there was a cake at that time, was that Sandy valued Dick's gentlemanly friendship and truly loved his company. We settled in that night at Dick's lovely spacious apartment, with Dick insisting we take his room while he slept in the den.

The following morning we went over to our place in the San Fernando Valley, where we had to get the manager to force the door open. First we both changed and dressed. I packed all that I thought we would need over at Dick's, then proceeded to pick up the place and straighten out things as best I could by clearing out the fallen Sheetrock. Clearly, we wouldn't be moving back here to lived. People were already moving out in huge numbers that day, with trucks, U-Hauls, and vans double-parking all around the building. I just wanted to get away with Sandy. I wanted to let the whole experience subside before making a rash move. It was going to take months, if not longer, before this place was going to be habitable again.

We got back to Dick's and he hadn't gone to work. He had a late lunch ready for us both. I fixed Sandy's feeding and we all sat together. Dick brought up the subject of school. "My God! Sandy, we haven't made plans about the classes. Dick, how are the phones? I've got to get on to Marty."

"Sure, right there in the kitchen," he directed.

Marty told me he had been over at the school all morning, that students were inquiring and he had told them he hadn't heard from us. "Well, how is the place?" I asked. "It looked OK to me yesterday. So what do you think?"

"That's up to you and Sandy," he said.

When I turned to relay to Sandy that Marty had been over there all morning, that everything was in shape, and that students had already been around, Sandy's response was simply, "So?"

I knew what that meant. I went back to the phone and told Marty that it was on for four o'clock. The day after the quake, more than half the students showed up. After all that we had been through, Sandy was back at class as if nothing had happened.

My Turn to Pull a John McCormack

The next day Jill came into the theatre all bent out of shape. A friend of hers had been killed in the quake, a young Irish kid newly here from Ireland living with his sister. The sister was in need of funds for the funeral. Jill was hell-bent on helping her. I asked her how it had happened.

"He was over on Valley Heart near Coldwater. Early that morning, he spotted a woman in a car with a baby. An electric wire from a disabled pole had dropped over the car and she was afraid to get out. He went to the rescue with a wooden pole to knock it away. Whatever happened, he was electrocuted and died instantly."

However it had happened, Jill wanted to help. She came to me and asked if I would sing. She had told the sister she knew an Irish tenor. They were planning a concert and already had five Irish rock bands from around the LA area lined up. I told Jill they didn't need me—they would all be young kids with no old farts like me there.

"Oh, yes, there will be. We're targeting the whole Irish community," she said. So I agreed. "If you think I wouldn't be out of place."

"An Irishman out of place there? Are you kidding?"

So I planned to sing six old Irish ballads, John McCormack standards, all the ones Pop used to sing. There must have been a reason I started working out last month, I thought. After not singing for close to thirty years—I didn't count teaching—I felt I had better get up in the morning after Dick left for work and do a little vocalizing with a pitch pipe. I noted my top register was much easier to achieve. It was as if I didn't really have to warm up and work up to it, as it were. I opened my mouth and it was just there with little effort. Even the forward placement of my voice seemed a bit unusual to me. As I remembered it, I used to work so hard when I was young, never knowing, always hoping. But now it wasn't work anymore—it was fun.

The fund-raiser was being held in Ambrose Hall next to the big Catholic church on Melrose between Sunset and Santa Monica Boulevards. It was Dick's church right over there in West Hollywood. The kids went wild over the rock bands. Did I feel like a fish out of water—until I stepped out onto the stage. Then I realized Jill had been right. The place was salt-and-peppered with old farts, excuse me, old folks like myself who seemed pleased to hear the old standards again. The people who had turned out for this affair were mostly family groups including the youngest child and the oldest grandfather. I spotted Jon Voight there kneeling next to Sandy while I was singing. He was one of the celebrities making an appearance as the accident had happened right in his Studio City neighborhood.

The Mysteries of the Voice

One morning after a quick jaunty workout, while walking back to the master bedroom to see how Sandy was doing, I put my hand in my pocket and pulled out a little green ribbon. It was identical to the one I had worn on my gray suit lapel four months earlier at my dad's wake. I was wearing my raggedy old, worn-out, weather-beaten, roustabout shorts, a get-up I wouldn't wear out anywhere, not even to take out the garbage. I wore them around the house just because I used to like them. I had never had them back east, so how in heaven's name had that ribbon made its way into that pocket? I stood there looking at it with only one word on my mind...Pop!

The following week I recorded a couple of songs. As I sat listening to them I could hear the difference, but I didn't want to verbalize what I was thinking. So I took a song and called my sister Anita and asked her to just listen. She did, to the whole thing from the first note to the last.

When it was over, I asked her, "What do you think?"

Her remark to me was, "I don't remember Pop singing that one. When did he record it? I have all the other ones he did." That was her statement precisely.

When I told her it was me, she said, "Get out. You have to play that for Carol!"

I did and got a similar reaction. I state all this for what it's worth. All I know is after a lifetime of singing—I was over sixty and as of this writing seventy-five—singing had never been so easy, relaxing, and pleasant. I don't want to beat a dead horse with the "whys" and "wherefores." It just happened.

42 Annus Mirabilis

April 28: A Red Letter Day for Sandy

The earthquake was barely behind us. We were still living at Dick Dunn's, making the trek over the hill to North Hollywood and the school. At the same time, things were all a bustle and a hustle as the big day approached. The Cancer Hope Foundation had been planning Sandy's gala for months. Ann Metcalfe was the professional fund-raiser in charge. The three kingpins spearheading this drive along with Dr. Bluming were Sydney Pollack, Gregory Peck, and Gordon Davidson, Director of the Dorothy Chandler Pavilion. Of all the people they could have picked, why a man like Davidson who had nothing to do with Sandy? He had never studied with Sandy. He had worked with Stella Adler, but he couldn't possibly have the understanding of and the devotion to the Meisner Technique nor the dedication to and love of Sandy that any former student had. I had no idea what the rationale was behind the choice, but then it wasn't up to me and I had absolutely nothing to do with it.

Ann told me that when she had approached Sydney, his first question was, "What does Sandy get out of this?" She replied, "How about a little recognition?" and then he went along with it, I guess. Gregory was there from the start to help with whatever he could do; he had great loyalty to Sandy and the Playhouse.

Ann Metcalfe had taken on this job with absolutely no staff at all. How it all came together and fell into place was a wonder. In the end all the letter writing, stamp-licking, and backbreaking preparation work was left to the school's recent graduates, a group led by Debra Anderson. The Hope Foundation and the LA Free-Net people, who barely knew Sandy, were also extremely helpful in pulling off the affair. I used to get midnight calls at Dick's from Ann in which she picked my brain about this or that. I was sorry I was of no use to her at all. This sort of thing was completely out of my element.

When she asked me what part I was going to take, I asked, "What do you mean?"

"Sydney or Gregory will be master of ceremonies, and the good doctor will talk, and someone will be presenting the award, you know. Can't you talk about Sandy? You're the one who really knows him."

"Ann, no way. I'm no public speaker. I've never done anything like that. If you want someone to speak about Sandy, there's only one person who can or should, and that's Arthur Seidelman. He's the only one who has remained a close friend of Sandy's throughout all these years. If I had my way, he would be the one to do that. As for me, what can I do? I'll tell you—all I do, and all I can do, besides talk too much, is sing. I'm a singer. But who wants to listen to me? I'm a nobody compared to all those stars who also sing. Forget it, Ann. I'll just get Sandy there in one piece. That'll be my job." That was all that was ever expected of me anyway. I did not involve myself in the preparations in any way. I had the school to run and the job of getting Sandy over the hilltop to class. And by this time I had my voice workouts at Seth's. That was enough to keep me busy.

I still wanted this event to come off for Sandy. I felt it was long overdue in Hollywood. His influence on this town was tremendous and far-reaching. No one had a notion as to the number of actors, extras, writers, directors, casting directors, department heads—people all the way from industry heads like Leslie Moonves at Warner Brothers TV, eventually head of CBS, down to the most insignificant day jobber—who had learned from Sandy. So many actors had gotten their start as beginners in Sandy's classes. Someone estimated that approximately 8,000 people passed through those classes, year in and year out. They were all molded and influenced by him.

It had all started more than sixty years before, in the thirties, in the Union Halls of the garment district on Seventh Avenue and on 14th Street. He continued honing his craft down through the years at the Neighborhood Playhouse, 20th Century-Fox, the American Musical and Drama Academy, the Bequia School, and then finally at the Meisner Carville School in North Hollywood, where he finished out his teaching days on the 16th of December '94. Cancer be damned, was he not deserving of some recognition? I should think so. It was long overdue.

Meetings were held in a posh conference room, with its standard-issue long table, on Wilshire Boulevard in Westwood. I attended, thanks to Ann, I am sure. Pollack presided, with Dr. Avrum, David Craig, Gregory Peck, Arthur Seidelman, Mark Rydell, Kathleen Nolan, Patricia Barry, Bill Allen, a few others, and of course Ann in attendance.

At one meeting the subject of entertainment came up. They settled on Mort Sahl who was going to darken his show in New York and fly out for the privilege of appearing. Lainie Kazan, who had been in my class so many years before, was doing bits of her nightclub act. Joel Grey's name came up, but we were told he wasn't about to perform in front of that crowd. It was decided that Sydney would open with the welcoming speech. Dr. Bluming would explain the Cancer Hope Foundation and Sandy's accomplishment, describing his battle with cancer through insurmountable odds

The Gala Committee with Sandy sitting, L to R Sydney Pollack, Arthur Seidelman, Gregory Peck, Kathleen Nolen, Mark Rydell, Patricia Barry, Jimmy

42 Annus Mirabilis

and the continued excellence of his life endeavors despite the enormous difficulties. Gregory would present the award at the end.

At this point Dr. Avrum asked, "And you, Jimmy, what will you do?"

All eyes were on me now. "Well, Doctor, all I can do is sing." I held my breath.

Sydney spoke first, "So, Jim, do you have your charts?"

Well, I didn't even know the meaning of the word in that context. I did feel the question a little condescending whether it was meant to be or not. At this point I felt a swift kick in the side of my calf from Kathleen who was sitting next to me. It gave me just the courage I needed. "Yes, Sydney, of course I do." And that was it. I was to sing in place of Joel Grey.

Sydney kept stressing the time factor. Each contribution to the evening should be short and sweet because these affairs could go on interminably and we wouldn't want that. Taking turns, Mark and Kathleen were to read out the names, male and female respectively in alphabetical order, of Meisner's actors from the Screen Actors Guild.

When the meeting was over, Kathleen took me to one side and said, "I'm glad you spoke up to him."

"Kathleen, what is he talking about, charts?"

She said, "Oh, you know, the charts bands use for their chords, like a musical score."

"My God," I said, "I'm not a rock band! I've never heard of charts. He's talking about my arrangements in my key. Of course I have my own arrangements. Nice try, whether he meant it or not."

The organizers even held a cocktail party. It was what I would call a teaser because the guest list was money, money, and more money. But isn't that what foundations are all about? Ann, her friend Dr. Ryan, and her student crew were responsible for getting the tickets out and sold. They decorated the hall with space-lights and flowers. A huge reproduction of Sandy's logo dominated the front of the banquet hall.

The "Living Daydream" gala took place on April 28, 1994, at the Century Plaza in Century City, where an audience from around the country and other parts of the world gathered to participate in conferring this honor on Sandy. Ironically, many of his students were working as we were celebrating and unable to attend. Yet Eli and Annie, Louise Lasser, Diane Keaton, as well as some teachers like Bob Modica attended from New York. Mary Steenburgen and Ted Danson came from Martha's Vineyard. Other actors came from Canada. Teachers from around the world came to pay their respects: June Whitaker from Vancouver, Yoshiko "Yoko" Nakaima from

Mort Sahl

Tokyo, and Roshan Taneja from Mumbai. I saw Tyne Daly run in to pay her respects, but she couldn't stay as she had obligations elsewhere. Of course, LA students, actors, celebrities, and teachers too numerous to mention were there. The banquet hall was filled with tables on all levels, with kudos due to the designer and decorators of the room that night. It was right out of a Hollywood dream!

Boolu, who came from New York, dressed in the room with Sandy and me. We had a room where Sandy could rest for the afternoon, dress, and be right on the spot when the festivities began. When we were dressed, Sandy and I went down to the lobby thirty minutes ahead of time for a photo shoot as the well-wishers were coming in. I got a chair and sat him in a strategic spot where the arrivals could go up to him and speak to him if they saw fit. One celebrity who shall remain nameless asked Rosie, "Do you really think Sandy is getting anything out of all this?" She was standing off at a distance and hadn't even spoken to him. I told Rosie she should have told Ms. Celeb to go up and ask him herself.

Perhaps it was hard for some who had known him in better days to see him for the first time in such a reduced state in his declining years. To them I had only one suggestion: "Get over yourselves. You all did love him once." Where was their compassion? The elderly do not stop feeling every emotion just because their bodies start to shut down.

Thank God that night the insensitive celebrity represented only a very few. Everyone else couldn't have been more gracious. Let me tell you, and you others of little faith, Sandy was enjoying every moment of the evening. It was Washington, DC, all over again. Many, as they came in, stopped and had a few words with Sandy, who sat there graciously smiling and nodding.

As the tables began to fill up, David Craig came over and offered, "May I help you to your table, Sandy?" I thought, why not? He was the one, I was sure, who had instigated this whole affair for Sandy with Dr. Avrum. David and Sandy went on ahead, and I brought up the rear with the folded-up wheelchair.

First they served a lovely gourmet meal, and Sydney did the welcoming speech. He compared Sandy to Paris, a moveable feast! Then Dr. Avrum followed, speaking about the HOPE Unit Foundation, Sandy, and the awards. He recounted one of Sandy's favorite recollections, the story about Eleanora Duse as Magda. It demonstrates Sandy's ability to recognize greatness,

Sandy, Jon Voight, Boolu & Sherri Lewis

and the people gathered there that night were acknowledging this great ability of his with their willingness to share their best efforts with the honoree. The Meisner-Longwell book, Sanford Meisner *On Acting*, quotes Sandy:

Duse played in a play called Magda. There's a scene in the last act. When she's a young girl she has an affair with a guy from the same village, and she has a child by him. Twenty-five years later, or thereabouts, she comes back to visit her family who live in this town, and her ex-lover comes to call on her. She accepts his flowers—I got this from Shaw—and they sit and talk. All of a sudden she realizes that she's blushing, and it gets so bad that she drops her head and hides her face in embarrassment. Now that's a piece of realistic acting! And Shaw confesses to a certain professional curiosity as to whether it happens every time she plays that part. It doesn't. But that blush is the epitome of living truthfully under imaginary circumstances, which is my definition of good acting. That blush came out of her. She was a genius!

Champagne Mumm of Reims, France, was so inspired by this story and impressed by Sandy's career that they chose a premium vintage of their blush champagne to become the first commemorative bottle honoring an individual in the 167-year history of the company. They supplied only 750 cases of 1988 Champagne Cordon Rose with an extra bonus: each bottle has Sandy's logo and an image of Duse on the label.

Mort Sahl performed, and Lainie Kazan was doing her act, and then there was to be yours truly. Just as I was beginning to prepare offstage, Richard Alfieri whispered into my ear that it must take one hell of a nerve to follow that class act, meaning Lainie. Well, I tell you, I froze. I don't think he meant anything unkind with the remark but it hit me the wrong way. After all, I hadn't sung professionally in thirty years. I must have thought he just might be right. And at that moment my professionalism escaped me. I drew a blank. Lainie was doing her last number. I thought it would never end; it seemed to go on for hours. I could not for the life of me remember the first line of my first song. I thought I would die. If I had had my wits about me, I would have walked over to the accompanist and checked. It was just that simple. But then I wasn't thinking straight. Instead I told the stage manager I had frozen and could not remember the first line.

He advised, "Forget it. When you get out there, it will come to you."

In the next second, it all came to me. I leaned over to him and said, "I got it! It's 'I often think of home.'"

"Right now, aren't we all?" he replied.

Lainie had been going on for some time, and the stage manager was concerned about keeping the show moving. Lainie introduced me and from that moment on it was between me and Sandy. Then I heard the ovation, with whistles and yells for more, and that was all I needed to hear.

The audience quieted down and I introduced Arthur Seidelman. As a director of stage, screen, and television, he spoke fondly of Sandy, the man, and had Sandy's brother Robert Meisner and Boolu stand to be recognized. I ran back through a side corridor to Sandy's table high up in the rear of the hall with all the other tables stretched out and around and down in front of him to the stage. I put him in the wheelchair for he was up next after Gregory Peck's presentation. I rolled him around through the side corridor so no one could see him all the way to the stage entrance. Sydney hadn't wanted Sandy to leave his table. He wanted the award brought to him at the table, Kathleen had told me.

When I relayed this plan to Sandy, he said, "No way. I am going up there."

I felt Sandy was right. No one down in the hall would have been able to see the presentation at his table. I believe Sydney felt Sandy would never be able to make it onto the stage. But Sydney was never able to spend time with Sandy to find out just what he was capable of, including his teaching. He just never took the time out of his ever so busy life to find out.

I remember a story I once heard. I don't know how accurate it is or even remember who told it to me, but it sheds a little light on what I'm referring to. It took place at a celebrity party, dinner, or gathering, whatever, in Beverly Hills. Early in the evening, Sydney was making for the door to leave when Marlon Brando intercepted him. "Sydney, where are you going so soon? The party's just beginning."

"Sorry, Marlon," Sydney explains, "I'm shooting tomorrow and I have to be up at the crack of dawn."

Marlon urges Sydney to stay. "Come on, Sydney. No, you don't. Stay and enjoy yourself. What's your rush? Look, Sydney, let me tell you something. I've been 'up there,' and I'm living proof there is nothing up there. So take off your coat and enjoy yourself."

I guess he never took the time to know Sandy well enough to be aware that when the time came that Sandy couldn't walk, talk, or teach, he would be the first to recognize it. If Sandy was anything, he wasn't a rip-off artist.

As Boolu and I passed Kathleen as we were going around to the stage with Sandy in the chair, she held up her right thumb saying, "Up the Irish." Gregory ended with a hilarious speech that lent a marvelously warm and family-familiar feeling to the end of the evening. It was only fitting that he should for we were family. We were all part of Sandy's family; at that moment we were all Sandy's kids.

Gregory Peck introduces Sandy

Sandy walked out onto the stage to Gregory on Boolu's arm. It was a sight I shall never forget. The house went mad, everyone up on their feet. As I watched the two of them up there arm in arm, my eyes filled with tears. Boolu then set the walker in front of Sandy so he could steady himself and left the stage to Gregory and Sandy. Gregory then reiterated the meaning and purpose of the award and presented it to Sandy. But it was much too heavy for Sandy to hold, so Boolu walked coolly out on stage and was right there to relieve him of the burden. Sandy's champagne, "Duse's Blush," was served to everyone by the waiters, and Gregory made a fitting toast ending with "hip-hip-hurray" like the kids we felt we were at that moment. The uproar was tremendous. I wonder now if that celeb in the vestibule still wondered if Sandy was getting anything out of this evening.

When Sandy turned with Boolu to walk off, the audience didn't want him to leave. The names of Sandy's students were to be read out by Kathleen and Mark, but Gregory worried it would take forever—the list was much too long to be read off one by one, they would be there all night. But the audience roared, "Read them, read them. We don't care. We'll stay all night!" I felt they would have. It was as if each and every one of them there that night wanted solid affirmation and recognition. Every one of them individually was a part of Sandy that night. I wondered if by now Sydney realized this was no ordinary Hollywood affair. This evening wasn't about fame or fortune. It was all about LOVE.

Then Conrad Janis, another student of Sandy's, struck up the band and people started dancing. I quickly rolled Sandy back through the passageway to his table by the exit from the room. Lines started forming both for Sandy and myself. Some were thanking Sandy and saying their good-byes and others were thanking me for caring for him all these years and remarking on my singing, most not having known I was a singer. It was all gratifying to me. Boolu asked if he could go out with some of the students along with Marty and Jill. It was too early for them to stop partying. I said, "Sure. Just stay at Marty's, and we'll pick you up in the morning."

Jimmy sings

Eventually the crowd thinned out. Sandy asked, "Well, what do you think?"

"I think they love you," I said, adding, "and well they should."

The following afternoon, Yoshiko from Tokyo came by with her two charming daughters to spend the afternoon. Dick Dunn came in from the office with a copy of Variety. He handed it to me opened to the second page. There it was in the "Army Archerd Column":

There wasn't a dry eye in the house when Sanford Meisner walked out onto the stage and Jimmy Carville sang 'Danny Boy.' Both Sandy and I were extremely grateful to all who made the evening a heartfelt, memorable occasion.

A Doctorate for the Man

The previous spring, Gene Terruso, an ex-student of Bill Esper's from Rutgers University in Newark, New Jersey, had attended the intensive class as a graduate student. Sandy had spent private time with him at the house. He was getting ready to take over as head of the Drama Department at Northern Illinois University in DeKalb. The school was setting up a complete drama department based exclusively on the Meisner Technique. The school had been getting so many requests solely for the Meisner Technique from prospective students at the regional interviews around the country that the president felt it prudent to revamp the department and specialize. Consequently, they wished to present Sandy with an Honorary Doctorate in the Humanities.

In '94 Sandy was approaching eighty-nine and still going at it in the classroom. Gene Terruso said of him in an article at the University:

He does not see acting as something that can be taught in absence of some talent in the actor, for he considers talent to be "the real inexorable primary tool." When asked to describe his teaching he said, "In all my teaching I try to help you get in touch with your self, your emotions, and once I've done that—if there is an actor there—the rest is up to you."

Meisner focuses on acting not as artifice or pretense, but as evocation and projection of genuine emotion and behaviors appropriate to the context of the script. If a scene isn't working a director might try to "fix" the scene. Meisner, however, works with the actor, striving to help them draw from and use their own emotions and experiences and to build on what other actors in the scene are bringing to it, to make the scene work. Meisner describes his guiding principle that "art expresses human experiences." In the process of "demystifying" acting, he has developed a series of progressive exercises to help the actor enhance his or her skills, and these are perhaps the most original aspect of his teaching.

Realizing Sandy would be unable to give an acceptance speech, they had asked Sydney Pollack to do it for him, but Sydney wasn't available so they then asked Tammy Grimes, who was willing. But she made too many petty demands such as limo service from Chicago to DeKalb and a first class hotel rather than the University's appropriate and perfectly good accommodation for visiting guests.

The president said, "Forget the stars. Ask Jimmy Carville, his assistant, to do it." When Gene Terruso asked me, I told him it wasn't for me, not my cup of tea at all.

"Well, it's high time you change that."

And I thought, you're right, damn it! I will come and do it because I would love to be able to do it. So I consulted Sandy, who merely asked, "Why not you?" That was that, it was settled.

So on May 14, 1994 we donned the caps and gowns, after all these years. I gave the acceptance speech for Sandy at the spring graduation of all the students receiving their degrees at Northern Illinois University. That humongous auditorium was full of recipients. When I told them Sandy felt silence could say a lot and it could also cover up a multitude of sins, they seemed to enjoy it. I closed with Sandy's final bit of advice to them, "To find in themselves those things human which are universal."

Jimmy & Sandy at NIU

A large party was held that night at the President's home, with all of NIU academia there. I must say it was unfamiliar territory for both Sandy and me, but it was most interesting and enjoyable.

We were not going to have any time in Chicago since we had to get back to classes ourselves. Val and George Rothschild came out to DeKalb for the presentation, and we were able to spend some time together there. When they were congratulating Sandy, I said, "Why not a doctorate? He's already a guru in India."

After Sixty Years, Time To Hang It Up

When it came time to send out interview notices for new students for the coming Intensive Class in June, we decided not to send them. I would like to think it was "we" and not just "me," for this man had been making his own decisions all his life. With such little precious time left, why take that remnant of autonomy from him now? I wanted to see him left with his dignity after such a long productive life. After twelve years of classical piano, Sandy had, at the age of nineteen, taken his first step onto the Broadway Stage in '24, seventy years earlier. Now after his sixty years of constant teaching, I felt it was time for him to retire because of his health. He seemed to agree with me readily this time. He reassured me quitting was just as much his idea as it was mine.

We notified prospective students that Sandy was retiring in December. The plans were for Sandy to continue our very last second year class through the summer without a break and on to the class fruition in December. I too would then retire, but from what I wasn't quite sure.

The Day We Leave, Dick Is Gone

My life had lightened up considerably with only one class to attend to now. I had stopped my voice workout at the age of sixty-five. Who was I kidding? Besides, as for singing just as an avocation, Bette Midler was right. The sessions were expensive and I didn't need the expense or the workout, not really, although they were fun while they lasted. You might say they brought back my youth a bit, but then so would a gay bar.

I was spending a lot of time with FEMA and our earthquake difficulties. I felt as if I were in Gian Carlo Menotti's opera *The Consul* with, "Papers, papers and more papers" ("All the Documents Must Be Signed"). Dick also seemed to me to be getting sicker by the day. I found myself caring for both him and Sandy, only Dick needed more care than Sandy. His doctor was calling me, checking to see whether Dick had taken his medicine or whether he was eating properly. His mind seemed to fade in and out at times. He went to the market one day and, crossing Santa Monica Boulevard and Doheney, a rather complicated intersection, he fell and someone brought him home. He couldn't be left alone. He got so bad I had to call 911. The firefighters came and took him to Cedars-Sinai. Even though he was weak, weaker than Sandy, the hospital kept him for only a few days and then let him come home.

In the meantime, I was realizing that Sandy and I would not be going back to the apartment on Riverside. So I was out looking for a place to move to. I was answering newspaper ads and talking to real estate agents, to whom I had an allergic reaction. To me, they were like piranhas. At the beginning of the last week of August, I found a three-bedroom house in of all places Northridge out in the boondocks where nobody wanted to live. It was quite far from the school. Still, the trip was only twice a week now and with our schedule we were traveling against traffic. With traffic light, I could cover the distance coming in on Route 217 from Roscoe Boulevard in under thirty minutes. The prospects looked good, the price was right, and Sandy liked the house and the quiet neighborhood. It wasn't fancy, but at our age who the hell cared about fancy?

The weirdest thing happened as we were coming back from Northridge after signing the lease. We would be moving in September 1. It had always been inevitable that we would be leaving Dick's place sooner or later. When we found a place, our biggest worry was Dick. The sicker he got, the more he depended on me. Moving out had never come up, but now the time had come. Dick could not possibly live alone. What was one to do, with his family living on the east coast?

By the time we reached the house, we still didn't have a semblance of a solution to the problem. When we got off the elevator, from which Dick's apartment was directly across the hall, the door was wide open. We walked in and there was Peggy MacKay who had been a soap opera actress for years and a longtime friend of Dick's. She informed us that Dick was dead and had just been taken to the morgue. Sandy took it hard and I settled him in the living room on a comfortable couch.

Peg called me into the kitchen where Sandy couldn't hear. "He doesn't have to know this, unless he already does. When I came in this afternoon, Dick was already dead on the floor of his den. He had been hemorrhaging profusely. I called 911 and proceeded to clean up the blood. It was all over the place. As they were tending to him, one of the cops told me to stop what I was doing. Didn't I know he had AIDS? Well, Jim, I didn't."

"But Peggy, he doesn't. Both Dick and his nurse told me he had hepatitis."

"Well, the last thing that cop told me was he had AIDS, not to touch that blood, and make sure I get an AIDS test," she said.

I called his doctor, the one I had talked to these past few months. When I asked him, "Did Dick have AIDS?," he said that it wasn't my business. I said, "I thought he had hepatitis?"

Then he asked, "Are you family?"

"No."

"Then ask them," he said. He would give me no information even though I told him I had been caring for Dick for the past seven months. He just hung up on me.

Did Dick have AIDS, I wondered? Or was the cop just assuming and jumping to conclusions, which would have been a hell of a thing to do. Yet I remembered a health nurse coming in saying he had hepatitis.

When I told Sandy, he said, "Don't get upset. Just go to the VA tomorrow and get checked to make sure." Which was exactly what we both did and the tests were negative.

What bothered me most about all this was how Dick's doctor handled me knowing I had been taking care of Dick all these many months. I asked Sandy, "What's happened to that profession?"

"Jimmy, forget it. They're doctors. It's all about court cases," Sandy said.

We stayed at the apartment for the week and attended the funeral service, which was well attended, at St. Ambrose over on Melrose. Peggy MacKay was also a parishioner there, and I believe she had a hand in the arrangements.

The gang from the school were instrumental in moving us out of the Valley Village Riverside apartment, which was just beginning to be reconstructed, a project that was going to take months. It didn't take us long to settle in to the place we rented on Stag Street—we were used to that. It was a cute little Valley-style house on a corner with a large walled-in yard. Sandy used to like me to wheel him about in his chair, to and fro all over the neighborhood through its tree-lined streets.

I felt, and believe he sensed it also, that there wasn't much time left. We were both making the most of the time remaining to us by just being alone together. He wasn't having any extreme difficulty, but he was quite frail, and, I noticed, getting weaker. He remained quite steady, so long as he took it easy.

At Eight-Nine a TV Role for Sandy

One fine fall day, the phone rang at our place out on Stag Street. It was my old friend Michael Greene. He was a student whom Sandy had suggested for a TV role when they were looking for a zany-type character. Sandy felt he could handle that request quite easily, but after they brought him to Hollywood it didn't work out. That had been years ago, and Michael had eventually become an agent in the industry out there.

"Jimmy," he said, "I'm not calling for you this time." He was always at me to start auditioning again. No way with Sandy in his present condition would I leave him just now... for any reason. "It's Himself I'm calling about," Michael went on. "How's he doing?" I told him he was going to class and only that. He was getting weaker by the day. "Well, I've got just the part for him. They're looking for an actor Sandy's age to play this ex-teacher wanting to reach his estranged son after twenty years, before he dies."

"Michael, you've got to be kidding. No way."

"Now, Jimmy, you hear me out," he said. "Throughout the whole scene, he's lying in bed and he doesn't even have to move, just lie there and do a deathbed scene. Jimmy, it's a classic. Look, Jimmy, it's for ER, the hottest show on TV right now. The head writer is Michael Crichton. It will be great, and if you can get him there, I know he could do it better than anyone. Come on, let me send you the script," he went on, ever the agent, I thought. "Just read it and see what you think then."

"Don't bother. But I'll tell you what you can do. Get me one of those fat little national commercials," I joked half-heartedly.

The next day the courier was there at the door. I sat down and read the script. It really wasn't asking for anything Sandy couldn't do. What instantly came to my mind was the only piece of film Eleanora Duse ever did. It was filmed in the early '20s. Sandy would ask the students to go to MOMA (The Museum of Modern Art) film department over on West 53rd Street and ask to be shown the short little flick of the Duse acting, the only example left, on silent film. It was an opportunity for us as students of the craft to witness truthful emotion under imaginary circumstances. Sandy felt, agreeing with George Bernard Shaw whom he valued as a critic, that Duse was one of the first besides Edmund Kean to embody this type of acting. In her day it was revolutionary. Sandy also felt she was unsurpassed to this day. I saw her in that old film and I was convinced. Then I thought, what if students ten or twenty years from now could witness Sandy in this death scene that I just read? I knew, as Michael did, that he could do it better than anyone.

I knew then it was imperative that I convince Sandy he must do it, if not for himself then for all the students for years to come to see he could put his money where his mouth was. It wasn't easy. He wouldn't even listen to me at first! I insisted, keeping it up until he relented. Finally, he agreed to at least go and see the casting director.

While we were in the casting director's office talking to him, several suits from the main office came in. There must have been four or five of them. I cannot tell you to this day who they were, but I could tell they were the power block of the show. I didn't know what they knew or where they were coming from. Sandy hadn't made up his mind, and they didn't know that. He was there because I wanted him there; he wasn't sold on this whole idea, not yet. The casting director knew it, but he was the only one. I was petrified. I felt this could get embarrassing. We were not yet all in the same ballpark, and knowing Sandy as I did, I feared we might never be.

The casting director was finessing the moment. Finally he asked Sandy outright if he would do it.

I held my breath as I heard Sandy say, "For how much?"

Everyone laughed a little. Then there was a pause and someone named a figure. There was another pause, and Sandy said, "For that...? I'll do it."

Then there was laughter again. I was the first to breathe a sigh of relief. Others expressed their pleasure at having him on board. Hands were shaken, and then all the power went back to work leaving Sandy and me to work things out with the casting director. Suffice it to say he gave a smashing performance with Noah Wyle who played the young doctor. At first Sandy had difficulty taking directions on the set from Christopher Chulack, so Chulack had me stand behind a pillar off-camera closer to Sandy. When Sandy heard my voice relaying the commands from Chris, he had no trouble taking directions off my voice. The whole experience was intensely compelling for all concerned that day. The depth of Sandy's emotion had all of us on the set mesmerized.

At one point, four men came walking onto the set, and everything immediately stopped dead. Everyone stood back and let them pass through to the room where Sandy rested when not needed on the set. The leader came in and introduced himself. It was Leslie Moonves, President of Warner Brothers Television and a former student of Sandy's. He walked over to where Sandy was sitting. "Hi, Sandy, it's Leslie. I heard you were here on the lot. I had to come down and tell you how pleased we are to have you here." The others were introduced, and a few niceties passed back and forth before they left.

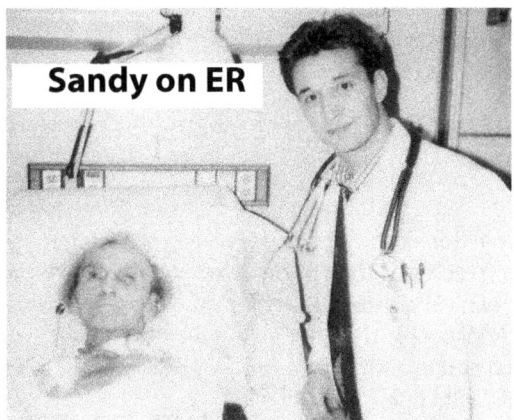

Sandy on ER

The aftermath of the shooting was the biggest surprise to me. The morning after the airing, a secretary from the ER office called and asked me to tell Sandy the TV ratings had gone off the charts. More than 45 million viewers had caught the show, the biggest rating since the grand finale of Cheers in the late '80s. The office had received a call from a man in Canada who was given only days to live. While watching the show he had been so moved by Sandy that he was asking about the text Noah had read to Sandy in the show. It was Walt Whitman's "Leaves of Grass." He wanted to have it read at his funeral, whenever. Everyone I knew was unanimously impressed and moved by Sandy's work.

Steven Spielberg sent a letter:

Dear Mr. Meisner,

We feel honored that you gave of your time and talent to ER and an episode of which I am personally proud. Your performance had my wife Kate and me in tears. It's a pleasure to see after so many years of teaching acting, the teacher finally gets to show the students that he's the best... and in front of almost 50 million American television viewers. I have great admiration and respect for all of your contributions over the years to the entertainment industry.

All my best,
Steven Spielberg

The icing on the cake occurred the following week. NBC bought the centerfold of Variety and had it colored bright red with white print. They thanked ER for topping the ratings chart, listing every single solitary worker from the inception of the show to date and also thanking them for their contribution. How and why it happened that particular show, who knew? All I can say is I was mighty pleased Sandy was allowed to be a part of it. No one was more pleased with the outcome than I. Did I know he could still manage it? I sure didn't. Oh, yes, I had my doubts that he could carry it off in his condition, but I wanted it so badly for him. Something just told me to trust. I just prayed my way through every shot. I couldn't tell you why I insisted in spite of all the doubts I might have had. There it was: he and the whole dang show came through with flying colors. Now we have this wonderful moment on tape for future students of the Meisner Technique or anyone else for that matter. "Sleepless in Chicago," episode 18 in the first year of ER's amazingly long run, first aired February 23, 1995, with Sanford Meisner playing Joseph Klein.

After Thirty-One Years, I Get to Teach a Few Classes

Around Thanksgiving that year, for the first time Sandy's teaching began to falter. Fortunately, we were at the end of term, and the only exercise left to teach was the Spoon River. I love this exercise and while I might not have been very good at it, other teachers do not always teach it according to Sandy's specific directions. Some of them seem to misinterpret its purpose or go at it in a little different way. Although it is a tough exercise, it is actually a delicate one.

Sandy once decided to stop teaching it altogether. "If the student eventually gets a chance to practice their craft by being fortunate in finding work," he said, "the purpose of this exercise will come along on its own, by osmosis, through experience." I felt the talented student deserved to get a crack at it regardless. Sandy told me go ahead and "take it on." I did, hoping that thereby I had eased them through those last few weeks of class.

Sandy's last class was held on Friday, December 16, 1994.

Retirement

We were both ready to relax and take it easy totally, and we had no intention of going any farther than Rosie's. I insisted that Boolu come out for the holiday so de tree a we could spend it together. I went out and bought our first Christmas tree ever and put it up outside on the terrace in front of our big picture window. It appeared to be an inside-outside tree. I decorated it with only tinsel and lit it with all green lights. It was still growing in a pot then and now it's almost fifty feet tall planted out front of our house on Huston.

We took Boolu down to Disneyland to catch the Christmas light parade. Kathleen Nolan went along with us. Let me tell you, this time I was as careful as all get-out with which rides I put Sandy on. But we had a good time anyway on the Saucers and Cups, Small World, and the Pirates of the Caribbean. Boolu and Kathleen, well, they went on everything they could manage to get on. We were like four kids on a high school outing. We waited for the big Disney Electrical Parade and then made for the exit when it was over.

Sandy said aside to me as we were leaving, "That Caribbean ride brought back fond memories," adding, "Do you think we will ever get back there again?"

"Sandy," I said, "just you wait and see. We will, we will. That place hasn't seen the last of us yet."

FEMA to the Rescue

One night while we were watching TV out on Stag Street, the program we were watching was interrupted by a public service announcement flashing across the screen. Essentially the announcement said that people who had been ousted, evicted, or forced out of their dwelling due to extreme damage from the earthquake were entitled to assistance from FEMA. If they were first-time buyers, they were eligible to purchase a dwelling, be it an apartment or a house, valued under $200,000 with no money down, with no closing fee, and at a fixed rate of 5.9% for thirty years. The only restriction was that your dwelling had to have been red-tagged as no longer livable. You were also required to prove that you were financially sound and able to meet the mortgage payments.

"Did you hear that, Sandy?" I asked.

"Yeah, but that lets me out. I'm not a first-time buyer. I owned one on Londonderry Drive years ago."

"Ah, but Sandy, I didn't. Under this deal, I qualify."

"So go for it," Sandy said. "That's a deal and a half."

My first hurdle was the time limit. This deal had been on the table since the previous August and it was only available until Martin Luther King Day on February 16. I had only a month and a half to file the papers, be approved, find a real estate agent, find a qualifying dwelling, and get an acceptable mortgage company to take me on. It wasn't going to be easy.

When I first applied, I was told my building hadn't been red-tagged; according to the building authority, my building had been green-tagged. I was told that some owners had paid under the table to get their building upgraded. The upgrade was fine for the owners but tough luck for someone like me applying for assistance from FEMA. We should have been red-tagged because we couldn't live there and I had proof from FEMA that we couldn't. They had earlier paid us a relocation fee. Once they saw my papers to that effect, they said they would check out the apartment themselves, even though it had a green tag.

What happened after the quake? Areas of our apartment complex were livable, but not our apartment. I could have moved into the livable area, but not Sandy in his physical condition. His doctor deemed it a health risk for his respiratory system, which was delicate at best, because of the construction required in and around the area. He had insisted Sandy be moved out, and we had documented it. I was there when the FEMA official finally came to the apartment to take pictures eleven months after the quake. He concluded that there was no way anyone could have been living there.

I now had FEMA approval in spite of the green tag. I got me an agent, a fabulous agent, Isa Persello from Woodland Hills who understood my urgency in finding a suitable house for Sandy and me. She really went all out with me. We scoured the area we would like to be in. Properties were at their lowest prices in years and they were plentiful. It was just a matter of deciding which one. We stumbled on a house in Sherman Oakes that was an exclusive, that is, in another agent's hands. This designation meant less for Isa Persello, but she knew it was perfect for us in every way and encouraged us to go ahead with it. Whatever happened to that piranha notion of mine? It was a foreclosure sale, and was it ever a sale! We could not have done better in the area. Isa took care of the escrow papers, found us a mortgage company, and we were in business.

Now these escrow people move at their own pace, and all we could do was wait. It was Friday, and Monday was Martin Luther King Day. When I didn't hear anything, I wrote the whole idea off. I knew everything would be closed on Monday.

"Well, Sandy, it was a nice try, but I guess we lost." Late in the day, Isa Persello came by with the papers. "Isa, what can we do now? It's after 5 PM. We missed it by a nose."

"No, we didn't," Isa replied. "I notified FEMA this morning and their agent accepted. The papers can be submitted on Tuesday because Monday is Martin Luther King Day. That isn't your fault. So don't worry, they will OK it on Tuesday."

We had the FEMA OK. Next it was up to the escrow people and our mortgage people. On April 29, Isa took the escrow and our mortgage papers to the Foreclosure Company, where she was given the keys to the house. These she brought over to us.

On Monday morning, May 1, 1995, we loaded all our clothes from our closets into the back of the car and drove over to our new house. As I drove up to the closed high wooden gate of the drive, I saw what looked like a notice tacked up on the fence. I got out of the car, took down the notice, took it back to the car, and read it to Sandy. "'This property is being put up on the auction block, on May 15, at such and such a time.' How can that be?"

"Good question, Jimmy. I guess you didn't buy it after all," said Sandy.

I went over to our mortgage company. I had just been over there signing the final papers the week before. The woman in the office thought there must have been some misunderstanding over in the foreclosure office and offered to call them. When she put down her phone, she explained what had happened. "Well, the house is still yours. There was a gross error over there as to who was in charge of unloading this property. One fellow thought the house was going to us at a giveaway price. So he figured why not try their luck at auction? They would do better there. But unbeknownst to him, another member of his company went ahead and signed the house over to us on that Friday before Martin Luther King Day. Consequently," our lady friend said, "the house is still yours, and you can just throw that notice away."

As I pushed him in his wheelchair back to the car, Sandy said, "I don't believe this. Is the house ours or isn't it?"

"Well, it's been another one of our roller coaster rides," I said.

"Let me know when it stops," Sandy returned. "I want to get off."

Nothing To Do, So What To Do? That Was The Question

Now that Sandy and I were finished at the school, even though he was physically weaker than ever, with a brain such as his he was beside himself. I on the other hand was busy as hell pulling our fixer-upper back into shape. You know, the usual changing a driveway here, a pink rose bed there, a red one over yonder, the Italian cypresses along the side, and inside a hardwood floor in the dining room. But the piece de resistance was to be a cobblestone fireplace, the construction of which couldn't be started until we were away. I was going at it hammer and tongs. To me it was like the early days on Bequia. But Sandy was going at it too, only it was at me. He was a nervous wreck just sitting there. I would put him in his wheelchair and roll him to wherever I was working just to make him feel part of what was going on. It really wasn't working. He liked what I was doing, but he was just an observer. No matter that every time I left the house to go to the paint store, Ace Hardware, or Home Depot, he insisted on coming along. He got a big kick out of riding through Home Depot; he loved that place. But...

When the idea of an Equity Waiver Theater for graduates came up, we thought it was a smashing idea. It was something Sandy could follow along, giving suggestions with little or no effort on his part. Sandy and I sat down and worked out the particulars, and the Sanford Meisner Center was born. We set about looking for a little seventy-seat house in the neighborhood.

Sandy told us: "This is what Paul and I envisaged for the Playhouse back in the '70s, but we were too long in the tooth by then to achieve it. When Tony Randall came to the Playhouse with the idea of a National Theater, we handed over the use of the school for this effort. After all he was a graduate and had been a member of the Board for years. I thought then, well, at last, someone with energy. However, it turned out that he wasn't planning for the graduates of the school. He was doing it all for himself. This was his vision alone. It had nothing to do with my work or the Playhouse. He was just using us and the school. I was desperately disappointed. I would have liked to see my work all come together on the stage as a unit like the Moscow Art Theater once was."

I knew what Sandy was talking about. I had seen a Moscow Art Theater production of Gogol's *Dead Souls* with Sandy in the '60s that Jean Dalrymple had brought to the New York City Center. The ensemble acting was a revelation to me.

We found a theater on Lankershim, just one block south of the Academy of Television Arts and Sciences on Magnolia.

So there we were, working on the house and working at the school, and Sandy was having a ball observing it all. Little could we foresee that come production time, he would be sitting front and center on the aisle, in the front row because of his weak vision, and right in the middle of all the action no matter who the director was. Sandy was in his element again.

Sandy's advice was to start out small and slowly, to take mini-steps while tending to the work all the way. "Never forget: it's about the work."

But a young actor needs to be discovered, find an agent, and work because without those things they are nothing and, consequently, no one, either in the business or in their own eyes. So how do you keep a company of actors together long enough to acquire any standard of note, especially without the wherewithal? The Group Theatre had run into the same problem all through the '30s, with defectors leaving for Hollywood one after another, from Franchot Tone, Edward Bromberg, Stella (Ardler) Adler, and Art Smith to Julie (John Garfield) Garfinkle. Sandy's advice, though it was right in theory, was inherently paradoxical, and therein lay the quandary. The Meisner Center would struggle with this problem for years to come.

For our first production, we had agreed on a One Act Festival. Sandy felt that was a good beginning. Three one-act plays would have and should have been ample. But one-act plays do not use too many actors, and we at the time had a stable full. So, with our herd, three one-acts over three nights of a weekend developed into three one-act plays per night over a three-day weekend. If your math is anything like mine, that multiplies into nine one-act plays over a weekend. And as it turned out, the run extended for nine weeks. It was terrific for the morale of the company, but whatever happened to small, slow, take mini-steps, and tend to the work? That was our first mistake. But not completely. It also cemented our loyalties, and every member was happy. They all got a chance to really act for a few moments every weekend for nine weeks, and that in itself was good.

The first night we played Bill Elverman's *After the Party*, Lanford Wilson's *The Great Nebula in Orion*, and Brian Kraft's *The Reality of Doing*. Saturday night we presented Victor Bumbalo's *Kitchen Duty*, Lanford Wilson's *Home Free*, and William Mastrosimone's *A Tantalizing*. On Sunday, we closed the weekend with Horton Foote's *A Young Lady of Property*, Martin Barter's *I'm Still Crying*, and Leonard Melfi's *Birdbath*. The reviews varied. Look, we were lucky to get reviewed at all, a new small company in the valley. One would have to thank Meisner's name for that. Perhaps the critics were looking for seasoned actors, which our actors weren't. But that didn't matter. After what they saw, they kept coming. We ran the first production until the 28th of June.

In August we went into rehearsal for *God's Country* by Steven Dietz directed by Martin Barter. It too had a big cast, obviously good for holding a non-paying company together. It opened on the 15th of September and ran until November 5 to very good reviews. I got Sandy to as many early rehearsals as possible. He attended all the dress and tech rehearsals right to the bitter end as well, and he never missed a company meeting. But as much as he was now back at the Center, he never interfered with Marty's classes. Eventually through unforeseen circumstances Alex Taylor became the teacher of the day.

I know that to Sandy being back at the theater was like being back in class again, and he was into every minute of it. He would sit there in his aisle seat in the front row, just glowing every opening night. Lest we forget, the man was now ninety years young and still able to function and relish every minute of it.

The Prodigal Son Returns

We were in rehearsal for *God's Country* when I got a call from CC, Boolu's aunt on his father's side who lived near him in Brooklyn. I had to laugh, well, smile, when I thought of all these relations in his life now compared to when he was nine and ten and desperately needed them and not a one of them around. Boolu spoke of her often, liked her, and spent Sundays there. She was calling me to tell me she felt Boolu was unhappy in Brooklyn.

Well, you could have knocked me over with a feather; this was the last thing I had expected to hear. I had to ask myself whether it was true or whether CC was just having a fight with Boolu's sister Sherry who benefited by Boolu living there. I told Sandy, "I have to get to the bottom of this one way or another. I'm going to call Sherry and just lay it on the line to her."

I got her on the wire and asked if she was on the outs with CC. "No," she said. "What is it?"

I related what CC had told me about Boolu. Sherry told me he had never said anything to her that would give her that impression. I asked her, "Is Boolu there?"

"Yes."

"Ask him if everything is all right."

She did and he said, "Yes."

"Ask him if he wants to come to LA."

She did and he said, "Yes."

"Ask him if he wants to come out and stay, and live out here with us?"

Sherry relayed again. "Jimmy, he 'tells' me yes, he wants to go out there."

"Tell him to pack all his things, even his Music Center. Tell him I will send him the ticket. If he wants to be out here, he should be." I added, "Tell him to give notice to everyone he's working for and be sure he tells Kate at Hunter College. Sherry, call me when he's ready to come."

He had been in that program at Hunter eleven and half years. Twelve teachers later, he was leaving. The department gave him a graduation celebration and a send-off party in the assembly hall on his last day there. They gave lovely speeches, and he was awarded his diploma from the department. He surprised them all by coming dressed in his West Indian outfit, wearing his open shirt and sash a la Harry Belafonte, and bringing along his conga drums. Through the course of the event, he got up on the stage, played his drums, danced, and sang West Indian songs. Kate said, "A joyful send-off party was had by all."

When we went to LAX to meet him, we got held up in that damn LA traffic and ended up late. I was so worried he wouldn't stay at the arrival lounge. I parked the car in the airport garage and took Sandy with me in his wheelchair. As we stood on the garage side of the street waiting for the light, I said to Sandy, "Well, he didn't stay in the arrival lounge."

"How do you know?"

"Because there he is with his luggage standing at the bus stop on the other side of the street."

I left Sandy there and went over to Boolu. "What are you doing out here?"

"Dey call your name on de mica-phone and dey tell me you not dere. So a lady took me to de luggage and said I should wait here, and I did."

I thought, that Guy is up there again. On the way home, I asked him why, when he had moved to Brooklyn, he hadn't just told us he wanted to come out to LA when we did.

He simply said, "I thought you didn't want me any more."

When I heard him say that, it was like a knife cutting through my heart. I couldn't get the thought out of my mind that he had held that feeling in his heart for three years. My God, how much that must have hurt him, yet he accepted and never complained.

He adjusted to California easily. He made friends with the young actors in the company and went out with them; he even had a pool-shooting buddy in Chris Mitchell. He made himself so useful around the theater that the members gave him an honorary membership. He also made friends in the neighborhood as was his way. Many of them knew Boolu but didn't have an inkling who Sandy and I were. Everyone at Pavilion, our supermarket, knew him, from the manager to the guy who swept up the place.

His coming out to LA couldn't have been more timely for me. The weaker Sandy got, the more difficult it was becoming for me. With Boolu there, life became a piece of cake. He was so helpful. I had had no idea how badly I needed him.

Meanwhile Back At The Ranch

God's Country rehearsals were going well. Sandy would sit in the front aisle seat while Boolu was always up in the last row on the right, both in rapt attention. Boolu loved anything and everything to do with performing. It made no difference whether it was Radio City, TV, movies, or our little theater. He was a real ham.

All in all the production was a good example of ensemble acting, and Sandy felt we were on our way. November 15 marked the opening of a production of a modern English farce, *The Farndale Avenue Housing Estate Townswomen's Guild Dramatic Society's Production of A Christmas Carol: A Comedy*. Sandy told the players just to have a ball, and they did. A fun time was had by all. Sandy and I caught the dress rehearsal before we left for Bequia.

The company went on to mount four more plays, which carried the company through the summer. Two of the plays that season were written by Lynn Mamet. You can see it was an ambitious bunch of kids we had gathered together. We went on presenting plays into the new millennium long after Sandy's death. Even Boolu eventually joined the company on stage, appearing as a taxi driver in a revival of Clifford Odets' Waiting for Lefty. Sandy would have been as proud as a peacock to see him on that stage, and in that particular show.

Alas, all good things must come to an end. That production of Waiting for Lefty was the last at the Sanford Meisner Theatre of the Arts. It starred Alex Taylor in the role of Agate Kellar originated by Elia Kazan in the 1935 production directed by Sanford Meisner. After the final performance on June 2, 2005, the Sanford Meisner Center as we all knew it changed when Martin Barter as artistic director ceased activities. The Meisner Carville School of Acting at the Center was also closed by around the same time though it is impossible to pinpoint an exact timing of its demise, as Marty continued on his own, teaching at his own center. But, according to the contract, it is not Sanford

Meisner's Center.

A few years later in the fall of '09, I, as executor of the Sanford Meisner Trust, founded the not-for-profit Sanford Meisner Institute. In my role as president, I appointed Alex Taylor, a former actor in the now defunct Sanford Meisner Theatre of the Arts, as Artistic Director-Teacher.

The Last Trip to Bequia for De Tree a We

The trip to Bequia was getting tougher, but with Boolu's help we were able to manage it. We were like a military traveling Medical Evac Unit, equipped to set up a Field Med Unit anywhere. The medical supplies required for a four-month stay were numerous. Sandy needed bandage dressing, gauze, and everything that goes with it to dress and service his G-tube for his stomach feedings, and suction supplies for his breathing stoma. His medicine alone filled a carry-on, with eye drops, potassium, Lasix, blood pressure and iron pills, and more. Then there was his liquid nourishment. All this gear just made his stay on the Island much safer. All the sea, sand, and sun made it a hell of a lot healthier for him, too. And what it did for his mental and emotional wellbeing was beyond calculation. He was home where he was happy.

"Why go through all this?" someone once asked me.

"That doesn't even deserve an answer," I replied. He was home, we were home. Where else should we be?

Boolu was tending to the everyday chores, running in and out to the Harbour. He worked mornings and took off after lunch. He was back at five to help prepare dinner. After dinner he was off again, who knew where? That was his time and I never infringed upon it. He seemed to be actively enjoying himself. It was a routine he was to follow for years to come. It was his way of handling his two lifestyles, his two cultures. They were clear and separate, and who was I to judge? It worked for him.

Christmas was busily working on Casa Sol, the new house I had designed for over the water tank and garage. I hoped one day down the road it would be an in-season rental. It would help with our retirement plan. Once Sandy's Social Security was cut off, because it damn sure would be, as would his retirement pension from the Playhouse which together amounted to around $2,000 a month, we would be reduced to my meager Social Security allotment. This wasn't Canada and there would be no such thing as a marriage or even a civil union. Our lifestyle, Boolu's and mine, was going to change drastically. But to hell with the Jerry Falwells of the world. They can keep the money. We will make out without their compassion and understanding. Understanding takes brains and theirs are warped.

Sandy spent mornings up on the terrace while I worked with Christmas and Bernard, our mason from St. Vincent. Boolu, Sandy, and I would have lunch, after which Boolu took off to points north or south, because that was the only choice he had on this narrow island. In the afternoon Sandy and I would make it over to Lower Bay. The sea was placid there and the waters clear as crystal. We would sit at the water's edge and look out over the Caribbean watching the sun complete its daily journey down, down into the western horizon, getting bigger by the minute as it turned from a golden yellow to a luscious orange. Some days, depending on the atmospheric gases, it would blush into a flaming red globe sending vibrating heat waves of shimmering light across the calm expanse of turquoise tapestry. Many times I sat there and wondered, how many more sunsets will we be allowed? Yet other times, the sunsets reminded us of times past and we would reminisce about Roatan in the western Caribbean. Another day it would be St. Martin in the north and that mauve-lavender twilight of the Leeward Islands. Our life was all reflective now; Sandy never verbalized this thought, perhaps he was afraid to. It was too much of a reminder of what little of all this remained for us.

Gone were the days of no electricity for a week or more. One could say the same for shortages of onions. There was no more fighting with the Prime Minister over a powdered milk embargo, no more smuggling Irish potatoes from Grenada. The dinners of Spam or corn beef because that was all Mrs. Derrick had, the smell of a kerosene hurricane lamp on the dining room table, gone, gone, all gone. It's true, we were still treated with visits over the weekend from Marie Kingston, Lou Keane, or Elaine Ollivierre, and even Sandy's niece, Ellen Wetherell, who was now living on her boat *Oh Life* in the Harbour. But so much more was all gone.

The French captain Joubert and the boat lady, Judy Kwaloff, Molly Burk, Rusty Ford, Rootie Derujinsky, Pat Field, Santa's helper Betsy Frisbee, Judy's Mac of Mac's Pizza, Jack from the bar with his foul mouth, as well as Nora and her Scrabble board, Anderson the Scot from Windsor now gone, leaving Brigitte all alone over behind Friendship Hotel, and Vi and Ralph Wallach and the Wears of Moon Hole, minus their library for they left that to us—all gone from the island, many dead. Even our Winnie, from whom by now I was divorced, and her lovely daughter Paulette, who had died of cancer. How their images fade. Well, really, not Winnie's, for Boolu and I have remained close to her over the years and we still see one another out in Queens where she is looked after by her daughter Hazel and her grandchildren. Unions now torn asunder—Tiare and Lee, Rita and Sam, Captain Thompson and Ethel, Son and Pat were "never no more." Many have gone and even more have come to fill the void. Ah, but it's not the same.

One afternoon looking across the bay from our house that was one of the first built in the area, I sat there counting the houses surrounding the Friendship Bay Hotel.

"Sandy, remember Trapazzo, Mallet, Vogel, Blenkinsopp, Lazar, Butts, Dwyer, Morton, Ford, and Fowley? Oh, yes, and the Brewsters? Well, they all came, built, and in their time they all did run. Sandy, they're all gone now, even Stan, Ron, and Brenda, not a single one left. Yet we're still here. And it's not as much fun."

"But God is good, isn't He?" Sandy replied. "We still have the sea, the sand, and the sun."

43 The Grim Reaper Slowly Pulls the Curtain

Hearth and Home

We could have stayed on Bequia longer that winter of '96; Sandy was up to it all right. I was torn by my need for a doctor's reassurance that we were doing the right thing by Sandy, that all that could be done for him in his present state was being done. Then, too, the Center needed a guiding hand—after all, even though the company had performed fifteen plays thus far, it was still in its infancy, not yet a year old.

We were never so close, de tree a we, as we were that year. I sensed, and I am sure Boolu did as well, what lay ahead. I could tell in Sandy's handgrip alone he too was well aware our time was now metered. How long we had was in the hands of a greater power. So we just carried on as we always had, including Sandy in everything we did, because that was the way he wanted it. Simply put, he may have felt that if he kept moving, the grim reaper wouldn't be able to catch up to him. Everywhere we went he went right along with us.

In June, we came back to the little homestead in Sherman Oaks to find all the plants in full bloom. El Nino had been kind. The rains that year had been plentiful, and the fruits of Boolu's labor were apparent all around the house. The roses were "beside themselves"; they were humongous. It isn't usual for an easterner to see roses six inches across and cypresses sprouting skyward. It was all so beautiful to come home to. But the biggest surprise was the fireplace that Steven Vaughn and his friend had built while we were away. It transformed the living room into a homey, hearth-warming center on those damp, chilly, winter nights. You see, we weren't used to them on Bequia. Sandy and I would sit there, staring at the bouncing flames and listening to the crackling embers as we had at 83rd Street thirty-odd years before.

The Center Of Our Lives

On the 2nd of October, we started rehearsing for Larry Cohen's *Fallen Eagle: The Untold Story of Charles A. Lindbergh*. Larry was a successful movie producer, director, and screenwriter. The play had a big cast with three parts for older men. I told Larry that Marty wouldn't have any trouble finding older graduates, but he did. Maybe if we'd been in New York it would have been easier. Older actors out in LA, if they're not doing frequent character parts, tend to drop out of the business altogether.

Larry didn't seem troubled by the situation. When I asked him why, he said, "Because you can do all three."

"You're joking, Larry," I replied. "We founded this theater for the kids, not the likes of me."

"I'm sure you did, but right now your theater needs three old cronies, and you're it—all three!"

All Sandy said was, "Jimmy, do 'em."

"When I wanted parts, I couldn't get arrested and now I'm handed them three at a time," I said.

"Remember I said to you-all, 'One of these days, you will all meet up with yourselves?' So let me be the first to introduce you. You are now Jimmy Carville, the character actor. And better late than never."

Well, you know, I played them and enjoyed every minute of the challenge. I played Jafsey, the Irish teacher from Fordham University who was the go-between in the Lindbergh kidnapping, Franklin Delano Roosevelt whose vocal tapes I studied, and Henry Ford whom I played as a Ross Perot type. My little Jafsey Vaudeville Act, the one that Jafsey went on the road with after he wrote his book, was a showstopper. That wasn't hard for an over-the-hill actor to take.

We had great houses throughout the run, from November 8 to December 15. Sandy was there every night, had to be since I was there every night. All Larry's friends and followers from the other side of the hill packed every performance to support him. The reviewers weren't too kind to Larry, I think because he had reduced the play from a screenplay and it had problems, especially in our tiny theater. Nevertheless the last two lines of the LA Times review read: "But all three parts played by Jimmy Carville were delightful."

Our Last Holiday Season

Christmas Eve was scheduled at Rosie's; we were expected as always whenever we were in town. But then Sandy started failing. He was very weak physically although he managed to get around, but almost imperceptibly his mind was wafting in and out of clarity. Keeping him on his oxygen helped a little but not much. I really doubted that he would make it up the stairs to Rosie's second-floor flat this year. Even if he did, what if he wasn't clearheaded? With some insensitive people, it could prove embarrassing, and I wanted to avoid that at any cost. So I told Rosie we might not make it, but she was insistent.

In the morning while suctioning out his stoma with the electric suction machine, I began to notice flecks of blood. It could have been bits of crusted mucous or maybe a strain from a coughing spasm. I just made a mental note of it and elected to watch it closely. Between Rosie's insistence and Sandy's insistence, I gave in, and de tree a we ever so slowly made it up the outside staircase to Rosie's. Sandy planted himself on the couch next to Rita and had no trouble with his clarity all evening. If he had, he did a damn good job of covering it up.

It was the usual Edelman Christmas party, but I noted some faces were missing this year. Time was taking its toll. Morey Amsterdam was gone, and we hadn't seen or heard from Patty Andrews and Wally Weschler since the earthquake. As on Bequia new faces filled the void. With all the activity at the theater, Boolu was kept busy with holiday parties. I spent my time at home keeping a close eye on Sandy. His blood pressure was low and his pulse was weak. Over New Year's weekend, I called Dr. Bluming who told me to bring him in on the 2nd of January unless he worsened, in which case to take him right in to Tarzana Hospital. I was beginning to worry.

I told Boolu that if he wanted to go out with some of the actors on New Year's, I would work that out for him. But he said, "No, I want to be with you two." We were staying at home in front of the TV and I didn't have to tell him why. At midnight Boolu went out on the street where our next-door neighbors and the gang from across the street were whooping it up. That seemed to satisfy him while Sandy and I eased ourselves into '97 with little exertion.

Our Last Few Days Together

On the 2nd of January, I took Sandy to his doctor's appointment. Dr. Bluming didn't see much difference. I described the blood in his mucous and the doctor examined his stoma but didn't make much of it. I felt it must just be me imagining things. We were sent home to come back on the 15th.

On Wednesday I took him to the weekly Theater Company meeting where he sat in his seat apparently clear as a bell. The blood seemed to increase each morning I suctioned his stoma. By the morning of Sandy's appointment on the 15th, I was truly concerned with what I was suctioning from the stoma. I decided to put it in a jar and bring it in to the good doctor just to let him see for himself. Sandy himself hadn't changed that much. He was still getting his oxygen, and he was up and about though he was taking things very easily. It was like watching a wind-up clock slow down ever so slowly when it needs a good sharp twist of the wrist.

Leaving Sandy in the waiting room, I went in to Dr. Avrum and showed him the jar, telling him, "This is from this morning alone."

He was not unaffected by what he saw. He said nothing at first, then, "I'm making an appointment for him with a trach and stoma specialist, a head and neck man over at St. Joseph's Medical Center in Burbank." Dr. Bluming implied Sandy was on borrowed time, and I above anyone knew that. I knew Dr. Avrum had never thought he would last this long, which was why he had held the gala the previous spring. But he added, "Look, Jim, he could still hang on for some time. He's such a fighter."

He suggested I should start thinking about how we were going to handle him as his faculties began to shut down and fail him altogether. He mentioned a few possibilities, that of a hospital nursing home, or a hospice, or home care under the auspices of the hospice people, or in-home health care that would come in a couple of times a week from the county. I didn't like the sound of "hospice." To me it smacked of letting him go, and all I could think was, why? He isn't in pain, and we can still communicate.

I told the doctor, "No homes and no hospices. He's staying with us for as long as we can handle him. We have three bedrooms at home. I'll turn one into a hospital room. We'll get a hospital bed and whatever else he will require. There's Boolu and me—we can watch him night and day. If we need a nurse, we'll get one. He's staying at home where I know he wants to be."

Our head and neck man found nothing out of the ordinary, which surprised the hell out of me. At our last meeting with Dr. Avrum on the 22nd of January, he asked what kind of care we were going to arrange for. I told him what I had already said, "He's staying at home, and no hospice."

"Then am I to assume that it's visiting nurse care?" he asked.

"Yes."

He told me he would notify the county and a supervisor would come around to the house with the necessary forms. It was still early in the day when we left his office. A feeling came over me that was hard to put into words. It was as if Sandy had met an impasse. His life from this day on would never be the same.

The company meeting was at four that afternoon. I asked him if he felt up to it. "Don't we always?" he answered. He had no idea as to what had transpired between Dr. Avrum and me.

I asked Boolu, "Are you hungry?" Sandy had been fed before we left the house.

"Almost." It was one of Boolu's favorite noncommittal replies.

So I said, "Let's drive over to the In'n'Out and pick up some cheeseburgers, french-fries, and a shake and go over to Balboa Park in the Sepulveda Basin for the afternoon."

I just had a premonition that this was going to be Sandy's last day out, how or why, I had no idea. Perhaps it was just the accumulation of everything that seemed to be conspiring against him. Everything was coming to a showdown, a slowdown, and, God I feared, a final shutdown. Yet he was still clearheaded and able to communicate and navigate. But he was becoming ever so passive, and that was what was getting to me.

We used to go to Balboa Park during our stay in Northridge. We used to watch the fishermen and the children playing whatever games children play in a park. We would feed the geese and ducks and watch them swim about. I felt he deserved one last day of all this peace and tranquility. It was all such a beautiful experience to partake of—the park and the day full of life, the sun high in its heaven. White fluffy-puffy clouds like gobs of marshmallow fluff floated slowly overhead. Soft breezes wafting in from the ocean over the

Santa Monica Mountains pushed the clouds across the vast expanse of the San Fernando Valley as they made their way to the high desert over yonder.

Later that afternoon we drove over to Lankershim in North Hollywood to attend the company meeting. The minutes were read; the usual everyday old business was brought up, discarded, or discussed. When the new business of a playwriting contest came up, Sandy was very much involved, advising, "Perhaps one-acts the first time around." That's right, Sandy, I thought to myself. Slow and easy and he's still going at it. That's exactly what we did for the rest of the week—we took it slow and easy. We never left the house, not even over the weekend.

The supervisor from the County Nurses Association came in on Monday morning. She explained the workings of the visiting nurse. We would be provided with one who would come twice a week at first and would be on call for emergencies. She gave me pamphlets to read and forms to fill out and sign. Then she examined Sandy.

Seeing all his paraphernalia, she said, "It looks like you've been at this for a while."

When I said, "Ever since August of '74," she laughed.

"The nurse will start at the end of the week," she said. "She'll be calling you." And she left.

On Wednesday he was much too weak to go to the company meeting. When he tried to get up off the bed that morning to go to the john, he toppled over on top of his walker, smashing his head into the mirrored sliding doors of his closet. The mirror, which wasn't really glass but a mirror compound of sorts, splintered without falling out of its encasement. It didn't cut him and because the door swayed inward when he struck it, it wasn't even much of a blow. I helped him to the bathroom. He was a dead weight and I had to hold him upright on the seat. I got him back into bed, put him immediately on oxygen, and took his vital signs. They were low but no lower than usual. What he needed was oxygen. I didn't administer it to him at night when he was sleeping, and I knew that back in bed with oxygen and rest he would rally, and he did.

Late that afternoon Sandy was feeling a little better. I planned to go to the meeting, leaving Boolu home with him. He wasn't having any of it. He wanted to dress and come with me.

"No way," I said. "Not today."

I was surprised he didn't insist. I could see he was tired and I told him to try to get some rest, I would be gone only an hour or so. As I left I told Boolu to check him out every once in a while. "If anything happens and there's a change, no matter what, call the theater—you have the number—and I'll be here in less than fifteen minutes." I had been known to make it in ten when the stoplights were with me.

The actors were surprised to see me there without Sandy. It was the first time I had been there alone. It was the first meeting he had missed, when he

43 The Grim Reaper Slowly

wasn't on Bequia, since the spring of '95. We were like the Bobbsey twins or more like Siamese twins: you see one, you get the other.

At the meeting I told the company that I felt he didn't have much time left. The reaction to a member was one of disbelief, some saying, "But he was here just last week and he was fine."

"Don't forget," I replied, "he's an actor." There were a few snickers, but I could see they were still not with me. As I left I stopped and told Marty it didn't look good. "Please stop by for a visit."

At home, I would feed him through the G-tube in bed and then he would get up into his wheelchair and join Boolu and me while we had dinner. For the first time, he was using his wheelchair in the house. Then he and I would sit in front of a crackling fire and watch TV, with me at the right end of the couch and him next to me in his wheelchair holding my hand. I say holding, but he wasn't holding, he was squeezing and hanging on with the grip of death. I just knew he was afraid he would slip away. He had once told me, and I remembered his words sitting there in front of the roaring fire, "Jimmy, I'm not afraid to die, I just want you to come with me." I know they were the truest words he ever spoke.

Saturday morning I called Marty to tell him I hadn't been kidding on Wednesday, that he should stop by, and I meant that day. I know he didn't believe me, but he came over late that afternoon anyway and sat on the bed and they talked. While Marty was making small talk, Sandy kept asking about the playwriting contest, just carrying on with work as usual, with all kinds of questions. "How many do you have so far?... How do you think the turnout will be?... Have you notified the colleges?... Who is going to judge and how many judges?"

He was so engaged that when Marty finally left he said, "I don't see what your concern is."

"I hope you're right."

After Marty left, Sandy got up in his wheelchair and joined Boolu and me again while we had our typical Saturday night dinner of franks, beans, and date-nut bread. Actually, they were pigs-in-a-blanket with cheese wrapped in crisp bacon. After dinner Boolu made a fire in the fireplace before going to his room. The TV was on but neither of us was watching it. We both just sat there and stared into the burning embers not saying a word. After thirty-six years who needed to talk? Everything had already been said many times over. After the eleven o'clock news, Sandy turned in. My right hand was cramped and purple.

When I awoke Sunday morning, he was already awake. "Are you in pain?" I asked.

"No."

"Are you hungry?" He nodded his head. "Let me suction you first and then I'll set up your feeding tube."

I went into the kitchen where Boolu was starting to fix breakfast. "Boolu," I said, "what do you say? Scrambled this morning?"

As I suctioned Sandy's stoma, I couldn't help but notice the amount of blood I was getting up. I made a mental note to save it to show to the nurse who was coming in that day for the first time.

I set Sandy up with his Jevity for the morning and went out to the kitchen and had breakfast with Boolu. Halfway through, I thought I had better go in and see how Sandy was doing and check the flow of the feeding tube. As soon as I walked in, I could see he had pulled out the feeding tube. The Jevity was running out over the bed linen. Normally, my nature being what it was, I would have yelled to high heaven at such a disaster, but I didn't. Somehow I knew instantly what was actually happening. I called pleasantly to Boolu to come and help me, that we had a little job to tend to. Then I saw Sandy had not only pulled out the feeding tube but had also yanked the G-tube with its inflated balloon out through the tiny stoma in his stomach. It must have taken quite a force on his part. I knew immediately he was through, he was finished.

He just lay there, looking up bewildered and vague. I ran to the bathroom, grabbed a towel and a new G-tube with gauze and tape, and instructed Boolu to insert it once he had finished cleaning the mess around him. I hurried to the phone to call the visiting nurse's office. She had been on her way to us, but had been diverted by an emergency call. "Well," I said, "there's an emergency here right now," and I hung up.

I rushed back to Boolu and Sandy. Boolu was calmly doing his job. I could tell Sandy was leaving us, so I ran back to the phone and dialed 911. They instructed me to lay him out on the floor. They would be right there. I went back to Sandy and kissed him on the forehead. Boolu was about finished. As we stood there by Sandy's side and I tried to grasp the reality of what was happening, we could see him pass away without a word.

"Boolu, he's gone." We took the quilt and stretched it out on the floor. We lifted him from the bed onto the quilt.

The firefighters were at the door in no time. As one knelt over him, he looked up at me standing next to the wall and said, "Sorry!"

"I know."

Friends

Boolu and I were in the kitchen, letting the firefighters do whatever firefighters do at a time like that. All the while I was frantically making calls. I called Dr. Avrum Bluming to tell him Sandy was gone and that the firefighters were here. He told me he would handle everything with the coroner. I told him Sandy wanted to be cremated; he said he would take care of that as well. I then called the visiting nurses to tell them to call off the nurse who hadn't come. It was too late now.

Then I called Marty to tell him. He could not believe it. "Well, you better believe it because this is the way it is." He said he would call Arthur and be right over.

I had no idea how all this was affecting Boolu. I hadn't thought about Boolu throughout until we sat at the kitchen table looking across at each other, waiting for the boys to come. I was so appreciative of their prompt response. I don't know how or whether I could have handled it if the firefighters had taken Sandy out with just Boolu at my side.

The coroner arrived. Arthur Seidelman and Richard Alfieri showed up with bags of groceries. "You won't be thinking about shopping for a while so perhaps this will tide you over," Richard said.

It was about an hour and a half before the firefighters and the coroner were finished and the necessary papers signed. They were taking Sandy away, away for the last time as I stood there with Boolu at my side, with our friends beside us, each of us saying our private, silent good-bye.

The Arrangements

So many things had to be done: decisions had to be made, arrangements tended to. Kim Garfield, our theater publicist, would handle the obits.

I had sat down the week before to do all that. I had just known somehow it was only days away. In fact I had already sent the release to a friend at the Associated Press on Friday; he had covered Sandy for the Channel 13 documentary in '90. I had told him it was just a matter of days. I wanted to hold the wake at the Center for only one day. It should be all day, from nine to nine. We would bank the stage with flowers and ferns. We could also hang a big picture of him. Stick it in front of a Chagall in one of our big gold frames. He won't mind for a couple of days, and neither will Chagall.

We could set a big TV screen off to the side and loop The *Theater's Best Kept Secret* over and over. We could add Sandy's gala tape to it.

No talks, no speeches, no people, just Sandy.

With Sandy's ashes in a simple gold box on a brass stand beneath his picture, they came in, sat down, and watched the TV, spending time with Sandy and their memories. I was quite satisfied; it was oh so peaceful with the stage banked with his favorite red and white roses and ferns mingled among bunches of big white chrysanthemums. Nancy Matthews, our theater electrician, topped it off with two huge brass candelabra from Warner Brothers that filled the back of the stage on either side of Sandy's picture. It couldn't have been more beautiful. I had said until nine, but it was more like ten before the day ended, and by then the vestibule was full of bouquets and floral wreaths from mourners.

The company took care of everything. Boolu and I didn't have to lift a finger. Sydney was interviewed on TV, and all the papers from coast to coast covered his passing thanks to the Associated Press. The New York Times... All I could say to them was a humble thank you. They did the man justice with their send-off; they really outdid themselves.

Late Sunday evening, a photographer from the Valley paper called and asked if she could come by to get a photo for their front-page article on Sandy. She came and took a shot of Boolu and me holding a large headshot of Sandy. The article reported the passing of a luminary who had been living in the San Fernando Valley and working at the Sanford Meisner Center on Lankershim Boulevard.

After the Sabbath, on Saturday night the 8th of February, Rabbi Debra Orenstein, a former student, flew in from Florida to perform the service. Only family and close friends attended. That was an easy guest list. All Sandy's relatives were on the east coast, so only Boolu, my brother Gerald who flew in from Boca in Florida for the service, and I were family. The friends were all those who had visited us in our home or had ever invited us to theirs. I do not believe we left anyone out.

On Sunday Boolu and I packed for Bequia and made for Connecticut and Rusty Ford's, bearing Sandy's ashes. On Wednesday the 12th the east coast memorial for Sandy was held at the Jazz Cathedral on Lexington Avenue and 54th Street, with a reception afterwards at the Neighborhood Playhouse. The church was full. I could see young actors peering in through the windows. The minister commented on the size of the turnout only wishing he had a congregation that size on a Sunday morning.

Unlike in California, speaker after speaker remembered Sandy. But the one who hit me in the solar plexus was his nephew, Danny. He reminisced back to the time at his house when he had told Sandy that he seemed distant and asked him why he wasn't closer with his family. Sandy's answer to Danny had been, "I pick my family." Danny continued, "Looking down at these front rows this morning, it's now obvious to me why." For all my family from all parts of the country were there. My ageable mom at ninety-three had got on the phone and called all twenty-nine of my siblings, in-laws, and out-laws to make damn sure they got there. She wanted everyone to be there to pay their respects to Sandy and to be with me and Boolu at this hour.

Sandy's problem with his family, aside from his father, had been that they put him on a pedestal, especially his mother and sister Ruth, and ended up intimidating the others with what a paragon he was. Ellen, Sandy's niece, remembers being so influenced by her mother and grandmother that she was actually frightened of Sandy when he made visits home. She was grateful for the time she later spent living on Bequia where she got to really know and love him for the man he truly was. This relationship with his family made Sandy uneasy and he regretted it profoundly. By contrast, with my family he was just one of the bunch. He truly liked it that way. He didn't aspire to greatness; he didn't need attention or fussing over. It was enough for Sandy just to be, and in that lay his greatness.

The next day Kathleen Nolan, Boolu, and I, after checking our bags for Bequia—and Sandy as well—at Grand Central Station baggage room, took off across town to the Actors Studio, where some of Sandy's much older former students from the '40s were still members. They were holding their own memorial for Sandy. Remember, Sandy had been at the Actors Studio with his actors long before Lee Strasberg pontificated there. Sidney Lumet was heard from and a note from Sydney Pollack was read. Eli Wallach also spoke. I told them that Sandy and Lee had gotten along over the years by just agreeing to disagree. Hadn't Lee wound up marrying one of Sandy's trained students, Anna? The place was full of red hearts and love: the following day was Valentine's Day.

The time came for us to have an early dinner, sleep over at Kathleen's, and wake up at the crack of day, February 14. We had to get out to Kennedy with our luggage, Sandy, and his death papers and board American Air for Barbados.

Bequia's Final Send-Off

By 7 PM we were seated at our dining room table having our first dinner there without Sandy, with Boolu sitting in Sandy's seat. Parnell was there and Aggie in the kitchen wanting to know the order of the day. "Well, the church service will be on Sunday afternoon. Sandy wanted his remains to be buried at the top of the winding path overlooking the house and the sea, just below the mini rain forest. We will have to finish the top part of the path tomorrow with flat fieldstone, and dig the grave."

"Let Christmas do that," said Parnell. "I have the wake to attend to."

"Wake? What wake?" I asked.

"Mr. Jimmy, this is Sandy-mon. He must have a proper send-off."

I thought, hasn't he had enough already? My God, both Boolu and I are exhausted.

"We do it Saturday night. Me and Aggie take care of everyting," he said. "You and Boolu take it easy."

I noticed Boolu's luggage upstairs over in the corner of the dining room. "What's this?"

And he informed me, "I'm sleeping in my daddy's bed."

"Be my guest." And up he went.

Well, Aggie and Parnell sure did take care of everything. Come Friday it was a hustle and bustle of activity up the hill behind the house. Parnell was in and out all day with food for Aggie to prepare. Saturday the booze and cases of beer came, and ice as well, washbasins full of it. Aggie and a plethora of her friends were a flurry of activity in the kitchen. Parnell had cleared the dining room of its furniture and improvised a makeshift bar in the corner. Judging from the amount of booze and food being slapped around in the kitchen, I could see they were expecting quite a crowd.

I said to Parnell, "This wake wasn't even announced over the radio, and we didn't get here in time to arrange all this. What makes you think a lot of people will be here?"

"Carville, everybody knows Sandy die, and everybody knows you're here. You just wait and see."

"Well, how long will this shindig go on tonight?" I asked. I was beat and we had the church service the next day.

"You know a West Indian wake go on all night till daybreak. You know that. Someone has to sit up with the family," he said.

My God! we're sitting shiva, I thought. "Thank them very much, Parnell, but I'll be fast asleep." This was something I hadn't planned on.

People started gathering after 6 PM, coming to Boolu and me expressing their condolences. By seven they had begun in earnest. Some, mostly older women, congregated in the living room, clustering around the rather large sitting room on couches and chairs. Off in a corner on the Steinway was a picture of Sandy. His ashes sat in front of it, with two candelabra on either side surrounded by sprays of salmon-colored bougainvillea. A woman stood in front of the heavy front doors leading them all in a hymn-sing. The men were scattered about sitting on benches on the terrace outside and up on the dining room terrace. Inside the dining room, around the bar being tended to by Parnell himself, were the serious drinkers. Aggie and her cohorts were frantically preparing chicken and rice pilau and salads, as well as macaroni and cheese and breads of various kinds all of which were to be served about midnight. People sat around with a drink of their choice talking to one another while the voices from the hymn-sing in the living room permeated the entire household.

It all started out familiarly enough. I recognized the hymns from the Anglican and Catholic hymnals. When one leader got tired, another stepped in and took over the baton and podium as it were. The singers seemed to switch on and off depending on the leader. Many denominations besides the major ones were represented: Seventh Day Adventists, Evangelicals, Baptists, and a few somewhat akin to Holy Rollers. Obviously missing were the Jehovah's Witnesses. Someone on Bequia had once told me that Jehovah's Witnesses didn't eat bread from two tables, only their own.

As the evening progressed, things became more raucous, even the hymn-sing. At one point I looked into the living room to see Parnell's mother, an Evangelical, leading the songfest. For want of shocktras or marimbas, she was shaking two large kitchen matchboxes. Boolu and I just roamed around talking to this one and that. Everyone there was a West Indian except Sam and Donna McDowell from Paget Farm. I suspect they felt a little out of place: I noted they left early. There was no doubt this was a true West Indian wake.

About 3 AM I asked Parnell, "How much longer can this go on?"

"I told you, till daybreak."

"No, Parnell. Boolu and I are about to drop. How can we get them to go home?"

"All you have to do is stop the booze and they will fade out," he said.

"Then please do. Lock up the grog and tell them we're all out." He did and within forty minutes the last of them were straggling, no staggering, down the drive. All gone that is, except Ernest Williams who passed out in the flower garden beyond the terrace and was left there until he awoke in the morning under a blazing sun.

At church that afternoon, Father Adams performed the service. Father had a new young fellow at the organ. I delivered the eulogy, and Boolu, after the congregation had settled in, carried Sandy's ashes down the center aisle and placed them on a brass stand at the altar-rail. The church was filled, mostly with Sandy's foreign friends from England, Ireland, Norway, Sweden, France, Belgium, Germany, Canada, and America, with a smattering of West Indians, the ones who hadn't sent him off last night. This church is where Sandy had played the organ for the school children twenty years ago, so he was no stranger to the place. The church was in the process of designing and creating a stained glass window in his honor.

The Eulogy

The bell tolled for Sanford Meisner just two weeks ago today. Many mourn his death. Some grieve their loss; others celebrate his life and his contribution to the entertainment world. If Sanford were standing here next to me today, I know what he would say. 'Jimmy, what's all the fuss about? I was just another acting teacher.'

But you see, he was much more than that. He taught his students a way of life. They were not only actors; there were writers, directors, casting directors, producers, and teachers. His influence was far reaching within the industry. We shall all miss and remember his sensitivity, kindness, and incisive understanding, from the lowliest walk-on to the lovely Princess Grace of Monaco. He was a giant among these people. They revered him. But they did not know the man who walked the shores of his adopted homeland among the people of Bequia. He was shy, unassuming, humble, and private. Not that he didn't know his worth. He was well aware that he was one of the best. Correction: Sandy was the best, and when coaxed, he grudgingly admitted it. But he never talked about it or himself. He was a very gracious person.

Though Sandy had a laryngectomy and lost his voice in 1974, his creativity remained undiminished. The essence of his human spirit, as he fought to overcome seemingly insurmountable physical odds, continued to flourish until the last minute when we were holding him in our arms.

Sandy's life was an inspiration to all of us. I am not here in his stead but merely here to convey his message to you. For the past thirty-five years I have been fortunate to serve as the humanitarian emissary for Sanford Meisner. As you all know, I assisted him in his work, where the need for his inspiration had been the greatest. Reflecting on acting and on life, Sandy's words speak for themselves:

Always be specific.

Every little moment has a meaning all its own.
Stay in the moment.
Listen, observe, listen. Really look, listen, concentrate.
Don't do anything until something happens to make you do it.
Act before you think: your instincts are more honest than your thoughts.
There is no such thing as genial charm.
An ounce of behavior is worth a pound of words.
There is no such thing as nothing. Silence can say a lot. It can also cover up a multitude of sins.
Don't take anything for granted.
Live fully, moment to moment. That is reality.

Sandy's treasure from Shaw in reference to Duse: "Behind every broad stroke there was a human idea."

Sandy's favorite from Goethe: "I wish the stage were as narrow as a tight rope, so that no incompetent would dare walk on it."

Find in yourself those things which are human, which are universal.

Thank you, Sandy!

A Resting Place for Sandy

At the end of the service, Father Adams said a few words. Since Sandy wasn't being buried in the cemetery, I assumed that was it and started to take Boolu and Sandy's ashes home to bury up the hill behind the house. At that point, Father informed me he was going home with us to give Sandy a proper burial service.

When we arrived at the house, I was surprised to see Parnell had arranged taxis and jeeps to bring out all those who wished to come for the interment. They all trudged up the drive, not an easy feat, and on up past the house to the narrow winding path that twisted and turned its way up through the little forest of trees to where the path stopped at the grave. The spot was just under the beautiful mini rain forest that lorded overhead, facing out over the house to Friendship Bay and the ocean. Boolu laid the brass box into the cement encasement Christmas had built. Father started the service as Christmas sealed the cement encasement and started to cover the grave with dirt. Then the West Indians began singing their hymns, which is their way. As Boolu saw the dirt burying Sandy, he broke down and cried. Father held him, trying to comfort him. Then the women passed through the line of people along the narrow path to lay their floral bouquets and wreaths. With Boolu crying and the women singing and people jostling to put their flowers on the little grave on the side of that steep hill enshrouded in trees, it was an intimate and emotional moment among close friends.

Marie, who arrived late because she had ridden out on her bike, like Noel Coward's Madame Arcati in Blithe Spirit, described it thus: "From the road at a distance the side of that very steep hill was the essence of a surrealist paint-

Sandy's final home

ing."

The scene was diffused through the trees. The narrowness of the path forced the line of people to twist and wind up and around that hill, everyone dressed in black or white with a smidgen of mauve as was the custom on the Island. She could hear the strains of "Nearer My God to Thee" wafting away on the sea breeze. Thus, on the afternoon of February 16, Sandy was finally laid to rest on the side of the hill above his home overlooking placid Friendship Bay and the massive Atlantic Ocean beyond.

Going down the hill my thoughts turned to all these people coming down to the house and I hoped to hell we still had enough grog and soft drinks after last night's siege. I cornered Aggie in the kitchen. "Do we have anything left from last night?"

"Not to worry, Mr. Jimmy. I put enough away last night to take care of this. I knew we were going to need something this afternoon."

Boolu recovered quickly and played the gracious host, passing out drinks with Parnell as Aggie circulated with what they call finger food today. Not wanting to overstay their welcome on such an occasion, people soon started drifting off and it wasn't long before we saw the last of them off down the drive.

Jimmy & Boolu

As Aggie was cleaning up in the kitchen and preparing dinner, Boolu and I walked out onto the terrace... looking over an expansive sea, beyond Friendship Bay and Hilary across to Baliceaux and Battowi', only the two of us you see. No more was there De Tree a We. There was just He & Me.

APPENDIX

Teachers Who Were Trained by Sandy

Many acting teachers claim to be teaching the Meisner Approach. Sanford Meisner's teachers in training, however, were few and far between. Below is a list of acting teachers he trained.

The first was David Pressman from his first class at the Playhouse in 1935. Then came:

- Charles Aidman (d-1993)
- Bill Alderson, LA
- Martin Barter, WA
- Robert Carnegie, LA
- Charles Conrad (d-1993)
- Jeff Corey (d-2002)
- William (Bill) Esper, NY
- Wynn Handman, NY
- Fred Kareman (d-2007)
- Richard LePore (d-1998)
- Ian McRae, Santa Cruz
- Robert X. (Bob) Modica, NY
- Ed Moore (d-1990)
- Sydney Pollack (d-2008)
- Richard Pinter, NY
- Mark Rydell, LA
- John Ruskin, LA
- Ron Stetson, NY
- Gene Terruso, LA
- Jim Tuthill, NY

Other Teachers

Many others who studied as actors with him are also teaching what Meisner taught them personally as actors. Individually focused training was one of Sandy's hallmarks. Others studied with his teachers he trained. Some of these teachers teach with more authenticity than others. By now, they are all over the globe.

- Janet Alhanti, NY
- Harold Baldridge, NY
- Herbert Berghof, NY
- Robert Emmett, CT
- Suzanne Esper, NY
- Nina Foch, LA
- James Price, NY
- Laurie Peters, NY
- Tom Radcliffe, UK
- Jose Santana, Santa Barbara, CA
- Marion Seldes, NY
- Tracy Sloat, Wichita, KS

Simon Gibbens, London, UK
Jeff Goldblum, LA
Lee Grant, LA
Johnny Jonson, NY
Fredric Mao, Hong Kong
John Mayo, Austin
Yoshiko (Yoko) Nakaima, Tokyo
Yoko Narahashi, Tokyo

Doug Taylor, CT
Barbara Ann Teer, NY
Roshan Teneja, Mumbai
Scott Trost, Shanghai
Martin Waldron, NY
Sheila Weber, Stamford, CA
June Whitaker, Vancouver, Canada
Greg Zittel, NY

Partial List of Meisner-Trained Actors

Over a period of 60 years, from 1935 until 1995, Sanford Meisner trained approximately 8000 actors. He turned out hundreds of future Broadway and Hollywood stars. Among them:

Mason Adams
Eddie Albert
Richard Alfieri
William Allyn
Elizabeth Ashley
Scott Bakula
Patricia Barry
Barbara Baxley
Herbert Berghof
Robert Blake
Doris Blum
Pat Boone
Richard Boone
Stockton Briggle
James Broderick
James Caan
Dyan Cannon
Jimmy Carville
June Carter Cash
John Cassavetes
Jack Cassidy
Marge Champion
Frances Chaney
Oona O'Neill Chaplin
Duane Clark
Montgomery Clift
Dabney Coleman

Mary Wells Lawrence
Shari Lewis & "Lamb Chop"
Christopher Lloyd
Michael Locassio
Dennis Longwell
Jack Lord
Sidney Lumet
David Mamet
Karl Malden
Vivian Matalon
Dylan McDermott
John McEvilley
Christopher Lawford
Darren McGavin
Ali McGraw
Biff McGuire
Steve McQueen
Adolph Green
Lorne Greene
Andre Gregory
Jennifer Grey
Joel Grey
Tammy Grimes
Annie Grindlay
George Grizzard
Gale Hansen
Marjorie Harris

Partial List of Meisner-Trained Actors (cont.)

Richard Conte
Tyne Daly
Kevin Dobson
James Doohan
Michael Douglas
Mary Doyle
Keir Dullea
Richard Dunn
Dominick Dunne
Robert Duvall
Rosemary Edelman
Timmy Everett
Sandy Faison
Peter Falk
Peggy Feury
Markus Flanagan
Geraldine Fitzgerald
Nina Foch
Nina Foneroff
Horton Foote
Bob Fosse
Meg Foster
Anthony Franciosa
John Frankenheimer
George Furth
Eva Gabor
John Garfield
Julie Garfield
Betty Garrett
Spencer Garrett
Jeff Goldblum
Akuyoe Graham
Farley Granger
Lee Grant
Kent Paul
Gregory Peck
Joan Pellet
Roberta Peters
John Pleshette
Suzanne Pleshette
Amanda Plummer
Sydney Pollack

Bonnie Oda Homsey
Dennis Hopper
Allison Janey
Annie Jackson
Conrad Janis
Johnny Johnson
Karl Johnson
Jennifer Jones
Shirley Jones
James Karen
Lainie Kazan
Diane Keaton
Susan Kellerman
Grace Kelly
Lisa Kirk
James Kirkland
Martin Landau
Louise Lasser
John Phillip Law
Dina Merrill
Ann Mitchum
Leslie Moonves
Robert Morris
Larry Moss
Rosemary Murphy
Leslie Nielson
Kathleen Nolan
Chuck Norris
Christopher Noth
Edmond O'Brien
Kevin O'Connor
Patrick O'Neal
Larry Parks
Robert Pastene
Mary Steenburgen
Frances Sternhagen
McLean Stevenson
Anna Strasberg
Elizabeth Sung
Roshan Taneja
Leigh Taylor-Young
Barbara Ann Teer

Partial List of Meisner-Trained Actors (cont.)

Antony Ponzini
Tom Poston
Princess Lee Radziwill
Tony Randall
Sally Jesse Raphael
Doris Roberts
Tracey Roberts
Cliff Roberts
Wayne Rogers
Melissa Rosenberg
Barbara Rush
Mark Rydell
Freddy Sadoff
Mort Sahl
Robert (Rob) Salvio
Gene Saks
Carol Saroyan
Arthur Seidelman
Marian Seldes
Suzanne Shepherd
Shirley Smith
Marlo Thomas
Kenneth (Ken) Tobey
Rip Torn
Tom Tryon
Manu Tupou
Brenda Vaccaro
Gloria Vanderbilt
Jo Van Fleet
Gwen Verdon
Jon Voight
Eli Wallach
Jessica Walters
Iris Whitney
Elizabeth Wilson
Marian Winters
Shelley Winters
Kirk Woller
Joanne Woodward
Gerrie Wormser
Gig Young
Efrem Zimbalist, Jr.

Names in bold indicate that the person won or was nominated for an Academy Award. A great many others on the list won other industry awards, such at Tonys, Emmys, Golden Globes, etc.

www.ingramcontent.com/pod-product-compliance
Lightning Source LLC
Chambersburg PA
CBHW071956150426
43194CB00008B/888